Race, Class, and Gender in a Diverse Society

A Text-Reader

Diana Kendall
Austin Community College

Allyn and Bacon

Boston ♦ London ♦ Toronto ♦ Sydney ♦ Tokyo ♦ Singapore

Editor in Chief, Social Sciences: Karen Hanson
Editorial Assistant: Jennifer Jacobson
Marketing Manager: Karon Bowers
Production Administrator: Annette Joseph
Editorial-Production Service: Communicáto, Ltd.
Manufacturing Buyer: Megan Cochran
Cover Administrator: Suzanne Harbison

Library of Congress Cataloging-in-Publication Data

Race, class, and gender in a diverse society : a text-reader / [edited
  by] Diana Kendall.
    p. cm.
  Includes bibliographical references and indexes.
  ISBN 0–205–19828–7 (alk. paper)
  1. Equality—United States. 2. Marginality, Social—United
States. 3. Minorities—United States—Social conditions. 4. Women—
United States—Social conditions. 5. Social classes—United
States. 6. United States—Social conditions. 7. United States—
Race relations. I. Kendall, Diana Elizabeth.
HN90.S6R35 1997
305'.0973—dc20   96–32295
                                             CIP

To Joe R. Feagin,
who continues to provide me and thousands of others
with new insights on the pressing and still unresolved problems
of U.S. racism, sexism, and invidious class distinctions

Contents

v

Part Three   ♦   Discrimination, Resistance, and Social Change   299

Preface

Race, Class, and Gender in a Diverse Society is a unique text-reader that provides contemporary students with a variety of perspectives on the interlocking nature of race, class, and gender at the micro- and macrolevels of society. This book contains the essential components of a comprehensive text and provides articles that demonstrate the interconnectedness of these three key systems of inequality. All articles were selected with two purposes in mind: (1) to reflect the diversity that is life in the United States today, and whenever possible, (2) to show how people are affected by the intertwining nature of race, class, and gender in daily life. Most articles are reprints of complete journal articles or entire chapters from recent books, which provide students with an in-depth look at the history, theory, and methods that inform social science research on pressing social issues, such as diversity and inequalities based on racism, sexism, and class oppression.

Distinctive Features

The following features are specifically designed to make *Race, Class, and Gender in a Diverse Society* accessible to students. The introductions to Parts One, Two, and Three include early stated theories and key concepts that are set forth in definition form and highlighted by bold type. Each article begins with a brief overview and with Looking Ahead—questions to help students focus on key issues and applicable theoretical perspectives. At the end of each article, Questions for Understanding and Critical Thinking are designed to assist students in retaining central ideas and developing critical-thinking skills. Suggestions for Further Reading also are provided for students at the conclusion of each of the three parts.

An *Instructor's Manual and Test Bank* provides teaching suggestions—such as class presentation and discussion suggestions, critical-writing assignments, further readings, and available films—and a selection of multiple-choice and essay questions. Professors who use *Race, Class, and Gender in a Diverse Society* in their classes are asked to send their own ideas and teaching tips to the editor for inclusion (and attribution) in future editions of the *Instructor's Manual.*

Organization

Race, Class, and Gender in a Diverse Society is divided into three main sections. Part One, A New Look at Race, Class, and Gender, provides a sociological foundation for examining how race, class, and gender shape people's personal and social realities at the microlevel and operate as interlocking systems of privilege/oppression at the macrolevel of society. Some articles in this section focus primarily on the development of a conceptual framework for examining race, class, and/or gender diversity and inequalities; others feature people's lived experiences as viewed through the prism of race, class, and gender. Some articles, such as the one by early African American sociologist W. E. B. Du Bois, provide historical insights on racism, sexism, and/or class oppression;

other articles highlight contemporary social issues, such as studies of cosmetic surgery (by Diana Dull and Candace West) and the nature of interactive service jobs in fast-food restaurants and insurance companies (by Robin Leidner).

Part Two, Learning about Diversity and Inequality, examines the development of racial-ethnic, class, and gender identities and how people learn—through families, peers, sports, and education—about diversity and inequality in society. The first five articles focus on compelling issues such as the social geography of race, the socialization of children of color to resist racism and discrimination, relationships between female socialization and eating problems, relationships between male socialization and organized sports, and the issue of racism and sports team names and mascots. The next five articles analyze education along lines of race, class, and gender to see how schooling may reproduce, rather than challenge, existing social inequalities. From elite boarding schools to working-class schools and job-training programs for central-city youths, issues of cultural and structural reproduction and resistance are examined by a variety of authors and scholars.

Finally, Part Three, Discrimination, Resistance, and Social Change, analyzes the process of discrimination as it is rooted in racism, sexism, and class oppression. Also discussed are the consequences of discrimination in people's lives, their resistance to oppression, and prospects for social change. Articles examine racism perpetrated against Asian Americans, harassment of women in public places, and discrimination and resistance among central-city residents and middle-class African Americans. The final articles call for an end to patriarchy and the renewal of hope for a *beloved community,* one in which race would be transcended or forgotten, in which no one would see skin color.

Brief Overview of Diversity and Inequality

Americans live and work in a highly diverse society, in which they often encounter the dynamic interplay of race, class, and gender, even when they are not consciously aware of it. Racial and ethnic diversity is increasing in the United States. African Americans, Latinos/Latinas, Asian Americans, and Native Americans comprise one-fourth of the U.S. population, while whites form a shrinking percentage of the population. By the year 2000, white Americans will make up 70 percent of the population, as compared to 80 percent in 1980. Latinos/Latinas will outnumber African Americans by the year 2010, and by 2050, whites will no longer be the numerical majority in the United States. The roots of the average U.S. resident will be in Africa, Asia, Latin America, the Pacific Islands, and the Middle East—not white Europe (Gross, 1996).

In recent years, class distinctions have increased rather than diminished. The gap between the rich and the poor has grown steadily, and many people in the U.S. middle and working classes are frustrated by their lack of economic gains, as reflected by a median household income that has remained flat (when adjusted for inflation) for the past 20 years. Some working-class families find themselves scraping by, as workers' real weekly wages have dropped almost 5 percent since 1979 and dramatic changes in the U.S. economy have contributed to higher rates of unemployment and underemployment. By contrast, the share of total wealth held by the richest 1 percent of U.S. families nearly doubled between 1979 and 1992. Although some people may not perceive increasing economic inequality as *class oppression,* some social analysts use this term to describe the subordination of members of the middle and lower classes by wealthy members of the capitalist class. Consider, for example, that today the ratio between the pay of a typical corporate chief executive officer (CEO) and an average U.S. worker is 225 to 1—up from 41 to 1 in the mid-1970s. By contrast, in Germany, the ratio is closer to 20 to 1 (Boroughs, 1996).

United States society is also characterized by gender inequality that results from economic, political, and educational discrimination. About two-thirds of all adults living in poverty are women. In 1993, single-parent families headed by women had a 46 percent poverty rate, as compared with a 9 percent rate for two-parent families. Women have a higher risk of being poor because they bear the major economic and emotional burdens of raising children when they are single heads of households, yet they earn only 70 to 75 cents for every dollar a male worker earns.

Women's positions in the U.S. workforce reflect their overall subordination in society: Most workplaces are gender segregated so that women and men are concentrated in different occupations, jobs, and work sites. In 1990, for example, 99 percent of all secretaries in the United States were women; 92 percent of all engineers were men (National Committee on Pay Equity, 1994). Although the degree of gender segregation in the professional labor market has declined since the 1970s, sexism and racism have remained deeply embedded in the social structure. For example, in Article 25, Elizabeth Higginbotham describes how African American professional women have been limited primarily to public-sector employment (e.g., as public school teachers, welfare workers, and public defenders) and excluded from private-sector employment in large corporations or major law firms. As a result, women, and especially women of color, have lower-paid, less-prestigious jobs, with little opportunity for advancement. In addition, most middle-class, married women in the United States combine paid work in the labor force and family work. Even with dramatic changes in women's workforce participation, little change has occurred in the sexual division of labor in many families.

Race, Class, and Gender in a Diverse Society examines theories, research, and real experiences that provide insights on the causes and consequences of race, class, and gender inequalities in the United States. Although similar problems exist in many nations, I have limited the focus of this book to the United States so that students can gain better understanding of how existing systems of power and privilege may be related to racism, sexism, and class oppression.

A Note about Language

As introductory sociology students learn, a key issue in sociology is whether language *creates* or simply *communicates* reality. At no point is this issue more pressing than when one attempts to analyze the experiences of people based on race, class, and gender. Ultimately, language both creates and communicates social realities; however, it also reflects current political ideologies and other deeply entrenched assumptions about domination and subordination in contemporary society.

The language of race, class, and gender is extremely important yet vague and often misleading. Consider, for example, the terms *race* and *ethnicity.* Although most social scientists view these terms as *social constructs,* not biological realities, they do not agree on whether race and ethnicity are interchangeable concepts (i.e., *racial-ethnic groups*) or significant distinctions *(racial and ethnic groups)* in sociological analysis. Looking at racial classifications in the U.S. Census for the past century, one can see how the meanings continue to change. Racial classifications and social realities about race have been linked in three ways: (1) Race is defined by perceived skin color—white or nonwhite; (2) racial purity is assumed to exist; and (3) official racial classifications may create a sense of group membership or "consciousness of kind" for people within arbitrary, externally imposed classification schemes, such as white, Latino/Latina, or Asian Americans. For example, the term *Asian American* is used to include a wide variety of cultures, including U.S. citizens of Pacific Island origins. Although such oversimplifications may be convenient, they also render specific racial or ethnic categories—such as *Pacific Islander Americans*—invisible.

People do not always accept externally imposed labels pertaining to their racial or ethnic roots. In Article 4, for example, Peruvian American scholar Suzanne Oboler explains how the widely used label *Hispanic* is rejected by many recent immigrants of Latin American descent who do not believe that it accurately reflects their own racial or ethnic roots.

Today, an emerging consciousness is causing politicians and social scientists to focus on *multiracial* or *mixed* racial categories. Demands are being made that a multiracial category (instead of *other*) be used by the U.S. Census Bureau in the year 2000 and on all other forms that classify the swiftly changing U.S. population, which is thought to include 1 to 2 million people of mixed race descent. The last big change in categories came in 1977, when the Office of Management and Budget established a system that counts whites, blacks, Hispanics, American Indians or Native Alaskans, and Asian or Pacific Islanders. Other changes undoubtedly will occur in the future as the composition of the U.S. population shifts (Gross, 1996).

Just as language pertaining to race and ethnicity may be ambiguous, terms used to describe gender and class are imprecise and often lead to confusion. When speaking of women, is one including the experiences of *all* women or of only *white* women? What is meant by *class* and *class oppression?* Does an *underclass* exist in the United States? Questions such as these will resurface in various articles.

Acknowledging these existing limitations of language, I have attempted to use consistent terminology throughout the introductions to Parts One, Two, and Three and in the brief overviews and questions relating to each article; however, the authors' terminologies stand in all articles.

Acknowledgments

I am indebted to each of the authors and scholars whose works make up this text-reader. Bringing their insights and scholarly research together in one place for you, the reader, has been my pleasure and privilege. Since I have not personally met each of the authors, I would like to take this opportunity to thank the following people (listed by the order of the articles) for allowing me to include their work in this anthology: Howard Winant, Ronald E. Hall, Suzanne Oboler, Felix M. Padilla and Lourdes Santiago, Stephen Richard Higley, Judith Lorber, Diana Dull and Candace West, Robin Leidner, Ruth Frankenberg, David H. Demo and Michael Hughes, Becky W. Thompson, Michael A. Messner, Ward Churchill, Caroline Hodges Persell and Peter W. Cookson, Jr., Gregory Mantsios, Jill Quadagno and Catherine Fobes, Ruben Navarrette, Jr., Emily W. Kane, Rita Chaudhry Sethi, Carol Brooks Gardner, Robin L. Jarrett, Joe R. Feagin, Kathryn M. Neckerman and Joleen Kirschenman, Elizabeth Higginbotham, Robert Jensen, and bell hooks.

I owe a debt of intellectual gratitude to Jeanne H. Ballantine, Catherine White Berheide, Elizabeth Higginbotham, and Marcia Texler Segal for an outstanding American Sociological Association teaching workshop on integrating race, class, and gender in the sociological curriculum. They made me aware that I was not alone in my quest to broaden the scope of teaching and research in sociology to include previously excluded people and perspectives. I also am indebted to Patricia Hill Collins, Margaret L. Andersen, and Paula S. Rothenberg for laying the foundation for inclusive thinking about race, class, and gender.

I am fortunate to have Karen Hanson at Allyn and Bacon as my editor in chief. Without her encouragement and patience, this text-reader would not have the depth of sociological explanation or the variety of articles that it now provides for students and instructors.

My most profound gratitude goes to my husband, Terrence Kendall, and the office staff at Kendall, Randle, Finch and Osborn, including Patricia Nuhn, without whom producing this book would have been impossible. From correspondence with authors and publishers to design and layout of the manuscript, Patricia cheerfully and professionally completed each task at hand.

Finally, *Race, Class, and Gender in a Diverse Society* is dedicated to Joe R. Feagin, Graduate Research Professor at the University of Florida, who has been my long-term friend and mentor from graduate school at the University of Texas at Austin. One hot Texas summer session, during a graduate seminar on race and ethnicity, Joe encouraged me to take a systematic look at race, class, and gender as systems of privilege and oppression, not just variables in sociological analysis. Almost 20 years later, I still rush to the bookstore to purchase his latest book and gain new insight on the still pressing—and unresolved—problems of racism, sexism, and invidious class distinctions that continue to haunt U.S. society as the end of this century approaches.

I invite professors and students to send their comments about *Race, Class, and Gender in a Diverse Society* to me in care of Austin Community College (Austin, TX). I also welcome e-mail messages at the following Internet address: dkendall@austin.cc.tx.us

References

Boroughs, Don L. 1996. "Winter of Discontent." *U.S. News & World Report* (January 22): 47–54.

Gross, Jane. 1996. "Changing How We Define Ourselves Racially." *Austin American Statesman* (January 14): H1, H4.

National Committee on Pay Equity. 1994. "The Wage Gap: Myths and Facts," in Alison M. Jagger (Ed.), *Living with Contradictions: Controversies in Feminist Social Ethics* (pp. 73–90). Boulder, CO: Westview Press.

PART ONE

A New Look at Race, Class, and Gender

AMONG THE MOST dramatic U.S. events of 1995 was the trial and acquittal of Orenthal James (O. J.) Simpson, the former professional football star, actor, and media celebrity who was charged with the murders of his ex-wife, Nicole Brown Simpson, and her friend, Ronald L. Goldman. Unprecedented national interest in the public announcement of the Simpson verdict on October 3, 1995, was described by one journalist:

> *The country stopped.*
>
> *Between 1 and 1:10 P.M. [EST] yesterday, people didn't work. They didn't go to math class. They didn't make phone calls. They didn't use the bathroom. They didn't walk the dog.*
>
> *They listened to the O. J. Simpson verdict. . . .*
>
> *It was an eerie moment of national communication, in which the routines and rituals of the country were subsumed by an unquenchable curiosity. Millions of people in millions of places seemed to spend 10 spellbound minutes doing exactly the same thing. (Kleinfield, 1995:A1)*

Immediately, people's reactions to the not guilty verdict jarred that brief moment and reflected deep divisions in public opinion—not only about Simpson's innocence or guilt but also about issues of race, class, and gender in the United States. In opinion polls, a majority of whites—even after the verdict—seemed to hold fast to the belief that Simpson was guilty, while a majority of African Americans believed in his innocence and indicated their profound distrust of law enforcement and a criminal justice system tainted by charges of racism, brutality, and injustice for persons of color.

Does the Simpson case shed light on issues of race, class, and gender in the United States? Communications professor Michael Eric Dyson suggests that many factors—not just race—were involved in this case:

> *I think in one sense this is an artificial and illusionary kind of case. O. J. Simpson is an extraordinary figure and an exception to the average [African American man] who is facing a capital crime. They don't have the kind of capital he has,*

they don't have the kind of money he has, they don't have the fame or celebrity
he has to deter his conviction. And I think what is being obscured here is that race
is central and dominant, but so are the issues of fame, so are the issues of
celebrity, and especially the issue of domestic violence. (1996)

Class and gender also are central and dominant issues. Dyson emphasizes that
not *all* African Americans or *all* whites viewed the case in the same manner:

Many African American women, who themselves were violated, identify with
O. J. against their own best self-interests. And I think that white women under-
stood domestic violence but they didn't understand how racism privileged their
own white bodies over black women's bodies. Black men understood the race di-
mension but they missed [the issue of] domestic violence. White men felt in their
guts that O. J. was guilty, but they don't understand how many black men and
women are pre-judged daily. And black women understood how race and gender
and class come together but often were forced to choose one over the other. This
case exemplifies the enormous entanglement of race, class, and gender and how
we have failed to generate a vocabulary that will help us analytically unmask the
problems that we face in this country. (1996)

As Dyson points out, the Simpson case highlights many unresolved—but
critical—questions about the unfinished business of race, class, and gender in
the United States. How can the interrelations among these systems of inequality best be conceptualized?

Sociologists emphasize that race, class, and gender must be explored as interlocking systems of oppression of race, class, and gender that produce social
positions characterized by intersectionality. Sociologist Patricia Hill Collins explains:

First, the notion of interlocking oppressions refers to the macro level connections
linking systems of oppression such as race, class, and gender. This is the model
describing the social structures that create social positions. Second, the notion of
intersectionality describes micro level processes—namely, how each individual
and group occupies a social position within interlocking structures of oppression
described by the metaphor of intersectionality. Together they shape oppression.
(1995:492)

From this perspective, race, class, and gender divisions are deeply embedded in
social structures and institutions—such as families, the economy and work, the
government and politics, and education—and affect all aspects of our lives.

In this book, we will examine race, class, and gender as both macrolevel
connections and microlevel processes. Despite their interlocking nature, Part
One will focus on race, class, and gender as distinct systems of inequality in order to establish a foundation for understanding their interlocking nature (see
Andersen and Collins, 1995; Collins, 1995).

An Overview of Race and Ethnicity

What is race? The concept of *race* has numerous meanings in contemporary societies. Some people use *race* to refer to skin color (the African American *race*); others use it to refer to a linguistic category (the Spanish-speaking *race*), a religious category (the Jewish *race*), or a national category (the German *race*). Still others refer to the entire human species as the human *race*.

As these definitions show, *race* is probably one of the least understood and most misused concepts in the English language. According to legal scholar Ian F. Haney Lopez, "Race may be America's single most confounding problem, but the confounding problem of race is that few people seem to know what race is" (1995:193).

In Article 1, sociologist Howard Winant points out that people in the United States experience greater anxiety and uncertainty over race than any other social or political issue because, as a society, people have not resolved the cultural and political meaning of race and its significance in shaping their social structure and collective psyche. According to Winant, no task is more urgent than developing a better theoretical perspective for understanding *race* and the pervasive U.S. race crisis.

Race

Today, most social scientists view race as a ***social construct***—**a classification of people based on social and political values.** From this social-definition perspective, a ***race*** **is a category of people who have been singled out, by others or themselves, as inferior or superior on the basis of subjectively selected physical characteristics such as skin color, hair texture, and eye shape.** According to sociologists, whatever significance race may have biologically is overwhelmed by its social significance.

In the contemporary United States, race permeates every institution, every relationship, and every individual. People are compelled to think racially, to use the racial categories and meaning systems into which they have been socialized (Omi and Winant, 1994). Race determines one's economic prospects; for example, a race-conscious market screens and selects people for manual jobs and professional careers, determines who receives financing for real estate and access to insurance, and even influences the price people pay for cars (Haney Lopez, 1995; Ayers, 1991). As a socially constructed reality, race perpetuates social inequality. If true racial equality existed in the United States, race would not be a consideration in the selection of leaders, in hiring decisions, or in the distribution of goods and services (Omi and Winant, 1994).

By contrast, some perspectives on race border on ***biological determinism***—**a belief that people possess certain unchangeable, genetically programmed physical or mental attributes that make them superior or inferior as human beings.** For example, in a recent, highly controversial book, *The Bell*

Curve, authors Richard J. Herrnstein and Charles Murray (1994) seek to revive the notion of *social Darwinism*—**a belief that certain societies and races have survived and prospered because of their superiority.** According to social Darwinism, members of some racial groups are destined to maintain their dominance over other, allegedly inferior, human races. In industrial societies, for example, the ills of poverty, welfare, and homelessness can be attributed to people's genetic inferiority. For Herrnstein and Murray, intelligence is genetically inherited, measurable (through IQ tests), and immutable—people cannot be smarter than they are born to be, regardless of environment or education. The authors point out that Asians (in Asia), on average, score higher than white Americans on IQ tests and that African Americans, on average, score 15 points lower than white Americans. They argue that, therefore, race and class differences primarily are related to genetic factors, not social inequalities.

Although scholars have critiqued *The Bell Curve* on theoretical and methodological grounds, the book touches an open nerve regarding U.S. race and class inequalities. It also strengthens the political agenda of conservative politicians and social analysts who want to see welfare reduced or eliminated, affirmative action in schools and workplaces ended or sharply curtailed, and educational programs such as Head Start trimmed back (Gould, 1995). Winant (the author of Article 1) argues that political debates dominated by charges of reverse discrimination and quotas in affirmative action plans are a racial reaction to the achievements and legacy of the black movement of the 1950s and 1960s, which ended the epoch of racial domination by challenging past racial practices and stereotypes and by ushering in a wave of social reform. However, according to Winant, this change has not brought an end to racial "exclusion, segregation, discrimination, malevolence, ignorance, and outright violence" (1994:29).

Although sociologists do not seek to negate or belittle all genetic research, they suggest that it is important to understand its limits. Biologically deterministic perspectives, such as those of Herrnstein and Murray, do not identify problems inherent in measuring human intelligence. Zoology professor Stephen Jay Gould explains:

> *Take a trait that is far more heritable than anyone has ever claimed IQ to be but is politically uncontroversial—body height. Suppose that I measure the heights of adult males in a poor Indian village beset with nutritional deprivation, and suppose the average height of adult males is five feet six inches. Heritability within the village is high, which is to say that tall fathers (they may average five feet eight inches) tend to have tall sons, while short fathers (five feet four inches on average) tend to have short sons. But this high heritability within the village does not mean that better nutrition might not raise average height to five feet ten inches in a few generations. Similarly, the well-documented fifteen-point average difference in IQ between blacks and whites in America, with substantial heritability of IQ in family lines within each group, permits no automatic conclusion that truly equal opportunity might not raise the black average enough to equal or surpass the white mean. (1995:5)*

The idea of social inequalities based on inherited physical differences is not new. As early as the 1600s, some Europeans began to establish hierarchical categories of people based on physical distinctions. Although not specifically referred to as *races* at this time, categories of people were hierarchically arranged based on their geographic origins and physical appearance. It is not surprising that Europeans placed themselves—white Europeans—at the top of the hierarchy while placing Africans at the bottom, allegedly due to skin color, a "primitive" culture, and their "slave" status (Jordan, 1969).

In the late eighteenth century, race came to be associated with *physical* characteristics transmitted by descent. Immanuel Kant referred to the human species as "the races of mankind," and some biologists, physical anthropologists, and other scientists initiated the use of *race* as a biological construct. In 1795, for example, German anatomist Johann Blumenbach classified and ranked human beings into five hierarchically arranged racial groups: the Caucasians (Europeans), the Mongolians (Asians), the Ethiopians (Africans), the Americans (Native Americans), and the Malays (Polynesians) (Gould, 1994). Later, the five categories were reduced to three:

1. *Negroid:* a grouping of human beings generally characterized by dark skin and black, very curly hair, who are assumed to have roots in geographic areas such as Africa, Melanesia, and New Guinea
2. *Caucasoid* (from the erroneous notion that the original home of the hypothetical Indo-Europeans was the Caucasus Mountains of Russia): a grouping of human beings generally characterized by lighter skin tones, tall stature, and straight or wavy hair, who are assumed to have roots in geographic areas such as Europe, Africa, the Near East, and India
3. *Mongoloid:* a grouping of human beings generally characterized by straight black hair, dark eyes with epicanthic folds, and relatively small stature, including the Eskimos, the North American Indians, and most of the peoples of Asia (based on *Webster's New World Dictionary,* 1988).

However, the notion of so-called pure races is meaningless. Even if pure races previously existed, centuries of migration, exploration, invasion, and interbreeding by members of diverse racial groups have rendered meaningless the notion of race as a discrete biological category.

Today, people within one racial category do not all share the same physical appearance or skin color. As social scientist Ronald E. Hall points out in Article 2, "The Color Complex: The Bleaching Syndrome," African Americans vary widely in skin color. Lightness or darkness of skin color may be a ***master status*—the most important socially defined position that a person occupies in a group or society**—that dichotomizes African Americans. According to Hall (1995:102), white racial domination contributes to African Americans' preference for light skin: "For African Americans, the utilization of light skin as a point of reference for attractiveness is plausible. Those who have light skin are believed to be most physically appealing given their visual proximity to the dominant race white population" (1995:102). Anywhere racial domination exists, physical characteristics such as skin color of the *dominated* group are stigmatized (Hall, 1995).

The Virginia case of *Hudgins v. Wright* (1806) is a historical example of the social and political significance given to so-called racial characteristics. In the nineteenth century, being a slave was an **ascribed status—a social position conferred on a person at birth.** A person born to a slave woman was a slave; one born to a free woman was free. The Wrights—an enslaved grandmother, mother, and daughter—sued for freedom on grounds that they were the descendants of a free maternal ancestor. Physical appearance was the only evidence the women could bring before the court to prove their status. (Under Virginia law, blacks were presumed to be slaves and had the burden of proving they were *not* slaves; white Americans and Native Americans were presumed to be free unless evidence indicated otherwise.) Accordingly, the presiding judge devised a racial test to determine if the Wrights were blacks (and thus slaves) or Native Americans (and thus free):

> *Nature has stampt upon the African and his descendants two characteristic marks, besides the difference of complexion, which often remain visible long after the characteristic distinction of colour either disappears or becomes doubtful; a flat nose and woolly head of hair. The latter of these disappears the last of all; and so strong an ingredient in the African constitution is this latter character, that it predominates uniformly where the party in equal degree descended from parents of different complexions, whether white or Indians. . . . So pointed is this distinction between the natives of Africa and the aborigines of America, that a man might as easily mistake the glossy, jetty clothing of an American bear for the wool of a black sheep, as the hair of an American Indian for that of an African, or the descendant of an African. Upon these distinctions as connected with our laws, the burden of proof depends.* (Hudgins v. Wright, *quoted in Haney Lopez, 1995:191–192)*

Based on the judge's criteria, the women were declared free because the hair of Hannah, one of the women, was "the long, straight, black hair of the native aborigines [Native Americans] of this country" (Haney Lopez, 1995). Thus, the fate of the Wrights—as free women or slaves—ultimately rested on hair texture. Cases such as *Hudgins v. Wright* demonstrate how race is a social and political construct.

Today, members of many racial-ethnic groups have identifiable physical characteristics that are not considered to be racial distinctions. Criteria for racial distinctions also may vary among societies. In Latin America, for example, racial distinctions may be based on hair texture, eye color, and height, whereas skin color and shape of lips may be more important criteria in the United States.

Social scientists focus on the social and political processes by which racial meanings are attributed and racial identities assigned in a society. Winant

(1994) uses the concept of *racial formation* to explain how race in contemporary societies should be viewed as an ever-changing complex of meanings shaped by sociopolitical conflict. According to Winant, race is not a fixed, concrete, and objective natural attribute; rather, it is socially and historically constructed. ***Racial formation theory* states that actions of the government substantially define racial and ethnic relations** (Omi and Winant, 1994). Governmental actions may range from race-related legislation (such as restrictive immigration quotas) to imprisonment of members of groups believed to be a threat to society. During World War II, for example, nearly 120,000 Japanese Americans were incarcerated for more than two years in U.S. internment camps located on remote military sites with guard towers and barbed-wire fences. The incarceration was a direct violation of the citizenship rights of many *Nisei* (second-generation Japanese Americans) who were born in the United States. Although the United States was at war with Japan, Germany, and Italy, only Japanese Americans (whose ancestors originated in Asia) were singled out for isolation; German Americans and Italian Americans (whose ancestors originated in Europe) were not thought to be a security threat to the country. U.S. General John DeWitt explained the forced evacuation of Japanese Americans as follows:

> *The Japanese race is an enemy race and while many second and third generation Japanese born on United States soil, possessed of United States citizenship, have become "Americanized," the racial strains are undiluted. . . . That Japan is allied with Germany and Italy in this struggle is not ground for assuming that any Japanese, barred from assimilation by convention as he is, though born and raised in the United States, will not turn against his nation when the final test of loyalty comes. It therefore follows that along the vital Pacific Coast over 112,000 potential enemies of Japanese extraction are at large today. There are indications that these are organized and ready for concerted action at a favorable opportunity. The very fact that no sabotage has taken place to date is a disturbing and confirming indication that such action will be taken.* (U.S. Army, Western Defense Command and Fourth Army, 1943:33–34; *quoted in Yinger, 1994:30*)

Although no evidence was ever presented that Japanese Americans posed a risk to the United States, many lost all they owned as a result of the internment (Takaki, 1993). Four decades later, the U.S. government issued an apology for its actions and agreed to pay $20,000 to each person who had been placed in an internment camp (Takaki, 1993; Daniels, 1993).

According to Winant (1994), racial domination of this type has been replaced by ***hegemony*—the ideological or cultural control of one racial group or class by another.** Hegemony is the means by which members of a societal ruling class convince people in other classes that ruling-class interests are universal interests shared by everyone. As a result, members of the ruling class must maintain—through education, the mass media, religion, and other social institutions—a popular system of ideas regarding these "shared" interests so that elites can retain their privileged position in society.

Today, racial hegemony in the United States is organized through the interplay of *racial projects,* **each of which is simultaneously an interpretation, representation, or explanation of racial dynamics and an effort to organize and distribute resources along particular racial lines.** Racial hegemony is achieved by the manufacture of consensus—through the manipulation of the context of cultural forms and major social institutions. Winant (1994:29) suggests that under hegemonic conditions, *opposition* and *difference* are not repressed, excluded, or silenced. Those who represent opposition or difference, but are able to gain access to the "halls of power," may be co-opted by the ruling class and mainstream culture, which tends to diminish original voices of protest. Race then becomes a political football in racial projects, ranging from the far right to radical democracy (see Article 1, Table 1).

Ethnicity

A concept closely related to race is ethnicity. An ***ethnic group* is a category of people distinguished, by others or by themselves, primarily on the basis of distinctive cultural or nationality characteristics** (Feagin and Feagin, 1996). Sociologists suggest that ethnic groups share five main characteristics:

1. Unique cultural traits (such as language, clothing, holidays, or religious practices
2. A sense of community
3. A feeling of ***ethnocentrism*—the belief that one's own culture and way of life are superior to all others**
4. Ascribed membership—a status conferred at birth
5. Territoriality—a tendency to occupy a distinct geographic area (such as Koreatown or Little Odessa) by choice or for self-protection

Examples of ethnic groups in the United States include Latinos/Latinas (e.g., Mexican Americans or Chicanas/Chicanos, Puerto Ricans, and Cuban Americans), white ethnics (e.g., Jewish Americans, Italian Americans, Irish Americans, German Americans, and Polish Americans), and white Anglo-Saxon Protestants (WASPs).

Like race, ethnicity is a social construct; people often are assigned to ethnic categories based on social and political values. In Article 4, Peruvian American scholar Suzanne Oboler points out the salience of ethnicity as a form of social and political classification. According to Oboler, official racial-ethnic classifications are public articulations of race-related value judgments. Widespread use of the word *Hispanic* to identify all Latin American immigrants, for example, is based on a faulty assumption that diverse categories of people are all alike and that they share the same cultural and national identity as *Hispanics.*

However, ethnic enclaves (such as Little Havana in Miami) highlight the diversity found *within* various racial-ethnic categories. These enclaves preserve a group's distinctive cultural characteristics (e.g., food habits, modes of dress, and entertainment), political orientation, and economic activities, at least for a period of time. Article 5, "Outside the Wall: Childhood Years and Family Life," by sociologist Felix M. Padilla and Lourdes Santiago provides insights on the strong sense of ethnic identity and community that Santiago experienced growing up in an area of Chicago where major cultural activities and structures of the Puerto Rican community were located.

Obviously, the concepts of ethnicity and racial groups tend to overlap. In addition to having assumed distinctive physical characteristics, racial groups often are believed to have unique *cultural* traits (e.g., African Americans and rap music, or Native Americans and religious ceremonies for purification), regardless of the validity of these assumptions. Similarly, some ethnic groups are singled out for their distinguishing *physical* characteristics (e.g., skin tone and color of hair and eyes among Latinas/Latinos). Scholars have pointed out that the physical characteristics commonly used to identify racial groups tend to be more visible than the cultural differences used to distinguish ethnic groups. These visible differences may result in higher levels of racially based stereotyping, prejudice, and discrimination in a society. In Article 2, Ronald E. Hall points out that African Americans and other racial and ethnic groups whose skin color is not similar to the dominant population have been expected to assume a passive social demeanor and otherwise not object to the contradictions of U.S. racial domination.

Dominant and Subordinate Groups

Social scientists use the term *minority group* to describe categories of people who have been the objects of collective discrimination perpetrated by members of a dominant group. A ***minority*** (or ***subordinate***) ***group*** is one whose members, because of physical or cultural characteristics, are disadvantaged and subjected to unequal treatment by the dominant group and who regard themselves as objects of collective discrimination** (Wirth, 1945). All persons of color and white women, for example, are considered to be minority group members in the United States.

The presence of minority groups assumes the existence of a ***majority*** (or ***dominant***) ***group**—one that is advantaged and has superior resources and rights in a society.** In the United States, whites with northern European ancestry (often referred to as *white Anglo-Saxon Protestants*) historically have been considered the majority group. In Article 6, "Privilege, Power, and Place: The Geography of the American Upper Class," geographer Stephen Richard Higley describes residential patterns and lifestyles of U.S. majority group members— elite white Anglo-Saxon Protestants whose names appear in the *Social Register.* According to Higley, personal, ethnic, and religious characteristics are extremely important for acceptance into—or rejection by—this dominant, upper-class group.

Although *minority group* and *majority group* are widely used terms in every-day life, many social scientists consider *dominant group* and *subordinate group* more accurate to identify power differentials between groups based on ascribed characteristics such as race/ethnicity, gender, religion, or sexual orientation. Al-though the Hindus of India make up about 80 percent of that nation's popula-tion (a numerical majority), for example, they face serious discrimination based on skin color and are more accurately viewed as a subordinate group (see Article 2).

An Overview of Class

Relationships based on racial-ethnic domination and subordination are one di-mension of *social stratification*—**a hierarchical arrangement of large social groups based on their control over scarce resources.** Class is another dimen-sion in the United States. A *class system* **is a system of social inequality in which people's status is determined by the ownership and control of re-sources and on the kinds of work people perform.** In a capitalist society, class location also affects *life chances*—**the extent to which persons have ac-cess to important scarce resources.**

Sociologists distinguish between a class system and a *caste system*—**a sys-tem of social inequality in which people's status is permanently determined at birth based on their parents' ascribed characteristics.** Castes are *closed* sys-tems of stratification; that is, upward or downward social mobility is almost im-possible, and privilege (or disadvantage) is passed on from one generation to the next. In a caste system, custom and law dictate that children of the privileged shall occupy the higher-level positions and maintain control of societal assets.

Caste systems may reinforce and perpetuate racial and ethnic inequality. For example, until recently, South Africa maintained a caste system based on *apartheid*—**the categorical separation of the races.** Although white South Africans (Afrikaners) constituted a numerical minority, they monopolized high-status, well-paid jobs and controlled the economy, government, military, and mass media. By contrast, black Africans—the numerical majority—primarily were consigned to jobs as manual laborers and servants. Racial segre-gation was enforced in all areas of life, including neighborhoods, schools, hos-pitals, and churches, and interracial marriages were forbidden.

In the United States, the African American experience has been compared to a caste system in which racial and ethnic inequalities are a permanent fea-ture of social life (see Dollard, 1957/1937; Berreman, 1960; Fredrickson, 1981). Historically, African Americans have experienced slavery, segregation, and an-timiscegenation laws prohibiting interracial sexual intercourse or marriage. To-day, racism and overt and covert patterns of discrimination continue to have a detrimental impact on African Americans of all social classes. In "The Souls of

Black Folk" (Article 3), early African American sociologist W. E. B. Du Bois describes blacks' castelike existence in the United States at the beginning of the twentieth century:

> *For the first time he [the African American] sought to analyze the burden he bore upon his back, that dead-weight of social degradation partially masked behind a half-named Negro problem. He felt his poverty; without a cent, without a home, without land, tools, or savings, he had entered into competition with rich, landed, skilled neighbors. To be a poor man is hard, but to be a poor race in a land of dollars is the very bottom of hardships. (Du Bois, 1989/1903:6)*

The residual effects of this experience continue today. African Americans remain far behind whites in measures of educational attainment, job opportunities, earned income, accumulated wealth, health care, life expectancy, and other critical determinants of life chances.

Unlike castes, classes are assumed to be open systems of stratification wherein people are able to enhance their life chances and lifestyles. Classes are characterized by *social mobility*—**the movement of individuals or groups from one level in a stratification system to another.** People may move upward or downward in the class structure through *intergenerational mobility*—**social movement from one generation to the next**—or *intragenerational mobility*—**social movement within a person's lifetime.** In Article 16, sociologist Gregory Mantsios describes the relationship between his working class background and his hopes for social mobility:

> *By high school most of us knew our fates were sealed. Sociologists could have told us all along that there is little class mobility in the United States. They could have told us that despite the wonderful rhetoric to the contrary, the rags to riches stories and the "we are all middle class" image of America were largely myths—but we were finding out for ourselves. (1995:241)*

Next, we will examine the classical perspectives of Karl Marx and Max Weber and the contemporary class models of Erik O. Wright and of Dennis Gilbert and Joseph A. Kahl. Focus will be on how class, as a series of social relationships, profoundly influences the social structure of society and people's interactions with each other.

Class Perspectives Based on Karl Marx

For Karl Marx (1818–1883), a *class* has these characteristics:

1. A distinct relationship to and role in the mode of production (e.g., ownership of the means of production, employment of wage labor, and economic interests)

2. A clear consciousness of its existence as a unified class with objective interests that are hostile to those of other classes
3. An organization of the class into a political party aimed at representing and fighting for its interests
4. A distinct set of cultural values and a separate style of life (Ollman, 1968; Hurst, 1992)

Based on these criteria, Marx suggested that capitalistic societies are comprised of two primary classes: the ***bourgeoisie*** (or ***capitalist***) ***class* that owns the means of production (e.g., the factories, tools, machines, and other resources used in production), and the *proletariat* (or *working class*) comprised of propertyless individuals who must sell their labor power to secure a livelihood.** According to Marx, capitalists constitute a dominant, or ruling, class that maintains its position through control of society's *superstructure*—the government, schools, churches, mass media, and other institutions responsible for the production and dissemination of ideas. Marx argued that "the ideas of the ruling class are in every epoch the ruling ideas" (Tucker, 1979:172).

According to Marx, class relationships involve inequality and exploitation. Workers are exploited because they must sell their labor power to capitalists, and in the process, forfeit control over their work and the labor process. Not only do workers no longer own the products they produce but capitalists also can expropriate a surplus value from their labor by paying the workers less than the resale value of what they produce. Consider a 10-hour work shift, for example: If the cost of the worker's pay is recovered after 6 hours' work, the capitalist appropriates the remaining 4 hours' production as surplus value—or a profit—the key element in a capitalist enterprise. And what do contemporary members of the working class get in return? According to Gregory Mantsios:

> *Most of them work at physically exhausting, mind-deadening jobs that require both physical strength and mental stamina. Many work a second job after hours or on weekends in order to get by. In some cases, they earn no more than the minimum wage. Even those who do earn considerably more cannot be sure that they will have employment throughout the year. For the construction workers . . . there will be only twenty-six weeks of work this year. (1995:233)*

Marx predicted that, due to capitalist exploitation, the workers would become alienated from the labor process and all other human beings, overthrow the capitalists, take over the state, and create a more egalitarian society.

Why has no workers' revolution occurred? According to scholars, as some workers grew tired of toiling for the benefit of capitalists, they banded together to form ***labor unions*—groups of employees who join together to bargain with employers over wages, benefits, and working conditions.** Mantsios notes that many of his evening students are able to enroll in college because they are members of unions that established educational funds to enable them to pursue a degree:

> *As I look around the room, I am struck by [the fact that] all this is made possible by labor unions—those institutions that have somehow become a dirty word in the U.S. . . .*
>
> *Yet it is these very organizations that are providing working people both with social services and self-respect. As many in the room will tell you, it is the union that fights for their rights, protects them from hazardous working conditions, and brings them a modicum of dignity in the workplace. It is also the union that fights for the social services so many poor and working people depend on and provides these services when government fails to do so or to do so adequately. (1995:232)*

Although Marx's analysis has been widely critiqued, it has been the foundation for other class perspectives, including the works of contemporary theorist Erik Olin Wright. According to Wright, four criteria are important for determining contemporary social classes:

1. Ownership of the means of production
2. Purchase of the labor of others (employing others)
3. Control of the labor of others (supervising others on the job)
4. Sale of one's own labor (being employed by someone else)

Based on these criteria, he identified four classes: the capitalist class, the managerial class, the small-business class, and the working class.

The *capitalist class* controls wealth and power through ownership of capital in the form of banks, corporations, factories, mines, news and entertainment industries, and agribusiness firms. Members of the capitalist class may possess inherited fortunes, own major corporations, or hold positions as top corporate executives with extensive stock holdings and substantial control over global investments, profits, and resources. In Article 6, Stephen Richard Higley points out that capitalist-class families currently listed in the *Social Register* are direct descendants of men who made great fortunes during the Gilded Age (1870–1910), a time of major capitalist expansion in the U.S. economy.

The *managerial class* has substantial control over the means of production and over workers because managerial-class jobs entail some workplace decision making and supervision of others. Like other workers, however, members of the managerial class sell their labor to earn a livelihood. Professionals (e.g., physicians, attorneys, architects, accountants, and engineers) in corporate settings may control their own work, but they generally do not own the means of production or have supervisory authority over many people.

Race and gender also are important determinants of managerial-class position. As sociologist Elizabeth Higginbotham notes in Article 25, "If one looks below the surface, one can identify how racism remains embedded in the social structure. Instead of being evenly split between the private and public sectors, the majority of professional and managerial Black women are employed in the public sector" (1994:119). For Higginbotham, higher rates of public sector employment among African American women may be attributed, at least in part, to less discrimination in hiring in this segment of the labor market.

The *small-business class* consists of the small-business owners and skilled craftspeople who may hire a small number of employees but largely do their own work. Some members own businesses such as "mom and pop" grocery stores, retail clothing stores, and jewelry stores. Others are self-employed doctors, lawyers, and other professionals who earn relatively high incomes from the sale of specialized information and services.

The *working class* is composed of a number of subgroups, one of which is blue-collar workers, some of whom are highly skilled and well paid while others are unskilled and poorly paid. Skilled workers include electricians, plumbers, and carpenters; unskilled blue-collar workers include workers in laundries and those who clean tables in restaurants. White-collar workers also are members of the working class; they do not own the means of production, do not control the work of others, and are relatively powerless in the workplace. The white-collar portion of the working class includes secretaries, clerks, and sales workers who take orders from others and work under relatively constant supervision. According to Wright, the working class is the most exploited class category because the workers do not control even their own work.

In sum, both Marx and Wright define a *class* as a common structural position in regard to ownership of the means of production. However, Wright extends his definition of *class* to include control over the labor power of others (e.g., supervision of people on the job).

Class Perspectives Based on Max Weber

Although Max Weber (1864–1920) agreed with Marx's analysis of the economic divisions between capitalists and workers, he believed that no one factor was sufficient for defining people's location in the class structure. As a result, Weber developed a multidimensional approach to class that emphasizes the interplay among wealth, prestige, and power in determining class location.

Wealth is the value of all of a person's or family's economic assets, including income, personal property, and income-producing property. Persons with great wealth are able to consume freely, control other people's livelihoods, and monopolize costly privileges (such as education) for their children. In Article 6, Stephen Richard Higley notes that wealth enables elites to "pass through life with very little significant contact with other social classes" (1995:18). And in Article 15, sociologists Caroline Hodges Persell and Peter W. Cookson, Jr. show how elite schools are a vehicle for transmitting intergenerational privilege to wealthy children. By contrast, the absence of wealth (i.e., poverty) dramatically diminishes life chances, as shown in Part 3, in articles such as Robin L. Jarrett's, "Living Poor: Family Life among Single Parent, African-American Women" (Article 22).

Wealth, prestige, and power are separate continuums on which people can be ranked from high to low. *Prestige* **is the respect or regard with which a person or status position is regarded by others.** According to Weber, persons with high levels of prestige—such as fame, respect, honor, and esteem—tend to socialize with each other and become self-protective against outsiders. *Power* **is the ability of people or groups to carry out their own goals despite opposition from others.** The powerful shape society in accordance with their own interests and direct the actions of others. Based on Weber's analysis of the class structure, sociologists Dennis Gilbert and Joseph A. Kahl (1993) developed the following model of U.S. classes:

1. *The upper (or capitalist) class* is the wealthiest and most powerful U.S. class; members own substantial income-producing assets and operate on the national and international scene.
2. *The upper-middle class* is made up of highly educated professionals, such as physicians, attorneys, dentists, and corporate managers, as well as persons who derive large profits from family-owned businesses.
3. *The middle class* includes white-collar workers, such as lower-level professionals and managers, and skilled blue-collar workers.
4. *The working class* is comprised of semiskilled factory workers, clerks, salespeople, some workers in the service sector, and persons in *pink-collar occupations*—**relatively low-paying, nonmanual semiskilled positions primarily held by women (e.g., day-care workers, checkout clerks, and waitpersons).**
5. *The working poor* includes families that live from just above to just below the poverty line; they work in unskilled jobs, seasonal migrant employment in agriculture, lower-paid factory jobs, and service jobs (such as counter help at fast-food restaurants). White women and all people of color are overrepresented among the working poor.
6. *The underclass* (a term in disfavor with many sociologists) is made up of people who have experienced long-term deprivation; they have low education, low employability, low income, and, eventually, low self-esteem (Gilbert and Kahl, 1993). Some are unable to work because of age or disability; others experience discrimination based on race or ethnicity, as sociologists Kathryn M. Neckerman and Joleen Kirschenman point out in "Hiring Strategies, Racial Bias, and Inner-City Workers" (Article 24). Single mothers also are overrepresented in the underclass; however, Robin L. Jarrett argues (in Article 22) that many single mothers living in poverty "assess their options and make choices that allow them to forge meaningful lives despite the harsh economic conditions in which they and their children find themselves" (1994:45)

Class perspectives based on Weber focus on prestige and power—as well as on people's economic interests—but they usually do not systematically examine how race, class, and gender are interlocking systems of privilege or oppression within the U.S. class system.

Representing Racial Issues in Class Terms

Some analysts use class explanations to account for most racial-ethnic inequalities. From this perspective, members of the capitalist class engage in racial-ethnic exploitation primarily for economic reasons. Based on the early work of sociologist W. E. B. Du Bois (see Article 3), sociologist Oliver C. Cox (1948) suggested that African Americans were not enslaved due to visible racial characteristics such as skin color but because they were the cheapest source of labor and the best workers for heavy labor in the mines and on plantations. According to Cox, slavery was a by-product of the class structure and the profit motives of capitalists.

Contemporary scholars, including sociologist William Julius Wilson (1980, 1981, 1987), have argued that class is more important than race in explaining racial-ethnic inequalities. Wilson suggests, for instance, that many African Americans in inner cities have been more adversely impacted by economic conditions and corporate decisions—such as a decision to close or relocate factories that previously provided secure, well-paid jobs—than by racial bias and discrimination. According to Wilson, racial bias has not been eliminated, but it is a less important factor than class for explaining the current situation of African Americans. Critics note, however, that Wilson's analysis may describe the situation of some middle-class African Americans but does not address the widespread racism faced by people of color regardless of class position (Willie, 1978; Landry, 1987).

In the 1990s, for instance, sociologist Joe R. Feagin (Article 23) demonstrated the continuing significance of race and public discrimination in the lives of middle-class African Americans. Also, Kathryn M. Neckerman and Joleen Kirshenman (Article 24) found evidence that racial bias severely limits employment opportunities for people of color in central-city areas.

Representing Class Issues in Racial Terms

While some analysts see racial-ethnic inequalities as a by-product of the class structure, others describe class issues in racial terms. In Article 1, Howard Winant argues that conservative/reactionary politicians attempt to disguise class issues in racial terms (e.g., quotas and reverse discrimination). In recent years, for example, the insistence of people of color on the continuing significance of race and racism was viewed as outdated and unfair by some analysts. When the Regents of the University of California System voted in 1995 to abolish affirmative action policies on campuses, they considered class-based criteria for admissions and hiring to be more acceptable. Based on Winant's article, decisions such as this are grounded in the false assumption that race (and gender) inequalities either no longer exist or that they can be reduced to class in-equality—a myth that he decries. According to Winant, contemporary issues of equality and fairness must be assessed in light of race, class, and gender, and in an environment that accepts and celebrates difference and diversity.

An Overview of Gender

Like race and ethnicity, gender is a social construct, not a biologically deter-mined reality. Economists Teresa Amott and Julie Matthaei explain:

> *Gender differences in the social lives of men and women are based on, but are not the same thing as, biological differences between the sexes. Gender is rooted in so-cieties' beliefs that the sexes are naturally distinct and opposed social beings. These beliefs are turned into self-fulfilling prophecies through sex-role socializa-tion: the biological sexes are assigned distinct and often unequal work and polit-ical positions, and turned into socially distinct genders. (1991:13)*

Amott and Matthaei suggest that a distinction must be made between sex and gender. *Sex* **is the biological and anatomical differences between females and males;** *gender* **is the culturally and socially constructed differences be-tween females and males** found in the meanings, beliefs, and practices asso-ciated with femininity and masculinity.

In Article 7, sociologist Judith Lorber suggests that people are uncomfort-able until they can successfully place another person in a gender status. As a re-sult, they tend to be confused and disturbed by lesbians and gays, bisexuals, transsexuals (persons who are genetically of one sex but have the gender iden-tity of the other sex and may alter their genitalia in order to have a body that is congruent with their own sense of gender identity), and transvestites (per-sons who dress in opposite-gender clothes but do not alter their genitalia). Ac-cording to Lorber, many transsexuals and transvestites carefully construct their gender status as women or men—whichever they want to be—by adhering to the appearance and behavioral norms of the desired sex. Since their appearance and mannerisms fall within the range of what is expected from members of the other sex, transvestites may "pass" for members of that sex.

Sex and gender as social constructs are closely related to societal attitudes about *sexual orientation*—**a preference for emotional-sexual relationships with members of the opposite sex** (heterosexuality), **the same sex** (homo-sexuality), **or both** (bisexuality) (Lips, 1993). Some lesbians, gay males, and bi-sexuals are the collective objects of prejudice and discrimination based on an ideology of *compulsion heterosexism*—the belief that heterosexuality is the only acceptable sexual orientation. Societies that define the male role narrowly ("Be a man—don't let somebody push you around") and devalue the female role ("Quit crying like a girl—don't be a sissy") tend to base these views on *homophobia*—**the fear and hatred of homosexuals and homosexuality.**

As previously discussed, most *sex* differences actually are socially constructed *gender* differences (Gailey, 1987). Social and cultural processes define what females and males are, what they should do, and what sorts of relations should exist between them (Ortner and Whitehead, 1981). As Lorber notes, gender is a learned identity, and people "do gender" without even thinking about it.

A Microlevel Analysis of Gender

When one examines gender at the microlevel, one focuses on how people learn *gender roles*—**the attitudes, behavior, and activities that are socially defined as appropriate for each sex.** In Part Two, we will examine gender-role socialization and its impact on the lives of women and men. An analysis by sociologist Becky W. Thompson (Article 12), for example, shows how girls' socialization—across lines of race, class, and religion—may contribute to eating problems, such as anorexia and bulimia, and to negative perceptions of self-worth. In Article 13, sociologist Michael A. Messner links boys' socialization in sports with narrow societal definitions of masculinity and deeply embedded beliefs that reinforce patriarchy, or male dominance.

Although gender roles may be long-lasting, they are not rigid and may change over time. In two-parent families, for example, many contemporary fathers are taking a larger role in child care due to their wives being employed. Today, about 20 percent of all preschool children (under age 5) are cared for by their fathers while their mothers are at work (U.S. Bureau of the Census, 1994). As men emphasize the nurturant components of parenting, they redefine some aspects of their *gender identity*—**a person's perception of the self as female or male.** However, modification of traditional gender roles may be involuntary for some men and women. Changing economic conditions in the United States have produced changes in some families. When corporations restructure (reorganize) or downsize (reduce the size of their workforce), for example, many middle-class jobs are eliminated. When U.S. corporations relocate their plants to other countries, many well-paid working-class jobs disappear, and workers and their families may find themselves in economically depressed areas of the country without a paycheck, without health insurance and other benefits, and with scarce employment opportunities. For a variety of reasons, the mothers of young children in two-parent families increasingly have entered (or reentered) the paid workforce in recent years. In 1993, for example, 60 percent of women with children under age 6 were in the labor force (U.S. Bureau of the Census, 1994).

Although changes in gender roles have occurred in some two-paycheck families, traditional gender roles still remain strong. Even when wives are employed full time, they still do about two-thirds of the housework, and their *second shift* of unpaid labor in the home typically consists of work that must be scheduled daily (e.g., feeding children dinner and getting them ready for bed).

By contrast, the chores husbands are most likely to perform do not have to be done daily (e.g., mowing the grass or having the car serviced) and allow for more flexible scheduling (e.g., taking children to the park) (Hochschild and Machung, 1989). Some women in two-paycheck families still do all of the household chores.

Gender identity is closely related to **body consciousness—how a person perceives and feels about his or her body.** In Article 8, sociologists Diana Dull and Candace West examine the gendered nature of body consciousness through their investigation of how people decide to undergo elective cosmetic surgical procedures to change facial or bodily features. The authors highlight the interlocking nature of gender, race, and class in these decisions. For example, Dull and West state that surgeons and patients make decisions about cosmetic surgery on the basis of what is supposedly normal and natural for women or men: Women's body consciousness is viewed as *essential* to their nature as women, whereas men's body consciousness is viewed as job-related or based on other extrinsic factors that do not relate to their nature as men. Some surgeons and patients view distinctive racial or ethnic features as *subjective* indicators that surgical intervention is necessary to enhance the appearance of people (particularly women) of color. An *objective* indicator regarding cosmetic surgery is the class background of the patient, who must be able to pay for the procedure since almost no cosmetic surgery is covered by insurance companies, health maintenance organizations (HMOs), or state-funded health-care programs.

A Macrolevel Analysis of Gender

As compared with microlevel analyses of gender roles and gender identity, macrolevel analyses of gender focus on structural features, external to the individual, that reinforce existing gender ideologies and perpetuate social inequalities. According to Judith Lorber (Article 7), gender is one of the major ways by which social life is organized in all sectors of society. Large-scale organizations and institutions are **gendered institutions—meaning that gender is used as a means to divide up work and allocate scarce resources.** In Article 9, sociologist Robin Leidner suggests that a specific job is given meaning based on its association with a particular gender. Leidner compares the experiences of interactive service workers in the "window crew" (primarily women) at McDonald's with life insurance agents (primarily men) at Combined Insurance Company of America. Although McDonald's and Combined Insurance Company have different products and organizational structures, work at both is routinized and gender segregated. *Routinization of labor* refers to the process by which the work performed by employees progresses according to predetermined rules under which workers need to know only one basic routine (Leidner, 1993:28).

According to Leidner, workers at both sites attempted to explain why their jobs were gender segregated and how their jobs were congruent with proper gender enactment. Workers at McDonald's, for example, explained the predominance of women on window crews by suggesting that women are more interested in dealing with people, that they have more nimble fingers for working the registers, and that they tend to look more presentable. By contrast, life insurance agents explained the predominance of male agents in their organization by asserting that women would be unlikely to succeed because the job requires a high level of determination and a so-called killer instinct—attributes the agents did not identify with women's gender roles.

Workers are not the only persons affected by gender-segregated jobs. As Leidner suggests, the public sees work done predominantly by women or by men as a confirmation that females and males have different natures and capabilities:

> *One of the most striking aspects of the social construction of gender is that its accomplishment creates the impression that gender differences in personality, interests, character, appearance, manner, and competence are natural, and not social constructions at all. Gender segregation of work reinforces this appearance of naturalness. When jobholders are all of the same gender, it seems as though people of that gender must be especially well suited to the work, even if at other times and places the other gender does the same work. (Leidner, 1993:194)*

Assumptions about so-called natural differences in men and women are maintained and reinforced by a *gendered belief system*—**all of the ideologies and assumptions regarding masculine and feminine attributes that are held to be valid in society.** Although the actual features of many jobs may not determine whether the work is defined as more appropriate for women or men, their gender appropriateness often is determined by beliefs held by workers, supervisors, and others regarding specific features of the jobs.

Perspectives on the Gendered Division of Labor

Social scientists offer a variety of explanations for the gendered division of labor in society. According to a classical *functionalist perspective,* distinct sex roles are essential not only for individuals and families but also for societal stability. Functionalists view society as a system made up of interdependent institutions (e.g., the family, education, religion, government, and the economy) that function together to preserve social order and stability. According to sociologist Talcott Parsons (1955), *instrumental* tasks (e.g., earning an income and making family decisions) usually are allocated to men, whereas *expressive* tasks (e.g., providing affection and emotional support for family members) are allocated to women. Division of labor by gender provides stability for family members and also ensures that important societal functions—including the reproduction and socialization of children—will be fulfilled. Writing four decades ago, Parsons did not examine issues such as class differences in gender roles, the gendered division of labor in the workplace, or the experiences of women and men of color. However, in Article 17, sociologists Jill Quadagno and Catherine Fobes document how the Job Corps—a core antipoverty program—taught young African American women from low-income backgrounds "a particular bourgeoisie family ideology in which women played a special role as dependent wife and mother" (Arnot, 1982:71, quoted in Quadagno and Fobes, 1995:186). Although the women received training that enhanced their occupational opportunities, the program also specifically prepared women—but not men—for the marriage and family market.

Another perspective that shares similar intellectual roots with functionalism is the *human capital model,* which asserts that the type of work people do and what they earn is a factor of their own choices (e.g., the amount of training, education, and experience—human capital—they accumulate) and the labor market need (demand) for and availability (supply) of certain kinds of workers at specific times. From this perspective, people bring different amounts of human capital with them to the labor market and are rewarded for the human capital they have acquired. But are people with the same amount of human capital sometimes rewarded differently in the job market? In Article 25, sociologist Elizabeth Higginbotham demonstrates that black professional women who have gained access to education in traditional male fields may not receive the same return on their human capital investment as white women. While black professional women are more likely to be employed in public sector jobs that pay lower salaries and are subject to budget cuts, white professional women are more likely to be employed in the private sector.

Conflict perspectives on the gendered division of labor differ significantly from theories based on functionalism and the human capital model. According to many conflict analysts, the gendered division of labor within families and the workplace results from male control and dominance over women and resources. In industrial societies, men hold most elite positions in corporations, the professions, the mass media, and the government. Through the institution of monogamous marriage, which was established to ensure the paternity of offspring (especially sons) to whom they wanted to leave their wealth, men of the capitalist class not only gained control over property and the distribution of goods but also over women.

Feminist perspectives are based on the belief that women and men are equal and should be valued equally and have equal rights. Many men, as well as women, advocate feminism and seek to identify ways in which norms, roles, institutions, and internalized expectations limit women's behavior. However, some feminist scholars also seek to demonstrate how women resist oppression in a society that tends to value men over women and masculine over feminine attributes. Branches of feminism include liberal feminists, radical feminists, socialist feminists, and black feminists.

For *liberal feminists,* gender equality is regarded as equal opportunity. Advocating reform *within* existing social structures, liberal feminists typically do not challenge patriarchy or capitalism. Instead, they advocate changes in laws that they believe will advance women's economic and political positions (e.g., equal employment and educational opportunities). In Article 19, sociologist Emily W. Kane notes, for example, that nineteenth-century U.S. feminists struggled for equal educational access as a route to expanding women's independence and opportunities. However, she also notes that a higher level of education among U.S. women and men today does not necessarily mean that they will challenge existing gender inequalities in the home or embrace group-based remedies—such as collective action and government policy—for gender inequality.

As compared with liberal feminists, *radical feminists* argue that patriarchy is the root of all human oppression, including racism and classism. Some analysts point out that patriarchy is grounded in biological differences between men and women. Pregnancy and child-care responsibilities make women dependent on men. However, radical feminist scholar Shulamith Firestone and others have suggested that patriarchy could be eliminated:

> *So that just as to assure elimination of economic classes requires the revolt of the underclass (the proletariat) and . . . their seizure of the means of **production**, so to assure the elimination of sexual classes requires the revolt of the underclass (women) and the seizure of control of **reproduction**: not only the full restoration to women of ownership of their own bodies, but also their (temporary) seizure of control of human fertility. . . . The end goal of feminist revolution must be . . . not just the elimination of male **privilege** but of the sex **distinction** itself: genital differences between human beings would no longer matter culturally.* (1984:140)

However, as scholar Robert Jensen suggests in Article 26, patriarchy will be abolished only when men—as well as women—begin to take feminism seriously and personally. According to Jensen, no man in mainstream contemporary U.S. culture escapes sexist training: "Sexism is institutionalized; sexist behavior and values are widely seen as normal or natural and continue unless there is active intervention to counter them" (1995:122). As a result, oppression goes unchecked if men are unwilling to reassess male privilege in light of their own early socialization and gender identity.

Socialist feminists suggest that employed women experience dual oppression: They face patriarchal exploitation at home and capitalistic exploitation in the workplace. Gendered job segregation is the primary mechanism by which male superiority is maintained in a capitalist society; a gendered division of labor enforces lower wages for women in the workplace (Hartmann, 1976). Consequently, women must do domestic labor either to gain a better-paid man's economic support or to stretch their own wages (Lorber, 1994). According to socialist feminists, gender equality will not occur until patriarchy and capitalism are eliminated and a socialist economy with equal pay and rights for women is established.

Black feminist perspectives are based on the belief that African American women experience a different world than other people because of multilayered oppression based on race/ethnicity, gender, and class (Collins, 1990). According to black feminist scholars such as Patricia Hill Collins, race, class, and gender are simultaneous forces of oppression for African American women. The experiences of African American women and other previously "silenced people" must be heard and examined within the context of particular historical and social conditions.

Feminists who analyze race, class, and gender suggest that equality will occur only when all women—regardless of race, ethnic group, class, age, religion, sexual orientation, or ability/disability—are treated more equitably (Andersen and Collins, 1995).

As we conclude our overview of race, class, and gender, recall their interlocking nature as you read the articles in Part One.

References

Amott, Teresa, and Julie Matthaei. 1991. *Race, Gender, and Work: A Multicultural Economic History of Women in the United States.* Boston: South End Press.

Andersen, Margaret L., and Patricia Hill Collins. 1995. *Race, Class, and Gender: An Anthology* (2nd ed.). Belmont, CA: Wadsworth.

Ayers, Ian. 1991. "Fair Driving: Gender and Race Discrimination in Retail Car Negotiations." *Harvard Law Review,* 104:817.

Berreman, Gerald D. 1960. "Caste in India and the United States." *American Journal of Sociology,* 66:120–127.

Collins, Patricia Hill. 1990. *Black Feminist Thought: Knowledge, Consciousness, and the Politics of Entitlement.* London: HarperCollins Academic.

———. 1995. "Symposium: On West and Fenstermaker's 'Doing Difference.'" *Gender & Society* 9(4)(August):491–494.

Cox, Oliver C. 1948. *Caste, Class, and Race.* Garden City, NY: Doubleday.

Daniels, Roger. 1993. *Prisoners Without Trial: Japanese-Americans in World War II.* New York: Hill & Wang.

Dollard, John. 1957/1937. *Caste and Class in a Southern Town.* Garden City, NY: Doubleday.

Du Bois, W. E. B. 1989/1903. *The Souls of Black Folk by W. E. B. Du Bois.* Introduction by Henry Louis Gates, Jr. New York: Bantam.

Dyson, Michael Eric. 1996. "Interview with O.J. Simpson: Life After the Verdict." (January 24) BET (Black Entertainment Television) Network. (See also: Dyson, Michael Eric. 1996. "Obsessed with O.J.: Meditations on an American Tragedy," in Michael Eric Dyson (Ed.), *Between God and Gangsta Rap: Bearing Witness to Black Culture* (pp. 25–39). New York: Oxford University Press.)

Feagin, Joe R., and Clairece Booher Feagin. 1996. *Racial and Ethnic Relations* (5th ed.). Englewood Cliffs, NJ: Prentice Hall.

Firestone, Shulamith. 1970. *The Dialectic of Sex.* New York: William Morrow.

———. 1984. "The Dialectic of Sex," in Allison M. Jaggar and Paula S. Rothenberg (Eds.), *Feminist Frameworks: Alternative Theoretical Accounts of the Relations between Women and Men* (2nd ed.) (pp. 136–143). New York: McGraw-Hill.

Fredrickson, George M. 1981. *White Supremacy: A Comparative Study in American and South African History.* New York: Oxford University Press.

Gailey, Christin Ward. 1987. "Evolutionary Perspectives on Gender Hierarchy," in Beth B. Hess and Myra Marx Ferree (Eds.), *Analyzing Gender: A Handbook of Social Science Research* (pp. 32–67). Newbury Park, CA: Sage.

Gilbert, Dennis, and Joseph A. Kahl. 1993. *The American Class Structure: A New Synthesis* (4th ed.). Belmont, CA: Wadsworth.

Gould, Stephen J. 1994. "The Geometry of Race." *Discover* (November):65–66.

———. 1995. "Mismeasure by Any Measure," in Russell Jacoby and Naomi Glauberman (Eds.), *The Bell Curve Debate: History, Documents, Opinions* (pp. 3–13). New York: Times Books.

Hall, Ronald E. 1995. "The Color Complex: The Bleaching Syndrome." *Race, Gender & Class,* 2(2) (Winter):99–109.

Haney Lopez, Ian F. 1995. "The Social Construction of Race," in Richard Delgado (Ed.), *Critical Race Theory: The Cutting Edge* (pp. 191–203). Philadelphia: Temple University Press. Reprinted from *Harvard Civil Rights–Civil Liberties Law Review* 29(1994):1.

Hartmann, Heidi. 1976. "Capitalism, Patriarchy, and Job Segregation by Sex." *Signs: Journal of Women in Culture and Society* 1(Spring):137–169.

Herrnstein, Richard J., and Charles Murray. 1994. *The Bell Curve: Intelligence and Class Structure in American Life.* New York: Free Press.

Higginbotham, Elizabeth. 1994. "Black Professional Women: Job Ceilings and Employment Sectors," in Maxine Baca Zinn and Bonnie Thornton Dill (Eds.), *Women of Color in U.S. Society* (pp. 113–131). Philadelphia: Temple University Press.

Higley, Stephen Richard. 1995. *Privilege, Power, and Place: The Geography of the American Upper Class.* Lanham, MD: Rowman & Littlefield.

Hochschild, Arlie Russell, with Anne Machung. 1989. *The Second Shift.* New York: Viking.

Hudgins v. Wright, 11 Va. 134 (1 Hen. & M.) (Sup.Ct.App.1806), quoted in Haney Lopez, 1995:191–192.

Hurst, Charles E. 1992. *Social Inequality: Forms, Causes, and Consequences.* Boston: Allyn and Bacon.

Jarrett, Robin L. 1994. "Living Poor: Family Life among Single Parent, African-American Women." *Social Problems,* 41(1):30–49.

Jensen, Robert. 1995. "Men's Lives and Feminist Theory." *Race, Gender, & Class,* 2(2)(Winter):111–125.

Jordan, Winthrop D. 1969. *White over Black.* Baltimore: Penguin.

Kleinfield, N. R. 1995. "A Day (10 Minutes of It) the Country Stood Still." *New York Times* (October 4):A1,A12.

Landry, Bart. 1987. *The New Black Middle Class.* Berkeley: University of California Press.

Leidner, Robin. 1993. *Fast Food, Fast Talk: Service Work and the Routinization of Everyday Life.* Berkeley: University of California Press.

Lips, Hilary M. 1993. *Sex & Gender: An Introduction* (2nd ed.). Mountain View, CA: Mayfield.

Lorber, Judith. 1994. *Paradoxes of Gender.* New Haven, CT: Yale University Press.

Mantsios, Gregory. 1995. "Living and Learning: Some Reflections on Emergence from and Service to the Working Class," in Janet Zandy (Ed.), *Liberating Memory: Our Work and Our Working-Class Consciousness* (pp. 231–248). New Brunswick, NJ: Rutgers University Press.

Ollman, Bertell. 1968. "Marx's Use of Class." *American Journal of Sociology,* 73:573–580.

Omi, Howard, and Howard Winant. 1994. *Racial Formation in the United States: From the 1960s to the 1990s.* New York: Routledge.

Ortner, Sherry B., and Harriet Whitehead (Eds.). 1981. *Sexual Meanings: The Cultural Construction of Gender and Sexuality*. Cambridge: Cambridge University Press.

Parsons, Talcott. 1955. "The American Family: Its Relations to Personality and to the Social Structure," in Talcott Parsons and Robert F. Bailes (Eds.), *Family, Socialization and Interaction Process* (pp. 3–33). Glencoe, IL: The Free Press.

Quadagno, Jill, and Catherine Fobes. 1995. "The Welfare State and the Cultural Reproduction of Gender." *Social Problems*, 42(2):171–190.

Takaki, Ronald. 1993. *A Different Mirror: A History of Multicultural America*. Boston: Little, Brown.

Tucker, Robert C. (Ed.). 1979. *The Marx-Engels Reader* (2nd ed.). New York: Norton.

United States Army, Western Defense Command and Fourth Army. 1943. *Japanese in the United States, Final Report: Japanese Evacuation from the West Coast*. Washington, DC: U.S. Government Printing Office.

U.S. Bureau of the Census. 1994. *Statistical Abstract of the United States, 1993*. Washington, DC: U.S. Government Printing Office.

Willie, Charles V. 1978. "The Inclining Significance of Race." *Society*, 15(July/August):10–15.

Wilson, William Julius. 1980. *The Declining Significance of Race* (2nd ed.). Chicago: University of Chicago Press.

———. 1981. "Race, Class, and Public Policy." *American Sociologist*, 16:125–134.

———. 1987. *The Truly Disadvantaged: The Inner City, the Underclass, and Public Policy*. Chicago: University of Chicago Press.

Winant, Howard. 1994. *Racial Conditions: Politics, Theory, Comparisons*. Minneapolis: University of Minnesota Press.

Wirth, Louis. 1945. "The Problem of Minority Groups," in Ralph Linton (Ed.), *The Science of Man in the World Crisis* (p. 38). New York: Columbia University Press.

Yinger, J. Milton. 1994. *Ethnicity: Source of Strength? Source of Conflict?* Albany: State University of New York Press.

ARTICLE 1 _____

In this article, sociologist Howard Winant emphasizes the importance of race in understanding U.S. society. He also explains the ***racial formation perspective***—**the view that in modern societies, race must be seen as an ever-changing complex of meanings shaped by sociopolitical conflict.** According to this approach, race is not a fixed, concrete, objective, natural attribute; rather, it is a *socially* and *historically* constructed attribute. Winant defines *race* as a concept that signifies and symbolizes sociopolitical conflicts and interests in reference to different types of human bodies. In the article, he shows how racial meanings are attributed and racial identities assigned in a given society.

According to Winant, U.S. racial history has shifted from domination to ***hegemony***—**the means by which members of a societal ruling class convince people in other classes that the ruling-class interests are universal interests shared by everyone.** As a result, members of the ruling class must maintain—through education, the media, and religion, for example—a popular system of ideas regarding these so-called universal interests so that they can retain their privileged position in society.

Howard Winant teaches in the Department of Sociology at Temple University where he has also served as director of the Latin American Studies Center. He is coauthor (with Michael Omi) of *Racial Formation in the United States from the 1960s to the 1980s* (1994) and author of *Stalemate: Political Economic Origins of Supply-Side Policy* (1988) and *Racial Conditions: Politics, Theory, Comparisons* (1994), from which this article was taken.

Looking Ahead

1. Why does the United States face a pervasive crisis of race?
2. How would you explain racial formation theory in your own words?
3. What effect did the black movement upsurge during the 1950s and 1960s have on the U.S. racial order?
4. Why do a wide variety of contemporary political groups seek to advance their own conception of the significance of race in contemporary U.S. society?

Source: Howard Winant, *Racial Conditions: Politics, Theory, Comparisons* (Minneapolis: University of Minnesota Press, 1994), pp. 22–36. Copyright © 1994 by Howard Winant. Reprinted by permission.

Where Culture Meets Structure

Race in the 1990s

◆ *Howard Winant*

The contemporary United States faces a pervasive crisis of race, a crisis no less severe than those the country has confronted in the past. The origins of the crisis are not particularly obscure: the cultural and political meaning of race, its significance in shaping the social structure, and its experiential or existential dimensions all remain profoundly unresolved as the United States approaches the end of the twentieth century. As a result, the society as a whole, and the population as individuals, suffer from confusion and anxiety about the issue (or complex of issues) we call race.

This should not be surprising. We may be more afflicted with anxiety and uncertainty over race than we are over any other social or political issue. Racial conflict is the very archetype of discord in North America, the primordial conflict that has in many ways structured all others. Time and time again what has been defined as "the race problem" has generated ferocious antagonisms: between slaves and masters, between natives and settlers, between new immigrants and established residents, and between workers divided by wage discrimination, by culture, even by psychosexual antagonisms (Roediger 1991). Time and time again this "problem" has been declared resolved, or perhaps supplanted by other supposedly more fundamental conflicts, only to blaze up anew. Tension and confusion in postwar racial politics and culture are merely the latest episode in this seemingly permanent drama.

The persistence of racial conflict, and of the anxiety and confusion that accompany it, has defied the predictions of most govern-ment officials, social critics, and movement leaders. Until quite recently, mainstream economists and Marxists, liberals and conservatives, ethnicity theorists and nationalists all expected the dissolution of race in some greater entity: free market or class struggle, cultural pluralism or nation-state. That race remains so central a factor both in the U.S. social structure and in the collective psyche, ought—at the very least—to inject a bit of humility into the discourses of all these sages.

Thus chastened, let us enter once more into the thickets of *racial theory.* No task is more urgent today. The mere fact that basic racial questions are at once so obvious and so obviously unanswered suggests how urgent is further theoretical work on race. Still, one must approach the effort modestly, for the concept of race in some ways is as large as social theory itself.

My strategy here is to examine contemporary U.S. racial dynamics from the standpoint of *racial formation theory,* an approach developed specifically to address the shifting meanings and power relationships inherent in race today. I begin with some basic propositions about racial formation. Then I look at recent U.S. racial history, which, I suggest, is in transition from a pattern of domination to one of *hegemony.* Next I discuss the range of contemporary racial projects, focusing on the contest for racial hegemony. Finally, I assess the system of racial hegemony in the 1990s.

RACIAL FORMATION THEORY

Racial formation theory was developed as a response to postwar understandings of race, both mainstream and radical, that practiced reductionism. By this I mean the explanation of racial phenomena as manifestations of some other, supposedly more significant, social relationship. Examples of racial reductionism include treatments of racial dynamics as epiphenomena of class relationships, or as the result of "national oppression," or as variations on the ethnicity paradigm established in the early twentieth century, after successive waves of European immigration.

In contrast to these approaches, racial formation theory looks at race as a phenomenon whose meaning is contested throughout social life (Omi and Winant 1986). In this account race is both a constituent of the individual psyche and of relationships among individuals, and an irreducible component of collective identities and social structures.

Because race is not a "natural" attribute but a socially and historically constructed one, it becomes possible to analyze the processes by which racial meanings are attributed, and racial identities assigned, in a given society. These processes of "racial signification" are inherently discursive. They are variable, conflictual, and contested at every level of society, from the intrapsychic to the supranational. Inevitably, many interpretations of race, many racial discourses, exist at any given time. The political character of the racial formation process stems from this: elites, popular movements, state agencies, cultural and religious organizations, and intellectuals of all types develop *racial projects*, which interpret and reinterpret the meaning of race.

The theoretical concept of racial projects is a key element of racial formation theory. *A racial project is simultaneously an interpretation, representation, or explanation of racial dynamics and an effort to organize and distribute resources along particular racial lines.* Every

project is therefore both a discursive and a cultural initiative, an attempt at racial signification and identity formation on the one hand, and a social structural initiative, an attempt at political mobilization and resource redistribution, on the other.

Interpreting the meaning of race is thus a multidimensional process in which competing "projects" intersect and clash. These projects are often explicitly, but always at least implicitly, political. Racial projects potentially draw both on phenomena that are "objective" or institutional and on those that are "subjective" or experiential. That such social structural phenomena as movements and parties, state institutions and policies, market processes, and so forth should be the source of political initiatives regarding race is hardly controversial. Racial formation theory, however, also finds the source of "projects" in less familiar social practices: in the manipulation and rearticulation of racial identities by their bearers, in the enunciation and transformation of racial "common sense," and in the various subversive, evasive, or parodic forms of racial opposition that closely resemble other forms of subordinated and postcolonial resistance (Scott 1985; Bhabha 1990a). In a later section of this essay I offer a "map," in table form, of contemporary U.S. racial projects.

RECENT U.S. RACIAL HISTORY: FROM DOMINATION TO HEGEMONY

From this theoretical vantage point, I propose now to examine, in what must necessarily be a fairly schematic account, the evolution of U.S. racial politics in the postwar period. To frame this account properly, let me present my key argument at the outset. The black movement upsurge of the 1950s and 1960s ended the epoch of racial domination and initiated the epoch of racial hegemony. The achievement of the movement was its initiation of sweeping political and cultural changes: it created new organizations, new political norms, new collective identities, new modalities of expression and representation; it challenged past racial practices and stereotypes; and it ushered in a wave of democratizing social reform, which ultimately extended well beyond the issue of race.

The Pre–Civil Rights Era

In the pre–civil rights era the U.S. racial order was maintained largely, though of course not exclusively, through *domination.* The most visible manifestations of this regime were all enforced by coercive means: segregation, racial exclusion, and physical violence culminating in extralegal terror. Periodic mob assaults on urban ghettos and barrios, deportations to Mexico in the Southwest, outright extermination and plunder of native peoples, anti-Asian pogroms, physical intimidation and murder by police, and of course the practice of lynching were all fairly characteristic of this epoch (McMillen 1989; Montejano 1987; Takaki 1990; Omi and Winant, 1986: 73–74). It was not until well into the twentieth century, and even then only in certain areas where racially defined minorities had been able to establish themselves in large numbers and to initiate negotiations between the white establishment and minority elites, that a measure of "protection," and even patronage and political influence, were sometimes available. But even these gains were highly limited and fragile.

The Political Effects of the Black Movement

The black movement upsurge changed all that. It permitted the entry of millions of racial minority group members into the political process—first blacks, and later Latinos, Asian Americans, and Native Americans. It initiated a trajectory of reform that exposed the limits of all previously existing political orientations—conservative, liberal, and radical. With very few exceptions, all these currents had colluded with the denial of fundamental political rights to members of racially defined minorities.

The aftermath of this prodigious movement upsurge was a racial order in which *domination was replaced by hegemony.* Political mobilization along racial lines resulted in the enactment of reforms that dramatically restructured the racial order, reorganized state institutions, and initiated whole new realms of state activity. The achievement of the franchise, the establishment of limited but real avenues of economic and social mobility, the destruction of de jure segregation, the reform of immigration law, and the institution of a measure of state enforcement of civil rights were but a few of the movement's more dramatic accomplishments.

The Cultural Effects of the Black Movement

Furthermore, by transforming the meaning of race and the contours of racial politics, the racially based movements also transformed the meaning and contours of American culture. Indeed, they made identity, difference, the "personal," and language itself political issues in very new ways. They made mainstream society—that is, white people—take notice of "difference"; they created awareness not only of different racial identities, but also of the multiple differences inherent in U.S. culture and society. In short, the new movements vastly expanded the terrain of politics and transfigured U.S. culture.

Thus, where U.S. culture previously had been monolithic and stratified, and indeed racially segregated ("race records," segregated media, etc.), it now became far more polyvalent, far more complexly articulated. Without being able to argue the point fully, I think it fair to assert that since the mid-1950s—I am taking as a fairly arbitrary demarcating point the advent of rock and roll—U.S. culture has adopted a far more pluralistic cast. With respect to race, this means that genres of music, art, and language retain their bases in particular communities while at the same time "crossing over" with far greater regularity than was previously the case. Cultural differences coexist without requiring any overarching synthesis, yet partial syntheses take place continually.

This does not mean that a "cultural revolution," along the lines proposed by Harold Cruse in the 1960s, has been or even could be achieved (Cruse 1968: 111–12). As in the political sphere, much of the increased presence of "darker" visions and "other" voices in the cultural sphere is the result of tokenism and co-optation. Pragmatic liberal practices advocating tolerance and diversity, rather than radical democratic practices celebrating difference, are the norm. Even granting all this, the present-day proliferation of artistic and popular cultural forms with roots in racially defined minority communities is quite astonishing when it is seen from a historical and comparative vantage point; much has changed in a few short decades. And this too must be judged an accomplishment of the movement.

The Racial Reaction

The achievements and legacy of the black movement were hardly greeted with universal acclaim. Various currents on the right strongly objected to the extension of an egalitarian racial awareness into everyday, indeed personal, life. Strong opposition arose to confront the newfound assertiveness and proliferation of cultural difference that the movement had fostered.

The very successes of the movement, however, set limits on the reaction that succeeded it. Because such movement themes as equality, group identity, and difference could not simply be rolled back, it became necessary, from the late 1960s onward, to rearticulate these ideas in a conservative ideological framework of competition, individualism, and homogeneity. In other words, since the movement's introduction of new political themes could not be undone, opponents had to learn how to manage these political themes as well.

This is why today's political debates about racial inequality are dominated by charges of "reverse discrimination" and repudiation of "quotas," why demands for "community control" have reappeared in opposition to school desegregation, and why high government officials claim that we are moving toward a "color-blind society." Cultural debates are dominated by the right's *rejection* of difference and "otherness" (whether racial, gender-based, sexual, or anything else). The right's strong defense of "traditional values," of individualism, and of mainstream culture, its discourse about family, nation, our "proud heritage of freedom," and so forth betokens intense resistance to the very idea of a polyvalent racial culture. Many of the notes struck by the right in contemporary cultural debates over race are, shall we say, white notes. They reflect a deep-seated fear, perhaps unconscious and only occasionally expressed, of the racialized other who has plagued the European for so long.

The "Decentering" of Racial Conflict

By the end of the 1960s the emancipatory effects of the black movement upsurge (and of its *sequelae* in other communities and constituencies) had been blunted by the racial reaction. Indeed, the dominant racial theory since World War II—ethnicity theory—which had once allied itself with the minority movements, reappeared as one of their chief theoretical antagonists: neoconservatism. Along with a reconstituted *far right,* the *new right* and *neoconservative* currents would emerge by the 1980s as three related but distinct right-wing racial projects.

Neoconservatism was largely an enterprise of intellectuals who sought to intervene in policy debates over race. Its chief concern was the threat to political and cultural traditions it discerned in racial minority demands for "group rights," or "equality of result." The *new right,* heir apparent of the 1960s backlash politics and the Wallace campaigns, was a far more grass-roots movement, linked to the religious conservatism fostered by some sectors of Catholicism and Protestant televangelism; it was a key component of every Republican presidential victory from 1968 to 1988. The *far right* was a more motley crew, consisting of the traditional assortment of bigots and race baiters, but also newly possessed of a modernized wing. The latter emerged in the mid-1980s when Klan leader and Nazi David Duke decided to swap his robe for a sport coat, get a blow-dried haircut, and undergo extensive plastic surgery, both on his face and in his rhetoric.

On the left, the movement upsurge fell victim to its own success. In the effort to adapt to the new racial politics they themselves had created, racial movements lost their unity and raison d'être. Working within the newly reformed racial state was more possible, and confronting it more difficult, than during the preceding period. Opposition to the backward and coercive racial order of the South had permitted a tenuous alliance between moderate and radical currents of the movement, an alliance that the winning of civil rights reforms ruptured. The "triumph" of liberal democracy failed to placate radicals who sought not only rights, but power and resources as well. The conferring of rights did not appreciably change the circumstances of a black youth in North Philly or a *vato loco* in East Los Angeles. What was heralded as a great victory by liberals appeared to radicals as merely a more streamlined version of racial oppression.

By the late 1960s, then, the U.S. racial order had largely absorbed the challenge posed by the civil rights movement, responding effectively—from the standpoint of rule—with a series of reforms. At the same time it had largely insulated itself from the more radical of its racial challengers—for example, revolutionary Marxist and nationalist currents—by drawing upon traditional coercive means, but also by exploiting the ideological weaknesses inherent in these viewpoints.

Over the following two decades what remained of the movement evolved into two loosely knit racial projects, those of the *pragmatic liberals* and of the *radical democrats.* In the former group I include the surviving civil rights organizations, the liberal religious establishment, and the Democratic party. In the latter group I include "grass-roots" organizations that continue to function at the local level, cultural radicals and nationalist groups that have avoided mystical and demagogic pitfalls, and survivors of the debacle of the socialist left who have retained their antiracist commitments.

This spectrum of racial projects, running from right to left, characterizes the United States today. In contrast to the earlier postwar period, the political logic of race in the United States is now "decentered," because the racial formation process operates in the absence of a coherent conflict. Only a comprehensive challenge to the racial order as a whole could generate such coherence. This decenteredness reflects not only the incomplete and fragmented character of the available racial projects, but also the complexity of contemporary racial politics and culture. None of the extant racial projects seems capable of presenting a durable and comprehensive vision of race. None can realistically address in even a minimally adequate way *both* the volatility of racial expression, meaning, and identities on the one hand, *and* the in-depth racialization of the social structure and political system in the United States. Indeed, such a totalizing vision of race may no longer be possible.

This decentered racial situation reflects an unprecedented level of societal uncertainty about race. The various racial projects listed here are merely efforts to advance one or another current, one or another political agenda, in a society wracked by racial anxiety and conflict. They may compete in the effort to construct a new racial hegemony, but they do not offer any real prospect of clarifying or resolving ambivalent racial meanings or identities. Despite occasional appearances to the contrary, the right-wing racial projects have no more gained racial hegemony than have those of the left. Rather, the state, business, media, and religious and educational institutions appear permanently divided, riven, inconsistent, and uncertain about racial conflicts and issues, much as we as individuals are confused and ambivalent.

THE SYSTEM OF RACIAL HEGEMONY: CONTEMPORARY U.S. RACIAL PROJECTS

Hegemony is a system in which politics operates largely through the *incorporation* of oppositional currents in the prevailing system of rule, and culture operates largely through the *reinterpretation* of oppositional discourse in the prevailing framework of social expression, representation, and debate. Of course, not everything in a hegemonic system works this way. For example, there is certainly plenty of room in contemporary U.S. racial politics and culture for exclusion, segregation, discrimination, malevolence, ignorance, and outright violence. Highlighting the hegemonic dimensions of present-day U.S. racial dynamics emphasizes the effects of several decades of racial formation processes and the qualitative shifts that have occurred in the meaning and structure of race since the movement upsurge of the 1960s.

Under hegemonic conditions, opposition and difference are not repressed, excluded, or silenced (at least not primarily). Rather, they are inserted, often after suitable modification, within a "modern" (or perhaps "postmodern") social order. Hegemony is therefore oxymoronic: it involves a splitting or doubling of opposition, which simultaneously wins and loses, gains entrance into the "halls of power" and is co-opted, "crosses over" into mainstream culture and is deprived of its critical content.

What is the logic of racial hegemony in the present-day United States? Today there can no longer be any single axis of racial domination and subordination. There can no longer be any explicitly segregationist politics, nor can there be forms of expressive culture reserved exclusively for whites. Just as these once-powerful forms of racial domination have been eroded or even destroyed, so too has opposition to them. Racial hegemony has gradually evolved from this situation, which is a crisis of the movement legacy of the 1960s.

Racial Hegemony and Racial Projects

The evolution of racial hegemony means that the outmoded antinomy of racial domination and racial subordination has been replaced by a range of racial projects whose "formation and superseding" (Gramsci) constitutes the process of racial formation in the United States.

In the contemporary United States, racial formation proceeds, and racial hegemony is organized, through the interplay of these projects. Hegemony operates through the adoption by the state, the media, large corporations, and other key societal institutions of political initiatives and cultural narratives drawn from competing racial projects. Through the state and the major parties, for example, racial policies are worked out across the entire national political agenda. Thomas Byrne Edsall and Mary D. Edsall describe some of the items on the agenda:

> *Considerations of race are now deeply imbedded in the strategy and tactics of politics, in competing concepts of the functions and responsibilities of government, and in each voter's conceptual structure of moral and partisan identity. Race helps define liberal and conservative ideologies, shapes the presidential coalitions of the Democratic and Republican parties, provides a harsh new dimension to concern over taxes and crime, drives a wedge through alliances of the working classes and the poor, and gives both momentum and vitality to the drive to establish a national majority inclined by income and demography to support policies benefiting the affluent and the upper middle class. (1991: 53)*

Race provides a key cultural marker, a central signifier, in the reproduction and expression of identity, collectivity, language, and agency itself. Race generates an "inside" and an "outside" of society, and mediates the unclear border between these zones; all social space, from the territory of the intrapsychic to that of the U.S. "national character," is fair game for racial dilemmas, doubts, fears, and desires. The conceptualization and representation of these sentiments, whether they are articulated in a track by Public En-emy or a television commercial for Jesse Helms, are framed in one or more racial projects.

By the 1980s, then, the racial order consisted of a range of conflicting *racial projects,* each descended from the days of racial domination and movement opposition, each seeking to advance its own conception of the significance of race in contemporary U.S. society. At the core of each project was a particular articulation of the culture and structure of race, of racial discourse and racial politics. This range of projects, which together constitute racial hegemony, can be "mapped," somewhat schematically, as shown in Table 1.

The linkage between culture and structure, which is at the core of the racial formation process, gives each project its coherence and unity. Indeed, once it is argued that the United States is inherently a "white man's country" (as in certain far right racial discourses), or that race is a spurious anachronism beneath the notice of the state (as in neoconservative positions), or that racial difference is a matter of "self-determination" (as in various radical democratic racial discourses), the appropriate political orientation, economic and social programs, and so forth follow quite naturally.

RACIAL HEGEMONY IN THE 1990s

Racial formation theory tells us that the racial order is in constant flux. Contested meanings and identities, conflict over political and economic resources, rivalries over territory and systems of cultural expression: these are the processes that continue to frame the complexities of race in the United States. Thus there is nothing eternal about the five racial projects outlined here. Indeed, they are presented somewhat schematically, in an effort to clarify divisions and antagonisms. In many respects the overlaps be-

TABLE 1 / Racial Hegemony in the United States (c. 1990)

CULTURE ← ARTICULATION → STRUCTURE

Project	Racial discourse: concept of identity, "difference" and the meaning of race	Political/programmatic agenda: orientation to the state, (in)equality, etc.
Far right	Represents race in terms of inherent, natural characteristics; rights and privileges assigned accordingly; traditional far right operates through terror; renovated far right organizes whites politically.	Open racial conflict; equality seen as a subversion of the "natural order"; the state is in the hands of the "race mixers." Whites need to form their own organizations, pressure the state for "white rights."
New right	Understands racial mobilization as a threat to "traditional values"; perceives racial meanings and identities as operating "subtextually"; engages in racial "coding"; articulates class and gender interests as racial.	Racial conflict focuses on the state; racial (in)equality determined by access to state institutions and relative political power.
Neoconservatism	Denies the salience of racial "difference," or argues that it is a vestige of the past, when invidious distinctions and practices had not yet been reformed; after the passage of civil rights laws, any collective articulation of racial "difference" amounts to "racism in reverse."	Conservative egalitarianism. Individualism, meritocracy, universalism. Rejection of any form of group rights; "color-blind" state.
Pragmatic liberalism	Racial identities serve to organize interests and channel political and cultural activities; as long as principles of pluralism and tolerance are upheld, a certain degree of group identity and racial mobilization can be accepted as the price of social peace.	Cultural and political pluralism; affirmative action as "goals, not quotas." State racial policy as moderating and eroding the legacy of discrimination.
Radical democracy	Racial difference accepted and celebrated; flexibility of racial identities; multiplicity and "decenteredness" of various forms of "difference," including race.	State racial policy as redistribution. Racial politics as part of "decentered" but interconnected pattern of "new social movements." Extension of democratic rights and of societal control over the state.

tween these five projects are as significant as the distinctions between them.

This last point is quite important, since ultimately, as Gramsci argued, hegemony is constructed out of differing social forces welded together in what he called a "historical bloc." For there are clear grounds for potential polarization in the five-part typology developed here: if racial hegemony today is in flux and divided among many initiatives, tomorrow it may be bifurcated among left and right currents.

Furthermore, the racial dimensions of political conflict and cultural representation are becoming ever more central as we approach the end of the twentieth century. Racial hegemony is converging in important respects with overall societal hegemony. In this situation the political and cultural currents that most effectively establish the link between racial "difference" and social inequality will win the contest for hegemony in the United States.

The right enjoys considerable privileges in this situation. Besides the institutional advantages realized during the Reagan and Bush years, right-wing racial projects have been able to portray minority racial identities, and minority insistence on the continuing significance of race and racism, as anachronistic, pernicious, and unfair. Left racial projects have only intermittently and partially succeeded in countering these views (as in the Jackson campaigns), and often appear mired in outmoded conceptions and proposals.

Indeed, at present throughout U.S. society, including in racially defined minority communities and on the left, there is an unwillingness to enter into discussions about race. This reluctance is not illogical: it is born of fear and bitter experience. But it is also politically dangerous. As the projects of the right advance a view of race that links difference and diversity to national weakness, economic decline, and widespread racist fears (Walters 1987), those on the left cannot refuse to debate the contemporary meaning of race and the programmatic alternatives before us. Such issues as the relationship among minority middle classes and "underclasses," the relevance of nationalist and integrationist traditions today, and, perhaps most centrally, the relationship between race and class must be extensively discussed in an atmosphere where dogma and orthodoxy are effectively resisted.

Race and Class

In the contemporary United States, hegemony is determined by the articulation of race and class. The ability of the right to represent class issues in racial terms is central to the current pattern of conservative racial hegemony. All three rightist projects—those of the far right, the new right, and the neoconservatives—partake of this logic. Conservative/reactionary politics today *disguises* class issues in racial terms. In so doing it builds on a thematic current that is as deep and wide as U.S. history itself. This theme can be called divide and conquer, dual/split labor markets, white-skin privilege, Eurocentrism, immigrant exclusion, or internal colonialism. Its clearest name is racism.

Conversely, any challenge to this current, any counterhegemonic initiative, must be *explicitly race-conscious* in its approach to issues of class or fall victim to the same hegemonic strategies that have doomed so many other progressive political initiatives. Traditional left politics have consistently failed to do this; they have steadily refused to afford race the centrality it receives on the right. Rather, left politics—both moderate and radical—has been steeped in class reductionism. In the particular conditions of U.S. politics, the subordination of race to class has never been viable; it is less logical in the contemporary period than ever before.

Making race consciousness explicit and central to class politics means recognizing the irreducibility of race in U.S. political and cultural life and thinking about class, inequality, and redistribution in ways that take racial divisions and conflicts into primary account. How might the racial projects of the left articulate the relationship of race and class? A full answer to this question must await large-scale political and cultural experimentation, but a more limited and schematic response is already possible.

First, such approaches cannot be mere inversions—whether innocent or cynical—of the new right uses of racial coding, nor of the neoconservative strategic denial of the significance of race. Left racial projects must affirm the ongoing reality of racial "difference" in U.S. cultural and political life. Indeed, in their radical democratic aspects at least, they must go further and create (or recreate) a recognition of racial difference that goes well beyond mere tolerance. One of the striking features of the contemporary racial situation is that many examples of such an appreciation exist in cultural life and in everyday experience—in music and art, sexual relationships, educational and religious settings, the media—without finding any political articulation at all.

Additionally, a radical democratic articulation of race and class must acknowledge that racial minority status still serves as a negative marker, a stigma, in the class formation process. Although significant minority middle classes have arisen since the 1960s, dark skin still correlates with poverty. Class position is in many respects *racially assigned* in the United States.

It follows from this that radical democratic challengers should reopen the question of discrimination as a racial process with class consequences. The reactionary redefinition of the nature of racial discrimination (in the "reverse discrimination" arguments of the 1970s and 1980s) as something that only happens to individuals and thus is disconnected from history and from any preponderant collective logic in the present conveniently suppresses the fact that discrimination drives all wages down.

Linking race and class in a manner that does not reduce race to class involves a *democratic challenge* to the fundamental authoritarianism of the right. It involves rethinking *populism* and the economic and cultural logics of *equality and fairness*. As a mass politics with strong themes of social injustice, exclusion, and resentment, U.S. populism has traditionally been directed at one of two main targets: on the one hand, at big business, the conglomerates, the trusts; on the other

hand, at racial minorities, the blacks, the "yellow peril," and so on.

Efforts to reconstruct the far right racial project along populist lines are indicative of the latter tendency. David Duke ran for president in 1988 on the ticket of the "Populist party," which was exhumed in the mid-1980s almost a century after its heyday of free silver, agrarian revolt, and southern lynching. This time around, the scapegoating of blacks is particularly central.

To counter this approach, a left populism will be needed. One such set of proposals, whose advocates have included William Julius Wilson and Orlando Patterson, involves the resuscitation of class-based New Deal policies (extensive public investment and job creation, expansion of the welfare state in a social democratic direction) combined with "race-specific" measures where discrimination per se is the issue (Wilson, 1987; Patterson 1979). Until recently, this sort of proposal would have appeared totally utopian, given the lethargy of the Democratic party, the perpetual fiscal crisis of the state, the absence of a strong and independent minority movement, and the political profits available to Republicans who played the racist card ("quotas," William Horton, etc.) in the 1980s. The 1992 electoral victory of Bill Clinton on a populist platform raised some hopes for more left-leaning initiatives, based on cuts in defense spending, a program of social investment, and the new president's promises to improve education and expand access to health care. On race, however, Clinton's orientation borrowed extensively from the right. He directed his attention almost exclusively toward the suburbs, and proved far more attentive to the needs of the middle class than to those of the poor. No significant effort to push Clinton's populism to the left has yet appeared.

If there is to be any progressive initiative, such left populist currents will have to be combined with an ethical trust, as Cornel West has recently argued (West 1991). In this view, social justice in all its forms—class-based, race-based, and gender-based—is achieved only through a combined political and moral vision. This suggests that the pragmatic liberal and radical democratic projects can learn from the right, just as the racial reaction learned from the minority movements of the 1960s.

In order to overcome right-wing populism's racist politics of resentment, notions of *equality and fairness* must be rethought in the combined light of race and class (and gender). Thinking of discrimination in terms of the restriction of the individual's rights and opportunities—in a "color-blind" way as the right-wing projects would have us do—becomes a lot more logical in a state committed to social and class justice. In a situation of tight labor markets such as the one Wilson proposes, the problem of "reverse discrimination" would be far less conflictual than it is in a situation where the gap between rich and poor is widening and middle-income people's "life chances" are eroding. Thus, linking race and class justice concerns would facilitate efforts to overcome historic patterns of racial discrimination without unduly threatening whites (Ezorsky 1991).

Similarly, the right-wing appeal to racial fears requires careful scrutiny. The right must employ the "politics of resentment" in this process; at a minimum, it must articulate these resentments and fears in "coded" racial terms, such as "quotas." David Duke, Lee Atwater, and Jesse Helms offered an authoritarian and exclusive program: to protect whites against nonwhites, against people they do not trust or understand. This authoritarian politics is open to a *democratic challenge:* it can be rearticulated as inclusion, not exclusion. Jesse Jackson demonstrated this with his rhetoric of "common ground" and his talk of "adding another patch to the quilt." By accepting and celebrating racial, gender, and sexual "difference" within a plural community, by offering and accepting a place under the "quilt," such a program reaffirms the themes mentioned earlier: equality, fairness, social justice, and an ethical society.

Racial hegemony is being reconstituted as overall hegemony; unfortunately, it is the right that is largely responsible for this trend and that stands to benefit the most from it. The task now is to provide an alternative, emancipatory account of the virtues of racial difference and racial diversity, and to reconstruct the links between the fate of racially defined minorities and the fate of U.S. society as a whole.

REFERENCES

Bhabha, Homi K. 1990. "DissemiNation: Time, Narrative, and the Margins of the Modern Nation," in Idem, ed., *Nation and Narration.* London: Routledge.

Cruse, Harold. 1968. *Rebellion or Revolution?* New York: Morrow.

Edsall, Thomas Byrne, and Mary D. Edsall. 1991. "Race." *Atlantic Monthly* (May).

Ezorsky, Gertrude. 1991. *Racism and Justice: The Case for Affirmative Action.* Ithaca, N.Y.: Cornell University Press.

Gramsci, Antonio. 1971. *Selections from the Prison Notebooks.* ed. Geoffrey Nowell-Smith and Quentin Hoare. New York: International Publishers.

McMillen, Neil R. 1989. *Dark Journey: Black Mississippians in the Age of Jim Crow.* Urbana: University of Illinois Press.

Montejano, David. 1987. *Anglos and Mexicans in the Making of Modern Texas, 1836–1986.* Austin: University of Texas Press.

Omi, Michael, and Howard Winant. 1994. *Racial Formation in the United States: From the 1960s to the 1990s.* 2nd ed. New York: Routledge.

———, and ———. 1986. *Racial Formation in the United States: From the 1960s to the 1990s.* New York: Routledge.

Patterson, Orlando, 1979. "The Black Community: Is There a Future?" in Seymour Martin Lipset, ed., *The Third Century: America as a Postindustrial Society.* Stanford, Calif.: Hoover Institution Press.

Roediger, David R. 1991. *The Wages of Whiteness: Race and the Making of the American Working Class.* New York: Verso.

Scott, James. 1985. *Weapons of the Weak: Everyday Forms of Peasant Resistance.* New Haven, Conn.: Yale University Press.

Takaki, Ronald. 1990. *Strangers from a Distant Shore: A History of Asian Americans.* New York: Penguin.

Walters, Ronald. 1987. "White Racial Nationalism in the United States," *Without Prejudice I* 1(Fall).

West, Cornel, 1991. "Nihilism in Black America," *Dissent* (Spring).

Wilson, William Julius. 1987. *The Truly Disadvantaged: The Inner City, the Underclass, and Public Policy.* Chicago: University of Chicago Press.

Winant, Howard. 1994. *Racial Conditions: Politics, Theory, and Comparisons.* Minneapolis: University of Minnesota Press.

Questions for Understanding and Critical Thinking

1. What steps occurred in U.S. racial history that contributed to the shift from a pattern of domination to one of hegemony?
2. What were the achievements and legacy of the black movement? How were the successes of the black movement greeted by others?
3. According to Winant, biological bases do not exist for distinguishing among people based on racial lines. If so, why are particular human features often singled out in the United States and other nations as being "racially significant"?
4. What does Winant believe conservative/reactionary politicians today gain by disguising class issues in racial terms?
5. What examples can you find in the media to support or refute Winant's five-part typology of U.S. *racial projects?*

ARTICLE 2

The following article by Ronald E. Hall examines pressures placed on African Americans to assimilate into a society characterized by racial domination. According to Hall, the Bleaching Syndrome is a response by some African Americans who have internalized light skin and other dominant race characteristics as the ideal point of reference for assimilation into U.S. society. Hall provides historical and contemporary explanations for the Bleaching Syndrome and suggests reasons why this societally induced syndrome is harmful to African Americans.

Ronald E. Hall, an assistant professor at the David Walker Research Institute, Michigan State University, is regarded as a leading scholar on skin color. In addition to authoring books such as *Color Complex, Cutanco-Chroma,* and *Black Male in America,* he testified as an expert witness for the first U.S. skin color court case, *Morrow v. IRS.*

Looking Ahead

1. How does Hall describe the "new consciousness" that he believes has been sparked in the United States?
2. What is the historical significance of the Bleaching Syndrome?
3. What is a *master status?* How is master status related to a person's skin color?
4. What are the effects of assimilation pressures on African Americans?

The Color Complex
The Bleaching Syndrome

◆ *Ronald E. Hall*

> *That may surprise you, but whites do the same thing.*
> *You have the blond hair and blue eyes and*
> *from there you go all the way down*
> *to the Greeks and the Italians.*
> *And they will tell you that.*
> *See, this is something that American culture has internalized.*
> *It began as black and white but it's much,*
> *much larger than that now because it's a cultural value.*
> *When people discriminate on the basis of skin color*
> *they're simply being American.*
>
> —Ronald E. Hall, *Star Tribune*, Feb. 6, 1993

Source: From Ronald E. Hall, "The Color Complex: The Bleaching Syndrome," in *Race, Gender & Class,* 2(2), Winter 1995, pp. 99–109. Reprinted by permission.

The current emphasis upon "diversity" in academia has brought about rapid and widely accepted curriculum changes which include more content regarding people of color (Norton, 1983; Garcia & Swenson, 1992). It is a reflection of the earlier protests and marches that have arguably been only too ineffective. Now after decades of struggle, those efforts have finally sparked a new consciousness. African Americans, previously segregated, commence to interaction in a less segregated environment with members of the racially dominant white population. For the most part, the impact of this consciousness has attracted little attention. It has no immediate implications for exact science or technology. It contains no solutions to other biases such as class and gender. But, if that impact escapes the attention of African Americans the future of their racial existence will be very likely put at risk.

The objective of this paper is then to inform African Americans and shed light upon some of the dynamics associated with racial domination. It will introduce the Bleaching Syndrome (Hall, 1990a) as a response by African Americans in their attempts to assimilate into a society characterized by such domination. It will also make available to scholars a theoretical framework for logically comprehending the impact of assimilation and racial domination upon the psyche of less powerful groups. And lastly, it will define and illustrate some of the consequences of the Bleaching Syndrome for those African Americans who internalize light skin and other dominant race characteristics as the ideal point of reference for normal assimilation into American society.

THE BLEACHING SYNDROME HISTORICALLY

The existence of the Bleaching Syndrome is historically rooted in the old "beauty" creams and folk preparations used by African Americans to make their skin lighter. According to Webster (Mish, 1989) "bleach" is a verb which means to remove color or to make white. A "syndrome" consists of a grouping of symptoms i.e.: behaviors that occur in conjunction and make up a recognizable pattern (Mish, 1989). In combination, historical folklore and English terminology operationally define the Bleaching Syndrome. It is also a metaphor that has universal application. Its relevancy to America is applicable because it is practical wherever racial domination exists. When applied to dark-skinned African Americans, its existence is proven in a most dramatic fashion. For it is they alone who have had to internalize racial ideals, such as light skin, that are often radically inconsistent with their outward appearances (Levine & Padilla, 1980). And the psychic conflict they suffer is exacerbated by America's general lack of tolerance for its growing diversity. The effort on the part of such persons to assimilate and simultaneously minimize the prevailing psychic conflict is made possible by an obsession with a "bleached" ideal. It is most evident among African Americans as relates to feminine beauty and the resulting impact upon marriage. No other aspect of racial domination is more revealing.

As a social phenomenon, the Bleaching Syndrome is not unprecedented. It is the legacy of such theoretical concepts which emphasize self presentation such as Dramaturgy (Adler, Adler & Fantana, 1987), Cooley's (1902) "looking glass self," and the more recent "Cool Pose" (Majors & Billson, 1992). But perhaps, W. E. B. DuBois, a sociologist, was one of the first scholars to specifically acknowledge the unique psychic conflict indicative of African Americans in their attempts to assimilate. He studied their response and labeled it "double consciousness" (cf. G. Myrdal, 1944). The implication of this "double consciousness" was that the ideal for white skin in America was extremely potent. It required other races or ethnic groups whose skin color did not approximate that of the dominant race population to assume a passive social demeanor or otherwise not object to the contradictions of racial domination. Survival and the ability to gain employment were greatly enhanced commensurate with the ability to defer. Knowing this, African Americans evolved a "bleached" presentation of self devoid of any offensive African American characteristics separate and apart from who they actually were within their own communities.

This peculiar form of social phenomena did not go unnoticed by social work. Sometime following the death of DuBois, Norton (1993), a social worker who recognized the importance of the person-in-the-environment approach, devised the "dual perspective." Similar to the "double consciousness" theory of DuBois, "dual perspective" is a response to racial domination indicative of African Americans in a color ranking society. It is the process they utilize to perceive, understand, and compare simultaneously the values, attitudes, and behavior of the larger societal system with those of the immediate family and community system (Norton, 1983). Given the nature of duality, both theories suggest an identity, valued by African Americans, separate and apart from that revealed to the dominant race population. In this respect the Bleaching Syndrome differs. It is linear in progression and best illustrated as a scale constructed on the basis of the "double/dual" models. At one end is identity for African Americans as defined by the dominant race—perhaps less valued by that dominant race. At the other end is the "bleached" ideal as defined by the same—perhaps less valued by African Americans. But those African Americans who aspire to normal assimilation in the context of racial domination invest their efforts in reaching the "bleached" ideal. By engaging in such efforts, they are more optimistic about the possibility of assimilation and the quality of life that goes with it. Such African Americans have been referred to in the community as "Oreos"—black on the outside and white on the inside (Kitano, 1985).

"MASTER STATUS" AND SKIN COLOR

African Americans

According to the domination model (Kitano, 1985) of assimilation, African Americans are regarded as "minorities" by the dominant race population. The most salient physical feature of African Americans is cutaneochroma (Hall, 1990b), hence referred to as skin color. In America, skin color may have an effect upon every phase of life, including job placement, earnings, and most importantly, self-concept (Vontress, 1970). It is a "master status" that distinguishes "minorities"—whose skin is dark—from members of the dominant white race population—whose skin in affect is light. So potent is this "master status" that it has recently become the grounds for legal suits between two African-American women of light and dark skin color (Morrow vs IRS, 1990; Hiskey, 1990). Ms. Morrow, the plaintiff, alleges that Ms. Lewis, an IRS defendant, assigned a poor work evaluation on the basis of Ms. Morrow's light skin color. It was Ms. Morrow's contention that Ms. Lewis, being dark-skinned, did in fact harbor prejudices against light-skinned African Americans. A resort to legal tactics is an indication that for them, assimilation has been particularly painful given the psychologically conflicting ideals of the process. That is, far too many African Americans have internalized racist ideals but unlike members of the dominant race population are prohibited from structural or normal assimilation into American society (Rabinowitz, 1978).

This leads to psychic conflict. Their willingness to assimilate, regardless, reflects an effort on the part of African Americans to improve their quality of life and live out the "American dream"—which for most African Americans has been tantamount to a myth. As a result, many African Americans may develop a disdain for dark skin because the disdain is an expression of dominant race ideals. It is regarded by the various American institutions as an obstacle that might otherwise afford African Americans the opportunity to fully assimilate. In order to reduce the psychic conflict and at the same time enable assimilation, some have manifested the Bleaching Syndrome.

According to a metaphoric statement by James Baldwin, the root of African American difficulty is directly related to skin color (cf. B. F. Jones, 1966). If this is indeed a fact, it then became a matter of the human condition for African Americans that skin color would eventually be utilized as one of the ideals of attractiveness and marriage. For example, African American females with more Caucasian features continue to be highly valued as they are believed to be more beautiful (cf. Neal & Wilson, 1989; Okazawa-Rey, Robinson, & Ward, 1987). This belief on the part of some African Americans is an old self destructive dominant race ideal that has remained quite significant over the years (Hertel & Hughes, 1988). It necessitated via the dominant white population that light-skinned, green-eyed Vanessa Williams be the first among her ethnic peers to adorn the crown of Ms. America (Hall, 1992c). Such a powerful acknowledgment of attractiveness is racist and creates for light-skinned African American women an advantage of wealth, marriage, and other assimilation criteria that darker-skinned African American females do not have. These advantages have long been apparent in their communities but seldom discussed openly or at a public forum (Lerner, 1972).

For African Americans, the utilization of light skin as a point of reference for attractiveness is plausible. Those who have light skin are believed to be most physically appealing given their visual proximity to the dominant race white population (Hernton, 1965). But that belief alone does not always determine overall appeal particularly for males because light skin may not always coincide with the group concept of masculinity. However, consistent with the greater attractiveness value placed upon light skin, according to Hall (1993d) and Majors and Billson (1992), African American males who have darker skin are viewed as more sinister and threatening by both the dominant white and dominated African American populations. One such male who exemplified this view is Willie Horton.

Willie Horton is a darker-skinned felon exploited by the Republican party in 1988 to help re-elect George Bush to the presidency (Schram, 1990). The threatening perception of his dark skin was assumed to exacerbate the most primal fears within the dominant race population. This no doubt was at least expected to impact voting trends and thus useful to Republicans in their effort to reclaim the presidency.

In a more recent incident, another darker-skinned African American male was accused of murdering a white pregnant woman by her white husband (Carlson, 1990). Much of the nation assumed the guilt of the accused based upon media hype and its larger than life photographs of the murder scene. Only after one of the accomplices involved in the frame-up came forward to reveal the truth was Mr. Bennett—the alleged perpetrator—released from police custody. The belief that Mr. Bennett was guilty was arguably a reflection of the culpability associated with the racist connotations of dark skin— frequently protested by people of color.

The belief that light skin is more attractive than dark skin is expressed in various ways (Huggins, 1942). Further proof of its attractiveness is contained in African American folk terms that designate the variations in skin color. They include for light skin such complimentary terms as "high-yellow," "ginger," "creme-colored," and "bronze" (Herskovits, 1968). Similar references are used to refer to features that are associated with having light skin. They include hair, which is "bad" if it is the kinky African type characteristic of those with dark skin and "good" if it is the straight Caucasian type associated with those whose skin is light. And before the "Black is beautiful" movement, the term "Black" more often than not designated something less attractive and more threatening particularly if it involved an African American male (Jones, 1980).

Because light skin is the ideal point of reference for attractiveness, dark skin is necessarily ugly and threatening. It is easily utilized in the subjective assessment of guilt. This has resulted in the exploitation and vilification of African American males everywhere. Hence, in comparison to those with lighter skin, those with darker skin are more often associated with crime and the general disruption of society (Hall, 1993d). And given the power of the dominant race population to impose its ideals via control of America's institutions, such association may to some extent be perpetuated by "bleached" African Americans as well.

Assimilation theory without domination views the selection of marriage partners as an indicator that race i.e.: skin color is not a barrier to full acceptance, while an alternate approach, hypergamy, sees marriage as a function of inequality in dominant and racially diverse societies (Shinagawa & Pang, 1988). For African Americans who manifest the Bleaching Syndrome, marriage then becomes a vehicle for the exchange of status characteristics. On that basis higher status persons are stigmatized if they are dark-skinned by others of equally high or higher status. Hypergamy among African Americans is thus a consequence of the status disparity between persons with light and dark skin. Both light-skinned males and females are regarded as more attractive but that is not necessarily reflected in marital patterns—particularly where the male is concerned. It may appear that African American males value light skin as a prerequisite to marriage more so than African American females. In fact African American females harbor similar attitudes which are less obvious given their tendency to marry up socio-economically which may make a dark-skinned male owning some wealth eligible. Thus, if a marriage between a light-skinned female and dark-skinned male does occur, it will require a disproportionate exchange of assets for the stigma associated with the assimilation of the dark-skinned spouse. When the prospects of marriage and physical attractiveness serve no purpose, the eventuality of psyche related ailments such as hypertension may follow (Roberts & Roberts, 1982; Boyle, 1970).

A seemingly contrasting preference for light skin among African Americans is not unique to that group. It is a universal fact of racial domination. Anywhere in the world where such domination is the preferred model of assimilation, the characteristics i.e.: skin color, of the dominated groups will be stigmatized. Particularly where colonialism has occurred, this is so. The Hindus of India offer a striking illustration of this fact which in many ways is synonymous with that of African Americans.

The Hindus of India

The Hindus of India comprise a religious group that constitutes about eighty percent of the nation's population (Buultjens, quoted in Franklin 1968). Proportionately, that makes them the dominant group via numbers. In skin color they are also among the darkest: some may even be darker-skinned than many African Americans (Guha, 1944). Yet those who live in the North of India have a prejudice against those in the South on the basis of their dark skin (cf. Franklin, 1968). Light skin may be valued as a consequence. Similar to African Americans, Hindus in India who manage to acquire some degree of wealth will also aspire to light-skinned Indians for marriage. In fact, the preference for light-skinned spouses is so potent that the rigidity of class boundaries is often overlooked by wealthy landowning families seeking light-skinned brides from among poorer members of their subcaste (cf. Franklin, 1968). The trait of light skin among ideal spouses is particularly apparent as the socio-economic status of Hindu individuals in India increases. This preference for light-skinned spouses can be easily verified by the matrimonial columns of some of the Hindu dailies. Among the most desirable traits a bride can have are virginity and light skin as evidenced by those placing ads (cf. Franklin, 1968).

For Hindu males, having dark skin is less of an obstacle if they are wealthy or have some unusual talent, but it is a stigma nonetheless. If he is smart or has some unusual wealth or talent a Hindu male may be eligible to take a light-skinned bride. This may be a source of pride for both he and his family. By marrying a light-skinned bride, a dark-skinned Hindu male can erase the stigma of his skin through off-spring and increase his status in Indian society. This practice is little different from the beauty standards and marital patterns of African Americans. In fact, in many Indian languages the words for fair and beautiful are synonymous (cf. Franklin, 1968). The common variable between the two groups is racial domination by whites who maintained a strong preference for light skin being indicative of their own. Although Hindus and other dark-skinned Indians dominate the population numerically, their continued preference for contrasting light skin is a testament to the impact of racial dominance upon the human psyche.

The internalization of light skin as a point of reference for attractiveness and marriage among African Americans and Hindu Indians reflects a trait of the dominant race population. It is an effective, albeit ultimately pathological vehicle to assimilation that predisposes both to psychic conflict. Perhaps due to their larger proportion in numbers, Hindus may be less imposed upon psychologically than African Americans. However, some such African Americans, for whatever reasons, may have a different reaction to the dynamics of assimilation and racial domination. They are under the same pressure to assimilate as other African Americans but are unable to reduce the resulting psychic conflict. Their suffering is characterized by the psyche related ailments verified in research most often as hypertension (Boyle, 1970).

THE PRESSURE OF ASSIMILATION

Hypertension is a major public health problem in America and it afflicts a disproportionate number of African Americans (Beckett, 1983). The fact that it has been virtually ignored as a disease may be attributed to whom it is associated with and that it is not necessarily life threatening. Fortunately, some health care professionals and other scholars have taken notice. Dr. Edwin Boyle (1970) is among the most respected. His work verified a quantitative relationship between blood pressure and skin color. He further noted the higher incident of hypertension among particularly dark-skinned African Americans.

Two separate studies were conducted to draw these conclusions. One was carried out in Charleston County, South Carolina and the other in Detroit, Michigan. Several variables related to hypertension were assessed such as age, sex, socio-economic status, stress, and genetics. None showed any promise of an explanation for the high incidence of hypertension among the darkest-skinned subjects. Other scholars extended the work of Boyle by concentrating specifically upon genes (Hamburg, Gielberman, Roeper, Schork & Schull, 1978). They noted the difference in higher hypertension rates for West Indians who migrated to the United States of America compared to African Americans born and raised. As a group, West Indians tend to have darker skin by comparison given the assumed larger pool of European genes concentrated among African Americans (Beckett, 1983). But just as West Indians were found to have higher rates of hypertension than African Americans, lower working class African Americans were found to have higher rates than their middle and upper class lighter-skinned counterparts. The common variable in both instances is skin color. Furthermore, the ratio between having African and European genes is also an indicator of the different sub-groupings among the various Americanized Africans, particularly as it relates to class (Beckett, 1983). The darker the skin, the greater the presumed ratio of African genes, and the likelihood of increased economic and social prejudice imposed by racial domination (Hertel & Hughes, 1988). In keeping with this gene based presumption, the lower working class African American is disproportionately darker-skinned than their middle and upper class counterpart. They would have the greatest difficulty for normal assimilation in America. As a result they find themselves in a "catch 22" situation. They obviously cannot offer light skin to a prospective mate to facilitate normal assimilation nor, if they are poor, can they attract a light-skinned mate for the same reason. Unless they can acquire

wealth or have some unusual talent that would make hypergamy possible, the marital potential of dark-skinned African Americans is then limited to others in a similar racially dominated situation that when paired continue the racist stigmatizing cycle of dark skin for off-spring. This can create a sense of hopelessness and dispair that may be the root cause of unbearable psychic conflict that cannot be alleviated by the Bleaching Syndrome (Kardiner & Oversey, 1951). It may also contribute to the disproportionate rates of hypertension among very dark-skinned African Americans. And unless African Americans and all people of color can create ideals conducive to themselves, not only their racial existence, but their mental health and assimilation expectations will be jeopardized.

CONCLUSION

As a response to racial domination vis à vis skin color, the Bleaching Syndrome for African Americans is pathological. It may temporarily allow them to reduce some measure of psychic conflict, but it is ultimately destructive. Its symptomology is less striking than the psyche related ailments like hypertension, etc., but it is no less critical. For those African Americans who opt to apply light skin as the point of reference for marriage and attractiveness, a slow but definite form of self-denigration is occurring. It gets passed via familial and other vital social systems. By all standards of self preservation this is counter-productive. The result will only encourage a continuation of racial domination by whites and increasingly less tolerance for America's racial diversity.

The Bleaching Syndrome is not to be confused as the sole prospect of assimilation. Domination is not without an alternative. Furthermore, American society's degree of diversity and multiculturalism distinguish it from every other society that has ever existed on earth. And once skin color assumes the same level of insignificance as any other physiological characteristic, a conducive and more healthy form of assimilation will move the civilization of mankind to its next level. Making that a reality for the dominant white population as well as for themselves can be the ultimate gift from African Americans to this nation.

REFERENCES

Adler, P., Adler, P., & Fontana, A. (1987). Everyday life in sociology. *Annual Review of Rociology,* vol 13, 217–235.

Beckett, A. K., (1983). *The relationship of skin color to blood pressure among Black Americans.* Unpublished master's thesis, Atlanta University, Atlanta.

Boyle, E. (1970). Biological patterns in hypertension by race, sex, body weight, and skin color. *American Medical Association Journal,* 213, 1637–1643.

Carlson, M. (1990, January). Presumed innocent, *Time,* pp 10–14.

Cooley, C. (1902). *Human nature and the social order.* New York: Scribner.

Cruden, R. (1969). *The Negro in reconstruction.* Englewood Cliffs, NJ: Prentice Hall.

Franklin, J. H. (Ed.), (1968). *Color and race.* Boston: Beacon.

Garcia, B., & Swenson, C. (1992). Writing the stories of white racism. *Journal of Teaching in Social Work,* 6(2): 3–17.

Guha, B. S. 1944. Racial elements in the population. *Oxford Pamphlets on Indian Affairs,* No. 22 (Bombay, 1944).

Hall, R. E. (1990a). *The Bleaching Syndrome.* Manuscript submitted for publication.

Hall, R. E. (1990b). The projected manifestations of aspiration, personal values, and environmental assessment cognates of cutaneo-chroma (skin color) for a selected population of African-Americans (Doctoral dissertation, Atlanta University, 1989). *Dissertation Abstracts International,* 50, 3363A.

Hall, R. E. (1992c). Bias among African-Americans regarding skin color: Implications for social work practice. *Research on Social Work Practice,* 2, 479–486.

Hall, R. E. (1993d). Clowns, buffoons, and gladiators: Media portrayals of African-American men. *The Journal of Men's Studies,* 1, 239–251.

Hamburg, E., Gielberman, L., Roeper, P., Schork, A., & Schull, W. (1978). Skin color, ethnicity, and blood pressure. *American Journal of Public Health,* 68, 1177–1182.

Herskovits, M. (1968). *The American Negro.* Bloomington: Indiana University Press.

Hernton, C. (1965). *Sex and racism in America.* New York: Grove.

Hertel, B., & Hughes, M. (1988). The significance of color remains. *Social Forces,* 68, 1105–1120.

Hiskey, M. (1990, February 1). Boss: Skin hue, firing unrelated. *The Atlanta Journal-Constitution,* pp 1, 4.

Huggins, N. (1942). *Key issues in the African-American experience.* New York: Harcourt Brace Jovanovich.

Jones, B. F. (1966). James Baldwin: The struggle for identity. *British Journal of Sociology,* 17, 107–121.

Jones, R. L. (Ed.). *Black pride in the seventies.* New York: Harper & Row.

Kardiner, A., & Oversey, L. (1951). *The mark of oppression.* New York: Norton.

Kitano, H. (1985). *Race relations.* Englewood Cliffs, NJ: Prentice-Hall.

Knox, D. (1985). *Choices in relationships.* St. Paul: West.

Lerner, G. (1972). *Black women in white America.* New York: Vintage.

Levine, E. S., & Padilla, A. M. (1980). *Crossing cultures in therapy.* Monterey, CA: Brooks/Cole.

Majors, R., & Billson, J. (1992). *Cool pose.* New York: Lexington.

Mish, F. C. (Ed.). (1989). *Webster's ninth new collegiate dictionary.* Springfield, MA: Merriam-Webster.

Morrow vs the Internal Revenue Service, 742 F. Supp. 670 (N.D. Ga. 1990)

Myrdal, G. (1944). *An American dilemma.* New York: Harper & Row.

Neal, A. M., & Wilson, M. L. (1989). The role of skin color and features in the Black community: Implications for Black women and therapy. *Clinical Psychology Review,* 9, 323–333.

Norton, D. (1983). Black family life patterns, the development of self and cognitive development of Black children. In Gloria J. Powell (Ed.). *The psychosocial development of minority group children.* New York: Brunner/Mazel, pp 181–193.

Norton, D. (1993). Diversity, early socialization, and temporal evelopment: the dual perspective revisited. *Social Work,* 38(1), 82–90.

Nye, F. I. (1980). Family mini theories as special instances of choice and exchange theory. *Journal of Marriage and the Family,* 42(3), 479–489.

Okazawa-Rey, M., Robinson, T., & Ward, J. V. (1987). Black women and the politics of skin color and hair. *Women and Therapy,* 6(1/2), 89–102.

Rabinowitz, H. (1978). *Race relations in the urban south.* New York: Oxford University Press.

Reuter, E. (1969). *The mulatto in the United States*. New York: Haskell House.

Roberts, R. E., & Roberts, C. R. (1982). Marriage, work and depressive symptoms among Mexican Americans. *Hispanic Journal of Behavioral Sciences*, 4, 199–221.

Russell, K., Wilson, M., & Hall, R. E. (1992). *The color complex*. New York: Harcourt Brace Jovanovich.

Schram, M. (1990, May). The making of Willie Horton. *The New Republic*, pp 17–19.

Shinagawa, L., & Pang, G. (1988). Intraethnic and interracial marriages among Asian-Americans in California, 1980. *Berkeley Journal of Sociology*, 33, 95–114.

Vontress, C. (1970). Counseling Black. *Personnel and Guidance Journal*, 48, 713–719.

Questions for Understanding and Critical Thinking

1. According to Hall, "African American males who have darker skin are viewed as more sinister and threatening by both the dominant white and dominated African American populations." What evidence might support this assertion? What evidence might refute it?

2. Is a preference for light skin unique among African Americans? Explain your answer.

3. What is the relationship between race, class, and hypertension? What other acute illnesses and chronic diseases reflect the linkage between class and race in the United States?

4. What reasons does Hall give for his assertion that the Bleaching Syndrome is ultimately destructive for African Americans?

ARTICLE 3 _____

Originally published in 1903, *The Souls of Black Folk* contributed to W. E. B. Du Bois's (1868–1963) emergence as a dominant political figure in the African American community. In this excerpt, we are introduced to Du Bois's concept of *double consciousness*—**the double life every "American Negro must live, as a Negro and as an American."** Du Bois used a veiled metaphor to describe the experiences of African Americans, whom he described as being "born with a veil, and gifted with the second-sight in this American world." According to Du Bois, African Americans' attempts to gain self-consciousness are impaired by negative images of themselves refracted in the gaze of white Americans. Consequently, African Americans must veil or mask their cultural selves whenever they cross or enter into the dominant white culture.

W. E. B. Du Bois, an early African American sociologist, founded one of the first U.S. sociology departments (at Atlanta University) and was a prolific writer on the problem of the "color line" in the twentieth century. Although Du Bois became extremely disenchanted with prospects for racial change in the United States and spent his last years in Ghana, his writings have had a profound impact on recent generations of race relations scholars.

Looking Ahead

1. What unasked question did Du Bois believe he continually faced?
2. Why did Du Bois believe that African Americans are "born with a veil, and gifted with second-sight in this American world?"
3. What forms of discrimination have African Americans historically experienced in the United States?
4. What did Du Bois view as a "concrete test of the underlying principles" of the United States?

The Souls of Black Folk

◆ *W. E. B. Du Bois*

Between me and the other world there is ever an unasked question: unasked by some through feelings of delicacy; by others through the difficulty of rightly framing it. All, nevertheless, flutter round it. They approach me in a half-hesitant sort of way, eye me curiously or compassionately, and then, instead of saying directly, How does it feel to be a problem? they say, I know an excellent colored man in my town; or, I fought at

Source: Excerpt from W. E. B. Du Bois, *The Souls of Black Folk* (New York: Bantam, 1989), pp. 1–9.

Mechanicsville; or, Do not these Southern outrages make your blood boil? At these I smile, or am interested, or reduce the boiling to a simmer, as the occasion may require. To the real question, How does it feel to be a problem? I answer seldom a word.

And yet, being a problem is a strange experience,—peculiar even for one who has never been anything else, save perhaps in babyhood and in Europe. It is in the early days of rollicking boyhood that the revelation first bursts upon one, all in a day, as it were. I remember well when the shadow swept across me. I was a little thing, away up in the hills of New England, where the dark Housatonic winds between Hoosac and Taghkanic to the sea. In a wee wooden schoolhouse, something put it into the boys' and girls' heads to buy gorgeous visiting-cards—ten cents a package—and exchange. The exchange was merry, till one girl, a tall newcomer, refused my card,—refused it peremptorily, with a glance. Then it dawned upon me with a certain suddenness that I was different from the others; or like, mayhap, in heart and life and longing, but shut out from their world by a vast veil. I had thereafter no desire to tear down that veil, to creep through; I held all beyond it in common contempt, and lived above it in a region of blue sky and great wandering shadows. That sky was bluest when I could beat my mates at examination-time, or beat them at a foot-race, or even beat their stringy heads. Alas, with the years all this fine contempt began to fade; for the words I longed for, and all their dazzling opportunities, were theirs, not mine. But they should not keep these prizes, I said; some, all, I would wrest from them. Just how I would do it I could never decide: by reading law, by healing the sick, by telling the wonderful tales that swam in my head,—some way. With other black boys the strife was not so fiercely sunny: their youth shrunk into tasteless

sycophancy, or into silent hatred of the pale world about them and mocking distrust of everything white; or wasted itself in a bitter cry, Why did God make me an outcast and a stranger in mine own house? The shades of the prison-house closed round about us all: walls strait and stubborn on the whitest, but relentlessly narrow, tall, and unscalable to sons of night who must plod darkly on in resignation, or beat unavailing palms against the stone, or steadily, half hopelessly, watch the streak of blue above.

After the Egyptian and Indian, the Greek and Roman, the Teuton and Mongolian, the Negro is a sort of seventh son, born with a veil, and gifted with second-sight in this American world,—a world which yields him no true self-consciousness, but only lets him see himself through the revelation of the other world. It is a peculiar sensation, this double-consciousness, this sense of always looking at one's self through the eyes of others, of measuring one's soul by the tape of a world that looks on in amused contempt and pity. One ever feels his twoness,—an American, a Negro; two souls, two thoughts, two unreconciled strivings; two warring ideals in one dark body, whose dogged strength alone keeps it from being torn asunder.

The history of the American Negro is the history of this strife,—this longing to attain self-conscious manhood, to merge his double self into a better and truer self. In this merging he wishes neither of the older selves to be lost. He would not Africanize America, for America has too much to teach the world and Africa. He would not bleach his Negro soul in a flood of white Americanism, for he knows that Negro blood has a message for the world. He simply wishes to make it possible for a man to be both a Negro and an American, without being cursed and spit upon by his fellows, without having the doors of Opportunity closed roughly in his face.

This, then, is the end of his striving: to be a co-worker in the kingdom of culture, to escape both death and isolation, to husband and use his best powers and his latent genius. These powers of body and mind have in the past been strangely wasted, dispersed, or forgotten. The shadow of a mighty Negro past flits through the tale of Ethiopia the Shadowy and of Egypt the Sphinx. Through history, the powers of single black men flash here and there like falling stars, and die sometimes before the world has rightly gauged their brightness. Here in America, in the few days since Emancipation, the black man's turning hither and thither in hesitant and doubtful striving has often made his very strength to lose effectiveness, to seem like absence of power, like weakness. And yet it is not weakness,—it is the contradiction of double aims. The double-aimed struggle of the black artisan—on the one hand to escape white contempt for a nation of mere hewers of wood and drawers of water, and on the other hand to plough and nail and dig for a poverty-stricken horde—could only result in making him a poor craftsman, for he had but half a heart in either cause. By the poverty and ignorance of his people, the Negro minister or doctor was tempted toward quackery and demagogy; and by the criticism of the other world, toward ideals that made him ashamed of his lowly tasks. The would-be black *savant* was confronted by the paradox that the knowledge his people needed was a twice-told tale to his white neighbors, while the knowledge which would teach the white world was Greek to his own flesh and blood. The innate love of harmony and beauty that set the ruder souls of his people a-dancing and a-singing raised but confusion and doubt in the soul of the black artist; for the beauty revealed to him was the soul-beauty of a race which his larger audience despised, and he could not articulate the message of another people. This waste of double aims,

this seeking to satisfy two unreconciled ideals, has wrought sad havoc with the courage and faith and deeds of ten thousand thousand people,—has sent them often wooing false gods and invoking false means of salvation, and at times has even seemed about to make them ashamed of themselves.

Away back in the days of bondage they thought to see in one divine event the end of all doubt and disappointment; few men ever worshipped Freedom with half such unquestioning faith as did the American Negro for two centuries. To him, so far as he thought and dreamed, slavery was indeed the sum of all villainies, the cause of all sorrow, the root of all prejudice; Emancipation was the key to a promised land of sweeter beauty than ever stretched before the eyes of wearied Israelites. In song and exhortation swelled one refrain—Liberty; in his tears and curses the God he implored had Freedom in his right hand. At last it came,—suddenly, fearfully, like a dream. With one wild carnival of blood and passion came the message in his own plaintive cadences:—

> *"Shout, O children!*
> *Shout, you're free!*
> *For God has brought you liberty!"*

Years have passed away since then,—ten, twenty, forty; forty years of national life, forty years of renewal and development, and yet the swarthy spectre sits in its accustomed seat at the Nation's feast. In vain do we cry to this our vastest social problem:—

> *"Take any shape but that,*
> *and my firm nerves*
> *Shall never tremble!"*

The Nation has not yet found peace from its sins; the freedman has not yet found in freedom his promised land. Whatever of good may have come in these years of change, the shadow of a deep disappointment rests upon the Negro people,—a disappointment all the more bitter because the unattained ideal was unbounded save by the simple ignorance of a lowly people.

The first decade was merely a prolongation of the vain search for freedom, the boon that seemed ever barely to elude their grasp,—like a tantalizing will-o'-the-wisp, maddening and misleading the headless host. The holocaust of war, the terrors of the Ku-Klux Klan, the lies of carpet-baggers, the disorganization of industry, and the contradictory advice of friends and foes, left the bewildered serf with no new watchword beyond the old cry for freedom. As the time flew, however, he began to grasp a new idea. The ideal of liberty demanded for its attainment powerful means, and these the Fifteenth Amendment gave him. The ballot, which before he had looked upon as a visible sign of freedom, he now regarded as the chief means of gaining and perfecting the liberty with which war had partially endowed him. And why not? Had not votes made war and emancipated millions? Had not votes enfranchised the freedmen? Was anything impossible to a power that had done all this? A million black men started with renewed zeal to vote themselves into the kingdom. So the decade flew away, the revolution of 1876 came, and left the half-free serf weary, wondering, but still inspired. Slowly but steadily, in the following years, a new vision began gradually to replace the dream of political power,—a powerful movement, the rise of another ideal to guide the unguided, another pillar of fire by night after a clouded day. It was the ideal of "book-learning"; the curiosity, born of compulsory ignorance, to know and test the power of the cabalistic letters of the white man, the longing to know. Here at last seemed to have been discovered the mountain path to Canaan; longer than the highway of Emancipation and law, steep and rugged, but straight, leading to heights high enough to overlook life.

Up the new path the advance guard toiled, slowly, heavily, doggedly; only those who have watched and guided the faltering feet, the misty minds, the dull understandings, of the dark pupils of these schools know how faithfully, how piteously, this people strove to learn. It was weary work. The cold statistician wrote down the inches of progress here and there, noted also where here and there a foot had slipped or some one had fallen. To the tired climbers, the horizon was ever dark, the mists were often cold, the Canaan was always dim and far away. If, however, the vistas disclosed as yet no goal, no resting-place, little but flattery and criticism, the journey at least gave leisure for reflection and self-examination; it changed the child of Emancipation to the youth with dawning self-consciousness, self-realization, self-respect. In those sombre forests of his striving his own soul rose before him, and he saw himself,—darkly as through a veil; and yet he saw in himself some faint revelation of his power, of his mission. He began to have a dim feeling that, to attain his place in the world, he must be himself, and not another. For the first time he sought to analyze the burden he bore upon his back, that dead-weight of social degradation partially masked behind a half-named Negro problem. He felt his poverty; without a cent, without a home, without land, tools, or savings, he had entered into competition with rich, landed, skilled neighbors. To be a poor man is hard, but to be a poor race in a land of dollars is the very bottom of hardships. He felt the weight of his ignorance,—not simply of letters, but of life, of business, of the humanities; the accumulated sloth and shirking and awkwardness of decades and centuries shackled his hands and feet. Nor was his burden all poverty and ignorance. The red stain of bastardy, which two centuries of systematic legal defilement of Negro women had stamped upon his race, meant not only the loss of ancient African chastity, but also the hereditary weight of a mass of corruption from white adulterers, threatening almost the obliteration of the Negro home.

A people thus handicapped ought not to be asked to race with the world, but rather allowed to give all its time and thought to its own social problems. But alas! while sociologists gleefully count his bastards and his prostitutes, the very soul of the toiling, sweating black man is darkened by the shadow of a vast despair. Men call the shadow prejudice, and learnedly explain it as the natural defence of culture against barbarism, learning against ignorance, purity against crime, the "higher" against the "lower" races. To which the Negro cries Amen! and swears that to so much of this strange prejudice as is founded on just homage to civilization, culture, righteousness, and progress, he humbly bows and meekly does obeisance. But before that nameless prejudice that leaps beyond all this he stands helpless, dismayed, and well-nigh speechless; before that personal disrespect and mockery, the ridicule and systematic humiliation, the distortion of fact and wanton license of fancy, the cynical ignoring of the better and the boisterous welcoming of the worse, the all-pervading desire to inculcate disdain for everything black, from Toussaint to the devil,—before this there rises a sickening despair that would disarm and discourage any nation save that black host to whom "discouragement" is an unwritten word.

But the facing of so vast a prejudice could not but bring the inevitable self-questioning, self-disparagement, and lowering of ideals which ever accompany repression and breed in an atmosphere of contempt and hate. Whisperings and portents came borne upon the four winds: Lo! we are diseased and dying, cried the dark hosts; we cannot write, our voting is vain; what need of education, since we must always cook and serve? And the Nation echoed and enforced this self-criticism, saying: Be content to be servants, and nothing more; what need of higher culture for half-men? Away with the black man's ballot, by force or fraud,—and behold the suicide of a race! Nevertheless, out of the evil came something of good,—the more careful adjustment of education to real life, the clearer perception of the Negroes' social responsibilities, and the sobering realization of the meaning of progress.

So dawned the time of *Sturm und Drang:* storm and stress to-day rocks our little boat on the mad waters of the world-sea; there is within and without the sound of conflict, the burning of body and rending of soul; inspiration strives with doubt, and faith with vain questionings. The bright ideals of the past,—physical freedom, political power, the training of brains and the training of hands,—all these in turn have waxed and waned, until even the last grows dim and overcast. Are they all wrong,—all false? No, not that, but each alone was over-simple and incomplete,—the dreams of a credulous race-childhood, or the fond imaginings of the other world which does not know and does not want to know our power. To be really true, all these ideals must be melted and welded into one. The training of the schools we need to-day more than ever,—the training of deft hands, quick eyes and ears, and above all the broader, deeper, higher culture of gifted minds and pure hearts. The power of the ballot we need in sheer self-defence,—else what shall save us from a second slavery? Freedom, too, the long-sought, we still seek,—the freedom of life and limb, the freedom to work and think, the freedom to love and aspire. Work, culture, liberty,—all these we need, not singly but together, not successively but together, each growing and aiding each, and all striving toward that vaster ideal that swims before the Negro people, the ideal of human brotherhood, gained through the unifying ideal of Race; the ideal of fostering and developing the traits and talents of the Negro, not in opposition to or contempt for other races, but rather in large conformity to the greater ideals of the American Republic, in order that some day on American soil two world-races may give each to each those characteristics both so sadly lack. We the darker ones come even now not altogether empty-handed: there are to-day no truer exponents of the pure human spirit of the Declaration of Independence than the American Negroes; there is no true American music but the wild sweet melodies of the Negro slave; the American fairy tales and folk-lore are Indian and African; and, all in all, we black men seem the sole oasis of simple faith and reverence in a dusty desert of dollars and smartness. Will America be poorer if she replaces her brutal dyspeptic blundering with light-hearted but determined Negro humility? or her coarse and cruel wit with loving jovial good-humor? or her vulgar music with the soul of the Sorrow Songs?

Merely a concrete test of the underlying principles of the great republic is the Negro Problem, and the spiritual striving of the freedmen's sons is the travail of souls whose burden is almost beyond the measure of their strength, but who bear it in the name of an historic race, in the name of this the land of their fathers' fathers, and in the name of human opportunity.

◆ ◆ ◆

Questions for Understanding and Critical Thinking

1. When was Du Bois first made to realize that he was "different from the others"? What effect did this realization have on him?
2. According to Du Bois, how did the harsh treatment received by African Americans affect their work as black artisans, ministers, doctors, and practitioners in other occupations?
3. What did Du Bois mean when he wrote that "to be a poor man is hard but to be a poor race in a land of dollars is the very bottom of hardships"?
4. Do you think Du Bois's concerns regarding double consciousness are valid today? What social changes have occurred to ameliorate the problem? What aspects of society have not changed sufficiently to eliminate the problem?

ARTICLE 4

Ethnic Labels, Latino Lives by Peruvian American scholar Suzanne Oboler explores the implications and the history and current use of the label *Hispanic* for a wide diversity of people of Latin American descent. She has investigated the widely held belief that all first-generation Latin American immigrants in the United States share the same cultural identity as Hispanics. Through interviews with 9 men and 13 women employed in the New York garment industry, Oboler shows why this assumption is inaccurate. She also demonstrates how race, class, and gender are interlocking dimensions of U.S. Latina/Latino identity.

Suzanne Oboler, who teaches Latin Studies and American Civilization at Brown University, has spent the past decade examining the meaning and implication of ethnic labels in people's lives. Her work focuses on the need to broaden access and develop strategies to ensure full participation and social justice for all in the United States.

Looking Ahead

1. Why do many Latin Americans view U.S. racial categories as misleading?
2. What influence did social class location in their country of origin have on Latinas' and Latinos' responses to being labeled *Hispanic* after they became residents of the mainland United States?
3. What terms other than *Hispanic* were preferred by some of Oboler's respondents?

Language, National Identity, and the Ethnic Label *Hispanic*

◆ *Suzanne Oboler*

Insofar as racial and ethnic distinctions in Latin America are not attributed the same significance as class, Latin Americans' "discovery" of the salience of race and ethnicity as a form of social classification in [the United States] is particularly significant to explore. While the men and women in this study could easily describe their perceptions of their situation in relation to their own past, most of them—particularly those with a working-class background—found it more difficult to articulate their position in the hi-

Source: From Suzanne Oboler, *Ethnic Labels, Latino Lives: Identity and the Politics of (Re)Presentation in the United States* (Minneapolis: University of Minnesota Press, 1995), pp. 129–144. Copyright © 1995 by the Regents of the University of Minnesota. Reprinted by permission.

erarchy of racial and ethnic classification and distinctions that they encountered in the United States. While some of the Latin American immigrants I interviewed tried to understand its rationale, others viewed it as an unresolved given. The following exchange among four Latin American women is telling in this respect:

> In the census you're not allowed to write down that you're white. It's so strange. I have a Colombian friend, he's really very white. He looked like an egg-white. He became an American citizen and when they asked him for his skin color, he wrote down "white." But they said to him: "You're not white," and they erased the color. "What color are you going to make me?" "Black," they said. Can you imagine that? A guy who's so white that he's virtually transparent! (Soledad, Colombia)

> Sure I can. But you know, my passport says I'm white. (Verónica, Dominican Republic)

> Well, it may say you're white, but you're not white here. (Milagros, Peru)

> That's right. Here they won't say you're white for anything! The only whites here are Americans. They won't put you down as white. (Soledad, Colombia)

> Why not? (Verónica, Dominican Republic)

> I don't know. It's the way they do things here. (Soledad, Colombia)

> It's because their race is white. So they think no one else can be white. (Dolores, Guatemala)

> Yes. It's their source of pride. (Milagros, Peru)

These women are critical of the fact that Hispanics are differentiated from "whites." At the same time, this exchange points to the fact that Latin Americans filter the racial categories in this country through their own racial categorizations. In so doing, however,

they implicitly acknowledge that perceptions in their societies do indeed adhere to the same type of racial criteria that prevails in the United States, although it is important to emphasize that these perceptions are interpreted in a different light in the dominant Latin American discourse. Hence, statements such as "They think no one else can be white" suggest the value that is attributed to "being white" in Latin America. So does their perception of "whiteness" as representing a "source of pride." Nevertheless, any similarities or comparisons should be drawn with caution, for in Latin America, race-related value judgments are publicly articulated in a different way than they are in U.S. society.

Indeed, every attempt is made to minimize the recognition of the effect of race in the organization of daily life in Latin America, to such an extent that the renowned Brazilian sociologist, Florestan Fernandes, once suggested that Brazilians' prejudice is rooted in their belief that they aren't prejudiced. This observation can be extended to represent, to varying degrees, the racial attitude present in Latin American countries.[1]

◆ ◆ ◆

To a large extent the meaning this group of immigrants attributed to the use of racial or ethnic forms of classification in this society was also influenced by the values stemming from their class positions in their own countries. These included not only class-based values but also the *culturally specific* racial prejudices that accompanied them in Latin America, given the close and gradated correlations between class and race there. Thus, for example, when asked to comment on whether his life had changed in the United States, Francisco, formerly a middle-class hearing specialist in his own country and now working in the garment industry, first established his class background, pointing out that there was considerable social distance between him and the other Latin Americans with whom he worked in the factory:

> They [Americans] exploit us with very low salaries, and they delude us into thinking that life is owning a car. Here it's common for people to have a car—you can get one dirt cheap; there's no status in it. You see, having an acceptable car, a good house does bring you status in any South American country. They delude people who could never have had a car in their own country. But the comforts of a good kitchen, of being able to wash your clothes, of having a dishwasher, a refrigerator, a good sound system, a television: none of that is really life. **There is no pride in acquiring any of it for anyone who comes here with an education.** (Francisco, Colombia; my emphasis)

In Latin America, having an "education" is one of the euphemisms for being middle class, and thus Francisco's discourse echoes a point raised by anthropologist Teófilo Altamirano in his study on the diversity of Peruvian immigrants in the United States:

> In concrete terms, the "American Dream" is associated with a comfortable lifestyle, with owning a house and car, with the benefits of the latest technology, with trips inside and out of the United States, with many dollars in the pocket and in the bank. In Peru, these aspirations are solely within the reach of the members of the upper and upper-middle classes.[2]

Having both distanced his aspirations and differentiated his (class-based) definition of "real life" from that of his working-class colleagues, Francisco proceeded to speak of the shift in his social status using the racial-ethnic hierarchy prevailing in the United States: that is, he compared his position and aspirations to those of the Latin American working-class immigrants with whom he

worked and *not to other middle-class immigrants like himself:*

> The fact is that they've got us [Latin Americans] poorer here. . . . **Our people** are coming here and are really being taken in by material factors. (Francisco, Colombia; my emphasis)

Terms such as "us" and "our people" clearly refer to an assumed Latin American "ethnic group"—regardless of the various nationalities and class positions it encompasses. Thus, Francisco used the classification based on ethnic grouping that prevails in U.S. society, rather than the Latin American emphasis on class, to discuss his perception of the social issues affecting him in this country.

Indeed, although in our discussion Francisco constantly separated himself socially from the other Latin Americans in the factory, he was also very conscious of the ways in which racial and ethnic categories in the United States obviate his own use of social class distinctions:

> My eyes have been opened in relation to Europeans here. I've found out that a lot of Europeans are illiterate. The problem is that we Latin Americans are not appreciated. We are considered the lowest race here. We are only here to work at the bottom. Because there's a bad policy here in the U.S. There are around 32 or 33 million of us and yet we are considered a minority. The percentage of Greeks, Germans, Poles, is very low, yet they have special privileges which we don't have. (Francisco, Colombia)

In the above statement, Francisco does not talk about the "special privileges" accorded to *all* Americans: Instead, he refers to "privileged" white European ethnic groups, whom he perceives as sharing his social, racial, and educational background, and excludes African Americans and other non-white citizens. Thus, he believes his own trajectory in this country should emulate "Greeks, Germans, Poles," because in his country, he shared what he perceives to be their white, middle-class values. He does not take into account their national origins or the specific immigrant history of their respective groups in this country.

Indeed a comparison between the ways that the previous class backgrounds of Francisco and María have shaped how they perceive their position in this society are quite telling. María discusses her successful position today in terms of a past situation that she identifies negatively:

> *"It's hard, life is really hard there [in the Dominican Republic]. . . . I've gone up in life here. I can't complain about this country. It's helped me a lot." (María, Dominican Republic)*

Francisco, on the other hand, speaks of his past in glowing terms, and does "complain about this country." Moreover, whereas María looks to the past in assessing her current situation, Francisco projects himself into the future, comparing his (low) status as a Latin American with "Greeks, Germans, Poles"—that is, with Americans who, as he states, "have special privileges which we don't have." In other words, Francisco has adopted the ethnic-racial discourse prevailing in this society as a strategy that, on one hand, differentiates him from other Latin American workers and, on the other, claims the same rights accorded to middle-class, assimilated Americans. In order to preserve his previous (higher) class position, he adopts ethnic and racial categories of discourse prevalent in the United States to articulate his position in his new society.

Both María's satisfaction with what she has achieved here and Francisco's evaluation of his situation in this society are linked to their respective past lived experiences. Francisco's demand for equal and full rights is in accordance with his class position in his old society and his desire to attain it once again in his new society. María's discourse, on the other hand, appears to be grounded more in her accommodation or resignation to a particular social status, which she perceives more positively here in the United States. In her words, "After paying all the bills, it's almost the same here [as the Dominican Republic], but you are more comfortable here." In contrast to Francisco, María identifies and compares her current status in relation to her home country rather than to United States society. Indeed, María's discourse—which includes the bringing of her family to this country—contrasts with Francisco's in that it emphasizes her successes: her expectations in terms of achieving a better life for herself and her family at least appear to have been fulfilled. As she put it, "Everything I used to think about [coming to the United States] when I was a little girl has become a reality for me. I achieved it on the basis of sacrifice and effort."

Francisco's expectations, on the other hand, are far from fulfilled. His references to the past serve primarily to point out how much better off he was in his old country. His discourse, unlike María's, includes a desire for incorporation into U.S. society, albeit projected into the future and defined by him in terms of equal access to the rights and privileges of the (white) middle classes in the United States.

Indeed, for poorer Latin Americans like María, accustomed as they are to perceive class belonging as the determinant of social mobility and status, social mobility in the United States may indeed be enhanced, at least potentially, whether or not they are "lumped" together with nonwhites and regardless of nationality. However, for those who, like Francisco, were better off before they immigrated, the road to incorporation into American society may be more costly, at least in terms of cultural perceptions. Once in the United States, all Latin Americans are "Hispanics," and thus all have to come to terms with this ethnic label assigned to them by the host society. At the same time, those like Francisco confront discrimination often for the first time and are further forced to recognize, through their own individual experience, the significance of racial and social prejudices, stereotypes, and labels that their own country's social organization historically allowed them to bypass, by virtue of their previous higher social status in their society's hierarchy.

◆ ◆ ◆

THE IMPACT OF SOCIAL CLASS IN DEFINING THE LABEL HISPANIC

. . . For a middle-class, college-educated immigrant like Francisco, incorporation into U.S. society involves access to the same rights and privileges of the (white) middle-class citizens. Francisco measured the extent of his potential or actual incorporation into U.S. society in terms of those (whites) he perceives as belonging, like himself, to the category of "first-class" citizens in this country. In so doing he shifted his categories of interpretation to include the ethnic and racial classifications prevailing in this society, abandoning his past as a measure of comparison. Many of the working-class people in this study tended, on the other hand, to measure their progress in the United States specifically against their life chances in their past society. Since their point of comparison is their homeland rather than their new society, at first sight, they seemingly pay little attention to the categories used to measure progress in this society or to the extent of their incorporation into U.S. society. Instead, they perceive themselves more in terms of having achieved the greater material comfort promised to them by the Ameri-

can Dream, long exported to their countries, that motivated their immigration in the first place.[3] Unlike the middle-class immigrants, then, it seems reasonable to suggest that many of the working-class participants in this study tended to perceive the very act of their immigration as a significant step toward fulfilling their dream for social mobility and an achievement in itself.

The Middle-Class Response

"They invented the word Hispanic to discriminate against us."

The culturally derived importance of establishing one's identity and position in social terms in Latin American society can lead middle-class immigrants to use U.S. categories about their origins to define their group's social position in the United States. In her interview, Soledad, the other middle-class, college-educated person in this study, insisted that each individual should be identified by her or his nationality. Nevertheless, like Francisco, she also immediately adopted the U.S. ethnic category, Hispanic, rather than that of her nationality to refer to Latin Americans in this country. Her perception of both its positive and negative value emerged in the following discussion among Soledad and three other Latin American women concerning the census questionnaire:

> *I'm Colombian, but I wrote down that I was Hispanic. (Soledad, Colombian)*
>
> *I think they wanted you to write it so that they know who speaks Spanish. (Verónica, Dominican Republic)*
>
> *Yes. But it's also to send more help to the Hispanic communities, like for bilingual schools and things like that. (Soledad)*
>
> *I remember that further down on that [census] form they had something about what race or tribe you belong to. (Verónica)*

Yes, there was a part that said, Dominican, Puerto Rican. (Soledad)

Well, I know that they separate Puerto Ricans. (Dolores, Guatemala)

I didn't see that. Why do they do that? (Milagros, Peru)

I don't know why. (Dolores)

Oh, I do. It's because they're undecided about Puerto Ricans. They don't really know if they're American or if they're Puerto Rican. See, they have a problem with Puerto Ricans because they can't believe that they can be Americans and still speak Spanish. So they catalogue them as Americans for some things, but for others they're Puerto Ricans. When they count for something they're Americans, but when they don't need them to count for anything they're **boricuas.** *But in different ways, they do that with all of us who speak Spanish. You know, if an American is running, he's just doing exercise, but if one of us is running, we've just committed a robbery. (Soledad)*

In the above conversation, Soledad first identified herself as Colombian but insofar as she recognized the discussion was within the context of the U.S. census, she then immediately translated her identity into the U.S. terminology, Hispanic. ("I'm Colombian, but I wrote down that I was Hispanic.") Her discussion of the greater social benefit to be derived from grouping all Latin American nationalities together as Hispanics—in terms of resource allocations for services such as bilingual schools and so on—shows that she is aware of the government's policies and the relationship between formal ethnic identification and the distribution of resources. However, while Soledad recognizes the social value of the term Hispanic, she is also aware of the stereotypes associated with it: first by implicitly alluding to her understanding of its source—the unresolved political condi-

tion and ambivalent position of Puerto Ricans in the United States—and then by attributing to language much of their difficulties ("They can't believe that they can be Americans and still speak Spanish"). Soledad ends her statement by extending her allusions to the prejudice she perceives against Puerto Ricans to encompass "all of us who speak Spanish" and provides an example of her perception of the prejudice against Hispanics as committing crimes in the United States.

Like Soledad, Francisco did not hesitate to include himself in the category of Hispanic as he discussed his position *as a Hispanic* relative to the rest of the population in this society. According to him, "there are around 32 or 33 million of us and yet we are considered a minority. . . . They do not appreciate us. Hispanics' labor must be among the lowest here. We are doing jobs that Americans don't want" (Francisco, Colombia). Similarly, he too seems to be aware of the importance of ethnicity in the organization of U.S. society and discusses the term itself, referring primarily to its negative attributes in this context:

They invented the word Hispanic to discriminate against us. It is used to separate us from a cultural point of view. It is used to separate us from a religious point of view. It is used to separate us from an economic point of view. It is used to separate us from an intellectual point of view. They do not recognize our merits. We have several Nobel prize winners. . . . But in this country, they don't acknowledge our achievements. (Francisco, Colombia)

Both Francisco and Soledad perceive the term Hispanic as signifying discrimination against Latin Americans and hence identify it as a term of segregation of "all of us" from mainstream U.S. society. Nevertheless, they use it to identify themselves within the U.S.

context, thus accepting the ethnic and racial categories in the country. At the same time, they both discussed the position of all Hispanics in the United States in broader sociological rather than personal terms, commenting on the negative implications of the term and comparing the position of Hispanics to that of other groups in this society. This is in marked contrast with the response of the working-class men and women for whom the term's negative connotation is perceived to have directly personal implications. As the next section demonstrates, they seek to distance themselves from being considered Hispanics by emphasizing their national rather than ethnic identity.

The Working-Class Response

"Hispanic? That's what they call us."

Unlike either of the middle-class people discussed above, the rest of the men and women in this study were not as prone to identify themselves explicitly as Hispanics. Like that of their middle-class counterparts, the point of departure in establishing their identity in this country stemmed from their past social status and position in their country of origin. But unlike Francisco and Soledad, the working-class immigrants measured their progress in the United States in terms of their society of origin, where it is not unlikely that, given their social standing, many of them would be considered, in Gilberto Velho's terminology, second- and third-class citizens. In this sense, they would view themselves as better off in this country—as the case of María exemplifies—and hence would be applying the categories reserved for measuring incorporation into their previous society, rather than this one.

It is not surprising then that when asked about the meaning of the term Hispanic, many, unlike Soledad and Francisco, initially dismissed the term altogether. Two of them flatly stated that they hadn't heard the word before. One identified it by explaining that she had "heard on the radio that that's what they call us."

Pointing to the word Hispanic on the union's school registration form, María acknowledged that she would check it off rather than any of the other ethnic identifiers on the form, but added:

> *I never even noticed that it had an "H" and an "I" in front of it. For some reason, I only saw the rest of the word "SPANIC." I assumed it referred to Spanish, to my language. That's why I'd mark that one. I think they use it because they want to know if you speak Spanish. (María, Dominican Republic)*

Moreover, most of the comments and explanations about the usage of the term invariably contained qualifiers such as "I think," "I believe," "maybe"—attesting to their lack of familiarity with the subject of our discussion, the meaning of the term Hispanic in the U.S. context and, particularly, with "their" (namely, Americans') intentions in formulating the concept.

While several explained the term Hispanic as reflecting language use, others made statements whose meaning in one way or another reflected the following comment by one informant: "Hispanic? Oh, yes, that's what *they* call us" (Dolores, Guatemala). However, the majority were reluctant to self-identify as Hispanics and hesitated to discuss the term, perceiving it as identifying a group of people whose negative attributes had absolutely no correspondence to themselves:

> *Hispanic? Yes, I know they call us that. I think the word Hispanic is used for everyone who speaks Spanish. But actually I don't know what it means. You see, there are dif-*

ferent conceptions of Hispanics. They think we are all alike. Sometimes they say, oh, yes, that's a Hispanic. We're not going to rent to him because he's Hispanic. They think that Hispanics are noisy; that they are badly educated; that they have no morals. Sometimes that's because they have no education. . . . Then others will say, oh yes, those are Hispanics. They're so dirty. They'll point to a building and say the people in there are pigs. Why? Because there are two or three families in a building who have the bad habit of throwing cans into the street, or making noise. So because of those two or three families, they call us all Hispanics. (Rosa, El Salvador)

According to Rosa, Hispanic is a term that "they" [Americans] use as a synonym for pigs, for people who are dirty, have bad habits, and are noisy. In trying to evade these negative connotations, it is not surprising that many find reasons to simply distance themselves from the term:

It's wrong to call us Hispanic. Because that word applies to the Spaniards. We're not Spaniards. We're from Latin America. (Alicia, Colombia)

In so doing, they signaled their deep disapproval of those they conceive of as Hispanics in this society:

Americans think that we come here to take away something that belongs to them. A lot of people give them that image. Many go into drugs, some don't work and so on. No wonder they think badly of Hispanics. (Verónica, Dominican Republic)

I know Americans think that we don't like to work, that we're disorganized and messy. It's because wherever there is something broken or dirty there's always a Hispanic. (Milagros, Peru)

Indeed, sometimes the discussion on the negative meaning attributed to the term Hispanics brings out prejudices that one national group might have about another:

I don't want to mention specific nationalities but it is true that there are people who put music on really loud; they drink beer and throw the cans out on the street. (Rosa, El Salvador)

Thus, not surprisingly, several informants like Alicia, quoted earlier, rejected the definition of Hispanic for themselves and for others from Latin America:

I will call myself by my nationality, no matter where I live. (Irene, Ecuador)

We should be called South Americans, or Central Americans. It depends on where you're from. (Julián, Peru)

Rosa explicitly linked her understanding of the meaning of the term Hispanic to her knowledge of the Spanish language:

When someone asks me what I am, I say I'm Salvadorean. I'm Central American from El Salvador, and that's it. (Rosa, El Salvador)

What if someone answers you by asking, "Then you are a Hispanic?"

No, I don't think that. I just think, "Oh well, maybe they call me that because I speak Spanish." Because the first thing I say to an American if I'm lost on the street, or if I have to go to an office is "Do you speak Spanish?" So, it probably comes from that. (Rosa, El Salvador)

Refusing to identify herself as a Hispanic, she thus negatively assesses its social value. Rosa's statement concerning Americans' use of the term Hispanic as being due to the fact that she always asks Americans "Do you speak Spanish?" sounds almost naive when contrasted to her harsher evaluation that the label results from the "lack of morals" of "two or three families." In this respect Rosa, like others in this study, shows her fear of having the connotations of the label imposed on her sense of self and life and, in so doing, openly distances herself from the label in personal rather than in the broad sociological terms adopted by Francisco and Soledad.

◆ ◆ ◆

ENDNOTES

1. Renato Ortiz, *Cultura e identidade nacional*, 36; Morner, *Race Mixture in the History of Latin America*; Richard Graham, ed., *The Idea of Race in Latin America, 1870–1940*; and Leslie Rout, *African Experience in Spanish America, 1512 to the Present*.

2. Teófilo Altamirano, *Los que se fueron: Peruanos en Estados Unidos*. Lima: Fondo Editorial de la Pontifica Universidad Católica del Peru, 1988.

3. G. Moura, *Tio Sam chega ao Brasil: A penetração cultural americana* (São Paulo: Brasilience, 1984); and Altamirano, *Los que se fueron*.

Questions for Understanding and Critical Thinking

1. How is language related to the construction of social and racial identities?
2. What measures do middle-class, college-educated immigrants use to determine the extent of their incorporation into U.S. society?
3. How do working-class people measure their progress in the United States?
4. Do you think some Latin American immigrants might have ambivalent feelings about their experiences in the United States? Why or why not?

ARTICLE 5 _____

In this article, Felix M. Padilla and Lourdes Santiago describe Santiago's childhood experiences in a Puerto Rican neighborhood in the United States where people had a strong sense of community but more limited opportunities and life chances when compared with elite persons listed in the *Social Register,* as described in Stephen Richard Higley's article (Article 6).

To write *Outside the Wall: Childhood Years and Family Life,* from which this article was taken, Felix M. Padilla, a sociology professor at Northeastern University, conducted extensive interviews with Lourdes Santiago, a Puerto Rican woman whose husband is serving a 70-year prison term for allegedly killing a rival gang member. Ms. Santiago currently participates in church activities and in other groups that support unity among prison inmates and their family members.

Looking Ahead

1. How was Santiago's childhood residence linked to her ethnic identity?
2. Why do nonresidents often see a neighborhood differently from persons who reside there?
3. How does Santiago view poverty in her neighborhood?
4. What kinds of racial injustice did Santiago and her family experience when they went outside their own neighborhood?

Outside the Wall
Childhood Years and Family Life

♦ *Felix M. Padilla and Lourdes Santiago*

For as long as I can remember we lived in the Humboldt Park area—what we call Division Street. Division Street is where the major cultural activities and structures of the Puerto Rican community were found. Like we used to say when we were youngsters, "Division Street was what was happening."

We lived in a different neighborhood before moving to Division Street. My brother remembers living on the South Side, near Sacramento and Roosevelt [streets]. I vaguely remember that because I was very young. But I do remember my father's youngest brother getting married there. I still remember the church. The few memories I still have of that neighborhood make it seem so different from the way it is now. People would sit on benches without having to worry about be-

Source: From Felix M. Padilla and Lourdes Santiago, *Outside the Wall: A Puerto Rican Woman's Struggle,* copyright © 1993 by Felix M. Padilla and Lourdes Santiago, pp. 32–42. Reprinted by permission of Rutgers University Press.

ing mugged or anything. That has changed totally now.

When my brother was eight or nine we moved to the north side, to Division Street. I think we came to live here because things were getting really bad in our old neighborhood. It was changing, and there were always frictions and fights between the black boys and Puerto Rican boys. So, my parents decided to leave. I'm not saying that my parents have anything against other racial groups, but from their conversations it was clear that they felt they weren't safe there anymore. They wanted to move where there were more Puerto Ricans. The fact that Division Street was emerging as a Puerto Rican neighborhood appealed to them a great deal. They believed that it would be more appropriate to raise their children among others of their kind. They felt that in a Puerto Rican neighborhood everyone knew how to deal with one another. Because we share the same culture, my parents assumed that, even in cases of friction, we would have the know-how for resolving them. And, since my parents did not speak English very well, they had difficulties understanding things people said to them in our other neighborhood.

People say that my neighborhood is terrible, but I'm glad to say that people can grow up and make something out of their life. I grew up here, and, though I married a gang member, we've come a long way, and we've learned that life teaches us a lot and we can turn things around. I would get very upset to hear people put down this neighborhood. There were the teachers in school who hated Division Street, the very same neighborhood where they taught. They were always making smart remarks about the 'hood and the people in it. Since I was young, I guess I couldn't understand why they would say those things. I knew that there were problems, but I still didn't see things as bad as they made them seem. Now

that I'm much older, I see things differently. However, since I'm still here, I guess I must like it.

When I was young I had this perception of Humboldt Park that this neighborhood, my neighborhood, was the extent of life. As far as I was concerned, this was it. I imagined that beyond this point, that beyond this area, there wasn't much more. Obviously, I knew there were other neighborhoods, parks, and schools, but I couldn't see anything other than the local store, the local grammar school, and the high school on the corner. Division Street was much of what I knew.

There was this older store owned by an older American couple but which is no longer there. The kids from the neighborhood came to know the couple very well. I'm sure this couple saw us in our mother's stomach. They saw us as babies. They knew us from the very beginning. We had this special respect for them, like if they were part of our family. To them we were not only customers; we were the kids from the neighborhood, their kids. It was special.

When I was in grammar school every day after school I would stop at the store along with the other kids. There were times when we would just stand in front and hang out. We would talk and gossip. Other times we would go inside and buy candy for a few pennies. Or sometimes we would go inside the store to browse around to see if any new candy had come in. I used to go there every day. Everyone stopped there from school. It was our hangout place. Every neighborhood where there is a grammar school you can find a store like the one that existed in ours. And kids adopt it as theirs.

And then there was a store owned by a Puerto Rican man—the store was very Puerto Rican. People would go and buy what they needed to cook with: their seasonings and their tomatoes and their lettuce. This is where people went to buy their rice and beans and all the other foods from the island. And you could go there and get your Spanish newspaper as well as catching up on the latest gossip because people were always standing outside and inside talking about the goings-on in the neighborhood, in their lives, in Puerto Rico. For some people the store was a very important source of information. They learned where to find a cheaper apartment or car, what happened with so-and-so and why so-and-so moved out or why so-and-so got divorced.

I remember the owner of the store as always being kind and caring. He extended credit to his customers. You could go there, buy some items, and say, "I'll pay you next week" *(apuntalo),* and the owner would say, "Okay." Of course, the credit sheet [the list on which debts are noted] for every customer would be very long. Buying on credit was one way of living and surviving.

My neighborhood was a world within itself. People could live here without having to have contact with the outside world. Why should they? Everything they needed was here. And, since we were mostly Latinos, it was like a big family. Because my mother didn't drive, and because of the fact that we attended school in the neighborhood and we were involved in church, there wasn't really much of anything else. That's what I used to think. Maybe in the summer we would go to the park, or my father would take us to Kiddyland. Later, after my mother divorced my father and remarried, my stepfather would take us out because he had friends, and in the summer we would go out to Lake Geneva in Wisconsin. I remember that we would drive to Lake Geneva and see a world that was totally different. This was the world of country life and living. I used to like the country. There were horses and cows. The air smelled different. Everything seemed so free.

I couldn't help but compare what I would see outside of Chicago to Humboldt Park. Where we lived was not very safe. On those few times when we went to the park with our parents we had to be careful at all times because the gangs were at war with one another. And then all of a sudden there is this environment where you could run around freely and play and go into the water. It was quite different. And, as a child, I used to wish that we could live there. But it was only a dream. It is not like I told my mother, "Let's move there," but, as working-class people, we simply could not afford to travel to many places outside the neighborhood, and when we did have a chance to go somewhere it didn't matter how the place was— we were always impressed by it. I see these places today and wonder how could I have reacted to them the way I did then. They do not look attractive; they seem so lifeless.

But my neighborhood was my neighborhood, and that's where I was and presumably was going to stay. There is no denying that neighborhood people were poor. This didn't matter to me because we were all in the same boat. We weren't any poorer or richer than other folks. We were all pretty much the same, and we weren't trying to outdo the other. I couldn't see any difference.

My mother always pointed out to us that, no matter how poor we were, if we were good with other people, that was how you became rich. What she was telling us was to always be proud of who we are, not to let anyone make us feel inferior just because we may not have what they have in terms of material possessions or even in education attainment. I have never felt ashamed for not having or owning what others possess. My dignity is what makes me rich and makes me feel good. Being good and fair to other people was my riches. I learned these wonderful lessons from my mother. I'm glad that she taught us those values because I have lived some very difficult times, and her lessons have carried me forward.

And, although the people in the neighborhood were poor, they treated each other with respect. People in the neighborhood treated one another as a family. Everybody knew each other. There was a lot of caring. There was a sharing of commitment for individuals and families. People knew everyone who moved in and out of the neighborhood. When something would happen there was always someone there to take care of it or to address the particular situation. It was known that people could rely on their neighbors. If you had a fight with the kid next door, the kid's mother would come over and work things out with your mother. When we were kids it was difficult doing things in the neighborhood because, if people saw you, they would immediately bring the news over to your house. Missing school when you were expected to be in class—that wonderful custom that so many kids try at least once in a lifetime—was a very risky thing to do. Dare you be seen by someone who knew your family, you were sure to get a beating from your mother or father because they would learn about it.

For Lourdes straying outside Division Street did not always produce positive outcomes. During visits to areas such as downtown Chicago she experienced directly the racial tension and antagonism of U.S. society. Individuals reacted to Lourdes and her family, as Puerto Ricans, with much racial indifference or even disdain. Lourdes and her family were made to feel like intruders, people who had stepped outside their boundaries. In other words, Lourdes experienced the unpleasant feeling associated with the question, stated openly or not: What are these Puerto Ricans doing here? These encounters reminded Lourdes and her family that, as Puerto Ricans, they were targets of racial prejudice and discrimination. Instead of succumbing to these threats, Lourdes and her family used them to further strengthen their ethnicity. Their commitment to the goodness and worthiness of their Puerto Rican ethnic tradition was reinforced by these acts of racial injustice.

Going downtown to State Street was a big deal. We had a tradition in our family that, in the winter, my cousin or aunt would take us downtown to window-shop. We used to go there to see the Christmas tree and to walk down State Street, to ride the train. It was fun. We would go to the store and see merchandise I knew I never would buy.

I also met with people there who were outright nasty. They would be all dressed up in fancy clothes, basically with their noses up in the air and walking and looking at you like, "What is this Puerto Rican kid doing here, walking downtown, out of her neighborhood?" I didn't care about their attitude because I was out to have a nice time and I thought I had every right to be there just like they did.

Going downtown was extremely hard on my mother because to this day she doesn't speak very much English. If she tried to communicate in a store when buying something, she always tried to ask for assistance. I could always see people being nasty and making fun of her. Although we would translate for her, I could still notice the pain and embarrassment she was suffering. My mother would tell us in Spanish, *"Esa persona es tan ignorante"* (That person is so ignorant).

My mother used these occasions to remind us about the importance of not letting people downgrade us. Since she couldn't answer back because of her language difference, she would still tell us to remain unmoved about what others say about us. She's very firm and strong when it comes to having people respect you. If she doesn't like something, she lets the person know. She is like that to this day. If she goes into a restaurant and the food is cold, she immediately tells the waiter, "My food should be hot—I'm paying for it." She doesn't accept anything that she's not supposed to get.

If my mother walks into a store and people begin to follow her around, she simply walks out. Even if that is the only store where she could find what she's looking for, she will walk away. This is another of her ways for dealing with people who treat her rude.

I find myself doing that sometimes, though I think I'm more outspoken. Before I used to accept things; hardly ever did I fight for anything. But not anymore. I've gone into stores, and people have followed me, and I find this very annoying, so I've walked right out.

A series of events contributed to the transformation of Lourdes's neighborhood into a site saturated with much intergang rivalry among youths. Residents who had lived in the neighborhood for a long time began moving away. Many returned to Puerto Rico, while others went to live with a son or daughter in a different neighborhood. Others simply moved their family to what they believed to be safer neighborhoods.

Puerto Rican youngsters from the second generation, who were in their teens a few years earlier, started turning to the gang in search of the identity, dignity, and monetary possessions they believed the larger society had denied them. As a teenager, Lourdes too was a member of this generation of young people who were changing the character of Division Street.

As the years went on, things began changing in the neighborhood. It starting getting a little bit worse. Some of the older residents, the older Puerto Rican residents who seemed to have lived there for years, began to move out because they didn't have any more kids. They decided to go live with a son or daugh-

ter who was married. Some retired and finally went home to Puerto Rico. For this last group the dream of going home to their beloved island was finally accomplished. They came to Chicago to work and to return someday; they did, though many were old. Others went back to Puerto Rico because they felt that the education system here was terrible and their kids could be better educated in Puerto Rico.

There was my neighbor from next door who decided to go back to Puerto Rico. That was hard for me, my sister, and brother because the daughters and sons were close with us. We were best of friends. Then the neighbor next to them, with whom we were very close too, bought a house and moved. The people on the first floor from where we lived left the neighborhood as well.

All of this happened within one single year. It was like removing the foundation of a house. You knew that the walls would crumble because they could not support themselves. It's funny that I had thought this way at that time since I was so young. But that's exactly how I saw what was happening. It was like an exchange taking place: the older people who had been there for many, many years were moving out, and younger people were coming in. This kind of exchange always spells some trouble.

Many of the young people who moved in were involved in gangs. I really believe that it was gang activity that made the people start moving out. In my view gang activities changed everything. The gangs were spreading throughout the neighborhood. There were the Cobras and Disciples in the same general area, while a few blocks away there were the Jivers and Spanish Lords. The kids were now fourteen or fifteen, and they were becoming members of the various neighborhood gangs. It seemed like there were thousands of these young people. They were members of my generation.

It is my belief that the coming of this generation of teenagers is responsible for the visibility of gang activity in our neighborhood. I remember that, while there were gangs before, you sometimes didn't notice them. But with the coming of all these kids it was quite obvious that gangs were developing into large organizations. We became aware that they were spreading throughout the neighborhood searching for drug-dealing markets. Gangs were creating their drug-dealing corners and making sure that oppositional gangs did not take over them. So, there developed a group of guys on that corner and this other corner who were saying, "I'm not moving out of here, this is my 'hood." What finally happened was that one gang began selling this product on this particular corner, another was selling the same product on another corner, and customers were going to only one. Before long the gangs who were competing for the same clientele starting fighting one another. And, of course, that is when the shootings and killings began. That's when people said, "This is not for me—I want out of here." And they began moving out of the neighborhood and going elsewhere.

My family moved out to a different area in the neighborhood, but after getting married I moved right back. I feel like I belong here. Even now, as I sit down with my coworkers, who know my experience of grief and pain, they ask me: "Why don't you move out? Why are you still there since his [my husband's] friends live in the neighborhood?" To me this is my neighborhood. I feel safe here. I don't think I can be this safe someplace else. Here I know everyone. When I walk down the street and people see me coming they say: "Oh, yeah, that's Lourdes. She's Doña Juanita's daughter." I'm very aware of the fact that many bad things happen as well, but I just feel comfortable.

Another thing is that I'm seeing that the people are coming back, and the youth that grew up here are buying property and reestablishing their roots. Not far from here are a couple of brothers who used to be gangbangers; they now own their buildings. Further down from these guys are four brothers who just bought their own house. That makes me feel good because they could have bought elsewhere. They decided to stay here and help to rebuild the neighborhood.

It's funny because I know these guys. I saw them growing up and doing the things that most kids were doing in those days. They used to write on the walls of buildings, but, now that they are home owners, they are making sure that nobody does this to their property. So, in essence they can help out a lot because, by enforcing the law of the neighborhood as they see things now, they're ensuring that their property is well maintained. This behavior makes other people in the neighborhood become more watchful of what they own.

◆ ◆ ◆

Questions for Understanding and Critical Thinking

1. Why did Santiago and her friends say, "Division Street was what was happening"?
2. How does an ethnic grocery store sometimes provide more than just groceries to area residents? Can you identify an ethnic grocery store in your community? Describe it.

3. How did Santiago's neighborhood change over time? What impact do such changes have on residents?
4. Why did Santiago decide to move back to the "old neighborhood" after she got married and moved away?
5. Is there a neighborhood that provides you with a sense of community? What part, if any, do you think class and race play as integral parts of a feeling of community?

ARTICLE 6 _____

In this article, geographer Stephen Richard Higley illustrates how people in the United States have sorted themselves residentially by social class and status. Understanding the geography of social class makes it possible to better understand how the life chances and lifestyles of persons differ by class. Through use of the *Social Register*—a highly selective address and telephone book that lists pertinent facts about some members of elite upper-class families (such as addresses of first, second, and third residences; membership in exclusive clubs and ancestral societies; and the colleges and universities they attended)—Higley demonstrates how geographic proximity is an essential pillar of upper-class identity and solidarity.

Previously an advertising and marketing executive in Chicago, Stephen Richard Higley currently teaches geography at Oklahoma State University.

Looking Ahead

1. What characteristics distinguish the U.S. upper class from other social classes?
2. Why did Higley use the *Social Register* in his research?
3. What national upper-class residential patterns did Higley identify?

Privilege, Power, and Place

The Geography of the American Upper Class

◆ *Stephen Richard Higley*

Modern conceptions of social class are rooted in the writings of Karl Marx and the great German sociologist, Max Weber. . . . Whereas the Marxian conception of social class is fundamentally determined by one's relationship to the means of production, Weber refined the Marxist definition to include the concept of status as well as class. Marx felt that the simplification endemic to capitalism would give rise to a class con-sciousness that would eventually lead to class conflict. On the other hand, Weber viewed class solidarity as dependent on a group awareness of a common fate, a consideration of one another as equals, and the development of joint action to pursue common interests. Weber's definition of class and status is best put in his own words:

> *Status groups are normally communities. They are, however, often of an amorphous*

Source: From Stephen Richard Higley, *Privilege, Power, and Place: The Geography of the American Upper Class* (Lanham, MD: Rowman & Littlefield, 1995), pp. 13–30, 63–96. Copyright © Rowman & Littlefield. Reprinted by permission.

kind, in contrast to the purely economically determined "class situation," we wish to designate as "status situation" every typical component of the life fate of men that is determined by a specific, positive, or negative, social estimation of honor. . . .

In content, status honor is normally expressed in the fact that above all else, a specific style of life can be expected from all those that wish to belong to the circle. Linked with this expectation are restrictions on "social intercourse" (that is intercourse that is not subservient to economic or any other of business's "functional" purposes). These restrictions may confine normal marriage to within the status circle and may lead to complete endogomous enclosure. . . .

Of course, material monopolies provide the most effective motives for the exclusiveness of a status group. . . . With an increased enclosure of the status group, the conventional preferential opportunities for special employment grow into a legal monopoly of special offices for the members. . . .

With some over-simplification, one might thus say that "classes" are stratified according to their relations to the production and acquisition of goods; where "status groups" are stratified according to the principles of their consumption of goods as represented by special "styles of life." (Weber 1946, 186–193)

Weber defines the group of families that are at the apex of society's social order as members of both the American upper class and the uppermost American status group. For the purposes of this paper, the term "upper class" will be used as a descriptive term that denotes both class and status.

Using the *Social Register* to define the American upper class fits neatly within the Weberian definition of class and status groups. From a class perspective, the American upper class exhibits a class solidarity derived from the group awareness that they share a common fate. They consider one another equals, and their voting behavior in support of the Republican Party and their charitable efforts are the most obvious manifestations of their ability for joint action in the pursuit of common interests.

The uppermost American status group also corresponds closely to the Weberian definition of a status group. Those that are listed in the *Social Register* are chosen primarily for the style of life (and, implicitly, the system of values) that they exhibit. The main purpose of the *Social Register* is to restrict social intercourse for the members by acting as a ready reference as to who is "in" and who is "out" of proper society. Although it is hard to confirm due to the *Social Register*'s policy of not responding to inquiries, the *Social Register* strives to "confine normal marriage to within the status circle" by requiring members that marry outside the *Register* to resubmit themselves and their bride or groom for membership. And the *Social Register* is but one element of the upper class's complete system of socialization. The American upper class has attempted to separate itself socially from the *hoi polloi* literally from birth to death. From favored maternity hospitals and attending physicians to specific retirement homes such as Dunwoody Village in Newtown Square, Pennsylvania, and Cathedral Village in Washington, D.C., the *Social Register* succinctly fulfills the Weberian definition of a status group. Between birth and retirement are a full array of socializing institutions: prep schools, Ivy League schools, debutante balls, and metropolitan clubs, to name a few.

According to Weber, social class is determined by an individual's relation to the production and acquisition of goods. The upper-class families listed in the *Social Register* are direct descendants of the men who made great fortunes during the Gilded Age (1870–1910). Baltzell's research on Philadelphia clearly shows the links between the original fortune makers and the *Social Register* listees of 1940 (Baltzell 1958, 17–24). Because the vast majority of new listings are born into the *Social Register* (rather than inducted as new members), undoubtedly the [current] listees are overwhelmingly descended from the same families. If social class is determined by one's relation to the production and acquisition of goods, the American upper class as defined by the *Social Register* is truly a social class as well as a status group.

Weber wrote extensively on the relationship of class and status, viewing status as ultimately dependent on class (Gilbert and Kahl 1987, 10). The short- and long-term economic success of the upper class is fundamentally important to maintaining the style of life that differentiates the upper class from the other classes in society. Once a family no longer has the economic resources to give its members the advantages that money can buy in the United States, the fall from social grace is swift and sure. The family that is reduced to "shabby gentility" is an often-used literary device that underlines the importance of liquid assets to continued good standing in American society.

The men and women that defined late-nineteenth- and early-twentieth-century American upper-class society were overwhelmingly white, Anglo-Saxon, and protestant. As the personal, ethnic, and religious characteristics were unofficially codified, social and generational seasoning became equally important for acceptance into upper-class society. No amount of improperly socialized new money could buy its way into "proper" upper-class society.

◆ ◆ ◆

THE ELEMENTS OF UPPER-CLASS COHESION

Weber (1946) stated, "status honor is normally expressed by the fact that above all else a specific style of life can be expected from all those who wish to belong to the circle." The American upper class has a large number of institutions and associational arrangements that have made it possible for members to pass through life with very little significant contact with other social classes. This section reviews the most important of these institutions: private boarding schools (prep schools), colleges, metropolitan and country clubs, and the Episcopal and Presbyterian churches. The role of debutante balls, service organizations, and charitable organizations as contributing factors in maintaining upper-class cohesion will also be explored. Finally, an in-depth look at the *Social Register* will examine the role of neighborhood and community in upper-class cohesiveness.

Private Preparatory Schools

Of all the institutions that inculcate upper-class values, private preparatory schools may have the greatest role (Cookson and Persell 1985, 13–30). . . . In the second half of the nineteenth century . . . boarding schools became the preferred method of educating young upper-class men and women. Boarding schools made it possible to completely control the social and educational environment of the students (Cookson and Persell 1985, 31–48). Parents could be assured that their child would be raised away from the distractions of the large cities and their hordes of newly arrived aliens. The prep schools were staffed with teachers who could be relied on to transmit the values of the upper class. The WASP ethic of civility, honesty, principle, and service was imparted within a totally structured environment. The schools, particularly the Episcopalian schools, were modeled after the public schools of England, complete with "forms" for grades and "headmasters" for principals.

◆ ◆ ◆

The boarding schools were but one of a series of institutions founded during this era to create social distance between old money and new money. Country clubs and metropolitan clubs were other examples. It was also during this time that books such as the *Social Register* and various blue books were published to provide a scorecard as to who was in and who was out in proper society.

More important than the social distancing function that prep schools provide is the common socializing force that they exert on young men and women of the upper class. C. Wright Mills felt that prep schools were an essential element in the calculus of preserving privilege. He wrote:

> *As a selection and training place of the upper classes, both old and new, the private school is a unifying influence, a force for the nationalization of the upper classes. The less important the pedigreed family becomes in the careful transmission of moral and cultural traits, the more important the private school—rather than the upper-class family—is the most important agency for transmitting the traditions of the upper social classes, and regulating the new admission of wealth and talent. It is the characterizing point in the upper class experience. (Mills 1956, 64–65)*

Although upper-class schools were originally conceived to buffer the old guard from the nouveau riche, the need to infuse the upper class with new talent and money and the need to socialize the parvenus into the

minutiae of upper-class culture led to the acceptance of some newly moneyed families. As sociologist Randall Collins notes, "Schools primarily teach vocabulary and inflection, styles of dress, aesthetic tastes, values and manners" (Collins 1971, 101). Levine's 1980 study found that, in general, it took one generation to socialize upper-class fortunes. The sons of fathers who acquired large fortunes in the early twentieth century often placed their children in the most prestigious boarding schools. The fathers were not above building a new library or classroom building to assure their son's entrance. In most cases the sons went on to Ivy League schools and became members of the upper-class secret societies and eating clubs. They were also likely to be listed in the *Social Register*. Gaining membership in upper-class secret societies and eating clubs would not present a problem because sponsorship would come easily from former schoolmates that were already members of the clubs.

◆ ◆ ◆

In summary, boarding schools offered a place where the upper class could rest assured that class-supportive values would be instilled in their young. Their children would be exposed to only those nouveau riche children that were "acceptable" and to none of the perceived evils of the city. They would make valuable social and business friendships that would be nourished in college and in the world of private clubs during their adult lives.

An Upper-Class College Education

Just as there are preferred upper-class boarding schools to attend, there are preferred universities for young men and women of the upper class. The three universities that are considered most desirable by upper-class parents are Harvard, Yale, and Princeton. These three are followed by any other school in the Ivy League (Brown University has become increasingly popular among students) or any number of small prestigious schools located primarily in New England (e.g., Williams, Amherst, or Trinity). If an upper-class family lives in a state with an academically prestigious public university, such as Wisconsin, Michigan, or California, it is increasingly considered appropriate to attend them. In addition, there are selected private regional universities that are considered acceptable if one is not accepted at one's first choice. Examples of these schools are Duke, Stanford, and Northwestern.

◆ ◆ ◆

The Ivy League schools have had a long and fruitful relationship with the sixteen most prestigious boarding schools. The relationship has evolved over time as the entrance requirements to the Ivy League schools have changed and become infinitely more rigorous. Harvard started the change in 1926 when it began a policy of pursuing superior students with or without the proper social credentials. To be sure, attendance at an elite prep school is still the most assured route to the Ivy League, but it is no longer the only one. The boarding schools have remade themselves in Harvard's image—demanding more from their students with the realization that a gentlemen's "C" would no longer assure entrance to Harvard, Princeton, or Yale. Those prep schools that did not upgrade their curriculums to meet Harvard's demands fell swiftly from upper-class favor (St. Mark's School in Southborough, Massachusetts, fell and returned to grace in this manner). The percentage of students at the sixteen most prestigious boarding schools that attended Harvard, Princeton, or Yale dropped precipitously from 67 percent in the 1930s to 21 percent in 1973. An analysis of

admissions to all the Ivy League schools done by Cookson and Persell showed that in the 1982 school year, 42 percent of the graduates of the sixteen most prestigious prep schools were accepted at Ivy League schools. This compares with 27 percent accepted from other leading prep schools and 26 percent accepted from the entire applicant pool.

In 1982, students that attended private schools made up approximately 10 percent of all students applying for college, yet at Harvard, Princeton and Yale, they made up 34, 40, and 40 percent, respectively, of the entering freshman class (Cookson and Persell 1985, 167–189). It is clear, then, that there is a real connection between the socially prominent boarding schools and the Ivy League schools.

Fraternities and Eating Clubs

Once a young man has been accepted at Harvard, Princeton, or Yale, he is confronted with a large university that is dominated in numbers, if not tone, by members of other social classes. The solution to the problem of having to mix with upper middle class (or worse) is a system of private clubs similar to the fraternities and sororities found on many American campuses. The system of private clubs is best described in the words of Baltzell:

> *An intricate system of exclusive clubs, like the fraternities on less rarified American campuses, serve to insulate the members of the upper class from the rest of the students at Harvard, Princeton and Yale. There are virtually "two nations" at Harvard. The private-school boys, with their accents, final clubs, and Boston debutante parties—about one-fifth of the student body—stand aloof and apart from the ambitious, talented, and less polished boys who come to Cambridge each year from public schools over the nation. (Baltzell 1958, 329–330)*

The private eating clubs of Princeton were formed in the years following Woodrow Wilson's 1906 ban on fraternities. Juniors and Seniors joined eating clubs that had a "pecking order" based on social status. Upper-class young men usually joined the Ivy Club or the Cottage Club. The exclusivity of the eating clubs was ended in the 1960s when the university compelled the clubs to accept all who had applied but had not been accepted.

At Harvard, Porcellian is the club of the most prestigious boarding schools such as St. Paul's and Groton. Other social clubs that are notable but of slightly less status are A.D., Fly, Spee, Delphic, and Owl. Porcellian's counterpart at Yale is the Fence Club. As at Harvard, there are a host of slightly less prestigious clubs to join. Perhaps the senior societies are even more important than the social clubs at Yale. The two most important are the elite and meritorious Skull and Bones Club (of which former President George Bush is a member) and the more socially exclusive Scroll and Key Club. The purpose of these clubs is to build class solidarity and personal alliances that will be translated into lifetime friendships and business relationships upon graduation (Baltzell 1958, 330–334).

At each critical juncture of a young person's life, the upper class has developed a series of supporting institutions to link individuals with a shared outlook and value system. By carefully molding young upper-class people into the established value system, the upper class assures its own continuity.

The Upper-Class World of Private Clubs

Upon graduation, young men and women begin their careers with yet another array of private clubs that will act as an extended class-oriented family. One can differentiate between two types of private clubs, the metropolitan dining clubs and the more familiar suburban country clubs. Baltzell maintains that the metropolitan clubs are much more important than country clubs in terms of the social ascription of status.

> *Unlike the American middle classes, and resembling the lower classes, in fact, the Philadelphia upper class is largely male dominated and patriarchal. The social standing of the male family head, the best index of which is his metropolitan club affiliation, usually determines the social position of the family as a whole. (Baltzell 1958, 336)*

The first American metropolitan club, following the British experience with such clubs, grew out of an informal gathering of the leading citizens to discuss daily affairs over coffee. In the days before reliable newspapers, it was a way to pass on news and keep informed of current events. The first club formed in the United States was the Philadelphia Club in 1835. It was closely followed by the Union Club of New York City, which was founded in 1836 (Baltzell 1958, 335–363).

◆ ◆ ◆

There have been several recent legal challenges to the all-male membership policies of metropolitan clubs. The Supreme Court has ruled against the males-only policies of the clubs. The main argument made by female complainants was that women are excluded from important business transactions that are discussed in the clubs. Aldrich maintains that the women's victory will be mainly Pyrrhic, as it is considered extremely bad form to discuss business in metropolitan clubs (Aldrich 1988, 122–123). However, Aldrich does not address the valuable alliances made in leisure that lead to business deals later, outside the confines of the club.

The suburban country club is less important than the metropolitan club, but it is significant in that the entire family are members and there are facilities and activities for all. The first American country club was established in 1882 in Brookline, Massachusetts; it is simply called The Country Club. These clubs are most frequently associated with golf, but they may include facilities for swimming, tennis, and, in some cases, polo. Americans are familiar with suburban country clubs, which have been enthusiastically established by the upper middle class throughout the country.

As in the case of metropolitan clubs, there is a status hierarchy among the country clubs. Due to the relatively small number of upper-class families, upper-class country clubs make up only a small portion of the private equity country clubs in the United States.

Yacht clubs are also an integral part of upper-class social life. Again, only a select few of the yacht clubs in America are favored by the American upper class. Similarly, there are a large number of historically oriented clubs, such as the well known Daughters of the American Revolution and more obscure clubs such as the American Association of the Sovereign Military Order of Malta.

The *Social Register* lists those clubs most frequented by the upper class; there are 194 listed in the 1988 edition.

Religion and the Upper Class

"However much details differ, stratification is found in all American communities, and religion is always one of its salient features" (Pope 1948, 89). Observers of the American scene have long commented on the status differentiation of protestant denominations. The upper class has had a long association with the Protestant Episcopal Church and to a lesser degree with the Presbyterian Church. The Episcopalian connection is a logical extension of the Anglophilia of the American upper class, as the church has a number of characteristics that make it attractive to upper-class men and women. The richness of the church's ritual, the classic traditionalism of most Episcopalian architecture, and the sophisticated, urbane, and intellectual nature of its leaders have great appeal to the upper class (Cookson and Persell 1985, 44–48). The Episcopalian Church was very close to an established church for some parts of colonial America and was, in fact, the established church of the state of Virginia until 1786. Although the church suffered during and immediately following the Revolutionary War due to its close association with England and her Loyalists, it quickly recovered its status as a church of the educated elite in the postwar period.

The appeal of the Episcopalian Church to the upper class overrode the appeal of other denominations. Quakerism in Philadelphia and Congregationalism and Unitarianism in Boston had long and deeply rooted favor among the upper classes. Yet, following the Civil War, most upper-class Philadelphians and Bostonians gravitated to the Episcopalian Church. In fact, there was a huge upsurge in Episcopalian membership in the post–Civil War period—the membership grew from 160,000 communicants in 1866 to 720,000 in 1900 (Baltzell 1958, 223–261).

Baltzell confirmed the alliance statistically by analyzing the church membership of those people in the upper class who were in both the 1940 edition of *Who's Who in America* and the 1940 Philadelphia *Social Register*. *Who's Who's* listing of church membership enabled Baltzell to determine religious affiliation for 226 upper-class heads of households. Although 35 percent did not acknowledge a church membership, 42 percent were affiliated with the Episcopalian Church (compared with 1.0 percent of the total U.S. population). An additional 13 percent of those in *Who's Who* listed the Presbyterian

Church as their place of worship (compared to 1.2 percent of the general population). Due the general privacy of religious information, it is difficult to verify Baltzell's findings. However, it is fair to say that the subjective information on the relationship is indeed overwhelming. Of course, not all Episcopalians are upper class. The actual number of upper-class families within the church is small compared to the total membership of Episcopalian churches; however, the church carries the distinctive imprint of upper-class support, philanthropy, and values.

Debutante Balls

The debutante season consists of a series of parties, teas, and dances held by upper-class families to formally announce the arrival and availability of their daughters for suitable matrimonial partners. Each major city holds a grand ball that is the highlight of the season. Debutante "coming-out" parties are yet another means of reinforcing class solidarity, as the young women and men that participate are carefully screened to ensure upper-class exclusivity. Because upper-class endogamy is highly valued, the debutante season is a formal process, the sole purpose of which is to encourage and create upper-class familial unions. Although there is often a philanthropic cause behind the tens of thousands of dollars spent for each coming out, none of the participants are under any illusion as to the real purpose behind the festivities. The debutante season strengthens the bonds of intrametropolitan upper-class social relationships just as shared summer resort holidays strengthen intermetropolitan alliances.

During the activism of the 1960s and 1970s, interest in the debutante experience declined among young upper-class women. However, the disinclination to participate has all but disappeared in the 1980s and

1990s and the debutante season continues to be an important upper-class ritual.

Service Clubs and Charitable Philanthropies of the Upper Class

Participating in service clubs or being on the board of major cultural, medical, or educational institutions is a time honored role for both upper-class men and women. The favored institutions realize that upper-class interest results in large donations and a certain social cachet that has tangentially beneficial fund-raising appeal to the other target of charitable fund-raising, the upper middle class. The involvement of the upper class provides a real benefit for the institution and allows individuals to derive a sense of contribution to society. The chosen charitable organizations invariably reinforce traditional areas of upper-class interests. In Chicago, for example, the favored organizations and institutions include the Chicago Symphony, the Lyric Opera, Northwestern Hospital, the Art Institute, and the Field Museum.

The Social Register

Prior to the Civil War, "society" in most large American cities, including New York City, was small enough that members of the upper class knew each other informally. Invitations to balls and other "serious" social events were handled either by personal secretaries or by the hostess herself. There were also self-appointed social arbiters whose dictates could help the unsure hostess in determining who was "in" and who was "out" of society.

The role of individual society kingmakers would soon be eclipsed with the appearance of the first *Social Register* in 1886. Hundreds of new fortunes were being made (and lost) during the last two decades of the nineteenth century, and a book was needed to take the place of personal knowledge as to a family's acceptability in polite society.

The first edition of the *Social Register* was a listing of society in Newport, Rhode Island. The next year, 1887, saw the first appearance of the New York City edition.

◆ ◆ ◆

The *Social Register* has remained the only social listing for . . . thirteen cities . . . since 1939.[1] In 1977, the twelve editions were combined into one large book—a reflection of the national solidarity of the upper class and also of cost considerations (Birmingham 1978). The *Social Register* has subsequently become an address and telephone book for the American upper class. Along with this basic information, the *Register* also lists which boarding school and which university members attended, the year in which he or she graduated, and their club memberships. Members may also list their children and the schools they are attending or their current addresses. It has several useful appendices: "Married Maidens," a listing of the maiden names of the wives (very helpful in a divorce-prone culture), and "Dilatory Domiciles," for those that are late in returning their annual questionnaires. There is also a separate volume published each summer called the *Summer Social Register.* The summer edition lists summer homes and also has a yacht registry that lists the home port, tonnage, and year built for each yacht. As the upper class has added winter homes in the post–World War II period, they have tended to list those addresses in the main *Social Register* (*Social Register* 1988).

The 1988 edition of the *Social Register* has 32,398 conjugal family listings. This is down from approximately 38,000 families in the 1984 edition. About 3,500 families were dropped in the 1985 edition and there have apparently been additional deletions since that date. As usual, there was no public com-

ment from the Social Register Association as to why individuals were dropped.

Getting into the *Social Register* and being dropped from the book have been subjects of endless speculation among the upper class and among gossip columnists. The best term to describe the process is idiosyncratic. There are three methods for obtaining membership. The most likely way to get in is to be born into it. The second is to marry into a listed family. However, a new bride or groom who is not in the *Register* must submit a new application to be accepted or rejected (without comment) by the "advisory committee." (The makeup of the committee has been the subject of much speculation, and some have questioned if there really is one.) The third way to gain a listing in the *Social Register* is to apply for membership. The prospective member fills out an application and if it passes initial review he or she must then supply the committee with four or five recommendations from current listees. The application then goes to the advisory committee and the applicant is either accepted or rejected without comment. It is believed that the number that gain membership through this process is extremely limited (Winfrey 1980).

◆ ◆ ◆

The largest groups that are systematically excluded from the *Social Register* are Jews, African Americans, and Asian Americans. Although there are one known Black and several Jewish members, the *Social Register* remains a compendium that is overwhelmingly white, Anglo-Saxon, and protestant American (*Newsday,* December 12, 1984, 10–11). A small percentage of the listees have French and Dutch surnames, but it is a challenge to find German, Scandinavian, or southern European surnames anywhere in the *Social Register.*

There are members of the upper class who have asked to have their names removed from the *Social Register* because of the *Register*'s discriminatory practices. Alfred Gwynne Vanderbilt and "Jock" Whitney were among the notable society people who asked to be deleted. It is politically astute for politicians to request that their names be deleted. George Bush had his name deleted before he received his complimentary listings as vice president and president. Former presidents and the chief justice of the Supreme Court are also given complimentary listings. There are many retired senators who are listed once it is "safe" to be associated with an organization that is so blatant in its discrimination.

The credibility of the *Social Register* as a listing of the American upper class is unassailable. Although it is by no means a complete listing, it is a large and excellent sampling. It is true that the core thirteen cities are overrepresented, but every writer that has examined the book has agreed with its value as an indicator of upper-class status. It has been used repeatedly as the authoritative

designator of the American upper class (Firey 1947; Baltzell 1958; Ingham 1978; Cookson and Persell 1985; Levine 1980).

The upper class has a distinct set of institutions that provide social and physical separation from the rest of society, and these institutions inculcate an intricate set of values and beliefs in both young and old. They affirm cultural and group solidarity within the upper class and clearly delineate class boundaries.

◆ ◆ ◆

NATIONAL PATTERNS

The 1988 *Social Register* contains 32,398 households. Of these, 6,660 (20.6 percent) list second homes, 377 (1.2 percent) list third homes and only 6 households list a fourth home. . . . The listing of first households (Table 1, Figure 1) clearly illustrates the concentration of upper-class households on the east coast of the United States.

TABLE 1 / *Social Register* First Homes by State

Rank/ State	No. of Homes	Rank/ State	No. of Homes	Rank/ State	No. of Homes
1. NY	5838	18. SC	303	35. HA	55
2. PA	4200	19. RI	288	36. WY	43
3. MA	3231	20. VT	281	37. NV	29
4. CA	2517	21. NC	247	38. MT	27
5. CT	2244	22. AZ	238	39. ID	26
6. FL	1689	23. DE	205	40. IN	26
7. MD	1629	24. GA	196	41. OK	24
8. NJ	1168	25. WA	138	42. UT	19
9. IL	989	26. LA	134	43. NE	17
10. VA	927	27. MI	131	44. MS	16
11. DC	913	28. KY	95	45. KS	13
12. OH	891	29. OR	95	46. IA	12
13. MO	778	30. TN	82	47. WV	11
14. TX	424	31. NM	75	48. AK	7
15. ME	389	32. WI	67	49. AR	7
16. NH	340	33. AL	66	50. SD	2
17. CO	307	34. MN	66	51. ND	1

FIGURE 1 / *Social Register* **First Homes, 1988**

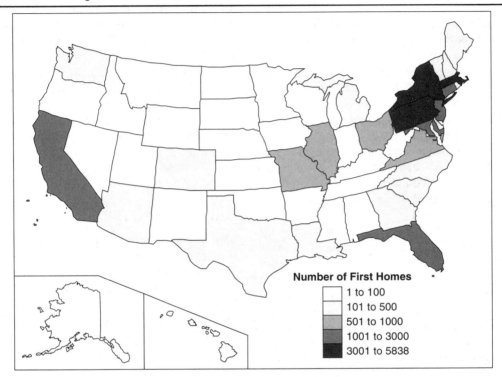

Number of First Homes

	1 to 100
	101 to 500
	501 to 1000
	1001 to 3000
	3001 to 5838

The eastern seaboard states from Maine to Virginia have 21,653 *Social Register* first homes, or 66.6 percent of the nation's upper class. The top ten states have over 75 percent of the total *Social Register* households (compared with 54 percent of the total United States population); the top twenty states have over 90 percent of the households.

◆ ◆ ◆

A somewhat imperfect matching of the 1988 *Social Register* with 1990 census data at the zipcode level is another illustration of the geographic density of upper-class families. Appendix A is a compilation of the forty zipcodes with the largest number of *Social Register* first homes. The forty zipcodes have a 1990 population of 1,014,180 residents (.4 percent of the U.S. population) and yet have

9,748 *Social Register* families (30.1 percent of the total number of *Social Register* first homes). Appendix A also shows that Gladwyne, Pennsylvania, a community located in Lower Merion Township near Philadelphia's Main Line has the highest concentration of *Social Register* families (11.6 percent of all households), and is closely followed by another Main Line community, Haverford (10.6 percent). . . .

In general, *Social Register* first homes are heavily concentrated on the eastern seaboard, in the largest metropolitan areas, and in suburban environments. Central city concentrations of upper-class families are most pronounced in New York City and Washington, D.C., and in the two southern cities of Charleston, South Carolina, and New Orleans. The large central cities with a small percentage of *Social Register* first homes are those cities that have seen their population decline since the 1950 census (e.g., Pittsburgh, Cleveland, and St. Louis).

Within the metropolitan areas, the *Social Register* first homes are highly concentrated in specific suburban communities that are locally considered to be at the apex of the social pyramid. Generally, there are specific communities that have historically been favored by the upper class. The high number of established older suburbs that are possibly in gentle decline can be contrasted with the growing, geographically peripheral communities of the nouveau riche. It appears that the smaller the metropolitan area, the more likely it is that the upper class is geographically concentrated. Cleveland and St. Louis upper classes are highly concentrated; in New York and Boston they are more diffused.

APPENDIX A: THE TOP FORTY ZIP CODES WITH THE LARGEST NUMBER OF *SOCIAL REGISTER* HOUSEHOLDS[2]

Rank	Zip Code	Location	Number of Households	Total # of Households	% of Tot.
1.	10021	Upper East Side-NYC	1,511	64,392	2.3
2.	10128	Upper East Side-NYC	582	28,755	2.0
3.	19118	Chestnut Hill, PA	501	7,955	6.3
4.	10028	Upper East Side-NYC	378	25,002	1.5
5.	06830	Greenwich, CT	373	9,350	4.0
6.	19010	Bryn Mawr, PA	371	7,854	4.7
7.	20007	Georgetown, DC	343	11,843	2.9
8.	19087	Wayne, PA	318	12,388	2.6
9.	33480	Palm Beach, FL	266	3,560	7.5
10.	10022	Upper East Side-NYC	264	20,323	1.3
11.	60045	Lake Forest, IL	262	5,902	4.4
12.	19041	Haverford, PA	252	2,373	10.6
13.	63124	Ladue, MO	235	4,035	5.8
14.	20016	Spring Valley-DC	232	13,573	1.7
15.	06840	New Canaan, CT	229	6,563	3.5
16.	21210	Roland Park-Baltimore	216	5,491	3.9
17.	08540	Princeton, NJ	214	13,833	1.5
18.	20008	Cleveland Park-DC	208	15,952	1.3
19.	02138	Cambridge, MA	182	12,935	1.4
20.	11560	Locust Valley, NY	174	2,387	7.3
21.	19035	Gladwyne, PA	170	1,469	11.6
22.	19085	Villanova, PA	157	1,762	8.9
23.	06820	Darien, CT	152	6,391	2.4
24.	02167	Chestnut Hill, MA	151	4,943	3.1
25.	02026	Dedham, MA	143	8,557	1.7
26.	20815	Bethesda, MD	141	11,329	1.2
27.	94118	Richmond-San Francisco	135	16,578	0.8
28.	60093	Winnetka, IL	135	7,143	1.9
29.	02146	Brookline, MA	132	26,337	0.5
30.	15143	Sewickly, PA	124	6,067	2.0
31.	63105	Clayton, MO	123	6,348	1.9

Continued

APPENDIX A / Continued

Rank	Zip Code	Location	Number of Households	Total # of Households	% of Tot.
32.	94109	San Francisco, CA	123	28,340	0.4
33.	94123	Marina-San Francisco	123	14,304	0.9
34.	19333	Devon, PA	122	2,426	5.0
35.	21212	Homeland-Baltimore	120	13,793	0.9
36.	19041	Manchester, MA	120	2,373	5.1
37.	21204	Ruxton, MD	120	14,870	0.8
38.	11771	Oyster Bay, NY	116	3,737	3.1
39.	94115	San Francisco, CA	116	15,410	0.8
40.	45208	Hyde Park, Cincinnati	114	9,437	1.2

ENDNOTES

1. The thirteen *Social Register* cities are Baltimore, Boston, Buffalo, Chicago, Cincinnati-Dayton, Cleveland, New York City, Newport, Philadelphia, Pittsburgh, San Francisco, St. Louis, and Washington, D.C.

2. The name used in this appendix is of the political unit or large city neighborhood with the largest # of *Social Register* households.

REFERENCES

Aldrich, Nelson W., Jr. 1988, *Old Money: The Mythology of America's Upper Class*. New York: Knopf.

Baltzell, E. Digby. 1958. *Philadelphia Gentlemen: The Making of a National Upper Class*. New York: Free Press.

Birmingham, Stephen. 1967. *The Right Places*. Boston: Little, Brown.

Collins, Randall, 1971. "Functional and Conflict Theories of Educational Stratification." *American Sociological Review* 36(December):1002–1019.

Cookson, Peter W. Jr., and Caroline Hodges Persell. 1985. *Preparing for Power*. New York: Basic.

Domhoff, G. William. 1983. *Who Rules America Now?* New York: Touchstone.

Firey, Walter, 1947. *Land Use in Central Boston*. Cambridge, Mass.: Harvard University Press.

Gilbert, Dennis, and Joseph A. Kahl. 1987. *The American Class Structure*. Chicago: Dorsey.

Ingham, John N. 1978. *The Iron Barons: A Social Analysis of an American Urban Elite, 1874–1965*. Westport, Conn.: Greenwood.

Levine, Steven B. 1980. "The Rise of American Boarding Schools and the Development of a National Upper Class." *Social Problems* 28(October):63–94.

Mills, C. Wright. 1956. *The Power Elite*. London: Oxford University Press.

Pope, Liston. 1948. "Religion and the Class Structure." *The Annals of the American Academy of Political and Social Science* 256:84–91.

Social Register 1988, Vol. CII. New York: Social Register Association.

Weber, Max. 1946. *From Max Weber: Essays in Sociology*, edited by H. H. Gerth and C. Wright Mills. New York: Oxford University Press.

Winfrey, C. 1980. "Society's 'In' Book: Does It Still Matter?" *New York Times* (February 2).

Questions for Understanding and Critical Thinking

1. Has the U.S. upper class changed significantly over the past two decades? Why or why not?
2. What does the geographic density of U.S. upper-class families reveal, if anything, about the upper class?
3. Do you think there is a relationship between people's residential choices and racial discrimination in the United States? Why or why not?

ARTICLE 7 _____

Gender studies scholar Judith Lorber of the City University of New York (CUNY) Graduate School takes a closer look at *gender* in this excerpt from her recent book, *Paradoxes of Gender*. As previously defined, *gender* refers to the meanings, beliefs, and practices associated with sex differences, which are referred to as *femininity* and *masculinity*. Lorber suggests that "much of what we take for granted about gender and its causes and effects either does not hold up or can be explained differently." As you read the article, think about your own assumptions about gender in light of Lorber's suggestion that everyone "does gender" without thinking about it.

Looking Ahead

1. Why does Lorber suggest that talking about gender "is the equivalent of fish talking about water"?
2. When does "gender construction" start for the individual?
3. How do people organize their lives around gender as a social construct?
4. What roles do gender, race, and class play in a society's system of stratification?

The Social Construction of Gender

◆ *Judith Lorber*

Talking about gender for most people is the equivalent of fish talking about water. Gender is so much the routine ground of everyday activities that questioning its taken-for-granted assumptions and presuppositions is like thinking about whether the sun will come up.[1] Gender is so pervasive that in our society we assume it is bred into our genes. Most people find it hard to believe that gender is constantly created and re-created out of human interaction, out of social life, and is the texture and order of that social life. Yet gender, like culture, is a human production that depends on everyone constantly "doing gender" (West and Zimmerman 1987).

And everyone "does gender" without thinking about it. Today, on the subway, I saw a well-dressed man with a year-old child in a stroller. Yesterday, on a bus, I saw a man with a tiny baby in a carrier on his chest. Seeing men taking care of small children in public is increasingly common—at least in New York City. But both men were quite obviously stared at—and smiled at, approvingly. Everyone was doing gender—the men who were changing the role of fathers and the other passengers, who were applauding them silently. But there was more gendering going on that probably fewer people noticed. The baby was wearing a white crocheted cap and white clothes. You couldn't tell if it was a boy or a girl. The child in the stroller was wearing a dark blue T-shirt and dark print pants. As they started to leave the train, the father put a Yankee baseball cap on the child's head. Ah, a boy, I thought. Then I noticed the gleam of tiny earrings in the child's ears, and as they got off, I saw the little flowered sneakers and lace-trimmed socks. Not a boy after all. Gender done.

Gender is such a familiar part of daily life that it usually takes a deliberate disruption of our expectations of how women and men are supposed to act to pay attention to how it is produced. Gender signs and signals are so ubiquitous that we usually fail to note them—unless they are missing or ambiguous. Then we are uncomfortable until we have successfully placed the other person in a gender status; otherwise, we feel socially dislocated. In our society, in addition to man and woman, the status can be *transvestite* (a person who dresses in opposite-gender clothes) and *transsexual* (a person who has had sex-change surgery). Transvestites and transsexuals construct their gender status by dressing, speaking, walking, gesturing in the ways prescribed for women or men—whichever they want to be taken for—and so does any "normal" person.

For the individual, gender construction starts with assignment to a sex category on the basis of what the genitalia look like at birth.[2] Then babies are dressed or adorned in a way that displays the category because parents don't want to be constantly asked whether their baby is a girl or a boy. A sex category becomes a gender status through naming, dress, and the use of other gender markers. Once a child's gender is evident, others treat those in one gender differently from those in the other, and the children respond to the different treatment by feeling different and behaving differently. As soon as they can talk, they start to refer to them-

selves as members of their gender. Sex doesn't come into play again until puberty, but by that time, sexual feelings and desires and practices have been shaped by gendered norms and expectations. Adolescent boys and girls approach and avoid each other in an elaborately scripted and gendered mating dance. Parenting is gendered, with different expectations for mothers and for fathers, and people of different genders work at different kinds of jobs. The work adults do as mothers and fathers and as low-level workers and high-level bosses, shapes women's and men's life experiences, and these experiences produce different feelings, consciousness, relationships, skills—ways of being that we call feminine or masculine.[3] All of these processes constitute the social construction of gender.

Gendered roles change—today fathers are taking care of little children, girls and boys are wearing unisex clothing and getting the same education, women and men are working at the same jobs. Although many traditional social groups are quite strict about maintaining gender differences, in other social groups they seem to be blurring. Then why the one-year-old's earrings? Why is it still so important to mark a child as a girl or a boy, to make sure she is not taken for a boy or he for a girl? What would happen if they were? They would, quite literally, have changed places in their social world.

To explain why gendering is done from birth, constantly and by everyone, we have to look not only at the way individuals experience gender but at gender as a social institution. As a social institution, gender is one of the major ways that human beings organize their lives. Human society depends on a predictable division of labor, a designated allocation of scarce goods, assigned responsibility for children and others who cannot care for themselves, common values and their systematic transmission to new members, legitimate leadership, music, art, stories, games, and other symbolic productions. One way of choosing people for the different tasks of society is on the basis of their talents, motivations, and competence—their demonstrated achievements. The other way is on the basis of gender, race, ethnicity— ascribed membership in a category of people. Although societies vary in the extent to which they use one or the other of these ways of allocating people to work and to carry out other responsibilities, every society uses gender and age grades. Every society classifies people as "girl and boy children," "girls and boys ready to be married," and "fully adult women and men," constructs similarities among them and differences between them, and assigns them to different roles and responsibilities. Personality characteristics, feelings, motivations, and ambitions flow from these different life experiences so that the members of these different groups become different kinds of people. The process of gendering and its outcome are legitimated by religion, law, science, and the society's entire set of values.

◆ ◆ ◆

GENDER AS PROCESS, STRATIFICATION, AND STRUCTURE

As a social institution, gender is a process of creating distinguishable social statuses for the assignment of rights and responsibilities. As part of a stratification system that ranks these statuses unequally, gender is a major building block in the social structures built on these unequal statuses.

As a *process*, gender creates the social differences that define "woman" and "man." In social interaction throughout their lives, individuals learn what is expected, see what is expected, act and react in expected ways, and thus simultaneously construct and

maintain the gender order: "The very injunction to be given gender takes place through discursive routes: to be a good mother, to be a heterosexually desirable object, to be a fit worker, in sum, to signify a multiplicity of guarantees in response to a variety of different demands all at once" (J. Butler 1990, 145). Members of a social group neither make up gender as they go along nor exactly replicate in rote fashion what was done before. In almost every encounter, human beings produce gender, behaving in the ways they learned were appropriate for their gender status, or resisting or rebelling against these norms. Resistance and rebellion have altered gender norms, but so far they have rarely eroded the statuses.

Gendered patterns of interaction acquire additional layers of gendered sexuality, parenting, and work behaviors in childhood, adolescence, and adulthood. Gendered norms and expectations are enforced through informal sanctions of gender-inappropriate behavior by peers and by formal punishment or threat of punishment by those in authority should behavior deviate too far from socially imposed standards for women and men.

Everyday gendered interactions build gender into the family, the work process, and other organizations and institutions, which in turn reinforce gender expectations for individuals.[4] Because gender is a process, there is room not only for modification and variation by individuals and small groups but also for institutionalized change (J. W. Scott 1988, 7).

As part of a *stratification* system, gender ranks men above women of the same race and class. Women and men could be different but equal. In practice, the process of creating difference depends to a great extent on differential evaluation. As Nancy Jay (1981) says: "That which is defined, separated out, isolated from all else is A and pure. Not-A is necessarily impure, a random catchall, to which nothing is external except A and the principle of order that separates it from Not-A" (45). From the individual's point of view, whichever gender is A, the other is Not-A; gender boundaries tell the individual who is like him or her, and all the rest are unlike. From society's point of view, however, one gender is usually the touchstone, the normal, the dominant, and the other is different, deviant, and subordinate. In Western society, "man" is A, "wo-man" is Not-A. (Consider what a society would be like where woman was A and man Not-A.)

The further dichotomization by race and class constructs the gradations of a heterogeneous society's stratification scheme. Thus, in the United States, white is A, African American is Not-A; middle class is A, working class is Not-A, and "African-American women occupy a position whereby the inferior half of a series of these dichotomies converge" (P. H. Collins 1990, 70). The dominant categories are the hegemonic ideals, taken so for granted as the way things should be that white is not ordinarily thought of as a race, middle class as a class, or men as a gender. The characteristics of these categories define the Other as that which lacks the valuable qualities the dominants exhibit.

In a gender-stratified society, what men do is usually valued more highly than what women do because men do it, even when their activities are very similar or the same. In different regions of southern India, for example, harvesting rice is men's work, shared work, or women's work: "Wherever a task is done by women it is considered easy, and where it is done by [men] it is considered difficult" (Mencher 1988, 104). A gathering and hunting society's survival usually depends on the nuts, grubs, and small animals brought in by the women's foraging trips, but when the men's hunt is successful, it is the occasion for a celebration. Conversely, because they are the superior group, white men do not have to

do the "dirty work," such as housework; the most inferior group does it, usually poor women of color (Palmer 1989).

Freudian psychoanalytic theory claims that boys must reject their mothers and deny the feminine in themselves in order to become men: "For boys the major goal is the achievement of personal masculine identification with their father and sense of secure masculine self, achieved through superego formation and disparagement of women" (Chodorow 1978, 165). Masculinity may be the outcome of boys' intrapsychic struggles to separate their identity from that of their mothers, but the proofs of masculinity are culturally shaped and usually ritualistic and symbolic (Gilmore 1990).

The Marxist feminist explanation for gender inequality is that by demeaning women's abilities and keeping them from learning valuable technological skills, bosses preserve them as a cheap and exploitable reserve army of labor. Unionized men who could be easily replaced by women collude in this process because it allows them to monopolize the better paid, more interesting, and more autonomous jobs: "Two factors emerge as helping men maintain their separation from women and their control of technological occupations. One is the active gendering of jobs and people. The second is the continual creation of sub-divisions in the work processes, and levels in work hierarchies, into which men can move in order to keep their distance from women" (Cockburn 1985, 13).

Societies vary in the extent of the inequality in social status of their women and men members, but where there is inequality, the status "woman" (and its attendant behavior and role allocations) is usually held in lesser esteem than the status "man." Since gender is also intertwined with a society's other constructed statuses of differential evaluation—race, religion, occupation, class, country of origin, and so on—men and women members of the favored groups command more power, more prestige, and more property than the members of the disfavored groups. Within many social groups, however, men are advantaged over women. The more economic resources, such as education and job opportunities, are available to a group, the more they tend to be monopolized by men. In poorer groups that have few resources (such as working-class African Americans in the United States), women and men are more nearly equal, and the women may even outstrip the men in education and occupational status (Almquist 1987).

As a *structure*, gender divides work in the home and in economic production, legitimates those in authority, and organizes sexuality and emotional life (Connell 1987, 91–142). As primary parents, women significantly influence children's psychological development and emotional attachments, in the process reproducing gender. Emergent sexuality is shaped by heterosexual, homosexual, bisexual, and sadomasochistic patterns that are gendered—different for girls and boys, and for women and men—so that sexual statuses reflect gender statuses.

When gender is a major component of structured inequality, the devalued genders have less power, prestige, and economic rewards than the valued genders. In countries that discourage gender discrimination, many major roles are still gendered; women still do most of the domestic labor and child rearing, even while doing full-time paid work; women and men are segregated on the job and each does work considered "appropriate"; women's work is usually paid less than men's work. Men dominate the positions of authority and leadership in government, the military, and the law; cultural productions, religions, and sports reflect men's interests.

In societies that create the greatest gender difference, such as Saudi Arabia, women are kept out of sight behind walls or veils, have no civil rights, and often create a cultural and emotional world of their own (Bernard 1981). But even in societies with less rigid gender boundaries, women and men spend much of their time with people of their own gender because of the way work and family are organized. This spatial separation of women and men reinforces gendered differences, identity, and ways of thinking and behaving (Coser 1986).

Gender inequality—the devaluation of "women" and the social domination of "men"—has social functions and a social history. It is not the result of sex, procreation, physiology, anatomy, hormones, or genetic predispositions. It is produced and maintained by identifiable social processes and built into the general social structure and individual identities deliberately and purposefully. The social order as we know it in Western societies is organized around racial ethnic, class, and gender inequality. I contend, therefore, that the continuing purpose of gender as a modern social institution is to construct women as a group to be the subordinates of men as a group. The life of everyone placed in the status "woman" is "night to his day—that has forever been the fantasy. Black to his white. Shut out of his system's space, she is the repressed that ensures the system's functioning" (Cixous and Clément [1975] 1986, 67).

THE PARADOX OF HUMAN NATURE

To say that sex, sexuality, and gender are all socially constructed is not to minimize their social power. These categorical imperatives govern our lives in the most profound and pervasive ways, through the social experiences and social practices of what Dorothy Smith calls the "everday/evernight world" (1990, 31–57). The paradox of human nature is that it is *always* a manifestation of cultural meanings, social relationships, and power politics; "not biology, but culture, becomes destiny" (J. Butler 1990, 8). Gendered people emerge not from physiology or sexual orientation but from the exigencies of the social order, mostly, from the need for a reliable division of the work of food production and the social (not physical) reproduction of new members. The moral imperatives of religion and cultural representations guard the boundary lines among genders and ensure that what is demanded, what is permitted, and what is tabooed for the people in each gender is well known and followed by most (C. Davies 1982). Political power, control of scarce resources, and, if necessary, violence uphold the gendered social order in the face of resistance and rebellion. Most people, however, voluntarily go along with their society's prescriptions for those of their gender status, because the norms and expectations get built into their sense of worth and identity as [the way we] think, the way we see and hear and speak, the way we fantasy, and the way we feel.

There is no core or bedrock human nature below these endlessly looping processes of the social production of sex and gender, self and other, identity and psyche, each of which is a "complex cultural construction" (J. Butler 1990, 36). *For humans, the social is the natural.* Therefore, "in its feminist senses, gender cannot mean simply the cultural appropriation of biological sexual difference. Sexual difference is itself a fundamental—and scientifically contested—construction. Both 'sex' and 'gender' are woven of multiple, asymmetrical strands of difference, charged with multifaceted dramatic narratives of domination and struggle" (Haraway 1990, 140).

ENDNOTES

1. Gender is, in Erving Goffman's words, an aspect of *Felicity's Condition:* "any arrangement which leads us to judge an individual's . . . acts not to be a manifestation of strangeness. Behind Felicity's Condition is our sense of what it is to be sane" (1983:27). Also see Bem 1993; Frye 1983, 17–40; Goffman 1977.

2. In cases of ambiguity in countries with modern medicine, surgery is usually performed to make the genitalia more clearly male or female.

3. See J. Butler 1990 for an analysis of how doing gender is gender identity.

4. On the "logic of practice," or how the experience of gender is embedded in the norms of everyday interaction and the structure of formal organizations, see Acker 1990; Bourdieu [1980] 1990; Connell 1987; Smith 1987.

REFERENCES

Acker, Joan. 1990. "Hierarchies, jobs, and bodies: A theory of gendered organizations," *Gender & Society* 4:139–58.

Almquist, Elizabeth M. 1987. "Labor market gendered inequality in minority groups," *Gender & Society* 1:400–14.

Bem, Sandra Lipsitz. 1993. *The Lenses of Gender: Transforming the Debate on Sexual Inequality.* New Haven: Yale University Press.

Bernard, Jessie. 1981. *The Female World.* New York: Free Press.

Bourdieu, Pierre. [1980] 1990. *The Logic of Practice.* Stanford, Calif.: Stanford University Press.

Butler, Judith. 1990. *Gender Trouble: Feminism and the Subversion of Identity.* New York and London: Routledge.

Chodorow, Nancy. 1978. *The Reproduction of Mothering.* Berkeley: University of California Press.

Cioux, Hélène, and Catherine Clément. [1975] 1986. *The Newly Born Woman,* translated by Betsy Wing. Minneapolis: University of Minnesota Press.

Cockburn, Cynthia. 1985. *Machinery of Dominance: Women, Men and Technical Know-how.* London: Pluto Press.

Collins, Patricia Hill. 1989. "The social construction of black feminist thought," *Signs* 14:745–73.

Connell, R. [Robert] W. 1987. *Gender and Power: Society, the Person, and Sexual Politics.* Stanford, Calif.: Stanford University Press.

Coser, Rose Laub. 1986. "Cognitive structure and the use of social space," *Sociological Forum* 1:1–26.

Davies, Christie. 1982. "Sexual taboos and social boundaries." *American Journal of Sociology* 87:1032–63.

Dwyer, Daisy, and Judith Bruce (eds.). 1988. *A Home Divided: Women and Income in the Third World.* Palo Alto, Calif.: Stanford University Press.

Frye, Marilyn. 1983. *The Politics of Reality: Essays in Feminist Theory.* Trumansburg, N.Y.: Crossing Press.

Gilmore, David D. 1990. *Manhood in the Making: Cultural Concepts of Masculinity.* New Haven: Yale University Press.

Goffman, Erving. 1977. "The arrangement between the sexes," *Theory and Society* 4:301–33.

Haraway, Donna. 1990. "Investment strategies for the evolving portfolio of primate females," in *Jacobus, Keller, and Shuttleworth.*

Jacobus, Mary, Evelyn Fox Keller, and Sally Shuttleworth (eds.). 1990. *Body/politics: Women and the Discourse of Science.* New York and London: Routledge.

Jay, Nancy. 1981. "Gender and dichotomy," *Feminist Studies* 7:38–56.

Mencher, Joan. 1988. "Women's work and poverty: Women's contribution to household maintenance in South India." In *Dwyer and Bruce.*

Palmer, Phyllis. 1989. *Domesticity and Dirt: Housewives and Domestic Servants in the United States, 1920–1945.* Philadelphia: Temple University Press.

Scott, Joan Wallach. 1988. *Gender and the Politics of History.* New York: Columbia University Press.

Smith, Dorothy. 1987. *The Everyday World as Problematic: A Feminist Sociology.* Toronto: University of Toronto Press.

_____. 1990. *The Conceptual Practices of Power: A Feminist Sociology of Knowledge.* Toronto: University of Toronto Press.

West, Candace, and Don Zimmerman. 1987. "Doing gender." *Gender & Society* 1:125–51.

Questions for Understanding and Critical Thinking

1. How much does gender influence a person's everyday beliefs and behavior? Explain your answer.
2. What specific examples from your own life can you point to that show how the social construction of gender shaped what appears to be your individual beliefs and behavior?
3. How are gendered norms and expectations enforced by society?
4. Why are the activities of women and men differently valued, even when their activities are very similar or the same?

ARTICLE 8

As sociologist Judith Lorber suggested in the previous article, "Everyone 'does gender' without thinking about it." In this article, sociologists Diana Dull and Candace West demonstrate how people "do gender" when they decide to undergo cosmetic surgical procedures in hopes of achieving aesthetic improvement through alterations of facial and bodily features. Through interviews with surgeons who perform cosmetic surgery and with individuals who have undergone such operations, Dull and West demonstrate how surgeons and patients uphold normative attitudes about so-called appearances for individuals in particular sex, racial, or ethnic categories.

At the time this article was written, Diana Dull was a graduate student at the University of California, Santa Cruz. Candace West, a sociology professor at the University of California, Santa Cruz, has written numerous articles on gender and inequality.

Looking Ahead

1. Why is cosmetic surgery typically viewed as more "normal, natural" for women as constrasted with men?
2. How can one determine the "objective" signs of aging?
3. What do the authors mean when they state that gender is an accomplishment?
4. How does cosmetic surgery serve as an institutional support for "doing gender"?

Accounting for Cosmetic Surgery

The Accomplishment of Gender

◆ *Diana Dull and Candace West*

Within the United States, physicians claim a professional mandate to define the nature and treatment of disease (Hughes 1958:78; Thorne 1973:36–37). For most surgeons, this mandate includes the right to evaluate patients' complaints, to determine what should be done about them, and to assess postoperative results.[1] For plastic surgeons, however, the mandate is not so clear. The field of plastic surgery encompasses two categories of operations: (1) reconstructive procedures, which restore or improve physical function

Source: From Diana Dull and Candace West, "Accounting for Cosmetic Surgery: The Accomplishment of Gender." © 1991 by the Society for the Study of Social Problems. Reprinted from *Social Problems*, Vol. 38, No. 1, Feb. 1991, pp. 54–70, by permission.

and minimize disfigurement from accidents, diseases, or birth defects, and (2) cosmetic procedures, which offer elective aesthetic improvement through surgical alterations of facial and bodily features (American Society of Plastic and Reconstructive Surgeons 1988). In the case of reconstructive surgery, the professional mandate rests on the surgeon's ability to improve physical function and minimize disfigurement. But in the case of cosmetic surgery, the evaluation of patients' complaints, the determination of what should be done about them, and the assessment of post-operative results must be negotiated in relation to *what* "aesthetic improvement" might consist of, and to *whom*. This, then, is the central dilemma of cosmetic surgery.

The disproportionate number of women who undergo cosmetic operations suggests the importance of gender to understanding how this dilemma is resolved. For example, in 1988 more than half a million people in the United States had cosmetic surgery, with the available evidence indicating that the vast majority were women.[2] Although official statistics do not distinguish between cosmetic and reconstructive operations, they do indicate a decided bias. In 1985, 61 percent of all rhinoplasty (nose surgery), 86 percent of all eyelid reconstruction, and 91 percent of all facelifts were performed on women (U.S. National Center for Health Statistics 1987). The American Society of Plastic and Reconstructive Surgeons estimates that 90,000 men opted for cosmetic surgery in 1988, but that number represents only 16 percent of the total cosmetic operations identified.

Our purpose in this paper is to examine how those involved in cosmetic operations resolve the central dilemma of cosmetic surgery. Our analysis of surgical screening and decision making focuses on how the medical profession comes to enter a terrain

that would seem so clearly beyond its mandate—that is, constructing appearances and performing surgery that, by its own definition, is unnecessary. We show how surgeons who perform cosmetic procedures justify their entry into this terrain and how people who elect such procedures make sense of their decisions to do so. Finally, in conjunction with these activities, we show how women are constituted as the primary frontier for this territorial expansion through the accomplishment of gender—in this context, the assessment of "good candidates" for surgery in relation to normative conceptions of men's and women's "essential natures" (Fenstermaker, West, and Zimmerman 1990; West and Fenstermaker forthcoming; West and Zimmerman 1987).

METHODS

Our primary data consists of interviews with surgeons who perform cosmetic surgery and with individuals who have undergone such operations. By law, any licensed medical doctor may perform cosmetic surgery, but we limited our study to surgeons certified to do so through boards recognized by the American Board of Medical Specialties. Eight of the ten surgeons in this sample are certified by the American Board of Plastic Surgery and two, by the American Board of Otolaryngology. We obtained these interviews through a snowball sample, yielding one woman and nine men surgeons, all white. With the exception of one surgeon outside California (whom we interviewed by phone), we conducted all our physician interviews in person at surgeons' offices. Each interview was recorded on audiotape and lasted approximately one hour.

Given the sensitive nature of the topic, we gave people who had undergone cosmetic surgery two interview options. The first option, chosen by 7 of the total 23, was to be interviewed on audiotape face to face. The second option, chosen by 16 of the 23, was to complete an open-ended questionnaire with a follow-up discussion over the phone if clarification was needed. In the analysis that follows, we found no differences among people's perspectives on cosmetic surgery according to which of the options they selected. These interviews were also obtained through a snowball sample.

Nineteen of the 23 persons interviewed were women whose surgical experiences included face lifting, upper and lower eyelid reduction, rhinoplasty, chin implantation, breast augmentation, breast reduction, and liposuction of the hips, thighs, and knees. Two of the interviews were with men who had undergone eyelid reduction or face lifting. Our secondary data consist of two further interviews with men who ultimately decided against cosmetic surgery. Given that both had seriously contemplated aesthetic rhinoplasty and were among only four men we were able to locate who had ever consulted plastic surgeons, we decided to include their views with those of our other interviewees—setting them off in our analysis as anomalous cases.[3] Four of the women and one of the men had undergone more than one surgery, and in at least two cases later operations were performed in order to correct the results of an earlier procedure.

At the time we interviewed them, individuals in this sample ranged in age from 24 to 67. Nine had had surgery before turning 35; seven more, between 35 and 50; and seven more, when they were 51 years or older. While facelifts were confined to those who were 50 and over, the other procedures were reported by people across different age groups.

Six people were single, two were divorced, and ten were married (with five failing to indicate marital status). Nine of them, including one who was single, had children. All of them were white; two identified their ethnicity as Jewish and one, as Italian. They held a variety of jobs, including those of dentist, bookkeeper, and administrative assistant. One, a retired medical assistant, had formerly been employed in the offices of two different cosmetic surgeons; another, also retired, had worked as a medical editor in a large health care facility.

Our analysis of these data is qualitative and inductive. In the tradition of grounded theory (Glaser and Strauss 1967), we did not set out to test specific hypotheses but rather to generate them from the entire corpus of material.

SURGERY AS A "NORMAL, NATURAL" PURSUIT

In routine descriptions of their circumstances and activities, people provide names, formulations, characterizations, excuses, explanations, and justifications for the circumstances and activities, thereby situating them in a social framework (Heritage 1984: 136–137). Among those who had undergone cosmetic surgery, many described their desires for such surgery as "normal" and "natural," explicitly comparing their inclination to buying makeup and having their hair done. They extolled the benefits of cosmetic surgery by characterizing their actions as what anyone would do. Hence, patients' descriptions of their activities were formulated as justifications for those activities. For example, a woman who underwent breast augmentation observed,

In this age, with all the technology possible, changing something less than perfect about one's looks seems so easy, so normal. It's unfair that cost keeps such a wonderful thing from so many people. . . . I would recommend this procedure to anyone.

A woman who underwent a facelift stated,

> *I mean, if it is your body and you want to have it done, why not? And if it helps your vanity, what's wrong with it? . . . Women buy makeup and have their hair done— what's the difference?*

We might expect such descriptions from people who have undergone cosmetic surgery, insofar as they are accounting for having done so in the course of being interviewed. However, such descriptions were not unique to former patients. Many surgeons also categorized cosmetic surgery as a "normal," "natural," pursuit. For example:

> **There is a certain natural order to things.** *(Emphasis added.) A person who is twenty-five years old does not need a facelift, but they need a breast augmentation.—Well, "need" is relative, obviously, but for purposes of discussion . . . there's a certain order of what you go through psychologically and what you might need. . . . If it makes them happy and gives them a boost, then it's no different than going on a two-week vacation as far as I'm concerned.*

Or, as another surgeon remarked, "It's not any vainer than wearing makeup or changing your hairstyle. If you think those things are vain, then plastic surgery is vain too."

To be sure, those descriptions contained numerous contradictions. First, some patients who characterized their surgery as what anyone would do nonetheless reported that they agonized over their decisions to have surgery. Second, surgeons and former patients who compared cosmetic surgery with other mundane activities often advanced claims with defensive overtones (for instance, assessing surgery as "no vainer than" other attentions to one's appearance). Third, even while surgeons and former patients referred to the desire for surgery as "normal" and "natural," they implied that

the desire was only "normal" and "natural" for women. They did not, for example, draw parallels between cosmetic procedures and shaving one's face or trimming one's beard. Thus, the claim that cosmetic surgery was a "normal," "natural" pursuit was a deceptively simple one.

"OBJECTIVE" INDICATORS

A more complex picture began to emerge as interviewees described "critiera" for particular surgical procedures as if these were objective indicators for surgery. As Zimmerman (1978:11) observes, we can examine "properties of social life which seem objective, factual, and transsituational" as "managed accomplishments or achievements of local processes." Such examination provides a preliminary understanding of how surgeons and former patients could reach the conclusion that cosmetic surgery was "normal" and "natural," namely, by formulating facial or bodily features as "objectively" problematic.

For example, like the surgeon who suggested that a 25-year-old person does not "need" a facelift, many patients alluded to "self-evident indicators" for surgery in accounts of their decisions. One woman "explained" her upper eyelid reduction by noting that

> *At about forty-five [your eyelids] start to come down. And that's when you start to notice that you're losing elasticity and you get the fold in your upper eye . . . by the time you get to be my age, it was certainly time to do it.*

The same woman described her subsequent decision to undergo liposuction under her chin by adding,

> *In your late fifties and sixties you start to get a lot of "crepeyness" in your neck. Just all of a sudden it's just there. And it's just, you know, not attractive. And your jowls, of*

course. Mine weren't that bad, but they were coming down.

In these excerpts, we find a concrete empirical description of the "natural order of things" described earlier. While this woman's description is perhaps more chronologically detailed than most, other patients were just as explicit in their references to "heavy eyelids," "droopy necks," and "baggy chins" as "objective" grounds for their decisions to have surgery.

Interestingly, surgeons were the ones who suggested that "objective" signs of aging—and their relationship to cosmetic surgery—might not be so objective. For example, when asked about the relationship between age and cosmetic surgery, many intimated that "age" was in the eye of the beholder. While a 20-year-old woman might look terrific to the person on the street, she may well look "too old" if she is competing in front of the camera:

> *The youngest lady I've done was a younger lady in her twenties who was a model and was losing it to the teenagers. So I did her face and eyes. . . . To you and me, she looked great. But to the camera and to the people who wanted to shoot the teenage look, she looked too old. . . . It was a modest facelift, but it was enough to put her right back there on the front page of the magazine. . . . She was perfectly realistic. She showed me her shots and shots of the kids and said, "This is where the industry is going, and I want to stay in it." You see, the perceived deformity relates to that person's particular situation in life. Their jobs or their perceived role.*

Although many surgeons acknowledged that procedures such as facelifts were more easily and effectively performed on someone who is young, one surgeon remarked,

> *You're never too old for it. The best answer to the question of when you need it or when you*

should do it, is when you need it. . . . I've done a facelift on a ninety-three-year-old.

Thus, the surgeons took patients' individual perceptions and livelihoods into account in their perspectives on "objective" signs of aging. Surgeons were not always so sociologically reflective when it came to other dimensions of identity such as race and ethnicity. For example, more than a few of them averred that patients' racial or ethnic features constituted "objective" problems. Through references to what people, particularly women, of color "have" and "need," these surgeons invoked race and ethnicity as factual, transsituational grounds for surgical interventions in appearance (cf. Zimmerman 1978):

> *I've had one Black patient . . . it was a lip reduction. . . . I guess there are more Black people that have big lips than white people. . . . I had a lot of Black patients back in [the South] . . . breast reduction was a tremendously common procedure . . . because . . . a lot of Black women have huge breasts. . . . The usual cosmetic procedures were, with the exception of rhinoplasty, very uncommon. You know, Black women don't usually have the aging changes that white women have—they don't get the fine wrinkles. . . . Orientals don't either.*

Or, as another surgeon remarked,

> *The Black people that I have operated on have had . . . mostly their noses [done]. The Black people have big flared nostrils and would like that smaller. The Orientals don't seem to have much of a bridge, so they, you know, [have] kind of a dish face.*

On the other hand, some surgeons implied that "problems" with racial and ethnic features were—at least in part—subjectively determined. They acknowledged, for example, that patients' conceptions of their racial features were often derived from their groups:

> *There are not that many Black flat women compared to Caucasians. . . . But another flipside—how many flat Asians do you see? Females? Lots! They're all over the place. For them, that's accepted. I do very few Asians. Very few Blacks. And my theory is that most of the Blacks don't need it. And my theory is for Asians, flat is still in.*

One surgeon contended that whatever a patient's racial or ethnic features, the surgeon's task was to improve the appearance of the individual patient, rather than to force fit it according to some universal criteria:

> *I saw a Black lady today who I had done her eyelids and a facelift. And she came back, and she wanted a forehead lift. And uh, you know . . . that was fine. . . . But this was just to make this lady look better. . . . Basically, it is just trying to make them look better, rather than to have them fit a mold.*

In this regard, the most complicated claims we heard were those that acknowledged "objective" differences between the racial or ethnic "characteristics" of different groups, but attributed desires for changes in such characteristics to the patients' individual perceptions—not to the characteristics themselves. Changes in such characteristics might result in a "different" appearance but not necessarily a "better" appearance:

> *I mean, if you've got a great big old honker, and it looks like somebody hit it with three passes of the sword and it comes down your face like a "Z" or a "W," you want to look better. . . . Now, contrariwise, if you just happen to have a big nose because you come from an Armenian background or some very recognizable ethnic appearance and you want to change it, that's cosmetic surgery. . . . Michael Jackson is leading the way*

on changing Negroid characteristics to Caucasian characteristics.

Patients' descriptions of their surgeries in relation to their ethnic backgrounds were more complex still. They expressed their desires for surgery through references to subtle alterations—rather than total transformations—of their "ethnic features." For example, one woman of Italian descent said that prior to her rhinoplasty,

> *I didn't like my nose in photographs. [Now] I have a cute profile and my nose is not tiny but in proportion to my face. . . . I think I look softer [now] and not as exotic as before.*

A Jewish woman said of her pre-operative consultation with a surgeon for rhinoplasty, "He wasn't going to give me a cute little WASPy nose, but one in proportion to my face. I was very satisfied." Through such carefully worded descriptions, patients implied that they were essentially satisfied with their "ethnic appearances," despite their desires to have particular features surgically changed. Notwithstanding these nuanced claims, we observed that surgeons and former patients only specified "problems" with racial and ethnic features in the marked case: in the case of individuals who were not white, Anglo Saxon, and Protestant. Some former patients referred to their "big Jewish" noses, but none ever referred to their "puny gentile" ones. Some surgeons alluded to "Caucasian" eyelids or lips, but only when contrasting them with "Oriental" or "Negroid" ones. Thus, even in these carefully worded descriptions, race and ethnicity were invoked as "objective," transsituational grounds for surgery.

Of course, patients' class backgrounds might also be seen as "objective" indicators for cosmetic surgery insofar as these determine who is—and who is not—able to afford it. Since insurance companies, health maintenance organizations, and state-funded health care programs exclude virtually all elective aesthetic procedures from their provisions for patients' care, prospective patients must be prepared to pay for their surgeries themselves.[4] A woman to whom $2,000 is "nothing" is in a far better position to finance her upper eyelid reduction than a person to whom $2,000 is a substantial—or inconceivable—outlay. For example, one patient reported that

> In South America, they say that everyone in the upper class has had this surgery. I mean, it's automatic, like you go to the dentist. And to me, it was like, you buy a car. You pay eight thousand to twelve thousand dollars for a car, and four years later, it's worth nothing. . . . So what's two thousand dollars? Nothing. And it's going to last a lot longer than a car.

Or, as another patient put it,

> It's sort of like wearing braces—it's sort of a status thing. Everybody's doing it. If one of [your] friends does it and looks good, well, how are [you] going to let her get away with that? [You're] going to have it done too. It is a status thing: "I had so and so do mine"—"Oh, did you? How did you like him? I had so and so do mine."

But our data indicate that while limited economic resources may *hinder* the pursuit of cosmetic surgery, they do not necessarily *prevent* that pursuit. For instance, one woman who underwent breast augmentation took out a personal loan for $3,000 to finance her operation, a loan she worked very hard to pay off for a year following her surgery. Another woman received her breast augmentation "as a present" from her husband for her thirty-second birthday after ten years of wanting it. Other people we interviewed scrimped and saved for their operations on their modest salaries as bank tellers or secre-taries. Thus, although class differences influenced people's perceptions of their operations as "luxuries" or "investments," they did not explain people's desires to pursue surgery in the first instance.

ASSESSING "GOOD CANDIDATES"

As surgeons described their screening procedures, they revealed a complex sequence of assessments with a course they did not determine by themselves. For example, most described their first task as finding out what patients "really want," as opposed, presumably, to what patients think they want or say they want. Some surgeons employ computerized questionnaires to help them elicit such information, but even then, they cannot rely on what patients tell them as prima facie evidence for surgery. Like surgeons who function without computers, they then assess whether patients' expectations are "realistic," that is, consistent with what surgeons expect they can do for patients. Though photographs may be employed as visual aids, it becomes clear that "having realistic expectations" results from extensive negotiations *between* surgeons and their prospective patients:

> The first thing I've got to find out is what the patient really wants. Then I have to find out whether the expectations are realistic or not. That sort of goes into what they want and what I can do for them. Once we've established that, then I tell them the way I do it . . . , and I give them real informed consent . . . , [discussing] potential complications, the kind of procedures and what they're going to be going through. Then they have to make up their mind whether they're going to go ahead with it.

As another surgeon put it, gauging whether a patient has realistic expectations is not a one-shot determination he makes by himself, but a "two-way interview" with the patient. If surgeons *can* establish that prospective patients "have realistic expectations," they can then solicit patients' informed consent and accept them as candidates for surgery. Even then, as many surgeons note, would-be patients have to make up their minds to go through with it.

What we see in such descriptions is the central dilemma of cosmetic surgery. As we noted earlier, where cosmetic procedures are concerned, the surgeons' mandate rests solely on their ability to provide elective "aesthetic improvement." Thus, surgeons involved in cosmetic procedures must negotiate the evaluation of patients' complaints, the determination of what should be done about them, and the assessment of postoperative results in relation to *what* "aesthetic improvement" might consist of, and *to whom*. Even individuals who are not deemed as "in need" of aesthetic improvement by the first surgeon they consult may be subsequently accepted as patients by another. Approximately one-third of the patients we interviewed said that they had consulted more than one surgeon prior to their operations, with several indicating that they had been refused surgery by the first surgeon they consulted. Our data suggest that the determination of *what* "aesthetic improvement" might consist of revolves in large part around patients' displays of "appropriate" levels of concern.

APPROPRIATE LEVELS OF CONCERN

All of the surgeons advanced the view that there were "appropriate" and "inappropriate" levels of concern for particular patient problems. They advanced this view with explicit references to when patients should exhibit concern—and how much concern patients should exhibit—for the specific problems that bring them to the surgeon's

office. They saw it as inappropriate, for example, for patients to wait until they were middle-aged before seeking surgical alteration of features that had bothered them all their lives:

> *Say they're fifty years old—why have they waited until now? There may be some good reason—maybe they couldn't afford it or they couldn't get the time off. But the reason may also be that this woman's husband is leaving her, and she thinks it may be her nose and puts undue attention on this one thing without paying attention to the other things—it can be very dangerous to operate on someone like that.*

Moreover, they saw it as very inappropriate for patients to display concern for problems that were insignificant in relation to the whole:

> *Say some absolutely gorgeous woman has some eeny-teeny little wrinkle right here and she's just invested her whole life to getting that wrinkle away—well, I know almost one hundred and ninety-nine percent that no matter what happens to that little wrinkle, she's going to fix on something else afterwards to uh, grope after. And those are real tough patients to help out.*

Of course, one of the dangers involved in doing surgery on patients who show "inappropriate" levels of concern is the possibility of subsequent suits for malpractice. Plastic surgeons are among the four types of surgical specialists (the others are neurosurgeons, obstetrician/gynecologists, and orthopedic surgeons) most likely to lose malpractice insurance due to lawsuits or negligence (Schwartz and Mendelson 1989). Among surgeons we interviewed, there was general consensus that "problem" patients (cf. Lorber 1975) who display "inappropriate" levels of concern are, most often, men. For example, when asked why so few men sought cosmetic surgery, surgeons responded,

> *I think that male patients are more difficult. They're harder to deal with. Ten years ago when I was beginning to train, the dictum was "you don't do male cosmetic surgery" because they're all problems. They all have enough emotional instability to one, either sue you, or two, be a surgical disaster.*

And,

> *I've turned a couple of males down. They were just totally unrealistic—totally secretive, which is fairly typical of males. Didn't have a good sense for what they wanted at all. Just totally edgy, jumpy sorts of people.*

Such descriptions suggest that surgeons rely on a proportionate analysis of patients' concerns in relation to patients' sex categories and surgeons' own perceptions of patients' problems. The claim that there are "appropriate" levels of concern for specific problems sustains the belief in objective, factual, transsituational grounds for aesthetic improvement—even as these are constructed from the particulars of the case at hand.

DOING IT FOR THEMSELVES

More complex still was the determination of *to whom* a particular surgical intervention might constitute an "aesthetic improvement." Surgeons implied that they determined this on the basis of evidence that prospective patients were seeking cosmetic surgery "for themselves." They described "good candidates" for surgery as those who think surgery will increase their self-esteem and improve their self-image, not those who think it will help them attract a younger lover or maintain their spouse's attention. Through these means, surgeons located the impetus for aesthetic improvement within

patients themselves. As one surgeon explained,

> *Married female patients, especially with breast enlargements, have a lot of antagonism from their husbands. . . . [A husband may say,] "You look fine to me, I don't know why you want to do this." The comment the ladies make is, "I don't feel good about myself, that's why I want to do it. I've had two or three babies, and I used to have a nice figure and now I don't, and I just don't feel good about myself and I'm having my breasts increased."*

However, surgeons' expressed preferences for patients who "do it for themselves" were not without contradiction. For instance, most surgeons acknowledged that it is perfectly reasonable for someone to seek surgery in order to meet the requirements of their job:

> *You know, I do a lot of theatrical people. . . . [Those] who earn a living by their appearance are pretty legitimate. I've had many of them tell me . . . that they wouldn't do this unless it were important for them to make a living.*

Moreover, many former patients indicated that they were influenced in their decisions to seek surgery by significant others. One woman who had undergone rhinoplasty at 14 years of age said,

> *My father was physically and psychologically abusive to me, and part of his abuse was about how ugly I was, how I didn't deserve to be alive, [and] how he wished I was dead. But a lot of it was on my looks, and I looked identical to him. I probably even had the same size nose as he did—that's where I got my nose—and he used to say that I looked so much like his mother. . . . He hated his mother.*

Another woman who had worked for two different plastic surgeons told the following story:

> The first doctor I worked for . . . one day he came into my office—this was after I had been there about three or four years—and he sat there and he looked at me and said, "One thing I have found out,"—And I looked at him and said, "And that is?"— And he said, "**Every** surgeon in town has done his girls." And I was the only girl! So he said, "When are we going to do you?" . . . Well, he never let me alone! Finally, I let him [perform a facelift]. I just figured, "Well, if it'll make him happy and it will help his practice, I'll do it . . ." because he needed an example to show patients. He was thrilled to have done me . . . , and I just loved him and his family, but I tell you, I would **not** have had it done.

Finally, surgeons' own accounts indicated that under some conditions, they might advise their would-be patients to consider particular surgical procedures that they did not "come in for." For example, one surgeon confided,

> I personally feel that the patient should tell me what procedures they want—what they feel a need for, that's what they should tell me. Now, if they ask me if there's anything else that I feel could use improvement, I'll give them an opinion.

Thus, our data show that patients "with realistic expectations" do not always generate those expectations from within. Surgeons' stated preferences for patients who are "doing it for themselves" obscure a range of outside influences (including friends, family members, and employers) on people's decision to seek "aesthetic improvement." Moreover, once in the surgeon's office, those considering surgery may be influenced by further recommendations as to what they might "need." Through these means, "patients with realistic expectations" are *created* as well as "found" (cf. Conrad 1976; Conrad and Schneider 1980).

REDUCING THE BODY INTO PARTS

For the surgeons and former patients we interviewed, a primary means of creating patients with realistic expectations was the reduction of would-be patients' faces and bodies to a series of component parts. To be sure, reductionism is a key to scientific, and therefore medical, reasoning, and surgeons are encouraged to develop the capacity for it in the course of their professional training. Given that surgical practice is predicated on the subdivision of patient "parts," it would be odd if the surgeons we interviewed did *not* display an orientation toward reductionism in their descriptions of their activities (cf. Guillemin and Holmstrom 1986; Scully 1980). But our data indicate that surgeons also look for evidence of this orientation in prospective patients. One surgeon explained his approach as follows:

> There's two groups of people. Ones that will come in and say, "Make me beautiful"— those are very poor candidates. And somebody [who comes in] and says, "I don't like my nose." And you say, "What don't you like?" And he says, "Well, I don't like the lump and it's too long"—if they can describe what bothers them, and you know that it can be surgically corrected, then those are excellent candidates for surgery.

Most former patients provided ample evidence of their orientation toward seeing their bodies in parts. For example, one woman described her "pre-rhinoplasty" appearance as follows:

> I had a very Roman nose, straight, kind of broad. I mean, it was perfect, but kind of

big. When the first guy operated, I had scars in here (pointing to nostrils in the drawing she has made of her nose). There was more of a stereotype of Jewish women [and] big noses. . . . So I thought, what better thing to do than have my nose made smaller?

Another woman specified the benefits of her facelift in this way:

I got what I wanted. A clear forehead, no heavy eyelids and bags under my eyes (my eyes weren't too bad to begin with [but] my forehead was heavily lined). No furrows around my mouth. No wrinkles. Neck is great.

Still another itemized the pluses and minuses of her breast augmentation by saying:

I am very pleased with the results. Sometimes I fluctuate on wondering if I should have chosen an even larger size in breasts, but I inevitably return to the same conclusion: that this is perfect proportionately. I see no scar whatsoever on the left nipple; there is a slight trace of scar along the edge of the right nipple, but I don't think anyone else would ever notice, it is so slight.

Here, patients demonstrate such well-honed abilities to reduce their bodies to parts that they can offer pre-and post-operative drawings of the parts in question, itemize the benefits of their procedures part by part, and even identify subtle traces of scars that no one else would notice. Clearly, reductionism plays an important part in these patients' own views of their experiences.[5]

We might ask why this orientation becomes so central to accounts of people who undergo cosmetic surgery and those who perform it. Our data suggest that reductionism is essential to problematizing the part (or parts) in question and establishing their "objective" need for repair. For example, throughout these interviews, surgeons and patients alike

alluded to technically normal features as "flaws," "defects," "deformities," and "correctable problems" of appearance. Surgeons referred to patients as "needing" facelifts and breast augmentations, while patients referred to the specific parts (or part of parts) that they had "fixed." Through such terminology, they constitute *cosmetic* surgery as a *reconstructive* project. Ultimately, they may even dissolve the distinction between the two categories of plastic surgery—suggesting, for example, that to someone with "an ugly nose or prominent ears," cosmetic surgery may be "just as important as reconstructing somebody after cancer removal." Thus, reductionism provides a means of resolving the central dilemma of cosmetic surgery—defining the nature and treatment of "disease." By jointly reducing patients' bodies to a series of parts and focusing on the parts that require "correction," surgeons and patients forge a *mutual* basis for evaluating patients' complaints, determining what should be done about them, and assessing post-operative results.

Of course, there were minor variations on this theme. For example, one surgeon argued that *patients* were the ones who perceived their features as deformed, not him:

*I'm perceiving it as a shape, a structure, as whatever you want to call it . . . this **person** perceives it as a deformity. I just perceive it as the way they look. And they're asking me, "Can you change the way I look to something I don't perceive as a deformity?" So I'm basically treating their attitude towards their own appearance.*

Two other surgeons characterized their work as "improving the patient's self-esteem" and "giving them more confidence." However, whether surgeons conceptualized the deformity as on the patient or in the patient's head, they took surgical means to repair it.[6]

There are several apparent inconsistencies in the evidence we have presented so far.

For example, if the pursuit of cosmetic surgery is—as surgeons and patients claim—"normal" and "natural," why are objective indicators needed to justify it? And if the objective grounds for surgery are sociologically variable, what sense does it make to describe them as "objective" in the first place? Finally, if surgeons prefer patients who are doing it for themselves, why do they accept patients whose decisions to have surgery are clearly influenced by others' (including surgeons') opinions on their problems? Below, we address what we see as the "missing link" in our analysis so far, namely, the accomplishment of gender.

THE ACCOMPLISHMENT OF GENDER

Elsewhere, we advance an ethnomethodological view of gender as an *accomplishment*, that is, an achieved property of situated social action (Fenstermaker, West, and Zimmerman 1990; West and Fenstermaker forthcoming; West and Zimmerman 1987). From this perspective, gender is not simply something one is; rather, it is something one does in ongoing interaction with others. Following Heritage (1984:179), we argue that to the extent that members of society know their actions are accountable, they will design their actions with an eye to how others might see and characterize them. Moreover, insofar as sex categories (e.g., "girl" or "boy," "woman" or "man") are omnirelevant to social life (Garfinkel 1967:111; Goffman 1977:324), they provide an ever-ready resource for characterizing social action (e.g., as consistent with women's or men's "essential nature"). Accordingly, "people involved in virtually *any* activity may hold themselves accountable and be held accountable for their performance of that activity *as women* or *as men*" (West and Fenstermaker forthcoming: 7).

In the data presented in this paper, we find that accounts of cosmetic surgery rest ultimately on the accomplishment of gender. For example, throughout our interviews with surgeons and former patients, we found implicit claims that what was "normal" and "natural" for a woman was *not* normal or natural for a man. Surgeons were united in the view that women's concerns for their appearance are *essential* to their nature as women. They observed that women are, after all, taught to look good and disguise their real or imagined "defects." Hence, they said, it is taken for granted that a woman "wants to primp and look as pretty as she can." Her desire may not be biologically ordained—as they noted, she *is* a product of our society and how she was brought up. But, they pointed out, by the time a woman has been "brought up," her consciousness of her appearance as a matter of self image is "intrinsic" to her nature *as a woman* (cf. Cahill 1982; 1986a; 1986b).

By contrast, surgeons characterized men's concerns for their appearance as extrinsic to their nature as men. They observed that men are taught "to deal with little defects here and there," and that therefore, "they don't have the psychological investment in it that women do." They further observed that men must rely on their wives to buy their clothes or tell them what looks good, and that men only attend to their appearance in instrumental fashion, for example, to attain a more prestigious job.

Women are more concerned about their appearance than men are as a basic rule. Now that is not something you can apply to every person. Obviously you'll see that the success level is related to their appearance level. People who don't take some care in how they appear don't seem to be in supervisory or professional positions. And I guess people, as they're educated, I guess, as they attempt to reach some goal in life, find that their appearance relates to achieving those goals. Women, conversely, are intrinsically . . . concerned about their appearance, not just in a goal-oriented fashion, but as a matter of self image.

Here, a surgeon notes that educated "people" (meaning men) may discover that their appearance has an impact on their "attempt to reach some goal in life," but he does not attribute that discovery to any natural order of things. In fact, a concern for appearance is so unnatural for men that, as another surgeon notes, some men may deliberately misrepresent it in surgeons' offices, for example, complaining that they "can't breathe" to cover up their wishes for "a better-looking nose."

Our interviews with former patients also suggested that what was "normal" and "natural" for a woman was not normal or natural for a man. As noted above, women referred to cosmetic surgery as what "anyone" would do, extolled its benefits for "everyone," and compared it to "wearing makeup" or "having your hair done." By contrast, the only grounds on which men characterized the pursuit of cosmetic surgery as "normal" were job-related concerns. One man, a cosmetologist who underwent upper eyelid reduction, felt his upper lids were a distraction in his work. Another, who had undergone a facelift, explained that as a dentist, he felt patients liked "younger persons working on them." Still another man we spoke with who underwent reconstructive rhinoplasty for a deviated septum—but decided against cosmetic alteration—stated that he would only consider cosmetic surgery if he "were disfigured or something." And a man who consulted a surgeon about cosmetic rhinoplasty—but then decided against it—told us,

I like my nose. It's a little on the large side, and I was teased about it when I was younger, but it's the nose I grew up

with. . . . Besides, would I lie to the kids I have some day? They're going to grow up with these noses and say, "Where did this come from?" My philosophy is that you work with what you've got.

Of course, the men in the last two excerpts were accounting for something they did not do, while those in the first two excerpts were accounting for something they did. We can, therefore, understand why the last two excerpts would emphasize good reasons for not having surgery, and the first two, good reasons for having it. But what is noteworthy in all four descriptions is the assumption that a desire for aesthetic improvement must be *justified* (either on the basis of job-related concerns or in the case of "disfigurement"). Clearly, it was not seen as "natural."

Our interviewees further distinguished women from men in their descriptions of "objective" indicators for surgery. Many surgeons acknowledged that our culture and its double standard of aging are responsible for women's and men's differential experiences as they get older. Thus, they explained the fact that a man with wrinkles looks "acceptable" while a woman with wrinkles does not on the basis of cultural conceptions, rather than any objective standard. Surgeons, however, relied *on those same cultural conceptions* to select candidates for surgery:

Our society has got a very strange double standard and it can be summarized that when a man gets old, he gets sophisticated, debonair [and] wise; but when a woman gets old, she gets old. A man with a wrinkly face doesn't necessarily look bad in our society. A woman with a wrinkly face looks old. So when a man comes in and he wants a facelift, I have to be able to get considerably more skin than I would on a woman. . . . And usually there is something else going on. . . . Usually, they're getting rid of their wife.

In requiring "considerably more [excess] skin" for men than women, the surgeon constructs an "objective indicator" for doing surgery—as well as "objective differences" between women and men.

Another surgeon contended that there *are* objective differences that make women more likely to "need" surgery:

> Men *don't seem to have the lipodystrophy [i.e., deposition of fat in tissue] that women do. They don't have subcutaneous fat layers and uh . . . I guess I've only done one man with love handles. . . . I think it is more of a gender-related difference than uh, psychological. . . . Men dermabrade their face with a razor every morning. You have thick hair follicles that support the skin so that it doesn't get wrinkled . . . like your upper lip, for instance. Men hardly ever have any problem with that and women, sometimes by age 50, need their lip peeled or something.*

Our concern here is *not* the physiological differences this surgeon attests to (although we note that he ignores potbellies in this description). Rather, we are interested in how these differences are invoked to legitimize one course of activity and discredit another. If women's bodies are seen as *essentially* "in need of repair," then surgery on women can be seen as a moral imperative instead of an aesthetic option. But if men "hardly ever have any problem with that," then surgery on men will require elaborate justification.

Such justification was apparent in our interviews with men who had undergone cosmetic surgery. For example, in contrast to the woman patient who said that "when your eyelids start to come down" and "you start to get that 'crepeyness' in your neck" it is simply "time to do it," one man said that *his wife's appearance* motivated him to have a facelift, as he did not want his wife "to look much younger." Here, he eschewed a description of "objective" signs of aging for an explanation of how he might appear in relation to his spouse. Another man stated that following his upper eyelid reduction, he "once again looked like [his] old self." As a result, he indicated he "felt better" and did not "get as tired," attributing the difference to psychological effect.

The notion of gender as an interactional accomplishment also advances our analysis of how race and ethnicity were constituted as "objective" grounds for surgery. References to Michael Jackson notwithstanding, the descriptions of most surgeons focused on what *women* in various racial and ethnic groups "have" and "need," not on men. Even while former patients relied on white, Anglo Saxon, Protestant features as the unmarked case, they described their postoperative benefits not only as looking "less exotic," but also, "prettier," and "more attractive to men."

In short, we contend that our interviewees' accounts would not have been possible without the accomplishment of gender. This is the mechanism that allows them to see the pursuit of elective aesthetic improvement as "normal" and "natural" for a woman, but not for a man. The accountability of persons to particular sex categories provides for their seeing women as "objectively" needing repair and men as "hardly ever" requiring it. The fact that gender is an *interactional* accomplishment explains why surgeons prefer patients who are "doing it for themselves" but actively participate in the construction of patients' preferences.

The evidence indicates that the selection of "good candidates" for cosmetic surgery relies not merely on the creation of patients with "appropriate" levels of concern and the reduction of patients' faces and bodies to a series of component parts. It also relies on the simultaneous accomplishment of gender. Following Berk (1985), we contend that there are actually *two* processes here: (1) the selection of "good candidates" for surgery, and (2) the accomplishment of gender. The "normal," "natural" character of each process is made sensible in relation to the other, and since they operate simultaneously, the relationship between the two processes and their outcomes "is virtually impossible to question" (West and Fenstermaker forthcoming:14). Thus, the assessment of "appropriate levels of concern" ensures patients who will agree with a surgeon's perceptions of their problems, and at the same time, it furnishes the opportunity to affirm the pursuit of cosmetic surgery as an essentially "gendered" activity:

> *A lot of guys come in and the classic one is that they want their nose fixed. And you look at the guy and he's got this big, God-awful nose. So does Anthony Quinn! Uh, a man can get away with that kind of nose. So what is normal for a man would not be . . . well, let's say what is **acceptable** for a man would not necessarily be acceptable for a woman.*

The point, then, is not merely that pursuing cosmetic surgery is seen as something women do, but that for a woman to seek it while a man does not displays the "essential" nature of each.

CONCLUSION

Sociologists have had little to say about cosmetic surgery. Although an impressive body of literature has documented the expansion of medicine into nonmedical terrain, this literature has focused primarily on the medicalization of deviance, redefining "badness" as "sickness" (Conrad and Schneider 1980; Ehrenreich and Ehrenreich 1978; Zola 1972), and the medicalization of natural processes, moving activities such as childbirth from home to hospital (Ehrenreich and English 1978; Reissman 1983; Wertz and Wertz

1977). Other research has treated the social and historical construction of the body as a subject of inquiry (Connell 1987; Glassner 1988; Turner 1984; Wilson 1987), but it has not yet addressed cosmetic surgery as a primary object of investigation. With the exception of feminist analyses of "the politics of appearance" (Chapkis 1986; Freedman 1986; Lakoff and Scherr 1984; Millman 1980), most scholarly interest in the topic has been limited to psychological studies of interpersonal attractiveness (Berscheid and Gangestad 1982; Berscheid and Walster 1969) and clinical studies of patients' motivations for surgery (Crikelair, Druss, and Symonds 1971; Edgerton and Knorr 1971).

In this paper, we have examined how surgeons who do cosmetic operations account for their activities and how people who elect such operations make sense of their decisions to do so. Our data indicate that surgeons and patients "explain" their involvement in these activities by extending the definition of reconstructive surgery to include cosmetic procedures. By reducing patients' faces and bodies to a series of component parts, surgeons and patients together establish the problematic status of the part in question and its "objective" need of "repair." This process affords them a mutual basis for negotiating the evaluation of patients' complaints, the determination of what should be done about them, and the assessment of post-operative results. But this process operates in tandem with the accomplishment of gender, allowing surgeons and patients to see the pursuit of cosmetic surgery as "normal" and "natural" for a woman and *not* for a man. Without the accountability of persons to sex categories, women could not be established as "objectively" in need of repair, nor men, as "objectively" acceptable.

We advance our findings as hypotheses rather than generalizations. Indeed, we present them in a spirit of invitation—with the hope of stimulating among sociologists a broader range of interest in the topic we sought to address. We do not know, for example, how prevalent these processes are among surgeons and patients at large. Nor do we know how these processes might operate in other clinical domains, such as orthodontia (for some suggestive leads, see Davis 1980) or cosmetic dentistry.

We do know that our findings contribute to the existing literature on medicalization by identifying a new frontier for expansion of the medical mandate. Beyond work on the appropriation of "bad" behavior and on the usurpation of natural processes, our findings point to the expropriation of the aesthetic realm as a third arena of medicalization. We also know that our findings yield a new direction for research on the social construction of the body: illustrating that bodies are not merely adorned and altered, but physically *reconstructed* in accord with prevailing cultural conceptions. Finally, we know that at least among the surgeons and patients we interviewed, accounting for cosmetic surgery depends on the accomplishment of gender (West and Zimmerman 1987). In offering accounts of their pursuit of surgery, patients enact their "essential natures" as women or men. In offering accounts of their surgical decision-making, surgeons uphold normative attitudes and activities for particular sex categories and, hence, become co-participants in the accomplishment of gender. In addition, surgeons act as technological facilitators of gender's accomplishment and as cultural gatekeepers in the fine tuning of gender's presentation. Thus, cosmetic surgery emerges as an institutional support for "doing gender."

ENDNOTES

1. The surgeon's mandate to assess post-operative results works in at least two ways. First, it affords surgeons the authority to appraise likely outcomes of operations in advance of their occurrence (and thereby, to determine whether operations should be performed). Second, it affords surgeons the authority to judge results of particular procedures after the fact (and thus, to pronounce procedures as "successful"). The latter mandate is especially important in cases of malpractice suits, where the expert testimony of other surgeons weighs heavily in litigation.

2. This figure should be treated as a conservative estimate, insofar is it only includes operations performed by the 2,550 active physician members of the American Society of Plastic and Reconstructive Surgeons. However, statistics on the actual incidence of cosmetic surgery are virtually impossible to maintain. For example, the U.S. National Center for Health Statistics reports figures independently of physicians' and surgeons' Board affiliations and society memberships, but it does not include operations performed outside hospitals. Since 95 percent of cosmetic procedures are said to be performed in private offices or clinics (American Society of Plastic and Reconstructive Surgeons 1988), the National Center for Health Statistics offers an even less reliable estimate of their actual incidence.

3. Ideally, we also would have obtained interviews with women who consulted plastic surgeons, but decided against cosmetic surgery. We were unable to locate such women through our snowball sample. However, insofar as the accomplishment of gender involves the *accountability* of persons to particular sex categories (not deviance or conformity per se), this "gap" in our data does not constitute a problem for our analysis.

4. Until July of 1990, military personnel and their families were an exception to this rule. Prior to that time, military physicians and surgeons performed aesthetic procedures on members of the U.S. Armed Forces under the general provisions for health care of those personnel "to sharpen their skills as surgeons in preparation for wartime duty" (*Parade Magazine* 1990:14). The Pentagon has introduced new regulations to prevent the use of appropriated funds except for "the correction of birth defects, the repairing of injuries, or the commmission of breast-reconstruction procedures following mastectomies."

5. Of course, the capacity for reductionism has received considerable attention in feminist analyses of the politics of appearance. Freedman (1986:25–29), for example, suggests that women develop an overall image of their bodies from the detailed scrutiny of particular parts. In cases where women suffer from "poor body image," they "generalize from one bad feature to their whole appearance, while ignoring the ways they are attractive" (25).

6. Here, we do not mean to be glib. But these surgeons' claims can be engaged in "surgery of the self image" are belied by their own participation in formulation

of patients' preferences and by their limited expertise in techniques of psychological assessment. For example, most surgeons said that "specific" psychiatric and/or psychological training had not been a part of their medical education and that patient selection was ultimately a "judgment call," based on their "gut feelings."

REFERENCES

American Society of Plastic and Reconstructive Surgeons
1988   Press Release: "Estimated number of cosmetic procedures performed by ASPRS members." Department of Communications, Arlington Heights, Ill.
Berk, Sarah F.
1985   The Gender Factory: The Apportionment of Work in American Households. New York: Plenum.
Berscheid, Ellen and Steve Gangestad
1982   "The social psychological implications of facial physical attractiveness." Clinics in Plastic Surgery 9:289–296.
Berscheid, Ellen and Elaine H. Walster
1969   Interpersonal Attraction. Reading, Mass.: Addison-Wesley.
Cahill, Spencer E.
1982   "Becoming boys and girls." Ph.D. dissertation, Department of Sociology, University of California, Santa Barbara.
1986a   "Childhood socialization as recruitment process: Some lessons from the study of gender development." In Sociological Studies of Child Development, ed. Patricia and Peter Adler, 163–186. Greenwich, Conn.: JAI Press.
1986b   "Language practices and self-definition: The case of gender identity acquisition." The Sociological Quarterly 27:295–311.
Chapkis, Wendy
1986   Beauty Secrets: Women and the Politics of Appearance. Boston: Southend Press.
Connell, R.W.
1987   "The Body and Social Practice." In Gender and Social Power: Society, The Person and Sexual Politics, 66–88. Stanford, Calif.: Stanford University Press.
Conrad, Peter
1976   Identifying Hyperactive Children: The Medicalization of Deviant Behavior. Lexington, Mass.: Lexington Books.
Conrad, Peter and Joseph W. Schneider
1980   Deviance and Medicalization: From Badness to Sickness. St. Louis, MO: Mosby.

Crikelair, George F., Richard G. Druss, and Francis C. Symonds
1971   "The problems of somatic delusions in patients seeking cosmetic surgery." Plastic and Reconstructive Surgery 48:246–250.
Davis, Peter
1980   The Social Context of Dentistry. London: Croom Helm Ltd.
Edgerton, Milton T. and Norman J. Knorr
1971   "Motivation patterns of patients seeking cosmetic surgery." Plastic and Reconstructive Surgery 48:551–557.
Ehrenreich, Barbara and John Ehrenreich
1978   "Medicine and social control." In The Cultural Crisis of Modern Medicine, ed. John Ehrenreich, 39–79. New York: Monthly Review Press.
Ehrenreich, Barbara and Deirdre English
1978   For Her Own Good: 150 Years of the Experts' Advice to Women. Garden City, N.Y.: Anchor/Doubleday.
Fenstermaker, Sarah, Candace West, and Don H. Zimmerman
1990   Gender inequality: New conceptual terrain." In Gender, Family and Economy: The Triple Overlap, ed. Rae Lesser Blumberg, 289–307. Beverly Hills: Sage.
Freedman, Rita
1986   Beauty Bound. Lexington, Mass.: D.C. Heath and Company.
Garfinkel, Harold
1967   Studies in Ethnomethodology. Englewood Cliffs, N.J.: Prentice Hall.
Glaser, Barney and Anselm Strauss
1967   The Discovery of Grounded Theory. Chicago: Aldine.
Glassner, Barry
1988   Bodies: Why We Look the Way We Do (and how we feel about it). New York: Putnam.
Goffman, Erving
1977   "The arrangement between the sexes." Theory and Society 4:301–331.
Guillemin, Jeanne H. and Lynda L. Holmstrom
1986   Mixed Blessings: Intensive Care for Newborns. New York: Oxford University Press.
Heritage, John
1984   Garfinkel and Ethnomethodology. Cambridge, England: Polity Press.
Hughes, Everett C.
1958   Men and Their Work. Glencoe, Ill.: The Free Press.
Lakoff, Robin T. and Raquel L. Scherr
1984   Face Value: The Politics of Beauty. Boston: Routledge & Kegan Paul.

Lorber, Judith
  1975   "Good patients and problem patients: Conformity and deviance in a general hospital." Journal of Health and Social Behavior 16:213–225.
Millman, Marcia
  1980   Such a Pretty Face: Being Fat in America. New York: Norton.
Parade Magazine
  1990   "Cosmetic surgery curbed." August 26, 1990:14.
Reissman, Catherine Kohler
  1983   "Women and medicalization." Social Policy 14:3–18.
Schwartz, William B. and D.N. Mendelson
  1989   "Physicians who have lost their malpractice insurance. Their demographic characteristics and the surplus-lines companies that insure them." Journal of the American Medical Association 262:1335–41.
Scully, Diana
  1980   Men Who Control Women's Health: The Miseducation of Obstetrician-Gynecologists. Boston: Houghton Mifflin.
Thorne, Barrie
  1973   "Professional education in medicine." In Education for the Professions of Medicine, Law, Theology and Social Welfare (a report for the Carnegie Commission on Higher Education), by Everett C. Hughes, Barrie Thorne, Agostino M. DeBaggis, Arnold

Gurin and David Williams, 17–99. New York: McGraw Hill.
Turner, Bryan S.
  1984   The Body and Society: Explorations in Social Theory. Oxford: B. Blackwell.
U.S. National Center for Health Statistics
  1987   Detailed Diagnoses and Surgical Procedures. Washington, D.C.: U.S. Government Printing Office.
Wertz, Richard W., and Dorothy C. Wertz
  1977   Lying In: A History of Childbirth in America. New York: Schocken Books.
West, Candace and Sarah Fenstermaker
  Forthcoming   "Power, inequality and the accomplishment of gender: An ethnomethodological view." In Theory on Gender/Feminism on Theory, ed. Paula England. New York: Aldine.
West, Candace and Don H. Zimmerman
  1987   "Doing gender." Gender & Society 1:125–151.
Wilson, Elizabeth W.
  1987   "Gender and Identity." In Adorned in Dreams: Fashion and Modernity, 117–133. Berkeley: University of California Press.
Zimmerman, Don H.
  1978   "Ethnomethodology." The American Sociologist 13:6–15.
Zola, Irving K.
  1972   "Medicine as an Institution of Social Control." Sociological Review 2:487–504.

Questions for Understanding and Critical Thinking

1. Why do more women undergo cosmetic operations than men? How do cultural norms contribute to their decisions to have elective surgery?

2. According to Dull and West, do people's racial or ethnic features sometimes constitute "objective" indicators for cosmetic surgery? Who decides what constitutes an "objective" problem that requires surgical improvement? Support your answers.

3. According to Dull and West, is what is "normal" and "natural" for a woman also normal and natural for a man? Why or why not?

4. Although the authors did not explicitly examine the class location of the patients and doctors in this study, you can think through this dimension for yourself. How do you think social class enters the picture for patients who have elective cosmetic surgery? How about for plastic and reconstructive surgeons who perform these operations?

ARTICLE 9

Two major U.S. corporations—McDonald's and Combined Insurance (a large firm headquartered in Chicago)—are examined in this article. Through interviewing and participant observation at each company, sociologist Robin Leidner uncovered the methods and consequences of employers' efforts to routinize *interactive service work*—jobs that involve direct interaction with customers or clients. Leidner also describes the distinctive features of interactive service jobs that show the interrelation of work, gender, and identity.

Robin Leidner teaches sociology at the University of Pennsylvania and is author of *Fast Food, Fast Talk: Service Work and the Routinization of Everyday Life,* a recent book that provides an in-depth analysis of the interactive service jobs discussed in this article.

Looking Ahead

1. How do interactive service jobs differ from other types of work?
2. What methods are used by employers to control workers' interactions?
3. How is gender salient in service jobs?
4. How did Combined Insurance and McDonald's differ in demands placed on workers?

Serving Hamburgers and Selling Insurance

Gender, Work, and Identity in Interactive Service Jobs

◆ *Robin Leidner*

All workers look for ways to reconcile the work they do with an identity they can accept, either by interpreting the work positively or by discounting the importance of the work as a basis of identity. [Sociologist Everett C.] Hughes, emphasizing the active process of interpretation, recommended examining the "social and social-psychological arrangements and devices by which men *[sic]* make their work tolerable, or even make it glorious to themselves and others" ([1951] 1984, 342). If the work cannot be construed as glorious, or even honorable, workers will look for ways to distance themselves from their jobs, assuring themselves that the work they are doing does not reflect their true

Source: From Robin Leidner, "Serving Hamburgers & Selling Insurance: Gender, Work, and Identity in Interactive Service Jobs," in *Gender & Society,* Volume 5, June 1991, pp. 154–177, copyright © 1991 by Sage Publications, Inc. Reprinted by permission of Sage Publications, Inc.

worth. One of the most important determinants of the meaning of a type of work, as well as of how the work is conducted and rewarded, is its association with a particular gender. Acceptance by a worker of the identity implied by a job is therefore determined in part by the degree to which the job can be interpreted as allowing the worker to enact gender in a way that is satisfying.

Much contemporary theory and research on gender shares an emphasis on its active and continual construction through social interaction (Garfinkel 1967; Goffman 1977; Kessler and McKenna 1978; West and Zimmerman 1987). [Sociologists Candace] West, and [Don] Zimmerman argue that "participants in interaction organize their various and manifold activities to reflect or express gender, and they are disposed to perceive the behavior of others in a similar light" (1987, 127). One of the most striking aspects of the social construction of gender is that its successful accomplishment creates the impression that gender differences in personality, interests, character, appearance, manner, and competence are natural—that is, that they are not social constructions at all. Gender segregation of work reinforces this appearance of naturalness. When jobholders are all of one gender, it appears that people of that gender must be especially well suited to the work, even if at other times and places, the other gender does the same work. Thus, [sociologist Ruth] Milkman's analysis of industrial work during World War II demonstrates "how idioms of sex-typing can be flexibly applied to whatever jobs women and men happen to be doing" (1987, 50).

In this article, I will argue that jobholders and their audiences may make this interpretation even under the most unlikely conditions: when the work might easily be interpreted as more suitable for the other gender, and when many aspects of the workers' presentations of self are closely dictated by superiors and are clearly not spontaneous expressions of the workers' characters, interests, or personalities. My analysis of the flexibility of interpretations of gender-appropriate work draws on research on the routinization of jobs that involve direct interaction with customers or clients—what I call "interactive service work" (see Leidner 1988). These sorts of jobs merit attention, since service work is increasingly central to the U.S. economy: The service sector is expected to continue to provide most new jobs through the year 2000 (Personick 1987; Silvestri and Lukasiewic 1987).

Interactive service jobs have several distinctive features that make them especially revealing for investigation of the interrelation of work, gender, and identity. These jobs differ from other types of work in that the distinctions among product, work process, and worker are blurred or nonexistent, since the quality of the interaction may itself be part of the service offered (Hochschild 1983). In many kinds of interactive service work, workers' identities are therefore not incidental to the work but are an integral part of it. Interactive jobs make use of workers' looks, personalities, and emotions, as well as their physical and intellectual capacities, sometimes forcing them to manipulate their identities more self-consciously than do workers in other kinds of jobs. The types of relations with service recipients structured by the jobs may also force workers to revise taken-for-granted moral precepts abut personal interaction. Workers who feel that they owe others sincerity, individual consideration, nonmanipulativeness, or simply full attention may find that they cannot be the sort of people they want to be and still do their jobs adequately (Hochschild 1983). While a variety of distancing strategies and rationalizations are possible (Rollins 1985), it may be difficult for interactive service workers to separate themselves from the identities implied by their jobs (Leidner 1988).

When interactive work is routinized, workers' interactions are directly controlled by employers, who may use scripting, uniforms, rules about proper demeanor and appearance, and even far-reaching attempts at psychological reorientation to standardize service encounters. The interactions are expressly designed to achieve a certain tone (friendliness, urgency) and a certain end (a sale, a favorable impression, a decision). Analysis of how employers try to combine the proper interactive elements to achieve the desired effects can make visible the processes by which meaning, control, and identity are ordinarily created through interaction in all kinds of settings. Workers' and service recipients' acceptance or rejection of the terms of the standardized interactions and their efforts to tailor the prescribed roles and routines to suit their own purposes are similarly revealing about the extent to which people sustain beliefs about who they are through how they treat others and are treated by them.

Gender is necessarily implicated in the design and enactment of service interactions. In order to construct routines for interactions, especially scripts, employers make many assumptions about what customers like, what motivates them, and what they consider normal interactive behavior. Some of the assumptions employers make concern how men and women should behave. Once these assumptions about proper gender behavior are built into workers' routines, service recipients may have to accept them in order to fit smoothly into the service interaction. My research on the routinization of service jobs was inspired in part by my astonishment at one such script: I learned that employees of Gloria Marshall Figure Salons were expected to ask their customers, "Have you and your husband discussed your figure needs?" (Lally-Benedetto 1985). The expectation that workers could toss out the term *figure needs* as if it were everyday speech was startling in itself, but I was especially intrigued by the layers of assumptions the question implied about the natures of women and men and the power relations between them.

As this example illustrates, scripts can embody assumptions about proper gendered behavior in fairly obvious ways. To do such jobs as intended, workers must "do gender" in a particular way (Berk 1985b; West and Zimmerman 1987). Even where the gender component is less obvious, workers in all kinds of jobs need to consider how their work relates to their own identities, including their gender identities. Whether workers take pride in the work itself or see it as stigmatizing, whether they work harder than is required or put in the least effort they can get away with, and whether they identify themselves with the job or seek self-definition elsewhere are related not just to job tasks and working conditions but to the extent that the jobs can be interpreted as honorable, worthwhile, and suitable for persons of their gender (Ouellet 1986).

This process of interpretation may be unusually salient and unusually open to analysis in routinized interactive service work. In such jobs, a convincing performance is important, and so employers are concerned about the degree to which workers enact their roles with conviction. The employers may therefore participate in reconciling workers' selves with the identities demanded by the work by providing positive interpretations of the work role or psychic strategies for dealing with its potentially unpleasant or demeaning aspects. In short, employers of interactive service workers may be unusually open in their attempts to channel workers' attitudes and manipulate workers' identities.

Gender is more salient in some service jobs than others, of course. There are routinized interactive service jobs for which the gender of employees and customers is not particularly relevant to how the jobs were constructed or how the interactions are carried out—telephone interviewing, for example, is apparently gender neutral and is done by men and women. However, the gender of workers is not irrelevant in these jobs, since respondents may react differently to men and women interviewers. Similarly, while airplane flight attendant is a job currently held by men as well as women, [sociologist Arlie Russell] Hochschild found that men flight attendants were more likely to have their authority respected and less likely to be subjected to emotional outbursts from passengers than were their women co-workers (Hochschild 1983). At the other extreme are jobs that are gender segregated and that would be virtually incomprehensible without extensive assumptions about how both workers and customers enact gender. The Gloria Marshall salon workers' job assumed that both workers and customers would be women. The script used by Playboy Bunnies, who were trained to respond to being molested by saying, "Please, sir, you are not allowed to touch the Bunnies" (Steinem 1983, 48), took for granted a male customer (see also Spradley and Mann 1975). Both scripts dictated "common understandings" about what men and women are like and how power is distributed between them.

I studied two jobs that fall between these extremes; they are neither gender neutral nor entirely saturated with assumptions about gender. I conducted fieldwork at McDonald's and at Combined Insurance Company of America. At McDonald's, my research centered on the food servers who dealt directly with the public (*window crew,* in McDonald's parlance), and at Combined Insurance, I studied life insurance agents.

These jobs were not strictly gender segregated, but they were held prominantly by either men or women, influencing how workers, employers, and customers thought about the jobs. Most, but not all, of McDonald's window crew were young women, and almost all of Combined Insurance's agents were men. Their gender attributes were not essential to their jobs. In fact, both jobs can be gender typed in the opposite direction—in its early years, McDonald's hired only men (Boas and Chain 1976), and in Japan, door-to-door insurance sales is a woman's job *(Life Insurance Business in Japan, 1987/88).*

Workers in both jobs tried to make sense of de facto job segregation by gender, interpreting their jobs as congruent with proper gender enactment. Examination of these two jobs and of how workers thought about them highlights a central paradox in the construction of gender: The considerable flexibility of notions of proper gender enactment does not undermine the appearance of inevitability and naturalness that continues to support the division of labor by gender. Although the work of the insurance agents required many of the same kinds of interactive behavior as the McDonald's job, including behavior that would ordinarily be considered feminine, the agents were able to interpret the work as suitable only for men. They did so by emphasizing aspects of their job that required "manly" attributes and by thinking about their interactive work in terms of control rather than deference. Their interpretation suggests not only the plasticity of gender idioms but the asymmetry of those idioms: Defining work as masculine has a different meaning for men workers than defining work as feminine has for women workers.

Because interactive service work by definition involves nonemployees in the work process, the implications of the gender constructions of the routines extend beyond the workers. When service jobs are done predominantly by men or predominantly by women, the gender segregation provides confirming "evidence" to the public that men and women have different natures and capabilities. This appearance is especially ironic when employers, treating their workers' selves as fairly malleable, reshape the self-presentations and interactional styles of the service workers. A brief account of my fieldwork and of the routinization of the two jobs precedes further discussion of how work, gender, and identity are enmeshed in these jobs.

ROUTINIZED INTERACTIONS

My data were gathered from participant observation and interviewing. I attended classes at McDonald's management training center, Hamburger University, in June 1986, and spoke with "professors" and trainees there. I conducted research at a local McDonald's franchise from May through November 1986, going through orientation and window-crew training, working on the window, interviewing window workers and managers, and hanging around the crew room to observe and talk with workers. At Combined Insurance, I went through the two-week training for life insurance agents in January 1987. Between January and March, I interviewed trainees and managers and spent one-and-a-half weeks in the field with a sales team, observing sales calls and talking to agents. Since insurance agents must be licensed and bonded, I did not actually sell insurance myself. I also conducted follow-up interviews with Combined Insurance managers in the summer of 1989. The workers and managers with whom I worked at both companies were aware that I was conducting research.

These two jobs were similar in a number of ways. Both were filled, by and large, with young, inexperienced workers, and both had extremely high rates of employee turnover. Neither job is held in high esteem by the public, which affected both customers' treatment of workers and the workers' willingness to embrace their roles (see Zelizer 1979, on the low prestige of life insurance agents). The companies, however, took training very seriously, and they carried the routinization of service interactions very far indeed. McDonald's and Combined Insurance each tried to exercise extensive control over their workers' presentation of themselves. However, they went about this task differently and placed different sorts of demands on their workers' psyches. The differences largely have to do with the kinds of relations that the companies established between workers and customers and are related to the gender typing of the work.

McDonald's

McDonald's has been a model of standardization for many kinds of service businesses, and its success, based upon the replication of standard procedures, has been truly phenomenal. The goal is to provide the same quality of food and service every day at every McDonald's, and the company tries to leave nothing to chance. Individual franchises have considerable leeway in some matters, including labor practices, but they are held to strict standards when it comes to the McDonald's basics of QSC—quality, service, and cleanliness.

At the McDonald's where I worked, all of the workers were hired at the minimum wage of $3.35. There were no fringe benefits and no guarantee of hours of work. As is typical at McDonald's, most men worked on the grill, and most women worked serving customers—about three-quarters of the window workers were women. About 80 percent of the restaurant's employees were Black, though Blacks were a minority of the city's population. Few of the workers were older than their early 20s, but most were out of high school—65 percent of my sample were 18 or over. The clientele, in contrast, was quite diverse in class, race, age, and gender.

The window workers were taught their jobs in a few hours and were fully trained in a couple of days. The job involved carrying out the "Six Steps of Window Service," an unvarying routine for taking and delivering orders. The modern cash registers used at this McDonald's made it unnecessary for window workers to remember prices or to know how to calculate change. The machines also reminded workers to "suggestive sell": For example, if someone ordered a Big Mac, french fries, and a shake, the cash register's buttons for apple pies, ice cream, and cookies would light up, to remind the worker to suggest dessert. (Garson [1988] provides a scathing view of McDonald's routinization and computerization.) These workers were closely supervised, not only by McDonald's managers, but also by customers, whose constant presence exerted pressure to be diligent and speedy.

The workers wore uniforms provided by McDonald's and were supposed to look clean-cut and wholesome—for instance, a young man with a pierced ear had to wear a Band-Aid on his earlobe. The lack of control workers had over their self-presentations was brought home clearly when a special promotion of Shanghai McNuggets began, and window workers were forced to wear big Chinese peasant hats made of Styrofoam, which most felt made them look ridiculous.

Workers were told to be themselves on the job, but they were also told to be cheerful and polite at all times. Crew people were often reprimanded for not smiling. Almost all of the workers I interviewed said that most customers were pleasant to deal with, but the minority of rude or unreasonable

customers had a disproportionate impact. Enduring customers' behavior, no matter how obnoxious, was a basic part of the job. Unfortunately for the workers, they completely lacked what Hochschild calls a "status shield" (1983, 163). Some customers who might have managed to be polite to higher-status workers seemed to have no compunction at all about snarling at McDonald's employees. The window crew could not escape from angry customers by leaving, and they were not allowed to argue or make smart-alecky remarks. Their only legitimate responses to rudeness or angry outbursts from customers were to control their anger, apologize, try to correct the problem, and in extreme cases, ask a manager to handle it.

The major task for the workers was to serve, and their major psychic task was to control or suppress the self. Workers were required to be nice to one person after another in a way that was necessarily unindividualized and to keep their tempers no matter how they were treated. What McDonald's demanded of its workers was a stripped-down interactive style, with some *pseudo-gemeinschaft* thrown in. The workers were supposed to be efficient, courteous, and friendly, but in short bursts and within a very narrow range. While they were told to be themselves, there was obviously not much range for self-expression.

Combined Insurance

Combined Insurance placed very different sorts of demands on its workers. The company's business is based on door-to-door sales in rural areas and small towns, and its profits depend on a high volume of sales of relatively inexpensive policies. Combined Insurance was founded in the 1920s by W. Clement Stone, and its agents still use many of the sales and self-conditioning techniques that he developed when he started out in the business—*The Success System That Never Fails* (Stone 1962). Almost all of the company's life insurance agents are men, most are white, and most are young—all of the members of the sales team I studied were in their early twenties. The prospects I called on with the agents were all white, about equally men and women, and quite varied in age.

The agents' initial training was more extensive than the McDonald's workers', involving two weeks of lectures, script memorization, and role playing. During sales school, trainees were taught what to say and do in almost hilarious detail. They memorized scripts for the basic sales presentations, for Rebuttals 1 through 5, corresponding to Objections 1 through 5, and for Interruption-stoppers. They were taught exactly how to stand while waiting for a door to be opened, how to position themselves and the potential customers (known as "prospects"), when to make and break eye contact, how to deliver the Standard Joke, and so on. A lot of class time was spent chanting the scripts in unison and rehearsing proper body movements, as well as in practicing responses to be used in various sales situations.

The trainer underlined the possibility of success through standardization with stories of foreign-born agents who succeeded even before they could speak English—they allegedly learned their sales presentations phonetically. It might seem that the message of these stories was that a parrot could succeed in this job, but in fact, the trainer argued that personal characteristics were vitally important to success, and the most important of these was a Positive Mental Attitude—what Stone called PMA. While McDonald's merely instructed workers to smile and behave pleasantly to customers, Combined Insurance tried to affect its employees' psyches quite fundamentally—to inculcate optimism, determination, enthusiasm, and confidence and to destroy habits of negative

thinking. The trainees were taught that through proper self-conditioning, they could learn to suppress negative thoughts altogether. The message for agents was somewhat paradoxical: You should do everything exactly the way we tell you to, but success depends on your strength of character.[1]

While McDonald's workers' main task was to serve people who had already chosen to do business with McDonald's, Combined Insurance's agents had to sell, to take prospects and turn them into customers. The agents' job was to establish rapport quickly with the people they called on (by "warming up the prospect"), to go through the basic sales presentation, to counter any objections raised by the prospects, and to persuade them to buy as much life insurance as possible. Naturally, most of the people they called on were strongly motivated to prevent them from going through this sequence, so their task was not easy. Since the agents' incomes were entirely based on commission, and their desire to handle their interactions successfully was of course very great, the detailed instructions for proper behavior provided by the company did not seem to strike them as ludicrous or intrusive.

Because the agents worked on their own, rather than in a central workplace, and because their interactions with customers could be much longer and cover a broader range than those of McDonald's workers, the agents were called on to use much more of their selves than the window workers were. They had to motivate themselves and keep up their enthusiasm, and they had to respond appropriately to a wide variety of situations, adjusting their behavior to suit the problems presented by each prospect. Although their basic routine was unvaried, they needed to be chameleon-like to a certain extent and adapt to circmstances. They were, like the McDonald's workers, required to control themselves, but their focus was always on controlling the prospect and the interaction. Virtually every detail of their routines was designed to help them do just that.

DOING GENDER WHILE DOING THE JOB

Although their jobs were largely segregated by gender, McDonald's and Combined Insurance workers interacted with both men and women as customers or prospects. Neither company suggested significantly different approaches to men and women service recipients; the Combined Insurance trainer recommended slightly varied techniques for persuading men and women to buy policies without first consulting their spouses. While the gender of the service recipient might well have influenced how the workers experienced their interactions, I did not find consistent patterns of variation in workers' behavior along this dimension.

At McDonald's, most of the window crew took the division of labor by gender for granted and did not seem to feel any need to account for it. Since there were no differences in the pay or prestige of window and grill work, and since there were exceptions to the pattern of gender segregation, few workers considered the division of labor by gender unfair.[2] When I asked the workers why they thought that there were more women than men working the window, about two-thirds of the 23 respondents said that they did not know, with about half offering a guess based on stereotypes about proper gender roles, whether or not they thought the stereotype was justified. About one-quarter of the sample, however, stated explicitly that they disapproved of the division of labor by gender, and three women said that they had asked a manager about it. The store's manager told me that women were typically assigned to start work on the window because "more females have an aversion to grill."

Two of the window workers, however (both Black men), thought that men might have an aversion to window because that job required swallowing one's pride and accepting abuse calmly:

Theo: [More women than men work window] because women are afraid of getting burned [on the grill], and men are afraid of getting aggravated and going over the counter and smacking someone.

Alphonse: I found the men who work here on window have a real quick temper. You know, all of them. And women can take a lot more. They deal with a lot of things, you know.

Although I never heard the masculinity of the few male window workers impugned, it was commonly taken for granted that men were naturally more explosive than women and would find it more difficult to accept abuse without answering back. The male window workers were usually able to reconcile themselves to swallowing insults, as the women were, either by dissociating themselves from their role or by telling themselves that by keeping their tempers they were proving themselves superior to the rude customers. Refusing to become riled when provoked is consistent with "the cool pose," which [sociologist Richard] Majors says Black men use to "fight to preserve their dignity, pride, respect and masculinity" by enacting an imperviousness to hurt (1989, 86). Thus, while the job did not allow workers to try to get the better of opponents, its demands were not seen as irreconcilable with enacting masculinity. However, no workers argued that men's capacity to tolerate abuse made them especially well-suited to the job, and the Black men quoted above made the opposite argument. Moreover, the job requirements of smiling and otherwise demonstrating deference are not in keeping with the cool pose. Those committed to that stance might well find such behavior demeaning, especially in interactions with white customers or those of higher status.

Other explanations given by workers of the predominance of women on window crew included assertions that women were more interested in dealing with people, that women "were more presentable" and looked better on window, that their nimble fingers suited them to working the registers, and that customers were more likely to find them trustworthy. Several of the workers who offered such stereotyped responses indicated that they did not believe that the stereotypes were sufficient justification for the predominance of women on the window crew.

It might easily have been argued that men were unsuited to work on the grill—cooking, after all, is usually considered women's work. As the work was understood at McDonald's, however, cooking presented no challenge to masculinity. Serving customers, which involved adopting an ingratiating manner, taking orders from anyone who chose to give them, and holding one's tongue when insulted, was more difficult to conceive as congruent with the proper enactment of manliness. Thus, while the crew people did not argue that window work was especially expressive of femininity, most found it unremarkable that women predominated in that job.

The work of Combined Insurance's agents, in contrast, was defined as properly manly, even though the job presented interactive imperatives that are generally identified with femininity, along with some stereotypically masculine elements. The life insurance sales force was almost entirely composed of men, and the agents on the sales team I observed felt strongly that women would be unlikely to succeed in the job.[3] Moreover, the 22-year-old manager of this sales team told me bluntly (without my

having raised the question) that he "would never hire a woman."[4] Since some aspects of the agents' job required skills that are not generally considered manly, the agents' understanding of the job as demanding masculine attributes meant that these skills had to be reinterpreted or de-emphasized.

Like many other kinds of interactive service jobs, including McDonald's window work, insurance sales requires that workers adopt an attitude of congeniality and eagerness to please. This in itself may strike some men as incompatible with the proper enactment of gender, as suggested by the cool pose, which associates masculinity with toughness and detachment (Majors 1989, 84). In *America's Working Man,* [sociologist David] Halle records that a few of the chemical workers he studied did not support Jimmy Carter's presidential candidacy because they "suspected that a man who smiled all the time might be a homosexual" (1984, 246). To them, behavior that is transparently intended to please others, to encourage liking, is not considered masculine. Toughness, gruffness, and pride are taken-for-granted elements of masculinity to many blue-collar men (Gray 1987; Willis 1977), and Combined's agents come largely from blue-collar or agricultural backgrounds. For such men, deferential behavior and forced amiability are often associated with servility, and occasions that call for these attitudes—dealings with superiors, for instance—may feel humiliating. Such behavior is not easy to reconcile with the autonomy and assertiveness that are considered central to "acting like a man." The rebellious working class "lads" [Paul] Willis studied were therefore concerned to find jobs with "an essentially masculine ethos," jobs "where you would not be expected to be subservient" (1977, 96). [Sociologists Richard] Sennett and [Jonathan] Cobb, drawing on their interviews with blue-collar men, interpret the low prestige ratings of many service jobs relative to blue-collar jobs as a response to the perceived dependence of service workers on other people, whose shifting demands they must meet (1972, 236).

Thus the glad-handing insincerity required of many sorts of businessmen may seem effete and demeaning to working-class men. The job of salesman, which is on the lower end of the white-collar hierarchy, would seem especially degrading from this point of view. Since success is largely dependent on ingratiating oneself with customers, playing up to others is an essential part of the agent's job, rather than just a demand of the social milieu. Salesmen must swallow insults, treat even social inferiors with deference, and keep smiling.

These aspects of the sales job were quite pronounced for Combined Insurance's life agents. The warming-up-the-prospect phase of the routine called for agents to figure out what topics might interest the prospects and display a flattering enthusiasm for those topics and for the prospects' accomplishments. Agents had to be willing to disguise their true feelings and to seem to accept the prospect's view of the world in order to ingratiate themselves. It was crucial that they not lose their tempers with prospects but remain polite and respectful at all times. Like most salespeople, they had to try to change prospective customers' minds while never seeming to argue with them and to stay pleasant even when rudely dismissed.

The skills required for establishing and maintaining rapport—drawing people out, bolstering their egos, displaying interest in their interests, and carefully monitoring one's own behavior so as not to offend—are usually considered womanly arts. In analyses of a small sample of conversations, [sociologist Pamela M.] Fishman (1978) found that women had to do much more interactive work than men simply to sustain dialogues;

men largely took for granted that their conversational attempts would succeed in engaging their partner's interest. Judging only by these interactive demands of insurance sales work, it would seem that women are especially well suited to be agents. We might even expect that the association of ingratiating conversational tactics with women would lead men to view the extensive interactive work required of salespeople as degrading, since it requires that they assume the role of the interactive inferior who must constantly negotiate permission to proceed. Given the additional attack on personal autonomy implicit in Combined Insurance's programming of employees to follow scripts, it would seem to be difficult for men to combine successful enactment of the role of Combined Insurance agent with the successful enactment of gender.

On the contrary, Combined Insurance's trainers and agents interpreted the agent's job as demanding manly attributes. They assigned a heroic character to the job, framing interactions with customers as contests of will. To succeed, they emphasized, required determination, aggressiveness, persistence, and stoicism. These claims were accurate, but qualities in which women excel, including sensitivity to nuance and verbal dexterity, were also important for success. While the sales training did include tips on building such skills, determination and aggressiveness were treated as the decisive factors for career success. It was through this need for toughness that the work was constructed as manly.[5]

Of course it was quite true that considerable determination, self-motivation, and persistence were required to do this job. The agents had to make numerous sales calls every day, despite the knowledge that many people would be far from glad to see them. They had to keep making calls, even after meeting with repeated rejection and sometimes hostility. And in sales interactions, they had to stick to their objectives even when prospects displayed reluctance to continue the conversation, as most did. Some agents and managers believed that women were unlikely to meet these job demands because they are too sensitive, too unaggressive, and not able to withstand repeated rejection. Josh, one of the agents, claimed, "Most girls don't have what it takes. They don't have that killer instinct." Josh had, however, recruited a woman he knew to join Combined's sales force. "She does have [the killer instinct], if I can bring it out," he said. Ralph, the sales manager, also acknowledged that there might be some exceptional women who could do the job. He amended his statement that he would never hire a woman by saying, "Only if she had a kind of bitchy attitude." "A biker woman" is the kind he meant, he said, "someone hardcore." Obviously, he did not believe it was possible to combine the traits necessary for success as an agent with femininity.[6]

One manager attributed women's assumed deficiencies not to their nature but to economics, arguing that women whose husbands provided an income were unlikely to have the requisite "burning need" to succeed that financial necessity provides. An obvious factor that would prevent most mothers from taking the job—at least one week a month was spent away from home—was not mentioned by any agents in explaining the dearth of women agents, though two managers did mention it. Two agents told me that they "wouldn't want their wives doing this" because of the unpleasant or potentially dangerous places agents must sometimes visit.

This emphasis on aggression, domination, and danger is only one possible construction of sales work. [Sociologists Nicole] Biggart (1989) and [Maureen] Connelly and [Patricia] Rhoton (1988) discuss in detail the very different ways that direct sales organizations that rely on a female labor force characterize sales work. These organizations, some of which are hugely successful, emphasize nurturance, helpfulness, and service both in relations with customers and among salespeople. Combined Insurance's training also encouraged agents to think of themselves as providing a service to prospective customers, largely in order to overcome trainees' reluctance to impose on others, and some of the agents I spoke with did use the service ideology to counter demeaning images of insurance sales as high-pressure hucksterism. For the most part, however, the agents emphasized the more "manly" dimensions of the work, though there is ample evidence that women can succeed in life insurance sales. For example, [sociologist Barbara J.] Thomas (1990) notes that after the Equitable Life Assurance Society made a commitment to recruiting and supporting women agents, the company's saleswomen outperformed salesmen in sales and commissions.

While most agents would not feel the need, on a daily basis, to construct an explanation for why there were so few women selling life insurance for their company, they did need to construct an interpretation of their work as honorable and fitting for a man if they were to maintain their positive attitudes and do well at their jobs, which required much more self-motivation than did McDonald's jobs. The element of competition, the battle of wills implicit in their interactions with customers, seemed to be a major factor that allowed the agents to interpret their work as manly. Virtually every step of the interaction was understood as a challenge to be met—getting in the door, making the prospect relax and warm up, being allowed to start the presentation, getting through the presentation despite interruptions, overcoming prospects' objections and actually making the sale, and perhaps even increasing the size of the sale. Since many prospects did their best to prevent the agents from continuing, going through these steps did not simply represent following a pre-scribed routine; it was experienced by agents as proof of their skill and victories of their wills. Each sales call seemed an uphill battle, as the interactions took place on the prospects' turf and prospects always had the option of telling the agent to leave.

The spirit of jousting was especially clear in some of the techniques taught for closing sales. As the trainer explained "The Assump-tive Close," the agents were supposed to "challenge customers"; it was up to the prospects to object if they did not want to go along with the sales. The routine allowed agents to limit the customers' options with-out seeming to do so, to let prospects believe that they were making decisions while the agents remained in control of the interac-tion. The pattern bears some resemblance to the seduction of an initially unwilling part-ner, and the satisfaction that the agents took in "winning" such encounters is perhaps similar to the satisfaction some men take in thinking of sexual encounters as conquests. The agents seemed to approach sales interac-tions with men in much the same spirit as those with women, however, though they often adjusted their presentation of self to suit a particular prospect's gender, age, and manner—subtly flirtatious, respectfully def-erential, or efficient and businesslike.

This sort of manipulation of interactions required a peculiar combination of sensitiv-ity to other people and callousness. The agent had to figure out which approach would work best at any given moment and avoid seeming cold or aggressive but still dis-regard the customers' stated wishes. The re-quired mix of deference and ruthlessness was well illustrated in an exchange that took place during a sales-team training session.

The agents were discussing how to deal with interruptions during a presentation: One of their superiors had advised ignoring them al-together, but the "training module" stated that it was insulting to fail to acknowledge a prospect's comment. When the sales man-ager instructed, "You have to let them know that you heard them," one of the agents fin-ished the sentence for him: "and that you don't give a shit."

All kinds of interactive service workers—including McDonald's window crew—try to exercise control over their interactions with customers, though not all of them are given organizational resources to help them do so (see, e.g., Whyte 1962, on waitresses, and Benson 1986, on department store sales-women). Women who can successfully dom-inate interactions at work might well take pleasure in doing so, as did Combined's life insurance agents. However, it is unlikely that these women's capacity to control other peo-ple would be taken as evidence that the work was womanly, unless it were reinterpreted in less aggressive terms, such as "skill in dealing with people."

If following a script could be given a manly cast when it involved asserting one's will through controlling an interaction, it was more difficult to do so when the interac-tions did not go the agents' way. Refusals were such a routine part of the job, however, that agents could accept most of them as in-evitable, not a result of lack of skill or deter-mination. In sales school, the trainers em-phasized that not everyone was going to buy—some people really do not need or can-not afford the product; some are just close-minded and would not listen to any sales-person. A greater challenge to the agent's definition of himself was presented by cus-tomers who were actively hostile. Some peo-ple were angry at being interrupted; some had a grievance against the company; some became furious if they felt that they were being manipulated. In any case, it was not unusual for agents to meet with loud insults, condescending sneers, and slammed doors. To accept this sort of treatment passively could certainly be seen as unmanly. However, the agents were expected to keep their cool, refrain from rudeness, and leave graciously. Some agents did tell me, with glee, of instances when they shouted obscenities once they got out the door, in response to particularly outrageous treatment from a customer. For the most part, however, passive acceptance of ill-treatment was reconciled with manly honor by defining it as maintaining one's control and one's positive attitude, a strategy similar to that used by male and female McDonald's workers. In this view, screaming back at a customer would not be considered standing up for yourself but letting the customer get the better of you, "letting them blow your attitude." Agents proved themselves to be above combative and insulting customers by maintaining their dignity and holding on to their self-concepts as winners, not by sinking to the customers' level.

Other attributes of the job, not directly connected with job routinization, also contributed to the salesmen's ability to define their jobs as compatible with properly enacting gender. The most important of these were the sense of independence agents felt and their belief that they could earn as much as they were worth. Within the limits of their work assignments, agents could set their own schedules, behave as they chose, and work only as hard as they felt like. Because of the importance of self-motivation to success, those who did well could feel justifiably proud, and those lacking in motivation could appreciate the freedom from pressure. The agents thus felt that their jobs provided some of the benefits of self-employment. They could live with the knowledge that many people looked down on them, put up

with insults, endure futile days of failure, and still maintain a sense that their work was compatible with manliness and social honor, as long as there was the possibility of "making it big."

DISCUSSION

Until the 1970s, most sociological work concerning the connection between workers' genders and their jobs mirrored the commonsense view that men and women hold different sorts of jobs because of differing physical capacities, psychological orientations, and family responsibilities. [Sociologist Rosabeth] Moss Kanter (1977) reversed the traditional argument that women's traits determine the sorts of jobs they hold, claiming instead that the structural features of most women's jobs determine characteristic attitudinal and behavioral responses, which are then interpreted as reflecting women's natures. She focused on power, opportunity, and numbers of like individuals in the workplace as the factors determining workers' responses to jobs. In her analysis, preexisting gender segregation leads workers, managers, and observers to believe incorrectly that gender explains how workers respond to their jobs. As [sociologist Sarah] Fenstermaker Berk (1985b) has argued, Moss Kanter understated the distinctive properties of gender and minimized the extent to which gender assumptions are built into jobs by work organizations (see also Acker 1990).

More recently, analysts have called attention to the ways that occupations are gendered—they are designed and evolve in particular ways because of the gender of typical incumbents (Cockburn 1985; Reverby 1987). Moreover, theorists have argued that gender is not simply imported into the workplace: Gender itself is constructed in part through work (Beechey 1988; Berk 1985a, 1985b). This argument applies both to the gender identities of individual workers and to cultural understandings of women's and men's natures and capacities and is supported by the cases of McDonald's and Combined Insurance.

Just how jobs are gendered and how doing these jobs affects workers' gender identities remain to be clarified, however. [Sociologist Cynthia] Cockburn describes the gendering of jobs and people as a two-way process: "People have a gender and their gender rubs off on the jobs they mainly do. The jobs in turn have a gender character which rubs off on the people who do them" (1985, 169). While acknowledging that the gender designation of jobs, tools, fields of knowledge, and activities may shift over time, she treats these designations as cultural givens. For example, Cockburn writes (1985, 70):

> *An 18th-century man no doubt felt effeminate using a spinning wheel, though he would have felt comfortable enough repairing one. Today it is difficult to get a teenage lad to use a floor mop or a typewriter because they contradict his own gender identity.*

Cockburn correctly perceives the relevance of work tasks to the workers' gender identity, but overstates the rigidity of the gender typing of those tasks: At McDonald's, mopping has largely become low-status men's work. I argue that despite the existence of culturally shaped gender designations of work activities, employers and workers retain the flexibility to reinterpret them in ways that support jobholders' gender identities. However, the gender designation of work is likely to have different kinds of significance for women and men.

Workers at both McDonald's and Combined Insurance were expected to adjust their moods and demeanor to the demands of their jobs and to learn to handle customers in ways that might be very different from their ordinary styles of interaction. To some extent, workers in both jobs had to take on the role of interactive inferior, adjusting themselves to the styles and apparent preferences of their customers. They were supposed to paste on smiles when they did not feel like smiling and to behave cheerfully and deferentially to people of every status and with every attitude. The workers were not permitted to respond to rudeness in kind but had to try to remain pleasant even in the face of insult.

This sort of behavior is usually associated with femininity, but in fact the two jobs were interpreted quite differently. At McDonald's, many workers and managers considered it natural, even self-evident, that women were best suited to deal with customers. At Combined Insurance, women were generally seen as ill equipped to handle such work. The insurance agents were able to define their job as masculine by emphasizing those aspects of the work that require "manly" traits (control and self-direction) and by reinterpreting some of the more "feminine" job requirements in ways that were not degrading. McDonald's workers' superiors emphasized that the crew's role was to serve, and attempts by window workers to assert their wills in interactions with customers were strongly discouraged. Combined Insurance's agents, on the other hand, were taught that their job was to establish and maintain control in interactions with prospects. They were told that they control their own destinies and were urged to cultivate the qualities of aggressiveness, persistence, and belief in themselves. While success might require that they take on a deferential manner, it was seen as a matter of skill in manipulating situations, not as servility, and therefore was not taken to be inconsistent with manliness. Similarly, accepting abuse calmly was interpreted as a refusal to let someone else dictate the terms of the interaction, not as a loss of control. This conceptualization of the work as an arena for enacting masculinity allowed the agents to accept working conditions that might otherwise have been seen as unacceptably frustrating and demeaning.

When [sociologist Everett C.] Hughes called attention to the "social and social-psychological arrangements and devices by which men make their work tolerable, or even make it glorious to themselves and others," he apparently meant "men" to include men and women. In fact, the case of Combined Insurance's agents suggests that defining a job as "men's work" is precisely how some men make their work tolerable or even glorious. [Paul] Willis (1977) and [Lawrence J.] Ouellet (1986) have shown how ideas about masculinity can transform what otherwise might be considered negative job features—danger, hard physical labor, dirt—into badges of honor. In other circumstances, work that seems "glorious" on its own merits—because it is understood to be important, highly skilled, responsible, powerful—is defined as masculine (see, e.g., Cockburn 1985). Identifying work as manly, then, can compensate male workers for hardships, but it also justifies privilege.

Some working-class boys and men insist that only jobs that are physically demanding, exhausting, or dangerous can be considered manly (cf. Halle 1984; Willis 1977), but in fact, the gender designation of particular job tasks is quite plastic, a matter of interpretation in which jobholders, employers, and customers may participate. The actual features of the work do not rigidly determine its gender designation. Nevertheless, the association of a job with manliness serves to elevate the work itself and allows men to construe success on the job as proof of masculinity. The importance of manly work for constructing and maintaining masculine identity may explain some of the resistance

of men working in gender-segregated occupations to women co-workers; they tend to define their work not just as particularly appropriate for men but as work that women would not be able to do (Cockburn 1983, 1985; Halle 1984; Swerdlow 1989; Willis 1977). The experiences of women entering previously male-dominated occupations bear out this interpretation. For example, [sociologist Jean Reith] Schroedel (1985, 20–21) quotes a female pipe fitter:

> *You see it is just very hard for them to work with me because they're really into proving their masculinity and being tough. And when a woman comes on a job that can work, get something done as fast and efficiently, as well as they can, it really affects them. Somehow if a woman can do it, it ain't that masculine, not that tough.*

The Combined Insurance agents sustained the belief that women could not handle their job, even though the work required some skills and qualities typically associated with women.

Interpreting work as womanly has a different meaning for women than interpreting work as manly has for men. Certain jobs, including nursing and elementary-school teaching, are understood to require some positively valued "female" traits, such as nurturance or sensitivity, and the identification of the work with femininity significantly determines how the work is organized (Melosh, 1982; Reverby 1987). Even when the work is seen as expressive of feminine capacities, however, it is not seen as offering proof of female identity in quite the same way that manly work supports male identity, because adult female identity has not traditionally been regarded as something that is achieved through paid work. In other words, while women in traditionally female-defined jobs might well take pleasure in doing work that supports their self-identification as feminine, they are unlikely to think of such work as a necessary part of their gender identity. Thus men and women respond differently to challenges to gender segregation of work. [Sociologist Christine] Williams (1989) found that women nurses did not feel threatened when men joined their ranks, though male marines much preferred to keep women out of the corps. Furthermore, while male nurses were concerned to differentiate their activities from those of their women co-workers, female marines did not feel that doing quintessentially masculine work was a challenge to their femininity.

Williams draws on the work of [sociologist Nancy] Chodorow (1978) to provide a psychoanalytic explanation for male workers' concern with defining their work as masculine and with maintaining gender segregation at work. She argues that because men, whose original identification is with a female caretaker, must achieve masculinity by distancing themselves from femininity, they are psychologically threatened when one proof of their masculinity is challenged by evidence that women can do the work they have defined as manly. Women, who need not alter their original identification with a female caretaker, have no corresponding need to prove their femininity: "What ones *does* has little bearing on how feminine one is" (Williams 1989, 140; emphasis in original). Whether or not the psychoanalytic explanation is valid, Williams persuasively demonstrates that gendered jobs have different meanings for men and women.

The different cultural valuation of behavior labeled masculine and feminine also contributes to the different meanings that enacting gender at work has for women and men. While the constant "doing" of gender is mandatory for everyone, many theorists have noted that the effects of this demand are asymmetrical, since doing masculinity generally means asserting dominance, while doing femininity often means enacting submission (Acker 1990; Berk 1985a). [Women's studies scholar Marilyn] Frye claims (1983, 33) that the female "cannot move or speak without engaging in self-deprecation. The male cannot move or speak without engaging in self-aggrandizement." Thus many men value the opportunity to do work that supports cultural understandings of masculinity and their own sense of manliness, but we cannot assume that job features that allow or require gender-appropriate behavior will necessarily be welcomed by women workers in the same way. In some cases, women may appreciate the opportunity to enact such "womanly" attributes as nurturance, helpfulness, or sexiness at work, because that behavior affirms their gender identity. On the other hand, servility may be congruent with femininity, but we would hardly expect female McDonald's workers to take the same pleasures in enacting it at work that Combined's agents take in asserting control.

Job features that allow or require gender-appropriate behaviors are not necessarily welcomed, then, but work routines that prevent workers from enacting gender in ways that they are comfortable with are resented and may contribute to workers' decisions to limit their investments of energy, effort, and self-definition in their jobs. Job features that allow gender enactment in ways workers find gratifying, on the other hand, may make up for deficiencies in more objective job benefits. In any case, the variation in the interpretations of similar job demands at McDonald's and Cominbed Insurance demonstrates that the actual features of the jobs do not themselves determine whether the work will be defined as most appropriate for men or women. Rather, these job features are resources for interpretation that can be drawn on by workers, their superiors, and other audiences.

Despite this flexibility in the interpretation of gender appropriateness, in these two work settings the association of the work with either women or men was made to seem natural—an expression of the essential natures of women and men. Even though the workers' behavior was largely dictated by routines they had no part in creating, and even where the job drew on traits associated with both femininity and masculinity, job segregation by gender was interpreted largely as an outgrowth of inherent gender differences in attitudes and behavior. In trying to make sense of the fact of gender segregation, many of the workers and managers I spoke with drew on taken-for-granted beliefs about the qualities and preferences of women and men. The prevalence of either men or women in a job became evidence that the job demanded specifically masculine or feminine qualities and that the jobholders must be best suited for the work. For the public, as well as for employers and workers, gender segregation of service jobs contributes to the general perception that differences in men's and women's social positions are straightforward reflections of differences in their natures and capabilities.

ENDNOTES

1. Combined Insurance has recently made changes in its life insurance products and sales techniques. Agents are now taught a more interactive sales routine ("needs selling") for a policy that can be tailored to suit customers' circumstances, allowing the agents somewhat greater flexibility. The company's largest division, which sells accident insurance, continues to follow Stone's original techniques closely. Positive Mental Attitude training is still stressed for all agents.

2. The job of "host," however, was viewed as less prestigious by some workers. That polite job title referred to those whose main responsibilities were to empty the trash and keep the lobby, windows, bathrooms, and dining areas clean. When one woman took this job, I heard two women window workers express their disapproval; they felt that "girls" should not have to do the dirty work of handling garbage.

3. I learned, in fact, that the two other women in my training class had lasted, respectively, only one day and three weeks in the field. Managers interviewed in 1989 reported that the number of women agents had increased since the new selling system was introduced, though women were still a small minority of the sales force. Reduced travel demands were one reason given for the job's increasing attractiveness to women. See also note 5.

4. The higher-level managers I interviewed did not endorse these discriminatory views, and some commented on the many successful women in the insurance industry. See Thomas (1990) for a discussion of the growth of women's employment in insurance sales. She shows that by 1980, women were 25 percent of the U.S. insurance agents.

5. Some managers believe that the new needs-selling approach is better suited to women agents because it requires a less domineering stance and allows women to draw on their understanding of families' needs.

6. Similarly, Williams (1989, 32) reports a backlash against women in the military among male soldiers during World War II. She argues that military men claimed that women soldiers must be unfeminine because the men did not want to accept the alternative explanation for the women's presence—that military service is not inherently masculine.

REFERENCES

Acker, Joan. 1990. Hierarchies, jobs, bodies: A theory of gendered organizations. *Gender & Society,* 4:139–58.

Beechey, Veronica. 1988. Rethinking the definition of work: Gender and work. In *Feminization of the labor force: Paradoxes and promises,* edited by Jane Jenson, Elisabeth Hagen, and Ceallaigh Reddy. New York: Oxford University Press.

Benson, Susan Porter. 1986. *Counter cultures: Saleswomen, managers, and customers in American department stores, 1890–1940.* Urbana: University of Illinois Press.

Berk, Sarah Fenstermaker. 1985a. *The gender factory: The apportionment of work in American households.* New York: Plenum.

_____. 1985b. Women's work and the production of gender. Paper presented at the annual meeting of the American Sociological Association, Washington, DC.

Biggart, Nicole. 1989. *Charismatic capitalism: Direct selling organizations in America.* Chicago: University of Chicago Press.

Boas, Max, and Steve Chain. 1976. *Big Mac: The unauthorized story of McDonald's.* New York: Mentor, New American Library.

Chodorow, Nancy. 1978. *The reproduction of mothering: Psychoanalysis and the sociology of gender.* Berkeley: University of California Press.

Cockburn, Cynthia. 1983. *Brothers: Male dominance and technological change.* London: Pluto.

_____. 1985. *Machinery of dominance: Women, men and technical know-how.* London: Pluto.

Connelly, Maureen, and Patricia Rhoton. 1988. Women in direct sales: A comparison of Mary Kay and Amway sales workers. In *The worth of women's work: A qualitative synthesis,* edited by Anne Statham, Eleanor M. Miller, and Hans O. Mauksch. Albany: State University of New York Press.

Fishman, Pamela M. 1978. Interaction: The work women do. *Social Problems* 25:397–406.

Frye, Marilyn. 1983. Sexism. In *The politics of reality.* Trumansberg, NY: Crossing Press.

Garfinkel, Harold. 1967. *Studies in ethnomethodology.* Englewood Cliffs, NJ: Prentice-Hall.

Garson, Barbara. 1988. *The electronic sweatshop.* New York: Simon & Schuster.

Goffman, Erving. 1977. The arrangements between the sexes. *Theory and Society* 4:301–31.

Gray, Stan. 1987. Sharing the shop floor. In *Beyond patriarchy: Essays by men on pleasure, power, and change,* edited by Michael Kaufman. Toronto: Oxford University Press.

Halle, David. 1984. *America's working man.* Chicago: University of Chicago Press.

Hochschild, Arlie Russell. 1983. *The managed heart: Commercialization of human feeling.* Berkeley: University of California Press.

Hughes, Everett C. [1951]. 1984. Work and self. In *The sociological eye.* New Brunswick, NJ: Transaction.

Kanter, Rosabeth Moss. 1977. *Men and women of the corporation.* New York: Basic Books.

Kessler, Suzanne J., and Wendy McKenna. 1978. *Gender: An ethnomethodological approach.* Chicago: University of Chicago Press.

Lally-Benedetto, Corinne. 1985. Women and the tone of the body: An analysis of a figure salon. Paper presented at the annual meeting of the Midwest Sociological Society, St. Louis, MO.

Leidner, Robin. 1988. Working on people: The routinization of interactive service work. Ph.D. diss., Northwestern University, Evanston, IL.

Life insurance business in Japan, 1987/88. Tokyo: Life Assurance Association of Japan.

Majors, Richard. 1989. Cool pose: The proud signature of Black survival. In *Men's lives,* edited by Michael S. Kimmel and Michael A. Messner. New York: Macmillan.

Melosh, Barbara. 1982. *"The physician's hand": Work culture and conflict in American nursing.* Philadelphia: Temple University Press.

Milkman, Ruth. 1987. *Gender at work: The dynamics of job segregation by sex during World War II.* Urbana: University of Illinois Press.

Ouellet, Lawrence J. 1986. Work, commitment, and effort: Truck drivers and trucking in small, non-union, West coast trucking companies. Ph.D. diss., Northwestern University, Evanston, IL.

Personick, Valerie A. 1987. Industry output and employment through the end of the century. *Monthly Labor Review* 10 (September):30–45.

Reverby, Susan M. 1987. *Ordered to care: The dilemma of American nursing, 1850–1945.* Cambridge: Cambridge University Press.

Rollins, Judith. 1985. *Between women: Domestics and their employers.* Philadelphia: Temple University Press.

Schroedel, Jean Reith. 1985. *Alone in a crowd: Women in the trades tell their stories.* Philadelphia: Temple University Press.

Sennett, Richard, and Jonathan Cobb. 1972. *The hidden injuries of class.* New York: Knopf.

Silvestri, George T., and John M. Lukasiewic. 1987. A look at occupational employment trends to the year 2000. *Monthly Labor Review* 10(September):46–63.

Spradley, James P., and Brenda J. Mann. 1975. *The cocktail waitress: Woman's work in a man's world.* New York: Wiley.

Steinem, Gloria. 1983. I was a Playboy bunny. In *Outrageous acts and everyday rebellions.* New York: Holt, Rinehart & Winston.

Stone, W. Clement. 1962. *The success system that never fails.* Englewood Cliffs, NJ: Prentice-Hall.

Swerdlow, Marian. 1989. Men's accommodations to women entering a nontraditional occupation: A case of rapid transit operatives. *Gender & Society* 3:373–87.

Thomas, Barbara J. 1990. Women's gains in insurance sales: Increased supply, uncertain demand. In *Job queues, gender queues: Women's movement into male occupations,* edited by Barbara Reskin and Patricia Roos. Philadelphia: Temple University Press.

West, Candace, and Don Zimmerman. 1987. Doing gender. *Gender & Society* 1:125–51.

Whyte, William F. 1962. When workers and customers meet. In *Man, work, and society,* edited by Sigmund Nosow and William H. Form. New York: Basic Books.

Williams, Christine. 1989. *Gender differences at work: Women and men in nontraditional occupations.* Berkeley: University of California Press.

Willis, Paul. 1977. *Learning to labor: How working class kids get working class jobs.* New York: Columbia University Press.

Zelizer, Viviana A. Rotman. 1979. *Morals and markets: The development of life insurance in the United States.* New York: Columbia University Press.

Questions for Understanding and Critical Thinking

1. How are the jobs at Combined Insurance and McDonald's divided by gender and race?
2. How did workers and managers in these two corporations view the division of labor by race and gender?
3. Why was the work of Combined Insurance's agents defined as "properly manly"?
4. Most people have been customers, employees, and/or managers at businesses that relied heavily on interactive service work. How did your experience in a setting such as McDonald's or Combined Insurance compare with Leidner's description of these highly routinized work environments?

PART ONE

Suggestions for Further Reading

Books

Blauner, Robert. 1972. *Racial Oppression in America*. New York: Harper & Row.

Delgado, Richard (Ed.). 1995. *Critical Race Theory: The Cutting Edge*. Philadelphia: Temple University Press.

Dyson, Michael Eric. 1996. *Between God and Gangsta Rap*. New York: Oxford University Press.

Firestone, Shulamith. 1971. *The Dialectic of Sex: The Case for Feminist Revolution*. New York: Bantam.

Franklin, Raymond S. 1991. *Shadows of Race and Class*. Minneapolis: University of Minnesota Press.

Gilbert, Dennis, and Joseph A. Kahl. 1993. *The American Class Structure: A New Synthesis* (4th ed.). Belmont, CA: Wadsworth.

Higley, Stephen Richard. 1995. *Privilege, Power, and Place: The Geography of the American Upper Class*. Lanham, MD: Rowman & Littlefield.

Jaggar, Alison M., and Paula S. Rothenberg. 1993. *Feminist Frameworks: Alternative Theoretical Accounts of the Relations Between Women and Men* (3rd ed.). New York: McGraw-Hill.

Leidner, Robin. 1993. *Fast Food, Fast Talk: Service Work and the Routinization of Everyday Life*. Berkeley: University of California Press.

Lorber, Judith. 1994. *Paradoxes of Gender*. New Haven, CT: Yale University Press.

McNall, Scott G., Rhonda F. Levine, and Rick Fantasia (Eds.). 1991. *Bringing Classes Back In: Contemporary and Historical Perspectives*. Boulder, CO: Westview.

Oboler, Suzanne, 1995. *Ethnic Labels, Latino Lives: Identity and the Politics of (Re)Presentation in the United States*. Minneapolis: University of Minnesota Press.

Omi, Michael, and Howard Winant. 1994. *Racial Formation in the United States: From the 1960s to the 1990s*. New York: Routledge.

Padilla, Felix M., and Lourdes Santiago. 1993. *Outside the Wall: A Puerto Rican Woman's Struggle*. New Brunswick, NJ: Rutgers University Press.

Winant, Howard. 1994. *Racial Conditions: Politics, Theory, Comparisons*. Minneapolis: University of Minnesota Press.

Wright, Erik O. 1989. *The Debate on Classes*. London: Verso.

Zandy, Janet (Ed.). 1995. *Liberating Memory: Our Work and Our Working-Class Consciousness*. New Brunswick, NJ: Rutgers University Press.

Journals

Gender & Society. Official Publication of Sociologists for Women in Society. Available from Sage Periodicals, Thousand Oaks, CA.

Journal of Black Studies. Available from Sage Periodicals Press, Thousand Oaks, CA.

Race, Gender & Class: An Interdisciplinary & Multicultural Journal. Jean Belkhir (Ed.). Institute for Teaching and Research on Women, Towson State University, Towson, MD. 21204-7097.

Social Problems. Published by the University of California Press for the Society for the Study of Social Problems.

PART TWO

Learning about Diversity and Inequality

My family was really very racist. It was just a very assumed kind of thing.

> —"Patricia Bowen," a white woman interviewed by Ruth Frankenberg
> (Article 10)

One memory that stays with me . . . is the night my stepfather brought his boss and the boss's wife to our apartment. The wife had recently purchased a gown that needed alteration and, knowing that my mother did this sort of thing, came over for a fitting. When, for the first time, I saw my mother get on her knees to pin up the boss lady's gown, I was suddenly filled with rage. I hated them for being so rich that they could bring my otherwise very tough and proud mother to her knees.

> —Sociologist Gregory Mantios's memories of his working-class childhood
> (Article 16)

My brothers were role models. I wanted to prove—especially to my brothers—that I had heart, you know, that I was a man, [meaning that] I didn't want to be a so-called scaredy-cat. You want to hit a guy even though he's bigger than you to show that, you know, you've got this macho image.

> —A 33-year-old black man interviewed by Michael A. Messner (Article 13)

AS THESE PERSONAL narratives suggest, most people initially construct their individual identities and form ideas about race, class, and gender through interaction with members of their families. This process is known as *socialization*—**the lifelong process of social interaction through which people acquire self-identities and learn to perform social roles deemed important by subgroups, communities, and society.**

An Overview of Race, Class, and Gender Socialization

Families and intimate relationships usually are the first and most profound **agents of socialization**—**the persons, groups, and institutions that teach**

129

people what they need to know in order to participate in society. Individuals are exposed to many agents of socialization throughout their lifetimes. The articles in Part Two show how four agents of socialization—families, peers, sports, and education—play an important role in race, class, and gender socialization.

As we examine this topic, it is important to remember several points. First, socialization is not limited to childhood; people continue to acquire new information and skills throughout life. Second, socialization is not simply a one-way process in which people learn how to fit into society. Sociologist Barrie Thorne emphasizes:

> *Adults are said to socialize children, teachers socialize students, the more powerful socialize, and the less powerful get socialized. Power, indeed, is central to all these relationships, but children, students, the less powerful are by no means passive or without agency. (1993:3)*

Third, socialization is not static and unalterable; it is related to social change. For example, in Article 13, sociologist Michael A. Messner points out that gender identity is developed through a complex process of interaction in which people not only learn appropriate gender scripts but also seek to modify them:

> *I view gender identity not as a "thing" that people "have," but rather as a* process of construction *that develops, comes into crisis, and changes as a person interacts with the social world. Through this perspective, it becomes possible to speak of "gendering" identities rather than "masculinity" or "feminity" as relatively fixed identities or statuses. (1990:416)*

Finally, in order to gain a better understanding of the interlocking nature of race, class, and gender as systems of privilege or oppression in society, the content of socialization must be analyzed as a social product generated within a particular political and socioeconomic structure (Curran and Renzetti, 1996).

The content of socialization influences how people's personal and collective identities develop, how they relate to other individuals, and how the groups of which they are a part relate to other groups within the society. Race, class, and gender socialization are specific aspects of the socialization process that contain messages and practices concerning the nature of being a member of a racial or ethnic category *(racial-ethnic socialization),* being male or female *(gender socialization),* or having a specific location in a class system *(class socialization).* Race, class, and gender socialization all involve: (1) personal and group identity, (2) intergroup and interindividual relationships, and (3) position in the social hierarchy. This socialization process includes direct statements regarding race, class, and gender; modeling behavior (where a child imitates the behavior of a parent or other caregiver); and indirect activities such as exposure to specific objects, contexts, and environments that represent one's group (Thornton et al., 1990). Socialization may legitimize social inequalities by reinforcing patterns of domination and subordination, or it may produce resistance and activism by subordinate group members who seek to bring about social change.

Families and Race, Class, and Gender Socialization

Families are significant agents of race, class, and gender socialization, as feminist scholar bell hooks explains:

> *Family is a significant site of socialization and politicization precisely because it is there that most of us learn our ideas about race, gender, and class. If we ignore family and act as though we can look to other structures for education for critical consciousness, we ignore the significance of early identity and value formation. (1994:72)*

In one's family, one learns about culture (including language, attitudes, beliefs, values, and norms) and develops a *social identity—***that part of a person's self-concept that derives from his or her knowledge of various group memberships (including racial-ethnic, class, religious, and regional subcultures) together with the value and emotional significance attached to those memberships.** In their study of socialization and racial identity among African Americans, for example, sociologists David H. Demo and Michael Hughes (Article 11) found that social identity is a key component of racial-ethnic socialization:

> *Structurally, being black in American society means occupying a racially defined status; associated with this status are roles in family, community, and society. One psychological consequence of being black is black group identity, the intensity of which should vary with the nature of role experience. (1990:364)*

However, persons who are members of the same racial-ethnic group do not necessarily share uniform social identities. As Demo and Hughes (1990) note, African American identity is a multidimensional phenomenon: Being African American means different things to different segments of the African American population. Similarly, recent studies of family influences on the socialization of Mexican American children (Knight et al., 1993a:106; Knight et al., 1993b) identified multiple components of ethnic identity:

1. *Ethnic self-identification:* The categorization of self as a member of one's ethnic group
2. *Ethnic constancy:* The knowledge that one's ethnic group membership is unchanging and permanent across time, settings, and transformations
3. *Ethnic role behaviors:* Engaging in the varying behaviors that manifest ethnic-cultural values, styles, customs, traditions, and language

4. *Ethnic knowledge:* The knowledge that certain role behaviors and traits, values, styles, customs, traditions, and language are relevant to one's ethnic group
5. *Ethnic preferences and feelings:* The feelings about one's own ethnic group membership and preferences for ethnic members, behaviors, values, traditions, and language.

Parental socialization is critical to the development of these components of children's racial-ethnic identities. Family characteristics—such as parents' cultural knowledge, language, generation of migration to this country, and extent of racial-ethnic group identity—influence the extent to which parents convey these components to their children (Knight et al., 1993a, Knight et al., 1993b).

Through teaching, role modeling, and nonverbal communication, all children receive some racial-ethnic socialization from members of their family. By about 4 years of age, most children have begun to crystallize racial-ethnic values and to be aware that a racial-ethnic hierarchy exists in society (Marger, 1994). However, the content of socialization varies between subordinate and dominant racial-ethnic groups. Parents in subordinate racial-ethnic groups tend to make their children aware of their own racial-ethnic culture, the dominant culture, and the nature of dominant/subordinate interactions. By contrast, dominant-group parents do not tend to provide their children with extensive information about the language or culture of racial-ethnic groups other than their own except through messages that may convey either ambivalence or fear (see Frankenberg, 1993).

Many parents of color socialize their children to live in a hostile environment by making them aware of the prejudicial attitudes and discrimination they are likely to encounter (see Hale-Benson, 1986; Jackson, McCullough, and Gurin, 1988). Studies show that about two-thirds of African American parents encourage children to confront and challenge racism, not merely to tolerate it (Bowman and Howard, 1985; Peters, 1985; Thornton et al., 1990). According to Demo and Hughes (1990), African American children whose parents promote racial awareness typically have stronger feelings of closeness to other African Americans and a stronger commitment to African American culture than do those whose parents reared them in an individualistic/universal manner (e.g., "be yourself, take care of yourself, you're as good as anyone else, work hard").

White parents also socialize their children about race, even though many whites do not think of themselves as having race. American studies scholar Ruth Frankenberg (Article 10) suggests that people may unintentionally socialize their children about race based on the social geography of race—the social meanings that are associated with the physical landscape where people live. According to Frankenberg, social geography has a strong influence on a person's self-identity, perception of others, and interaction (or lack of interaction) with other people. For example, she compares the experiences of Beth Ellison (who grew up in a white, middle-class neighborhood located some distance from people of color) with those of Sandy Alvarez (who grew up in a working-class neighborhood where she had close relationships with people of color) and finds that a so-called landscape structured by racism plays an important part in people's racial-ethnic and class socialization.

The social geography of race and class also has a significant influence on children of the upper class. You will recall that Stephen Richard Higley's article in Part One (Article 6) described how wealthy white elites tend to be clustered in a relatively few U.S. Zip Codes where their children primarily associate with other members of the upper class. Through socialization, upper-class parents instill the values and lifestyle of their class in their children. Parents who have higher levels of education are more likely to expose their children to a wide variety of books and educational materials, to computers, and to global travel at an early age (Cookson and Persell, 1985). In turn, these opportunities make it possible for upper-class children to attend elite boarding schools and prestigious colleges and universities that help to reproduce the family's class position into the next generation (see Article 6). As bell hooks (1994) points out, class is more than one's economic standing—it determines values, standpoints, and interests. The class identity and world view of children is strongly linked with the family's class location.

However, children of the upper class may not become fully aware of their relative class positions in society until they see how people in other classes live. Consider, for example, George Pillsbury—heir to the Pillsbury Flour Company family fortune—who grew up on a private estate, spent his free time at the country club, and attended St. Paul's, an elite boarding school. According to Pillsbury, he never saw people living in poverty until he enrolled at Yale University in New Haven:

> *I confronted a lot of anger and resentment that I never dealt with at St. Paul's. . . . It was the first time I'd ever lived in the city—a real city with housing projects with poor people. I began to see poverty where I never had before. . . . I saw the inequities and felt them personally for the first time. I felt a lot of guilt at first, but then it became an emotional and intellectual process toward dedicating myself to positive social change. (quoted in Sedgwick, 1985:120)*

Unlike Pillsbury, children in middle- and working-class families often become aware of class differences as their parents attempt to prepare them for the workplace and life as the parents know it. Although scholars acknowledge that extensive **anticipatory socialization—preparation for future roles—**takes place within the home, a lack of consensus exists as to the extent that parents reproduce their own class in the next generation.

Some analysts suggest that class differences in the content of socialization have declined in recent years, especially between the middle and working class, whereas others believe the differences persist. According to sociologist Melvin L. Kohn (1969, 1990), class (as measured by parental occupation) is one of the strongest influences on what and how parents teach their children. For example, middle- and upper-middle-class parents (who tend to have more freedom and flexibility at work) may allow their children greater freedom to make their own decisions, instill in them ideas of monetary and social success, and emphasize the importance of thinking and behaving in socially acceptable ways—all values to which these parents subscribe. As Kohn notes, "Parents' values for their children are values for themselves" (1969:73).

In contrast, Kohn (1969) suggests that working-class parents (who typically are closely supervised at work and are expected to follow orders unquestioningly) tend to emphasize the importance of obedience and conformity in their children. Today, many working-class parents have only a limited amount of time and energy to devote to taking care of their children and socializing them for future roles, as Gregory Mantsios describes in Article 16:

> *[Working-class parents] raise a family and keep house without the benefit of paid helpers. They cook, clean, shop, and take care of their children on their own in the little time that is left after a day at work. Time and economic class are inevitably intertwined: everything takes longer when you are pressed for money. Whether it is the time needed to shop comparatively or the time it takes to use public transportation, getting through everyday life is fraught with inconvenience or peril, or both. (1995:233)*

The problem of economic marginality especially affects the socialization of the working poor—those who are employed full time, the year around, and still live at or below the poverty line. According to social analysts John E. Schwarz and Thomas J. Volgy:

> *The darker side of life in the world of underpaid workers often is seen as well in inadequate child care and the frustrations that it can cause. When both mother and father work and manage to scrape together enough only for survival, another cruel irony awaits: neither can afford to stay at home, neither can raise the children, and even with both parents working, they cannot afford child care. (1992:127)*

Parents in low-income and poverty-level families also may unintentionally socialize their children to believe that it will be impossible for them to acquire a high level of education or to aspire to a well-paid job (Ballantine, 1993). In his study of the teenagers who lived in a housing project, for example, sociologist Jay MacLeod describes family problems that affected the socialization of the "Hallway Hangers," a group of 8 to 18 youths, primarily white boys of Italian or Irish descent:

> *The Hallway Hangers share certain family characteristics that may affect their aspirations. Foremost among these are the duration of these families' tenancy in public housing. With the exception of [two boys], all the Hallway Hangers and their families have lived in the projects for many years. . . . Like most of the project residents, the educational attainment of these boys' parents and older brothers and sisters is very low. . . . The sporadic employment record of family mem-*

bers is another common characteristic. For those who are able to find employment at all, it is typically menial, low paying, and unstable. Other less widespread commonalities between the families of these boys include the fathers' absence from the household, the large size of the families, and the numerous encounters of family members with the law. (1995:53)

MacLeod found that a number of the Hallway Hangers have been socialized in such a way as to reproduce their existing class location, as evidenced by their responses to MacLeod's question "What kind of work does your mother [do your parents] want you to do for a living?":

Boo-Boo: *Anything. She doesn't really care, as long as I'm working.*
Frankie: *She don't . . . care. I mean, I'm sure she cares, but she don't push nothing on me.*
Slick: *She wants me to make a buck so I can move for myself.*
Steve: *Anything, man. Somethin'. I dunno. Just a . . . job.*
Jinks: *They don't talk about it. They hardly ever talk about it. Just as long as I'm not out of work. My mother hates when I'm unemployed. (1995:57)*

MacLeod suggests:

If the Hallway Hangers view their predicament as a race in which they, as members of the lower class, must jump a number of hurdles, while the rest of the pack can simply sprint, [they] believe a strong finish, given their handicap, is out of the question and drop out of the race before it begins. (1995:81)

Family-class location also is intertwined with children's racial-ethnic and gender socialization. In Article 12, sociologist Becky W. Thompson shows how family-class location influences the socialization of young women, especially regarding food consumption and supposedly ideal weight and size:

When Joselyn was young, her family was what she called "aspiring to be middle class." For people of Joselyn's parents' generation, having chubby, healthy children was a sign the family was doing well. But, as the family moved up the social ladder, Joselyn's father began to insist that Joselyn be thin. (1994:32)

Some of the women in Thompson's study reported that, as their parents sought upward social mobility or to "assimilate with Anglo culture," they decided that their daughters should adhere to appearance standards based on a culture of thinness. According to Thompson, racism and class inequality influence feminine beauty standards in the socialization process:

To understand why a girl's relatives want her to be thin, we need to know what forms of economic, racial, ethnic, and religious discrimination they have encountered. Underlying an attempt to make a girl thin is an often unspoken assumption that while the family might not be financially stable, or it cannot fully shield her from racism, or it does not speak English without an accent, her small size may make her life and their's somewhat easier. (1994:44)

To gain a better understanding of why women and men may be subjected to different socialization about such things as "ideal" appearance norms, one must first look at how early gender socialization occurs in families.

Before a baby is born, parents usually have an idea about whether they want a girl or a boy. From birth, parents may talk to and play with children on the basis of gender labels. Children's clothing and toys reflect parents' gender expectations: Boys' clothing commonly features male activities and characters, whereas girls' clothing usually is more feminine (floral fabrics, lace, and bows) and features female characters. Boys and girls are given gender-appropriate toys and encouraged to participate in games and recreational activities associated with their gender.

In the process of socialization, families may reproduce gender roles by assigning different household chores to boys and girls. Maintenance chores (e.g., mowing the lawn and taking out the garbage) are assigned to boys while domestic chores (e.g., babysitting, shopping, cooking, and washing dishes) are assigned to girls (Burns and Homel, 1989). Assigning chores on the basis of gender may contribute to people's perceptions about the appropriateness of a gendered division of labor in families and the workplace. While girls may learn how to take care of *people,* especially younger brothers and sisters, boys may learn how to work with *things* such as cars and computers. Early gender-role socialization may lead to an unequal distribution of household work and to different career paths in adulthood.

However, gender differences in chore assignments are heavily influenced by a family's social class, racial-ethnic background, and size. Children from upper-class families may have few, if any, chores to do because such activities are taken care of by a paid staff. Upper-class families that seek to foster responsibility in children typically assign both females and males to take care of a horse, dog, or other family pet (Sedgwick, 1985). Children from middle- and upper-income families typically are less likely to be assigned gender-linked chores than those from lower-income backgrounds. Some analysts have suggested that gender-linked chore assignments occur less frequently in African American families, where both sons and daughters tend to be socialized toward independence, employment, and child care (Hale-Benson, 1986); however, the patriarchal beliefs of some African American fathers have been the focus of some analysts, including black feminist scholar bell hooks:

Like many precocious girls growing up in a male-dominated household, I understood the significance of gender inequality at an early age. Our daily life was full of patriarchal drama—the use of coercion, violent punishment, verbal harassment, to maintain male dominance. As small children we understood that our father was more important than our mother because he was a man. This knowl-

edge was reinforced by the reality that any decision our mother made could be overruled by our dad's authority. . . . It was only when I entered college that I learned that black males had supposedly been "emasculated," that the trauma of slavery was primarily that it had stripped black men of their right to male privilege and power, that it had prevented them from fully actualizing "masculinity." . . . In the real world of my growing up I had seen black males in positions of patriarchal authority, exercising forms of male power, supporting institutionalized sexism. (1994:119–120)

Clearly, patriarchal authority patterns are evident in many homes across lines of race/ethnicity and class; however, more inclusive research is needed on gender socialization in families of color. Until recently, scholars focused almost exclusively on white families as the norm for *all* families. In studies of African American families, analysts tended to minimize gender distinctions in social relations or to use the experience of African American men as a point of reference for all African American people (hooks, 1994).

Regardless of race or ethnicity, families clearly have a major impact on the socialization of children. This is also true regarding the second agent of socialization that we will examine: peer groups. Peers often contribute to people's positive or negative feelings about themselves and others based on gender, race, and class.

Peers and Race, Class, and Gender Socialization

As soon as children are old enough to have acquaintances outside the home, most begin to rely heavily on their peer group as a source of information and approval. A ***peer group* is a group of people who are linked by common interests, equal social position, and (usually) similar age.** Numerous studies have found that children and young people acquire ideas and attitudes about race, class, and gender from peer-group interactions (e.g., Cohen, 1993; Sadker and Sadker, 1994).

Peers may reinforce prevailing stereotypes about gender-appropriate behavior. During the preschool years, same-sex peers have a powerful influence on how children see their gender roles (Maccoby and Jacklin, 1987). Boys commonly receive more pressure from their peers to do masculine things than girls receive from other girls to do feminine things. Studies of peers and gender socialization also have shown that competing with one's peers in sports has a significant impact on boys' perceptions of masculinity. In Article 13, sociologist Michael A. Messner suggests that peer groups often socialize boys concerning self-worth, especially in regard to winning or losing at sports. Boys learn that, to get the kind of attention and connection they crave, they must be "better than the other guys—beating them—that is the key to acceptance" (1990:422). By contrast, girls' peer groups typically encourage more cooperative play and less competition.

Girls, more than boys, are able to cross the so-called gender divide by wearing "boy clothes" such as jeans. Boys who want to wear dresses or play games with girls are likely to be shunned by other boys. Such gendered distinctions in clothing and activities highlight the cultural message that male activities and behavior are more acceptable—and more important—than those of females (Wood, 1994).

As girls reach adolescence, peer groups may reinforce a culture of thinness and encourage girls to participate in activities such as beauty pageants, which glorify "whiteness, youth, heterosexuality, and able-bodiedness" (Thompson, 1994:44–45). In sociologist Becky W. Thompson's study (Article 12), for example, some of the girls learned that, to be accepted by their peers, they had to look like WASPs (white Anglo-Saxon Protestants)—to have straight blonde hair and be passive and quiet. Some were humiliated by their peers because of their weight. One girl (called "Taters"—a big potato) noted that, at a "slave auction" where girls were auctioned off for a high school fundraiser, "When it was my turn, no one was bidding. . . . It was just the most humiliating thing in my life" (1994:37).

Peers also may be a source of prejudice and discrimination based on religion. Two Jewish women in Thompson's (1994) study recalled negative experiences with Protestant classmates: One had been told that Jewish people had horns; both had been called names and excluded from friendship groups. Such encounters tend to have a long-term effect on people's perceptions of themselves and others, as evidenced by the fact that the respondents related these events to Thompson decades after they had occurred.

Some peer groups may be short in duration and still have long-term effects on people, but other peer groups endure for many years. For example, in their study of elite boarding schools, Caroline Hodges Persell and Peter W. Cookson, Jr. (Article 15) found that upper-class young people from various regions of the country developed friendships in elite boarding schools and built long-term social networks that continued through their college years and helped them to acquire upper-class marriage partners and adult business deals.

At the other end of the class spectrum, by contrast, government programs such as the Job Corps—a core antipoverty program geared primarily for low-income central-city youth—have acknowledged the significance of peer-group influence by seeking to establish new and better peer groups for young people in the program. In Article 17, sociologists Jill Quadagno and Catherine Fobes describe how the Job Corps removed young people from central cities to job-training sites "where kids would have an opportunity to get . . . into an environment that was different—a more healthful environment away from their families and away from their gangs" (1995:176). In keeping with organizers' plans for moral reform as well as vocational training, the program sought to replace participants' previous peer groups with new peers who had shared in self-improvement courses and clubs dealing with such things as art and books. At least theoretically, the Job Corps was designed to help students improve their lives and to gain upward mobility. A similar goal often is expressed for sports as a means of socialization in the United States.

Sports and Race, Class, and Gender Socialization

In contemporary societies, sports plays an increasingly important role in race, class, and gender socialization. With regard to racial-ethnic divisions in society, sociologist Jay Coakley (1990) suggests that sports has served as a source of tension management for many years. Early Italian immigrants in New York, for example, engaged in sporting events such as boxing as a way to channel their pent-up energy into positive avenues and "to defuse the exuberant adolescent brawling that sometimes threatened to explode into ethnic violence" (Mangione and Morreale, 1992:373).

Sports also may serve as a vehicle for upward social mobility, especially for working-class and poverty-level children of color (Coakley, 1990). Although some African Americans and Latinos/Latinas have become high-paid professional athletes, the odds of central-city youths becoming sports stars are not good (e.g., about 1 in 47,600 African Americans and about 1 in 2,500,000 Latinos will become professional football players). Whites are more likely than any other racial or ethnic group to become professional athletes in all sports except football and basketball (Leonard and Reyman, 1988).

Although sports may socialize some people for social stability and upward mobility, it also may contribute to intergenerational race and class reproduction. According to conflict theorists, professional sports reflects the interests of the wealthy and powerful wherein athletes are capitalist tools, in the guise of sports heroes who endorse products and sell people on unrealistic—and unnecessary—goals of consumerism.

Class reproduction may also occur in amateur sports. In their study of elite boarding schools, Caroline Hodges Persell and Peter W. Cookson, Jr. (Article 15) found that having sports ability and experience in scarce areas such as ice nockey, crew, and squash provides some upper-class students with an advantage in gaining admission to highly selective colleges and universities. While affluent students in elite private boarding schools are more likely to participate in sports such as crew and squash, public school students from middle- and lower-income family backgrounds are more likely to play baseball, basketball, or football. Sociologists generally have found a strong relationship between amateur sports involvement and socioeconomic status: the higher the status, the higher the involvement (Coakley, 1990).

Some students of color believe that athletics provides them with an opportunity to be judged on their own merits, not on the color of their skin. "Thomas M.," an African American athlete who attended a predominantly white, middle-class school, explained how he felt about athletic achievement:

> *I came from a very poor family, and I was very sensitive about that. . . . When people would say things like "Look at him—he has dirty pants on," I'd think about it for a week. [But] I'd put my pants on and I'd go out on the football field with the intention that I'm gonna do a job. And if that calls on me to hurt you, I'm gonna do it. It's as simple as that. I demand respect just like everybody else. (Messner, 1992:57)*

Sports socialization may diminish intergroup tension or exacerbate it by perpetuation of racial-ethnic *stereotypes*—**overgeneralizations about the appearance, behavior, or other characteristics of all members of a group.** Racial-ethnic stereotypes abound in sports, as Ward Churchill, a Native American scholar and activist, points out in Article 14. According to Churchill, use of Native American names, images, and mascots by numerous sports teams is a racist practice that perpetuates a negative image of native peoples. For example, names of professional teams such as the Washington *Redskins* and mascots with feathers, buckskins, beads, spears, and warpaint project a "savage" image of Native Americans. As Jay Coakley (1990) stresses, use of such stereotypes symbolizes a lack of understanding of native people's culture and heritage and is offensive to all Native Americans. Churchill poses this important question: What would happen if stereotypic portrayals of other racial-ethnic groups—such as African Americans, Jewish Americans, Polish Americans, or white Anglo Saxon Protestants—were used in a similar manner? Would greater resistance take place?

In addition to learning racial-ethnic stereotypes through sports socialization, children may also learn gender-based stereotypes and a gendered division of labor. According to sociologist Judith Lorber, "Sports illustrate the ways bodies are gendered by social practices and how the female body is socially constructed to be inferior" (1994:41). Most sports are rigidly divided into female and male events, and gender-based stereotypes influence the types of sports in which females and males are encouraged to participate.

During childhood, children spend more than half of their nonschool time in play and sports, but the activities they participate in tend to differ by gender. As previously discussed, boys are socialized to participate in highly competitive, rule-oriented games with a larger number of participants than games played by girls. Girls have been socialized to play exclusively with others of their own age, in groups of two or three, in activities such as hopscotch and jump rope that involve a minimum of competitiveness (Lever, 1978).

From elementary school through high school, boys play football and other competitive sports while girls are cheerleaders, members of the drill team, and homecoming queens. In a recent study, sociologist Donna Eder (with Evans and Parker, 1995) documents how a lack of official support for female athletics limits its cultural significance among middle school students. Some male coaches were openly critical of attempts by female coaches to enhance the visibility of female athletics:

> *Paulson [a basketball coach] made a comment, "Douglas, did you hear that the girl's team was thinking of using [the high school gym]? They want to have their games there." Douglas acted really surprised and said, "What for? Why should they want to play over there?" Paulson said something about better coverage and visibility, and Douglas laughed and said, "Do you think they're going to fill it up?" This was somewhat sarcastic and, I guess, a reflection of the lack of atten-*

dance at girls' games. . . . Douglas went on to describe what he had seen, saying, "Their offense . . . is like a gym class; two people do something and the other three stand around." (Eder, 1995:34)

According to Eder, lack of faculty and administrative support for female athletics limits their cultural significance in school and thus encourages girls to seek out the higher-status activity of cheerleading instead. In Eder's study, the most popular female groups in school were cheerleaders and their friends. However, different attributes are encouraged and rewarded in male athletes as compared to female cheerleaders. As sociologist Michael A. Messner notes in Article 13, sports are a means of constructing a masculine identity, and for male athletes, achievement, aggression, and competition are highly valued:

During the drills Coach Adams emphasized being meaner than they had been before. He said that he wanted animals but that he had a bunch of "nice boys." When he said "nice boys," he paused and softened his voice [Steve's notes] (Eder, 1995:61–62).

By contrast, female cheerleaders were encouraged to demonstrate poise, a bubbly personality, attractiveness, and a continual smile, even when they were in pain:

When they were doing a stunt, [the coach] said she wanted them to smile through the pain. Later on, when they were practicing the stunts in front of the eighth-graders, Karla [an eighth-grade cheerleader] continually reminded them to smile as they worked on their jumps. The way Karla put it was, "Smile the whole time." (Eder, 1995:105)

Across class lines, girls who were not cheerleaders were indirectly influenced by the athlete-cheerleader culture at school, especially in regard to appearance norms:

Although appearance concerns were found at all status and class levels in this school, the nature of the concerns varied somewhat by social class. Girls from middle-class backgrounds spent much more time fixing their hair and trying to imitate the hairstyles of cheerleaders and other esteemed girls and women. . . .

Unfortunately, girls at all social class levels further create an arena for viewing girls as objects. Since girls and women are so used to being judged by superficial criteria and noticed primarily for their appearance, a related form of objectifying girls is likely also to seem normal—sexual objectification. (Eder, 1995:122–123)

Just as cheerleading may contribute to existing gender bias in society, sociologist Michael A. Messner (1990) found that male athletes may develop a "conditional self-worth" based on whether they win or lose that can have a long-term influence on their ability to construct intimate relationships with others (see Article 13). As Messner notes, however, males may have different experiences based on race and class:

> It is not some singular "masculinity" that is being constructed through athletic careers. . . . "The world" is a very different place for males from different racial and socioeconomic backgrounds. Because males have substantially different interactions with the world, based on class, race, and other differences and inequalities, we might expect the construction of masculinity to take on different meanings for boys and men from differing backgrounds. (1989:441)

Girls and women also may have different experiences with sports based on their racial-ethnic and class background. Some females have engaged in resistance processes, such as placing a high value on toughness and practicing self-defense (Eder and Parker, 1987). Those who engage in supposedly masculine sports (such as bodybuilding) may either ignore their critics or attempt to redefine the activity or its result as feminine or womanly by not letting their bodies get overbuilt or by posing like fashion models (Klein, 1993).

In the future, more girls and women will participate in sports formerly thought to be male activities. However, even with these changes, women athletes will face contradictory statuses of being both women and athletes. According to one study, women college basketball players dealt with this contradiction by dividing their lives into segments. On the basketball court, the women "did athlete," as they pushed, shoved, fouled, ran hard, sweated, and uttered obscenities. Off the court, the players "did woman" by showering, dressing nicely, applying make-up, and styling their hair after the game, even if they were only getting on a van for a long ride home (Watson, 1987). Resistance to gender-stereotyped roles in sports and in education is an uphill battle because of existing structural and cultural barriers based on race, class, and gender inequalities.

Education and Race, Class, and Gender Socialization

During the early years of formal education, teachers exert a powerful influence over students; many children spend more hours per day with their teachers than they do with their own parents. In addition to teaching specific knowledge and skills, schools have a profound effect on children's self-images, beliefs, and values. From kindergarten through college, teachers and professors provide important messages about race, class, and gender that may reinforce, or subvert, beliefs taught by family or peers.

How does education influence people's identities and intergroup relations? In Article 19, sociologist Emily W. Kane describes two divergent perspectives on education. One approach suggests that education may be viewed as an enlightening experience: Through the knowledge and values it conveys, education teaches democratic ideals, encourages tolerance, reduces prejudice, and fosters intergroup harmony. According to the enlightenment perspective, education serves as a great equalizer in society that helps people recognize social inequality, endorse equality, and support efforts to achieve it (Jackman and Muha, 1984). A second approach is offered by reproduction theorists who argue that education may legitimize, rather than challenge, social inequality (Bowles and Gintis, 1976). Reproduction theory is based on the assumption that social institutions (including education) perpetuate (or reproduce) the social relationships and beliefs needed to maintain existing relations of production in a capitalist society. Although some reproduction theories focus on the structural requirements of the capitalist economic system, others focus on cultural factors that members of the upper classes may use for their own benefit, often at the expense of persons in the lower classes. From this perspective, educational systems encourage a meritocratic and individualistic orientation ("I made it; why can't you?") that justifies existing social inequalities, especially economic inequality.

As sociologists Jill Quadagno and Catherine Fobes explain in Article 17, reproduction theory argues that the primary functions of schools are the reproduction of the dominant ideology, its forms of knowledge, and the circulation of skills needed to reproduce the social division of labor. However, reproduction theory has been criticized for being overly deterministic because it largely ignores *human agency*.

Recently, resistance theory has sought to fill this void by shifting the focus to how people respond to situations in which they find themselves. According to sociologist Henry A. Giroux, resistance is a response to the educational system rooted in "moral and political indignation" (1983:98–99). Only behavior that is based on a struggle against, rather than submission to, domination qualifies as resistance. For example, skipping school or not doing homework does not qualify.

What do these perspectives say about how education is linked with race, class, and gender socialization? Based on the insights of French sociologist Pierre Bourdieu, cultural theorists argue that social reproduction in education occurs through students' possession of differing amounts of ***cultural capital— the general cultural background and social assets (including values, beliefs, attitudes, and competencies in language and culture) that are passed from one generation to the next*** (Bourdieu and Passeron, 1990). According to Bourdieu, parents in each class transmit distinctive cultural capital to their children. Upper-class children, for example, typically acquire high levels of cultural capital through their family's cultural activities, such as visiting museums and art galleries, attending concerts, and reading books. For example, upper-class boarding school students (as described in Article 15 by sociologists Caroline Hodges Persell and Peter W. Cookson, Jr.) accumulate cultural capital in their families and at elite boarding schools. Along with academic skills, cultural capital prepares them for success and power:

> *The cultural capital that prep school students accumulate in boarding schools is a treasure trove of skills and status symbols that can be used in later life. Armed, as it were, by the classical curriculum, the prep school graduate is prepared to do battle in the marketplace of ideas, competently, if not necessarily brilliantly. (Cookson and Persell, 1985:30)*

Although knowledge of the dominant culture is rewarded by educational systems, schools typically do not teach such competencies to working-class and poverty-level children. Since students who succeed in school are rewarded (at least theoretically) with the best job opportunities, the class structure is reproduced into the next generation by the presence or absence of cultural capital. The identity and self-esteem of students also are affected by the lack of cultural capital, as sociologist Gregory Mantsios (Article 16) relates from his own working-class background:

> *For the most part, I hated school. I thought it was a boring and hostile place. I also had trouble with the English language and that didn't help matters. My mother spoke in Greek at home and insisted that I do the same, even as she frantically tried to master English. . . .*
>
> *School was dominated by the ideologies and personalities of the white middle class. We were fed values and lifestyle models which were simultaneously presented as universal and lacking in ourselves. What counted was white not black or brown, American not immigrant, middle class not poor or working class. So different was less, inferior, inconsequential, and inadequate and we all quickly learned to see the enemy within us. We were developing prejudices and self-hate that would take a lifetime to overcome. (1995:237–241)*

Mantsios's experience shows how working-class children, especially those from subordinate racial-ethnic backgrounds, may start school with distinct disadvantages that have nothing to do with intelligence or capabilities.

Some educational and job-training programs have attempted to provide cultural capital to poor youths in the form of a middle-class value system. As Quadagno and Fobes point out in Article 17, one of the purposes of the Job Corps was to provide cultural capital for central-city youths so that they would acquire the appropriate values and workplace skills needed to get and keep a job. However, in this instance, the meanings of cultural capital differed for young men and young women: "For young men the emphasis was on transmitting skills that would enhance their employability; training for young women emphasized values and behaviors that would change their approach to family life" (1995:179). According to Quadagno and Fobes, the Job Corps reproduced gender stratification in two ways: (1) *structurally* by replicating a gendered division of labor and (2) *culturally* by instilling an ideological framework that sustains that division of labor. Job-training programs may represent a route to upward mobility for those who otherwise would lack opportunities; however, such programs may reproduce race, class, and gender inequalities when subordinate group members are not granted equal access to training and when the training provided perpetuates existing inequalities.

According to the theory of cultural capital, school assessment and evaluation programs that appear to be fair to all students actually may legitimize economic inequality by treating the possession of cultural capital as a sign of intelligence and natural ability. Instead of acquiring more upper-class cultural capital in school, many children from working-class and poverty-level families are exposed to a *hidden curriculum*—**the process by which dominant cultural values and attitudes (such as the importance of obedience to authority figures, punctuality, and good work skills) are informally transmitted through implied demands found in rules, routines, and regulations** (Snyder, 1971). Class differences are apparent in where and how the hidden curriculum is transmitted. For example, schools for working-class students tend to emphasize procedures and rote memorization without providing students with adequate opportunities to make decisions or to ask questions. Students may be evaluated on these criteria as much, or more, than on academic subject matter. For example, Gregory Mantsios (Article 16) remembers that his public school report card listed six grading categories: (1) social behavior, (2) work habits, (3) health habits, (4) language arts, (5) math, and (6) other areas (social studies, science, music, art). As he recently stated, "There was little doubt in my mind that these reflected the school's priorities. Reading recent accounts of inner city schools, I am not sure that priorities are very different today, despite the rhetoric" (1995:238). By contrast, teachers in schools attended primarily by middle- and upper-middle-class students tend to stress the importance of processes—such as computational skills and decision making—in getting the right answer. Schools for affluent students, however, focus on creative activities in which students are encouraged to express their own ideas and engage in critical thinking.

Not only does the hidden curriculum tend to reproduce social class inequalities but it is also a source of *gender bias,* **which consists of showing favoritism toward one gender over the other.** Although unspoken, many teachers communicate the message that boys are more important than girls. Even though gender bias usually occurs unintentionally, girls, over time, may learn through classroom activities and treatment by teachers and peers that they are less able than boys to achieve in certain areas (such as math and science). Recent research has shown that girls receive less attention and less of a teacher's time than do boys (Sadker and Sadker, 1994). Boys are called on more frequently in class (even when they do not volunteer) and receive more praise for their contributions. Boys are praised for their problem-solving skills and are more likely than girls to be asked follow-up questions in class discussions. By contrast, girls are praised for attributes such as personal appearance and neat, punctual papers (Sadker and Sadker, 1994).

Throughout their years of schooling, students are evaluated and compared with one another by teachers and guidance counselors who make assumptions about their abilities and future opportunities. Students often are grouped in categories based on notions about their perceived academic abilities. In-class ability grouping is used in elementary schools, based on the assumption that it is easier to teach students with similar abilities. Most middle schools and high schools employ *tracking*—**the assignment of students to specific courses and educational programs based on their test scores, previous grades, or both**—as a means of sorting students. Tracking systems typically are identified with labels such as *college preparatory, vocational, general education, special,* and *alternative.* Within each track, courses may be distinguished as *advanced, basic,* or *remedial* based on the level of difficulty and the proficiency they require of students.

As author Ruben Navarrette, Jr., suggests in Article 18, ability grouping and tracking affect students' academic achievements and thus their career choices. In Navarrette's case, his second-grade teacher decided to divide the class into six groups based on individual ability. Each group was assigned a geometric symbol to differentiate it from the others; Navarrette was a hexagon—the symbol for the smartest kids in the class. According to Navarrette, ability grouping and distinctions identified by geometric symbols were not lost on 7-year-old children: "Even in second grade, my classmates and I knew who was smarter than whom. And on the day on which we were assigned our respective shapes, we knew that our teacher knew, too" (1993:256).

Based on their geometric shapes, the children were assigned different books, and each group had different amounts of work to do. The process worked the way the teacher imagined that it would: Students did learn at their own pace. Some children learned faster than others; however, as Navarrette later realized, some did not learn at all. Tracking—along with the cultural capital that he acquired from a middle-class family background—enabled Navarrette to attend Harvard University, but it also left some of his classmates, especially many other Mexican Americans, without an adequate education. According to Navarrette:

> *Finally I face the truth: I have, in my academic lifetime, experienced a form of racial injustice reminiscent of the sort of outright discrimination that, years ago, crippled the lives of so many members of my parents' and grandparents' generations. It is newer and more subtle, and so more insidious. Let the academics class it "intraracial differentiation." Let the rest of us understand it to simply mean teachers, particularly elementary school teachers, passing an early judgment about the learning ability of their students with regard to race. And while this sort of thing is not historically unique, what is new is that, in this case, teachers are distinguishing between students of the same race. . . . Teachers' lounge distinc-*

tions [have taken] on a new dimension: Smart Mexican, Dumb Mexican. *(1993:260–261)*

As Navarrette's story demonstrates, tracking may have very different outcomes based on race and class. Students from middle- and upper-middle-class families are more likely to be tracked into programs for the supposedly gifted and talented, accelerated courses, and college prep courses. Students from working-class and poverty-level backgrounds are clustered on the lower tracks in remedial ("bonehead") and vocational courses. Since students of color are more likely to be from working-class and poverty-level families, they are overrepresented in the lower tracks, which have high dropout rates.

Some analysts have concluded that working-class and poverty-level students are in such courses because they have less ability, less ambition, and they know that less will be demanded of them. However, scholars have found this assumption erroneous; rather, children from low-income family backgrounds often have had more limited educational opportunities—less qualified teachers, lower-quality texts and laboratory equipment, few (if any) computers, and less stimulating activities in the classroom environment (Ballantine, 1993).

For children of color, these problems are further exacerbated by unequal funding of schools in central cities and by racial segregation and resegregation (see Kozol, 1991; Ballantine, 1993). Even in supposedly integrated schools, tracking and ability grouping tend to produce resegregation at the classroom level. Today, courses for low-ability students and special education classes disproportionately enroll students of color, especially African Americans and Latinos/Latinas. Unfortunately, studies show that achievement differences in African American and white students increase with each year of schooling. The achievement gap between African American and white first-graders is smaller than the gap between similar students in the twelfth grade. Some analysts suggest that this is evidence that schools reinforce, rather than eliminate, disadvantages of race and class (Mickelson and Smith, 1995). As educator Jody Cohen explains, "Schooling provides requisite information and affirmation for members of the dominant culture. Members of minority cultures, however, may find schooling irrelevant or even hostile to their development of cultural identities" (1993:293).

Differences in tracking also are evident between male and female students across racial-ethnic lines. According to recent studies, gender-segregated education—especially in mathematics, science, computer technology, athletics, and vocational education—is diminishing; however, harmful remnants remain (Sadker and Sadker, 1994). Although girls and boys initially take similar courses in math, including algebra and geometry, the gender divide becomes very apparent in advanced courses (such as calculus), which tend to be populated primarily by male teachers and students (Tocci and Engelhard, 1991). In science and computer technology courses, the gender divide occurs even sooner: Boys are much more involved in such courses in middle school and high school than are girls (Kramer and Lehman, 1990; Nelson and Watson, 1990–1991; Levin, Sabar, and Libman, 1991).

Sexist instruction in courses such as science, math, and computer technology may contribute to girls' perception that these courses make them feel stupid. In their analysis of 30 physical science and 30 chemistry classes, education scholars Gail Jones and Jack Wheatley (1990) find that boys received more encouragement from teachers to talk in class and to volunteer for demonstrations and experiments. In contrast, girls were more likely to be observers and to be self-conscious and quiet. More blatant forms of sexism were observed by researchers who analyzed coeducational physical science classrooms where male teachers tended to reinforce traditional gender stereotypes by encouraging and rewarding male students while belittling and minimizing the accomplishments of female students.

Self-selection out of courses by girls and women due to the perceived environment of the classes and overt discrimination by male students and teachers has a long-term effect on women's careers. Without prerequisite courses in high school science and math, college courses are out of reach, and without the college courses, women are filtered out of many high-paying careers that remain overwhelmingly populated by men (Sadker and Sadker, 1994).

Likewise, a direct link exists between vocational courses in high school and the jobs women and men will hold after graduation. Vocational education for girls primarily has included the fields of home economics, clerical and secretarial work, and health care (Wellesley, 1992; Smith, 1991). Boys, on the other hand, may learn skilled crafts such as woodworking, auto mechanics, and computer repair. By high school, girls who attempt to cross the gender divide may not fare as well as their younger counterparts mentioned earlier. For example, a Vietnamese American high school student gave this account of a shop class:

> I took a full-year shop class in high school. I was the only girl in the class, that is, the only girl by the end of the year. There was another girl at the beginning, but the two of us were—well, I wouldn't exactly say harassed, but it's true. After just a few days, the other girl transferred out of the course. I'm quite stubborn, so I stayed in the course the entire year. The boys literally pushed me around, right into tables and chairs. They pulled my hair, made sexual comments, touched me, told sexist jokes. And the thing was that I was better in the shop class than almost any guy. This only caused the boys to get more aggressive and troublesome. . . . Throughout the entire year no teacher or administrator ever stopped the boys from behaving this way. (quoted in Sadker and Sadker, 1994:127)

Gender bias in schools contributes to feelings of inadequacy and negative self-images in girls and women. It also sends a message to students that women's and men's work is different and differentially rewarded by society. From this standpoint, education may become a *self-fulfilling prophecy*—a situation in which a false belief or prediction produces behavior that makes the originally false belief come true.

Although education may serve to enlighten people and to provide them with greater opportunities for success, it also may reproduce existing inequalities based on gender, race, and class. In her research on the effect of education on men's versus women's beliefs about gender inequality, for example, Emily W. Kane (Article 19) points out that people's attainment of more years of formal education does not necessarily mean that they will readily acknowledge that inequalities exist in society or that they will willingly embrace strategies that might eradicate the inequalities. In regard to gender inequality, Kane notes, "While men and women share some interests based on other social positions, including social class, gender stratification also generates different interests for men and women as groups" (1995:78). Thus, instead of being the great equalizer or a force for enlightenment, education may transmit ideologies that support existing structural and cultural inequalities—based on gender, race, and class—and perpetuate existing systems of economic stratification.

In this section, we have examined how various agents of socialization influence people's social identities and how inequalities based on race, class, and gender may be reproduced intergenerationally. In Part Three, we will investigate the relations of domination and subordination as they evidence themselves in patterns of prejudice, discrimination, and resistance in public places, the workplace, families, and all other aspects of everyday life.

References

Ballantine, Jeanne H. 1993. *The Sociology of Education: A Systematic Analysis* (3rd ed.). Englewood Cliffs, NJ: Prentice-Hall.

Biagi, Shirley. 1994. *Media/Impact: An Introduction to Mass Media* (2nd ed.). Belmont, CA: Wadsworth.

Bourdieu, Pierre, and Jean-Claude Passeron. 1990. *Reproduction in Education, Society and Culture.* Newbury Park, CA: Sage.

Bowles, Samuel, and Herbert Gintis. 1976. *Schooling in Capitalist America: Education and the Contradictions of Economic Life.* New York: Basic Books.

Bowman, Philip, and Cleopatra Howard. 1985. "Race-Related Socialization, Motivation, and Academic Achievement: A Study of Black Youth in Three-Generation Families." *Journal of the American Academy of Child Psychiatry,* 24:134–141.

Burns, Ailsa, and Ross Homel. 1989. "Gender Division of Tasks by Parents and Their Children." *Psychology of Women Quarterly,* 13(1):113–125.

Coakley, Jay J. 1990. *Sport in Society: Issues and Controversies* (4th ed.). St. Louis: Times Mirror/Mosby.

Cohen, Jody. 1993. "Constructing Race at an Urban High School: In Their Minds, Their Mouths, Their Hearts," in Lois Weis and Michelle Fine (Eds.), *Beyond Silenced Voices: Class, Race, and Gender in United States Schools* (pp. 289–308). Albany: State University of New York Press.

Cookson, Peter W., Jr., and Caroline Hodges Persell. 1985. *Preparing for Power: America's Elite Boarding Schools.* New York: Basic Books.

Curran, Daniel J., and Claire M. Renzetti. 1996. *Social Problems: Society in Crisis* (4th ed.). Boston: Allyn and Bacon.

Demo, David H., and Michael Hughes. 1990. "Socialization and Racial Identity among Black Americans." *Social Psychology Quarterly,* 53(4):364–374.

Eder, Donna, and Stephen Parker. 1987. "The Cultural Production and Reproduction of Gender: The Effect of Extracurricular Activities on Peer-Group Culture." *Sociology of Education,* 60:200–213.

_____ , with Catherine Colleen Evans and Stephen Parker. 1995. *School Talk: Gender and Adolescent Culture.* New Brunswick, NJ: Rutgers University Press.

Frankenberg, Ruth. 1993. *The Social Construction of Whiteness: White Women, Race Matters.* Minneapolis: University of Minnesota Press.

Giroux, Henry A. 1983. *Theory and Resistance in Education.* London: Heinemann Educational Books.

Hale-Benson, Janice E. 1986. *Black Children: Their Roots, Culture and Learning Styles* (rev. ed.). Provo, UT: Brigham Young University Press.

hooks, bell. 1994. *Teaching to Transgress: Education as the Practice of Freedom.* New York: Routledge.

Jackman, Mary R., and Michael J. Muha. 1984. "Education and Intergroup Attitudes: Moral Enlightenment, Superficial Democratic Commitment or Ideological Refinement?" *American Sociological Review,* 49:751–769.

Jackson, James, Wayne McCullough, and Gerald Gurin. 1988. "Family, Socialization Environment, and Identity Development in Black Americans," in Harriette McAdoo (Ed.), *Black Families* (2nd ed.) (pp. 242–256). Beverly Hills: Sage.

Jones, M. Gail, and Jack Wheatley. 1990. "Gender Differences in Teacher-Student Interactions in Science Classrooms." *Journal of Research in Science Teaching,* 27(9):861–974.

Kane, Emily W. 1995. "Education and Beliefs about Gender Inequality." *Social Problems,* 42(1):74–90.

Klein, Alan M. 1993. *Little Big Man: Bodybuilding Subculture and Gender Construction.* Albany: State University of New York Press.

Knight, George P., Martha E. Bernal, Marya K. Cota, Camille A. Garza, and Katheryn A. Ocampo. 1993a. "Family Socialization and Mexican American Identity and Behavior," in Martha E. Bernal and George P. Knight (Eds.), *Ethnic Identity: Formation and Transmission Among Hispanics and Other Minorities* (pp. 105–129). Albany: State University of New York Press.

_____ , _____ , Camille A. Garza, and Marya K. Cota. 1993b. "A Social Cognitive Model of the Development of Ethnic Identity and Ethnically Based Behaviors," in Martha E. Bernal and George P. Knight (Eds.), *Ethnic Identity: Formation and Transmission Among Hispanics and Other Minorities* (pp. 213–234). Albany: State University of New York Press.

Kohn, Melvin L. 1969. *Class and Conformity: A Study in Values.* Homewood, IL: Dorsey Press.

_____ , Atsushi Naoi, Carrie Schoenbach, Carmi Schooler, and Kazimierz M. Slomczynski. 1990. "Position in the Class Structure and Psychological Functioning in the United States, Japan, and Poland." *American Journal of Sociology* 95:964–1008.

Kozol, Jonathan. 1991. *Savage Inequalities: Children in America's Schools.* New York: Crown.

Kramer, Pamela, and Sheila Lehman. 1990. "Mismeasuring Women: A Critique of Research on Computer Ability and Avoidance." *Signs: Journal of Women in Culture and Society,* 16(1):158–172.

Leonard, Wilbert M., and Jonathan E. Reyman. 1988."The Odds of Attaining Professional Athlete Status: Refining the Computations." *Sociology of Sport Journal,* 5:162–169.

Lever, Janet. 1978. "Sex Differences in the Complexity of Children's Play and Games." *American Sociological Review,* 43:471–483.

Levin, Tamar, Naama Sabar, and Zipora Libman. 1991. "Achievements and Attitudinal Patterns of Boys and Girls in Science." *Journal of Research in Science Teaching,* 28(4):315–328.

Lorber, Judith. 1994. *Paradoxes of Gender.* New Haven, CT: Yale University Press.

Maccoby, Eleanor E., and Carol Nagy Jacklin. 1987. "Gender Segregation in Childhood." *Advances in Child Development and Behavior,* 20:239–287.

MacLeod, Jay. 1995, *Ain't No Makin' It: Aspirations and Attainment in a Low-Income Neighborhood.* Boulder, CO: Westview.

Mangione, Jerre, and Ben Morreale. 1992. *La Storia: Five Centuries of Italian American Experience.* New York: HarperPerennial.

Mantsios, Gregory. 1995. "Living and Learning: Some Reflections on Emergence from and Service to the Working Class," in Janet Zandy (Ed.), *Liberating Memory: Our Work and Our Working-Class Consciousness* (pp. 231–248). New Brunswick, NJ: Rutgers University Press.

Marger, Martin N. 1994. *Race and Ethnic Relations: American and Global Perspectives.* Belmont, CA: Wadsworth.

Messner, Michael A. 1989. "Masculinities and Athletic Careers." *Gender & Society,* 3:71–88.

———— . 1990. "Boyhood, Organized Sports, and the Construction of Masculinities." *Journal of Contemporary Ethnography,* 18(4):416–444.

———— . 1992. *Power at Play: Sports and the Problem of Masculinity.* Boston: Beacon Press.

Mickelson, Roslyn Arlin, and Stephen Samuel Smith. 1995. "Education and the Struggle Against Race, Class, and Gender Inequality," in Margaret L. Andersen and Patricia Hill Collins (Eds.), *Race, Class, and Gender* (2nd ed.) (pp. 219–304). Belmont, CA: Wadsworth.

National Council of La Raza. 1994. "Distorted Reality: Hispanic Characters in TV Entertainment." (September).

Navarrette, Ruben, Jr. 1993. *A Darker Shade of Crimson.* New York: Bantam Books.

Nelson, Carole, and J. Allen Watson. 1990–1991. "The Computer Gender Gap: Children's Attitudes, Performance, and Socialization." *Journal of Educational Technology Systems,* 19(4):345–353.

Peters, Marie. 1985. "Racial Socialization of Young Black Children," in Harriette McAdoo and John McAdoo (Eds.), *Black Children* (pp. 159–173). Beverly Hills: Sage.

Quadagno, Jill, and Catherine Fobes. 1995. "The Welfare State and the Cultural Reproduction of Gender." *Social Problems,* 42(2):171–190.

Sadker, Myra, and David Sadker. 1994. *Failing at Fairness: How America's Schools Cheat Girls.* New York: Scribner.

Schwarz, John E., and Thomas J. Volgy. 1992. *The Forgotten Americans.* New York: W. W. Norton.

Sedgwick, John. 1985. *Rich Kids.* New York: William Morrow.

Smith, Douglas. 1991. "Classroom Interaction and Gender Disparity in Secondary Vocational Instruction." *Journal of Vocational Education Research,* 16(3):35–58.

Snyder, Benson R. 1971. *The Hidden Curriculum.* New York: Knopf.

Thompson, Becky W. 1994. *A Hunger So Wide and So Deep: American Women Speak Out on Eating Problems.* Minneapolis: University of Minnesota Press.

Thorne, Barrie. 1993. *Gender Play: Girls and Boys in School.* New Brunswick, NJ: Rutgers University Press.

Thornton, Michael C., Linda M. Chatters, Robert Joseph Taylor, and Walter R. Allen. 1990. "Sociodemographic and Environmental Correlates of Racial Socialization by Black Parents." *Child Development,* 61:401–409.

Tocci, Cynthia, and George Engelhard. 1991. "Achievement, Parental Support, and Gender Differences in Attitudes Toward Mathematics." *Journal of Educational Research,* 84:(5):280–286.

Watson, Tracey, 1987. "Women Athletes and Athletic Women: The Dilemmas and Contradictions of Managing Incongruent Identities." *Sociological Inquiry,* 57:431–446.

Wellesley College Center for Research on Women. 1992. *How Schools Shortchange Girls.* Washington, DC: American Association of University Women Educational Foundation.

Wood, Julia T. 1994. *Gendered Lives: Communication, Gender, and Culture.* Belmont, CA: Wadsworth.

ARTICLE 10 _____

According to scholar Ruth Frankenberg, "Race shapes white women's lives. In the same way that both men's and women's lives are shaped by their gender, and that both heterosexual and lesbian women's experiences in the world are marked by their sexuality, white people and people of color live racially structured lives. In other words, any system of differentiation shapes those on whom it bestows privilege as well as those it opposes" (1993:1). In this excerpt from her book, *White Women, Race Matters: The Social Construction of Whiteness,* Frankenberg examines the social geography of race in the lives of five women.

   At the time Ruth Frankenberg wrote the book from which this article is taken, she was an American studies professor at the University of California at Davis.

Looking Ahead

1. What is the "social geography" of race?
2. How did the social geography of race influence women who had an "apparently all-white childhood"?
3. What effect does racial segregation have on people's awareness of race?
4. Why do many people see others through a racial lens but not consciously see race, cultural difference, or racism?

Growing Up White
The Social Geography of Race

◆ *Ruth Frankenberg*

> *My family was really very racist. It was just a very assumed kind of thing.*
>
> —Patricia Bowen

> *Ever since I was a baby, Black people have been around, the person who taught me to walk was a Black woman, that was a maid for our family . . . pretty much all throughout my childhood, there was a maid around.*
>
> —Beth Ellison

I was so unaware of cultural difference that I probably wouldn't have noticed they were different from me.

    —Clare Traverso

The main things I remember . . . are some friends. . . . The Vernons were two sisters and they had a little brother too, just like our family, and they were Black. And the Frenches . . . they were white.

    —Sandy Alvarez

I never looked at it like it was two separate cultures. I just kind of looked at it like, our family and our friends, they're Mexicans and Chicanos, and that was just part of our life.

    —Louise Glebocki

This [article] begins with childhood, looking in detail at five white women's descriptions of the places in which they grew up and analyzing them in terms of what I will refer to as the "social geography" of race. *Geography* refers here to the physical landscape —the home, the street, the neighborhood, the school, parts of town visited or driven through rarely or regularly, places visited on vacation. My interest was in how physical space was divided and who inhabited it, and, for my purposes, "who" referred to racially and ethnically identified beings.

The notion of a *social* geography suggests that the physical landscape is peopled and that it is constituted and perceived by means of social rather than natural processes. I thus asked how the women I interviewed conceptualized and related to the people around them. To what extent, for example, did they have relationships of closeness or distance, equality or inequality, with people of color? What were they encouraged or taught by example to make of the variously "raced" people in their environments? *Racial* social geography, in short, refers to the racial and ethnic mapping of environments in physical and social terms and enables also the beginning of an understanding of the conceptual mappings of self and other operating in white women's lives.

The five women upon whom I focus . . . do not represent the full range of experiences of the thirty women I interviewed, and the landscapes of childhood will in fact be a recurrent theme in this [article]. Rather than taking these particular narratives as representative in their content, I draw on them here to begin the process of "defamiliarizing" that which is taken for granted in white experience and to elaborate a method for making visible and analyzing the racial structuring of white experience. This method, it seems to me, takes the question of white women and racism well beyond that of the individual and her beliefs or attitudes to something much broader and more grounded in the material world. For it becomes possible to begin examining the ways racism as a system shaped these women's daily environments, and to begin thinking about the social, political, and historical forces that brought these environments into being.

All five of the women in this group were between twenty-five and thirty-six years old at the time of the interviews, their childhoods and teenage years spanning the mid-1950s, 1960s, and early 1970s. One woman, Beth Ellison, grew up middle class, the other four—Pat Bowen, Clare Traverso, Sandy Alvarez, and Louise Glebocki—in working-class homes. Pat grew up in Maryland, Beth in Alabama and Virginia; Sandy and Louise are from the Los Angeles area, and Clare is from a small town outside San Diego, California.

These women's stories all bear the marks of an era of challenges and transformations in terms of race, racism, and antiracism. Sandy's mother, for example, was a political activist involved in struggles for integration. By contrast, as we will see, Beth's mother was ambivalent in the face of challenges to the racial status quo in her all-white, middle-class neighborhood. All five women spent at least part of their childhoods in racially desegregated schools, indicative of the effects of the civil rights movement on the patterning of children's daily lives. As will be abundantly clear, however, the women's material and conceptual environments were shaped in complex ways by long histories of racism. Regional histories also differentiated the racial and ethnic landscapes of these women's childhoods. Thus, for southerners Pat Bowen and Beth Ellison, the people of color with whom they had contact were mainly African American (or, in the language of the time, Black). Clare Traverso grew up on the U.S.-Mexican border, in a town with Native Americans and Mexican Americans. And both Sandy Alvarez and Louise Glebocki grew up in racially heterogeneous (Latino, Asian, Black, and white) working-class Los Angeles neighborhoods.

As adults, these five women were also distinctive in the extent to which they had thought about, or acted on, antiracism. Two of them, Sandy Alvarez and Clare Traverso, taught in high schools whose students were predominantly Asian and Latino; for each of them, teaching was to some extent tied to social change. Thus, for example, Sandy had tried (with limited success) to raise faculty consciousness about racism, and Clare had worked to make student literacy a vehicle for empowerment. Louise Glebocki was active in a left party. And while neither Pat Bowen nor

Beth Ellison described herself as an activist, both had thought a great deal about the interracial dynamics with which they had grown up. In addition, Louise and Sandy were both in long-term primary relationships with Chicano men. One of the five, Beth, was lesbian, the others heterosexual.

These women were, then, unusual in certain ways, both politically and in their life choices. Their accounts of childhood, however, resonated with those of more conservative interviewees, and, like the others', their experiences ran the gamut from explicitly articulated and de facto segregation to what I will refer to as "quasi integration." There was, then, no predictive relationship between ways of growing up and adult perspectives. (Indeed, even Sandy, whose mother was an active integrationist, described her sister as having become "racist" in her adult attitudes.)

Race was, in fact, lived in as many different ways as there were women I talked with. Nonetheless, patterns emerged as I analyzed the interviews. I clustered the childhood narratives around four types or modes of experience, not because each narrative fell clearly into one or another mode, but because there were enough common threads to make the similarities worth exploring, and because the contrasts between modes were significant enough to require analysis. Of the four modes, one seemed at first to be characterized by an absence of people of color from the narrator's life, but turned out, as I will suggest, to be only *apparently* all white." Second, there was a racially conflictual mode. Third, there were contexts in which race difference was present, but unremarked, in which race difference functioned as a filter for perception while not always being consciously perceived. Finally, some white women described experiences I have interpreted as quasi-integrated, that is, integrated but not fully so, for reasons that should become clear below. One of the five women I focus on in this chapter is drawn from each of the first three modes and two from the quasi-integrated group.

BETH ELLISON: AN "APPARENTLY ALL-WHITE" CHILDHOOD

Many of the women whose childhoods were apparently all white shared suburban middle-class childhoods. Beth, born in 1956, grew up in a white, middle-class, professional suburb in a town in Virginia. Today, she describes herself as a feminist. She is an artist who makes a living as a retail worker. Beth said of her childhood:

> I was born in Alabama and spent my real early years in New Orleans. I was five when we moved to Virginia. I remember living in a professional subdivision, our neighbors were all doctors and lawyers. . . . It was a white neighborhood. . . . The only specifically racist thing I remember from growing up in Virginia was when a Black doctor and his family moved into the neighborhood . . . at that time I guess maybe I was fourteen and I still didn't think about racism . . . I wasn't interested in politics . . . but I vaguely remember neighbors banding together to see if they could keep this family from moving in and I remember thinking that was disgusting, but I was more concerned with my life and being a young teenager.

In the telling of this incident, racism is categorized as "politics," and as separate from daily life as a teenager. Beth's self-description in this sense highlights a key difference between whites' experience of racism and the experience of people of color: racism is frequently pushed to the forefront of consciousness of people of color, as a construct that organizes hardship and discrimination. The statement that the only *specifically* racist incident was the attempted exclusion of a Black family from the neighborhood sug-

gests a view of racism as limited to willed, concerted activity. Yet the very existence of a neighborhood whose residents are all white itself bespeaks a history of racist structuring of that community. Elements of that history might include both the "redlining" of neighborhoods by realtors to keep Black people from buying property in them and also the economic dimensions of racism that would place affluent neighborhoods beyond the reach of most Black families. The incident that drew Beth's attention to racism was, in short, only the tip of the iceberg.

There *were* Black people not too far away, for Beth says:

> I saw a lot of Black people around . . . on the street and . . . in class and downtown, but . . . I don't remember there being many Black and white people hanging out together, I just don't remember seeing that. And also I didn't pay real close attention to it, either. . . . Now that we're talking about this, I remember seeing a lot of Black people around, and I remember not really hanging out with them . . . it wasn't any kind of conscious decision but it was just not what I did.

With or without a conscious decision, Beth's experience of friendship and community was racially structured in multiple ways.

Beth said that there were no parts of town that she avoided when she was growing up. In her hometown in Virginia, the poorest—and Black—part of town was on the way to the downtown record and bookstores, and Beth traversed it regularly. So, unlike some other women in the "all-white" group, Beth did not perceive people of color as a threat or a group to avoid; rather, their presence or absence was not a salient issue.

If Beth felt no anxiety, however, her mother seemed to oscillate between what Beth called a "humanist" belief in at least a limited integration and the sense that she needed to keep her children apart (and, in her perception, *safe*) from Black children and adults. This is illustrated in Beth's description of school integration, which for her began in fifth grade:

> I would have been about ten when schools were desegregated [in 1965]. I don't remember anyone in my family being upset about it, or my mother trying to withdraw me from school or anything. . . . I was . . . a little bit excited about it because it was something new. . . . My mother tried really hard to be— she's kind of a humanist, so I don't remember her saying anything like "Don't hang out with Black kids."

But later, in high school, Beth was involved in an incident in which she was pushed up against the wall of the gym changing room by a Black girl. This resulted in her parents moving her to a segregated private school. Beth comments:

> We didn't talk about it at the time, but as I look back on it now . . . it seems evident to me that they did this because it wasn't a school where there would be, uh, what they might consider rowdy Black girls for me to have to contend with.

Beth's mother showed a similar ambivalence on the question of residential integration. On the one hand, Beth did not think her mother had taken part in the effort to keep the Black family out of her neighborhood. Her response was very different, however, when Beth, at twenty, moved to a poor, racially mixed part of the same town:

> I do remember my mother being really concerned and I don't know if that's because there were a lot of Black people living there or because it was an extremely poor part of town where you'd be more inclined to be ripped off . . . [but she] wouldn't let my younger brother come visit me.

So Beth grew up in a context in which Black people were the "significant others" of color, and where race and income were intertwined. Being white and middle class meant living somewhere different from Black people. The social distance between white and Black people—which was considerable—was produced and reproduced through the conscious efforts of white people, including Beth's mother and neighbors, and through the more diffuse effects of the interplay of the class structure with racism. White people like Beth's mother deliberated over the permissibility and safety of living in the same terrain as Black people, seemingly projecting their fear or dislike of Black people when they made such decisions. Less visible here are the forms of white people's personal and structural violence toward African Americans that marked both residential and school desegregation and the period of civil rights struggle in general.

In any event, Beth received mixed messages. Her environment was shaped by at least three factors. First, there was a preexisting arrangement of racial segregation and inequality, reproduced, for example, by the all-white private school. Second, Beth's mother's verbal messages about segregation espoused ideas about equality or what Beth called "humanism." Third, and contrasting with her humanism, there were Beth's mother's actions in response to Beth's experiences and choices, which, as Beth tells it, frequently leaned in the direction of segregationism and hostility toward Black people. The result was that, without trying, Beth could continue to live a mostly racially segregated life.

For Beth, the structure of racial inequality was at times simply lived in; at other times, it was both lived and seen. If the consequences for *herself* of a racially structured environment were not always obvious to Beth, however, the impact on others of race and class hierarchy was at times very clear.

She said of the two communities she knew well as she was growing up:

Beth: *In [the town in Virginia] it seems like it was mostly poor neighborhoods where Black people lived, but there were also a lot of poor white people that lived there too. But in [the town in Alabama], there was a Black part of town and a white part of town. There was the rich part of the white part of town, the middle class, and then the poor white section. And then there was shantytown, and it was literally shacks.*

RF: *So the shantytown was really the Black part of town?*

Beth: *Yeah . . . these tiny little shacks that looked like they'd been thrown together out of plywood and two-by-fours. The difference was incredible, because you could drive for one minute in your car and go through rich, beautiful neighborhoods to . . . what looked squalid to me.*

Comparing Beth's words here with her memories of her own neighborhood, it is striking that Beth was much more sharply aware of racial *oppression* shaping Black experience than of race *privilege* in her own life. Thus, Beth could be alert to the realities of economic discrimination against Black communities while still conceptualizing her own life as racially neutral—nonracialized, nonpolitical.

For Beth and the other women who grew up in apparently all-white situations, there were in fact at least one or two people of color not too far away. It is in fact conceptually rather than physically that people of color were distant. In this regard, one startling feature of several descriptions of apparently all-white childhoods was the sudden appearance in the narratives of people of color as employees, mainly Black, mainly female, and mainly domestic workers. What is striking here is not the presence of domestic workers as such but the way in which they were talked about. For, oddly, these Black

women were *not* summoned into white women's accounts of their lives by means of questions like "Were there any people of color in your neighborhood?" or "Who lived in your household when you were growing up?" Rather, they arrived previously unheralded, in the context of some other topic.

Black women domestic workers appeared in Beth's narrative when I asked her if she remembered the first time she became conscious of race difference, or conscious that there were Black and white people in the world. Beth responded that her first consciousness of race as a difference was when she was about four years old, when her mother chastised her for referring to a Black woman as a "lady." Here, of course, we are seeing race not just as difference but as hierarchy. Beth said:

> *Ever since I was a baby, Black people have been around, the person who taught me to walk was a Black woman, that was a maid for our family . . . pretty much throughout my childhood, there was a maid around.*

She added that, although she had not really noticed at the time, she realized now that when her mother remarried, the family stopped employing anyone to do housework. Thus Black domestic workers, despite involvement in Beth's life on the very intimate level of teaching her to walk, seemed on another level to have been so insignificant as not to have merited mention earlier in our conversation. Nor had she noted their departure from the household after a certain point in her life.

The forgotten and suddenly remembered domestic worker recurred in several of these white, middle-class neighborhoods. Tamara Green, raised "solidly middle class" in suburban Los Angeles, said:

> *I totally forgot until I just started thinking about it—we had housekeepers who, all but*

one from the time we lived in California, were Latin American, Mexican, Colombian, Honduran, Salvadoran. There was one British Honduran who was Black. And I had a close relationship with one of them.

Why is the story told in this particular way? It may be the status of domestic workers from the standpoint of white middle-class women, or the status of people of color from the purview of a white and middle-class childhood, that made these women invisible and stripped them of subjectivity in the landscapes of childhood. But whether or not it is race per se that determined how the domestic worker of color appeared in the interviews, it is primarily through employer-employee, class-imbalanced relationships that women from apparently all-white homes encountered women of color. If not themselves in positions of clear authority, these white middle-class women must have seen their parents in such positions, able to summon and dismiss the racially different Other at will. It is perhaps in this sense of control and authority that the home was indeed all white, and the neighborhood similarly so.

PATRICIA BOWEN: RACE CONFLICT AND "SEGREGATION"

I grew up in a town that was semi-southern . . . a fairly small town, and pretty much in a working-class family. The town was very racist, it was very segregated. Everyone was aware of race all the time and the races involved were pretty much white and Black people.

Patricia Bowen grew up in Maryland in the 1960s, in a town where race conflict and racism were in the forefront of daily life. Pat described her town as "segregated," yet, as we will see, she and her family had more interaction with people of color (specifically, Black people) than either Beth or Clare (whose narrative follows). Segregation, in

Pat's experience, was a complex system of interactions and demarcations of boundary rather than complete separation. In fact, Black and white people lived close together:

[We] lived on a street that was all white, and there were no Black people on that street. But the back of our house—our front door faced an all-white street, the back door faced an all-Black street. . . . It was completely separate.

The boundary between white and Black was thus very clear. And differences between the streets were also evident to Pat: the houses on the Black people's street were poorer, more "shacky" (her term), and there were more children playing outside.

In this setting, both the presence and the absence of Black people were sharply indicated. They were very noticeably absent from the street in front, yet in some sense almost more visible than whites, given the children playing in the street beyond the back door. Added to this sharp distinction was a feeling of fear:

We were kind of told that it wasn't safe to walk down the Black street. . . . [Black children would] yell at you . . . I never got hurt but [they] threatened you a little bit. . . . So I grew up learning that Black people were dangerous.

Pat never came to any harm on the "Black street," and in fact often used it as a shortcut: the idea of danger was introduced by adults and by the threats (apparently never carried out) of the Black children, but in fact Pat went in fear rather than in danger. As an explanation for the threats, Pat suggested that the Black children "weren't used to whites walking through"—yet it sounded as though Pat and her friends routinely cut through the street. One is tempted to interpret the situation as another aspect of boundary demarcation, or as a gesture of turf maintenance on the part of Black children frustrated at their treatment by their white neighbors. In any event, in Pat's experience, difference, opposition, and threat lived right on the back doorstep.

As Pat describes others in her family, however, it seems that for them the issue was not fear so much as maintaining a complex balance of association with and differentiation from Black people. Black and white people used the same stores. As the person in charge of the household, Pat's grandmother took care of shopping. As a result, Pat explained, her grandmother knew many of the Black women in the other street. She would chat and even visit their homes but always maintained a separateness:

Pat: *She'd tell me proudly or just very self-righteous, "Well, you know, I would never sit down when I go in their house. I would go over and talk to them, but I wouldn't sit down." You know, because to sit down would imply some equal relationship and she wouldn't do that. They would come up to the back door.*
RF: *Instead of the front door?*
Pat: *Yes.*

This elaborate and contradictory boundary maintenance was undertaken by other relatives, too:

My uncle was pretty young . . . , a teenager when I lived there. He and his friends would kind of play with boys who were Black, but again they didn't really consider them friends in the same way. . . . Black culture was really cool, they would imitate them all the time, and the funny thing was they spoke exactly like them . . . it was pretty much the accent something like they had anyway. The way they danced was really cool and everyone listened to Black music all the time . . . , but at the same time there was this "niggers, niggers, niggers," it was this weird contradiction.

The direct teaching Pat received from family members about racism was equally mixed. On the one hand, she said:

My mother was more liberal . . . so she would always tell me not to say 'nigger,' that Black people weren't any worse than white people.

On the other hand:

I remember this one incident. . . . When I was about eight or nine and walking with my uncle down the street and kind of mutually bumping into a Black woman. I just said, "Excuse me," and he said, "Don't ever say excuse me to a nigger. If you bump into them or they bump into you, it's always their fault." And I said, "How is it their fault if I bumped into them?"

Notice here Pat's resistance or at least her puzzlement in the face of explicitly racist socialization. Like Beth, Pat was not always an unquestioning recipient of her environment.

The potential for complexity in responses to racially structured environments was dramatized in Pat's descriptions of two relationships she had with young Black teenagers in her junior high school years:

There are some things about friendships that I developed with Blacks at that time that are kind of interesting. There were two in particular that I really remember. One was a guy in my junior high . . . who was kind of a leader, very charismatic person, and he started hassling me a lot, he wanted to pick on me and he would tease me and kind of threaten me, pull my hair or whatever and I was terrified of him. This went on for a while and then one Halloween my friends and I were out trick-or-treating—we were teenagers and were tagging along with the little kids. . . . We saw him with a friend also trick-or-treating and we laughed. It was a kind of bonding because we were both these obnoxious teenagers out trick-or-treating, trying to get candy with the kids. So I had a feeling he kind of really liked me after that. . . . The relationship kind of switched from him threatening me to being a real friendly relationship. I wasn't afraid of him any more.

But the way that got played out is a lot of jokes about racism acted out, like he would pretend to threaten me or tease me in front of people, like Black and white people who were there, and I would play with him back, and everyone would be nervous and thought a fight was going to break out. . . . It was something where we would never really talk or become friends, but it was a neat little thing.

And Pat had a similar experience with a Black girl:

She was a very, very large woman and she would pretend to threaten me sometimes and I remember some Black girls going "ooh" because I was much smaller than she was. We'd play around with that.

In playing with the segregation system like this, Pat and her friends were taking at least a small step toward subverting it. By acting out their roles as enemies but not really fighting, they signaled that they knew what they were caught in; the dramatization was a kind of stepping aside from their assigned roles, although this did not, of course, change them. For Pat, one could say that this kind of play involved *acting* being white simultaneously with *being* white.

However, white people's fear of people of color—which played a part in many narratives—involved another, much less self-conscious inversion of social reality. For if Pat's African American friends were playing with the racial order by pretending to threaten her, that threat itself inverts the institutionalized relations of racism wherein African Americans actually have much more

to fear from white people than vice versa. Commonplace as is white people's fear of people of color, and especially of Black people, it is important to step back from it and realize that it is socially constructed and in need of analysis. I will return to this issue later.

Most of the time Pat and others around her lived out the rules of segregation without subverting them. The same girlfriend with whom Pat "played" racial tension also experienced it directly in an incident that Pat described:

There were three of us that hung around together, . . . Janet, who was Black, and my friend Sandra and me. Sandra—again, like I had this whole liberal interpretation I got from my mother about Black people and race. Sandra was just more—"nigger"—she would whisper that word and things like that—yet we were both friends with Janet. . . . I remember one night—this is really an awful, painful thing—we were at Janet's house just hanging around, she was drinking Coke out of a can and she passed it to my friend Sandra, and Sandra . . . said no, and we all knew it was because she wouldn't drink out of a can after a Black person, but yet this was our friend that we hung around with. I remember Janet just looking really sad, but also accepting, like it hurt her. . . . I guess it never occurred to me not to drink the Coke.

Pat, Sandra, and Janet were all around twelve years old at the time of their friendship. It is worth noting that Pat did not state the race of her white friend, Sandra; as is often the case, white stands for the position of racial "neutrality," or the racially unmarked category. . . . Pat further commented on this incident that "we never really talked about race, it was just too taboo a subject."

Taboo or not, race difference and racism seemed never to be far from the forefront of

Pat's experience. Her life was structured very visibly by race hierarchy. Curiously, however, segregation bespoke the presence rather than the absence of people of color. This might partly have been a result of the fact that Pat was working class: Pat pointed out that middle-class whites in the town would probably have had less contact with African Americans than she did, and in fact one can speculate that, had Pat been middle class, the racial social geography of her childhood might have resembled Beth's.

Boundary demarcation of physical space —being in the same street or house, sitting or standing, making physical contact, sharing a drink—seemed to be of major concern for the white people Pat described, probably precisely because of the proximity of white and Black people in the context of an ideology and practice of white superiority. However, boundary maintenance was an issue in other women's stories too, evidenced, for example, in Beth's all-white neighborhood. In addition, as I will discuss in the context of other narratives, the taboo on interracial sexual relationships, possibly the most intimate form of refusal of racial boundaries, came up in conversations with many of the women I interviewed.

CLARE TRAVERSO: RACE DIFFERENCE AS A FILTER FOR PERCEPTION

In contrast to this very clear and immediate awareness of race difference, the situation described by Clare Traverso was a complex mix of noticing and not noticing people of color. Whether Clare saw people of color as different from or the same as herself was at times also unclear. Clare was born in 1954 and grew up in a small, rural town not far from San Diego. The town, said Clare, was

kind of like a redneck town, actually. . . . Very conservative politically. People off to
themselves, don't want to be bothered with government or politics or other people, love to drink beer and drive around and stuff like that.

Clare's parents were "fundamentalist Christian, but not moral majority" people who had moved to California from South Dakota with their children. Clare, the fifth child of six, was born in California. Describing how her time was spent as a child, Clare explained:

We lived sort of off into the hills. We didn't really go into town much. . . . The amount of times I went out to eat before I went to college was maybe five times. . . . See, my parents had more traditional values from the Midwest—always saving money and . . . we never went on vacations. I went on two, but they were back to South Dakota to visit my relatives.

Consequently, aside from school and, later, church-related activities, Clare spent a lot of time during her early years playing on the land around her family's house. Nonetheless, she was able to describe the racial composition of the town:

The town itself is located right next to an Indian reservation. . . . There was also a small Mexican American population that went to our high school, but I would say probably no Blacks. Maybe one or two.

One may note that Clare's standpoint here is clearly different from that of the African American townspeople themselves, for whom it would be impossible to confuse existence with nonexistence. What Clare's cloudy memory on this point perhaps indicates is the lack of importance accorded to Black people in the community by whites.

Clare's first contact with people of color was when she began traveling on the school bus. At that point, her response, like Pat's, was fear:

> *The bus I rode, there were these . . . Mexican American families, lived on the hill across from us, so they rode our bus, and they always had the reputation for being really tough. And I was really scared of this one girl, I remember, because she used to get in fights with this other girl.*

Clare speculated that her fear was probably bolstered by her brother, who was in class with one of the "tougher" Mexican American boys. Again like Pat's, Clare's fear did not come from experience of personal attack so much as from a sense of different behavior perceived as louder or rowdier than her own:

> *They used to yell, flip people off—I came from a more sheltered environment. My parents never did things like that.*

In a sense, the explanation—my *parents* never behaved that way—suggests that, unconsciously, a cultural explanation is being advanced for the difference in behavior: it is placed in the realm of things taught. Although the fact that this group was Mexican American is clearly a part of the anecdote, once the children were off the bus and in school, Mexicanness became less important as a feature of conscious differentiation:

RF: *So your [kindergarten] class was all white?*
Clare: *I'm pretty sure it was—probably—oh, wait, I had one little friend, Ralph Vasquez. Their whole family was Mexican American, my sister went through school with one girl in that family. . . . But I never really thought of them as, like, different from me. I don't think I was aware of them being culturally different.*

A similar pattern appeared in Clare's description of her Native American school-

mates later on in school. On the one hand, she said:

> *I was so unaware of cultural difference that I probably wouldn't have noticed they were different from me.*

On the other hand, she remembered Native Americans in school as a distinct group, noting that they were in the remedial classes. Differences were thus both seen and not seen, or perhaps seen but only partially. Race difference entered into Clare's conscious perception of her environment only on those rare occasions when it carried a real or imagined threat to herself (as when she was afraid on the school bus). The ways in which racism did seem to cause hardship for students of color, by contrast, were perceived only dimly, accessible to memory but not remembered as having made a strong impact on Clare at the time. For, presumably, racism accounted for the location of the Native American students in remedial classes and, more indirectly, perhaps for their intragroup fights too.

The composition of Clare's friendship group in high school further supports this picture of a daily life that was in effect patterned by race: structured around the student council and a church youth group, it was all white. What shaped Clare's descriptions of all three groups—whites, Mexican Americans, and Native Americans—was on the one hand the absence of a conscious conceptualization of cultural and racial difference per se, but on the other hand, the *experience* of a racially structured environment, not understood as such at the time. In sum, Clare saw individuals in her immediate community through a racial lens, but did not consciously see race, cultural difference, or racism.

Clare came to awareness of all three concepts as she grew older but, interestingly, in relation to communities other than her own:

Clare: *In sixth grade I started learning Spanish and learning a bit about Latin culture, Latin*

America. My awareness of race came through that rather than Mexican American people.

RF: *So what did you learn about Latin America?*

Clare: *Pyramids, music, sometimes we'd listen to the radio. I was fascinated by the Aztecs and the Incas.*

Latin America thus appeared to Clare as a site of more real or authentic cultural difference, and as the proper adjunct to learning Spanish. Cultural difference was at a distance and in the past rather than nearer to home. At the same time, in a contradictory vein, Clare commented that Spanish seemed like the appropriate language to study in school, rather than German or French, "because we were living around and across the border from people who spoke it."

If Latin culture was conceived as being far away, it was clear that the Spanish language was closer at hand. In this nearer context, though, difference referred to social inequality more directly than to cultural difference. The Mexican border was less than a two-hour drive from Clare's home, and for some, although not for Clare's family, border towns like Tijuana were places to visit on day trips. Clare *did* visit across the border in rather different circumstances, as described in the following story. Note the implication that Mexican Americans or Chicanos somehow do not really count as members of a Latino, Spanish-speaking culture. Again the issue is one of the perceived inauthenticity of Latinos on the U.S. side of the border:

Clare: *Even though I had Spanish in high school, I didn't really speak it—once when we went down to Tecate at Christmastime to give away clothes and we spoke a little bit of Spanish to real people who spoke it. . . . This Spanish teacher I had . . . every year they used to collect all these clothes and bring it*

down and give it away to people in Tecate. I think we did that twice. And you'd give away the clothes to people, the poor people there.

RF: *So how do you do that?*

Clare: *You just walk up to people and say, "Hey, do you need something?"*

RF: *Just like that?*

Clare: *Yeah, it was kind of weird, really. . . . We would walk around—and, yeah, we had trucks or cars or something. . . . Our teacher knew someone there. I think he knew the mayor. . . . I felt really odd about giving things away like that, even though they didn't have anything and I know they needed things. They needed food and clothes. You could tell by the way their houses were, just like little shacks, really—dirt floors . . . I remember feeling a real contrast between myself and them. . . .*

RF: *Do you remember any comments, from your parents, or from school?*

Clare: *I'm sure they thought it was good. . . . We all felt happy that we'd helped poor people out.*

In this incident Clare was unwittingly inscribed into the power relations involved in any act of charity. While the sharing of wealth in almost any form is of course useful, here the process was controlled entirely by the givers. The receivers were dependent on the mercy of the schoolchildren who, at their teacher's behest, walked the streets asking, "Do you need anything?" This power imbalance may in part have accounted for Clare's feeling that something was not quite right about the situation. In going to Tecate, Clare became starkly aware of the imbalance of resources on opposite sides of the border. But it was not clear from our conversation how, if at all, this imbalance was explained to her. It is likely that in this context the United States would be identified as generous and "good" rather than as partially responsible for Mexico's poverty.

Remember that this expedition took place in the context of learning a language. As adjuncts to the language, Clare was taught about ancient and distant *cultures* (exemplified by her fascination with the Aztecs and Incas), along with present-day, physically nearer *poverty*. This pattern replicates the classic colonialist view of the conquered society: a view of past glories and present degradations (from which, within a colonialist ideology, it is the conqueror's duty to save the poor native).

Further, authentic difference of any kind was placed firmly outside Clare's home community. Asked about the possibility of practicing Spanish with Mexican American fellow students, Clare was unsure whether any of them spoke Spanish. She summed up this contradictory situation thus:

> *I think I was so—like I say, we never went to Mexico, we never had contact with other races, really, and if they were there I wasn't aware that they were from another race, I mean vaguely, only looking back on it.*

Toward the end of high school, social studies classes analyzing global inequality and her sister's involvement in the movement against the Vietnam War gave Clare a political outlook and a set of values that she felt were more "liberal" than those of most people in her family and hometown. Again the focus was largely outside her immediate community, however. The same was true of the process whereby Clare began to see *herself* as a culturally specific being:

> *I went away to college [in Minnesota] and I met . . . all these people who had a real sense of "I am Swedish," "I am Norwegian." And then when I went to [stay in] Mexico. That was the two strongest things, I think.*

The social geography of race for Clare differed from Beth's in the greater number of people of color she encountered and the ab-sence of the racially divided employer-employee relationships in the family. Her story also differed from Pat's in that racial difference was not in the forefront of consciousness, nor was there visible ongoing conflict.

One feature common to all three stories is white women's fear of people of color. As I have suggested, this fear needs careful analysis, both because of its prevalence and because it is an inversion of reality. In general, people of color have far more to fear from white people than vice versa, given, for example, the ongoing incidence of white supremacist terrorism around the United States, which targets African and Asian Americans, Latinos, Native Americans, and Jewish Americans (in addition to gay men and lesbians); and the problematic relationship with the police that leaves many communities of color with, at the very least, a sense that they lack legal and physical protection.

White people's fear of people of color is an inversion that can be contextualized in a number of ways. Most importantly, it must be understood as an element of racist discourse crucially linked to essentialist racism, or the idea that people of color are fundamentally Other than white people: different, inferior, less civilized, less human, more animal, than whites. Further, U.S. history is marked by many moments when the power of racist imagery constructing men of color as violent, dangerous, or sexually threatening has been renewed, as rationale or pretext for white hostility, in the context of political and economic conflicts between particular communities of color and white Americans. Thus, for example, a key aspect of white women's fear of Black men has to do with the persistent, racist image of the Black man as rapist. As Angela Davis has clarified, the production of this myth took place alongside the abolition of slavery and efforts by Black and white people toward reconstruction of the southern economy and polity along more racially egalitarian lines. The lynching of Black people was a means of social and political repression; accusations of rape were used as alibis for what were in effect politically motivated death squads. A discourse ostensibly about threat or danger was in fact a rationale for repression or control.

Similarly, it was in tandem with white, "nativist" movements for immigration control and economic protectionism that, from the late nineteenth century into the first decades of the twentieth, first Chinese, then Japanese, then Filipino male immigrants were represented in the white-owned press as sexually lascivious and physically violent. Most recently in the United States, in the context of the Los Angeles rebellion of May 1992, newspaper and television reports once again described African American protestors as "savage," "roving bands," engaged in a "feeding frenzy" of looting. More generally in the present, I would further speculate, white people's fear of men and women of color may have to do with the projection or awareness of the anger of individual people of color at white racism.

Beyond these few examples of contextualization, white people's fear of people of color and the distinctively gendered dimensions of it require far more extensive discussion than is possible here. It is also crucial to ask what "interrupts" or changes white people's fear of people of color: for those who are not afraid, what made, or makes, the difference? I do not know how to answer this question, but I register it here as an important one for us as white women to address.

QUASI INTEGRATION: SANDY ALVAREZ AND LOUISE GLEBOCKI

Sandy Alvarez and Louise Glebocki both grew up in contexts that I choose to call quasi-integrated, which is to say, seemingly or apparently integrated. I qualify "integration" in this way because it seems to me that true integration would require a broader antiracist social context than existed in the United States while Sandy and Louise were growing up. It might involve, for example, that no area of physical space be marked by racial hierarchy and that racist ideas be entirely absent—a situation that is impossible in the United States as it is presently constituted. As Sandy's and Louise's narratives show, neither woman's life circumstances in any sense placed her outside the system of racism. Their experience of close peer relationships with men and women of color nonetheless marks them off from the women I have discussed so far.

Both grew up in working-class families in Los Angeles. Sandy was born in 1948. She teaches English as a second language, in a high school. Her husband is Chicano and she has two small children. Louise was born in 1958. She cleans houses, not a job she enjoys but one that she feels is "OK for now." She described herself as always learning, growing, and active. She and her partner of seven years were about to get married at the time of the interview. Like Sandy's husband, he is Chicano.

Sandy Alvarez

Sandy said of the neighborhood where she lived before she was five years old:

The main things I remember . . . are some friends. . . . The Vernons were two sisters and they had a little brother too, just like our family, and they were Black. And the Frenches . . . they were white. . . . I'm only mentioning race because of this interview . . . as a kid it wasn't until I went to elementary school that I really became aware that these people were different races. Before that you just played with everybody.

From the beginning, Sandy had friends from various ethnic and racial groups. At five, she moved to a community, still in Los Angeles, that was, in her words, "equal thirds Japanese, Mexican, and white, with two Black families," and her friends reflected this mix. Sandy says that she played with Japanese boys and with the only girl in the neighborhood, who was in Sandy's terminology "Anglo." Her school friends were Mexican and white. Her "crushes" (again to use her word) and boyfriends were Anglo, Mexican, Guamanian. A Black woman who was Sandy's neighbor is to this day "like a second mother":

[She] is one of my dearest friends. She always thought of me as her daughter. She never had a daughter, and couldn't have any more kids. She really loves me and I really love her, and it's a real close relationship.

Looking at the differences between Sandy's experience and Beth's, the first and obvious precondition for Sandy's more racially mixed childhood is that people of color and whites were living nearer to each other. In addition, people responded to physical proximity in a particular way; it need not have led to the mixed friendship groups Sandy describes. The complex relationships between Pat and the Black children in her neighborhood contrast with the visiting back and forth between the Vernons and Sandy's household. The Vernon children would often stay overnight at her house.

The other major difference between Sandy as a child who grew up "integrated" and the other women I interviewed is her parents' standpoint. I asked Sandy what her mother thought of her having friends who were Black. She responded:

Well, my mother is really—she's a radical, politically. . . . The church we went to . . . the community had turned primarily Black and it was an all-white church and [my par-

ents] were really into helping to integrate the church.

Clearly, Sandy's mother was a woman unlikely to object to her children having Black friends—and for preschoolers, parental cooperation is key to social interaction. Less obvious but also extremely interesting was Sandy's awareness that her childhood was in this respect unusual, so that she cited her mother's activism to account for it. Given that it took work to integrate the church, Sandy's parents may well have been different from other whites in the neighborhood. Later in the interview, Sandy made explicit her sense of being different:

I don't know that a lot of people have had the integrated experience that we've had growing up, where it wasn't just our acquaintances but our real good friends and all our peers were of different races.

How are race and cultural difference conceptualized in this context? As she suggested earlier, Sandy felt that it was not until she was about six that she became aware of racial differences between herself and her peers. She explained:

In second grade . . . there are just two pictures in my mind, and I just remember a Black boy, about my age. I don't remember if he was just one of the things that made me aware . . . I just remember becoming aware different kids were different races. And this one girl that I'll never forget. I was really aware she was culturally different, because—she may not have been Mexican, she could have been Filipina, I don't know which culture—somehow I think she was Mexican because the neighborhood was about a third Mexican. But she'd wear her hair up in a bun, and, um, she must have been Asian, because she had those big chopsticks in her hair and in the playground she fell down and one went right inside her skull and they had to take her to emergency hospital. And, uh, I was just aware that was a big cultural difference, that I would never wear those in my hair.

Here, the specifics of cultural difference are perhaps more imaginary than real in any substantive sense. Sandy, drawing on her early memories and perceptions, did not know to which ethnic group the little girl belonged. The key here is not whether Sandy could answer this question correctly but her struggle as a child to make some sense of cultural difference. The two points to note here are, first, that Sandy was registering how cultural and race differences shape appearance and experience; and, second, that Sandy's awareness that her schoolmates and friends were culturally and racially different did *not* evoke fear, as it did for Clare and Pat.

It was not until many years later, Sandy said, that she was conscious of others seeing her as white and therefore belonging to a privileged group. When I asked her whether her awareness of race changed as she grew older, she said:

Sandy: *As you grow older you see how others perceive you, look at yourself. Before that you just act, you are who you are. In that sense [here she mentions a recent adult experience of feeling judged for being white] that's the only change.*

RF: *So in junior college and at university you were still "acting," rather than thinking about how you were acting?*

Sandy: *Yes.*

RF: *At any point in your life did you think of yourself as white?*

Sandy: *From elementary school on up I guess I was aware of that.*

Here, strikingly, whiteness is described as having been noted without any negative or positive charge—in contrast with most contexts, where white either stands for superiority or is neutralized and assumed. Else-

where—and this may be the most common experience for young white feminists of the 1980s—"white" is a concept learned simultaneously with a negative connotation of privilege. . . . For Sandy in this early period, however, "white" or "Anglo" merely described another ethnic group. One cannot help but see this as connected to the multiracial peer context within which she experienced her ethnicity: one in which, at least within the confines of home, elementary school, and the neighborhood, racial and ethnic identities were not hierarchically ordered.

However, it is important not to present a falsely utopian picture of Sandy's experience. Although her friendship groups were racially mixed, from preschool to college, she pointed out that there was racial tension and division elsewhere in the schools she attended. Nor was she immune to racist ideology. For example, she told me that a Black male school friend had asked her out on a date. She explained that she did not accept because she could not bring herself to face the stares she knew they would receive as an interracial, especially as a Black and white, couple. Sandy was not convinced by the myth that says only "bad" white women date Black men, but she was afraid to challenge it in public.

In other words, growing up in a racially mixed context did not mean that racism was absent, nor that the environment was not racially structured. Rather, Sandy was placed in a specific relationship to race difference and racism.

Louise Glebocki

Louise Glebocki, who was born in 1958, did not come from a family that used the languages of integration or antiracism, but she grew up with a more thoroughgoing connection with a community of color than the rest of the women I interviewed. Like Sandy,

Louise described growing up in Los Angeles. Having spent her first six years on the East Coast of the United States, Louise, with her mother and two older sisters, came west, moving

> *into a barrio, basically around all Spanish-speaking people. . . . Besides Mexicanos, the others that lived there were poor whites. . . . It was just a poor, small community.*

Right from the start, Louise and her sisters began having boyfriends. And more of Louise's boyfriends and female friends were Mexicano, or in other terms Chicano, than white:

Louise: *I remember I had a white boyfriend and then a Chicano one. But more I started hanging around more with the Chicanos. But both—always.*

RF: *How come you hung out more with the Chicanos?*

Louise: *To me they were more—at that point I did have white friends too. I don't know, there was just something real honest about them, and real friendly, and real close relationships formed, I remember, around a couple of girlfriends I had. Just visiting their families was a really nice atmosphere—kind of like ours. Because for a white family, while we were poor, we grew up [around] a lot of people. We had a lot of relatives in the L.A area. It was always a lot of activity, and hustle and bustle. And a lot of times I guess, among the whites, even if they were poor, it was kind of like more snobby, more uppity.*

In short, Louise viewed Chicano families as similar to her own, rather than different from it. Louise was also commenting here on class and people's perceptions of themselves. She suggested, in effect, that there was a link between class position and cultural style, linking her own working-class position with a liveliness shared with Chicano families. The suggestion is that other poor whites acted differently, aspiring to a style of life associated with a higher class position. Louise preferred the Chicanos' way of life, viewing it as more down to earth, more honest, and more like her own. Of course, Louise's words are adult ones: it is hard to know exactly what form these thoughts would have taken in the consciousness of a younger person.

In fact, Louise's extended family was not only similar to the Chicanos, part of it actually *was* Chicano. For as Louise explained, a number of her mother's sisters and brothers had Mexican American partners:

RF: *Did it feel to you like you were in a bicultural family, or a family with two cultures? . . .*

Louise: *I never looked at it like it was two separate cultures. I just kind of looked at it like, our family and our friends, they're Mexicans and Chicanos, and that was just part of our life.*

More than any of the other women described here, Louise had a childhood in which a community of color played a central role. The following description from Louise's narrative underlines three things: first, the closeness of Louise's connection to Chicano or Mexican American culture; second, the fact that at the same time, Louise and her relatives were clear that she was white; and third, the extent to which white culture remained, at least linguistically, Louise's point of reference:

RF: *If you would go to your aunt's house or your uncle's house, would there be things about how their house was and how they raised their kids, things that they would have on the walls or would do, that came from the fact that it was a partly Mexican and partly white household?*

Louise: *Yeah. Like I remember my aunt, she was married to this Mexican dude. And his background was really, strongly into the whole Mexican scene. . . . He was real strong in terms of what he was. I mean, he would never want to be anything else but Mexican. And he had a real strong "machismo." He had something like thirteen kids in his previous marriage. . . . And she really took all that in. In fact, she's still constantly like that . . . her attitude is, well, a woman should be a woman, and in her place—the whole mentality was, I don't know, really a trip.*

But I remember like, with these relatives, the Chicanos, they would always joke around, you know, around us being Polish, and white. There would be a lot of joking about it and stuff, oh you know, "You honkies gotta learn more" and stuff.

And in terms of their house? They'd play a lot of Mexican music, and a lot of regular music, and have stuff on the Indians up on the walls, and from Mexico.

There are interesting contradictions and complexities here. On the one hand, Louise said that she did not conceptualize the two cultures as separate, yet it is clearly possible for her to do so descriptively. The sense of Chicano culture as more sexist (assuming that "machismo" connotes sexism in Louise's usage of it) is jarring, given Louise's statement that Chicano culture was better, more "in tune with reality." The distinction between Mexican and "regular" music suggests that the dominant culture remained the reference point in her description. However, Louise was also conscious of her whiteness in this description, as, it seems, were her Chicano relatives. The use of the usually negative "honkies" to describe Louise and her white family members suggests that no one lost sight of the wider context of race conflict, either. "Taming" the word *honkie* by joking about it suggests a context in which it has been possible to situationally subvert and play with external hierarchies.

Curiously, despite this mix of relatives on her mother's side of the family, Louise's father had very different ideas, including, as Louise put it, "racist tendencies." For example:

My parents had been saving money, and they wanted to buy a house. . . . I'm pretty sure one of the things my dad really emphasized was . . . a nice, white community.

Although the family moved to a white section of a small town in the Los Angeles area, their situation did not change much

because our school just ended up being pretty poor, and the majority was Chicanos, and a lot of them were people who had just come over from Mexico, so there was a lot of Spanish-speaking people. And there was a whole section of whites, too, but it wasn't this pure, middle-class, white area, it was once again a real mixture.

Through school and into adulthood, Louise continued to be close friends with Chicanos, as much as or more than with whites. . . . But like Sandy, she may well have been unusual in this, for she described increasing racial and cultural conflict among students throughout her school career:

When we were in elementary school, everybody was together, playing. By junior high, things started really dividing up, into groups of people. Hey! By high school—to me, the school system really helped set it down. You had your sections. By that time, you had a whole section of these white racists that were into surfing—very outspoken on being racist. I just started seeing a whole lot of divisions—a whole lot of different lifestyles coming together and just crashing. . . . Low riders, . . . gangs. Things started becoming more segregated, more separate.

Louise described the "surfers'" attempts to recruit her to their side, and her refusal to move over: "I saw myself with pride as an antiracist white."

She also saw herself as Polish, identified as such by her surname:

We had to put up with . . . a lot of racist, Polish jokes, but I looked at it—I just laughed, you know, I just looked at it like, "It doesn't bother me! I feel great!"

In Louise's life, then, despite her own connections to Chicano culture, explicit racial conflict was as visible in her environment as in Pat Bowen's in Maryland. Louise responded to it, though, by means of a much more explicit antiracism.

Despite the extent to which Sandy and Louise grew up with close ties with Chicano (and in Sandy's case, also Black and Asian) people as well as whites or "Anglos," there are reasons to argue that experiences like Sandy's and Louise's represent only a partial or qualified integration. Nor can they be anything else in a racist society, if racial integration is taken to mean the absence of race hierarchy and racist ideas. In fact, Sandy's was an integrating family rather than a family living in an integrated environment. This was also true for two of the other women whose childhoods were marked by what I call a quasi integration. Their parents were also radicals, and both of them felt it necessary to offer this fact to explain a state of affairs they know to be abnormal (although desirable) in a racist society. All of these women encountered racial hierarchy and racist mythology once they were outside a limited, protected space.

CONCLUSION

In all of these narratives, landscape and the experience of it were racially structured—whether those narratives seemed to be marked predominantly by the presence or the absence of people of color. This is of course not to say that race was the only organizing principle of the social context. Class intersected with race in differentiating Pat's and Beth's relationships with Black communities and as part of the context for the quasi-integrated experiences of Louise and Sandy. Controls on sexuality link up with racism to create hostility toward relationships between African American men and white women.

Once a person is in a landscape structured by racism, a conceptual mapping of race, of self and others, takes shape, following from and feeding the physical context. Thus, for example, Sandy experienced the term "Anglo" initially without any negative or positive connotation; Clare both saw through the lens of racial stratification in her own environment *and* did not perceive racial stratification as such. Even the presence or absence of people of color seemed to be as much a social-mental construct as a social-physical one: recall the invisible African American and Latina domestic workers in some apparently all-white homes.

This analysis has some implications for a definition of racism. First of all, it clarifies and makes concrete some of the forms—some subtle, some obvious—that race privilege and racism may take in the lives of white women: educational and economic inequality, verbal assertions of white superiority, the maintenance of all-white neighborhoods, the "invisibility" of Black and Latina domestic workers, white people's fear of people of color, and the "colonial" notion that the cultures of peoples of color were great only in the past. In this context, it would be hard to maintain the belief that race only affects the lives of people of color. Moreover, racism emerges not only as an ideology or political orientation chosen or rejected at will but also as a system of material relationships with a set of ideas linked to and embedded in those material relations.

The racial structuring of white experience as it emerged in each of these narratives is complex. It is contradictory: the two women most explicitly raised to espouse racist ideas, Beth Ellison and Pat Bowen, found moments and situations, however fleeting, in which to question the racist status quo. Conversely, Sandy Alvarez and Louise Glebocki, raised to find ways in which to challenge racism, were nonetheless not outside its reach: racism as well as antiracism shaped their environments, and both women drew at times on white-centered logics in describing and living their lives.

These women's accounts of their environments were also mobile. All five indicated in various ways that, with hindsight, they had become more cognizant of the patterning of their earlier experiences: phrases like "now that we're talking about this I remember" and "I was so unaware of cultural difference that" signal both lack of awareness of racism *and* moments of recognition or realization of it. "Experience" emerged here as a complicated concept. As the narratives showed, there are multiple ways in which experiences can be named, forgotten, or remembered through changing conceptual schemata. . . . Race shaped the lives of all the women I interviewed in complex ways, at times explicitly articulated and at other times unspoken but nonetheless real.

Questions for Understanding and Critical Thinking

1. Why are relationships of closeness or distance and issues of equality or inequality between people of color and white people important as children grow up?
2. Is it possible to predict a relationship between people's ways of growing up and their perspectives as adults? Why or why not?
3. How did class intersect with race in differentiating some of the women's relationships with African American communities?
4. Would Frankenberg's findings regarding the social geography of race have been similar if men had been included in her study? Why or why not?

ARTICLE 11 _____

In this article, sociologists David H. Demo and Michael Hughes investigate the primary socialization experiences of a national sample of African American adults to ascertain how parental messages may influence people's racial identity. Note the three distinct dimensions of African American identity that the authors identify and see how they support the hypothesis that group identity is shaped by the content of parental socialization. What is the relationship between societal racial inequality and African American social identity and self-perception according to Demo and Hughes?

David H. Demo teaches in the Department of Human Development and Family Studies at the University of Missouri, Columbia. Michael Hughes is a faculty member in the Department of Sociology at Virginia Polytechnic Institute.

Looking Ahead

1. What is racial socialization and why is it important?
2. What part does the social class of the family play in children's socialization?
3. What conclusions do Demo and Hughes reach pertaining to determinants of African American identity and self-perception?

Socialization and Racial Identity among Black Americans

◆ *David H. Demo and Michael Hughes*

Studies of black group identity generally have taken two approaches. One is to examine the effects of group identification and group consciousness on other variables such as political participation (Miller, Gurin, Gurin, and Malanchuk 1981), racial militancy (Marx 1967; Tomlinson 1970), personal efficacy (Gurin and Epps 1975; Hughes and Demo 1989), and minority group self-esteem (Hughes and Demo 1989; Kardiner and Ovesey 1951; Pettigrew 1964). The second is to identify the socioeconomic and demographic determinants of black identity (Allen, Dawson, and Brown 1989; Broman, Neighbors, and Jackson 1988). Few scholars, however, have examined the influence of various social factors over the life course on racial identity of black adults. The central objective of this study is to examine the impact of socialization experiences and social

Source: From David H. Demo and Michael Hughes, "Socialization and Racial Identity among Black Americans," in *Social Psychology Quarterly,* 1990, 53(4), pp. 364–374. Reprinted by permission of the American Sociological Association.

structural arrangements in both childhood and adulthood on various dimensions of racial identity among black adults.

BACKGROUND

Black Identity

As sub-units of the self-concept, identities are "meanings a person attributes to the self as an object in a social situation or social role" (Burke 1980, p. 18). Structurally, being black in American society means occupying a racially defined status; associated with this status are roles in family, community, and society. One psychological consequence of being black is black group identity, the intensity of which should vary with the nature of role experiences.

The literature on racial identity (e.g., Broman et al. 1988; Gurin, Miller, and Gurin 1980) uses this concept fairly consistently to refer to "the feeling of closeness to similar others in ideas, feelings, and thoughts" (Broman et al. p. 148). Yet as suggested in Cross's (1985) discussion of black reference group orientation and Allen et al.'s (1989) study of the African American belief system, black group identity is clearly multidimensional and includes not only in-group factors such as closeness to other blacks and black separatism, but also racial group evaluation.

Factors That Influence Black Identity

Yancey, Ericksen, and Juliani (1976) and Taylor (1979) argue that ethnicity is an emergent phenomenon arising from structural conditions and processes in American society, and that sociologists "have generally failed to identify the *internal* forces of the black community which have contributed to this emergent phenomenon" (Taylor 1979, p. 1403, author's emphasis).

Two recent empirical studies demonstrate the importance of social and demographic factors for racial identity among black adults. Broman et al. (1988) found that people who were older, southern, rural, and less educated scored higher on an index measuring closeness to other blacks. Allen et al. (1989) found that socioeconomic status was related negatively to closeness to other blacks and black autonomy but positively to favorable evaluations of blacks as a group. They also found that religiosity and exposure to black-oriented media were related less strongly, but positively, to black identity variables. Neither of these studies considers the importance of social background, socialization, or social interaction variables that may be important determinants of black identity.

Childhood Socialization The family context is generally regarded as the most influential socialization setting for forming the child's emerging sense of self, values, and beliefs (e.g., Gecas 1981). The significance of familial relations is evident in the amount, scope, and intensity of parent-child interaction; in the ongoing, reciprocal processes of attachment, identification, modeling, and role-playing; and in the impact of familial relationships on children's dispositions toward self and others (Demo, Small, and Savin-Williams 1987; Gecas and Schwalbe 1986). Through these processes socialization serves to transmit values, norms, morals, and beliefs from one generation to the next.

Peter's analysis of racial socialization in black families suggests that "building self-respect and pride concerning their racial identity undergirds every parent's child-rearing philosophy" (1985, p. 165). Although the literature discusses problems of racial socialization (e.g., Boykin and Toms 1985), there is little empirical evidence regarding the *content* of parental socialization or its role in the development of racial identity.

Interracial interaction during the pre-adult years also structures interpersonal experiences in ways that may influence racial identity profoundly. Rosenberg (1975, 1979) demonstrated that dissonant racial contexts affect racial group identification adversely by increasing exposure to prejudiced communications and to out-group norms, values, and attitudes. Similarly, McGuire, McGuire, Child, and Fujioka (1978) showed that awareness of one's ethnicity decreases as the ethnic group becomes less distinct (or more integrated) in the social environment. Thus we would expect interracial contact to influence black identity negatively.

The social class of the family of origin may be particularly important because it structures opportunities and resources for children, the types of schools they attend, the friends they have, and the values and attitudes to which they are exposed (Gecas 1979). Following the literature on social structure and personality, however, we would expect much of the effect of parents' social class on racial identity to be indirect, operating through microsocial interaction processes such as parental socialization and interracial contact.

Adult Socialization. The empirical literature on determinants of racial group identification among black adults is even more limited than that among children. One important reason is that socialization theory and research have focused on children and generally have neglected the social psychological processes shaping the identity of adults. An important question is the degree to which adult social structure and social process variables affect black identity independent of childhood background and socialization variables. Analysts of the life course point to the

crucial impact of adult roles on personality (Clausen 1986; Elder 1981; Gecas and Mortimer 1987). Adults' cognitive processes also are more advanced and more sophisticated than children's; they are characterized by dialectical reasoning (Basseches 1984) and peak intellectual abilities (Horn and Donaldson 1980; Schaie 1983). Thus the social and cognitive-developmental processes bearing on adults' identity and self-concept are different from the processes bearing on those of children (Suls and Mullen 1982).

Studies suggest that the quality of interpersonal relations with family and friends, religious involvement, socioeconomic status, interracial interaction, and age should be important determinants of black identity.

Family and Friends: An important context for the formation of adult attitudes toward self and others is interpersonal relations with family and friends (Demo et al. 1987; Gecas and Mortimer 1987). A recent study (Hughes and Demo 1989) demonstrated that the quality of social relationships with family and friends is an important determinant of self-esteem (also see Hoelter 1982) as well as of racial self-esteem (what we refer to in this paper as racial group evaluation), and is correlated positively with measures of black separatism and feelings of closeness to other blacks.

Religious Involvement: Another important interpersonal dimension of black socialization is religious involvement. The church provides opportunities for blacks to occupy important and respected positions that may be denied them in the wider society; it also creates experiences and relationships that bolster self-respect, evaluations of one's racial group (Hughes and Demo 1989), and psychological well-being (Ortega, Crutchfield, and Rushing 1983).

Socioeconomic Status: As noted above, two recent studies (Allen et al. 1989; Broman et al. 1988) show that socioeconomic status is related negatively to feelings of closeness to other blacks. In addition, Allen et al. (1989) found that socioeconomic status was related negatively to black autonomy and positively to evaluations of blacks as a group. These findings suggest that integration into the social and economic mainstream of American society has important consequences for various dimensions of black identity, but these effects could be due to variables other than socioeconomic status.

Adult Interracial Interaction: Work by Rosenberg and Simmons (1972) and Rosenberg (1979) suggests that as blacks move out of isolated environments and interact more frequently with whites and members of other groups, they are detached to some degree from traditional black culture, and group identification is weakened. Broman et al. (1988) demonstrate that education, urban residence, and residence in regions other than the south and the northeast are associated with weakened group identification among black adults.

Age: Age locates blacks in particular sociohistorical contexts. Porter and Washington (1979) and Cross (1985) suggest that social changes stemming from the black movement may strengthen racial identity and may have the greatest effect on younger blacks. Although some evidence supports this view (Krystall, Friedman, Howze, and Epps 1970; Toomer 1975), a more recent study reports stronger racial identification among older blacks (Broman et al. 1988).

The Problem

Empirical studies of identity development in childhood are limited because they employ only a limited range of explanatory factors and are not very helpful in understanding adult identity. Empirical studies of adult black identity have shown what demographic variables are related to black identity but have not illuminated the impact of family background and childhood experience. Further, there are no studies that examine both childhood and adult experiences as they relate to adult racial identity.

In particular, we do not know how the following factors affect adult black identity: parents' socioeconomic status, content of parental socialization, preadult interracial contact, quality of family and friendship relations, and adult interracial contact. In our analysis we examine these factors along with religious involvement, current socioeconomic status, gender, and age. The two primary questions we ask concern 1) the effects of family background and socialization on black identity, and 2) whether family background and socialization variables account for the previously documented relationship between socioeconomic status and black identity.

DATA AND METHODS

The Sample

The National Survey of Black Americans (NSBA) data were collected in 1979–80 by the Survey Research Center, Institute for Social Research, University of Michigan; a multistage sampling procedure was used. The response rate was approximately 69 percent. The NSBA is a nationally representative sample involving interviews with 2,107 black Americans 18 years of age and older. Robert Taylor (1986) observed that the demographic composition of the sample is comparable to that of the general black population except that the sample contains an overrepresentation of women (61%), is slightly older, and is less western. Other details concerning the data set and sampling procedure may be found in Jackson and Gurin (1987, pp. i–vii);

a demographic profile of the sample is available in Broman et al. (1988).

Variables

Dependent Variables: Black Identity. Because racial identity is multidimensional (Cross 1985; Porter and Washington 1979; also see Allen et al. 1989), in the present study we use three measures that tap black identity in somewhat different ways.

Feelings of Closeness to Other Blacks: Our measure of black identity is based on a measure developed by Gurin et al. (1980) for use in their study of racial group identification among black adults, and is nearly identical to the measure used by Broman et al. (1988). Respondents were asked how close they felt to eight different classifications of black people: 1) poor, 2) religious, 3) young, 4) middle-class, 5) working-class, 6) older, 7) elected officials, and 8) professional people. Scores were summed for each respondent and then were averaged across the eight items. The alpha reliability coefficient for the scale is .82. [Ed. note: A reliability coefficient is a measure of the extent to which the results of the research should be correct.] If responses were missing on three or fewer of the items, we entered the mean response of the items with valid responses for the missing data.

Black Separatism: This scale, also used by Allen and Hatchett (1986) and Hughes and Demo (1989), measures commitment to African culture and the degree to which blacks should confine their social relationships to other blacks. A virtually identical scale is used by Allen et al. (1989) and is termed "black autonomy." Respondents were asked whether they agreed with the following: 1) black children should learn an African language, 2) blacks should always vote for black candidates when possible, 3) black women should not date white men, 4) black

people should shop in black-owned shops whenever possible, 5) black men should not date white women, 6) black parents should give their children African names. The responses were coded as follows: 1 = strongly disagree, 2 = disagree, 3 = agree, and 4 = strongly agree. Because the two questions on dating were correlated very strongly, they were combined into a single item by averaging the responses. The resulting five items were averaged for each respondent. These items yield an alpha reliability coefficient of .61. Our estimate of the reliability of this scale is lower than that presented by Allen and Hatchett (1986) because we combine the two highly correlated items on dating into one variable. If responses were missing on two or fewer of the five items, we entered the mean response on the items with valid responses for the missing data.

Black Group Evaluation: The operationalization of this variable is not standardized. Porter and Washington (1979) use the term "racial self-esteem" to refer to "how the individual feels about the self as black, i.e., about his group identity" (p. 54). Similarly, we operationalize black group evaluation as the belief that most black people possess positive characteristics and do not possess negative characteristics. The measurement amounts to an overall evaluation of black people as a group; Allen and Hatchett (1986) used the same items to examine what they term black group perception. The question was worded: "How true do you think it is that most black people _____?" The question was completed with the following characteristics: 1) keep trying, 2) love their families, 3) are ashamed, 4) are lazy, 5) neglect their families, 6) are lying and trifling, 7) are hardworking, 8) do for others, 9) give up easily, 10) are weak, 11) are proud of themselves, 12) are honest, 13) are selfish, 14) are strong. Responses were coded as follows: 1 = true, 2 = somewhat true, 3 = a little true, and

4 = not true at all. We recoded responses so that all items were in the positive direction. The alpha reliability coefficient for this scale is .80.

Socialization Variables

Family and Friendships: We used three items assessing closeness of and satisfaction with family relationships and one item assessing the respondent's role as a friend. Four response categories were provided for each question: 1) "Would you say your family members are very close in their feelings to each other, fairly close, not too close, or not close at all?" 2) "How satisfied are you with your family life, that is, the time you spend and the things you do with members of your family?" 3) "Given the chances you have had, how well have you done in taking care of your family's wants and needs?" 4) "Given the chances you have had, how well have you done at being a good friend?"

Religious Involvement: The items are as follows: 1) "How often do you usually attend religious services?" 2) "How religious would you say you are?" 3) "How often do you read religious books or other religious materials?" The alpha reliability coefficient for this scale is .71.

Interracial Contact: The items in the survey measuring interracial contact show the respondent's level of involvement with white people over his or her lifetime. Respondents were asked to judge the racial composition of eight social settings in their life: 1) grammar or elementary school, 2) junior high school, 3) high school, 4) college, 5) neighborhood while growing up, 6) present neighborhood, 7) church or place of worship usually attended, 8) present workplace, if employed. Responses were coded as follows: 1 = all blacks, 2 = mostly blacks, 3 = about half blacks, 4 = mostly whites, 5 = almost all whites. From these items we constructed two measures of interracial contact: 1) a preadult interracial contact scale (Items 1, 2, 3, 4, and 5), and 2) an adult interracial contact scale (Items 6, 7, and 8). For each scale we calculated the average score over the items containing valid data for each respondent. If there were no valid responses across the eight items, we coded the variable as missing data for that respondent.

Parental Socialization: In order to develop a measure of how respondents were socialized by their parents concerning what it is to be black in America, we examined responses to a complex set of questions included in the NSBA. Respondents were asked open-ended questions concerning the most important things they had told their children to help them know *what it is to be black* and *how to get along with white people.* Respondents whose socialization by their parents differed from their socialization of their own children, respondents who had not taught their own children anything about these matters, and respondents with no children were asked directly what their parents had taught them about what it is to be black and what other things they had been told about getting along with whites.[1] If respondents stated that they socialized their own children in the same way as they were socialized as children, we took their indication of their own children's socialization as an indication of how they had been socialized.

Initially we constructed two measures; one indicated what the respondent had been taught about what it is to be black, and the other indicated other things the respondent had been told about getting along with whites. For both variables we used the NSBA classification scheme (see Jackson and Gurin 1987) and collapsed the responses further into four categories: 1) respondent was taught to take an *individualistic and/or universalistic* attitude without specific racial references: work hard, excel, take a positive attitude toward self, be a good citizen, all are equal; 2) respondent was taught to take a positive group-oriented *integrative/assertive* attitude: racial pride, importance of black heritage, acceptance of being black, importance of getting along with whites, try to understand whites, stand up for rights; 3) respondent was taught a group-oriented *cautious/defensive* attitude: social distance, deference, white prejudice, whites have the power; and 4) respondent was taught nothing about being black or getting along with whites.

We constructed three dummy variables (1 = individualistic/universalistic, 0 = other; 1 = integrative/assertive, 0 = other; and 1 = cautious/defensive, 0 = other) for each of the two basic parental socialization variables (what respondent had been taught about *what it is to be black,* and what other things respondent had been taught about *getting along with whites*), creating a total of six dummy variables. Because the two original questions are linked (the second one asks about what "other" things respondent was taught), we constructed three final variables for the analysis by summing 1) the two individualistic/universalistic variables, 2) the two integrative/assertive variables, and 3) the two cautious/defensive variables.[2]

Age: Age is the self-reported age of the respondent in years.

Adult Socioeconomic Status: Our measure of current socioeconomic status combines the z-score for respondent's education (which was recorded in 18 one-year categories from 0 through 17 or more, inclusive) with the z-score for respondent's occupational prestige (see Hughes and Demo 1989), weighting each equally.

Parents' Socioeconomic Status: Respondents were asked: "When you were growing up, what was the main job of your father?" They also were asked: "How many years of school did your father complete?" The same questions were asked about the respondent's mother. The survey does not provide the three-digit occupation code for parents' occupations, so no occupational prestige scores could be assigned. Instead, after the interview, parents' occupations were coded into 31 categories ordered roughly by prestige. Education was coded as for the respondent.

Unfortunately, there were so many missing data on parents' education that we could not use this variable directly in determining parents' socioeconomic status. Instead we relied on the occupational prestige of the parent with the higher rating. If the rating was missing for one parent, we used the rating for the other. We reclassified both father's and mother's occupation into eight ranked occupational prestige categories. Because Glenn's (1963) analysis demonstrated the primacy of education as a prestige indicator among black Americans, we confirmed the prestige orderings for both father's and mother's occupation by examining the correlation between education and the occupational prestige indicator for those cases in which education was available. The correlation (r) between mean parental education and our occupational prestige indicator is .50 for mothers and .46 for fathers.

The eight categories are as follows: 1) farmers, 2) service workers and unskilled laborers, 3) operatives, including transport, 4) craftsmen, foremen, government protective service workers (police, etc.), and members of the armed forces, 5) small business persons, 6) clerical and sales workers, 7) managers, 8) professionals.

FINDINGS

Table 1 presents the correlation matrix along with means and standard deviations. The major point illustrated by these data is the multidimensionality of black identity. Although our three indicators of black identity

TABLE 1 / Correlations, Means, and Standard Deviations, Aspects of Black Identity

	(1)	(2)	(3)	(4)	(5)	(6)	(7)	(8)	(9)	(10)	(11)	(12)	(13)	(14)	(15)	(16)	(17)
(1) Black separatism	1.00																
(2) Closeness to other blacks	.278**	1.00															
(3) Black group evaluation	.076**	.089**	1.00														
(4) Individualistic/universalistic	.031	.031	.054*	1.00													
(5) Integrative/assertive	.015	.093**	.012	-.197**	1.00												
(6) Cautious/defensive	.066*	.062**	-.026	-.187**	-.193*	1.00											
(7) Interracial contact (preadult)	-.195**	-.241**	.045	.026	.020	-.101**	1.00										
(8) Parents' SES	-.127**	-.162**	.028	.036	-.001	-.096**	.244**	1.00									
(9) Family closeness	.037	.202**	.125**	.053*	.042	-.004	-.033	.010	1.00								
(10) Family satisfaction	.115**	.263**	.057**	.060**	.063**	-.015	-.147**	-.108**	.245**	1.00							
(11) Caring for family	.068**	.200**	.032	.044*	.009	.018	-.126**	-.058*	.116**	.253**	1.00						
(12) Being good friend	.061**	.212**	.057*	.044*	.007	.011	-.016	.031	.081**	.156**	.263**	1.00					
(13) Interracial contact (adult)	-.163**	-.173**	.140**	.018	.022	-.063**	.348**	.172**	.007	-.133**	-.048*	-.101	1.00				
(14) Religious involvement	.080**	.349**	.011	.064**	.074**	.082**	-.182**	-.131**	.155**	.179**	.196**	.159**	-.083**	1.00			
(15) Adult SES	-.225**	-.244**	.132**	.025	-.012	-.065**	.305**	.353**	.062**	-.169**	-.055	-.012	.340**	-.104**	1.00		
(16) Female	-.040	-.099	-.019	-.038	-.020	-.030	.003	-.004	-.025	-.006	.107**	.050*	-.100**	.208**	.30	1.00	
(17) Age	.163**	.292**	-.012	.058**	-.018	.124**	-.289**	-.269**	.073**	.222**	.231	.092**	-.197**	.368**	-.424**	.020	1.00
Mean	2.96	3.36	3.05	.387	.424	.322	1.83	3.04	3.48	3.39	4.54	4.72	2.01	2.38	.02	.62	43.15
Standard Deviation	.72	.51	.44	.59	.61	.57	.90	1.95	.74	.75	.65	.51	.76	.88	.49	.49	17.71

Ns range between 1849 and 2087.

*p ≤ .05

**p ≤ .01

are related positively to each other, as one would expect, the correlations are not so high as to suggest that all three variables are tapping the same underlying dimension. For example, black group evaluation has correlations of .076 and .089, respectively, with black separatism and feelings of closeness to other blacks.

In Table 2 we present the results of stepwise regression analyses in which preadult socialization influences were entered first, followed by adulthood variables. For all three indicators of black identity, age is unrelated; socioeconomic status of family of origin is unrelated when adult socialization variables are included in the analysis. The latter finding is consistent with our expectation that the influence of early socioeconomic conditions would be indirect, operating through adult social experiences.

When we examine feelings of closeness to other blacks, the data show that the strongest correlates include two preadult influences: integrative/assertive parental socialization and interracial contact. Three aspects of adult socialization are quite important: interpersonal relations with family and friends, religious involvement, and so-

TABLE 2 / Standardized Regression Coefficients Showing the Impact of Socialization and Social Structural Variables on Dimensions of Black Identity and Black Group Evaluation

	Closeness to Other Blacks		Black Separatism		Black Group Evaluation	
	(Preadult variables)	(All variables)	(Preadult variables)	(All variables)	(Preadult variables)	(All variables)
Preadult Variables						
Parental socialization						
Individualistic/universalistic	.084**	.018	.057*	.041	.067*	.054*
Integrative/assertive	.136**	.081**	.068**	.057*	.008	.002
Cautious/defensive	.086**	.038	.059*	.043	.000	.000
Interracial contact	−.235**	−.117**	−.170**	−.098**	.023	−.022
Parents' SES	−.080**	−.008	−.071**	−.012	.026	−.018
Adulthood Variables						
Quality of family and friendship						
Family closeness		.108**		.018		.084**
Family satisfaction		.106**		.031		.035
Caring for family		.056*		.012		.002
Being good friend		.124**		.046		.068**
Interracial contact		−.038		−.084**		.132**
Religious involvement		.234**		−.007		−.023
Adult SES		−.130**		−.142**		.113**
Female		−.076**		−.037		.000
Age		.043		.036		.055
R^2	.094**	.261**	.048**	.088*	.006	.053**
N	(1559)		(1556)		(1558)	

*p < .05
**p < .001

cioeconomic attainment. Adult interracial contact is unrelated to feelings of closeness to other blacks. The findings and conclusions presented by Broman et al. (1988) and Allen et al. (1989) are supported strongly by the fact that adult socioeconomic status is related negatively to closeness and separatism and positively to black group evaluation after background, socialization, and social relationship variables are controlled.

Examining the data for both feelings of closeness and black separatism reveals some similarities in the correlates of these two indicators. When preadult and adulthood variables are entered in the analysis, it is evident that blacks who were reared in an integrative/assertive manner ("don't be prejudiced, recognize all races as equal, treat whites the way you want to be treated") identified more closely with black people, their history, and their culture than did blacks who were reared in an individualistic/universalistic manner ("be yourself, take care of yourself, you're as good as anyone else, work hard") or in a cautious/defensive manner ("whites believe they are superior, blacks don't have the chances whites have, don't ever put your trust in whites"). Preadult interracial contact, however, is related inversely to feelings of closeness and black separatist attitudes; this finding supports Rosenberg's (1975, 1979) contention that dissonant racial contexts detract from blacks' feelings of group identification and attachment.

These two indicators also show important differences. In contrast to feelings of closeness, black separatism is unaffected by religious involvement or interpersonal relations with family and friends. Further, interracial contact during adulthood is related negatively to black separatism, a phenomenon paralleling the effect of integration earlier in the life course.

The only primary socialization variable that is related significantly to black group evaluation is individualistic/universalistic socialization. Examining adulthood variables, we found that close social relationships with family and friends are associated with positive group evaluation, as are interracial contact and socioeconomic attainment. These results contrast sharply with our findings regarding feelings of closeness, which are influenced (negatively) by interracial contact in the childhood and adolescent years. This finding suggests marked differences in the impact of preadult and adult experiences on dimensions of racial identity.

DISCUSSION AND CONCLUSIONS

The three distinct dimensions of black identity examined in this study are affected differently by predictor variables. This suggests that it is reasonable to conceptualize black identity as a multidimensional phenomenon, and that being black means different things to different segments of the black population.

The findings also support the hypothesis that group identity is shaped by the content of parental socialization. Compared to blacks who do not remember their parents telling them anything about being black or getting along with whites, those who were reared in an integrative/assertive manner or a cautious/defensive manner had stronger feelings of closeness to other blacks and a stronger commitment to black separatism. Individualistic or universalistic messages from parents enhanced black group evaluation weakly but positively among adults in our sample. There is also evidence that parental socialization has broader consequences in that cautious/defensive messages were related inversely to interracial contact during both preadult and adult years.

Our findings regarding parental socialization and interpersonal relationships in black families substantiate the important role of black families in providing social support and familial bonds (Hill 1972; McAdoo 1978; Stack 1974; Taylor 1986). The data show that feelings of closeness and black group evaluation are enhanced by positive interpersonal relations with family and friends, and thus confirm the importance of these resources to black Americans.

Using the same data set that we analyzed, Broman et al. (1988) report that age is an important variable in that older blacks have stronger racial identification. Yet the results of our regression analysis involving age and other predictors of feelings of closeness (nearly identical to the racial identification scale used by Broman et al.) show that age is unrelated to dimensions of group identity. This finding suggests that the effects of age are explained by religious involvement and close family relations, both of which are stronger among older blacks. In analyses not presented here but similar to those presented in Table 2, we found that compared to their elders, younger blacks assign greater importance to being black; this result supports the findings of other investigators (Krystall et al. 1970; Toomer 1975) and suggests that some dimensions of black identity may be associated with age. These inconsistencies across studies provide further evidence of the multidimensionality of black identity and suggest that if we are to understand the formation of racial identity over the life course, we must understand more fully the nature of its different dimensions.

The relationships between interracial interaction and black identity variables suggest that the impact of interracial interaction depends on its timing in the life course. Such contact during childhood and adolescence—when youths are striving to attain a sense of who they are and what they stand for—has a negative impact on the in-group variables, namely closeness and black separatism. In contrast, interracial relationships during adulthood promote positive black group evaluation. One explanation for the latter finding is that racial integration in neighborhoods and workplaces represents the fulfillment of individual and group goals, thus bolstering racial pride. A second explanation is suggested by the work of McGuire et al. (1978), who show that members of minority groups are more aware of their distinctiveness and their ethnicity than are members of majority groups. The heightened salience of one's ethnicity, coupled with the self-esteem motive, may lead blacks (and others) to evaluate positively the characteristics of their group. Further evidence of this view is provided by Lau (1989), who demonstrates that "the more strongly other people treat a person as part of a group, the more strongly will that group become a part of the person's social identity" (p. 222).

The pattern of effects for socioeconomic status parallels the pattern for interracial interaction. Both variables have a generally negative effect on closeness and separatism variables but a positive effect on black group evaluation. These findings suggest that institutional racial inequality may promote black identity in the sense of increasing in-group concerns, but that it tends also to promote a negative evaluation of blacks as a group. If there are declines in institutional inequality that are associated with socioeconomic advancement and decreasing racial segregation, the character of black identity should change such that less emphasis is placed on in-group concerns and more on positive group characteristics.

The negative impact of inequality on black group evaluation echoes our earlier finding that institutional inequality and discrimination inhibit the development of personal efficacy among black Americans (Hughes and Demo 1989). These findings are important because numerous studies have examined self-esteem and have concluded that racial inequality has little or no impact on black self-perception. The accumulating evidence suggests that self-esteem is too narrow a focus to warrant such a conclusion, and that although self-esteem may be insulated from macrosocial systems of social inequality, other aspects of black identity and self-perception are affected adversely.

ENDNOTES

1. Although first-, second-, and third-mentioned responses were included in the data, we used only first-mentioned responses in our analyses because of the paucity of second- and third-mentioned responses.

2. In our development of these three categories of racial socialization, we were guided in part by Boykin and Toms (1985, p. 46), who discuss the "triple quandary" facing black adults in their socialization of children: "socialization in the mainstream of American society, socialization informed by oppressed minority status, and socialization linked to a proximal Black cultural context that is largely noncommensurate with the social dictates of mainstream American life." Our scheme thus distinguishes socialization patterns that promote racial awareness (integrative/assertive and cautious/defensive) from those which emphasize a nonracial orientation (individualistic/universalistic) and distinguish those which mostly emphasize mainstream involvement (integrative/assertive and individualistic/universalistic) from those with a more alienated orientation (cautious/defensive). We also distinguish between positive and generally integrative racial awareness (integrative/assertive) and that which is more detached (cautious/defensive).

REFERENCES

Allen, Richard L., Michael C. Dawson, and Ronald E. Brown. 1989. "A Schema-Based Approach to Modeling an African-American Racial Belief System." *American Political Science Review* 83:421–41.

Allen, Richard L. and Shirley Hatchett. 1986. "The Media and Social Reality Effects: Self and System Orientations of Blacks." *Communication Research* 13:97–123.

Basseches, Michael. 1984. *Dialectical Reasoning and Adult Development*. Norwood, NJ: Ablex.

Boykin, A. Wade and Forrest D. Toms. 1985. "Black Child Socialization: A Conceptual Framework." Pp. 33–51 in *Black Children: Social, Educational, and Parental Environments*, edited by Harriette Pipes McAdoo and John Lewis McAdoo. Beverly Hills: Sage.

Broman, Clifford L., Harold W. Neighbors, and James S. Jackson. 1988. "Racial Group Identification among Black Adults." *Social Forces* 67:146–58.

Burke, Peter J. 1980. "The Self: Measurement Requirements from an Interactionist Perspective." *Social Psychology Quarterly* 43:18–29.

Clausen, John A. 1986. *The Life Course: A Sociological Perspective*. Englewood Cliffs, NJ: Prentice-Hall.

Cross, William E., Jr. 1985. "Black Identity: Rediscovering the Distinction between Personal Identity and Reference Group Orientation." Pp. 155–71 in *Beginnings: The Social and Affective Development of Black Children*, edited by Margaret B. Spencer, Geraldine K. Brookins, and Walter R. Allen. Hillsdale, NJ: Erlbaum.

Demo, David H., Stephen A. Small, and Ritch C. Savin-Williams. 1987. "Family Relations and the Self-Esteem of Adolescents and Their Parents." *Journal of Marriage and the Family* 49:705–15.

Elder, Glen H., Jr. 1981. "History and the Life Course." Pp. 77–115 in *Biography and Society*, edited by D. Bertaux. Beverly Hills: Sage.

Gecas, Viktor. 1979. "The Influence of Social Class on Socialization." Pp. 365–404 in *Contemporary Theories about the Family*, Volume 1, edited by Wesley R. Burr, Reuben Hill, F. Ivan Nye, and Ira L. Reiss. New York: Free Press.

————. 1981. "Contexts of Socialization." Pp. 165–99 in *Social Psychology: Sociological Perspectives*, edited by Morris Rosenberg and Ralph H. Turner. New York: Basic Books.

Gecas, Viktor and Jeylan T. Mortimer. 1987. "Stability and Change in the Self-Concept from Adolescence to Adulthood." Pp. 265–86 in *Self and Identity: Individual Change and Development*, edited by T. M. Honess and K. M. Yardley. New York: Routledge and Kegan Paul.

Gecas, Viktor and Michael L. Schwalbe. 1986. "Parental Behavior and Dimensions of Adolescent Self-Evaluation." *Journal of Marriage and the Family* 48:37–46.

Glenn, Norval D. 1963. "Negro Prestige Criteria: A Case Study in the Bases of Prestige." *American Journal of Sociology* 68:645–57.

Gurin, Patricia and Edgar G. Epps. 1975. *Black Consciousness, Identity, and Achievement*. New York: Wiley.

Gurin, Patricia, Arthur H. Miller, and Gerald Gurin. 1980. "Stratum Identification and Consciousness." *Social Psychology Quarterly* 43:30–47.

Hill, Robert. 1972. *The Strengths of Black Families*. New York: Emerson Hall.

Hoelter, Jon. 1982. "Race Differences in Selective Credulity and Self-Esteem." *Sociological Quarterly* 23:527–37.

Horn, J. L. and G. Donaldson. 1980. "Cognitive Development in Adulthood." Pp. 445–529 in *Constancy and Change in Human Development,* edited by O. G. Brim, Jr. and J. Kagan. Cambridge: Harvard University Press.

Hughes, Michael and David H. Demo. 1989. "Self-Perceptions of Black Americans: Self-Esteem and Personal Efficacy." *American Journal of Sociology* 95:132–59.

Jackson, James S. and Gerald Gurin. 1987. *National Survey of Black Americans, 1978–80* (Machine-readable codebook). Ann Arbor: Inter-University Consortium for Political and Social Research, Institute for Social Research, University of Michigan.

Kardiner, Abram and Lionel Ovesey. 1951. *The Mark of Oppression: Explorations in the Personality of the American Negro.* New York: Norton.

Krystall, E., N. Friedman, G. Howze, and E. Epps. 1970. "Attitudes toward Integration and Black Consciousness: Southern Negro High-School Students and Their Mothers." *Phylon* 31:104–13.

Lau, Richard R. 1989. "Individual and Contextual Influences on Group Identification." *Social Psychology Quarterly* 52:220–31.

Marx, Gary T. 1967. *Protest and Prejudice: A Study of Belief in the Black Community.* New York: Harper.

McAdoo, Hariette P. 1978. "Factors Related to Stability in Upwardly Mobile Black Families." *Journal of Marriage and the Family* 40:762–78.

McGuire, William J., Claire V. McGuire, P. Child, and T. Fujioka. 1978. "Salience of Ethnicity in the Spontaneous Self-Concept as a Function of One's Ethnic Distinctiveness in the Social Environment." *Journal of Personality and Social Psychology* 36:511–20.

Miller, Arthur H., Patricia Gurin, Gerald Gurin, and Oksana Malanchuk. 1981. "Group Consciousness and Political Participation." *American Journal of Political Science* 25:494–511.

Ortega, Suzanne T., Robert D. Crutchfield, and William A. Rushing. 1983. "Race Differences in Elderly Personal Well-Being." *Research on Aging* 5:101–18.

Peters, Marie Ferguson. 1985. "Racial Socialization of Young Black Children." Pp. 159–73 in *Black Children: Social, Educational, and Parental Environments,* edited by Harriette Pipes McAdoo and John Lewis McAdoo. Beverly Hills: Sage.

Pettigrew, Thomas F. 1964. *Profile of the Negro American.* Princeton: Van Nostrand.

Porter, Judith R. and Robert E. Washington. 1979. "Black Identity and Self-Esteem." *Annual Review of Sociology* 5:53–74.

Rosenberg, Morris. 1975. "The Dissonant Context and the Adolescent Self-Concept." Pp. 97–116 in *Adolescence in the Life Cycle,* edited by Sigmund E. Dragastin and Glen H. Elder, Jr. New York: Wiley.

———. 1979. *Conceiving the Self.* New York: Basic Books.

Rosenberg, Morris and Roberta G. Simmons. 1972. *Black and White Self-Esteem: The Urban School Child.* Washington DC: American Sociological Association.

Schaie, K. W. 1983. "The Seattle Longitudinal Study: A 21-Year Exploration of Psychometric Intelligence in Adulthood." Pp. 64–135 in *Longitudinal Studies of Adult Psychological Development,* edited by K. W. Schaie, New York: Guilford.

Stack, Carol. 1974. *All Our Kin.* New York: Harper and Row.

Suls, Jerry and Brian Mullen. 1982. "From the Cradle to the Grave: Comparison and Self-Evaluation across the Life-Span." Pp. 97–125 in *Psychological Perspectives on the Self,* Volume 1, edited by Jerry Suls. Hillsdale, NJ: Erlbaum.

Taylor, Robert Joseph. 1986. "Receipt of Support from Family among Black Americans: Demographic and Familial Differences." *Journal of Marriage and the Family* 48:67–77.

Taylor, Ronald. 1979. "Black Ethnicity and the Persistence of Ethnogenesis." *American Journal of Sociology* 84:1401–23.

Tomlinson, T. 1970. "Ideological Foundation for Negro Action: A Comparative Analysis of Militant and Non-Militant Views of the Los Angeles Riots." *Journal of Social Issues* 26:93–119.

Toomer, J. 1975. "Beyond Being Black: Identification Alone Is Not Enough." *Journal of Negro Education* 44:184–99.

Turner, Ralph. 1976. "The Real Self: From Institution to Impulse." *American Journal of Sociology* 81:989–1016.

Yancey, William L., Eugene P. Ericksen, and Richard N. Juliani. 1976. "Emergent Ethnicity: A Review and Reformulation." *American Sociological Review* 41:391–403.

Questions for Understanding and Critical Thinking

1. What is the "structural" meaning of being African American in U.S. society?
2. How did prior research on racial socialization contribute to the study conducted by Demo and Hughes?
3. Why is information on determinants of racial group identification among African American adults limited?
4. What can be gained from an examination of the step-by-step processes that scholars such as Demo and Hughes use to acquire firsthand knowledge about their topic?

ARTICLE 12 _____

In her study of women and eating problems such as anorexia and bulimia, sociologist and African American studies scholar Becky W. Thompson shows how the socialization of girls and women is shaped by race/ethnicity, class, religion, sexual orientation, and nationality. According to Thompson, "an expansive understanding of socialization requires scrutiny of the power of racism and classism as they inform standards of appearance."

This article is taken from Thompson's book, *A Hunger So Wide and So Deep: American Women Speak Out on Eating Problems,* in which she also explores how women can resist societal pressures and regain trust in their bodies and appetites. Thompson has taught African American studies and sociology at Wesleyan University and coedited books (with Sangeeta Tyagi) on multicultural education and racial identity.

Looking Ahead

1. What part does gender socialization play in girls' expectations about their weights and appetites?
2. How does gender socialization differ by race, religion, and class?
3. Why does Thompson suggest that not all white girls are socialized in the same manner?
4. What cultural messages do girls receive regarding heterosexuality?

Childhood Lessons

Culture, Race, Class, and Sexuality

◆ *Becky W. Thompson*

If there is one story that is an integral part of the folklore of growing up female, it is the chronicle of the onset of menstruation. These accounts are often embarrassing—a thirteen-year-old girl has to ask her father to tell her what to do, another is sure that people can tell from her face what is going on in her body—and many, like that of the young teenager who gets a red cake with red candles from her mother to celebrate her first period, are funny. Usually told only in the company of other women, these stories of a rite of passage are often filled with pain, ingenuity, and humor—and sometimes joy.

Equally revealing stories about the development of female identity in the United States spring from lessons girls learn about their body sizes and appetites. Whether they are fat or thin, Latina or Jewish (or both), lesbian or heterosexual, girls are barraged by complicated messages about their bodies, skin, hair, and faces. Not surprisingly, girls who do not fit the standard mold—who look like tomboys, whose skin is dark, who have nappy hair, who are chubby or just plain big, who develop early or develop late—are most aware of negative assessments, and their stories are commonly filled with shame and confusion.

Although there is no single message to girls about weight and food that crosses regional, religious, and cultural lines in the United States, early lessons about weight and appetite often leave indelible marks on their lives. Growing up on a working farm may protect a girl from the pressure to diet, but she may learn elsewhere that a big appetite is not acceptable for girls and women. While being raised in the Dominican Republic may help a young girl value women of all sizes, if she emigrates to the United States, the pressures to assimilate culturally and linguistically may make her especially determined to be thin.

Increasingly, one of the few experiences common to growing girls in the United States is the pressure to diet. This pressure not only reveals strictures about body size, it also telegraphs complicated notions about race, culture, and class. A girl's body may become the battleground where parents and other relatives play out their own anxieties. Just as stories about a first menstruation tell us about a family's social traditions and the extent to which the girl's body is respected within them, lessons about weight and eating habits tell us an enormous amount about culture, race, religion, and gender. It is through these familial and cultural lenses that young girls make judgments about their bodies and their appetites. The nuances in the socialization of girls show why—across race, class, and religion—they may become vulnerable to eating problems and demonstrate how many girls begin to use food to cope with trauma.

GROWING UP LATINA

By the year 2020 the single largest minority group in the United States will be Latino people—including the descendants of people who were in what is now the United States before it was "discovered," people who fled El Salvador and Guatemala in the 1970s and 1980s, Puerto Rican people, and a host of others. Latinos share a history of struggling against colonialism and racism, and they share a common language. Other generalizations are often erroneous.

There is no single Latino ethic about body size and eating patterns. Even to profess that there is a common Puerto Rican expectation about women's body size would conflate significant generational and regional differences.[1] The notion that Latinas as a group are somehow protected from or ignorant of cultural pressure to be thin simply does not hold up in the face of their diversity. Nor can it be said that any particular group of women is isolated from the culture of thinness; the mass media have permeated even the most remote corners of the United States. The pressures of assimilation and racism may make some Latinas especially vulnerable to strictures about weight.

The task, then, is to identify both how ethnic, racial, and socioeconomic heterogeneity among Latinos and Latinas influences their socialization and how these factors may make Latinas susceptible to developing eating problems. One of the Latina women I interviewed, Elsa, was raised by German governesses in an upper-class family in Argentina. Another, Julianna, was cared for by her grandmother in a middle-class family in the Dominican Republic. The other three are Puerto Rican women who grew up in the United States and whose backgrounds ranged from working- to upper-middle-class; among these women, the degree of assimilation varied markedly depending on whether Spanish was their first language, the degree of contact with other Latinas, and the extent to which they identified as Puerto Ricans.

What the Latina women learned about weight and size was influenced by nationality. Julianna, who grew up in a small town in the Dominican Republic, was taught that

> *people don't think that fat is bad. You don't undermine fat people. You just don't. . . . The picture of a woman is not a woman who has a perfect body that you see on TV. A woman is beautiful because she is a virgin or because she is dedicated to her husband or because she takes care of her kids; because she works at home and does all the things that her husband and family want her to do. But not because she is skinny or fat.*

In the Dominican Republic, female beauty is closely linked to being a good wife and mother and obeying gendered expectations about virginity and monogamy. Thinness is not a necessary criterion for beauty, regardless of a woman's class. By contrast, the Argentinian woman, Elsa, said that a woman's weight was the primary criterion for judging her worth. The diets and exercise her father enforced among his wife and daughters were "oppressive and Nazi-like." But judgments about weight varied with class and degree of urbanization:

> *The only people who see being fat as a positive thing in Argentina are the very poor or the very rural people who still consider it a sign of wealth or health. But as soon as people move to the bigger cities and are exposed to the magazines and the media, dieting and figures become incredibly important.*

None of the Puerto Rican women I talked with benefited from the acceptance of size that the Dominican woman described. Laura, who lived in Puerto Rico with her family for four years when she was a child, recalls that "Latina women were almost expected to be more overweight. Latin women living in Puerto Rico were not uncomfortable with extra weight. To them it wasn't extra. It wasn't an issue." This didn't help Laura appreciate her own chunky size because her family's disdain for fat people was much more influential. Her father was British and her mother liked to "hang out with wealthy white women," both factors that impeded Laura's ability to adopt the Puerto Rican community's values.

Another Puerto Rican woman, Vera, who grew up in Chicago, was chunky as a child and learned that people around her disapproved of her size. Vera remembers painful scenes at school and in clothing stores that taught her she should be embarrassed by her body size. Although she was an amazingly limber and energetic student in her ballet class, her mother took her out of it because Vera wasn't thin enough.

AFRICAN-AMERICAN GIRLS AND COMMUNITY LIFE

Rosalee grew up in Arkansas in a rural African-American community where, as she described it, "home grown and healthy" was the norm. She remembers that her uncles and other men liked a "healthy woman": as they used to say, "They didn't want a neck bone. They liked a picnic ham." Among the people in her community, skin color and hair were more important than weight in determining beauty. Unlike most of the other women I interviewed, Rosalee didn't think about dieting as a way to lose weight until she was a teenager. Because her family didn't always have money, "there were times when we hardly had food anyway so we tended to slim down. And then . . . when the money was rolling in . . . we celebrated. We ate and ate and ate." When poverty is a constant threat, Rosalee explained, "dieting just isn't a household word." This did not stop Rosalee from developing an eating problem when she was four years old as a response to sexual abuse and being a witness to beatings. Trauma, not size, was the primary factor.

Carolyn, a middle-class woman who grew up in an urban area, remembered that her African-American friends considered African-American women of varying weights to be desirable and beautiful. By contrast, among white people she knew, the only women who were considered pretty were petite. Both the white and the African-American men preferred white girls who were petite.

The women who went to schools in which there were only a few African-American students remember thinness as dominant. By contrast, those who went to racially mixed or predominantly African-American schools saw more acceptance of both big and thin women. One of the many hazards for black students who attend overwhelmingly white schools is pressure to adopt cultural values—including thinness—that may not reflect African-American values.[2]

The women who attended private, predominantly white schools were sent by parents who hoped to open up opportunities unavailable in public schools. As a consequence, both Nicole and Joselyn were isolated from other African-American children. Their parents discouraged them from socializing with neighborhood African-American children, who in turn labeled them arrogant, thus furthering their isolation. Both were teased by neighborhood children for being chubby and light-skinned. At school they were teased for being fat and were excluded by white people in ways both subtle and overt. Racist administrators and teachers

granted the girls neither the attention nor the dignity they deserved. Joselyn, who attended Catholic schools, remembered both racial and religious intolerance: "Sister Margaret Anna told me that, basically, what a black person could aspire to at that time was to Christianize the cannibals in Africa." Neither Nicole nor Joselyn had a public context in which her racial identity was validated. As Nicole said, "By second or third grade I was saying I wished I was white because kids at school made fun of me. I remember . . . getting on the bus and a kid called me a brown cow." As the women were growing up, their weight and their race were used to ostracize them.

INTERSECTION OF RACE AND CLASS

Most of the African-American and Latina women were pressured to be thin by at least one and often all of their family members. For some, these pressures were particularly virulent because they were laced with racism. Rosalee, who grew up on a farm in the South, got contradictory messages about weight and size from her family. Like most of the African-Americans in her community, Rosalee's mother thought thin women were sickly and took her young daughters to the doctor because they weren't gaining enough weight. But her father told her she "had better not turn out fat like her mother." Rosalee and her mother often bore the brunt of his disdain as he routinely told them that African-American women were usually fatter and less beautiful than white women. Rosalee says:

> *I can remember fantasizing that "I wish I was white." . . . It seemed to be the thing to be if you were going to be anything. You know, [white women] were considered beautiful. That was reinforced a lot by my father, who happened to have a strong liking for*

white women. Once he left the South and he got in the army and traveled around and had more freedom, he became very fond of them. In fact, he is married to one now. He just went really overboard. I found myself wanting to be like that.

Although she was not familiar with dieting as a child, she feared weight gain and her father's judgments. At puberty, she began to diet. Her father's sexism and prejudice against black women meant that she was raised with contradictory messages about weight. At the same time, she was learning about the dominant standard of beauty that emphasizes a fair complexion, blue eyes, and straight hair. About the lessons many black girls learn about straightening their hair and using lightening creams, Rosalee says:

It was almost as if you were chasing after an impossible dream. I can remember stories about parents pinching their children's noses so they don't get too big. I laugh about it when I am talking about it with other people but on the inside I don't laugh at all. There is nothing there to reinforce who you are, and the body image gets really confused.

Some of the Latinas' and African-Americans' relatives projected their own frustrations and racial prejudices onto the girls' bodies. Joselyn, an African-American woman, remembers her white grandmother telling her she would never be as pretty as her cousins because they had lighter skin. Her grandmother often humiliated Joselyn in front of others, making fun of Joselyn's body while she was naked and telling her she was fat. As a young child Joselyn began to think that although she couldn't change her skin color, she could at least try to be thin.

When Joselyn was young, her grandmother was the only family member who objected to her weight. Then her father also

began to encourage his wife and daughter to be thin as the family's social status began to change. When Joselyn was very young, her family was what she called "aspiring to be middle class." For people of Joselyn's parents' generation, having chubby, healthy children was a sign the family was doing well. But, as the family moved up the social ladder, Joselyn's father began to insist that Joselyn be thin:

When my father's business began to bloom and my father was interacting more with white businessmen and seeing how they did business, suddenly thin became important. If you were a truly well-to-do family, then your family was slim and elegant.

Her grandmother's racism and her father's determined fight to be middle class converged, and Joselyn's body became the playing field for their conflicts. While Joselyn was pressured to diet, her father still served her large portions and bought treats for her and the neighborhood children. These contradictory messages confused her. Like many girls, Joselyn was told she was fat from the time she was very young, even though she wasn't. And, like many of the women I interviewed, Joselyn was put on diet pills and diets before puberty, beginning a cycle of dieting, compulsive eating, and bulimia. She remembers her father telling her, "You know you have a cute face, but from the body down, you are shot to hell. You are built just like your old lady."

Another African-American woman also linked contradictory messages about food to her parents' internalized racism. As Nicole explains it, her mother operated under the "house-nigger mentality," in which she saw herself and her family as separate from and better than other African-American people. Her father shared this attitude, saying that being Cherokee made him different. Her parents sent Nicole to private schools and a "very white Anglican upper-class church" in which she was one of a few black children. According to Nicole, both parents "passed on their internalized racism in terms of judgments around hair or skin color or how a person talks or what is correct or proper."

Their commandments about food and body size were played out on Nicole's body in powerful ways. Nicole's father was from a working-class rural Southern family. Her mother, by contrast, was from a "petit bourgeois family," only one of three black families in a small New Hampshire town. While Nicole's father approved of her being, as he said, "solid," her mother restricted her eating to ensure that Nicole would grow up thin. Each meal, however, was a multicourse event. Like Joselyn, Nicole was taught that eating a lot was a dangerous but integral part of the family tradition:

> When I was growing up, I thought that breakfast was a four- or five-course meal the way you might think dinner is. I thought that breakfast involved fruit and maybe even juice and cereal and then the main course of breakfast, which was eggs and bacon and toast. On Sundays we had fancy breakfasts like fish and hominy grits and corn bread and muffins. So breakfast had at least three courses. That is how we ate. Dinner was mostly meat and potatoes and vegetables and bread. Then my father would cajole my mother into making dessert. There were lots of rewards that all had to do with food, like going to Howard Johnson or Dunkin' Donuts.

At the same time, Nicole's mother put her on a diet when she was three and tortured her about her weight. Nicole became terrified of going to the doctor because she was weighed and lectured about her weight. Yet, after each appointment, her mother took her to Dunkin' Donuts for a powdered jelly doughnut. When her father did the grocery shopping, he bought Nicole treats, which her mother snatched and hid, accusing her father of trying to make her fat. When she was left alone, Nicole spent hours trying to find the food. In her mother's view, Nicole's weight and curly hair were what kept her from being perfect: her body became the contested territory onto which her parents' pain was projected.

The confusion about body size and class expectations that troubled some of the African-American women paralleled the experiences of two Puerto Rican women. Vera attributed her eating problems partly to the stress of assimilation as her family moved from poverty to the working class. When Vera was three, she was so thin that her mother took her to a doctor who prescribed appetite stimulants. By the time she was eight, though, she remembered her mother comparing her to other girls who stayed on diets or were thin. Vera attributed her mother's change of heart to pressure from family members:

> Even though our family went from poverty to working class, there were members of my extended family who thought they were better than everyone else. As I grew up, the conversation was, "Who is going to college? Who has a job working for Diamonds?" It was always this one-upmanship about who was making it better than who. The one-upmanship centered on being white, being successful, being middle class . . . and it was always, "Ay, Bendito [Oh, God]! She is so fat! What happened?"

Vera's mother warned her that she would never make friends if she was fat. Her mother threatened to get a lock for the refrigerator door and left notes on it reminding Vera not to eat. While Vera's mother shamed her into dieting, she also felt ambivalent when Vera did not eat much. When Vera dieted, her mother would say, "You have to eat. You have to eat something. You can't starve your-self." The messages were always unclear.

Ruthie also remembers changes in the family ethic about size and eating that she attributes to assimilation with Anglo culture. In keeping with Puerto Rican tradition, Ruthie's mother considered chubby children a sign of health and well-being. According to Puerto Rican culture, Ruthie says, "if you are skinny, you are dying. What is wrong with you?" When Ruthie was ten to twelve years old, her mother made her take a food sup-plement and iron pills that were supposed to make her hungry. Ruthie did not like the supplement and felt fine about the size of her body. But how Ruthie looked was very important to her mother: "My mother used to get these dresses from Spain. She used to show everyone our closets. They were im-peccable. Buster Brown shoes and dresses. She thought if I were skinny it would reflect badly on her." Ruthie questioned whether her mother cared about Ruthie or was actu-ally worried about what the family and neighbors would say. When Ruthie became a teenager, her mother's attitude about weight changed:

> When I was little, it was not okay to be skinny. But then, at a certain age, it was not okay to be fat. She would say, "Your sister would look great in a bikini and you wouldn't." I thought maybe this was be-cause I felt fat. . . . Being thin had become something she valued. It was a roller coaster.

Ruthie attributed this change to her mother's acceptance of Anglo standards, which she tried to enforce on Ruthie's eating and body size.

The women's experiences dispel the no-tion that African-American and Latina wo-men—as a group—are less exposed to or in-fluenced by a culturally imposed thinness than white women. The African-American women who saw community acceptance of different sizes did not escape pressure to be thin from family members. While growing up in a rural area and attending predomi-nantly black schools did protect two of the girls from pressures to diet, childhood trau-mas resulted in eating problems. For the women of color whose parents' internalized racism, an emphasis on thinness was partic-ularly intense. Rosalee explains:

> For a black woman dealing with issues of self-esteem, if you don't get it from your family, you [are punished] twice because you don't get self-esteem from society either. If you come from a dysfunctional or abusive family, there [are] just not a lot of places to go that will turn things around for you.

This reality underscores why some women of color may be more, rather than less, vulner-able than white women to eating problems.

WHITE GIRLS IN THEIR FAMILIES AND COMMUNITIES

As is true of the women of color, ethnic, reli-gious, and national diversity among white women makes it difficult to generalize about a monolithic socialization process. With the exception of a Sephardic Jewish woman who grew up outside the United States, none of the white women I talked with escaped pres-sure to diet and be thin. Ethnic and religious identity, however, did influence their eating patterns and their attitudes about their bod-ies. Anti-Semitism and ethnic prejudice shaped the way some of the girls interpreted strictures about weight and eating. Like most of the women of color, the white women had little access to communities in which women of different sizes were valued. Mes-sages that white girls received both in their homes and in their communities promoted dieting and thinness.

All of the American Jewish women I in-terviewed were taught that they needed to be thin. Although none were fat as children, all had parents who were afraid they would become fat and took what they saw as precautions. One family bought only enough food for one day at a time, reasoning that they would not overeat if no "extra" food was available. Two Jewish women who went to predominantly Protestant schools said belonging to a religious minority exacerbated pressures about body size. Both felt like outsiders because they were Jewish, and their Protestant classmates perceived them as talking, dressing, and looking different.

As for many of the Latinas and African-American women, the discrimination Jewish children experienced was most overt when they were in the minority. Sarah learned that some of her Protestant classmates thought that Jewish people had horns. Both Sarah and Gilda were called names and excluded from friendship groups. Gilda, who is a Sephardic Jew, remembers that when she began to attend school in the United States, other children spit on her and called her "kike":

It was the craziest thing I had ever experienced. I hadn't experienced it from people I was told we were at war with [in North Africa]. If anything, the Arab women and mothers were more supportive. They would take us in.[3]

Children in the United States called her father the "Tasmanian devil" and made fun of her accent. The Jewish girls coped with discrimination by minimizing the ways they felt different from or inferior to others, including trying to hide their body sizes. Sarah explained that "in the school I attended, where I was only one of a handful of Jewish kids, I never felt like I fit in. I didn't have the right clothes, I didn't look the right way. I didn't come from the right family." When she was as young as eleven, Sarah began to feel "that I had to lose weight or that some-

thing wasn't right." Although she wasn't fat, in her mind, she was.

Of the five Jewish women, Gilda—who grew up in North Africa and France before settling in the United States—was the only one exposed to a wholehearted acceptance of food. For Gilda's father, who was raised in North Africa, family meals were a central, celebrated aspect of maintaining North African and Jewish culture:

First of all food and Friday night and Shabbes. Friday night for my father is a very important time. . . . We have a traditional [North African] meal with vegetables and different salads and [North African] spices. The whole flavor, the whole mood of the evening is not American at all. On holidays, Passover, we read the Haggadah in French, Arabic, Hebrew, and English. By page thirty, you are ready to die of hunger and exhaustion.

Eating together as a family was an important aspect of this tradition. Although Gilda learned that being a very thin child was not acceptable and that eating was a primary way her father celebrated his culture and religion, she remembered her mother always being on a diet, even though she was never more than slightly overweight. Gilda's father became angry with her when, as an adolescent, Gilda refused to eat with the family and did not keep kosher meals. Contradictory messages from her father and mother and differences between North African and U.S. standards caused confusion about weight and size.

The white women who were raised in Christian families were taught that being thin was crucial for females. Dawn, a middle-class white woman raised in a strict Catholic family, was taught from a young age that "a woman's worth was in her size." Antonia's ideas about eating and weight were deeply affected by her Italian-American ethnic identity. Like some of the Jewish women and women of color, Antonia felt like an outsider at school from kindergarten on, a feeling that was compounded by thinking she was overweight. At school she learned that to be accepted socially, she had to look and act like the "WASPs"—to have straight blond hair and be passive and quiet. She remembers that "I used to get called loud. I talked a lot. Very active. And I was very aggressive. I used to wrestle with the boys a lot. I stood out from other people." Because she was fat, she was often humiliated by other children at school. One of the boys called her "taters" (a big potato). At a high school prom fundraiser—a "slave auction," where girls were auctioned off—"when it was my turn, no one was bidding. To this day, . . . I can't even really remember the actual sequence of events. It was just the most humiliating thing in my life." When Antonia was eleven, her mother put her on a diet and a doctor prescribed amphetamines. During adolescence she tried to diet but her heart was not in it. In her mind, no amount of dieting would take away her assertive, emotional, and athletic ways, so what was the point in trying to lose weight anyway?

GROOMING GIRLS TO BE HETEROSEXUAL

While messages to girls about their bodies and appetites are shaped by race, class, ethnicity, and religion, no such diversity exists when it comes to learning about heterosexuality. In both subtle and overt ways, girls— across race, class, ethnicity, and religion— learn that being heterosexual is natural and inevitable. These expectations add up to what poet and writer Adrienne Rich has termed "compulsory heterosexuality": a largely invisible but enormously powerful force that orchestrates the range of what is considered acceptable female sexuality.[4] Ele-

ments of this enforced heterosexuality include pressure to marry and have children, male control of female sexuality, and an economic system that makes it difficult for many women to support themselves without marrying—plus prejudice and discrimination against gay men and lesbians and limitations on how emotionally close people of the same gender can be without facing reprisals. As girls reach their teenage years, they are punished if their friendships with other girls become intimate. They are also expected to show an interest in the opposite sex.[5] As Johnnetta Cole writes, women in the United States are "being measured against an objectified notion of female sexuality which is eternally young, never fat but 'well developed,' heterosexual, submissive to 'her man,' and capable of satisfying him sexually. It is striking how this ideal image cuts across racial, ethnic and class lines."[6]

The idea that heterosexuality is a necessary condition of "normal development" is often not overt or explicit unless girls begin to show signs of not being sufficiently heterosexual. For example, a Puerto Rican lesbian told me:

> My mother would say, there is nothing you can't do, if you want. But yet, in other subtle ways, she would encourage me to be a nurse. She wouldn't come right out and say, you can't be a doctor. She'd say I was supposed to be ladylike.

Being ladylike and having a traditionally female career was a prerequisite for marriage. Being thin was also integral to this heterosexual expectation.

All of the women I interviewed were taught that heterosexuality was essential. Many traced strictures about their bodies and appetites partly to this imperative. Implicit messages were commonly conveyed in the form of how girls were expected to look, how they were permitted to use their bodies athletically, how they should dress, and how much they were allowed to eat. For many girls, these rules were most fiercely applied as they approached puberty. Tomboys who grew up riding bicycles, playing handball, and wrestling with boys were often summarily reprimanded as they approached puberty. As they were informed that they should start wearing dresses and go to the junior high dances, they were also encouraged to "eat like a lady" and pass up second helpings. In some families, boys were allowed to eat all they wanted while girls were not. The rationale for this double standard was that girls should be smaller than boys in order to be attractive to the opposite sex. Some girls remembered hating these restrictions. They missed being physically active, and they resented having to get by with less food.

As they approached their teen years, many were taught that having boyfriends depended upon being thin. One African-American woman remembers initiating her first self-imposed diet because her boyfriend liked thin women. All of his sisters encouraged it, too. When an Argentinean woman was eleven years old her mother told her, "You should really make an effort and diet. You won't be popular around the boys. You are going to have trouble finding a husband. You look terrible. What a pity. You have a nice face but look at your figure." Laura, a Puerto Rican woman, remembers her mother and father both teaching her that she needed to lose weight or run the risk of being an "old maid." Integral to her socialization was the message that being successful heterosexually depended upon being thin:

> One day when I was eleven my parents and I were sitting on the beach in Puerto Rico. There was this blond woman walking down the beach with about ten men around her. She was in a bikini and my father and mother said, "She is not very attractive but she is thin. Look at all those men around her." They pointed out this other woman, who was heavy. She was by herself. She had a very beautiful face. They said, "See, she is beautiful. But she is not thin. She is by herself." It was right out front. That began at eleven years old. You are worthless unless you are thin.

The lessons about heterosexuality often went hand in hand with lessons about weight and dieting. Not surprisingly, those who questioned their heterosexuality at a young age were often best able to identify how these strictures reinforced each other. One of the characteristics of dominant ideology—including compulsory heterosexuality—is that it is understood as significant only when it is transgressed. This is also the power of dominant ideology, since it is often consciously felt only by those who contest it, who are encouraged—and sometimes forced—to accept it. For example, one woman who was not interested in boys during high school and had crushes on girls remembers that the "in group" of girls at school constantly talked about their boyfriends, diets, and losing weight. She partly wanted to be like them and thought that dieting would make her feel included in their friendship circle. Another woman's grandmother and mother taught her that "if you were thin, then all of your problems should be erased. You could be happily married, you could satisfy a man, anything you wanted could be yours if only you could be thin."

None of the girls grew up in homes where heterosexuality was questioned. This taken-for-granted aspect of their socialization meant that all the models for sexuality pivoted on attracting men; there were no alternatives. Consequently, there was no room for the idea that women's appetites and body sizes could be defined according to their own standards rather than norms based on rigid definitions of masculinity and femininity.

WHOSE BODY IS THIS, ANYWAY?

Given the complex and sometimes contradictory messages that girls get as they are growing up, it is no wonder that many come of age distrusting their appetites and their bodies. The process highlights many feminist assertions about eating problems, and understanding the impact of gender discrimination takes us a long way toward seeing that many girls must reckon with the question, Whose body is this, anyway?

Girls are bombarded with complicated ideas about their bodies not just within their families; pressures in their communities, schools, and churches also play a vital role. Feminists rightfully recognize that it is impossible to understand girls' attitudes toward their bodies without scrutinizing what goes on both inside and outside their families. This comprehensive scope is especially important for a multiracial focus, since some women of color may get contradictory messages in their communities and in their homes.

Taking community pressures into consideration also counters the psychoanalytic tendency to reduce eating problems to psychic problems caused by mother-daughter dynamics. The psychoanalytic notion that a girl's anorexia is a "reaction to a hostile mother" or a manifestation of a child's unconscious ambivalence toward her mother is problematic when it is seen through a feminist, sociocultural lens.[7] Rather than placing blame solely on mothers, feminists explain that anorexia may be a girl's logical solution to a world in which women's bodies are treated like objects and ridiculed. While nonfeminist theorists may root a girl's anorexia in unconscious conflicts with her mother, feminists argue that it is necessary to look at the entire family. Mothers are not the only ones implicated in encouraging girls to diet and distrust their appetites: fathers, siblings, and other relatives are often responsible as well. Fathers may ridicule girls as their bodies develop, tell them that they should not be "fat like their mother," demand that they diet, and link weight loss to the family's social success.

Whether they're African-American, Latina, or white, most girls grow up learning that being thin is valued—especially for women. All of the women I interviewed talked about being aware of this pressure at some point in their lives. They all experienced the physiological and psychological stress of dieting—which researchers have implicated in the onset of bulimia and anorexia.[8] Family pressure to curb their appetites, use diet pills, and diet did render many vulnerable to anorexia and bulimia. Many of the women were put on diets or were given diet pills before adolescence—perhaps disrupting their metabolisms and making it more rather than less difficult to lose weight. (We now know that persistent dieting can lower the resting metabolism, which can result in weight gain rather than loss.)[9] Diet pills also jeopardize physical strength and sleeping patterns. One woman had routinely cleaned her room in the middle of the night, not knowing that her insomnia was linked to the mescaline in her diet pills. It wasn't until she was in college and saw friends' frenetic activity when they were taking speed that she realized that her childhood hyperactivity was drug-induced. Another woman collapsed and had a seizure in reaction to diet pills. She was rushed to the hospital and prescribed a strong depressant. She remembers being "totally freaked out. I was shaking. I couldn't talk. It was like my tongue had swollen in my mouth and I was completely stoned. . . . That was . . . my first introduction to dieting."A third woman remembers feeling like she was going to pass out playing softball and running track because she had so little food in her body.

Many of the women responded to enforced dieting by sneaking or stealing food and then bingeing secretly. The woman who was hospitalized came home, ate an enormous amount of chicken, and slept for twenty-four hours because she hadn't slept in three weeks. The woman who worried about fainting at sports practice binged as a way of compensating for being deprived of food. Some of the women stole money from their mothers' purses to buy food when they were as young as six and seven. In response to constant teasing about her weight, one woman remembers thinking, "I will show you. I can be as fat as I want. I will still have friends. I would go eat. Stuff myself. I would go get candy. Steal candy. Candy bars. Hide them in my pocket."

Many of the women say that they lost weight but eventually gained back more than they had lost. The presentation of dieting as an inevitable requirement of growing up female initiated a cycle of dieting, bingeing, and purging that, once it was begun, was hard to stop. Enforced dieting undermines a girl's bodily integrity—her ability to control what goes in and out of her body—by making it difficult for her to control her desire to binge. It whittles away her sense of being able to control how much or when she eats, which compromises her belief that she is in charge of her body.

Many of the women had a difficult time developing an accurate sense of their body size and shape as a result of their families' inaccurate and inconsistent assessments. Many who were put on diets would be considered "normal" according to insurance charts. Often what was identified as fat was actually their developing breasts and hips—suggesting that the psychoanalytic assumption that a girl develops eating problems as a result of

her own fear of having an adult female body is in at least some cases unwarranted. In fact, *others'* fears of girls' growing bodies can serve as the catalyst for dieting and disruption of their normal processes of development.

Because the development of hips and breasts was misnamed as fat, the women often lost a realistic sense of their body sizes and shapes. Dawn says, "At age eleven or twelve, when I started to develop, I remember being fascinated. Loving my body. Standing in front of the mirror and looking. Posing with no clothes on. Loving the shape of my waist." During the same year, Dawn remembers, her mother turned to her and said, "You have to be careful. You are starting to put on weight"; "I don't even think I weighed 105 pounds," says Dawn now. In response to this warning,

> I started to realize that actually my hips were a little bigger than they should be. I had already been concerned around food because my sister has always been a little overweight. I got messages from very, very young that a woman's worth is in [her] size.

Stories of parents' confusing observations about their daughters' weight are common. Another woman, Vera, says:

> I was not a fat child. My mother had me believe I was. But I wasn't. I used to look at other girls and compare myself to them. I would think, I am not as thin as her, but I am not as fat as her.

As she tried to develop a realistic understanding of her body's contours, her mother continued to confuse her. Her mother told her that she was so fat she would have to wear a nurse's uniform to her eighth-grade graduation because a uniform store was the only place where they made white clothes big enough for her. The comment devastated her. Actually, though, her mother had already sent for a beautiful dress from

Mexico—a size nine, certainly not large for a thirteen-year-old girl who had already been through puberty. She also remembers, when she was fifteen, walking down the street with her mother, who pointed to a woman who weighed 300 pounds:

> When she walked her behind went boom-boom-boom-boom. She was an incredibly obese person. My mother said, "You look just like her. Your body is exactly like hers." I can remember going home and standing in front of the mirror and looking and looking and looking. In my mind I was totally warped as to what I looked like. I was probably wearing [a size] eleven or thirteen. When I would lose a little weight I would wear a nine.

Another woman was told by all of her sisters and her mother that she was the fattest one of them all. She was the last to be served at each meal and was picked on for being overweight. She cried her way through most meals. It wasn't until she was an adult that she realized by looking at pictures that she was not a fat child and that, in fact, her mother was obese.

Dieting was the initial way many of the women had tried to cope with confusion about their body sizes. If they were not able to figure out if they were fat, many reasoned that it wouldn't hurt to diet. Paying close attention to their eating began as an attempt to assert some control over their bodies. At least initially, this helped avoid being teased about an "unacceptable" body size and allowed them to counteract what they were being blamed for.

Dieting often backfired. What began as a way to control eating frequently resulted in bingeing and, in some cases, purging. Other traumas exacerbated these cycles. Many of the women have had to adjust to major changes in their body sizes at least once and often many times during their lives. Extreme weight fluctuation not only can cause physical damage but also impairs a woman's ability to know her actual size. Sudden weight gain and loss leaves a woman little time to adjust to changes in her body dimensions.

AMERICAN DREAMS AND UNSATISFIED HUNGERS

The childhood lessons that African-American, Latina, and white women learn illuminate pressures about body size and appetites that have not yet been examined in research or focused on by the media. Jewish and black parents may assume that although they cannot protect their daughters from anti-Semitism and racism, encouraging thinness at least shields them from discrimination against fat people. An African-American or Latino parent who tells a child not to eat and then feeds her confuses the child as she learns to feed herself, yet the feeding may also indicate a cultural tradition of nurturing through food. When a Puerto Rican mother gives her five-year-old daughter a food supplement to make her gain weight, then ridicules her when she gains weight as an adolescent, pressures of assimilation may account for the mother's change of heart.

To understand why a girl's relatives want her to be thin, we need to know what forms of economic, racial, ethnic, and religious discrimination they have encountered. Underlying an attempt to make a girl thin is an often unspoken assumption that while the family might not be financially stable, or it cannot fully shield her from racism, or it does not speak English without an accent, her small size may make her life and theirs somewhat easier. Some African-American women and Latinas I interviewed related pressure to be thin to their parents' hopes to be middle class, and middle-class standing depended upon upholding this aesthetic. The dual strain of changing class expectations and racism may explain why some of the women of color linked an emphasis on thinness to class pressures while the white women did not. Class does not, by itself, determine whether or not the women were expected to be thin. Supposing that it does implies that poor women—both women of color and white women—are somehow culturally "out of the loop," an assumption that is both demeaning and inaccurate. But changes in class did fuel some parents' desire to control their daughters' appetites.

Pressures on parents do not justify their attempts to mold their daughters' bodies, but understanding why women across race and class develop eating problems requires clarifying what constitutes the "culture" in the culture-of-thinness model. Many people accept the notion that body size is, in fact, something that can be controlled, given enough self-discipline. This ideology makes dieting appear to be a logical strategy. When caretakers demand that their daughters be thin, some may do so believing that they have more control over weight than over other more complex and insidious forces that they have little power to change.

Doing justice to the social context in which eating problems arise also explains why the culture-of-thinness model needs to be considered along with other destructive social forces. Although thinness is an institutionally supported criterion for beauty, imperatives about age, color, and sexuality matter as well. An often-cited 1980 study documents the emergence of the culture of thinness by showing a marked decrease in the weight of centerfold models in *Playboy* magazine and the winners of the Miss America Pageant between 1959 and 1978.[10] This study quantifies a relationship between the social emphasis on thinness and the increase in eating problems but does not point out that, until recently, women in *Playboy* and the Miss America Pageant have been almost exclusively white, young, and heterosexual. Although the study shows that both the magazine and the pageant support a tyranny of slenderness, an integrated analysis would also elucidate tyranny based on the glorification of whiteness, youth, heterosexuality, and able-bodiedness. An expansive understanding of socialization requires scrutiny of the power of racism and classism as they inform standards of appearance. While white skin will not protect a fat woman from weight discrimination, it does protect her from racial discrimination. The resilience of the stereotype of the fat black "mammy" shows the futility and damage of considering standards of beauty as simply gendered. Interpreting socialization inclusively shows the myriad pressures affecting girls' opinions of their bodies. This approach also paves the way for seeing why girls—across race, class, religion, and ethnicity—may turn to food as a reaction to injustice.

ENDNOTES

1. Iris Zavala Martinez explains that statistics and stereotypes often treat Puerto Rican women as if they were a homogeneous group. In her essay on the economic and "socio-emotional" struggles of Puerto Rican women, Martinez writes, "Such treatment fosters a myth that ignores class differences, racial variations, and differences in places of birth and cultural background, as well as in educational process or language preference." In response to this distorted picture Martinez cautions that "only when the portrayals become richer, more sensitive to the multitude of such interacting characteristics, will the dynamic, complex and changing world of Puerto Rican women come fully into view." See Iris Zavala Martinez, "En La Lucha: Economic and Socioemotional Struggles of Puerto Rican Women in the United States," in *For Crying Out Loud*, ed. Rochelle Lefkowitz and Ann Withorn, pp. 109–22 (Boston: Pilgrim, 1986), p. 112.

2. Elsie J. Smith, "The Black Female Adolescent: A Review of the Educational, Career and Psychological Literature," *Psychology of Women Quarterly* 6, no. 3 (Spring 1982).

3. The country she referred to has been replaced with North Africa to protect her anonymity.

4. Adrienne Rich, "Compulsory Heterosexuality and Lesbian Existence," in *Blood, Bread, and Poetry* (New York: Norton, 1986). Compulsory heterosexuality is supported in the workplace and in families when women are channeled into "women's jobs" that pay poorly, allow for limited vertical advancement, provide few benefits, and are fashioned on serving men (secretary, maid, stewardess). The way that compulsory heterosexuality is enforced is also influenced by a woman's class. For example, while a single working-class mother may need to marry for financial reasons—which makes marriage compulsory—women who are independently wealthy do not have to marry to survive financially. While they may be spared this economic necessity to marry, they may still be psychologically convinced that getting married and having children are inevitable and natural for all women. Compulsory heterosexuality also varies with generation, ethnicity, religion, and nationality. Women who grew up before the emergence of the gay and lesbian liberation movement of the late 1960s endured an isolation and animosity many younger lesbians have been partially spared. Growing up in a rural community in which there is little or no positive reflection of oneself exacts a toll that is often softened in a large city like New York or Los Angeles. Religious differences also influence heterosexist stipulations. Women raised in Pentecostal or other conservative Protestant churches (Mormon, Baptist, Methodist, etc.), in Orthodox Jewish, or in Roman Catholic families face a degree of rejection and exile from their faith communities that far surpasses that faced by women raised in more sexually tolerant religious traditions (Unitarian, Quaker). Latina, African-American, and Asian-American lesbians not only confront racism among white people—including gay men and lesbians—but also must reckon with homophobia among heterosexual Latinos, African-Americans, and Asians. Finding "home" on the borders of these communities is an intricate process of protecting oneself from oppression experienced in triplicate. See Oliva Espin, "Issues of Identity in the Psychology of Latina Lesbians," in *Lesbian Psychologies: Explorations and Challenges*, ed. Boston Lesbian Psychologies Collective (Chicago: University of Illinois Press, 1987), pp. 35–56; Cherríe Moraga and Gloria Anzaldúa, eds., *This Bridge Called My Back: Writings by Radical Women of Color* (Ithaca, N.Y.: Kitchen Table, 1983).

5. While heterosexuality—sexual and emotional relationships between men and women—does not inherently limit women, compulsory heterosexism is injurious since it enforces men's sexual and physical control over them, is institutionally supported rather than freely chosen, and does not allow for the full range of human relationships. Compulsory heterosexuality is partly enforced within families through a socialization process in which daughters and wives serve their fathers and husbands. In many households, girls learn that their mothers are expected to care for themselves, their children, and their husbands. Female children are typically expected to do more household work and caretaking than is expected of boys. Enforced sexuality may also include the message that girls must provide for male relatives sexually. Both battery and sexual abuse are components of compulsory heterosexuality in that they "assure male physical and economic access and control over women" (Rich, "Compulsory Heterosexuality," p. 50).

6. Johnnetta Cole, ed., *All American Women* (New York: Free Press, 1986), pp. 15–16.

7. For representative samples of psychoanalytic explanations for the conflicts underlying eating problems, see Robert Linder, *The Fifty Minute Hour: A Collection of True Psychoanalytic Tales* (New York: Holt, Rinehart & Winston, 1955); John Sours, *Starving to Death in a Sea of Objects: The Anorexia Nervosa Syndrome* (New York: Aronson, 1980).

8. For feminist and medical research that shows that psychological and physiological effects of dieting may lead to bulimia and anorexia, see A. Keys, J. Brozek, A. Henschel, O. Michelsen, and H. L. Taylor, *The Biology of Human Starvation* (Minneapolis: University of Minnesota Press, 1950); Ruth Striegel-Moore, Lisa Silberstein, and Judith Rodin, "Toward an Understanding of Risk Factors for Bulimia," *American Psychologist* 41, no. 3 (1986); Valerie Smead, "Eating Behaviors Which May Lead to and Perpetuate Anorexia Nervosa, Bulimarexia and Bulimia," *Women and Therapy* 3, no. 2 (Summer 1984): 37–49; David Garner, Wendi Rockert, Marion Olmsted, Craig Johnson, and Donald Coscina, "Psychoeducational Principles in the Treatment of Bulimia and Anorexia Nervosa," *Handbook of Psychotherapy for Anorexia Nervosa and Bulimia*, ed. David M. Garner and Paul Garfinkel (New York: Guilford, 1985), pp. 513–72.

9. For research documenting correlations between dieting and weight gain, see Johanna Dwyer, "Nutritional Aspects of Anorexia Nervosa and Bulimia," in *Theory and Treatment of Anorexia Nervosa and Bulimia*, ed. Steven Wiley Emmett (New York: Brunner/Mazel, 1985), pp. 20–51; Lisa Schoenfielder and Barb Wieser, eds., *Shadow on a Tightrope: Writings by Women about Fat Liberation* (Iowa City: Aunt Lute, 1983).

10. D. Garner, P. Garfinkel, D. Schwartz, and M. Thompson, "Cultural Expectations of Thinness," *Psychological Reports* 47 (1980): 483–91.

Questions for Understanding and Critical Thinking

1. How does childhood socialization affect women's perceptions about their weights and appetites?
2. Why do views regarding thinness differ among Latinas? Among African Americans? Among white Americans?
3. What is "enforced heterosexuality"? How is this notion related to gender socialization and eating problems?
4. Why does Thompson believe a relationship exists between familial socialization and discrimination that family members have experienced?
5. Based on your own experience, do you think your gender socialization has contributed to your expectations about your own body size, weight, and overall appearance?

ARTICLE 13 _____

Are men naturally more competitive, aggressive, and violent than women? In this article, sociologist Michael A. Messner suggests how the narrow definitions of masculinity that boys learn in sports connect with other forms of social dominance. According to Messner, class and racial-ethnic differences affect how boys and men construct masculine identities within the institution of organized sports.

Michael A. Messner teaches in the Department of Sociology and the Program for the Study of Women and Men in Society at the University of Southern California.

Looking Ahead

1. Why are boyhood, organized sports, and the construction of masculinities so intertwined in the United States?
2. What part do family influences play in the socialization of young males for sports?
3. How does the importance placed on winning contribute to conditional self-worth among young boys and men?
4. How are race and class related to commitment to sports?

Boyhood, Organized Sports, and the Construction of Masculinities

◆ *Michael A. Messner*

The rapid expansion of feminist scholarship in the past two decades has led to fundamental reconceptualizations of the historical and contemporary meanings of organized sport. In the nineteenth and twentieth centuries, modernization and women's continued movement into public life created widespread "fears of social feminization," especially among middle-class men (Hantover, 1978; Kimmel, 1987). One result of these fears was the creation of organized sport as a homosocial sphere in which competition and (often violent) physicality was valued, while "the feminine" was devalued. As a result, organized support has served to bolster a sagging ideology of male superiority, and has helped to reconstitute masculine hegemony (Bryson, 1987; Hall, 1988; Messner, 1988; Theberge, 1981).

The feminist critique has spawned a number of studies of the ways that women's sports has been marginalized and trivialized

Source: From Michael A. Messner, "Boyhood, Organized Sports, and the Construction of Masculinities," in *Journal of Contemporary Ethnography,* Vol. 18, No. 4, pp. 416–444, copyright © 1990 by Sage Publications, Inc. Reprinted by permission of Sage Publications, Inc.

in the past (Greendorfer, 1977; Oglesby, 1978; Twin, 1978), in addition to illuminating the continued existence of structural and ideological barriers to gender equality within sport (Birrell, 1987). Only recently, however, have scholars begun to use feminist insights to examine men's experiences in sport (Kidd, 1987; Messner, 1987; Sabo, 1985). This article explores the relationship between the construction of masculine identity and boyhood participation in organized sports.

I view gender identity not as a "thing" that people "have," but rather as a *process of construction* that develops, comes into crisis, and changes as a person interacts with the social world. Through this perspective, it becomes possible to speak of "gendering" identities rather than "masculinity" or "femininity" as relatively fixed identities or statuses.

There is an agency in this construction; people are not passively shaped by their social environment. As recent feminist analyses of the construction of feminine gender identity have pointed out, girls and women are implicated in the construction of their own identities and personalities, both in terms of the ways that they participate in their own subordination and the ways that they resist subordination (Benjamin, 1988; Haug, 1987). Yet this self-construction is not a fully conscious process. There are also deeply woven, unconscious motivations, fears, and anxieties at work here. So, too, in the construction of masculinity. Levinson (1978) has argued that masculine identity is neither fully "formed" by the social context, nor is it "caused" by some internal dynamic put into place during infancy. Instead, it is shaped and constructed through the interaction between the internal and the social. The internal gendering identity may set developmental "tasks," may create thresholds of anxiety and ambivalence, yet it is only through a concrete examination of people's interactions with others within social institutions that we can begin to understand both the similarities and differences in the construction of gender identities.

In this study I explore and interpret the meanings that males themselves attribute to their boyhood participation in organized sport. In what ways do males construct masculine identities within the institution of organized sports? In what ways do class and racial differences mediate this relationship and perhaps lead to the construction of different meanings, and perhaps different masculinities? And what are some of the problems and contradictions within these constructions of masculinity?

DESCRIPTION OF RESEARCH

Between 1983 and 1985, I conducted interviews with 30 male former athletes. Most of the men I interviewed had played the (U.S.) "major sports"—football, basketball, baseball, track. At the time of the interview, each had been retired from playing organized sports for at least five years. Their ages ranged from 21 to 48, with the median, 33; 14 were black, 14 were white, and two were Hispanic; 15 of the 16 black and Hispanic men had come from poor or working-class families, while the majority (9 of 14) of the white men had come from middle-class or professional families. All had at some time in their lives based their identities largely on their roles as athletes and could therefore be said to have had "athletic careers." Twelve had played organized sports through high school, 11 through college, and seven had been professional athletes. Though the sample was not randomly selected, an effort was made to see that the sample had a range of difference in terms of race and social class backgrounds, and that there was some variety in terms of age, types of sports played, and levels of success in athletic careers.

Without exception, each man contacted agreed to be interviewed.

The tape-recorded interviews were semi-structured and took from one and one-half to six hours, with most taking about three hours. I asked each man to talk about four broad eras in his life: (1) his earliest experiences with sports in boyhood, (2) his athletic career, (3) retirement or disengagement from the athletic career, and (4) life after the athletic career. In each era, I focused the interview on the meanings of "success and failure," and on the boy's/man's relationships with family, with other males, with women, and with his own body.

In collecting what amounted to life histories of these men, my overarching purpose was to use feminist theories of masculine gender identity to explore how masculinity develops and changes as boys and men interact within the socially constructed world of organized sports. In addition to using the data to move toward some generalizations about the relationship between "masculinity and sport," I was also concerned with sorting out some of the variations among boys, based on class and racial inequalities, that led them to relate differently to athletic careers. I divided my sample into two comparison groups. The first group was made up of 10 men from higher-status backgrounds, primarily white, middle-class, and professional families. The second group was made up of 20 men from lower-status backgrounds, primarily minority, poor, and working-class families.

BOYHOOD AND THE PROMISE OF SPORTS

Zane Grey once said, "All boys love baseball. If they don't they're not real boys" (as cited in Kimmel, 1990). This is, of course, an ideological statement: In fact, some boys do *not* love baseball, or any other sports, for that matter. There are millions of males who at an early age are rejected by, become alienated from, or lose interest in organized sports. Yet all boys are, to a greater or lesser extent, judged according to their ability, or lack of ability, in competitive sports (Eitzen, 1975; Sabo, 1985). In this study I focus on those males who did become athletes—males who eventually poured thousands of hours into the development of specific physical skills. It is in boyhood that we can discover the roots of their commitment to athletic careers.

How did organized sports come to play such a central role in these boys' lives? When asked to recall how and why they initially got into playing sports, many of the men interviewed for this study seemed a bit puzzled: after all, playing sports was "just the thing to do." A 42-year-old black man who had played college basketball put it this way:

> It was just what you did. It's kind of like, you went to school, you played athletics, and if you didn't, there was something wrong with you. It was just like brushing your teeth: it's just what you did. It's part of your existence.

Spending one's time playing sports with other boys seemed as natural as the cycle of the seasons: baseball in the spring and summer, football in the fall, basketball in the winter—and then it was time to get out the old baseball glove and begin again. As a black 35-year-old former professional football star said:

> I'd say when I wasn't in school, 95% of the time was spent in the park playing. It was the only thing to do. It just came as natural.

And a black, 34-year-old professional basketball player explained his early experiences in sports:

> My principal and teacher said, "Now if you work at this you might be pretty damned

good." So it was more or less a community thing—everybody in the community said, "Boy, if you work hard and keep your nose clean, you gonna be good." Cause it was natural instinct.

"It was natural instinct." "I was a natural." Several athletes used words such as these to explain their early attraction to sports. But certainly there is nothing "natural" about throwing a ball through a hoop, hitting a ball with a bat, or jumping over hurdles. A boy, for instance, may have amazingly dexterous inborn hand-eye coordination, but this does not predispose him to a career of hitting baseballs any more than it predisposes him to a life as a brain surgeon. When one listens closely to what these men said about their early experiences in sports, it becomes clear that their adoption of the self-definition of "natural athlete" was the result of what Connell (1990) has called "a collective practice" that constructs masculinities. The boyhood development of masculine identity and status—truly problematic in a society that offers no official rite of passage into adulthood—results from a process of interaction with people and social institutions. Thus, in discussing early motivations in sports, men commonly talk of the importance of relationships with family members, peers, and the broader community.

FAMILY INFLUENCES

Though most of the men in this study spoke of their mothers with love, respect, even reverence, their descriptions of their earliest experiences in sports are stories of an exclusively male world. The existence of older brothers or uncles who served as teachers and athletic role models—as well as sources of competition for attention and status within the family—was very common. An older brother, uncle, or even close friend of the family who was a successful athlete appears to have acted as a sort of standard of achievement against whom to measure oneself. A 34-year-old black man who had been a three-sport star in high school said:

My uncles—my Uncle Harold went to the Detroit Tigers, played pro ball—all of 'em, everybody played sports, so I wanted to be better than anybody else. I knew that everybody in this town knew them—their names were something. I wanted my name to be just like theirs.

Similarly, a black 41-year-old former professional football player recalled:

I was the younger of three brothers and everybody played sports, so consequently, I was more or less forced into it. 'Cause one brother was always better than the next brother and then I came along and had to show them that I was just as good as them. My oldest brother was an all-city ballplayer, then my other brother comes along he's all-city and all-state, and then I have to come along.

For some, attempting to emulate or surpass the athletic accomplishments of older male family members created pressures that were difficult to deal with. A 33-year-old white man explained that he was a good athlete during boyhood, but the constant awareness that his two older brothers had been better made it difficult for him to feel good about himself, or to have fun in sports:

I had this sort of reputation that I followed from the playgrounds through grade school, and through high school. I followed these guys who were all-conference and all-state.

Most of the men, however, saw their relationships with their athletic older brothers and uncles in a positive light; it was within these relationships that they gained experience and developed motivations that gave them a competitive "edge" within their same-aged peer group. As a 33-year-old black man describes his earliest athletic experiences:

> My brothers were role models. I wanted to prove—especially to my brothers—that I had heart, you know, that I was a man.

When asked, "What did it mean to you to be 'a man' at that age?" he replied:

> Well, it meant that I didn't want to be a so-called scaredy-cat. You want to hit a guy even though he's bigger than you to show that, you know, you've got this macho image. I remember that at that young an age, that feeling was exciting to me. And that carried over, and as I got older, I got better and I began to look around me and see, well hey! I'm competitive with these guys, even though I'm younger, you know? And then of course all the compliments come—and I began to notice a change, even in my parents—especially in my father—he was proud of that, and that was very important to me. He was extremely important . . . he showed me more affection, now that I think of it.

As this man's words suggest, if men talk of their older brothers and uncles mostly as role models, teachers, and "names" to emulate, their talk of their relationships with their fathers is more deeply layered and complex. Athletic skills and competition for status may often be learned from older brothers, but it is in boys' relationships with fathers that we find many of the keys to the emotional salience of sports in the development of masculine identity.

RELATIONSHIPS WITH FATHERS

The fact that boys' introductions to organized sports are often made by fathers who might otherwise be absent or emotionally

distant adds a powerful emotional charge to these early experiences (Osherson, 1986). Although playing organized sports eventually came to feel "natural" for all of the men interviewed in this study, many needed to be "exposed" to sports, or even gently "pushed" by their fathers to become involved in activities like Little League baseball. A white, 33-year-old man explained:

> I still remember it like it was yesterday—Dad and I driving up in his truck, and I had my glove and my hat and all that—and I said, "Dad, I don't want to do it." He says, "What?" I says, "I don't want to do it." I was nervous. That I might fail. And he says, "Don't be silly. Lookit: There's Joey and Petey and all your friends out there." And so Dad says, "You're gonna do it, come on." And in my memory he's never said that about anything else; he just knew I needed a little kick in the pants and I'd do it. And once you're out there and you see all the other kids making errors and stuff, and you know you're better than those guys, you know: Maybe I do belong here. As it turned out, Little League was a good experience.

Some who were similarly "pushed" by their fathers were not so successful as the aforementioned man had been in Little League baseball, and thus the experience was not altogether a joyous affair. One 34-year-old white man, for instance, said he "inherited" his interest in sports from his father, who started playing catch with him at the age of four. Once he got into Little League, he felt pressured by his father, one of the coaches, who expected him to be the star of the team:

> I'd go O-for-four sometimes, strike out three times in a Little League game, and I'd dread the ride home. I'd come home and he'd say, "Go in the bathroom and swing the bat in the mirror for an hour," to get my swing

level. . . . It didn't help much, though, I'd go out and strike out three or four times again the next game too [laughs ironically].

When asked if he had been concerned with having his father's approval, he responded:

Failure in his eyes? Yeah, I always thought that he wanted me to get some kind of [athletic] scholarship. I guess I was afraid of him when I was a kid. He didn't hit that much, but he had a rage about him—he'd rage, and that voice would just rattle you.

Similarly, a 24-year-old black man described his awe of his father's physical power and presence, and his sense of inadequacy in attempting to emulate him:

My father had a voice that sounded like rolling thunder. Whether it was intentional on his part or not, I don't know, but my father gave me a sense, an image of him being the most powerful being on earth, and that no matter what I ever did I would never come close to him. . . . There were definite feelings of physical inadequacy that I couldn't work around.

It is interesting to note how these feelings of physical inadequacy relative to the father lived on as part of this young man's permanent internalized image. He eventually became a "feared" high school football player and broke school records in weightlifting, yet,

As I grew older, my mother and friends told me that I had actually grown to be a larger man than my father. Even though in time I required larger clothes than he, which should have been a very concrete indication, neither my brother nor I could ever bring ourselves to say that I was bigger. We simply couldn't conceive of it.

Using sports activities as a means of identifying with and "living up to" the power and status of one's father was not always such a painful and difficult task for the men I interviewed. Most did not describe fathers who "pushed" them to become sports stars. The relationship between their athletic strivings and their identification with their fathers was more subtle. A 48-year-old black man, for instance, explained that he was not pushed into sports by his father, but was aware from an early age of the community status his father had gained through sports. He saw his own athletic accomplishments as a way to connect with and emulate his father:

I wanted to play baseball because my father had been quite a good baseball player in the Negro leagues before baseball was integrated, and so he was kind of a model for me. I remember, quite young, going to a baseball game he was in—this was before the war and all—I remember being in the stands with my mother and seeing him on first base, and being aware of the crowd. . . . I was aware of people's confidence in him as a serious baseball player. I don't think my father ever said anything to me like "play sports" . . . [but] I knew he would like it if I did well. His admiration was important . . . he mattered.

Similarly, a 24-year-old white man described his father as a somewhat distant "role model" whose approval mattered:

My father was more of an example . . . he definitely was very much in touch with and still had very fond memories of being an athlete and talked about it, bragged about it. . . . But he really didn't do that much to teach me skills, and he didn't always go to every game I played like some parents. But he approved and that was important, you know. That was important to get his ap-

proval. I always knew that playing sports was important to him, so I knew implicitly that it was good and there was definitely a value on it.

First experiences in sports might often come through relationships with brothers or older male relatives, and the early emotional salience of sports was often directly related to a boy's relationship with his father. The sense of commitment that these young boys eventually made to the development of athletic careers is best explained as a process of development of masculine gender identity and status in relation to same-sex peers.

MASCULINE IDENTITY AND EARLY COMMITMENT TO SPORTS

When many of the men in this study said that during childhood they played sports because "it's just what everybody did," they of course meant that it was just what *boys* did. They were introduced to organized sports by older brothers and fathers, and once involved, found themselves playing within an exclusively male world. Though the separate (and unequal) gendered worlds of boys and girls came to appear as "natural," they were in fact socially constructed. Thorne's observations of children's activities in schools indicated that rather than "naturally" constituting "separate gendered cultures," there is considerable interaction between boys and girls in classrooms and on playgrounds. When adults set up legitimate contact between boys and girls, Thorne observed, this usually results in "relaxed interactions." But when activities in the classroom or on the playground are presented to children as sex-segregated activities and gender is marked by teachers and other adults ("boys line up here, girls over there"), "gender boundaries are heightened, and mixed-sex interaction

becomes an explicit arena of risk" (Thorne, 1986; 70). Thus sex-segregated activities such as organized sports as structured by adults, provide the context in which gendered identities and separate "gendered cultures" develop and come to appear natural. For the boys in this study, it became "natural" to equate masculinity with competition, physical strength, and skills. Girls simply did not (could not, it was believed) participate in these activities.

Yet it is not simply the separation of children, by adults, into separate activities that explains why many boys came to feel such a strong connection with sports activities, while so few girls did. As I listened to men recall their earliest experiences in organized sports, I heard them talk of insecurity, loneliness, and especially a need to connect with other people as a primary motivation in their early sports strivings. As a 42-year-old white man stated, "The most important thing was just being out there with the rest of the guys—being friends." Another 32-year-old interviewee was born in Mexico and moved to the United States at a fairly young age. He never knew his father, and his mother died when he was only nine years old. Suddenly he felt rootless, and threw himself into sports. His initial motivations, however, do not appear to be based on a need to compete or win:

> *Actually, what I think sports did for me is it brought me into kind of an instant family. By being on a Little League team, or even just playing with all kinds of different kids in the neighborhood, it brought what I really wanted, which was some kind of closeness. It was just being there, and being friends.*

Clearly, what these boys needed and craved was that which was most problematic for them: connection and unity with other people. But why do these young males find *organized sports* such an attractive context in which to establish "a kind of closeness" with others? Comparative observations of young boys' and girls' game-playing behaviors yield important insights into this question. Piaget (1965) and Lever (1976) both observed that girls tend to have more "pragmatic" and "flexible" orientations to the rules of games; they are more prone to make exceptions and innovations in the middle of a game in order to make the game more "fair." Boys, on the other hand, tend to have a more firm, even [in]flexible orientation to the rules of the game; to them, the rules are what protects any fairness. This difference, according to Gilligan (1982), is based on the fact that early developmental experiences have yielded deeply rooted differences between males' and females' developmental tasks, needs, and moral reasoning. Girls, who tend to define themselves primarily through connection with others, experience highly competitive situations (whether in organized sports or in other hierarchical institutions) as threats to relationships, and thus to their identities. For boys, the development of gender identity involves the construction of positional identities, where a sense of self is solidified through separation from others (Chodorow, 1978). Yet feminist psychoanalytic theory has tended to oversimplify the internal lives of men (Lichterman, 1986). Males do appear to develop positional identities, yet despite their fears of intimacy, they also retain a human need for closeness and unity with others. This ambivalence toward intimate relationships is a major thread running through masculine development throughout the life course. Here we can conceptualize what Craib (1987) calls the "elective affinity" between personality and social structure: For the boy who seeks and fears attachment with others, the rule-bound structure of organized sports can promise to be a safe place in which to seek nonintimate attachment with others

within a context that maintains clear boundaries, distance, and separation.

COMPETITIVE STRUCTURES AND CONDITIONAL SELF-WORTH

Young boys may initially find that sports gives them the opportunity to experience "some kind of closeness" with others, but the structure of sports and athletic careers often undermines the possibility of boys learning to transcend their fears of intimacy, thus becoming able to develop truly close and intimate relationships with others (Kidd, 1990; Messner, 1987). The sports world is extremely hierarchical, and an incredible amount of importance is placed on winning, on "being number one." For instance, a few years ago I observed a basketball camp put on for boys by a professional basketball coach and his staff. The youngest boys, about eight years old (who could barely reach the basket with their shots) played a brief scrimmage. Afterwards, the coaches lined them up in a row in front of the older boys who were sitting in the grandstands. One by one, the coach would stand behind each boy, put his hand on the boy's head (much in the manner of a priestly benediction), and the older boys in the stands would applaud and cheer, louder or softer, depending on how well or poorly the young boy was judged to have performed. The two or three boys who were clearly the exceptional players looked confident that they would receive the praise they were due. Most of the boys, though, had expressions ranging from puzzlement to thinly disguised terror on their faces as they awaited the judgments of the older boys.

This kind of experience teaches boys that it is not "just being out there with the guys—being friends," that ensures the kind of attention and connection that they crave; it is being *better* than the other guys—*beating* them—that is the key to acceptance. Most of the boys in this study did have some early successes in sports, and thus their ambivalent need for connection with others was met, at least for a time. But the institution of sports tends to encourage the development of what Schafer (1975) has called "conditional self-worth" in boys. As boys become aware that acceptance by others is contingent upon being good—a "winner"—narrow definitions of success, based upon performance and winning become increasingly important to them. A 33-year-old black man said that by the time he was in his early teens:

> It was expected of me to do well in all my contests—I mean by my coaches, my peers, and my family. So I in turn expected to do well, and if I didn't do well, then I'd be very disappointed.

The man from Mexico, discussed above, who said that he had sought "some kind of closeness" in his early sports experiences began to notice in his early teens that if he played well, was a *winner*, he would get attention from others:

> It got to the point where I started realizing, noticing that people were always there for me, backing me all the time—sports got to be really fun because I always had some people there backing me. Finally, my oldest brother started going to all my games, even though I had never really seen who he was [laughs]—after the game, you know, we never really saw each other, but he was at all my baseball games, and it seemed like we shared a kind of closeness there, but only in those situations. Off the field, when I wasn't in uniform, he was never around.

By high school, he said, he felt "up against the wall." Sports hadn't delivered what he had hoped it would, but he thought if he just tried harder, won one more championship trophy, he would get the attention he truly craved. Despite his efforts, this at-

tention was not forthcoming. And, sadly, the pressures he had put on himself to excel in sports had taken most of the fun out of playing.

For many of the men in this study, throughout boyhood and into adolescence, this conscious striving for successful achievement became the primary means through which they sought connection with other people (Messner, 1987). But it is important to recognize that young males' internalized ambivalences about intimacy do not fully determine the contours and directions of their lives. Masculinity continues to develop through interaction with the social world—and because boys from different backgrounds are interacting with substantially different familial, educational, and other institutions, these differences will lead them to make different choices and define situations in different ways. Next, I examine the differences in the ways that boys from higher- and lower-status families and communities related to organized sports.

STATUS DIFFERENCES AND COMMITMENTS TO SPORTS

In discussing early attractions to sports, the experiences of boys from higher- and lower-status backgrounds are quite similar. Both groups indicate the importance of fathers and older brothers in introducing them to sports. Both groups speak of the joys of receiving attention and acceptance among family and peers for early successes in sports. Note the similarities, for instance, in the following descriptions of boyhood athletic experiences of two men. First, a man born in a white, middle-class family:

> I loved playing sports so much from a very early age because of early exposure. A lot of the sports came easy at an early age, and because they did, and because you were

successful at something, I think that you're inclined to strive for that gratification. It's like, if you're good, you like it, because it's instant gratification. I'm doing something that I'm good at and I'm gonna keep doing it.

Second, a black man from a poor family:

Fortunately I had some athletic ability, and, quite naturally, once you start doing good in whatever it is—I don't care if it's jacks—you show off what you do. That's your ability, that's your blessing, so you show it off as much as you can.

For boys from both groups, early exposure to sports, the discovery that they had some "ability," shortly followed by some sort of family, peer, and community recognition, all eventually led to the commitment of hundreds and thousands of hours of playing, practicing, and dreaming of future stardom. Despite these similarities, there are also some identifiable differences that begin to explain the tendency of males from lower-status backgrounds to develop higher levels of commitment to sports careers. The most clear-cut difference was that while men from higher-status backgrounds are likely to describe their earliest athletic experiences and motivations almost exclusively in terms of immediate family, men from lower-status backgrounds more commonly describe the importance of a broader community context. For instance, a 46-year-old man who grew up in a "poor working class" black family in a small town in Arkansas explained:

In that community, at the age of third or fourth grade, if you're a male, they expect you to show some kind of inclination, some kind of skill in football or basketball. It was an expected thing, you know? My mom and my dad, they didn't push at all. It was the general environment.

A 48-year-old man describes sports activities as a survival strategy in his poor black community:

Sports protected me from having to compete in gang stuff, or having to be good with my fists. If you were an athlete and got into the fist world, that was your business, and that was okay—but you didn't have to if you didn't want to. People would generally defer to you, give you your space away from trouble.

A 35-year-old man who grew up in "a poor black ghetto" described his boyhood relationship to sports similarly:

Where I came from, either you were one of two things: you were in sports or you were out on the streets being a drug addict, or breaking into places. The guys who were in sports, we had it a little easier, because we were accepted by both groups. . . . So it worked out to my advantage, cause I didn't get into a lot of trouble—some trouble, but not a lot.

The fact that boys in lower-status communities faced these kinds of realities gave salience to their developing athletic identities. In contrast, sports were important to boys from higher-status backgrounds, yet the middle-class environment seemed more secure, less threatening, and offered far more options. By the time most of these boys got into junior high or high school, many had made conscious decisions to shift their attentions away from athletic careers to education and (nonathletic) career goals. A 32-year-old white college athletic director told me that he had seen his chance to pursue a pro baseball career as "pissing in the wind," and instead, focused on education. Similarly, a 33-year-old white dentist who was a three-sport star in high school, decided not to play sports in college, so he could focus on getting into dental school. As he put it,

> *I think I kind of downgraded the stardom thing. I thought it was small potatoes. And sure, that's nice in high school and all that, but on a broad scale, I didn't think it amounted to all that much.*

This statement offers an important key to understanding the construction of masculine identity within a middle-class context. The status that this boy got through sports had been *very* important to him, yet he could see that "on a broad scale," this sort of status was "small potatoes." This sort of early recognition is more than a result of the oft-noted middle-class tendency to raise "future-oriented" children (Rubin, 1976; Sennett and Cobb, 1973). Perhaps more important, it is that the *kinds* of future orientations developed by boys from higher-status backgrounds are consistent with the middle-class context. These men's descriptions of their boyhoods reveal that they grew up immersed in a wide range of institutional frameworks, of which organized sports was just one. And—importantly—they could see that the status of adult males around them was clearly linked to their positions within various professions, public institutions, and bureaucratic organizations. It was clear that access to this sort of institutional status came through educational achievement, not athletic prowess. A 32-year-old black man who grew up in a professional-class family recalled that he had idolized Wilt Chamberlain and dreamed of being a pro basketball player, yet his father discouraged his athletic strivings:

> *He knew I liked the game. I loved the game. But basketball was not recommended; my dad would say, "That's a stereotyped image for black youth. . . . When your basketball is gone and finished, what are you gonna*

do? One day, you might get injured. What are you gonna look forward to?" He stressed education.

Similarly, a 32-year-old man who was raised in a white, middle-class family, had found in sports a key means of gaining acceptance and connection in his peer group. Yet he was simultaneously developing an image of himself as a "smart student," and becoming aware of a wide range of nonsports life options:

> *My mother was constantly telling me how smart I was, how good I was, what a nice person I was, and giving me all sorts of positive strokes, and those positive strokes became a self-motivating kind of thing. I had this image of myself as smart, and I lived up to that image.*

It is not that parents of boys in lower-status families did not also encourage their boys to work hard in school. Several reported that their parents "stressed books first, sports second." It's just that the broader social context—education, economy, and community—was more likely to *narrow* lower-status boys' perceptions of real-life options, while boys from higher-status backgrounds faced an expanding world of options. For instance, with a different socioeconomic background, one 35-year-old black man might have become a great musician instead of a star professional football running back. But he did not. When he was a child, he said, he was most interested in music:

> *I wanted to be a drummer. But we couldn't afford drums. My dad couldn't go out and buy me a drum set or a guitar even—it was just one of those things; he was trying to make ends meet.*

But he *could* afford, as could so many in his socioeconomic condition, to spend countless hours at the local park, where he was told by the park supervisor

> that I was a natural—not only in gymnastics or baseball—whatever I did, I was a natural. He told me I shouldn't waste this talent, and so I immediately started watching the big guys then.

In retrospect, this man had potential to be a musician or any number of things, but his environment limited his options to sports, and he made the best of it. Even within sports, he, like most boys in the ghetto, was limited:

> We didn't have any tennis courts in the ghetto—we used to have a lot of tennis balls, but no racquets. I wonder today how good I might be in tennis if I had gotten a racquet in my hands at an early age.

It is within this limited structure of opportunity that many lower-status young boys found sports to be *the* place, rather than *a* place, within which to construct masculine identity, status, the relationships. A 36-year-old white man explained that his father left the family when he was very young and his mother faced a very difficult struggle to make ends meet. As his words suggest, the more limited a boy's options, and the more insecure his family situation, the more likely he is to make an early commitment to an athletic career:

> I used to ride my bicycle to Little League practice—if I'd waited for someone to pick me up and take me to the ball park I'd have never played. I'd get to the ball park and all the other kids would have their dad bring them to practice or games. But I'd park my bike to the side and when it was over I'd get on it and go home. Sports was the way for me to move everything to the side—family problems, just all the embarrassments—and think about one thing, and that was sports.

> . . . In the third grade, when the teacher went around the classroom and asked everybody, "What do you want to be when you grow up?", I said, "I want to be a major league baseball player," and everybody laughed their heads off.

This man eventually did enjoy a major league baseball career. Most boys from lower-status backgrounds who make similar early commitments to athletic careers are not so successful. As stated earlier, the career structure of organized sports is highly competitive and hierarchical. In fact, the chances of attaining professional status in sports are approximately 4:100,000 for a white man, 2:100,000 for a black man, and 3:1 million for a Hispanic man in the United States (Leonard and Reyman, 1988). Nevertheless, the immediate rewards (fun, status, attention), along with the constricted (nonsports) structure of opportunity, attract disproportionately large number of boys from lower-status backgrounds to athletic careers as their major means of constructing a masculine identity. These are the boys who later, as young men, had to struggle with "conditional self-worth," and, more often than not, occupational dead ends. Boys from higher-status backgrounds, on the other hand, bolstered their boyhood, adolescent, and early adult status through their athletic accomplishments. Their wider range of experiences and life chances led to an early shift away from sports careers as the major basis of identity (Messner, 1989).

CONCLUSION

The conception of the masculinity-sports relationship developed here begins to illustrate the idea of an "elective affinity" between social structure and personality. Organized sports is a "gendered institution"—an institution constructed by gender relations. As such, its structure and values (rules, formal organization, sex composition, etc.) reflect dominant conceptions of masculinity and femininity. Organized sports is also a "gendering institution"—an institution that helps to construct the current gender order. Part of this construction of gender is accomplished through the "masculinizing" of male bodies and minds.

Yet boys do not come to their first experiences in organized sports as "blank slates," but arrive with already "gendering" identities due to early developmental experiences and previous socialization. I have suggested here that an important thread running through the development of masculine identity is males' ambivalence toward intimate unity with others. Those boys who experience early athletic successes find in the structure of organized sports an affinity with this masculine ambivalence toward intimacy: The rule-bound, competitive, hierarchical world of sports offers boys an attractive means of establishing an emotionally distant (and thus "safe") connection with others. Yet as boys begin to define themselves as "athletes," they learn that in order to be accepted (to have connection) through sports, they must be winners. And in order to be winners, they must construct relationships with others (and with themselves) that are consistent with the competitive and hierarchical values and structure of the sports world. As a result, they often develop a "conditional self-worth" that leads them to construct more instrumental relationships with themselves and others. This ultimately exacerbates their difficulties in constructing intimate relationships with others. In effect, the interaction between the young male's preexisting internalized ambivalence toward intimacy with the competitive hierarchical institution of sport has resulted in the construction of a masculine personality that is characterized by instrumental rationality, goal-orientation,

and difficulties with intimate connection and expression (Messner, 1987).

This theoretical line of inquiry invites us not simply to examine how social institutions "socialize" boys, but also to explore the ways that boys' already-gendering identities interact with social institutions (which, like organized sport, are themselves the product of gender relations). This study has also suggested that it is not some singular "masculinity" that is being constructed through athletic careers. It may be correct, from a psychoanalytic perspective, to suggest that all males bring ambivalences toward intimacy to their interactions with the world, but "the world" is a very different place for males from different racial and socioeconomic backgrounds. Because males have substantially different interactions with the world, based on class, race, and other differences and inequalities, we might expect the construction of masculinity to take on different meanings for boys and men from differing backgrounds (Messner, 1989). Indeed, this study has suggested that boys from higher-status backgrounds face a much broader range of options than do their lower-status counterparts. As a result, athletic careers take on different meanings for these boys. Lower-status boys are likely to see athletic careers as *the* institutional context for the construction of their masculine status and identities, while higher-status males make an early shift away from athletic careers toward other institutions (usually education and nonsports careers). A key line in inquiry for future studies might begin by exploring this irony of sports careers: Despite the fact that "the athlete" is currently an example of an exemplary form of masculinity in public ideology, the vast majority of boys who become most committed to athletic careers are never well-rewarded for their efforts. The fact that class and racial dynamics lead boys from higher-status backgrounds, unlike their lower-status counterparts, to move into nonsports careers illustrates how the construction of different kinds of masculinities is a key component of the overall construction of the gender order.

REFERENCES

Birrell, S. (1987) "The woman athlete's college experience: knowns and unknowns." *J. of Sport and Social Issues* 11:82–96.

Benjamin, J. (1988) *The Bonds of Love: Psychoanalysis, Feminism, and the Problem of Domination.* New York: Pantheon.

Bryson, L. (1987) "Sport and the maintenance of masculine hegemony." *Women's Studies International Forum* 10:349–360.

Chodorow, N. (1978) *The Reproduction of Mothering.* Berkeley: Univ. of California Press.

Connell, R. W. (1987) *Gender and Power.* Stanford, CA: Stanford Univ. Press.

Connell, R. W. (1990) "An iron man: the body and some contradictions of hegemonic masculinity," In M. A. Messner and D. F. Sabo (eds.) *Sport, Men and the Gender Order: Critical Feminist Perspectives.* Champaign, IL: Human Kinetics.

Craib, I. (1987) "Masculinity and male dominance." *Soc. Rev.* 38:721–743.

Eitzen, D. S. (1975) "Athletics in the status system of male adolescents: a replication of Coleman's *The Adolescent Society.*" *Adolescence* 10:268–276.

Gilligan, C. (1982) *In a Different Voice: Psychological Theory and Women's Development.* Cambridge, MA: Harvard Univ. Press.

Greendorfer, S. L. (1977) "The role of socializing agents in female sport involvement." *Research Q.* 48:304–310.

Hall, M. A. (1988) "The discourse on gender and sport: from femininity to feminism." *Sociology of Sport J.* 5:330–340.

Hantover, J. (1978) "The boy scouts and the validation of masculinity." *J. of Social Issues* 34:184–195.

Haug, F. (1987) *Female Sexualization.* London: Verso.

Kidd, B. (1987) "Sports and masculinity," pp. 250–265 in M. Kaufman (ed.) *Beyond Patriarchy: Essays by Men on Pleasure, Power, and Change.* Toronto: Oxford Univ. Press.

Kidd, B. (1990) "The men's cultural centre: sports and the dynamic of women's oppression/men's repression," In M. A. Messner and D. F. Sabo (eds.) *Sport, Men and the Gender Order: Critical Feminist Perspectives.* Champaign, IL: Human Kinetics.

Kimmel, M. S. (1987) "Men's responses to feminism at the turn of the century." *Gender and Society* 1:261–283.

Kimmel, M. S. (1990) "Baseball and the reconstitution of American masculinity: 1880–1920," In M. A. Messner and D. F. Sabo (eds.) *Sport, Men and the Gender Order: Critical Feminist Perspectives.* Champaign, IL: Human Kinetics.

Leonard, W. M. II and J. M. Reyman (1988) "The odds of attaining professional athlete status: refining the computations." *Sociology of Sport J.* 5:162–169.

Lever, J. (1976) "Sex differences in the games children play." *Social Problems* 23:478–487.

Levinson, D. J. et al. (1978) *The Seasons of a Man's Life.* New York: Ballantine.

Lichterman, P. (1986) "Chodorow's psychoanalytic sociology: a project half-completed." *California Sociologist* 9:147–166.

Messner, M. (1987) "The meaning of success: the athletic experience and the development of male identity," pp. 193–210 in H. Brod (ed.) *The Making of Masculinities: The New Men's Studies.* Boston: Allen & Unwin.

Messner, M. (1988) "Sports and male domination: the female athlete as contested ideological terrain." *Sociology of Sport J.* 5:197–211.

Messner, M. (1989) "Masculinities and athletic careers." *Gender and Society* 3:71–88.

Ogelsby, C. A. (Ed.) (1978) *Women and Sport: From Myth to Reality.* Philadelphia: Lea & Farber.

Osherson, S. (1986) *Finding Our Fathers: How a Man's Life Is Shaped by His Relationships with His Father.* New York: Fawcett Columbine.

Piaget, J. H. (1965) *The Moral Judgment of the Child.* New York: Free Press.

Rubin, L. B. (1976) *Worlds of Pain: Life in the Working Class Family.* New York: Basic Books.

Sabo, D. (1985) "Sport, patriarchy and male identity: new questions about men and sport." *Arena Rev.* 9:2.

Schafer, W. E. (1975) "Sport and male sex role socialization." *Sport Sociology Bull.* 4:47–54.

Sennett, R. and J. Cobb (1973) *The Hidden Injuries of Class.* New York: Random House.

Theberge, N. (1981) "A critique of critiques: radical and feminist writings on sport." *Social Forces* 60:2.

Thorne, B. (1986) "Girls and boys together . . . but mostly apart: gender arrangements in elementary schools," pp. 167–184 in W. W. Hartup and Z. Rubin (eds.) *Relationships and Development.* Hillsdale, NJ: Lawrence Erlbaum.

Twin, S. L. [ed.] (1978) *Out of the Bleachers: Writings of Women and Sport.* Old Westbury, NY: Feminist Press.

Questions for Understanding and Critical Thinking

1. How has feminist scholarship contributed to the understanding of socialization for masculinity?
2. Why do organized sports play such a central role in athletes' lives?
3. Based on your own experiences, do you agree with Messner's assessment that role models are important in gender socialization for sports? Why or why not?
4. Why do males from lower-status backgrounds often develop higher levels of commitment to sports careers than males from higher-status backgrounds?
5. How does race affect boys' decisions to compete in athletic events and pursue sports careers?

ARTICLE 14 _____

Racial socialization may take place covertly through people's continual exposure to negative images and stereotypes regarding members of a subordinate
racial-ethnic group. In this article, Native American scholar Ward Churchill
discusses the controversy surrounding the names of professional sports teams
such as the Washington Redskins and the Atlanta Braves (the latter being
known for its fans' use of the famous "Tomahawk Chop"). Churchill argues
that the use of these racist images and stereotypes perpetuates the subordination of Native Americans, who, for centuries, have been the objects of prejudice and discrimination in all aspects of life.

Ward Churchill teaches American Indian Studies and Communications at
the University of Colorado–Boulder, where he serves as associate director of
the Center for Studies of Ethnicity and Race in America. He also is codirector
of the American Indian Movement of Colorado and vice chairperson of the
American Indian Anti-Defamation Council.

Looking Ahead

1. What does Churchill think people should do if they genuinely are interested
   in honoring Native Americans?
2. Why have many Native Americans protested the use of native names, images, and symbols as sports team mascots?
3. What would happen if images of other racial-ethnic groups were used by
   sports teams in the same way as those of Native Americans?

Indians R US?
Let's Spread the "Fun" Around

The Issue of Sports Team Names and Mascots

◆ *Ward Churchill*

If people are genuinely interested in honoring Indians, try getting your gov-
ernment to live up to the more than 400 treaties it signed with our nations.
Try respecting our religious freedom which has been repeatedly denied in
federal courts. Try stopping the ongoing theft of Indian water and other

Source: From Ward Churchill, *Indians R US?* (Monroe, ME: Common Courage Press, 1994), pp.
65–72. Copyright © 1994 by Ward Churchill. Reprinted by permission of Common Courage
Press, Box 702, Monroe ME 04951.

natural resources. Try reversing your colonial process that relegates us to the most impoverished, polluted, and desperate conditions in this country. . . . Try understanding that the mascot issue is only the tip of a very huge problem of continuing racism against American Indians. Then maybe your ["honors"] will mean something. Until then, it's just so much superficial, hypocritical puffery. People should remember that an honor isn't born when it parts the honorer's lips, it is born when it is accepted in the honoree's ear.

—Glenn T. Morris
Colorado AIM

During the past couple of seasons, there has been an increasing wave of controversy regarding the names of professional sports teams like the Atlanta "Braves," Cleveland "Indians," Washington "Redskins," and Kansas City "Chiefs." The issue extends to the names of college teams like Florida State University "Seminoles," University of Illinois "Fighting Illini," and so on, right on down to high school outfits like the Lamar (Colorado) "Savages." Also involved have been team adoption of "mascots," replete with feathers, buckskins, beads, spears, and "warpaint" (some fans have opted to adorn themselves in the same fashion), and nifty little "pep" gestures like the "Indian Chant" and "Tomahawk Chop."

A substantial number of American Indians have protested that use of native names, images, and symbols as sports team mascots and the like is, by definition, a virulently racist practice. Given the historical relationship between Indians and non-Indians during what has been called the "Conquest of America," American Indian Movement leader (and American Indian Anti-Defamation Council founder) Russell Means has compared the practice to contemporary Germans naming their soccer teams the "Jews," "Hebrews," and "Yids," while adorning their uniforms with grotesque caricatures of Jewish faces taken from the nazis' antisemitic propaganda of the 1930s. Numerous demonstrations have occurred in conjunction with games—most notably during the November

15, 1992, match-up between the Chiefs and Redskins in Kansas City—by angry Indians and their supporters.

In response, a number of players—especially African-Americans and other minority athletes—have been trotted out by professional team owners like Ted Turner, as well as university and public school officials, to announce that they mean not to insult, but instead to "honor," native people. They have been joined by the television networks and most major newspapers, all of which have editorialized that Indian discomfort with the situation is "no big deal," insisting that the whole thing is just "good, clean fun." The country needs more such fun, they've argued, and "a few disgruntled Native Americans" have no right to undermine the nation's enjoyment of its leisure time by complaining. This is especially the case, some have contended, "in hard times like these." It has even been contended that Indian outrage at being systematically degraded—rather than the degradation itself—creates "a serious barrier to the sort of intergroup communication so necessary in a multicultural society such as ours."

Okay, let's communicate. We may be frankly dubious that those advancing such positions really believe in their own rhetoric, but, just for the sake of argument, let's accept the premise that they are sincere. If what they are saying is true in any way at all, then isn't it time we spread such "inoffensiveness" and "good cheer" around among *all* groups so that *everybody* can participate *equally* in fostering the round of national laughs they call for? Sure it is—the country can't have too *much* fun or "intergroup involvement"—so the more, the merrier. Simple consistency demands that anyone who thinks the Tomahawk Chop is a swell pastime must be just as hearty in their endorsement of the following ideas, which—by the "logic" used to defend the defamation of American Indians—should help us all *really* start yukking it up.

First, as a counterpart to the Redskins, we need an NFL team called "Niggers" to "honor" Afroamerica. Halftime festivities for fans might include a simulated stewing of the opposing coach in a large pot while players and cheerleaders dance around it, garbed in leopard skins and wearing fake bones in their noses. This concept obviously goes along with the kind of gaiety attending the Chop, but also with the actions of the Kansas City Chiefs, whose team members—prominently including black team members—lately appeared on a poster looking "fierce" and "savage" by way of wearing Indian regalia. Just a bit of harmless "morale boosting," says the Chiefs' front office. You bet.

So that the newly-formed "Niggers" sports club won't end up too out of sync while expressing the "spirit" and "identity" of Afroamericans in the above fashion, a baseball franchise—let's call this one the "Sambos"—should be formed. How about a basketball team called the "Spearchuckers"? A hockey team called the "Jungle Bunnies"? Maybe the "essence" of these teams could be depicted by images of tiny black faces adorned with huge pairs of lips. The players could appear on TV every week or so gnawing on chicken legs and spitting watermelon seeds at one another. Catchy, eh? Well, there's "nothing to be upset about," according to those who love wearing "war bonnets" to the Super Bowl or having "Chief Illiniwik"

dance around the sports arenas of Urbana, Illinois.

And why stop there? There are plenty of other groups to include. "Hispanics"? They can be "represented" by the Galveston "Greasers" and San Diego "Spics," at least until the Wisconsin "Wetbacks" and Baltimore "Beaners" get off the ground. Asian Americans? How about the "Slopes," "Dinks," "Gooks," and "Zipperheads"? Owners of the latter teams might get their logo ideas from editorial page cartoons printed in the nation's newspapers during World War II: slant-eyes, buck teeth, big glasses, but nothing racially insulting or derogatory, according to the editors and artists involved at the time. Indeed, this Second World War–vintage stuff can be seen as just another barrel of laughs, at least by what current editors say are their "local standards" concerning American Indians.

Let's see. Who's been left out? Teams like the Kansas City "Kikes," Hanover "Honkies," San Leandro "Shylocks," Daytona "Dagos," and Pittsburgh "Polacks" will fill a certain social void among white folk. Have a religious belief? Let's all go for the gusto and gear up the Milwaukee "Mackerel Snappers" and Hollywood "Holy Rollers." The Fighting Irish of Notre Dame can be rechristened the "Drunken Irish" or "Papist Pigs." Issues of gender and sexual preference can be addressed through creation of teams like the St. Louis "Sluts," Boston "Bimbos," Detroit "Dykes," and the Fresno "Faggots." How about the Gainesville "Gimps" and Richmond "Retards," so the physically and mentally impaired won't be excluded from our fun and games?

Now, don't go getting "overly sensitive" out there. *None* of this is demeaning or insulting, at least not when it's being done to Indians. Just ask the folks who are doing it, or their apologists like Andy Rooney in the national media. They'll tell you—as in fact they *have* been telling you—that there's been no harm done, regardless of what their victims think, feel, or say. The situation is exactly the same as when those with precisely the same mentality used to insist that Step'n'Fetchit was okay, or Rochester on the *Jack Benny Show,* or Amos and Andy, Charlie Chan, the Frito Bandito, or any of the other cutesey symbols making up the lexicon of American racism. Have we communicated yet?

Let's get just a little bit real here. The notion of "fun" embodied in rituals like the Tomahawk Chop must be understood for what it is. There's not a single non-Indian example deployed above which can be considered socially acceptable in even the most marginal sense. The reasons are obvious enough. So why is it different where American Indians are concerned? One can only conclude that, in contrast to the other groups at issue, Indians are (falsely) perceived as being too few, and therefore too weak, to defend themselves effectively against racist and otherwise offensive behavior. The sensibilities of those who take pleasure in things like the Chop are thus akin to those of schoolyard bullies and those twisted individuals who like to torture cats. At another level, their perspectives have much in common with those manifested more literally—and therefore more honestly—by groups like the nazis, aryan nations, and Ku Klux Klan. Those who suggest this is "okay" should be treated accordingly by anyone who opposes nazism and comparable belief systems.

Fortunately, there are a few glimmers of hope that this may become the case. A few teams and their fans have gotten the message and have responded appropriately. One illustration is Stanford University, which opted to drop the name "Indians" with regard to its sports teams (and, contrary to the myth perpetuated by those who enjoy insulting Native Americans, Stanford has experienced *no* resulting drop-off in attendance at its games). Meanwhile, the local newspaper in Portland, Oregon, recently decided its long-standing editorial policy prohibiting use of racial epithets should include derogatory sports team names. The Redskins, for instance, are now simply referred to as being "the Washington team," and will continue to be described in this way until the franchise adopts an inoffensive moniker (newspaper sales in Portland have suffered no decline as a result).

Such examples are to be applauded and encouraged. They stand as figurative beacons in the night, proving beyond all doubt that it is quite possible to indulge in the pleasure of athletics without accepting blatant racism into the bargain. The extent to which they do not represent the norm of American attitudes and behavior is exactly the extent to which America remains afflicted with an ugly reality which is far different from the noble and enlightened "moral leadership" it professes to show the world. Clearly, the United States has a very long way to go before it measures up to such an image of itself.

Questions for Understanding and Critical Thinking

1. Do you think that the use of Native American names, images, and symbols as sports team mascots is just "good, clean fun" or is it racist, as Churchill suggests? Why or why not?
2. What effect do such images and stereotypes have on young children who are spectators at sporting events? Explain your answer.
3. Have television and other media contributed to widespread knowledge of these derogatory images of Native Americans? Explain your answer.
4. According to Churchill, is there any reason to be optimistic that things might change in the future? Why or why not?

ARTICLE 15 _____

According to sociologists Caroline Hodges Persell and Peter W. Cookson, Jr., the upper class is reproduced through elite education. From interviews and observations at 42 private boarding schools, Persell and Cookson find that elite schools confer special status rights on their students. Through chartering and bartering, officials at such schools contribute to the reproduction of the upper class in the United States.

    Caroline Hodges Persell teaches in the Department of Sociology at New York University. Peter W. Cookson, Jr., teaches sociology at Adelphi University in Garden City, New York.

Looking Ahead

1. How do Persell and Cookson define *chartering* and *bartering?*
2. What has been the historical relationship between elite boarding schools and Ivy League colleges?
3. How do the educational processes described by Persell and Cookson contribute to social class reproduction in the United States?

Chartering and Bartering
Elite Education and Social Reproduction

◆ *Caroline Hodges Persell and Peter W. Cookson, Jr.*

The continuation of power and privilege has been the subject of intense sociological debate. One recurring question is whether the system of mobility is open or whether relationships of power and privilege are reproduced from one generation to the next. If reproduction occurs, is it the reproduction of certain powerful and privileged families or groups (cf. Robinson, 1984)? Or, does it involve the reproduction of a structure of power and privilege which allows for replacement of some members with new recruits while preserving the structure?

The role of education in these processes has been the subject of much dispute. Researchers in the status attainment tradition stress the importance for mobility of the knowledge and skills acquired through education thereby emphasizing the meritocratic and open basis for mobility (e.g., Alexander and Eckland, 1975; Alexander et al., 1975; Blau and Duncan, 1967; Haller and Portes,

Source: From Caroline Hodges Persell and Peter W. Cookson, Jr., "Chartering and Bartering: Elite Education and Social Reproduction." © 1985 by the Society for the Study of Social Problems. Reprinted from *Social Problems,* Vol. 33, No. 2, December 1985, pp. 114–129, by permission.

1973; Otto and Haller, 1979; Kerckhoff, 1984; Sewell et al., 1969, 1970; Wilson and Portes, 1975). On the other hand, theorists such as Bowles and Gintis (1976) suggest education inculcates certain non-cognitive personality traits which serve to reproduce the social relations within a class structure; thus they put more emphasis on non-meritocratic features in the educational process.

Collins (1979) also deals with non-meritocratic aspects when he suggests that educational institutions develop and fortify status groups, and that differently valued educational credentials protect desired market positions such as those of the professions. In a related vein, Meyer (1977) notes that certain organizational "charters" serve as "selection criteria" in an educational or occupational marketplace. Meyer defines "charter" as "the social definition of the products of [an] organization" (Meyer 1970:577). Charters do not need to be recognized formally or legally to operate in social life. If they exist, they would create structural limitations within a presumably open market by making some people eligible for certain sets of rights that are denied to other people.

Social observers have long noted that one particular set of schools is central to the reproduction and solidarity of a national upper class, specifically elite secondary boarding schools (Baltzell, 1958, 1964; Domhoff, 1967, 1970, 1983; Mills, 1956). As well as preparing their students for socially desirable colleges and universities, traditionally such schools have been thought to build social networks among upper class scions from various regions, leading to adult business deals and marriages. Although less than one percent of the American population attends such schools, that one percent represents a strategic segment of American life that is seldom directly studied. Recently, Useem and Karabel (1984) reported that graduates of 14 elite boarding schools were much more likely than non-graduates to become part of the "inner circle" of Fortune 500 business leaders. This evidence suggests that elite schools may play a role in class reproduction.

Few researchers have gained direct access to these schools to study social processes bearing on social reproduction. The research reported here represents the first systematic study of elite secondary boarding schools and their social relations with another important institution, namely colleges and universities.

The results of this research illustrate Collins' view that stratification involves networks of "persons making bargains and threats . . . [and that] the key resource of powerful individuals is their ability to impress and manipulate a network of social contacts" (1979:26). If such were the case, we would expect to find that upper class institutions actively develop social networks for the purpose of advancing the interests of their constituencies.

By focusing on the processes of social reproduction rather than individual attributes or the results of intergenerational mobility, our research differs from the approaches taken in both the status attainment and status allocation literature. Status attainment models focus on individual attributes and achievements, and allocation models examine structural supports or barriers to social mobility; yet neither approach explores the underlying processes. Status attainment models assume the existence of a relatively open contest system, while reproduction and allocation models stress that selection criteria and structural barriers create inequalities, limiting opportunities for one group while favoring another (Kerckhoff, 1976, 1984). Neither attainment nor allocation models show how class reproduction, selection criteria, or structural opportunities and impediments operate in practice.

Considerable evidence supports the view that structural limitations operate in the labor market (e.g., Beck et al., 1978; Bibb and Form, 1977; Stolzenberg, 1975) but, with the exception of tracking, little evidence has been found that similar structural limitations exist in education. Tracking systems create structural impediments in an open model of educational attainment (Oakes, 1985; Persell, 1977; Rosenbaum, 1976, 1980), although not all research supports this conclusion (e.g., Alexander et al., 1978; Heyns, 1974).

In this paper we suggest that there is an additional structural limitation in the key transition from high school to college. We explore the possibility that special organizational "charters" exist for certain secondary schools and that a process of "bartering" occurs between representatives of selected secondary schools and some college admissions officers. These processes have not been clearly identified by prior research on education and stratification, although there has been some previous research which leads in this direction.

EMPIRICAL LITERATURE

Researchers of various orientations concur that differences between schools seem to have little bearing on student attainment (Averch et al., 1972; Jencks et al., 1972; Meyer, 1970, 1977). Indeed, Meyer (1977) suggests the most puzzling paradox in the sociology of American education is that while schools differ in structure and resources, they vary little in their effects because all secondary schools are assumed to have similar "charters." Meyer believes that no American high school is specially chartered by selective colleges in the way, for instance, that certain British Public Schools have been chartered by Oxford and Cambridge Universities. Instead, he suggests that "all American high schools have similar status rights, (and therefore) variations in their effects should be small" (Meyer, 1977:60).

Kamens (1977:217–218), on the other hand, argues that "schools symbolically redefine people and make them eligible for membership in societal categories to which specific sets of rights are assigned." The work of Alexander and Eckland (1977) is consistent with this view. These researchers found that students who attended high schools where the social status of the student body was high also attended selective colleges at a greater rate than did students at other high schools, even when individual student academic ability and family background were held constant (Alexander and Eckland, 1977). Their research and other work finding a relationship between curricular track placement and college attendance (Alexander et al., 1978; Alexander and McDill, 1976; Jaffe and Adams, 1970; Rosenbaum, 1976, 1980) suggest that differences between schools may affect stratification outcomes.

Research has shown that graduation from a private school is related to attending a four-year (rather than a two-year) college (Falsey and Heyns, 1984), attending a highly selective college (Hammack and Cookson, 1980), and earning higher income in adult life (Lewis and Wanner, 1979). Moreover, Cookson (1981) found that graduates of private boarding schools attended more selective colleges than did their public school counterparts, even when family background and Scholastic Aptitude Test (SAT) scores were held constant. Furthermore, some private colleges acknowledge the distinctive nature of certain secondary schools. Klitgaard (1985: Table 2.2) reports that students from private secondary schools generally had an advantage for admission to Harvard over public school graduates, even when their academic ratings were comparable. Karen (1985) notes that applications to Harvard from certain private boarding schools were placed in special colored dockets, or folders, to set them apart from other applications. Thus, they were considered as a distinct group. Not only did Harvard acknowledge the special status of certain schools by color-coding their applicants' folders, attendance at one of those schools provided an advantage for acceptance, even when parental background, grades, SATs, and other characteristics were controlled (Karen, 1985).

NETWORKS AND THE TRANSMISSION OF PRIVILEGE

For these reasons we believe it is worth investigating whether certain secondary schools have special organizational charters, at least in relation to certain colleges. If they do, the question arises, how do organizational charters operate? Network analysts suggest that "the pattern of ties in a network provides significant opportunities and constraints because it affects the relative access of people and institutions to such resources as information, wealth and power" (Wellman, 1981:3). Furthermore, "because of their structural location, members of a social system differ greatly in their access to these resources" (Wellman, 1981:30). Moreover, network analysts have suggested that class-structured networks work to preserve upper class ideology, consciousness, and life style (see for example Laumann, 1966:132–36).

We expect that colleges and secondary schools have much closer ties than has previously been documented. Close networks of personal relationships between officials at certain private schools and some elite colleges transform what is for many students a relatively standardized, bureaucratic procedure into a process of negotiation. As a result, they are able to communicate more vital information about their respective needs, giving selected secondary school students an inside track to gaining acceptance to desired colleges. We call this process "bartering."

SAMPLE AND DATA

Baltzell (1958, 1964) noted the importance of elite secondary boarding schools for upper class solidarity. However, he was careful to distinguish between those boarding schools that were truly socially elite and those that had historically served somewhat less affluent and less powerful families. He indicates that there is a core group of eastern Protestant schools that "set the pace and bore the brunt of criticism received by private schools for their so-called 'snobbish,' 'undemocratic' and even 'un-American' values" (Baltzell, 1958:307–308). These 16 schools are: Phillips (Andover) Academy (MA), Phillips Exeter Academy (NH), St. Paul's School (NH), St. Mark's School (MA), Groton School (MA), St. George's School (RI), Kent School (CT), The Taft School (CT), The Hotchkiss School (CT), Choate Rosemary Hall (CT), Middlesex School (MA), Deerfield Academy (MA), The Lawrenceville School (NJ), The Hill School (PA), The Episcopal High School (VA), and Woodberry Forest School (VA). We refer to the schools on Baltzell's list as the "select 16."[1]

In 1982 and 1983, we visited a representative sample of 12 of the select 16 schools. These 12 schools reflect the geographic distribution of the select 16 schools. In this time period we also visited 30 other "leading" secondary boarding schools drawn from the 1981 *Handbook of Private Schools'* list of 289 "leading" secondary boarding schools. This sample is representative of leading secondary boarding schools nationally in location, religious affiliation, size, and the sex composition of the student body. These schools are organizationally similar to the select 16 schools in offering only a college preparatory curriculum, in being incorporated as non-profit organizations, in their faculty/student ratios, and in the percent of boarders who receive financial aid. They differ somewhat with respect to sex composition, average size, the sex of their heads, and number of advanced placement courses (see Table 1). However, the key difference between the select 16 schools and the other "leading" schools is that the former are more socially elite than the latter. For instance, in one of the select 16 boarding schools in 1982, 40 percent of the current students' parents were listed in *Social Register.*[2]

All 42 schools were visited by one or both of the authors. Visits lasted between one and five days and included interviews with administrators, teachers and students. Most relevant to this study were the lengthy interviews with the schools' college advisors. These interviews explored all aspects of the college counseling process, including the nature and content of the advisors' relationships with admissions officers at various colleges. At a representative sample of six of the select 16 schools and a representative sample of 13 of the other "leading" schools a questionnaire was administered to seniors during our visits.[3] The questionnaire contained more than 50 items and included questions on parental education, occupation, income, number of books in the home, family travel, educational legacies as well as many questions on boarding school life and how students felt about their experiences in school. Overall, student survey and school record data were collected on 687 seniors from the six select 16 schools and 658 seniors from other leading schools. Although not every piece of data was available for every student, we did obtain 578 complete cases from six select 16 schools and 457 cases from ten leading schools.[4] School record data included student grade point averages, Scholastic Aptitude Test (SAT) scores, class rank, names of colleges to which students applied, names of colleges to which students were accepted, and names of colleges students will attend. This material was supplied by the schools after the seniors graduated, in the summer or fall of 1982 and 1983. With this population actual enrollment matches school reports with high reliability. The record data have been linked with questionnaire data from the seniors and with various

TABLE 1 / Comparison of Population and Two Samples of Boarding Schools[a]

	Total population (N = 289)	Other boarding school sample (N = 30)	Select 16 sample (N = 12)
Percent with college preparatory curriculum	100	100	100
Percent with no religious affiliation	65	70	67
Percent incorporated, not-for-profit	83	90	83
Average faculty/student ratio	0.17	0.15	0.15
Average percent of boarders aided	15	16	18
Percent of schools which are all-boys	28	17	33
Percent of schools which are all-girls	17	28	0
Percent coeducational schools	55	55	67
Percent with male heads	92	73	100
Average number of advanced courses	3.5	4.8	6.7
Average size	311	322	612

[a]Computed from data published in the *Handbook of Private Schools* (1981).

characteristics of the college. The colleges students planned to attend, were coded as to academic selectivity, Ivy League, and other characteristics not analyzed here.[5]

CHARTERING

Historical evidence shows that the select 16 schools have had special charters in relation to Ivy League colleges in general, and Harvard, Yale, and Princeton in particular. In the 1930s and 1940s, two-thirds of all graduates of 12 of the select 16 boarding schools attended Harvard, Yale, or Princeton (Karabel, 1984). But, by 1973, this share had slipped noticeably to an average of 21 percent, although the rate of acceptance between schools ranged from 51 percent to 8 percent (Cookson and Persell, 1978: Table 4). In the last half century, then, the proportion of select 16 school graduates who attended Harvard, Yale, or Princeton dropped substantially.

This decrease was paralleled by an increase in the competition for admission to Ivy League colleges. According to several college advisors at select 16 boarding schools, 90 percent of all applicants to Harvard in the 1940s were accepted as were about half of those in the early 1950s. In 1982, the national acceptance rate for the eight Ivy League schools was 26 percent, although it was 20 percent or less at Harvard, Yale and Princeton (*National College Data Bank,* 1984).

The pattern of Ivy League college admissions has changed during this time. Ivy League colleges have begun to admit more public school graduates. Before World War II at Princeton, for example, about 80 percent of the entering freshmen came from private secondary schools (Blumberg and Paul, 1975:70). In 1982, 34 percent of the freshman class at Harvard, 40 percent of Yale freshmen, and 40 percent of Princeton freshmen were from non-public high schools (*National College Data Bank,* 1984).

This shift in college admissions policy, combined with increased financial aid and an inflationary trend in higher education that puts increased emphasis on which college one attends, contributes to the large number of applications to certain colleges nationally. Thus, while in the past decade the number of college age students has declined, the number of students applying to Ivy League colleges has increased (Mackay-Smith, 1985; Maeroff, 1984; Winerip, 1984).

In view of these historical changes, is there any evidence that the select 16 schools still retain special charters in relation to college admissions? When four pools of applications to the Ivy League colleges are compared, the acceptance rate is highest at select 16 schools, followed by a highly selective public high school, other leading boarding schools, and finally the entire national pool of applications (Table 2).[6]

While we do not have comparable background data on all the applicants from these various pools, we do know that the students in the highly selective public high school have among the highest academic qualifications in the country.[7] Their combined SAT scores, for example, average at least 150 points higher than those of students at the leading boarding schools. On that basis they might be expected to do considerably better than applicants from boarding schools: which they do at some colleges but not at Harvard, Yale or Princeton.

The most revealing insights into the operation of special charters, however, are provided by a comparison between select 16 boarding schools and other leading boarding schools—the most similar schools and the ones on which we have the most detailed data.

Students from select 16 schools apply to somewhat different colleges than do students from other leading boarding schools. Select 16 school students were much more

TABLE 2 / Percent of Applications That Were Accepted at Ivy League Colleges from Four Pools of Applications

College name	Select 16 boarding schools[a] (1982–83)	Other leading boarding schools[b] (1982–83)	Selective public high school[c] (1984)	National group of applicants[d] (1982)
Brown University				
Percent accepted	35	20	28	22
Number of applications	95	45	114	11,854
Columbia University				
Percent accepted	66	29	31	41
Number of applications	35	7	170	3,650
Cornell University				
Percent accepted	57	36	55	31
Number of applications	65	25	112	17,927
Dartmouth				
Percent accepted	41	21	41	22
Number of applications	79	33	37	8,313
Harvard University				
Percent accepted	38	28	20	17
Number of applications	104	29	127	13,341
Princeton University				
Percent accepted	40	28	18	18
Number of applications	103	40	109	11,804
University of Pennsylvania				
Percent accepted	45	32	33	36
Number of applications	40	19	167	11,000
Yale University				
Percent accepted	40	32	15	20
Number of applications	92	25	124	11,023
Overall percent accepted	42	27	30	26
Total number of applications	613	223	960	88,912

[a]Based on school record data on the applications of 578 seniors.

[b]Based on school record data on the applications of 457 seniors.

[c]Based on data published in the school newspaper.

[d]Based on data published in the *National College Data Bank* (1984).

likely to apply to one or more of the eight Ivy League and at least one of the other highly selective colleges than were students from other leading boarding schools (Table 3). Among those who applied, select 16 students were more likely to be accepted than were students from other boarding schools, and, if accepted, they were slightly more likely to attend.

Before we can conclude that these differences are due to a school charter, we need to control for parental SES[8] and student SAT

TABLE 3 / Boarding School Students' College Application, Chances of Acceptance, and Plans to Attend

	Ivy League colleges % (N)	Highly selective colleges % (N)
A. Percent of boarding school samples who applied		
Select 16 boarding schools	61 (353)	87 (502)
Other leading boarding schools	28 (129)	61 (279)
B. Percent of applicants who were accepted		
Select 16 boarding schools	54 (191)	84 (420)
Other leading boarding schools	36 (47)	64 (178)
C. Percent of acceptees who plan to attend		
Select 16 boarding schools	79 (151)	81 (340)
Other leading boarding schools	53 (25)	77 (137)

TABLE 4 / Percent of Students Who Applied to the Most Highly Selective Colleges Who Were Accepted, with SAT Scores, SES, and School Type Held Constant

	Student combined SAT scores					
	High (1580–1220)		Medium (1216–1060)		Low (1050–540)	
Student socioeconomic status	Select 16 schools % (N)	Other leading boarding schools % (N)	Select 16 schools % (N)	Other leading boarding schools % (N)	Select 16 schools % (N)	Other leading boarding schools % (N)
High	87 (93)	70 (33)	80 (73)	64 (36)	65 (34)	53 (30)
Medium	89 (100)	71 (28)	85 (66)	76 (46)	44 (18)	35 (51)
Low	92 (72)	72 (25)	78 (51)	69 (32)	55 (33)	33 (49)

Based on student questionnaires and school record data on 1035 seniors for whom complete data were available.

scores.[9] This analysis is shown in Table 4. One striking finding here is the high rate of success enjoyed by boarding school students in general. At least one-third and as many as 92 percent of the students in each cell of Table 4 are accepted. Given that the average freshman combined SAT score is more than 1175 at these colleges and universities, it is particularly notable that such a large proportion of those with combined SAT scores of 1050 or less are accepted.

In general, high SAT scores increase chances of acceptance, but the relationship is somewhat attenuated under certain conditions. Students with low SAT scores are more likely to be accepted at highly selective colleges if they have higher SES backgrounds, especially if they attend a select 16 school. These students seem to have relatively high "floors" placed under them, since two thirds of those from select 16 schools and more than half of those from other schools were accepted by one of the most selective colleges.[10]

The most successful ones of all are relatively low SES students with the highest SATs attending select 16 schools—92 percent of whom were accepted. Students from relatively modest backgrounds appear to receive a "knighting effect" by attending a select 16 school. Thus, select 16 schools provide mobility for some individuals from relatively less privileged backgrounds. To a considerable degree all students with high SATs, regardless of their SES, appear to be "turbocharged" by attending a select 16 school compared to their counterparts at other leading schools.

At every level of SATs and SES, students' chances of acceptance increase if they attend a select 16 school. Such a finding is consistent with the argument that a chartering effect continues to operate among elite educational institutions. The historical shifts toward admitting more public school students on the part of Ivy League colleges and the increased competition for entry, described above, have meant that more effort has been required on the part of select 16 schools to retain an advantage for their students. We believe that certain private boarding schools have buttressed their charters by an increasingly active bartering operation.

BARTERING

Normally, we do not think of the college admissions process as an arena for bartering. It is assumed that colleges simply choose students according to their own criteria and needs. Few students and no high schools are thought to have any special "leverage" in admissions decisions. Our research revealed, however, that select 16 boarding schools—perhaps because of their perennial supply of academically able and affluent students—can negotiate admissions cases with colleges. The colleges are aware that select 16 schools attract excellent college prospects and devote considerable attention to maintaining close relationships with these schools, espe-

cially through the college admissions officers. Secondary school college advisors actively "market" their students within a context of tremendous parental pressure and increasing competition for admission to elite colleges.

SELECT 16 COLLEGE ADVISORS AND IVY LEAGUE ADMISSIONS DIRECTORS: THE OLD SCHOOL TIE

Of the 11 select 16 school college advisors on whom data were available, 10 were graduates of Harvard, Yale, or Princeton. Of the 23 other leading boarding school college advisors on whom data were available, only three were Ivy League graduates, and none of them was from Harvard, Yale, or Princeton. College advisors are overwhelmingly white men. At the select 16 schools only one (an acting director) was a woman, and at other schools five were women. Some college advisors have previously worked as college admissions officers. Their educational and social similarity to college admissions officers may facilitate the creation of social ties and the sharing of useful information. Research shows that the exchange of ideas most frequently occurs between people who share certain social attributes (Rogers and Kincaid, 1981).

College advisors at select 16 schools tend to have long tenures—15 or more years is not unusual. On the other hand, college advisors at other schools are more likely to have assumed the job recently. A college advisor at one select 16 school stressed the "importance of continuity on both sides of the relationship." Thus, it is not surprising that select 16 schools hold on to their college advisors.

Select 16 college advisors have close social relationships with each other and with elite college admissions officers that are cemented through numerous face-to-face meetings each year. All of the select 16 schools are on the east coast, whereas only 70 percent of the other leading boarding schools are in that region. However, even those leading boarding schools on the east coast lack the close relationships with colleges that characterize the select 16 schools. Thus, geography alone does not explain these relationships.

The college advisors at most of the boarding schools we studied have personally visited a number of colleges around the country. Boarding schools often provide college advisors with summer support for systematic visits, and a number of geographically removed colleges offer attractive incentives, or fully paid trips to their region (e.g., Southern California). These trips often take place during bitter New England winters, and include elegant food and lodging as well as a chance to see colleges and meet admissions officers.

However, the college advisors at select 16 schools are likely to have visited far more schools (several mentioned that they had personally visited 60 or 70 schools) than college advisors at other schools (some of whom had not visited any). They are also much more likely to visit regularly the most selective and prestigious colleges.[11]

Numerous college admissions officers also travel to these boarding schools to interview students and meet the college advisors. The select 16 schools have more college admissions officers visit than do other schools; more than 100 in any given academic year is not unusual. College advisors have drinks and dinner with selected admissions officers, who often stay overnight on campus. As one college advisor noted, "We get to establish a personal relationship with each other." Moreover, Ivy League colleges bring students from select 16 schools to their campus to visit for weekends.

By knowing each other personally, college advisors and admissions officers "develop a relationship of trust," so that they can evaluate the source as well as the content of phone calls and letters. We observed phone calls between college advisors and admissions officers when we were in their offices. Several college advisors mentioned, "It helps to know personally the individual you are speaking or writing to," and one college advisor at a select 16 school said, "I have built up a track record with the private colleges over the years."

Virtually all of the select 16 school college advisors indicated that in the spring—before colleges have finished making their admissions decisions—they take their application files and drive to elite colleges to discuss "their list." They often sit in on the admissions deliberations while they are there. In contrast, the other schools' college advisors generally did not make such trips. Such actions suggest the existence of strong social networks between select 16 school college advisors and elite college admissions officers.

HOW THE SYSTEM WORKS: "FINE-TUNING" THE ADMISSIONS PROCESS

Bartering implies a reciprocal relationship, and select 16 schools and elite colleges have a well-developed system of information exchange. Both sides have learned to cooperate to their mutual benefit. College advisors try to provide admissions officers with as much information about their students as possible to help justify the acceptance of a particular applicant. Select 16 schools have institutionalized this process more than other schools. The most professional operation we found was in a select 16 school where about half the graduating class goes to Harvard, Yale or Princeton. There, the college advisor interviews the entire faculty on each member of the senior class. He tape records all their comments and has them transcribed. This produces a "huge confidential dossier which gives a very good sense of where each student is." In addition, housemasters and coaches write reports. Then the college advisor interviews each senior, dictating notes after each interview. After assimilating all of these comments on each student, the college advisor writes his letter of recommendation, which he is able to pack with corroborative details illustrating a candidate's strengths. The thoroughness, thought, and care that goes into this process insures that anything and everything positive that could be said about a student is included, thereby maximizing his or her chances for a favorable reception at a college.[12]

Information also flows from colleges to the secondary schools. By sitting in on the admissions process at colleges like Harvard, Princeton, and Yale, select 16 school college advisors say they "see the wealth and breadth of the applicant pool." They get a first-hand view of the competition their students face. They also obtain a sense of how a college "puts its class together," which helps them to learn strategies for putting forward their own applicants.

By observing and participating in the admissions process, select 16 school college advisors gain an insider's view of a college's selection process. This insider's knowledge is reflected in the specific figures select 16 advisors mentioned in our conversations with them. One select 16 school college advisor said that a student has "two and one half times as good a chance for admission to Harvard if his father went there than if he did not." Another said, "while 22 percent in general are admitted to Ivy League colleges, 45 percent of legacies are admitted to Ivy League colleges." In both cases, they mentioned a specific, quantified statement about how being a legacy affected their students' admissions probabilities.[13] Similarly, several select 16 college advisors mentioned the percent-

ages of the freshman class at Harvard and Yale that were from public and private schools, and even one mentioned how those percentages have changed since 1957. College advisors at other schools do not lace their conversations with as many specific figures nor do they belong to the special organization that some of the select 16 schools have formed to share information and strategies.

The special interest group these schools have formed is able to negotiate with the colleges to their students' advantage. For instance, the college advisors explained that select 16 school students face greater competition than the average high school student and carry a more rigorous course load.[14] Therefore, this group persuaded the colleges that their students should not receive an absolute class rank, but simply an indication of where the students stand by decile or quintile. Colleges may then put such students in a "not ranked" category or report the decile or quintile rank. No entering student from such a secondary school is clearly labeled as the bottom person in the class. To our knowledge, only select 16 schools have made this arrangement.

Armed with an insider's knowledge of a college's desires, select 16 school college advisors seek to present colleges with the most appropriate candidates. As one select 16 school college advisor said, "I try to shape up different applicant pools for different colleges," a process that has several components. First, college advisors try to screen out hopeless prospects, or as one tactfully phrased it, "I try to discourage unproductive leads." This is not always easy because, as one said, "Certain dreams die hard." College advisors in other schools were more likely to say that they never told students where they should or should not apply.

One select 16 school requires students to write a "trial college essay" that helps the college advisor ascertain "what kind of a student this is." From the essay he can tell how well students write, determine whether they follow through and do what they need to do on time, and learn something about their personal and family background. With faculty and student comments in hand, college advisors can begin to assemble their applicant pools. One thing they always want to learn is which college is a student's first choice, and why. This is useful information when bartering with colleges.

Some college advisors are quite frank when bartering, for example, the select 16 college advisor who stressed, "I am candid about a student to the colleges, something that is not true at a lot of schools where they take an advocacy position in relation to their students. . . . We don't sell damaged goods to the colleges." College advisors at other schools did not define their role as one of weeding out candidates prior to presenting them to colleges, although they may do this as well. It would seem then that part of the gate-keeping process of admission to college is occurring in select 16 secondary schools. College advisors, particularly those with long tenures at select 16 schools, seem quite aware of the importance of maintaining long-term credibility with colleges, since credibility influences how effectively they can work for their school in the future.

While the children of certain big donors (so-called "development cases") may be counseled with special care, in general the college advisors have organizational concerns that are more important than the fate of a particular student. Several select 16 school college advisors spoke with scorn about parents who see a rejection as the "first step in the negotiation." Such parents threaten to disrupt a delicate network of social relationships that link elite institutions over a considerable time span.

At the same time, college advisors try to do everything they can to help their students

jump the admissions hurdle. One select 16 school college advisor said:

> I don't see our students as having an advantage (in college admissions). We have to make the situation unequal. We do this by writing full summary reports on the students, by reviewing the applicants with the colleges several times during the year, and by traveling to the top six colleges in the spring. . . . [Those visits] are an advocacy proceeding on the side of the students. The colleges make their best decisions on our students and those from [another select 16 school] because they have the most information on these students.

Another select 16 college advisor said, "We want to be sure they are reading the applications of our students fairly, and we lobby for our students." A third select 16 college advisor made a similar statement, "When I drive to the [Ivy League] colleges, I give them a reading on our applicants. I let them know if I think they are making a mistake. There is a lobbying component here."

Select 16 college advisors do not stop with simply asking elite college admissions officers to reconsider a decision, however. They try to barter, and the colleges show they are open to this possibility when the college admissions officer says, "Let's talk about your group." One select 16 college advisor said he stresses to colleges that if his school recommends someone and he or she is accepted, that student will come. While not all colleges heed this warranty, some do.

One select 16 college advisor said, "It is getting harder than it used to be to say to an admissions officer, 'take a chance on this one,' especially at Harvard which now has so many more applications." But it is significant that he did not say that it was impossible. If all else fails in a negotiation, a select 16 college advisor said, "we lobby for the college to make him their absolute first choice on the waiting list." Such a compromise represents a chance for both parties to save face.

Most public high school counselors are at a distinct disadvantage in the bartering process because they are not part of the interpersonal network, do not have strategic information, and are thus unable to lobby effectively for their students. One select 16 advisor told us about a counselor from the Midwest who came to an Ivy League college to sit in on the admissions committee decision for his truly outstanding candidate—SATs in the 700s, top in his class, class president, and star athlete. The select 16 college advisor was also there, lobbying on behalf of his candidate—a nice undistinguished fellow (in the words of his advisor, "A good kid") with SATs in the 500s, middle of his class, average athlete, and no strong signs of leadership. After hearing both the counselors, the Ivy League college chose the candidate from the select 16 school. The outraged public school counselor walked out in disgust. Afterwards, the Ivy League college admissions officer said to the select 16 college advisor, "We may not be able to have these open meetings anymore." Even in the unusual case where a public school counselor did everything that a select 16 boarding school college advisor did, it was not enough to secure the applicant's admission. Despite the competitive environment that currently surrounds admission to elite colleges, the admissions officers apparently listen more closely to advisors from select 16 boarding schools than to public school counselors.

CONCLUSIONS AND IMPLICATIONS

The graduates of certain private schools are at a distinct advantage when it comes to admission to highly selective colleges because of the special charters and highly developed social networks these schools possess. Of course, other factors are operating as well.

Parental wealth (which is not fully tapped by a measure of SES based on education, occupation, and income), preference for the children of alumni, Advanced Placement (AP) coursework, sports ability especially in such scarce areas as ice hockey, crew or squash, and many other factors also influence the process of college admission. Elite boarding schools are part of a larger process whereby more privileged members of society transmit their advantages to their children. Attendance at a select 16 boarding school signals admissions commmittees that an applicant may have certain valuable educational and social characteristics.

Significantly, neither the families nor the secondary schools leave the college admissions process to chance or to formal bureaucratic procedures. Instead, they use personal connections to smooth the process, and there is reason to believe that those efforts affect the outcomes. The "knighting effect" of select 16 schools helps a few low SES, high SAT students gain admission to highly selective colleges, evidence of sponsored mobility for a few worthy youngsters of relatively humble origins. Our findings are consistent with Kamens' (1974) suggestion that certain schools make their students eligible for special social rights. Furthermore, the interaction between social background, SATs, and select 16 school attendance suggests that both individual ability and socially structured advantages operate in the school-college transition.

These results illustrate Collins' (1979) view that stratified systems are maintained through the manipulation of social contacts. They show one way that networks and stratification processes are interconnected. College access is only one aspect of the larger phenomenon of elite maintenance and reproduction. Elite boarding schools no doubt contribute as well to the social contacts and marriage markets of their graduates. What this instance shows is that reproduction is not a simple process. It involves family and group reproduction as well as some structural replacement with carefully screened new members. There is active personal intervention in what is publicly presented as a meritocratic and open competition. The internal processes and external networks described here operate to construct class privileges as well as to transmit class advantages, thereby helping to reproduce structured stratification within society.

If this example is generalizable, we would expect that economically and culturally advantaged groups might regularly find or create specially chartered organizations and brokers with well-developed networks to help them successfully traverse critical junctures in their social histories. Such key switching points include the transition from secondary school to college, admission to an elite graduate or professional school, obtaining the right job, finding a mentor, gaining a medical residency at a choice hospital (Hall, 1947, 1948, 1949) getting a book manuscript published (Coser et al., 1982), having one's paintings exhibited at an art gallery or museum, obtaining a theatrical agent, having one's business considered for venture capital or bank support (Rogers and Larsen, 1984), being offered membership in an exclusive social club, or being asked to serve on a corporate or other board of directors (Useem, 1984).

In all of these instances, many qualified individuals seek desired, but scarce, social and/or economic opportunities. Truly open competition for highly desired outcomes leaves privileged groups vulnerable. Because the socially desired positions are finite at any given moment, processes that give an advantage to the members of certain groups work to limit the opportunities of individuals from other groups.[15] In these ways, dominant groups enhance their chances, at the same time that a few worthy newcomers are

advanced, a process which serves to reproduce and legitimate a structure of social inequality.

ENDNOTES

1. Others besides Baltzell have developed lists of elite private schools, including Baird (1977), Domhoff (1967, 1970, 1983), and McLachlan (1970).

2. We were not able to compute the percent of students in *Social Register* for every school because most schools do not publish the names of their students. Hence, we were not able to look their families up in *Social Register*. We do know that less than .000265 percent of American families are listed in *Social Register*. See Levine (1980) for an historical discussion of the social backgrounds of students at several of the select 16 schools.

3. We asked to give the student questionnaires at nine of the 12 select 16 schools and six of those nine schools agreed. At the other leading schools, we asked to give the questionnaires at 15 and 13 schools agreed.

4. Three leading schools did not supply the college data.

5. Following Astin et al. (1981:7), we measured selectivity with the average SAT scores of the entering freshmen.

6. The entire national applicant pool includes the relatively more successful subgroups within it. If they were excluded, the national acceptance rate would be even lower.

7. Students admitted to this selective public high school must be recommended by their junior high school to take a competitive entrance exam, where they must score very well. The school was among the top five in the nation with respect to the number of National Merit Scholarships won by its students, and each year a number of students in the school win Westinghouse science prizes. This school was selected for purposes of comparison here because academically it is considered to be among the very top public schools in the nation. However, it does not have the social prestige of the select 16 boarding schools.

8. SES was measured by combining father's education, father's occupation, and family income into a composite SES score. These SES scores were then standardized for this population, and each student received a single standardized SES score.

9. The combined verbal and mathematics scores were used.

10. We performed separate analyses for boys and girls to see if sex was related to admission to a highly selective

college when type of boarding school, SATs, and SES were held constant, and generally it was not. Girls who attend either select 16 or other leading boarding schools do as well or better in their admission to college as do their male counterparts, with the single exception of girls at select 16 schools in the top third on their SATs and SES. In that particular group, 92 percent of the boys but only 77 percent of the girls were accepted at the most highly selective colleges. Since that is the only exception, boys and girls are discussed together in the text of the paper.

11. Our field visits and interviews with college advisors at two highly selective public high schools and three open admissions public high schools show that college advisors at even the most selective public high schools generally do not personally know the admissions officers at colleges, particularly at the most selective and Ivy League colleges, nor do they talk with them over the phone or in person prior to their admissions decisions.

12. Such a procedure requires considerable financial and personnel resources. Select 16 schools have more capital-intensive and professional office services supporting their college admissions endeavor than other schools. Most of them have word processors, considerable professional staff, and ample secretarial and clerical help.

13. We did not ask students what colleges their parents attended so we could not control for college legacy in our analysis. Further research on the admissions process should do so.

14. One way select 16 schools establish their reputation as rigorous schools is through the numbers of their students who succeed on the Advanced Placement (AP) Exams given by the College Entrance Examination Board. Compared to other secondary schools, select 16 schools offer larger numbers of advanced courses (Table 1), encourage more students to take them, coach students very effectively on how to take the test, and maintain contacts with the people who design and read AP exams so that they know what is expected and can guide students accordingly. (See Cookson and Persell, 1985, for more discussion of these processes.) Other schools are much less likely than select 16 ones to have teachers who have graded AP exams or to know people who have helped to write the tests.

15. See Parkin (1979) for a discussion of social closure as exclusion and usurpation.

REFERENCES

Alexander, Karl L., Martha Cook and Edward L. McDill 1978 "Curriculum tracking and educational stratification: some further evidence." American Sociological Review 43:47–66.

Alexander, Karl L. and Bruce K. Eckland 1975 "Contextual effects in the high school attainment process." American Sociological Review 40:402–16.

———— 1977 "High school context and college selectivity: institutional constraints in educational stratification." Social Forces 56:166–88.

Alexander, Karl L., Bruce K. Eckland and Larry J. Griffin 1975 "The Wisconsin model of socioeconomic achievement: a replication." American Journal of Sociology 81:324–42.

Alexander, Karl L. and Edward L. McDill 1976 "Selection and allocation within schools: some causes and consequences of curriculum placement." American Sociological Review 41:963–80.

Astin, Alexander W., Margo R. King, and Gerald T. Richardson 1981 The American Freshman: National Norms for Fall 1981. Los Angeles: Laboratory for Research in Higher Education, University of California.

Averch, Harvey A., Steven J. Carroll, Theodore S. Donaldson, Herbert J. Kiesling, and John Pincus 1972 How Effective Is Schooling? A Critical Review and Synthesis of Research Findings. Santa Monica, CA: The Rand Corporation.

Baird, Leonard L. 1977 The Elite Schools. Lexington, MA: Lexington Books.

Baltzell, E. Digby 1958 Philadelphia Gentlemen. New York: Free Press.

———— 1964 The Protestant Establishment. New York: Random House.

Beck, E. M., Patrick M. Horan, and Charles M. Tolbert II 1978 "Stratification in a dual economy." American Sociological Review 43:704–20.

Bibb, Robert C. and William Form 1977 "The effects of industrial, occupational and sex stratification on wages in blue-collar markets." Social Forces 55:974–96.

Blau, Peter and Otis D. Duncan 1967 The American Occupational Structure. New York: Wiley.

Blumberg, Paul M. and P. W. Paul 1975 "Continuities and discontinuities in upper-class marriages." Journal of Marriage and the Family 37:63–77.

Bowles, Samuel and Herbert Gintis 1976 Schooling in Capitalist America. New York: Basic Books.

Collins, Randall 1979 The Credential Society. New York: Academic Press.

Cookson, Peter Willis, Jr. 1981 "Private secondary boarding school and public suburban high school graduation: an analysis of college attendance plans." Unpublished Ph.D. dissertation, New York University.

Cookson, Peter W., Jr. and Caroline Hodges Persell 1978 "Social structure and educational programs: a comparison of elite boarding schools and public education in the United States." Paper presented at the annual meeting of the American Sociological Association, San Francisco.

_____ 1985 Preparing for Power: America's Elite Boarding Schools. New York: Basic Books.

Coser, Lewis A., Charles Kadushin, and Walter W. Powell 1982 Books: The Culture & Commerce of Publishing. New York: Basic Books.

Domhoff, G. William 1967 Who Rules America? Englewood Cliffs: Prentice-Hall.

_____ 1970 The Higher Circles. New York: Vintage.

_____ 1983 Who Rules America Now? Englewood Cliffs: Prentice-Hall.

Falsey, Barbara and Barbara Heyns 1984 "The college channel: private and public schools reconsidered." Sociology of Education 57:111–22.

Hall, Oswald 1946 "The informal organization of the medical profession." Canadian Journal of Economics and Political Science 12:30–41.

_____ 1948 "The stages of a medical career." American Journal of Sociology 53:327–36.

_____ 1949 "Types of medical careers." American Journal of Sociology 55:243–53.

Haller, Archibald O. and Alejandro Portes 1973 "Status attainment processes." Sociology of Education 46: 51–91.

Hammack, Floyd M. and Peter W. Cookson, Jr. 1980 "Colleges attended by graduates of elite secondary schools." The Educational Forum 44:483–90.

Handbook of Private Schools 1981 Boston: Porter Sargent Publishers, Inc.

Heyns, Barbara 1974 "Social selection and stratification within schools." American Journal of Sociology 79:1434–51.

Jaffe, Abraham and Walter Adams 1970 "Academic and socio-economic factors related to entrance and retention at two- and four-year colleges in the late 1960s." New York: Bureau of Applied Social Research, Columbia University.

Jencks, Christopher, Marshall Smith, Henry Acland, Mary Jo Bane, David Cohen, Herbert Gintis, Barbara Heyns, and Stephan Michelson 1972 Inequality. New York: Basic Books.

Kamens, David 1974 "Colleges and elite formation: the case of prestigious American colleges." Sociology of Education 47:354–78.

_____ 1977 "Legitimating myths and educational organization: the relationship between organizational ideology and formal structure." American Sociological Review 42:208–19.

Karabel, Jerome 1984 "Status-group struggle, organizational interests, and the limits of institutional autonomy: the transformation of Harvard, Yale, and Princeton 1918–1940." Theory and Society 13:1–40.

Karen, David 1985 "Who gets into Harvard? Selection and exclusion." Unpublished Ph.D. dissertation, Department of Sociology, Harvard University.

Kerckhoff, Alan C. 1976 "The status attainment process: socialization or allocation?" Social Forces 55:368–81.

_____ 1984 "The current state of social mobility research." Sociological Quarterly 25:139–53.

Klitgaard, Robert 1985 Choosing Elites. New York: Basic Books.

Laumann, Edward O. 1966 Prestige and Association in an Urban Community: An Analysis of an Urban Stratification System. Indianapolis: Bobbs-Merrill.

Levine, Steven B. 1980 "The rise of American boarding schools and the development of a national upper class." Social Problems 28:63–94.

Lewis, Lionel S. and Richard A. Wanner 1979 "Private schooling and the status attainment process." Sociology of Education 52:99–112.

Mackay-Smith, Anne 1985 "Admissions crunch: top colleges remain awash in applicants despite a smaller pool." Wall Street Journal (April 2):1, 14.

Maeroff, Gene I. 1984 "Top Eastern colleges report unusual rise in applications." New York Times (February 21):A1, C10.

McLachlan, James 1970 American Boarding Schools: A Historical Study. New York: Charles Scribner's Sons.

Meyer, John 1970 "The charter: conditions of diffuse socialization in school." Pp. 564–78 in W. Richard Scott (ed.), Social Processes and Social Structure. New York: Holt, Rinehart.

_____ 1977 "Education as an institution." American Journal of Sociology 83:55–77.

Mills, C. Wright 1956 The Power Elite. London: Oxford University Press.

National College Data Bank. 1984 Princeton: Peterson's Guides, Inc.

Oakes, Jeannie 1985 Keeping Track: How Schools Structure Inequality. New Haven, Yale University Press.

Otto, Luther B. and Archibald O. Haller 1979 "Evidence for a social psychological view of the status attainment process: four studies compared." Social Forces 57:887–914.

Parkin, Frank 1979 Marxism and Class Theory: A Bourgeois Critique. New York: Columbia University Press.

Persell, Caroline Hodges 1977 Education and Inequality. New York: Free Press.

Robinson, Robert V. 1984 "Reproducing class relations in industrial capitalism." American Sociological Review 49:182–96.

Rogers, Everett M. and D. Lawrence Kincaid 1981 Communications Networks: Toward a New Paradigm for Research. New York: Free Press.

Rogers, Everett M. and Judith K. Larsen 1984 Silicon Valley Fever: The Growth of High-Tech Culture. New York: Basic Books.

Rosenbaum, James E. 1976 Making Inequality: The Hidden Curriculum of High School Tracking. New York: Wiley.

_____ 1980 "Track misperceptions and frustrated college plans: an analysis of the effects of tracks and track perceptions in the national longitudinal survey." Sociology of Education 53:74–88.

Sewell, William H., Archibald O. Haller, and Alejandro Portes 1969 "The educational and early occupational attainment process." American Sociological Review 34:82–91.

Sewell, William H., Archibald O. Haller, and George W. Ohlendorf 1970 "The educational and early occupational status achievement process: replication and revision." American Sociological Review 35:1014–27.

Social Register 1984 New York: Social Register Association.

Stolzenberg, Ross M. 1975 "Occupations, labor markets and the process of wage attainment." American Sociological Review 40:645–65.

Useem, Michael 1984 The Inner Circle: Large Corporations and the Rise of Business Political Activity in the U.S. and U.K. New York: Oxford University Press.

Wellman, Barry 1981 "Network analysis from method and metaphor to theory and substance." Working Paper Series 1B, Structural Analysis Programme, University of Toronto.

Wilson, Kenneth L. and Alejandro Portes 1975 "The educational attainment process: Results from a national sample." American Journal of Sociology 81:343–63.

Winerip, Michael 1984 "Hot colleges and how they get that way." New York Times Magazine (November 18):68ff.

Questions for Understanding and Critical Thinking

1. Why do Persell and Cookson believe that graduates of certain private schools are at a distinct advantage when it comes to admission to highly selective colleges?

2. Do you think the practices described in this article constitute a form of affirmative action for children from elite families? Why or why not?

3. Do practices such as educational chartering and bartering contribute to inequalities of race and gender—as well as to class reproduction—in the United States? Why or why not?

ARTICLE 16 _____

As director of Worker Education at Queens College, City University of New York, sociologist Gregory Mantsios has worked as a scholar in the areas of class, education, and the labor movement. He also has helped a new generation of working-class students acquire a college education. In this article, Mantsios gives a first-person narrative about his experiences with class and racial socialization and the development of a working-class identity.

Looking Ahead

1. Why does Mantsios disagree with stereotypic portrayals of working-class people and of labor unions?
2. According to Mantsios, how does social class "rein in the spirit"?
3. What relationship exists between race, class, and the educational experiences of working-class students?
4. Why does Mantsios believe that knowledge is empowering for the working class?

Living and Learning

Some Reflections on Emergence from and Service to the Working Class

◆ *Gregory Mantsios*

It is six-thirty in the evening. It's already been a long day: ten hours of meetings, telephone calls, and paperwork. The classroom I am now in is beginning to fill up with a new crop of students. They are here for their first college orientation. Unlike their more traditional counterparts across campus, these students are not recent high school graduates. They are older and, in fact, many of them have never been to high school, earning instead a high school equivalency diploma by taking a standardized exam.

As the director of Worker Education for Queens College, it's my job to tell these students about college requirements, tuition rates, and grading policies. It's also my job to tell them why a college education is important and what it will mean for their lives now and in the future.

No matter how many times I do this, it never comes easy. As I look around the room, it's not myself I see sitting in those classroom chairs but rather my parents and their contemporaries—not as they are now, but as they were when I was a teenager. It seems odd; I cannot imagine them in a college classroom either then or now.

Some of the students in the room are in their early thirties, many considerably older. Some speak perfect English, many speak broken English. Some are white, most are black or Latino. Some are native New Yorkers, others recently migrated from the South. Many are recent immigrants from Eastern Europe, Asia, or Latin America. By day, these students work in garment shops, on construction sites, in warehouses, on assembly lines, and in high-rise office buildings. By night, they enter the world of the "nontraditional student" in a fairly traditional college setting. It's been a long day for them, too.

Why are these working adult students enrolling in college when so many others like them do not? It is because they are members of unions that have established educational funds to enable them to enroll in a college degree program either on a tuition-free basis or at minimal cost. Eight unions participate in the program, enrolling nearly six hundred students. Some unions provide reimbursement to students who successfully complete their course work, others provide full or partial scholarships. One union provides full tuition, fees, and book expenses for fifty of their members, all garment workers, to attend classes in this program. The Education Director of the garment workers is with me at the orientation to address his member-students.

As I look around the room, I am struck by two things. First, that all this is made possible by labor unions—those institutions that have somehow become a dirty word in the U.S. While big business and conservative politicians blame unions for all of society's economic ills, progressive politicians scramble to distance themselves from unions for fear of damaging their political careers. Yet it is these very organizations that are providing

working people both with social services and with self-respect. As many in the room will tell you, it is the union that fights for their rights, protects them from hazardous working conditions, and brings them a modicum of dignity at the workplace. It is also the union that fights for the social services so many poor and working people depend on and provides these services when government fails to do so or do so adequately.

The union has brought these members to our college program. It not only provides the educational funds that make it possible for union members to attend college, it has actively recruited, counseled, and cajoled its members into taking advantage of this educational benefit. The union leader who is addressing his member-students at the orientation ends his talk with the words, "Knowledge is power: seize the power."

The second thing that strikes me is that I am facing a group of people who are commonly portrayed in our society as lazy, unproductive, and selfish. Our movies and television serials depict them as crude, our comics stereotype and mimic them as dumb, and our news media suggest that they are a greedy lot that have outpriced themselves in the global labor market. Workers always seem to get a bum rap in a class society.

The everyday life of the worker-student in front of me is a hard one. Most of them work at physically exhausting, mind-deadening jobs that require both physical strength and mental stamina. Many work a second job after hours or on weekends in order to get by. In some cases, they earn no more than the minimum wage. Even those who do earn considerably more cannot be sure that they will have employment throughout the year. For the construction workers in the room, there will be only twenty-six weeks of work this year.

They raise a family and keep house without the advantage of paid helpers. They cook, clean, shop, and take care of their children on their own in the little time that is left after a day at work. Time and economic class are inevitably intertwined: everything takes longer when you are pressed for money. Whether it is the time needed to shop comparatively or the time it takes to use public transportation, getting through everyday life is fraught with inconvenience or peril, or both. Finding the time and the energy to take college courses seems like a Herculean task. This is a life that is in sharp contrast to those who shape our cultural stereotypes and who are fond of making pronouncements about the problems with the U.S. labor force.

But the hardened faces that fill this room are filled with hope as well as with hardship. And hope, like hardship, has a class character. I often ask new students what motivated them to return to school. Some have very specific goals in mind, but most have limited and vague aspirations: to pick up some skills, to get a better job, to earn a little more money, and increasingly, to get out of a dying industry.

While their younger, middle-class counterparts are often filled with great ambitions for accomplished careers, successful business ventures, and recognized professional achievements, such aspirations are rare with working adult students. These students want a decent job and the ability to carry on an intelligent conversation and they hope we can help them with both. I remember reading an account of one working-class student who put it this way, "I just want to be average."[1] Class also has a way of reining in the spirit.

It sometimes astounds me that such a vague promise of a better life through education inspires considerable sacrifice among the poor and working class. One student told me, "I slaved all my life to send my kids to college, now it's my turn."

Another student said, "The union is terrific; it gave me an opportunity to go to school and better myself and I would be a fool not to take advantage of it."

But it's not all that simple: both unions and education have a spotted history. And what really troubles me is the ambivalence of those workers not in the room—the ones who don't attend union meetings, read the union newspaper, or take advantage of union services. Perhaps worse still, I think about the workers we spoke to and failed to recruit to the program. If unions are so great, why is it then that they so often fail to interest, let alone mobilize workers? And if education is so great, why do so many drop out of school in the first place and then fail to continue their studies, even when someone else is paying for it?

For every worker touched by the labor movement, there are countless others who think unions are irrelevant at best, corrupt and counterproductive at worst. For every student enthusiastic about his or her studies, there are countless others who have dropped out of or even been destroyed by the educational system. Not all have fared well by unions or by education. All this makes me reflect on my own past and I cannot help but feel that the ambivalence both towards unions and towards education is justified.

I was immersed in a class struggle, of sorts, almost from the day I was born. My father, a fur worker who immigrated from Greece, was by all accounts a good, decent, kind, hard-working man. He died of a bleeding ulcer before I was ten months old.

My mother is a sensitive but tough woman who had a particularly difficult life. Her mother died of pneumonia six years after arriving in the U.S. from Greece with my grandfather. My mother was two years old at the time. Her father returned to Greece to raise his two young children with the help of his sister. Within days of arriving in his homeland, he was taken prisoner by Turkish soldiers and was never seen again. My mother and her brother continued to live in Greece with their aunt. Eighteen years later, her brother returned to the U.S. and in four years' time had earned enough money to bring over my mother. For the next five years, they lived with relatives in a Harlem flat. My mother did factory work to contribute to the household. At age twenty-nine, five years after arriving in the United States, my mother married my father.

Married for barely two years and with an infant son, my mother had to face the unexpected death of my father and deal with the sudden loss of a loved one for the third time in her life. Rather than raise her son in a strange land without any money or employment, she gave me up for adoption to a wealthy uncle of hers who had made money in real estate speculation and who she believed could provide me with both comfort and security. His own son had recently died in the Second World War and I was the replacement. The terms of the agreement included a stipulation that my mother never divulge her true identity to me. After six months of heartache, my mother secretly returned to her uncle's house and kidnapped me back. Her aunt and uncle adopted another child a year later. I wasn't told any of this until I was in my twenties.

My mother raised me with the help of her brother, who moved in with us to share the rent and expenses. He was a warm, vivacious man who sold insurance to the Greek community in Jamaica, Queens. Eventually he was to become a leader in the community: a local activist who emerged as a compromise candidate between Jews and Blacks for District Leader in the local Democratic Party. His service to the community would influence me in more ways than I knew at the time.

Like most girl children in Greece, my mother had been taught to sew at an early age. Since this was the only marketable skill she possessed that would allow her to stay home and take care of me while earning a living, she sought work in the garment industry. One of my earliest memories is of riding the subway with my mother every Wednesday morning. She carried a large cardboard box tied with a cord and held with a wooden handle. We walked several blocks from the station and entered one of the hundreds of garment storefronts that lined the side streets of midtown Manhattan. The large plate glass windows in the front were covered with dingy yellow plastic sheets to protect the already-badly-faded dresses on display. I found it hard to believe, even at that age, that this was a place of business.

We walked to the back of the store, past dozens of women operating sewing machines, greeted the shop owner, and placed our cardboard box on a large table for the owner to open and examine. The boss was friendly enough, but examining my mother's work was a serious and stern matter. He spread dozens of fur collars out on a table, lifting and turning each one as he ran his hands through them, his eyes squinting as he examined every stitch. These were the fur collars, soon to be attached to women's coats, that were so popular in the fifties and it was my mother's job to take a piece of unfinished fur and make it into a clean, smooth, elegant collar. After the boss nodded his approval, a worker from the shop carried away the merchandise and presented us with a new cardboard box filled with another week's work.

Back in our apartment, my mother sat for hours working those collars. In the winter, she sat on a footstool by the window: in the summer she took her work out to the fire escape where, propped on some cushions, she worked until sunset. She was happier working outside because among other things, she knew intuitively that the fur hair and microscopic fur dust visible only at certain angles in the bright sunlight would settle and accumulate throughout our apartment, presenting a health hazard to us both. She wrapped everything in plastic and mopped constantly. To this day, more than thirty years after she gave up "homework," my mother wraps everything—everything—in plastic. For the "privilege" of doing her work at home and on her own time, my mother was paid less than the shop floor workers, had no job security or benefits.

Unions have always opposed "homework" because it undercuts wages and undermines the union. But without "homework" at the time, I don't know how we would have survived. Naturally, my mother didn't care much for unions.

After ten years as a widow, my mother broke the traditional Greek taboo and remarried. My stepfather, like my father, was kind, gentle, and hardworking. He worked as a merchant marine for twenty-four years before jumping ship in New York. Born in the same town as my mother's family, he settled in the states at the age of forty-five. Equipped with no knowledge of English, but with a penchant for hard work, he spent his life in the U.S. working in restaurant kitchens. For years he jumped out of windows and hopped over fences to avoid immigration inspectors. As an "illegal alien" he worked off the books at or below minimum wage. He was always paid in cash. Years later when he finally gained citizenship, he got his first real paycheck. It was at that time, too, that he first became a union member. Ironically, it was his boss who signed him up for the union, telling him he was required to do so. For my father, it just meant one more deduction from his pay.

One memory that stays with me from this period is the night my stepfather brought his boss and the boss's wife to our apartment. The wife had recently purchased a gown that needed alteration and, knowing that my mother did this sort of thing, came over for a fitting. When, for the first time, I saw my mother get on her knees to pin up the boss lady's gown, I was suddenly filled with rage. I hated them for being so rich that they could bring my otherwise very tough and proud mother to her knees.

The neighborhood we lived in was situated between a stable working-class community to the north and a dirt-poor black community to the south. It was a commercial and transient district of storefront businesses and residents who lived on the margins of society. We had more than our share of neighborhood drunks and "white trash." There were half a dozen transient hotels that doubled as houses of prostitution. It was a tough neighborhood even by today's standards. Guns and drugs were around, even if not as abundant as they are now; switchblades, brass knuckles, and burglar's tools were also quite popular at the time. Most of the kids I knew on our block wound up dead or in jail.

I started working at a relatively young age and took on a number of jobs. I worked as a stock boy, bellhop, messenger, and later as a janitor, cab driver, and gem runner (transporting diamonds and other precious materials to and from the jewelry district). I also spent one summer making pizza and another one hawking beers at ball games. None of these jobs were unionized.

Here I was working in unskilled, low-wage jobs and part of a community most in need of a voice and an advocate and yet the labor movement failed to reach me—failed to touch me in any way. And these were the days of "big labor" with a public image that rivaled that of "big business." It all seemed irrelevant to me at the time. It's ironic that it wasn't until I started teaching in college and making a decent salary for the first time in my life that I went to my first union meeting and walked my first picket line.

The advantages of schooling, like the advantages of unionism, were late in coming to me. For the most part, I hated school. I thought it was a boring and hostile place. I also had trouble with the English language and that didn't help matters. My mother spoke in Greek at home and insisted that I do the same, even as she frantically tried to master English. She went to night school to improve her English and sent me to after-school classes to improve my Greek. In afternoon school and at home, I was learning the ways and customs as well as the language of the Greeks.

Based on appearances, my primary school experience should have been a positive one. Public School 170 was literally a little red school house at the top of a grassy hill. There were only two classes for each grade, making for a relatively small and intimate school community. The school was racially integrated and had a rich ethnic and linguistic mix: Russians, Poles, Latinos, Asians, Jews, and Greeks. The kids also came from what appeared to me to be economically diverse backgrounds: workers and shop owners, apartment dwellers and homeowners. (In my mind, the sons and daughters of shop owners were rich kids. They were, after all, the children of businessmen and property owners, even if their business was a coffee shop and the home they lived in a row house.)

The school, however, was far from idyllic. The building was old, outmoded, and in constant need of repair. The playground was a barren parking lot with a gravel surface that ensured bloodied kneecaps whenever anyone fell. The third floor was reserved for a girls' vocational high school program. Within a decade, the school would be demolished completely and replaced by a much larger modern school building.

Semi-annual report cards at PS 170 listed six grading categories, in the following order: (1) social behavior, (2) work habits, (3) health habits, (4) language arts, (5) math, (6) other areas (social studies, science, music, art). There was little doubt in my mind that these reflected the school's priorities. Reading recent accounts of inner city schools, I am not sure, that priorities are very different today, despite the rhetoric.[2]

There was one message that predominated throughout my early school experience: it was my teachers telling me "this is the way we do things." Language arts meant grammar skills, spelling quizzes, penmanship evaluation. All this was counterposed in my head with the way I was used to doing things in Greek. There was absolutely nothing in those six years to inspire me about the written word. Primary schools in those days were called grammar schools, for good reason.

Math, too, was taught in a mechanistic and unimaginative way. Social studies, to the extent that it was taught at all, was a collection of dates, names, places, and facts, none of which either spoke to me or interested me. On the one hand, all this was foreign and disorienting to me; on the other hand, the listening, memorizing, and repeating over and over was the most tedious thing I had ever experienced. I alternated between feeling intimidated and being bored to death.

No matter what my mother said, school just didn't seem that important. Economic class does have a way of determining what a kid thinks is important. I remember the day in fifth grade when school officials were conducting their annual in-class eye exams. For two years I had been cheating my way through those exams to avoid having to wear glasses. My teacher had suspected for some time that I couldn't read the blackboard, so she asked me, once again, to identify the letters on the eye chart, this time reading backwards. I flunked. It is ironic because I never cheated on class tests: that just wasn't worth the bother. Cheating on eye exams was a matter of survival. I was going to be in for some pretty rough times in the neighborhood.

With glasses, my schoolwork improved. My strategy, however, remained the same and revolved around getting by. Like so many others, I just wanted to be average. Once in six years I said something brilliant about a math problem on the board, astonishing both my teacher and myself. Overall, I was content with being mediocre and this characterized what would remain a fairly lackluster academic career for many years to come.

Much more was going on, however, because in addition to the basic academics, I was learning how to be an American: I was learning how to fit in. It was not only a matter of learning how to dress, speak, and look, I was also learning what to like and what to dislike. And it was not simply a matter of accepting and conforming to a lifestyle and set of values, but of internalizing them. I remember, quite vividly, the day in sixth grade when I changed, forever, the way I pronounce my last name. I traded in the harsh sounding "Mann-choz" of northern Greece, for a much softer sounding "man-sios" because it sounded a lot like the way Jayne Mansfield pronounced the beginning of her last name. I also remember responding to the question "what are you?" by telling people I was Catholic, because that sounded less foreign and because someone told me that Greek Orthodoxy was closer to Catholicism than to Protestantism. This was, of course, years before Hollywood and Olympic Airlines were to create images of Greek Zorbas and dancing in the aisles that would endear Greeks to a significant portion of the U.S. population. As for me, I ended up feeling shame and guilt both for being foreignlike and for wanting not to be. I just wanted to be average.

For others, the black, Latino, and Eastern European kids, it was worse. While I was presented with models that held out the hope of assimilation, they were presented with models that challenged their very being. Everything we were being taught made who they were and what they were beyond redemption. These were the days of fierce battles to maintain racial segregation: they were also the days of the cold war, evil empires, and school shelter drills. Without a conscious attempt on the part of the school system to teach tolerance and respect for differences, everything we were taught reflected and reinforced the prejudice and intolerance we saw around us. Teachers were obsessed with eradicating Black English in the school, textbooks provided us not with black history but with glimpses of "exceptional" blacks, and administrators adopted a patronizing tone when addressing black kids: all of this confirmed the messages we were getting from outside. Ordered to duck under our desks to avoid annihilation by Russian missiles at the sound of special school bells, it was no wonder we were afraid even to talk to our Russian classmates. Much of the racist sentiments and most of the anti-immigrant sentiments we picked up had less to do with race and ethnicity than it did with class. No one had to tell me that Polish jokes were really jokes about class: they were about everything we did not want to be. I would chuckle nervously, knowing I was about an inch away from rock bottom.

School was dominated by the ideologies and personalities of the white middle class. We were fed values and lifestyle models which were simultaneously presented as universal and lacking in ourselves. What counted was white not black or brown, American not immigrant, middle class not poor or working class. So different was less, inferior, inconsequential, and inadequate and we all quickly learned to see the enemy within us. We were developing prejudices and self-hate that would take a lifetime to overcome.

Some of us could harbor fantasies of being "average" more easily than others. As white kids, we believed our second-class status was temporary: if we worked hard, perfected our social skills, and entered the middle class, we too would be average. But skin colors, like gender, are irreversible. And if you were unfortunate enough to be handicapped by class, race, and gender, like most of the girls on the third floor, then you were surely doomed. Boys could learn to make decent money working with their hands; the girls on the third floor were learning to type and cut hair.

Most of us eased the pain and got back our self-confidence on the street, not in the classroom. Tough kids who behaved in class earned the privilege of going outside to clean blackboard erasers. Some reward. Kids that didn't give up and withdraw, became defiant and confrontational. The classroom increasingly became a battleground.

The battle was lost in Mr. Zago's junior high school class. Mr. Zago taught by the force of sheer terror and his routine was a fairly simple one. He would slowly walk around the room, stop at a desk, call out your last name, and ask you a question. If you knew the answer, he would move on to another student. If you didn't have the right answer, he would slam a yardstick on your desk, an inch from your face and hands. He would then tell you to stand up, berate you, and ask you a series of additional questions, each one a little harder than the one before it. After humiliating you at your desk, he would have you go to the blackboard and ask you to write out answers to still tougher questions. You would find yourself sinking deeper and deeper into a nightmarish pit from which there was no escape. The ordeal usually lasted ten or fifteen minutes. At least one student was put through the ordeal each day. Mr. Zago's boot camp approach to teaching got me to do my homework, but I forgot everything he taught me the last day of class.

By high school most of us knew our fates were sealed. Sociologists could have told us all along that there is little class mobility in the U.S. They could have told us that despite the wonderful rhetoric to the contrary, the rags to riches stories and the "we are all middle class" image of America were largely myths—but we were finding out for ourselves.

The older kids on the block weren't making it. At best, they were stuck in the same type of dead-end jobs our parents had. As for my own generation of kids, we were now armed with cars, drugs, and a swelling sense of machismo and anger. Our childhood pranks were increasingly turning to criminal activities. One kid was arrested for car theft, another for selling drugs. Still another fell to his death jumping roof tops. Through it all, I survived. In the neighborhood, I avoided arrest: in school, I managed to stay average. When I decided to go to college, my friend Ray beamed, "The rest of us aren't going to make it, Greg, but you will." At that moment, I felt both that I had betrayed my friends and that I had an enormous responsibility to them. This was not a social responsibility: it was an individual responsibility to make it for myself.

I reached my lowest point in college. I was enrolled in a Western Civilization course, a degree requirement that could have been and should have been one of the most interesting courses of my academic career. Up to then, I had been taking remedial courses and struggling with the mechanics of math and the English language just to get C grades. The Western Civ course was a bust. I couldn't focus on the lectures and I couldn't concentrate on my readings. My mind would drift and I would daydream or struggle to keep my eyelids open. I couldn't connect either to the teacher or the readings. I forced myself, tortured myself, to study and after a lot of cramming, I managed to get a D. This pulled my grade average down to where I was within fractions of flunking out. All the self-doubts and all the ambivalence about going to college reached a crisis point. My friends were doing other things: I had abandoned them for this? I wasn't cut out for this sort of thing. It seemed that the only question left for me was whether to drop out or let the school throw me out.

My Western Civ professor is now a colleague of mine at Queens College. He doesn't remember me, of course, and I have never mentioned any of this to him. I have had few encounters with him, but when I was seated opposite him at a reception a couple of years ago, I had an urge to reach across the table and shake him.

What kept me going through all this? Certainly thinking about the alternatives—death, jail, dead-end jobs, and the army—helped. The urging and the model of perseverance offered by my mother helped too. So did my ties to an ethnic community beyond my immediate neighborhood. These ties provided a sense of ethnic pride, broadened my circle of friends, and offered additional role models.

There were also some positive experiences in my earlier schooling, though not by curriculum design, that helped me keep things in perspective. In sixth grade I had a teacher who would send his son into school to substitute for him when he couldn't make it. The son, who had a bohemian quality to him, brought his guitar to class and sang folk songs. It was the first time I appreciated the beauty and power of language. The music and lyrics touched me in ways that no poetry book ever did.

◆　◆　◆

Around this time, one of my teachers assigned *The Other America* by Michael Harrington.[3] This was the first book I ever read from cover to cover. I read it out on the fire escape. For once, I felt someone was paying attention to those of us who were not part of the "affluent society." It was a revelation that not only were there others like us, but that there were others in situations much worse than ours. Why hadn't anyone said this before? Why were the only images of America presented in the classroom and in the media those of an affluent middle class? Much later, I was to become a colleague of Harrington at Queens College. He continued to inspire me and became a friend.

My eighth grade social studies teacher, Mr. Gatto, was the first teacher to have a real influence on me. He taught a wonderful class, assigned interesting readings, and demonstrated a caring manner, even when he was tough. One day he pulled several boys aside, including one of the toughest, meanest kids in the class. Mr. Gatto convinced us to join his theater club. I had never been to the theater and it seemed the strangest of all suggestions. I still don't know how he paid for it, but he took us to Saturday afternoon matinees. After a performance of *The Great White Hope,* he took us backstage to meet James Earl Jones. I never forgot that performance or that day and I have been going to the theater ever since.

Listening to folk songs in class and going to the theater with a teacher were not major happenings, and yet they had a profound effect on me. Folk songs of the beat generation provided me with an alternative perspective at a fairly young age and such a perspective, whether it comes from a counterculture or a political movement, is critical for those trying to survive poverty and deprivation in a society which prides itself on its abundance. Theater, on the other hand, exposed me to a middle-class art form that was appealing: its social commentary stimulated me to think about the world as well as about personal and social issues. I learned to appreciate cultural expressions, even if they were mainstream or what I considered "high culture." Theater was fun, moving, meaningful, even self-critical at times. Maybe middle-class life, values, and talents had something to offer after all. That such trivial events could have such a major impact, is indicative both of the paucity of the educational system and the resiliency of the human spirit.

Folk and theater, however, were only seeds: my real awakening came in college. After my Western Civilization course, I knew I had one more semester left. If I didn't pull my average up immediately, I would be out of college on my rear end. I registered for a sociology course with Mike Brown, a demanding but very popular teacher. (I always thought it tragic, that at most large, urban public colleges, the system of letting seniors and juniors register first meant that freshmen and sophomores got closed out of the best classes at the most critical juncture of their academic career.) Mike was very exciting and dynamic and exposed me to a completely different way of seeing the world. In his class, I read C. Wright Mill's classic *The Sociological Imagination* and learned what was probably the most important lesson of my life.[4] I learned that far from being individual and personal problems, most of the troubles that I and my friends and neighbors faced were broad social issues. They were systemic issues that demanded structural and public policy changes. I was beginning to learn that if I were to understand my own experiences, I would have to locate them in society and in history. By the end of the course, I was convinced that our compassions were skewed, our priorities reversed, and our institutions fundamentally flawed. I was also convinced that society need not be this way. Mike didn't offer any easy solutions, nor did he suggest models to emulate: he did offer ideas and experiences to draw on to make a better world. I was developing vision.

I never worked as hard as I did in that course. From that point on I got nothing but straight A's. Some teachers and courses were more interesting and more socially relevant than others, but it didn't matter. I was determined to learn as much as I could and to develop my own perspective.

Identifying with society's underdogs wasn't difficult for me. Although it had not been an easy lesson for me to learn, my uncle had been teaching me all along to identify with the "common people." He had become a Democratic Party stalwart because, as he was quick to tell me, the Democrats best represented the interests of poor people, immigrants, minorities, and working people. When he stayed up all night listening to the election returns, it conveyed the impression that the interests of the "common people," if not the Party, mattered. Now it was all coming together.

It wasn't, however, simply a matter of identifying with the underdog: I was developing an important set of principles to guide me. I remember visiting family in South Carolina: they were not much better off than we were and they were certainly just as nice. But when my sweet, vivacious older cousin sternly reprimanded me for unknowingly walking to the back of the bus with "What are you, a nigger lover?", I knew she was speaking not only for herself, but for the other white working-class people on the bus as well. Now I was learning to distinguish between good working-class instincts and bad. I was also learning that when my neighborhood friends spoke to and of women in insulting and degrading ways, that there was something fundamentally wrong both with them and with a society that encourages such attitudes and practices. I was developing a class loyalty that was informed and principled—a class loyalty that made sense.

My classmates and I were being influenced by the social movements around us. I was learning from the civil rights movement and the women's movement as well as the antiwar and anti-imperialist movements. I am convinced that these movements would never have reached me if I had not been exposed to their ideas in college.

It wasn't long before I became a social activist, myself. I became active in campus organizing, and later I joined the government's ACTION program, and became a full-time community organizer. I was learning important organizational and interpersonal skills. I was also learning from the Left, the Old Left as well as the New Left.

My understanding of and identification with labor unions were tied to academe as well. A former classmate of mine moved to California and became an organizer for the farmworkers' grape boycott. While visiting her, I worked briefly on the boycott myself and was deeply moved by the moral and political strengths of the farmworkers' cause. I spent many an afternoon in front of supermarkets convincing customers to shop elsewhere. I was part of a very effective team of picketers and we turned back hundreds of would-be shoppers. When the boycott as a whole proved to be effective, it gave me a tremendous sense of collective power.

A year later, having earned a master's degree in Urban Studies, I got my first full-time teaching job at William Paterson College in New Jersey. Within a few weeks of my appointment, I got caught up in a statewide faculty strike over salary and class size. This too, was an effective strike with considerable student and community support. Shortly afterwards, I was elected to union office and became increasingly involved in union activities. After two years on the faculty, I was fired for my union activities.

My interest in labor unions was growing and I sought out and found ways to connect my new interest with my academic work. I was asked to teach an "Introduction to Labor Studies" course to a group of electrical apprentices enrolled at Empire State College.

This was a group of young working-class men and a few women, not unlike my neighborhood friends. Just about everyone of them hated being in class, or so they told me on the first day. In most cases, they had chosen to become class-A electricians (construction) precisely because they wanted to work with their hands rather than continue with school. After signing them up for their apprenticeship and at the union's request, the industry board overseeing the apprenticeship program imposed a two-year college requirement. While the industry board provided full tuition for these apprentices, this endeared them neither to the union nor to my class. They were a very rowdy bunch, but over time they began to give me the benefit of the doubt. Together we read quite a bit of labor history. It was only one of the topics I planned to cover, but it grabbed them the most and we stuck with it for the entire semester. They, too, had been taught that poor and working people were inconsequential in our society. Now, we were learning about the courageous working-class heroes and heroines who fought for the rights and benefits most working men and women take for granted today: the minimum wage, the forty-hour week, and the right to be treated with dignity and respect. From those apprentices, I was also learning how to bring my academic knowledge and skills to my community. The following semester, I was appointed director of the program: a program that was to grow to nearly fifteen hundred students at its peak.

Compared to the apprentices, the Queens College students in the room with me now are older, perhaps wiser. Most have already been in the labor force for quite some time. What do I tell these worker-students about college and about the college career they are about to embark on? I tell them that, done right, higher education, like union struggle, can be an empowering and liberating experience. I tell them that education doesn't have to be boring, rote, or degrading: not ticky tacky, not little boxes, not all the same.

I tell them that education can be inspiring, enriching, and self affirming: that in college they will learn to think critically and creatively; that when they are exposed to middle-class, male, Eurocentric ideas and values they will be identified as such and that other values and ideas will be presented as equally legitimate; that they will struggle with ideas and learn to articulate well-thought-out arguments; that they will build their self-confidence: that they will be exposed to teachers who will infect them with their enthusiasm; that they will be challenged and that they will grow, individually and collectively.

I also tell them that I sincerely hope that we fulfill our promise to them: that we have created a special worker education program that provides them with pro-active counseling, special tutoring, small classes, and exciting and caring teachers: that we have designed a special worker education curriculum which, in addition to some of the more traditional course requirements in the liberal arts and sciences, includes such course requirements as Writing and the Literature of Work; Latin American Literature; African-American Literary Traditions; and Work, Class, and Culture: that in addition to the college's fifty majors, they can choose special courses of study in Public Policy or Labor Studies: that we have created a new bachelor's degree in Applied Social Sciences with the explicit purpose of organizing a course of study around finding solutions to social problems and around developing strategies for social change; that our faculty and staff are committed to providing them with the knowledge and skills not only to make them better informed and more effective worker-citizens, but to become advocates in their communities and leaders in their workplace.

Yes, ambivalence toward education and toward unions may be justified. But we are doing our part and they must do their part to make these institutions more responsive and effective. Our Labor Resource Center at Queens College was established to encourage discourse on the future of the labor movement. It organizes workshops and conferences with the active participation of rank and file members as well as union leaders. At the same time, the college's Academic Senate provides a forum for discussion and debate on policies and practices. It is a particularly interesting forum because administrators like myself can attend and speak on the floor of the Senate, but cannot vote. Decisions about college policy, including admissions criteria, degree requirements, and retention standards, are voted on by representatives elected by the students and faculty: one-third students, two-thirds faculty. I make a point of telling them that they have a right and a responsibility to help shape college policy. It is a responsibility to make higher education and unions into viable instruments for social change and for a better world.

And yes, knowledge is empowering. But there is another motto to ponder: "Discimus ut serviamus." It is the college's motto, and though it is buried in the college bulletin so that hardly anyone knows it, and rarely uttered so that those who know it forget it, and written in Latin so that those who see it may not understand it, it is particularly relevant: "We learn so that we may serve." It is a motto to be taken to heart by anyone emerging from the working class.

ENDNOTES

1. Mike Rose, *Lives on the Boundary* (New York: Penguin Books, 1989), p. 28.
2. See, Jonathan Kozol, *Savage Inequalities: Children in America's Schools* (New York: Crown Publishers, 1991).
3. Michael Harrington, *The Other America: Poverty in the United States* (New York: Penguin Books, 1962).
4. C. Wright Mills, *The Sociological Imagination* (Oxford: Oxford University Press, 1959).

Questions for Understanding and Critical Thinking

1. Why was Mantsios's early life so influential in his later career? How have experiences in your childhood been influential in your educational choices and future career plans?

2. What factors are involved in the process of "learning how to be an American"? Do recent immigrants still go through this process today? Why or why not?

3. Why was the process of "Americanization" more difficult for African American, Latino/Latina, and eastern European children than it was for Mantsios, whose family roots were in northern Greece?

4. How do professors' own life experiences affect their college teaching? Can you think of situations where your professors have revealed personal information about themselves that is reflected in the courses they teach?

ARTICLE 17 _____

According to sociologists Jill Quadagno and Catherine Fobes, gender stratification has been perpetuated by the *welfare state*—a situation in which the government takes over responsibility for welfare by offering specific categories of people certain services and benefits, such as housing, health care, education, and income. This article examines how the Job Corps—a core antipoverty program—reproduced gender inequality.

Jill Quadagno teaches sociology at Florida State University where she is affiliated with the Pepper Institute on Aging and Public Policy. Catherine Fobes was a sociology graduate student at Florida State University when she coauthored this article.

Looking Ahead

1. What evidence do Quadagno and Fobes present to show how the welfare state organizes class relations? Gender relations?
2. Why did Job Corps organizers believe that it was important to provide poor youths with new peer groups and cultural capital in the form of a middle-class value system?
3. What contributions did the Job Corps make to the training of women and men? What were its major limitations?

The Welfare State and the Cultural Reproduction of Gender
Making Good Girls and Boys in the Job Corps

◆ *Jill Quadagno and Catherine Fobes*

INTRODUCTION

Theories of the Welfare State

In theorizing the welfare state, social scientists recognize that it not only performs the obvious functions of providing income and social services but that it also operates as a system of stratification. As Esping-Anderson (1990:55) argues, "Welfare states are key institutions in the structuring of class and the social order. The organizational features of the welfare state help determine the articulation of social solidarity, divisions of class, and status differentiation."

Source: From Jill Quadagno and Catherine Fobes, "The Welfare State and the Cultural Reproduction of Gender." © 1995 by the Society for the Study of Social Problems. Reprinted from *Social Problems*, Vol. 42, No. 2, May 1995, pp. 171–190, by permission.

Much of the research on the welfare state has examined how it organizes class relations. The central question has been to explain whether or when the welfare state merely reproduces the existing class structure or whether or when it ameliorates inequality (Gough 1979; Korpi 1989; Baldwin 1990; Offe 1984). Feminist theorists, however, argue that the focus on class relations has ignored inequality based on gender. Recent feminist research has examined the effect of the welfare state on gender relations (Quadagno 1990; Shaver and Bradshaw 1993; Orloff 1993; Skocpol 1992; Gordon 1990; Jenson 1991; Shaver 1990; Nelson 1990; Fraser 1990; Mink 1990). As Orloff (1993:303) explains:

> *Theorists may disagree about the causes of gender inequality and women's subordination, but few would deny that the character of systems of public social provision affects women's material situations, shapes gender relationships, structures political conflict and participation and contributes to the formation and mobilization of specific identities and interests.*

When analyzing how the welfare state influences gender relations, most feminist theorists conclude that it reproduces male dominance. There are several mechanisms that lead to this outcome. Some social programs, like social insurance systems, reproduce market inequality through eligibility rules that link benefits to prior wages (Harrington Meyer 1990; Sainsbury 1989; Shaver and Bradshaw 1993). The welfare state also reproduces gender inequality by providing greater rewards for benefits earned through paid work effort than for those bestowed on the basis of family membership. The latter do not incorporate women into the welfare state "as citizens like men, but as members of the family, a sphere separate from . . . civil society and the state" (Pateman 1988:235–36). Finally,

welfare policies may reproduce gender inequality by *failing* to intervene. Women are less competitive in the labor market if they are unable to take paid leave after the birth of a child or to find affordable, high-quality child care. The tension between familial and market demands reduces women's earning power and increases their economic dependence on men (Maume 1991; Presser and Baldwin 1980). Through such mechanisms, the welfare state reinforces the gendered division of labor in the household and in the market.

In explaining how the welfare state reproduces gender stratification, feminist theorists have largely disregarded cultural factors. They examine the structural factors that create or maintain inequality in the market but overlook the cultural "codes and rules which guide and regulate traffic, with instructions on which boundaries may be transversed under what conditions" (Gerson and Peiss 1985:319). Theories of cultural reproduction link these more structural arguments to the ideologies, meaning systems, and informal rules that also produce and maintain stratification systems (Bourdieu 1984).

Theories of Cultural Reproduction and Resistance

Most of the theorizing on cultural reproduction emerges from studies of educational institutions. Reproduction theorists identify cultural reproduction as the discourses, ideologies, materials, and practices that reproduce class inequality and that shape class destinies (Bowles and Gintis 1976; Apple 1979; Bourdieu 1973). They claim that contrary to the liberal view of the educational institution as the great equalizer—i.e., a vehicle for individual development, social mobility, and empowerment of the disadvantaged—the primary functions of schools are the reproduction of the dominant ideology, its forms of knowledge, and the circulation of skills needed to reproduce the social division of labor (Giroux 1983). As Paul Willis (1983:110) explains:

> *Education (is) not about equality, but inequality. . . .*
>
> *Education's main purpose of the social integration of a class society could be achieved only by preparing most kids for an unequal future, and by insuring their personal underdevelopment. Far from productive roles in the economy simply waiting to be 'fairly' filled by the products of education, the 'Reproduction' perspective reversed this to suggest that capitalist production and its roles required certain educational outcomes.*

While reproduction theories have been invaluable in identifying the reproduction of class relations, in contributing to a broader understanding of the political nature of schooling, and in analyzing the relationship between the educational institution and capitalist society, they have been highly criticized (Giroux 1981, 1983; Willis 1977, 1981). One of the major problems is their ahistorical emphasis on domination at the expense of human agency. Patterned after structural-functionalist versions of Marxism that stress that history is made "behind the backs" of members of society, they fail to capture how human agents come together within specific historical and social contexts to resist domination and struggle for change (Giroux 1983). In a word, they have been shaped by a type of determinism where "people [become] puppets in a ballet of cosmic categories" (Connell et al. 1981:104). The idea "that people do make history, including its constraints, has been neglected" (Giroux 1983:259). By overemphasizing domination at the cost of agency, reproduction theories ignore the complex contradictions and conflicts within social institutions; they fail to illuminate the dynamics of teachers, parents,

and students' accommodation and resistance both inside and outside schools; and, they rarely take into account other forms of oppression, specifically those based on gender, race, and ethnicity (Giroux 1981, 1983).

Recent research on schooling in the United States, Europe, and Australia has both challenged and attempted to move beyond reproduction theories by emphasizing history, human agency, conflict, struggle, and resistance (Giroux 1981, 1983; Willis 1981; Holland and Eisenhardt 1990; Anyon 1983; Arnot 1982; Mac An Ghaill 1989; Fernandes 1988). Loosely labeled as "resistance theory," these theories suggest that cultural reproduction is an historically concrete, dialectical process. First, cultural reproduction is not an iron law of transmission, but a mutable, historically variant creative process (Giroux 1983; Willis, 1977, 1981; Scott 1990). This means that cultural reproduction is an ever repeated creative process that, in different material or political circumstances, produces different outcomes. Sexual categories, for instance, are not rigidly determined. Rather, they are socially constructed out of political struggles, giving rise to different interest groups that stand to gain or lose depending on the ascendance of one form (Holland and Eisenhart 1990).

Secondly, resistance theorists claim that the reproduction of dominant relations can help create a social space for human beings to dialectically create, resist, and accommodate themselves to dominant ideologies and practices (Fernandes 1988; Scott 1990; Genovese 1972; Giroux 1983; Anyon 1983). Victims of oppressive systems, for example, rarely totally accept or reject these systems. Rather, they can engage in a process whereby they resist the repressive features of oppressive systems within patterns of accommodation. This means that they accept what can not be avoided and simultaneously fight individually "and as a people for moral as well as physical survival" (Genovese 1972:659). Thus, resistance theorists argue that cultural reproduction is never fully complete because it is dialectically confronted by oppositional cultures that transform or subvert the reproductive process (Giroux 1983; Willis 1977).

Theories of cultural reproduction have helped identify that stratification systems are reproduced, in part, through the distribution and legitimation of dominant ideologies, discourses, meanings, and material practices. Resistance theory has challenged and expanded this theoretical framework by elucidating contradictions within social institutions, by emphasizing the historical and creative dimensions of cultural reproduction and resistance, and by capturing the dynamic process of human agency. These theories provide a solid foundation for a close examination of the cultural reproduction of gender.

The Cultural Reproduction of Gender

Much of the empirical research on cultural reproduction has demonstrated how structural factors help reproduce a gendered division of labor. In a study of British high schools, for example, Kelly (1985) documented how such mechanisms as sex-stereotyped examples used by teachers, textbooks that provide no illustrations of women engaged in scientific activities, and differential treatment of students by teachers encouraged male dominance of the physical sciences (physics, chemistry, biology). Similarly, Skeggs (1988:134) concluded that vocational courses in Britain were centered around the assumption "that the primary role for women was outside of the labor market in the family." Because courses bore only a tenuous relationship to the labor market, they prepared the students for work "as unpaid domestic laborers, willing to sustain

and regulate their own families and provide unpaid community care" (Skeggs 1988:136).

The way sex stereotyped expectations are reproduced through the curriculum is only part of the process of cultural reproduction. More important are practices directed toward constructing masculinity and femininity. As Connell et al. (1982:174) argue, "That football is often played by boys and rarely by girls is a trivial point; what counts is the way it serves as a focus for a whole programme of constructing masculinity and subordinating some forms of it to others." In other words, what matters are the cultural, ideological systems that reproduce gender inequality. For example, in a study of gender differences in extracurricular activities, Eder and Parker (1987) found that the lack of official support for female athletics limited its cultural significance among middle school students and encouraged girls to seek out the higher status activity of cheerleading instead. They discovered that male athletes and female cheerleaders were exposed to very different values through these activities. Whereas male athletes were taught to value achievement and competition, among female cheerleaders, poise, personality, general appearance, smiling, and the ability to "sparkle" (convey a bubbly personality) were emphasized. Further, resistance processes in this study were suggested by girls who rejected cheerleading, girls who placed a high value on toughness, girls who used ritual insults, and girls who practiced self-defense strategies (Eder and Parker 1987). Thus, research suggests that gender stratification occurs on two levels. The structural level concerns the mechanisms that reproduce the sexual and social division of labor. The cultural level emphasizes the ideologies, meaning systems, and informal practices that create and reproduce—but also resist—these stratifying mechanisms (Fernandes 1988).

In this paper we seek to address theoretical arguments about cultural reproduction and resistance in the context of the welfare state. We argue that the welfare state reproduces gender stratification structurally by replicating a gendered division of labor and culturally by inculcating an ideological framework that sustains the division of labor. We document forms of female resistance and we show that while welfare state policy did reproduce gender stratification, it paradoxically provided emancipatory possibilities for men who were not of the dominant race.

We illustrate our arguments through an historical study of Lyndon Johnson's War on Poverty, the only major expansion of the welfare state in the second half of the twentieth century. A key program of the War on Poverty was the Job Corps, a youth training program emphasizing basic skills and preparation for jobs in the skilled trades. The Job Corps represents an opportunity to link theories of the welfare state with theories of cultural reproduction, because it was an educational program that operated through an agency, the Office of Economic Opportunity, that was created to by-pass mainstream political institutions and transform the welfare state (Quadagno 1994). The question we explore is how that process of transformation differed in regard to the organization, goals, curriculum and ideologies in the men's and women's Job Corps Centers.

Our evidence comes primarily from the historical documents of the War on Poverty housed in the National Archives, especially Record Group 381 from the Office of Economic Opportunity, and Record Group 86, Women's Bureau, Department of Labor. Also relevant are newspaper articles, congressional hearings on the Economic Opportunity Act and oral histories of key figures in the War on Poverty from the collection of the Lyndon Baines Johnson Library, Austin, Texas.

STRUCTURAL DETERMINANTS OF GENDER INEQUALITY

The Exclusion of Women

Feminist theorists of the welfare state contend that gender inequality is reproduced when the state fails to provide programs that enhance women's ability to compete in the labor market. Initially, it seemed that the Job Corps would exclude women entirely. During hearings on the economic opportunity bill in March 1964, program planners made clear their views that the Job Corps would train young men (Graham 1990). They argued that women's centers would only drain funds targeted to men and complicate implementation of the program. Rep. Edith Green's (D-OR) suggestion that women be included met considerable resistance. As Green recalled, "When I suggested that the Job Corps ought to be for girls as well as boys, I got a lot of static from the Johnson administration. They really did not like to be challenged, and especially by a woman."[1] Green was a key member of the House Committee on Education and Labor, however, and before the bill left the committee, she acquired an understanding that women would constitute at least one-third of total enrollment.

On August 20, 1964, Johnson signed into law the Economic Opportunity Act. Title I authorized the establishment of a Job Corps "to prepare for the responsibilities of citizenship and to increase the employability of young men and young women aged sixteen through twenty-one by providing them in rural and urban residential centers with education, vocational training, useful work experiences. . . ."[2]

The Act specified that one-third of Job Corps trainees be female. By the following spring, several Women's Job Corps Centers were operating. On April 6, 1965, the St. Petersburg, Florida, center became the first to open, followed by centers in Cleveland, Los Angeles, and Charleston, West Virginia. However, after one year of operation, only 2,393 of the 27,300 recruits—less than 10 percent— were female. Green complained that the Job Corps was biased against girls, and in response, Congress directed the Office of Economic Opportunity, which ran the Job Corps, to accommodate 10,000 girls.[3] By 1967 there were 122 centers operating, with 103 allocated to men. In all 31,000 men and 9,000 women were being trained (Levin 1977).

Although the women's centers satisfied the commitment to training women, they differed considerably in the type of training offered. While young men received training for the better-paying skilled trades, young women were channeled into traditional female jobs. Further, women but not men were trained in homemaking skills. The curriculum of the Job Corps Centers supports an argument from feminist theories of the welfare state: that the welfare state can replicate male dominance by reproducing a gendered division of labor. By channeling women into low-paying jobs and by training them to become family caregivers, the Job Corps reinforced the gender segregation of the labor market and the patriarchal structure of the family.

Reproducing the Gendered Division of Labor

In planning the Job Corps Centers, different standards were established for male and female recruits. Training centers for men, located in both rural or urban areas, provided basic education in reading and math, as well as intense job training for entry-level skills in the well-paying skilled trades. Curriculum planning to meet these objectives included detailed lists of jobs broken down into specific skills, and an analysis of the training experiences and basic education needed to provide these skills.[4] For example, a corpsman being trained as an auto mechanic needed basic reading skills to read a driver's manual, lubrication charts, or repair manuals. His training also included instruction in how to maintain pick-up trucks and wheel tractors. His curriculum would include learning electrical systems, cooling systems, brake systems, fuel systems, engine repair and overhaul, transmission and differential, tune-ups, trouble shooting, manual reading, and part ordering. Young men being trained as carpenters could specialize in hand tools, power tools, rough carpentry, finish carpentry, and cabinet making. They would learn such specific skills as how to use tools and such general skills as framing, sheathing, flooring, siding, and roofing.[5] Clearly, the urban centers were designed to provide young men the specific training and work experience needed for obtaining employment in the skilled labor market.

The rural conservation centers developed from the Job Corps Task Force's idealistic vision of a program "where kids would have an opportunity to get out of cities and into an environment that was different—a more healthful environment away from their families and away from their gangs."[6] These centers were oriented more toward basic remedial education. However, trainees still received work experience for more than a hundred jobs. These included laborer, equipment operator, mechanic, draftsman, welder, soil scientist, land surveyor, brickmason, gardener, carpenter, truck driver, rigger, salesman, land surveyor, painter, power machine operator, lumberman, snow surveyor, custodian, clerk, mail carrier, typist, and entomologist.

While the Job Corps was open to all deprived youth, the criteria used to screen applicants biased the programs toward African Americans. Initial screening focused on 10 criteria. Applicants had to be between 16 and 21 years old and be a permanent resident of the United States. They received priority for being unemployed, being a high school drop-out and having no marketable skills. Applicants also had to show evidence of environmental deprivation, defined by the following criteria: living in substandard housing; living in a high crime area; having low family income or having the primary wage earner be unemployed or on public assistance; having parents with less than a fifth-grade education; having parents in unskilled work or farm labor or having moved residences frequently.

The criteria for entry into the programs differed by gender, however. In addition to the characteristics listed above, female applicants were considered environmentally deprived if they had "no opportunity for marriage to men capable of providing more than a poverty-level income."[7] Male but not female applicants had to pass a medical examination that screened for homosexuality, drug or alcohol addiction, severe emotional disturbances, and mental retardation. Skills expectations also differed by gender. Male applicants were given a basic reading and math test, females applicants were not.[8] Implicit in the recruitment guidelines was the assumption that men were to be controlled, educated, and trained for skilled jobs, while women were to be prepared for marriage.

As the Job Corps Task Force planned the women's centers, it depended on the Women's Bureau within the Department of Labor to supply background data. The Women's Bureau, which was run by women active in the trade union movement, championed the needs of working women. It supplied the Task Force data indicating that the labor force participation of women was on the rise, that young women aged 16 to 19 lacked job skills, and that a high percentage of women who headed families, especially black families, were in poverty. However, few of these insights were incorporated into the curriculum of the women's centers (Zelman 1980). Although women did receive basic education and occupational training, the emphasis was on "intensive training in home and family life and the development of values, attitudes, and skills that (would) contribute to stable family relationships and a good child-rearing environment."[9] Fulfilling these objectives would allow Job Corps graduates to acquire and hold jobs at the entry level or above and would provide "education in home and family life . . . knowledge in homemaking and child care responsibilities, [which would enable] them to assume responsibility for running a home."[10]

To achieve the vocational objective, each trainee was offered training in one of 11 job clusters. These clusters included business and clerical; retail; services such as beauty shop assistant, food preparation, household service, clothing service, child care service; health occupations; recreation; education; and art.[11] According to the Task Force members, training in these areas would provide tremendous opportunities for employment in an expanding service-oriented economy and reinforce the "natural links between women's innate capacities for human relationships and their homemaking and child care skills and the many jobs to be filled."[12]

Vocational objectives could also be achieved on a more informal basis through the daily operation of the center. According to program guidelines, "laboratories" included the kitchen, dining room, laundry room, clothing area, and sewing room. The laboratories should include "a mixture of modern and conventional/traditional" equipment, because the "girls would undoubtedly use modern appliances at places of employment," but "some of them would return to, or establish, homes without such modern conveniences." Training in the laboratories meant that the women washed and ironed their own linens, mended their own clothing, and prepared and served their own meals. By contrast, Job Corps men were not expected to perform personal care tasks such as cooking or laundry. Rather corpsmen could get their laundry and dry-cleaning done at Corps-approved establishments with costs borne by the Job Corps.[13]

The Historical Context of the Job Corps

Why did the Job Corps emphasize training for high-paying skilled jobs for men and homemaking for women? One reason is that by the mid-1960s, employment equality for women had yet to emerge as a major political issue. Although the Civil Rights Act of 1964 included women in its Title IV provisions banning employment discrimination by sex, the intent of legislators was to open the labor market to African Americans (Burstein 1985). Further, the women's movement, which would soon sweep the nation, was still in its nascent stages, and recognition of the increasing labor force participation of women was largely unknown. The specific interest in making young, African-American women into competent wives and mothers, however, reflected more direct intent based on a thesis about the black family that had been circulating through the Johnson administration.

In 1965 Daniel Patrick Moynihan, a key planner on the Job Corps Task Force, published a report contending that the fundamental problem with African-American communities was family structure. High rates of unemployment among black males and government programs such as Aid to Families with Dependent Children encour-

aged female-headed households and weakened the stature and authority of black males. As Moynihan (1965:93) explained, "Ours is a society which presumes male leadership in private and public affairs but in the Negro family the dependence on the mother's income undermines the position of the father." The only solution, according to Moynihan, was for the government to guarantee that "every able-bodied Negro man was working, even if this meant that some jobs had to be redesigned to enable men to fulfill them." Only a massive federal effort could terminate the pathology afflicting African-American communities. The goal of federal policy, according to Moynihan, should be "the establishment of a stable Negro family structure" (Moynihan 1965:43).

Sargent Shriver, director of the Office of Economic Opportunity, was clearly influenced by the Moynihan thesis. In an exchange with Green about adding women to the Job Corps, he defended the male-only policy as a means of turning young men into breadwinners:

Mr. Shriver: The principal purpose of these centers was to give young men, who we hope will be heads of families and wage earners, an opportunity . . . to learn the necessary skills . . . for employment during the rest of their lives.

Mrs. Green: Are there not as many young women in that age group, or probably more because military service absorbs a large number of young men?

Mr. Shriver: There probably are, but the thought was to start with those who would have as their principal necessity in life . . . the earning of a living and supporting a family. . . . We started with men because we felt the need was greatest there.[14]

Secretary of Defense Robert McNamara agreed. Training young girls was a good idea, but the need for training "primary bread-winners" was "much greater" (Zelman 1980: 81).

The initial planning for the Job Corps illustrates how the welfare state can reproduce gender inequality. At first, only men were to be provided job training opportunities. When women were added, they were trained for jobs that would replicate a sex-segregated labor market and were given skills that would teach them to become family care-givers. However, the Job Corps agenda was formulated in a context in which gender expectations were derived from views about race. Objectives of white, middle-class reformers for the poor, and especially poor African Americans, were not only concerned with changing the opportunity structure available to youths but also with transforming what they considered to be black culture.

Cultural Reproduction and Gender Inequality

Cultural theorists argue that stratification systems are not only maintained by structural conditions but also by cultural boundaries (Lamont and Fournier 1992). These boundaries are constructed around the possession of "cultural capital," which is transmitted across generations through the family and maintained by sociopolitical forces (DiMaggio and Mohr 1985; Nash 1990). The concept of cultural capital as originally articulated by Bourdieu and Passeron (1977) suggests that children from the dominant class enter schools with key social and cultural cues, while working-class children must acquire these skills to negotiate the educational experience after they enter school. Elements of cultural capital, which range from personal style, linguistic competence, familiarity with elements of high culture like books, music or art to technical, economic or political expertise, are treated by the schools as signs of intelligence. In other words, the schools are not passive but play an active role in making the cultural capital of the elite valuable.

Since Bourdieu and Passeron's original formulation, others have more fully specified the functions of cultural capital. According to Lamont and Lareau (1988:56), one of the most important dimensions of the theory is "the idea of cultural capital . . . as a basis for exclusion from jobs, resources and high status jobs." In addition to training deprived youths for jobs, the Job Corps also included a moral reform campaign (Clarke 1987). The task of the moral reformers was to provide cultural capital to the culturally deprived by converting them to a morally and socially superior lifestyle.

Specifically, the Job Corps sought to encourage the poor, and especially poor African Americans, to adopt white middle-class values and behaviors. Through a broad training program, middle-class reformers planned to provide the poor with cultural resources that would enhance opportunities for social mobility. This ideology derived from the "culture of poverty" thesis, which reflected a larger strand of liberalism of the period: the idea that the poor were helpless and passive, and that the leadership of liberal intellectuals could break the cycle of deprivation and degradation that characterized their lives (Katz 1989).

First articulated by anthropologist Oscar Lewis, the "culture of poverty" thesis consisted of the assumption that the cultural environment of the poor fostered self-defeating attitudes and behaviors that perpetuated poverty. These included a strong present-time orientation, an inability to delay gratification and to plan for the future, a sense of fatalism and resignation, improper speech patterns, incompetence in patterns of middle-class interpersonal communication, low levels of aspirations, and maternal dominance (Lewis

1966). When members of the Job Corps Task Force began planning the programs, they sought to alter the behavioral traits of the poor that locked them into this "culture of poverty" by distributing cultural capital. However, meanings of cultural capital differed for young men and young women. For young men the emphasis was on transmitting skills that would enhance their employability; training for young women emphasized values and behaviors that would change their approach to family life.

Distributing Cultural Capital to Men

The Men's Job Corps Centers sought to provide poor youths with cultural capital in the form of a middle-class value system that would improve their ability to get and keep a job. An important goal was to teach young men to value "work, courtesy and excellence . . . the wise use of freedom, willingness to subordinate personal desires for the larger good of a group, to hold in check momentary impulse in order to secure a long-range good, being truthful, fair, honest, and patriotic."[15] By participating in the Job Corps, trainees "would improve their health through regular hours of work, study and sleep, gain confidence through successful job experiences and learn promptness and reliability."[16] In the long run, young men who were out of school and unemployed and "who (found) the exit from a life of poverty blocked by lack of opportunity" would have a chance "to improve their skills and capacities."[17] As Job Corps director Otis Singletary explained:

> One of the criticisms I remember that came out . . . about Camp Kilmer was "what you guys are really trying to do is change these kids' life styles." Instead of taking that as an accusation, I took that as a statement of fact. My answer was: "Exactly. Precisely."[18]

Thus, central to training in the Men's Job Corps were the concepts of self-control and occupational responsibility. The values and behaviors they were taught would increase their opportunities in the labor market.

Distributing Cultural Capital to Women

The Women's Job Corps Centers were also concerned with providing cultural capital, but the form taken emphasized altering women's roles in the familial transmission of self-defeating values. Task Force members argued that the backgrounds of these poor, young women could not "provide the soil in which the seeds of insight and self-confidence flourish," nor "the basis of learning the arts of communication, for developing tastes and innate capacities, or for bridging the gap of alienation between the world of poverty and the world of rising expectations and prosperity."[19] As daughters from poor, fatherless families, they grew up lacking "the necessary process of sexual identification" and a distorted "image of the husband-wife relationship into the patterns that so often prompt promiscuity, delinquency and anti-social behavior. . . . Caring for the younger children (because the mothers work) often falls to the older daughters and further restricts their chances for educational advancement" (quoted in Zelman 1980:83). For these women, "the poorest of the poor," the Job Corps represented an opportunity to "raise their own horizons, improve their earning capacity, learn how to break the dead-end habit patterns of poverty and pass this knowledge on to their children." In this way, the "endless circle of frustration in which they, their parents and grandparents" subsisted could be broken.[20] As the Guidelines for Program Development explained:

> Since many enrollees will have suffered from the effects of broken homes, impoverished or

strife-torn family life . . . it is imperative that experiences be provided which develop insights into interpersonal relationships; opportunities to learn how to plan and prepare nutritious meals; skills in child care and guidance; and the effective management of money in the home.[21]

Through the cultural reconstruction of poor young women, the cycle of poverty would be broken. How could this goal be achieved?

Theories of cultural capital recognize that the process of transmitting styles of interaction and social skills is gendered (Collins 1992). Men specialize in dealing with the market, while women reproduce family status through "household status presentation," a term that refers to the cleanliness of the house, the style of furniture, and the presentation of food. These presentations vary by social class, and thus become a means of translating class into status group membership (Collins 1992:213). An important objective of the Women's Job Corps was teaching trainees the art of household status presentation. "Preparing and serving food [was] an important aspect of the girls' training . . . meals were to be served at small tables seating four to six with tablecloths used, at least, at the evening meal and Sunday dinner."[22] In the child care area the girls would learn the fundamentals of child care and guidance, while the family living area provided a setting for activities "fostering wholesome family relationships."[23]

Health and recreation education followed home and family life as a training priority that would provide consumption and status production skills owned by middle-class women.[24] Job Corps planners believed that trainees possessed few skills and little or no motivation for recreation or wise use of leisure time, because many were school dropouts who had been in conflict with authorities. Recreation education was invaluable as a tool to encourage "creativity, improved communications, inner security, personal values, and socially acceptable attitudes and behavior patterns." Coeducational activities, for example, which were "a necessary part of learning the role of women, should include dances, skating parties, picnics and the like to reinforce the heterosexual role." A physical fitness program could serve "as a means of releasing tensions, hostilities and aggressions." Art clubs, book clubs, bird study, and other nature activities would increase the young women's self-respect and help them "develop a sense of belonging to a group."[25]

The Women's Job Corps program included specific incentives and disciplinary procedures to instill these behaviors in trainees. Under an incentive system, a trainee would receive a larger allowance if she showed exceptional behavior in the classroom or in the residential area. No girl would be served in the cafeteria if she wore slacks and rollers in her hair. Other disciplinary regulations included no food in rooms, no pets, no closed doors, no daytime TV and no weapons.[26]

Goals for the Women's Job Corps vacillated between preparation for home and family life and preparation for the job market. The home and family life program would qualify the girls as sub-professionals in home and family services, help them develop wholesome attitudes toward job perception, develop professional attitudes and ethics regarding work habits and relationships with employers, and assist in maintaining acceptable standards of personal grooming, as well as the efficient use of time and energy on the job.[27] As Deputy Director Monty Harlow explained to a newspaper reporter, "If these girls are going to be employable, they will have to know to accept responsibility, respect authority, and even dress and fix their hair."[28] At the same time, training would alleviate "the economic indices of alienation, antisocial behavior, lack of educational and vocational skills and the accompanying inadequate standards of living."[29] Training was designed "to reduce possible conflict between home and family orientation of young women and decisions affecting vocational choice and preparation" by training in the maintenance of the home and the raising and support of the family and in marketable skills in the area of home and family services.[30] The implication was that homemaking skills were transferable to the market and that young women would take jobs in female-dominated service jobs.

Empirical research on the issue of cultural reproduction usually faces one major limitation. Researchers rarely report directly on the motivations of educational planners. Rather, they presume intent, either by retrospectively considering outcome or by relegating intentions to abstract assumptions about domination and hegemony. Tracing a program from the planning stages through implementation demonstrates the complex calculations about race, gender, and class that motivate program planners. Operating from a vision of the poor, and especially of poor African-American women trapped in a culture of poverty, Job Corps planners conceived them as lacking aspirations, imbued with hostility and alienation. As mothers passed these traits from generation to generation, neither they nor their offspring could function effectively in the home or in the market. The solution was to imbue them with attributes of white, middle-class femininity and to train them for jobs that would reinforce a gendered division of labor.

RESISTANCE TO MORAL REFORM

Resistance theorists generally agree that students bring to school a value system and a behavioral repertoire that provides a basis for resistance to ideological domination (Giroux 1983). Yet, a central debate in resistant theory concerns how to identify these observed behaviors. The primary question has been to explain whether defiant behavior by youths can be considered resistant when the result of that behavior merely reproduces the status quo (Willis 1977; Fernandes 1988; Scott 1990; Anyon 1983). Scholars maintain that resistance at the level of the reproduction of the sexual and social division of labor is commonly

> *translated into the development of strategies which aim at counter-attacking the structural determinants which channel the students, in a differential and stratified way, to degrees, levels and branches of education according to their social origin and sex (Fernandes 1988:174).*

However, resistance at the level of ideological inculcation is a very complex and contradictory process because it can exhibit reproductive and resistant aspects simultaneously (Fernandes 1988). As Fernandes (1988:175) argues, it is therefore necessary "to take into account whether the direction of the main resultant leads to resistance against ideological inculcation, or on the contrary, to reinforcement of the dominant ideology(-ies)." However, this outcome is difficult to measure empirically, especially given the intricacies of female resistance in the face of gender, class, and racial hierarchies (Anyon 1983; Arnot 1982; Holland and Eisenhardt 1990; Mac An Ghaill 1989).

A major problem with most empirical research on resistance is that the analysis takes place within the school setting. External elements of class, race, and gender repression are taken as given. Here we present a case study from the files of the Office of Economic Opportunity of a Women's Job Corps Center in St. Louis, Missouri, to illustrate the limitations the external environment places on both the possibilities for cultural reproduction and on the potential for resistance. Our case also highlights the complexity of identifying and interpreting patterns of resistance.

Racial Barriers to Moral Reform

Although the Job Corps Task Force had idealistic visions of what the centers could accomplish, racial barriers posed formidable obstacles to these objectives. The biggest barrier was the resistance white communities raised about locating Job Corps centers in their midst. Anticipating resistance, Job Corps staff met with local Chambers of Commerce, women's groups, and religious organizations to prepare the communities for the centers. Despite such preparations, many communities still vehemently objected. The outcome was that many urban Job Corps centers were installed in segregated, inner-city neighborhoods. One of the largest Women's Job Corps Centers was established in St. Louis, Missouri, on the four-acre site of the former Missouri Baptist Hospital.[31] The Missouri center illustrates the concrete problems that arose in attempting to implement visionary ideals.

Located in a poor, black neighborhood in the heart of the city, the former hospital was in a state of disrepair. The rooms to be used as classrooms were vacant, without "instructional equipment, desks, blackboards, visual aids, textbooks or teaching materials." Several of the rooms had ventilation problems, the fourth floor was in total disarray, and much of the old hospital equipment was still in place. When an inspection took place on October 6, 1966, no one had been hired to direct and coordinate preparations for opening the center, and no detailed plans for the vocational training program existed. Still, the program was to be fully operational by Dec. 3, 1966.[32] In November, the center

accepted its first trainees, even though the building was only partially equipped and "looked shabby and sinister."[33]

The location of the center in what was considered the worst area in St. Louis—a neighborhood known for its high incidence of prostitution, drug sales, and burglaries—created safety problems for residents and staff. Numerous assaults on the women en route to and from the center were reported. One corpswoman was stabbed in the abdomen, four to five rapes were reported each week, and a staff member and two corpswomen were assaulted by a group of men as they were leaving the parking lot.[34]

The reality of daily life in an urban ghetto differed immensely from middle-class visions of home and family life. Racial segregation thus undermined possibilities for transmitting what program planners believed was valuable cultural capital. The risks of rape and assault faced by the women also demonstrated the intersection of racial and gendered forms of domination. The antagonism of white communities to Job Corps Centers with high proportions of African-American trainees forced the location of the centers in dangerous neighborhoods, exposing the women to male violence.

Interpreting Behavior as Resistance

Because working-class subjects are not always passive recipients, what is viewed by middle-class reformers as norm-violating behavior may instead be forms of resistance. As Fernandes (1988:171) contends:

> *(T)he oppositional attitudes and behaviors developed by working-class, racial and ethnic minority students towards teachers and schools (include) the rejection of intellectual work (which) is usually translated into a violation of school norms, lack of discipline, dropping out . . .*

The problem, however, is how to determine whether a given behavior that violates school rules is, in fact, a form of resistance. Does it seriously challenge the status quo or merely reproduce it (Holland and Eisenhardt 1990)? Some of the empirical research on resistance among school girls suggests that it takes the form of exaggerated femininity and assertive sexuality (Anyon 1983; Holland and Eisenhart 1990; Gilbert and Taylor 1991). Other research indicates that female resistance violates conventional femininity (Kessler et al. 1985) or manifests itself in "hidden" forms of protest like alcoholism or mental illness (Cloward and Piven 1979; Anyon 1983).

In the Missouri Center, exaggerated feminine behaviors weren't the issue. Rather, the oppositional behaviors were more clearly defiance of the rules. Drinking, which was a major disciplinary issue, represented the most obvious form of resistance. Girls snuck alcohol in their rooms, and some drank excessively on social outings in the community. One advisor, a Washington University psychology major, expressed her frustration with the drinking problem: "I'd rather help some of these girls with grooming, get them to decorate their rooms, organize some kind of student government and teach them how to have a good time without getting drunk."[35] Other discipline problems included fighting among the girls, thefts of personal items, violation of curfews, and pregnancies among the recruits. Getting pregnant also served a pragmatic function—getting dismissed from training and going home.

Identifying resistance poses a tremendous challenge for ethnographic researchers, who must rely upon their interpretations of behavior. The challenge for archival work is even greater, for the researcher is often limited to offical records rather than direct reports from subjects. In the Women's Job Corps one could interpret the behaviors noted here as forms of resistance within patterns of accommodation to the white middle-class female role. However, it is not clear that the trainees engaged in these behaviors as a form of rebellion against the training program, nor is it apparent that they understood why they behaved in rebellious ways. Resistance is difficult to identify, and its meaning may be highly colored by the researcher's interpretation.

The Effect of Job Training

Despite a training program that seemed geared toward moral reform, many young women did learn real job skills. By February 1967, after a few weeks of classroom training, 14 young women from the Missouri Center had been placed in on-the-job training positions in state agencies. Six were assigned to the Army Records Center for training in typing, switchboard, key punch, and general office routine work. Another four who also received training in office work were placed at the Federal Building. Four corpswomen were being trained as PBX operators at Cochran Hospital. Job Corps staff also worked with placement agencies in the St. Louis area to locate more on-the-job training opportunities for the trainees.[36]

These jobs presented poor, young African-American women with an opportunity for upward mobility. However, the salary scales of these jobs were significantly less than those for men. Overall, the average hourly wages of men graduating from the urban centers was $2.02 an hour and from the conservation centers, $1.85 an hour. Women graduating from Job Corps Centers received an average wage of $1.50 an hour. Although women received lower salaries than men even within similar occupational groupings, the greatest wage disparity resulted from differences in occupation. Males entering the machine trades started at $2.16 an hour, in structural work $2.35 an hour; women entering clerical work started at $1.58 an hour, in services $1.51.[37] Thus, the Job Corps enhanced occupational opportunity for women even while reproducing a gendered labor market.

Meanwhile, as a result of the recruitment process, nearly 60 percent of male Job Corps trainees were African American (Weir 1988). As these young men entered the job market in search of employment in the skilled trades, they confronted racial discrimination by the skilled trade unions. Discrimination was particularly intense in the Building and Construction Trades union, which formed the most powerful bloc in the AFL-CIO (Davis 1986). In 1964 less than one percent of the union's membership was African American (Quadagno 1994).

The refusal of the skilled trade unions to admit African Americans threatened to undermine federal job training efforts. What good was job training if graduates couldn't get jobs? At first the Johnson administration designed a compromise agreement that involved voluntary integration of the unions. But by 1965 the civil rights movement had targeted employment as the key civil rights issue, and demonstrations at federal construction sites highlighted racial discrimination by trade unions. When the skilled trade unions refused to comply with these voluntary agreements, the federal government devised the first affirmative action regulations, which set target goals for minority hiring and timetables for meeting them (Quadagno 1992, 1994). Thus, the Men's Job Corps empowered African-American men, providing them with legal weapons to use in the pursuit of equal employment opportunity.

DISCUSSION

Job training is an important though often overlooked component of the welfare state.

It represents a route to upward mobility for those who would otherwise lack such opportunities. The potential opportunities are constrained, however, when women or minorities are not granted equal access to job training and when the training provided perpetuates existing forms of inequality.

Between 1960 and 1970 the labor force participation rates of women aged 20 to 24 rose from around 45 percent to more than 55 percent (U.S. Department of Labor 1986). When the decade began, the index of sex segregation was 44. The rapid infusion of young women into the labor force presented an opportunity to equalize employment conditions. Indeed such an agenda was mandated by the Civil Rights Act of 1964, which banned discrimination in employment on the basis of race or gender and established an Equal Employment Opportunity Commission to implement it. Yet by 1970 the index of sex segregation remained unchanged (Reskin and Hartmann 1986).

Sex segregation of the labor force is an undeniably complex phenomenon resulting from such diverse forces as discrimination by employers and unions, institutionalized personnel practices, informal barriers in the work place and sex-role socialization. However, labor market outcomes are directly affected by education. Graduating from a trade or industrial program is a direct link to an apprenticeship, the primary avenue for entry into the skilled trades (Reskin and Hartmann 1986).

The Job Corps provided a potential link to union apprenticeships. After some controversy, women were included in the program. However, their training experience was organized around the premise that poverty was caused by joblessness among African-American men, not that women were relegated to jobs that paid wages below the poverty line. Rather than alleviating sex segregation, the Job Corps perpetuated it. It provided African-American men with real job skills that empowered them in their battle to integrate the skilled trade unions. By contrast, the curriculum for women only provided training for low-wage service jobs.

The Job Corps was not unique in perpetuating a gendered conception of the labor force. Its predecessor, the Manpower and Development Training programs, operated along similar assumptions. Under MDTA, training funds went to women as well as men (Harlan and Steinberg 1989). By 1964 among all trainees, 39 percent were female. However, nearly all of the training experiences for women were in traditional female occupations with the largest proportion being trained as stenographer/typists and nurses aides.[38] Similarly, the Work Incentive Program established by the 1967 Social Security Amendments was designed to provide training for persons receiving AFDC. Although more than 80 percent of AFDC recipients were women, WIN's explicit priority was for male household heads (Quadagno 1990; Reskin and Hartmann 1986). The Comprehensive Employment Training Act of 1973 (CETA) condensed all the major War on Poverty training programs into a single program. Preference in eligibility standards for household heads and veterans explicitly favored men. Like MDTA, training opportunities for women were primarily in traditional women's jobs. Thus, instead of enhancing employment for women and eliminating discrimination, which was made illegal in 1964, MDTA, WIN, and CETA reinforced the sex segregation already existing in the labor force.

CONCLUSION

Orloff (1993:318–19) identifies two criteria for assessing the impact of welfare state programs on gender inequality: whether they promote access to paid work and whether they enhance the ability of women to form and maintain an autonomous household. Access to paid work is "the extent to which states promote or discourage women's paid employment." This includes the potential of paid work to provide women with some autonomy vis-à-vis marriage or dependence on parents. The capacity to form and maintain an autonomous household generally indicates an individual's freedom from the compulsion to enter into potentially oppressive relationships in a number of spheres. The capacity to form and maintain an autonomous household is important because, among other reasons, "it relieves women of the compulsion to enter or stay in a marriage because of economic vulnerability" (Orloff 1993:321). How did the Job Corps fare on these criteria? To what extent did the Job Corps foster access to paid work and promote economic autonomy?

Insofar as the Job Corps did train women for work in business, clerical, and retail services, it promoted women's paid employment. However, at the same time, women and not men were specifically prepared for the marriage and family market. While men were being trained for high-skilled waged labor positions—freed from the responsibility of doing their own laundry and cooking—women were instructed in household status presentation, child care, and the performance of domestic and personal care. Thus, while the Job Corps did enhance occupational opportunities for women, the forms the programs took simultaneously reproduced a gendered division of labor and inculcated an ideological framework that concentrated women's labor—paid and unpaid—in the realm of domestic status production and consumption, and men's labor in the sphere of highly skilled waged material production.

The Job Corps was not organized around the goal of training young men and young women to form and maintain autonomous households. Guided in part by the assumptions of heterosexual marriage and the family wage strategy, the programs sought to eliminate the "culture of poverty" by encouraging the formation of male breadwinner/female caregiver households. Male graduates fared better economically than their female counterparts (earning, on average, 35–50 cents more per hour), and thus had a greater economic capacity to form an autonomous household. By preparing male trainees for jobs in the skilled trades, the Job Corps not only promoted their access to paid work, but indirectly became a vehicle for them to pursue equal employment opportunity. As job training became enveloped in the struggle for civil rights, these young African-American men successfully challenged racial discrimination in the craft unions (Quadagno 1992). Thus, the Job Corps became a program to enhance the autonomy of African-American males vis-à-vis the labor and marriage markets.

Job training for young African-American women, by contrast taught "a particular bourgeois family ideology in which women played a special role as dependent wife and mother" (Arnot 1982:71). Instead of liberating women from men, the gendered entrance requirements, the gendered curriculum, and the gendered distribution of cultural capital contributed to the reproduction of women's dependence on male waged labor. Yet, this attempt to transform African-American women's culture into a traditional, white, middle-class culture did not happen without some resistance. While it is not entirely clear whether female oppositional behaviors were a direct form of rebellion against the training program, our evidence suggests the cultural reproduction and resistance to ideological inculcation are mediated by complex interrelations and interactions of race, gender, and class.

ENDNOTES

1. Edith Green Oral History, Lyndon Baines Johnson Library, Austin, Texas, p. 66.

2. Public Law 88-452, 88th Congress, S. 2642, August 20, 1964, 78 Stat. 508.

3. National Archives (hereafter NA), RG 381, Office of Economic Opportunity, Records of David Squire, Box 799, File: Centers—Women's. "More Job Corps aid for girls." *Washington, D.C. News*, June 15, 1966; "Potential women's centers sites." *Washington, D.C. News*, July 11, 1966.

4. NA, RG 381, Box 781, File: 7.02. Work Program Chart.

5. NA, RG 381, Box 781, File: 7.02. Vocation and Curriculum Guidelines for Job Corps Conservation Centers.

6. Lyndon Baines Johnson Library, Austin, Texas. Oral history of Vernon R. Alden, Dec. 18, 1985, p. 18–19.

7. NA, RG 381, Box 783, File: 8.02. Staffing Functions.

8. NA, RG 381, Box 783, File: 8.02. Handbook for Job Corps Screening Agency. A potential trainee could be excluded for a history of assaultive behavior or criminal convictions but not for such behaviors as truancy, curfew violations, being a runaway, or being expelled from school.

9. NA, RG 381, Box 783, File: 8.02. Annex A, The Job Corps Program.

10. NA, RG 381, Box 799, File: Centers—Women's. "Establishment of Job Corps training centers for women." Nov. 16, 1964, p. 6.

11. NA, RG 381, Box 799, File: Centers—Women's. "Establishment of Job Corps training centers for women." Nov. 16, 1964, p. 14–15.

12. NA, RG 86, Women's Bureau, Files of Mary Hilton, Box 6, File: Economic Opportunity Office. "The Women's Job Corps—An attack on persistent poverty." p. 7.

13. NA, RG 381, Box 781, File: 7.02. Bulletin No. 37.

14. *Hearings on H.R. 10440*, Economic Opportunity Act of 1964, before the Subcommittee on the War on Poverty Program of the Committee on Education and Labor, House of Representatives, 1964, 88th Congress, 2nd Session, pp. 64–65.

15. NA, RG 381, Box 781, File: 7.02. Rural Center Administrative Manual.

16. NA, RG 381, Box 781, File: 7.02. Conservation Center Administration Manual.

17. NA, RG 381, Box 783, File: 8.02. Selection. Annex A, The Job Corps Program.

18. Otis Singletary Oral History. Lyndon Baines Johnson Library, Austin, Texas, p. 20.

19. NA, RG 86, Box 6, File: Economic Opportunity Office. "The Women's Job Corps—An attack on persistent poverty." p. 1.

20. NA, RG 86, Box 6, File: Economic Opportunity Office. "The Women's Job Corps—An attack on persistent poverty." p. 1.

21. NA, RG 381, Subject Files of David Squire, Box 802, File: Labor. The Job Corps Program Requirements.

22. NA, RG 381, Box 799, File: Centers—Women's. "Establishment of Job Corps training centers for women." Nov. 16, 1964, p. 31.

23. NA, RG 86, Box 6, File: Economic Opportunity Office. "Recommended guidelines for home and family education in the women's training centers." Prepared by Dr. Annabell Sherman, p. 2.

24. NA, RG 86, Box 6, File: Economic Opportunity Office. "Recommended guidelines for basic education in the Women's Training Centers Job Corps" prepared by Patricia Gill, p. 4.

25. NA, RG 86, Box 6, File: Economic Opportunity Office. "Recommended guidelines for recreation education in the Women's Training Centers Job Corps." Prepared by Dr. Peggy Frank.

26. NA, RG 381, Box 41, File: WJC, Missouri. "St. Louis Corps Center." July 5, 1967, p. 7.

27. NA, RG 86, Box 6, File: Economic Opportunity Office. "Recommended guidelines for home and family education in the Women's Training Centers." Prepared by Dr. Annabelle Sherman, p. 5.

28. Charlene Prost, "Keeping peace among girls in Job Corps Center." *St. Louis Post-Dispatch,* March 3, 1967.

29. NA, RG 86, Box 6, File: Economic Opportunity Office. "Recommended guidelines for basic education in the Women's Training Centers Job Corps." Prepared by Patricia Gill, p. 1.

30. NA, RG 86, Box 6, File: Economic Opportunity Office. "Recommended guidelines for vocational education in the Women's Training Center." Prepared by Patricia Gill, p. 2.

31. NA, RG 381, OEO Inspection Reports, Box 41, File: WJC, Missouri. "Job Corps Center for Women to be set up in St. Louis."

32. NA, RG 381, OEO Inspection Reports, Box 41, File: WJC, Missouri. "St. Louis Job Corps for Women, basic education." By Irvin H. Himmele.

33. Charlene Prost, "Shabby rooms greet girls at job center." *St. Louis Post-Dispatch,* March 2, 1967.

34. NA, RG 381, Box 41. File: WJC, Missouri. "St. Louis Job Corps Center." July 5, 1967, p. 8.

35. Charlene Prost, "Discipline is difficult in Job Corps." *St. Louis Post-Dispatch,* March 3, 1967, p. 1.

36. NA, RG 381, Box 41, File: WJC, Missouri. "Job Corps women begin on-job-training."

37. NA, RG 381, Box 799, File: Centers—Men. Job Corps Placement by Occupational Category, Oct. 10, 1966.

38. NA, RG 86, Women's Bureau, Mary Hilton, Box 7, File: Female Enrollments. MDTA Institutional Courses; Sex and Color of Trainees Enrolled Under the MDTA, April 30, 1964.

REFERENCES

Anyon, Jean
1983 "Intersections of gender and class: Accommodation and resistance by working-class and affluent females to contradictory sex-role ideologies." In Gender, Class and Education, eds. Stephen Walker and Len Barton, 19–27. London: Falmer Press.

Apple, Michael W.
1979 Ideology and Curriculum. Boston: Routledge and Kegan Paul.

Arnot, Madeleine
1982 "Male hegemony, social class and women's education." Journal of Education 164: 64–89.

Baldwin, Peter
1990 The Politics of Social Solidarity: Class Bases of the European Welfare State. New York: Cambridge University Press.

Bourdieu, Pierre
1973 "Cultural reproduction and social reproduction." In Knowledge, Education, and Cultural Change, ed. Richard Brown, 71–112. London: Tavistock.
1984 Distinction: A Social Critique of the Judgment of Taste. Cambridge, Mass.: Harvard University Press.

Bourdieu, Pierre, and Jean Claude Passeron
1977 Reproduction in Education, Society, and Culture. Beverly Hills, Calif.: Sage.

Bowles, Samuel, and Herbert Gintis
1976 Schooling in Capitalist America. New York: Basic Books.

Burstein, Paul
1985 Discrimination, Jobs and Politics. Chicago: University of Chicago Press.

Clarke, Alan
1987 "Moral protest, status defence and the anti-abortion campaign." British Journal of Sociology 38:235–253.

Cloward, Richard A., and Frances Fox Piven
1979 "Hidden protest: The channeling of female innovation and resistance." Signs: Journal of Women in Culture and Society 4: 651–669.

Collins, Randall
1992 "Women and the production of status cultures." In Cultivating Differences: Symbolic Boundaries and the Making of Inequality, eds. Michele Lamont and Marcel Fournier, 213–231. Chicago: The University of Chicago Press.

Connell, R. W., G. W. Dowsett, S. Kessler, and D. J. Ashenden
1981 "Class and gender in a ruling-class school." Interchange 12:102–117.

Connell, R. W., D. J. Ashenden, S. Kessler, and G. W. Dowsett
1982 Making the Difference: Schools, Families and Social Division. Sydney, Australia: George Allen Unwin.

Davis, Mike
1986 Prisoners of the American Dream. London: Verso.

DiMaggio, Paul, and John Mohr
1985 "Cultural capital, educational attainment and marital selection." American Journal of Sociology 90:1231–1261.

Eder, Donna, and Stephen Parker
1987 "The cultural production and reproduction of gender: The effect of extracurricular activities on peer-group culture." Sociology of Education 60:200–213.

Esping-Anderson, Gosta
1990 The Three Worlds of Welfare Capitalism. Princeton, N.J.: Princeton University Press.

Fernandes, Joao Viegas
1988 "From the theories of social and cultural reproduction to the theory of resistance." British Journal of Sociology of Education 9:169–180.

Fraser, Nancy
1990 "Struggle over needs: Outline of a socialist-feminist critical theory of resistance." In Women, the State and Welfare, ed. Linda Gordon, 199–225. Madison, Wis.: The University of Wisconsin Press.

Genovese, Eugene
1972 Roll, Jordan, Roll: The World the Slaves Made. New York: Vintage.

Gerson, Judith, and Kathy Peiss
1985 "Boundaries, negotiation, consciousness: Reconceptualizing gender relations." Social Problems 32:317–331.

Gilbert, Pam, and Sandra Taylor
1991 Fashioning the Feminine: Girls, Popular Culture and Schooling. Sydney, Australia: Allen and Unwin.

Giroux, Henry
1981 Ideology, Culture and the Process of Schooling. Philadelphia: Temple University Press.
1983 "Theories of reproduction and resistance in the new sociology of education: A critical analysis." Harvard Educational Review 53:257–293.

Gordon, Linda, ed.
1990 Women, the State and Welfare. Madison, Wis.: The University of Wisconsin Press.

Graham, Hugh Davis
1990 The Civil Rights Era: Origins and Development of National Policy. New York: Oxford University Press.

Gough, Ian
1979 The Political Economy of the Welfare State. London: Macmillan.

Harlan, Sharon, and Ronnie Steinberg
1989 Job Training for Women: The Promise and Limits of Public Policies. Philadelphia: Temple University Press.

Harrington Meyer, Madonna
1990 "Family status and poverty among older women: The gendered distribution of retirement income in the United States." Social Problems 37:553–559.

Holland, Dorothy, and Margaret Eisenhart
1990 Educated in Romance: Women, Achievement, and College Culture. Chicago: University of Chicago Press.

Jenson, Jane
1991 "Making claims: Social policy and gender relations in postwar Sweden and France." Paper presented at the Annual Meeting of the Canadian Sociology and Anthropology Association, June 1991, Kingston, Ontario.

Katz, Michael
1989 The Undeserving Poor, From the War on Poverty to the War on Welfare. New York: Pantheon.

Kelly, Alison
1985 "The construction of masculine science." British Journal of Sociology of Education 6:133–154.

Kessler, S., D. Achenden, R. W. Connell, and G. W. Dowsett
1985 "Gender relations in secondary schooling." Sociology of Education 58:34–48.

Korpi, Walter
1989 "Power, politics and state autonomy in the development of social citizenship." American Sociological Review 54:309–328.

Lamont, Michele, and Annette Lareau
1988 "Cultural capital, allusions, gaps and glissandos in recent theoretical developments." Sociological Theory 6:153–168.

Lamont, Michele, and Marcel Fournier
1992 Cultivating Differences: Symbolic Boundaries and the Making of Inequality. Chicago: The University of Chicago Press.

Levin, Henry
1977 "A decade of policy developments in improving education and training for low-income populations." In A Decade of Federal Anti-Poverty Programs, ed. Robert Haveman, 123–188. New York: Academic Press.

Lewis, Oscar
1966 La Vida, A Puerto Rican Family in the Culture of Poverty—San Juan and New York. New York: Random House.

Mac An Ghaill, Mairtin
1989 "Beyond the white norm: The use of qualitative methods in the study of black youths' schooling in England." Qualitative Studies in Education 2:175–189.

Maume, David
1991 "Child-care expenditures and women's employment turnover." Social Forces 70: 495–508.

Mink, Gwendolyn
1990 "The lady and the tramp: Gender, race, and the origins of the American welfare state." In Women, the State and Welfare, ed. Linda Gordon, 92–122. Madison, Wis.: The University of Wisconsin Press.

Moynihan, Daniel Patrick
1965 The Negro Family: The Case for National Action. U.S. Department of Labor: Office of Policy Planning and Research.

Nash, Roy
1990 "Bourdieu on education and social and cultural reproduction." British Journal of Sociology 11:431–447.

Nelson, Barbara
1990 "The origins of the two-channel welfare state: Women's compensation and mother's aid." In Women, the State and Welfare, ed. Linda Gordon, 123–151. Madison, Wis.: The University of Wisconsin Press.

Offe, Claus
1984 The Contradictions of the Welfare State. Cambridge, Mass.: MIT Press.

Orloff, Ann
1993 "Gender and the social rights of citizenship: The comparative analysis of state policies and gender relations." American Sociological Review 58:303–328.

Pateman, Carol
1988 "The patriarchal welfare state." In Democracy and the Welfare State, ed. Amy Gutmann, 231–260. Princeton: Princeton University Press.

Presser, Harriet, and Wendy Baldwin
1980 "Child care as a constraint on employment: Prevalence, correlates and bearing on the work fertility nexus." American Journal of Sociology 85:1202–1213.

Quadagno, Jill
1990 "Race, class and gender in the U.S. welfare state: Nixon's failed Family Assistance Plan." American Sociological Review 55:11–28.
1992 "State transformation and social movements: Labor unions and racial conflict in the War on Poverty." American Sociological Review 57:616–634.
1994 The Color of Welfare: How Racism Undermined the War on Poverty. New York: Oxford University Press.

Reskin, Barbara, and Heidi Hartmann
1986 Women's Work, Men's Work: Sex Segregation on the Job. Washington, D.C.: National Academy Press.

Sainsbury, Diane
1989 "Welfare state variations, women and equality: On varieties of the welfare state and their implications for women." Paper presented to the ECPR Workshop on Equality Principles and Gender Politics, Paris, April 10–15.

Scott, James C.
1990 Domination and the Art of Resistance. New Haven: Yale University Press.

Shaver, Sheila
1990 "Gender, social policy regimes and the welfare state." Paper presented at the Annual Meeting of the American Sociological Association, August 11–15, Washington, D.C.

Shaver, Sheila, and Jonathan Bradshaw
1993 "The recognition of wifely labour by welfare states." Discussion Paper No. 44. University of New South Wales: Social Policy Research Centre.

Skeggs, Beverly
1988 "Gender reproduction and further education: Domestic apprenticeships." British Journal of Sociology of Education 9: 131–148.

Skocpol, Theda
  1992 Protecting Soldiers and Mothers. Cambridge, Mass.: Harvard University Press.
U.S. Department of Labor
  1986 Bureau of Labor Statistics, Employment and Earnings, January, 1986. Washington, D.C.: U.S. Government Printing Office.
Weir, Margaret
  1988 "The federal government and unemployment: The frustration of policy innovation from the New Deal to the Great Society." In The Politics of Social Policy in the United States, eds. Margaret Weir, Ann Shola Orloff, and Theda Skocpol, 149–190. Princeton: Princeton University Press.

Willis, Paul
  1977 Learning to Labor: How Working Class Kids Get Working Class Jobs. New York: Columbia University Press.
  1981 "Cultural production is different from cultural reproduction is different from social reproduction is different from reproduction." Interchange 12:48–67.
  1983 "Cultural production and theories of reproduction." In Race, Class and Education, eds. Len Barton and Stephen Walker, 107–138. London: Croom-Helm.
Zelman, Patricia
  1980 Women, Work and National Policy: The Kennedy-Johnson Years. Ann Arbor, Mich.: UMI Press.

Questions for Understanding and Critical Thinking

1. How do feminist theories of the welfare state differ from other perspectives on this phenomenon?
2. What key arguments are set forth by theories of cultural reproduction and resistance?
3. Why did white communities resist locating Job Corps centers in their areas? Do you think such resistance still would exist today? Why or why not?
4. How did discrimination against African American Job Corps trainees by skilled trade unions affect the civil rights movement and formulation of affirmative action regulations?

ARTICLE 18 _____

In this excerpt from his book, Ruben Navarrette, Jr., describes his experience as a "Hexagon"—the highest ability group in his second-grade class. Navarrette argues that public school tracking—especially of African American, Latino/Latina, and Native American children in racially integrated learning environments—is a form of racial injustice.

   Ruben Navarrette, Jr., is a graduate of Harvard University and recently has been enrolled in graduate studies in education at the University of California, Los Angeles.

Looking Ahead

1. How were the experiences of "Hexagons" different from those of "Circles," "Squares," and "Triangles" in Navarrette's second-grade class?
2. Do recent studies support Navarrette's concerns about tracking? In what way?
3. Why did Navarrette feel lonely and isolated during his 12 years of public schooling?

A Darker Shade of Crimson

Odyssey of a Harvard Chicano

♦ *Ruben Navarrette, Jr.*

My educational journey began in the early 1970s. Richard M. Nixon had just been re-elected president and the term "Watergate" signified no more than the name of an obscure office complex in Washington. The images of the Vietnam War still permeated the evening news. There was violence and division everywhere, from Kent State to Munich. And a wounded country began its delicate recovery from the social upheaval of the 1960s.

   In Cambridge, a handful of Mexican-American students, pioneers who had endured and survived an exploratory expedition, graduated from Harvard College and began the precarious journey home. Meanwhile, three thousand miles away, a five-year-old Mexican-American boy in a kindergarten classroom nibbled graham crackers and milk and, by excitedly answering his teacher's questions, unknowingly began an equally precarious journey away from home.

   One fateful day, in the second grade, my teacher decided to teach her class more efficiently by dividing it into six groups of five students each. Each group was assigned a geometric symbol to differentiate it from the others. There were the Circles. There were the Squares. There were the Triangles and Rectangles.

I remember being a Hexagon.

I remember something else, an odd coincidence. The Hexagons were the smartest kids in the class. These distinctions are not lost on a child of seven. Child psychologists suggest that children usually conclude their first year of schooling already well aware of which of their classmates are smart and which are not so smart. Even in the second grade, my classmates and I knew who was smarter than whom. And on the day on which we were assigned our respective shapes, we knew that our teacher knew, too.

As Hexagons, we would wait for her to call to us, then answer by hurrying to her with books and pencils in hand. We sat around a table in our "reading group," chattering excitedly to one another and basking in the intoxication of positive learning. We did not notice, did not care to notice, over our shoulders, the frustrated looks on the faces of Circles and Squares and Triangles who sat quietly at their desks, doodling on scratch paper or mumbling to one another. Obediently, they waited their turn at the reading table, anticipating their few minutes of attention. Occasionally, the teacher would look up from our lesson and command order to the rest of the class.

"Could I have all my Circles be quiet . . ."

We knew also that, along with our geometric shapes, our books were different and that each group had different amounts of work to do. The textbook company maximized profit by printing not one but a series of six different reading books, each one more difficult than the one preceding it in the series. The Circles had the easiest books and were assigned to read only a few pages at a time. The Triangles had books that were a lit-

tle more difficult than those of the Circles, and they were expected to read a few more pages in them. Not surprisingly, the Hexagons had the most difficult books of all, those with the biggest words and the fewest pictures, and we were expected to read the most pages.

The result of all this education by separation was exactly what the teacher had imagined that it would be: Students could, and did, learn at their own pace without being encumbered by one another. Some learned faster than others. Some, I realized only as a doctoral student at a pristine university, did not learn at all.

What I had been exposed to, and in truth had benefited from, in that dusty elementary school was the educational practice of ability-grouping, or tracking. And if my classmates and I were being tracked by teachers and guidance counselors, then I was certainly on the right one. Fourth grade honors led to fifth grade honors which led to sixth grade honors. At the brink of entering junior high school, a crucial point in my educational development, my sixth grade teacher recommended to junior high officials that I be placed in a pre-algebra class instead of one for general math. That simple distinction enabled me to take, in subsequent years, courses in algebra, geometry, advanced algebra, trigonometry, math analysis, and finally calculus—that elite course that winked approvingly from my transcript at the Harvard admissions officer.

From grade school to high school, teachers and counselors and principals understood that I was intelligent. Not one of them was brave enough to question my ability, to second-guess the scribblings of their colleagues on my cumulative file.

So, in truth, it was tracking, along with the support of my family and my own effort and talent, that had ultimately carried me from a small farming town to the most prestigious university in the country. And now, it was tracking that was responsible for the new assortment of "goodies"—the doctoral program, the administrative policy exceptions, and, of course, the excessive fellowship that filled my bank account. It was no accident, no quirk of fate that I now found myself in such elite company. In essence, my ascension to the heights of academic privilege was orchestrated almost twenty years earlier by well-intentioned grade school teachers and an assortment of odd geometric shapes.

Confronted with this new, old reality, I initially thought of writing my old second grade teacher, then retired, a thank you note for indirectly saving my academic life. Still, the more that I learned about the insidious nature and harmful consequences of tracking, consequences even for its benefactors, the less I felt like thanking anyone.

For me, the most distressing lesson about ability grouping was the disparate effect that it seems to have on certain students.

In the 1980s, a number of studies examining tracking in an array of elementary and secondary schools found that African-American, Latino, and Native-American students were typically among those most adversely affected by the practice. Researchers invariably found that, in racially integrated learning environments, disproportionate numbers of minority students were relegated by teachers and guidance counselors to slow-learner, low-achieving, and vocational classes than were their Asian-American and white classmates.

The findings were not unlike those of a subsequent 1992 report by the American Association of University Women that concluded, among other things, that elementary and secondary school teachers typically track their female students away from careers in math and science. Encompassing twenty years of research, the report also found that teachers give significantly less classroom at-tention to girls than to boys, call upon them for answers to questions much less frequently than they do boys, and sometimes even chastise girls for calling out the correct answers while rewarding boys for the same type of behavior.

Whether disparate academic treatment is predicated upon racial or gender differences, researchers agree, an inevitable consequence of teachers differentiating between children based on perceived academic ability is that, within the classroom, less-favored groups of students receive an implicit label of inferiority and are considered less intelligent than more-favored groups.

Squares and Circles, we knew, were not as smart as Hexagons.

More troublesome still, the research suggests, is that less-favored students themselves eventually realize that they carry such a label and that, understandably, such a realization proves detrimental to their fragile and developing notions of self-esteem.

Even at seven, Circles knew *why* they were Circles, as well as what was expected, and not expected, from them.

All of this, researchers conclude, eventually results in a damaging loss of self-confidence and self-respect in impacted students and consequently, in staggering statistics of meagre educational performance like drop-out rates and low test scores for Latino students.

Hexagons answered the teacher's command by excitedly running to her with books and papers in hand . . . Not much was expected from Circles, Squares, and Triangles, so not much was received from them either.

As autumn yields to winter in Los Angeles, the memory of my early academic life is becoming clearer and clearer.

I see myself as a little boy. I am in the second grade. I am lucky. I am a Hexagon. I will be cared for. I call out the right answer. My teacher smiles her approval and I smile back. I do not notice the others, the Circles and Squares and Triangles daydreaming in their boredom. I do not notice something else—a curious observation that will ultimately define the character of my life. I am an oddity.

Yes, I am a Hexagon. I am also the only Mexican-American Hexagon.

In a classroom, in a school, and in a town which were all over half Mexican-American, I was the only one. The lucky one. The lonely one. For the next ten years in public school, I will occasionally be taunted by some of the same Mexican friends with whom I was once intimate, those with whom I shared harmless elementary school vices. They will view me with a mixture of suspicion and respect and awe. They will call me "Brain" as I walk through hallways in junior high school. Mimicking adults, some of them will even practice ethnic division. They will accuse me, by virtue of my academic success, of "trying to be white." Whatever that means.

Above all, they will recognize early on that, similar skin color and a familiar surname notwithstanding, we are *not* the same. They will know, in their hearts, that we have not been given the same education and they will resent me and others like me for conspicuously gorging on opportunity while they go hungry. And they will be right to feel that way. All that I will understand at the time is that I feel embarrassed for having been set aside from those friends so similar to me. And because we all know that what initially fueled the separation was one teacher's assessment that I was not only different but smarter than them, that sense of embarrassment will gradually be compounded with a bitter dose of guilt.

It is the exact same guilt that now finds me in Los Angeles, a twenty-four-year-old graduate student in education examining for the first time the road that took me there. The guilt returns to me with a vengeance. It reaches out from my textbook and strangles me with my own complicity in a tragic drama that has spanned nearly twenty years. A drama of win some, lose some.

Finally I face the truth: I have, in my academic lifetime, experienced a form of racial injustice reminiscent of the sort of outright discrimination that, years ago, crippled the lives of so many members of my parents' and grandparents' generations. It is newer and more subtle, and so more insidious. Let the academics call it "intraracial differentiation." Let the rest of us understand it to simply mean teachers, particularly elementary school teachers, passing an early judgment about the learning ability of their students with regard to race. And while this sort of thing is not historically unique, what is new is that, in this case, teachers are distinguishing between students of the same race.

The phenomenon revolves around the frustrated concession by educators that since they cannot teach them all, they should settle for a few success stories. The new educational mission drifts away from the romantic ideal of enlightening the masses and toward the more manageable, more cynical, goal of merely searching out a few bright stars to pierce the darkness of racial stereotype. Teachers' lounge distinctions takes on a new dimension: *Smart Mexican, Dumb Mexican.*

In that scenario, I was always the Smart Mexican. For twelve years of public schooling, I was groomed to take college-prep courses and apply for academic scholarships by the very same people who were telling the dark-skinned Mexican boy sitting next to me that he would be lucky to graduate from high school. Maybe the boy did graduate. Eventually. Barely. Restrained by his own low self-esteem, he struggled helplessly in the same schoolwork in which I excelled. Ironically, given our shared ethnicity, my classmate's difficulty only made my academic success even more extraordinary by comparison. Again I was praised.

To the bureaucrats in the Harvard admissions office who studied my college application, I was a most alluring novelty—a Mexican-American valedictorian in a school system with a 50 percent drop-out rate for Hispanic students. Graciously, they invited me to join their elite family. Shamelessly, I did. Unknowingly, I went to Harvard in the name of the less fortunate, in place of the educational casualties embodied by the dire statistics on the evening news. I went to "represent" them to the America's elite ruling class, to upper-class children of privilege who would foolishly view me as being typical of the millions of Latinos in the United States.

And so, truth be known, I am not a victim of the injustice of intraracial differentiation. I am actually its beneficiary. I have benefited from the very sort of educational inequity that I went to graduate school with the hope of eliminating. I was allowed to excel in the American educational system by virtue of the same form of ability-grouping that had undermined the educational progress of so many other Mexican-American students like me.

This realization comes to me only now, as a doctoral student lost on the final leg of my educational trek. As I run along the Pacific shoreline and feel warmth of the southern California sun on my skin before my afternoon class, the tranquility of the moment fades. Only discomfort remains.

Making matters worse, by now my complicity in the drama has thickened. My fellow doctoral students, most of them white teachers who are much older than me, have warmly accepted me into their ranks. One day, in a class discussion of the possible reasons for the academic difficulties of minority students, someone suggests that Latinos cannot learn at the same pace as many of their classmates. Someone else agrees, blaming the parents. "Didn't former Secretary of Education Lauro Cavazos once say as much?" Someone else blames economics. "Poor students from high schools in East Los Angeles can't be expected to compete with the kids at Beverly Hills High." Someone else blames bilingualism. "Isn't having to keep both Spanish and English in their heads confusing for Mexican kids?" And a home environment devoid of hope. "What do you expect given where they come from?" And, of course, being teachers as well as students, they all blame low salaries for educators.

What they do not blame, not one of them, is an educational system implicated in three generations of racial discrimination. What they do not blame are teachers who are content with educating only a few of the young people with whose conception of self they have been entrusted. What they do not blame is tracking, the insidious practice of subtle and not-so-subtle differentiation that makes their admittedly difficult jobs much easier.

I am one of them. Their classmate, colleague, and confidant. More than that, I am what I am *because* of them. They smile at me as they tell me, implicitly, that people like my parents, like my old friends, like the new girlfriend back home whose immeasurable love is sustaining me, are incompetent and unintelligent and unmotivated and hopeless. They wink and nod at me, perhaps taking comfort from the assumption that I am different from the cultural caricature that they envision when they hear the word "Chicano." In a sense, they are right. In adolescence, I did not gang-bang, smoke pot, impregnate my girlfriend, or drop out of high school.

I am a Chicano, but a *Harvard* Chicano. The cultural influence of Harvard has followed me to graduate school; indeed, it has paved my way to graduate study.

◆ ◆ ◆

Questions for Understanding and Critical Thinking

1. How did class interact with race/ethnicity in Navarrette's educational experiences?
2. Why does Navarrette believe Harvard University admitted him to its undergraduate program?
3. If tracking was beneficial for Navarrette, why is he critical of this practice?
4. According to Navarrette, why do some Latinos/Latinas have academic difficulties in public schools today?

ARTICLE 19 _____

In this article, sociologist Emily W. Kane examines competing claims regarding the role of education in intergroup relations generally and its role in shaping gender ideology in particular. According to Kane, her findings are consistent with the argument that education reproduces rather than challenges social inequality.

Emily W. Kane teaches sociology at the University of Wisconsin, Madison.

Looking Ahead

1. How do enlightenment and reproduction approaches explain the effect of education?
2. What is the role of education in shaping gender ideology?
3. Why does Kane believe that education is more strongly associated with some beliefs about gender inequality than with others?

Education and Beliefs about Gender Inequality

◆ *Emily W. Kane*

INTRODUCTION

The relationship between education and intergroup attitudes has received a great deal of attention, and the interpretation of that relationship lies at the heart of a controversy regarding the nature of relations between dominant and subordinate groups. In addition, education has long been emphasized as a central factor in encouraging nontraditional gender attitudes. However, how education shapes different types of beliefs about gender inequality, and whether education has a similar impact on men's and women's beliefs, have not been thoroughly examined. Such an examination has important implications for understanding the role of education in shaping dominant and subordinate group members' beliefs about gender inequality in particular and about social inequality more generally. Viewing beliefs about gender inequality as expressions of the broader ideology or belief-system surrounding gender inequality, I use public opinion data from a national probability sample of

Source: From Emily W. Kane, "Education and Beliefs about Gender Inequality." © 1995 by the Society for the Study of Social Problems. Reprinted from *Social Problems*, Vol. 42, No. 1, February 1995, pp. 74–90, by permission.

the United States to investigate whether the impact of education varies across a broad array of gender-related ideological domains. I also investigate whether the role of education differs for men versus women.

Almost all of the literature on education and intergroup attitudes focuses on dominant group attitudes, especially tolerance, prejudice, and democratic values. While it has been established that education is associated with such attitudes, many different explanations have been offered for that relationship. These explanations can be classified into two broad groups[1] that offer two very different approaches to understanding intergroup relations. The first group of approaches, which emphasize education as enlightenment, assumes that education can change the fundamental nature of inequality. The second group assumes education's impact is limited in such a way as to make it unrelated to any truly fundamental change, implying that education reproduces rather than challenges inequality.[2] I argue that approaches emphasizing education as reproducing inequality, through their attention to the group interests generated by social inequality, more accurately capture the effect of education, especially its effect on dominant group beliefs. I address both dominant *and* subordinate group beliefs about gender inequality and consider the potentially different meanings education has for members of these groups, thereby offering a more comprehensive analysis of education's role in shaping beliefs about social inequality.

EDUCATION AND ENLIGHTENMENT

The argument that education enlightens has been offered in a variety of forms. For example, Lipset's (1960) notion of working-class authoritarianism maintains that people are anti-democratic until they are socialized by educational institutions stressing democratic values. Stouffer (1955) focuses on the relationship between education and tolerance, noting that education increases people's willingness to allow civil liberties for advocates of viewpoints with which they disagree. Others have highlighted the role of education in reducing prejudice, treating prejudice as irrational and education as a mechanism for increasing rationality and reducing categorical thinking (see, for example, Borhek 1965). These perspectives share a common emphasis on the ability of education, through the knowledge and values it conveys, to foster intergroup harmony. This notion continues to be applied most often to understanding dominant group beliefs about racial and class inequality, although it is evident in the gender attitude literature as well (see, for example, Klein 1984; Smith and Fisher 1982; Welch 1975).

Beginning with the implicit assumption that dominant groups gain little from stratification, and therefore rejecting any notion of conflicting group interests, proponents of these approaches see the prospect of an end to irrational intergroup tensions through education. If the effect of education is one of enlightenment, as proposed by these approaches, one would expect education to be associated with rejection of social inequality across a wide range of beliefs about inequality. As education increases, recognition of the existence of social inequality, as well as endorsement of social equality and efforts to achieve it, should increase as well. Enlightenment should also be evident across intergroup contexts, with education similarly encouraging rejection of, for example, racial, class, and gender inequality.

EDUCATION AND REPRODUCTION OF INEQUALITY

The second set of approaches views the effect of education quite differently. While acknowledging the empirical relationship between education and attitudes like prejudice and tolerance, approaches in this second category share the assumption that education does not change the most important aspects of intergroup relations, and may actually legitimate rather than challenge inequality.

Bowles and Gintis (1977) posit that educational institutions encourage a meritocratic and individualistic orientation that justifies and works to reproduce existing social inequalities, especially economic inequality. Education as it is practiced in the United States, they claim "... prevents the formation of the social bonds and critical consciousness whereby existing social conditions might be transformed" (1977:104). Jackman and Muha (1984) also argue that by encouraging competitive, individual effort and emphasizing individual achievement, education promotes individualistic interpretations of social outcomes, and attention is thereby "diverted away from issues of outright distributional equality and channelled into the more individualistic realm of equality of opportunity" (1984:762). They note that education may be associated with some recognition of social inequality among dominant group members, but that it also is associated with a commitment to individualism that obscures the systematic benefits dominants receive and leaves inequalities intact. These approaches assume inequality has its basis in real interests and that education, since it does not change those interests, does not change the basis of inequality. As Jackman and Muha put it, "... education cannot be seen as a liberating agent, since it does not release people from the concerns and interests imposed by the social fabric, nor does it render people insensible to those interests" (1984:752).

To view education as reproducing inequality suggests that education may affect some types of beliefs about inequality but not others. For example, education might be associated with increased recognition of inequality. But, depending on the structure of social interests, it may not necessarily be associated with increased endorsement of the goal of equality or of efforts to achieve it. In addition, Bowles and Gintis's (1977) emphasis on education as legitimating economic inequality suggests that its impact may vary across intergroup contexts rather than being similar for beliefs about all forms of social inequality.

BELIEFS ABOUT GENDER INEQUALITY

Looking more specifically at beliefs about gender inequality, it is important to consider what these two competing approaches imply about the role of education in shaping gender ideology. Testing the approaches requires addressing a broad array of beliefs about gender inequality, going well beyond the emphasis on only role-related attitudes which is common in public opinion literature on gender relations. I consider attitudes within six conceptual domains of central interest to scholars of intergroup attitudes and to feminist analysts of gender relations.

1. *Gender-role orientations* have long been staples in the study of gender attitudes because they reflect a key practice that structures gender inequality: role differentiation.

2. *Beliefs about the origins of gender stratification* are also central components of gender ideologies, in light of the importance of biological determinism in traditional legitimations of gender inequality.

3. The unequal distribution of social power by gender, rather than only the division of roles, is at the heart of gender stratification and therefore *beliefs about men's and women's relative power* are also important to address.

The reproduction approach emphasizes education as solidifying an individualistic ideology, which necessitates exploring attitude domains relevant to group-based remedies for gender inequality as well, including attitudes toward collective action by women and gender-related policy orientations.

4. For example, subordinated groups' involvement in group-based social movements is often considered a prerequisite for any substantial change in inequality, which highlights the relevance of *attitudes toward gender-related collective action*.

5. *Policy orientations* reflect goals for change and the willingness to devote social resources to achieving equality. Therefore, some analysts of intergroup attitudes have argued that policy attitudes offer a more stringent test of commitment to change than do more general measures.

6. Finally, it is important to consider *perceptions of men's and women's group interests*, since attention to such interests is a key distinction between the enlightenment and reproduction approaches.

The enlightenment approach suggests that education should increase both awareness and criticism of gender inequality, as well as a commitment to eliminate that in-equality. The view that education reproduces inequality by encouraging an individualistic and meritocratic orientation, on the other hand, implies that the effect of education on beliefs about inequality should vary across forms of social inequality. While education might increase awareness of class inequality, it should not increase criticism of such inequality nor endorsement of efforts to eliminate it. In the context of gender relations, however, education may promote awareness and even criticism of gender inequality, since criticism would not be inconsistent with a meritocratic outlook. But education should not encourage acceptance of group-based efforts to achieve gender equality, such as collective action and government policies on behalf of women, and could even have a negative effect on acceptance of such efforts. Rejection of the notion of group-based interests and remedies is central to the individualistic ideology legitimating economic inequality (and protecting the interests of economically-dominant classes), and education's role in supporting that rejection should shape attitudes toward gender inequality as well. Table 1 summarizes the effects of education on beliefs about gender inequality predicted by the two approaches across attitude domains.

TABLE 1 / Predicted Effects of Education by Attitudinal Domain

	Enlightenment	Reproduction
Domain:		
Roles	+	+
Origins	+	+
Power/Influence	+	+
Collective Action	+	0 or −
Policy	+	0 or −
Group Interests	+	0 or −

Note: + = positive effect (i.e., education associated with increasingly egalitarian and/or critical beliefs), 0 = no effect, − = negative effect.

A key distinction between the enlightenment and reproduction approaches appears in their views of group interests and thus their predictions regarding the uniformity of education effects across various beliefs about inequality. The enlightenment approach predicts education effects across belief domains, while the reproduction approach predicts such effects in some domains but not others.

Following the reproduction approach, I expect that education will be positively associated with non-traditional gender-role orientations and a rejection of biological explanations for gender inequality, because both of these attitudinal domains address allowing for individual choice rather than biological destiny. In addition, I expect education to be positively associated with criticism regarding men's and women's social power, given that this may qualify as recognition of inequalities and could still, as Bowles and Gintis's approach suggests, be combined with a tendency to reject efforts to reduce inequality. The other attitudinal domains—attitudes toward collective action by women, gender-related policy orientations, and perceptions of men's and women's group interests—focus more on group-based remedies or conflictual interpretations. For these the reproduction approach suggests that education will have little relationship with critical attitudes, or may even be negatively associated.

EXPECTATIONS REGARDING EDUCATION AND MEN'S AND WOMEN'S BELIEFS ABOUT GENDER INEQUALITY

In my analyses, I address not only a variety of belief domains but also the effect of education on men's versus women's beliefs about gender inequality. Efforts to explain the impact of education on intergroup attitudes have tended to focus exclusively on dominant group attitudes. I address both dominant and subordinate group attitudes in order to document education effects more fully and, more importantly, in order to illuminate the role of group interests in shaping the effects of education. While men and women share some interests based on other social positions, including social class, gender stratification also generates different interests for men and women as groups. Thus, examining education effects separately for men and women allows further exploration of the role of group interests in shaping the relationship between education and beliefs about inequality. Following Jackman and Muha's (1984) assertion that education does not "render people insensible" to their interests, I expect that the effect of education on men's beliefs about gender inequality will follow the pattern predicted by the reproduction approach. Women, on the other hand, do not share men's structural position or all of men's group interests relative to gender stratification. Therefore, I expect education to be associated somewhat more consistently with criticism of gender inequality among women, following a pattern more like the one predicted by the enlightenment approach. This expectation is consistent with the findings of studies that document that education affects both men's and women's attitudes (see, for example, Fleming 1986; Gurin 1985; and Klein 1984) but tends to have a greater impact on women's attitudes (Baxter and Lansing 1980; Davis and Robinson 1991; Huber, Rexroat, and Spitze 1978; Kluegel and Smith 1986; Schreiber 1978; Smith and Kleugel 1984). There are a variety of reasons to expect a more consistent association between education and beliefs about gender inequality among women relative to men.

First, education may take on a very different meaning for women and men. Women traditionally have been excluded from advanced schooling, and in the contemporary United States many still argue that their limited participation in graduate programs and in scientific and technical training hinders the achievement of gender equality. Such educational inequality, and the ideology of female inferiority that was used to justify it, led nineteenth century U.S. feminists to struggle for equal educational access as a route to expanding women's independence and opportunities (Delamont 1978a, b). In this sense, education may both enlighten women and also empower them to analyze their structural position more critically. Studies of women's gender-role attitudes suggest that education is indeed associated with more egalitarian attitudes (e.g., Mason, Czajka, and Arber 1976; Morgan and Walker 1983; Tallichet and Willits 1986; Thornton, Alwin, and Camburn 1983). The enlightenment approach implies that education provides *knowledge* and *values* that foster awareness of social inequalities and commitment to reducing them. This process could occur for both men and women, although attention to group interests suggests that its effects might be more limited among men. But the additional process of *empowerment* is also a potential source of education effects among women. By providing not only knowledge and values (i.e., enlightenment) but *also* access to independence, status, and opportunities in general, education may allow women the freedom to criticize their own subordinate group status. It is not possible to disentangle the processes of enlightenment and empowerment in the cross-sectional data presented here. However, even if the association between education and beliefs about gender inequality were consistent with the pattern predicted by the enlightenment approach for both men and women, the processes shaping that pattern would probably vary by gender.

Along with men's and women's different interests relative to gender inequality in gen-eral, education also has different effects on men's versus women's interests. These differences offer additional reasons to expect that education will have a more consistent effect on women's beliefs about gender inequality than it has on men's. By increasing their independence from men and their specific occupational opportunities, education may increase women's interests in gender equality. And education may have a lesser effect on women's interests in class inequality than it does on men's. In the context of class inequality, education tends to offer access to greater class privilege and social status. Many individuals who have higher education will become members of an economically dominant class, and therefore may develop similar economic interests. However, in the context of gender relations education is not as uniformly associated with social dominance and interests. Men with higher levels of education tend to be in a dominant position on two dimensions of stratification (gender and class), which is all the more reason to expect that the pattern of education effects among men might follow the prediction of the reproduction approach. But even highly educated women remain subordinated within the system of gender stratification, despite the fact that they may enter a more dominant economic position. In addition, while education is associated with increased earnings among women, that association is stronger among men: Education offers greater earnings returns for men than for women (U.S. Department of Labor 1988). Therefore, to the degree that education solidifies a commitment to individualism as a justification for social inequality, women may have less interest in accepting that justification.

However, there are also reasons to believe that there will be limits to any greater effect of education on women's versus men's beliefs about gender inequality. Despite the greater economic returns to education for men, formal schooling still provides certain educational and status advantages to women, and these could offer women the opportunity to avoid or ignore some of the limitations imposed on them by gender stratification. By allowing them access to even some privileges of dominant group members, education may increase women's interest in the status quo and therefore discourage them from criticizing social inequality, including gender inequality. In addition, Bowles and Gintis (1977) argue that the promotion of an individualistic and meritocratic ideology is part of the experience of education. Even if that ideology has its material basis in the interests of dominant groups, they argue that the U.S. educational system promotes it to all students. Therefore, education might discourage women almost as much as men from endorsing group-based efforts toward social equality, including gender equality. Finally, the paternalistic structure of gender relations, as evidenced in the generally unequal interpersonal relationships that attach men and women, may discourage women from translating the knowledge, values, or empowerment they gain from education into widespread criticism of gender inequality. Rossi argues that because of the intimate relationships between men and women, women may fear conflict with men if they "press hard for . . . equality" (1969:5). Similarly, Lerner notes that given men's status as a dominant group, the woman who struggles against gender stratification "fears the threat of loss of communication with, approval by, and love from the . . . men in her life" (1986:226).

The enlightenment approach may fail to capture the influence of education on dominant group members' beliefs by failing to acknowledge their interest in maintaining inequality. But it may more accurately capture the effect of education on subordinate group beliefs, albeit through a process that involves enlightenment, empowerment, and the expression of group interests. However, the competing influence of education in conferring some of the privileges of dominant group members and promoting individualism, as well as the paternalistic structure of gender relations, may mute the enlightening/empowering effect of education on women's beliefs about gender inequality. As a result, while I expect education effects among women to correspond more closely with the enlightenment approach than they do among men, I still expect to see some evidence of the pattern predicted by the reproduction approach even among women.

DATA AND METHODS

The data for this research are drawn from a public opinion survey administered by telephone to a national probability sample of adults in the United States (N = 1,750). The sample is representative of currently working telephone numbers in the continental United States, with one adult selected at random for each contacted household. The items analyzed appeared on a continuous national survey, designed such that the accumulation of sample telephone numbers over several months represents a probability sample of numbers over that period. The survey was conducted between September 1990 and June 1991,[3] by the Letters and Science Survey Center at the University of Wisconsin, Madison.

The attitudinal measures analyzed here can be categorized into the six groups noted previously. All measures are coded such that higher scores represent more egalitarian or critical beliefs about gender inequality. In the tables that follow, respondents who offered "don't know" responses or refused to answer on a given measure are excluded from the analysis for that measure. This results in a varying loss of cases across measures, with an average loss of about 8 percent of cases. The measures are described briefly; the full text of all items and additional details of recoding are shown in the Appendix.

Roles

Gender-role orientations form the first group, and I consider two measures in this domain: home roles and work roles. Each of these combines two individual items focusing on preferences for equality of roles and on beliefs about actual role practices. The resulting measures range from the traditional belief that women and men ought to have different roles to the egalitarian and critical belief that women and men should have equal roles but actually do not.

Origins

Two items measure beliefs about the origins of gender stratification, addressing natural versus social explanations for women's abilities in homemaking (home origins) and for occupational inequality (work origins).

Influence

Perceptions of relative power are captured in a single measure that addresses the perceived discrepancy between men's and women's influence, with high scores indicating that women's influence is too limited and men's too great (relative influence).

Collective Action

I combine two items in this domain, each of which contrasts individual with collective strategies for overcoming gender inequality. The resulting measure, collective action, represents the number of items on which a respondent endorses collective action (either by women alone or by women and men together).

Policy

The two items addressing policy orientations tap satisfaction with existing governmental efforts on gender issues. These are combined in a single measure, government effort, with high scores indicating that the government is doing too little.

Group Interests

The final attitudinal domain, perceptions of group interests, focuses on whether men and women are viewed as having distinct interests and whether those interests are viewed as conflicting. The items in this domain ask respondents to identify who they believe benefits and who is hurt by two gender-related social arrangements: occupational segregation by gender within the labor force and women's responsibility for the home through the division of public and domestic labor. These items address whether such practices are considered beneficial to men, women, everyone or no one and whether they are considered harmful to men, women, everyone or no one. The two employment-related items are combined to form a measure of the degree to which occupational segregation is perceived as generating group interests for men and women (work interests). Low scores indicate no perception of gender interests; a middle category represents the belief that men benefit *or* women are harmed; and high scores indicate the conflictual belief that men benefit *and* women are harmed. A parallel measure addresses the interests generated by the division of public and domestic labor (home interests).

RESULTS

Table 2 shows distributions for the various beliefs about gender inequality by gender.

TABLE 2 / Men's and Women's Beliefs about Gender Inequality: Distributions and Tests of the Significance of Gender Differences

	Men	Women
Roles, Home		
Traditional	9.2%	8.3%
Moderate	15.1	13.0
Egalitarian/Critical	75.8	78.7
N =	743	905
Roles, Work		
Traditional	8.7%*	5.8%*
Moderate	43.0	35.8
Egalitarian/Critical	48.3	58.4
N =	779	921
Origins, Home		
Natural	52.5%*	40.8%*
Social	47.5	59.2
N =	751	887
Origins, Work		
Natural	25.0%*	16.1%*
Social	75.0	83.9
N =	667	856
Relative Influence		
Men's much too little	3.3%*	1.5%*
Men's somewhat too little	6.5	4.1
Men's and women's equal	38.9	24.5
Women's somewhat too little	24.9	24.7
Women's much too little	26.4	45.2
N =	768	907
Collective Action		
Work individually	22.7%	19.3%
Mixed	47.1	46.5
Organize collectively	30.2	34.2
N =	724	875
Gov't Effort		
Too much	5.5%*	2.2%*
Somewhat too much	8.6	4.5
About right	24.5	15.7
Somewhat too little	29.5	32.6
Too little	31.9	45.0
N =	706	828
Interests, Home		
No gender interests	78.7%	76.5%
Men benefit or women hurt	15.2	16.1
Men benefit and women hurt	6.2	7.5
N =	753	859
Interests, Work		
No gender interests	65.7%*	60.5%*
Men benefit or women hurt	23.7	25.1
Men benefit and women hurt	10.6	14.4
N =	747	855

*p < .05

Note: Significance of gender differences based on chi-square tests, two-tailed.

These distributions suggest that most Americans are at least moderately egalitarian and critical regarding gender roles. Most believe that gender roles should be more egalitarian than they actually are, both at home and at work. While men and women show similar response patterns for the home-roles measure, women are more likely than men to express egalitarian/critical attitudes regarding work-related role inequality. For the origins measures, more than 50 percent of men and about 40 percent of women express the belief that women's homemaking abilities are natural in origin, but few respondents perceive work-related gender inequalities as natural. In terms of power inequality, about 50 percent of men and 70 percent of women express at least some dissatisfaction with women's social influence relative to men's, although women express stronger grievance in this regard.

Respondents tend to prefer individual to collective strategies, with only about one-third of men and women expressing a preference for collective action on both items comprising this measure. The modal response regarding government efforts is to consider such efforts at least somewhat insufficient, and women are more likely than men to express that belief. Finally, most respondents do not perceive either the division of labor or occupational segregation as generating gender interests: More than 60 percent of men and women perceive neither benefits to men nor harm to women stemming from these social arrangements. Fewer than 15 percent perceive men and women as having conflicting interests relative to the division of labor or occupational segregation.

While gender differences in these beliefs are not striking in magnitude, women do tend to be more critical of gender stratification than men. The presence of at least some gender difference in responses to these items seems, of course, consistent with the differ-

ent structural positions of men and women relative to gender stratification. But how does the association between education and beliefs about gender inequality vary by attitudinal domain and by gender? To address this question, I present regression coefficients estimating the impact of education separately for men and for women, and coefficients estimating the impact of the interaction between gender and education, net the effects of other factors. Ordinary Least Squares (OLS), ordered logistic,[4] and logistic regression equations are used, depending on each dependent variable's range. The education measure is composed of five categories: less than a high school education; high school degree; some college; a college degree; or a graduate/professional degree beyond college. All analyses were also conducted using a series of education dummy variables, representing the various categories, in order to check for nonlinear education effects. The series of dummy variables indicated a generally linear effect of the education categories for almost all of the attitude variables, so the results from the single education measure presented here are not substantially different from those documented by the dummy variables.

Education coefficients are estimated separately for men and women, with controls for other factors that are confounded with education and that also could be expected to affect the development of gender-related beliefs.[5] The controls include: age (continuous measure); class identification (poor, working, middle, or upper-middle class); employment status (currently employed or not); family income (measured in $10,000 categories, with the final category representing those with incomes more than $120,000); race (non-white, white);[6] and interviewer gender (to control for the possibility that interviewer gender is affecting men's and women's expressed beliefs about gender inequality). The only independent variable with notable levels of missing data is family income. Therefore, for the other independent variables, cases with missing data are excluded from the regression analyses. For family income, missing cases are coded to zero and all equations include a dummy variable representing missing data on that variable. Along with education coefficients from separate equations for men and women, I also present coefficients estimating the effect of the interaction between gender and education to summarize the presence or absence of a greater impact of education on women's attitudes (from equations estimated for both men and women combined, adding terms representing the interaction between gender and all other independent variables).

In general, the pattern of education effects evident for men in Table 3 is consistent with the reproduction approach. Education is significantly associated with the role-related measures, the origins measures, and the influence measure. It is not significantly associated with attitudes toward collective action, policy orientations, or perceptions of group interests. As education increases, men are more likely to acknowledge that domestic labor is not shared equally, that women may be discriminated against in the labor force, that gender inequalities are socially constructed, and that men's influence is too great while women's is too little. All of these patterns qualify as greater recognition of gender inequalities among more highly-educated men. The absence of increasing criticism with education in the domains focusing on action (collective action and policy) and on the group interest measures, on the other hand, may qualify as avoiding group-based remedies and conflictual interpretations.

The pattern of education effects is similar for women. Contrary to my expectation, there is only limited evidence that education is more consistently predictive of women's beliefs about gender inequality than men's.

For seven of the nine measures the education coefficient is larger for women than for men, but for only two of these is the interaction between education and gender statistically significant. Significant interactions are evident for the measure addressing the origins of gender inequality at work, and for the measure regarding the group interests served by occupational gender segregation, an attitudinal domain that addresses group-based and non-harmonious interpretations for gender stratification.

To the degree that any differential impact of education on women's beliefs is evident, it appears for employment-related issues. Within the origins domain, the differential effect is for the work-related and not the home-related measure. Within the group interests domain, it appears for the measure regarding occupational segregation rather than the division of public and domestic labor. Higher education offers women access to new employment opportunities. This may increase their expectations for occupational equality and increase their criticism when such expectations are frustrated by continuing gender inequalities in employment. In addition, education may increase women's interests in occupational equality, given that it increases their qualifications for potential job opportunities, regardless of their current income or employment status. Education also offers some degree of status and credibility independent of its effects on employment opportunities, which may be a source of empowerment for more highly-educated women. For men, higher education may increase knowledge regarding gender inequality, but there is no reason to expect it would increase their interest in occupational equality as it does for women. This may temper the positive association between education and critical attitudes toward work-related gender inequality among men relative to women.

TABLE 3 / Regression Coefficients Estimating Effects of Education for Men and Women (Net of the Effects of Age, Race, Class Identity, Family Income, Employment Status, and Interviewer Gender)

	Men	Women	Interaction
Roles, Home (OL)	.20*	.24**	.03
s.e.	(.09)	(.08)	(.12)
N =	727	878	1605
Roles, Work (OL)	.27**	.34**	.07
s.e.	(.07)	(.07)	(.10)
N =	763	892	1655
Origins, Home (L)	.22**	.30**	.07
s.e.	(.08)	(.07)	(.10)
N =	736	861	1597
Origins, Work (L)	.22*	.43**	.21*
s.e.	(.09)	(.10)	(.13)
N =	653	832	1485
Relative Influence	.16**	.13**	− .03
s.e.	(.04)	(.03)	(.05)
N =	755	880	1635
Collective Action (OL)	.02	− .01	− .04
s.e.	(.07)	(.06)	(.09)
N =	710	851	1561
Gov't Effort	.03	.06	.04
s.e.	(.04)	(.03)	(.05)
N =	692	809	1501
Interests, Home (OL)	.08	.10	.02
s.e.	(.10)	(.07)	(.12)
N =	737	836	1573
Interest, Work (OL)	.01	.17**	.17*
s.e.	(.08)	(.06)	(.10)
N =	733	829	1562

*p < .05

**p < .01

Notes:

(OL) = ordered logit coefficient, (L) = logit coefficient, all others OLS.

Significance tests for education coefficients are two-tailed. The interaction variable is the product of a gender dummy variable on which women are coded 1 and the education measure, and tests for these coefficients are one-tailed (predicted direction positive).

This differential effect of education by gender is less evident for home or family-related issues, such as the origins of home-making abilities and the interests served by the division of public and domestic labor. Household labor research indicates that married women's employment status does not strongly influence the degree to which they are responsible for housework (for example, Berk and Berk 1980; Ross 1987), which suggests that gender inequality in the family may be particularly entrenched.[7] In that light, it is not surprising that education may empower women to criticize employment-related gender inequality more than it does men, while the impact of education on family-related beliefs is more similar for men and women. Perhaps the intimate and paternalistic structure of gender relations in the family discourages women from outpacing men in the extent to which they translate any knowledge, power, and status they gain from education into criticism of home-related inequality. Gender relations in employment, on the other hand, are less intimate, and education may affect women's interests regarding gender inequality at work more than it affects their interests regarding gender inequality at home. Therefore, for employment-related issues women may feel more free to outpace men in the extent to which they translate the empowerment accompanying education into criticism of gender inequality.

It is also possible that the differential effect of education by gender for some employment-related measures reflects the content of different curricula experienced by men and women. Perhaps, for example, college-educated women are more likely to major in disciplines that might heighten their awareness of labor force inequality. To provide a limited test of this possibility, I estimated the interaction between gender and education separately for dummy variables representing the education categories (data not shown). A curricular explanation implies that education should interact with gender more substantially for those who have attended college than for high school graduates, since college students can select into varying curricula while high school students often cannot. I found no evidence of larger education by gender interactions at the college-educated level, but it would be helpful to incorporate curricular measures into future studies so that this possibility could be tested more fully.

DISCUSSION AND CONCLUSIONS

The analyses presented here indicate that education is more strongly associated with some beliefs about gender inequality than with others. Education effects are evident for role-related issues, beliefs about the origins of gender stratification, and perceptions of men's and women's influence, and in all of these domains education is associated with more egalitarian or critical gender-related attitudes. Education effects are less evident for issues with more clearly group-oriented or conflictual content like attitudes toward collective action, policy orientation, and perceptions of men's and women's group interests. These results lend credence to the reproduction approach to understanding the relationship between education and intergroup attitudes: Education may encourage criticism of inequality on some dimensions, but it does not encourage the extension of that criticism to endorsement of group-based interpretations and remedies.

If men's gender attitudes were mainly a reflection of knowledge, as the enlightenment approach suggests, we would expect them to be more consistently modified by education. If, on the other hand, stratification attitudes reflect each group's interests, then we would not expect such a consistent impact of education on dominant group attitudes. This latter approach better accounts for the pattern evident here: Men's attitudes toward several aspects of gender inequality (collective action, policy orientation, and group interests) are unrelated to education. For women, most of the attitudinal domains addressed here are at least somewhat more closely related to education than they are for men, which also suggests that the association between education and beliefs about gender inequality reflects not just knowledge alone, but also reflects interests and power. However, the interaction between education and gender is significant only for two employment-related measures.

The knowledge, power, and employment-related interests associated with education among women may encourage them, more than men, to recognize the social origins and harmful effects of gender inequality in employment. However, women are not significantly more likely than men to translate education into criticism of gender inequality in the home. Even as education increases women's criticism of gender inequality, it does so within clear limits. Those limits suggest that two aspects of gender ideology are particularly entrenched: attitudes toward gender inequality in the home and attitudes toward group-based remedies for gender inequality. Education increases women's awareness of gender inequities in occupations more than men's, but the same is not evident for home-related inequities. And education does not appear to counter the U.S. tendency toward individualism for women any more than for men: The impact of education on attitudes toward collective action and government policy is not significantly greater for women than for men. Education may present a quandary for subordinate group members, offering them the resources to reject the legitimacy of stratification but leaving unchallenged the orientation toward individual effort that discourages any broad group-based or conflictual claims.

Jackman and Muha suggest that education changes the way in which dominant group members articulate and understand the ideology legitimating inequality, a process they term "ideological refinement." In comparing race, class, and gender stratification, they claim that ". . . ideology takes a different shape—and education plays a different role—depending on the extent of challenge from subordinates" (1984:765). Gender inequality is characterized by the absence of any such broad challenge from subordinates.[8] They argue that under these circumstances, education may equip dominants to recognize inequality but also to construe it as harmless and avoid concrete action toward change. While my analyses cannot address the cognitive processes Jackman and Muha

(1984) posit, the pattern of education effects I have documented for men is consistent with their argument. But why then, with the exception of some employment-related attitudes, is the same pattern of education effects evident for women? Perhaps men's social dominance, which privileges their world view over women's, as well as the stake more highly-educated women have in economic inequality and therefore in resisting group-based claims in general, explain the appearance of this similar pattern of education effects among women. In addition, it is possible that women's interpersonal and material dependence on men also discourages them from translating education into group-based or conflictual claims. It would be useful to explore the effect of education on dominant and subordinate group attitudes in other intergroup contexts. Both Rossi's (1969) and Lerner's (1986) arguments that women who struggle against gender inequality must fear interpersonal sanctions from the men in their lives suggest that intergroup contexts marked by less interpersonal intimacy and dependence, such as racial stratification, might be characterized by even greater variation in the effect of education on dominant versus subordinate group members' beliefs about inequality.

The analyses I have presented indicate that education clearly affects beliefs about gender inequality, but the distribution of beliefs documented here is by no means an overwhelming rejection of gender stratification. In addition, education appears to play competing roles simultaneously, encouraging a critical analysis of existing gender inequalities while also allowing for an individualist interpretation of the social order. Education alone does not prompt uniformly critical beliefs about gender inequality among either men or women, and instead plays a role consistent with the assertion that education may reproduce rather than challenge social inequalities.

APPENDIX: TEXT AND RECODING OF ATTITUDE ITEMS

Home Roles: Combines the following items:[9] scored 0 if respondent believes child care should be mainly a woman's responsibility, 1 for the belief that men and women should share and actually do, and 2 for the belief that they should share but women are actually responsible.

1. If a man and a woman have children, do you think that taking care of the children *should be* mainly a woman's responsibility or that it should be a man's responsibility as much as a woman's?

2. And how do you think most men and women *actually* divide child care: Do you think most women are actually responsible for taking care of children or do you think most men actually take equal responsibility?

Work Roles: Combines the following items: correlation between the items as shown below: −.25. Recoded to score 0 if respondent does not agree that women should have equal job opportunities, 1 for agreement that job opportunities should be equal along with agreement that opportunities actually are equal, and 2 for agreement to equal opportunities coupled with disagreement that opportunities actually are equal.

3. In general, women in this country *should be* given equal job opportunities with men (do you agree strongly, agree somewhat, disagree somewhat, or disagree strongly with that statement?).

4. In general, women in this country *actually are* given equal job opportunities with men (same response options as #3).

Note: For subsequent items, codes for each response shown in parentheses.

Origins, Work

5. Men have more of the top jobs because they are born with more drive and ambition than women (0). OR Men have more of the top jobs because our society discriminates against women (1).

Origins, Home

6. By nature, many women are better than men at making a home and caring for children (0). OR Our society, not nature, teaches women to be better than men at homemaking and child care (1).

Relative Influence: A sum of the following items (range 0 to 4); correlation between the two items: .46.

7. Thinking of women as a group, would you say women have too much influence (0), just about the right amount of influence (1), or too little influence (2) in society?

8. And, thinking about men as a group, would you say men have too much influence (2), just about the right amount of influence (1), or too little influence (0) in society?

Collective Action: A sum of items 9 and 10 (range 0 to 2); correlation between the two items: .27.

9. The best way to handle problems of discrimination is for each woman to make sure she gets the best training possible for what she wants to do (0). OR Only if women organize and work together can anything really be done about discrimination (1).

10. If women want to change their position in America, which of the following do you think is the best way for them to do it: Women should organize as a group with men and women (1), OR each woman should work to get ahead on her own (0), OR women should organize as a group with other women (1).

Note: Almost all respondents who received a score of 1 on this summary measure endorsed collective action on item 10 but not item 9.

Gov't Effort: The sum of items 11 and 12 (range 0 to 4); correlation between the two items: .35.

11. Think of how much the federal government is doing to make sure women have the same job opportunities as men; would you say the federal government is doing too much (0), about the right amount (1), or too little (2) about this?

12. Next, think of how much the federal government is doing to provide day care centers for the children of working parents; would you say the federal government is doing too much (0), about the right amount (1), or too little (2) about this?

Interests, Home: Items 13 and 14 are summed (range 0 to 2); correlation between the two items: .39. The INTERESTS items were preceded by a brief explanatory text not shown here.

13. Most women take primary responsibility for the care of the home and children while most men take primary responsibility for supporting the family financially. Who benefits from this—men (1), women (0), everyone (0) or no one (0)?

14. Who is hurt by this—men (0), women (1), everyone (0) or no one (0)?

Interests, Work: Items 15 and 16 are summed (range 0 to 2); correlation between the two items: .34.

15. There are more women in certain kinds of jobs such as nurses and secretaries while there are more men in other kinds of jobs such as engineers and doctors. Who benefits from this—men (1), women (0), everyone (0) or no one (0)?

16. And who is hurt by this—men (0), women (1), everyone (0) or no one (0)?

ENDNOTES

1. There are also approaches that treat the relationship between education and intergroup attitudes as a measurement artifact, which I do not address here. See for example, Jackman (1973), Sullivan, Piereson, and Markus (1979).

2. Davis and Robinson (1991) offer a similar distinction between education as enlightenment versus repro-

duction. However, they address a more limited array of beliefs about gender inequality and their analysis focuses on a variety of predictors of such beliefs cross-nationally rather than on an in-depth exploration of education effects.

3. Both the independent and dependent variables were assessed for time effects across the 10 months during which interviews were conducted, and no substantial effects were evident.

4. The ordered logistic regression model assumes that the effects of independent variables are similar across cutpoints in the dependent variable distribution. Tests of the applicability of this assumption were conducted, and the coefficients for education were similar across cutpoints.

5. This set of controls includes both factors exogenous to education and endogenous to it, and therefore the resulting education coefficients estimate the direct effects of education. Given that both Bowles and Gintis (1977) and Jackman and Muha (1984) stress the role of education in carrying dominant values of individualism and meritocratic orientation net of the indirect effects it may have in bestowing economic advantages, and that the enlightenment approach highlights only the experience of education, the focus on direct effects is necessary. However, to explore the implications of focusing only on the direct effects of education, I also estimated its indirect effects via class identification, employment status, and family income (still controlling for age and race to remove any spurious component of the association between education and beliefs about gender inequality), following Alwin and Hauser's (1975) suggested procedure. For the model specified here, across the various dependent variables, 80 to 97 percent of the total effect of education on both men's and women's beliefs about gender inequality is direct (data not shown).

6. I also checked for interactions between education and race among women, given the suggestion that education may have a unique effect on women of color, whose background and experiences are often at odds with what is valued by traditional educational institutions (Belenky et al. 1986; Rich 1991). Race and education did not generally interact significantly in predicting beliefs about gender inequality, and women of color expressed greater criticism of gender inequality across education categories than did white women.

7. The trend over time in attitudes toward family *roles* has been toward increasing egalitarianism (Mason and Lu 1989), like the trend in attitudes toward employment roles (Spitze and Huber 1980).

8. Jackman and Senter (1980, 1983) compare attitudes toward racial, class, and gender inequality, and document that openly conflictual attitudes and disagreement between dominants and subordinates are least evident in gender relations.

9. The correlation between these two items, as they are coded below, is almost zero (−.05), due to very low variation on the first item (over 90 percent of respondents believe the responsibility should be men's as much as women's).

REFERENCES

Alwin, Duane F., and Robert M. Hauser
1975 "The decomposition of effects in path analysis." *American Sociological Review* 40:37–47.

Baxter, Sandra, and Marjorie Lansing
1980 Women and Politics: The Invisible Majority. Ann Arbor: The University of Michigan Press.

Belenky, Mary Field, Blythe McVicker Clinchy, Nancy Rule Goldberger, and Jill Mattuck Tarule
1986 Women's Ways of Knowing. New York: Basic Books.

Berk, Richard A., and Sarah Fenstermaker Berk
1980 Labor and Leisure at Home. Beverly Hills, Calif.: Sage.

Borhek, J.
1965 "A theory of incongruent experience." *Sociological Review* 8:89–95.

Bowles, Samuel, and Herbert Gintis
1977 Schooling in Capitalist America. New York: Basic Books.

Davis, Nancy J., and Robert V. Robinson
1991 "Men's and women's consciousness of gender inequality." *American Sociological Review* 56:72–84.

Delamont, Sara
1978a "The contradiction in ladies' education." In The Nineteenth Century Woman: Her Cultural and Physical World, eds. Sara Delamont and Lorna Duffin, 134–163. New York: Barnes and Noble.
1978b "The domestic ideology and women's education." In The Nineteenth Century Woman: Her Cultural and Physical World, eds. Sara Delamont and Lorna Duffin, 164–187. New York: Barnes and Noble.

Fleming, Jeanne J.
1986 "Women against men?: Gender as a base of support for change in women's rights and roles." In Women and Politics: Activism, Attitudes, and Office-Holding, eds. Gwen Moore and Glenna Spitze, 105–117. Greenwich, Conn.: JAI Press.

Gurin, Patricia
1985 "Women's gender consciousness." *Public Opinion Quarterly* 49:143–163.

Huber, Joan, Cynthia Rexroat, and Glenna Spitze
1978 "A crucible of opinion on women's status: ERA in Illinois." *Social Forces* 57:549–565.

Jackman, Mary R.
1973 "Education and prejudice or education and response set?" *American Sociological Review* 38:327–339.

Jackman, Mary R., and Michael J. Muha
1984 "Education and intergroup attitudes: Moral enlightenment, superficial democratic commitment or ideological refinement?" *American Sociological Review* 49:751–769.

Jackman, Mary R., and Mary Scheuer Senter
1980 "Images of social groups: Categorical or qualified?" *Public Opinion Quarterly* 44:341–361.
1983 "Different, therefore unequal: Beliefs about trait differences between groups of unequal status." *Research in Social Stratification and Mobility* 2:309–335.

Klein, Ethel
1984 Gender Politics. Cambridge, Mass.: Harvard University Press.

Kluegel, James R., and Eliot R. Smith
1986 Beliefs About Inequality. New York: Aldine de Gruyter.

Lerner, Gerda
1986 The Creation of Patriarchy. New York: Oxford University Press.

Lipset, Seymour Martin
1960 Political Man. London: Heinemann.

Mason, Karen Oppenheim, John L. Czajka, and Sara Arber
1976 "Changes in U.S. women's sex-role attitudes, 1964–1974." *American Sociological Review* 41:573–596.

Mason, Karen Oppenheim, and Yu-Hsia Lu
1988 "Attitudes toward women's familial roles: Changes in the United States, 1977–1985." *Gender & Society* 2:39–57.

Morgan, Carolyn Stout, and Alexis J. Walker
1983 "Predicting sex role attitudes." *Social Psychology Quarterly* 46:148–151.

Rich, Adrienne
1991 "Taking women students seriously." In The Gender Reader, eds. Evelyn Ashton-Jones and Gary A. Olson, 328–335. Boston: Allyn and Bacon.

Ross, Catherine E.
1987 "The division of labor at home." *Social Forces* 65:817–833.

Rossi, Alice S.
1969 "Sex equality: The beginnings of ideology." *The Humanist* Sept./Oct.:3–16.

Schreiber, E. M.
    1978   "Education and change in American opinions on a woman for president." Public Opinion Quarterly 42:171–182.
Smith, M. Dwayne, and Lynne J. Fisher
    1982   "Sex-role attitudes and social class." Journal of Comparative Family Studies 13:77–88.
Smith, Eliot, and James R. Kluegel
    1984   "Beliefs about women's opportunity: Comparison with beliefs about blacks and a general perspective." Social Psychology Quarterly 47:81–95.
Spitze, Glenna, and Joan Huber
    1980   "Changing attitudes toward women's non-family roles." Sociology of Work and Occupations 7:317–335.
Stouffer, Samuel
    1955   Communism, Conformity, and Civil Liberties. New York: Doubleday.
Sullivan, John L., James Pierson, and George E. Marcus
    1979   "An alternative conception of political tolerance." American Political Science Review 73:781–794.

Tallichet, Suzanne E., and Fern K. Willits
    1986   "Gender-role attitude change of young women: Influential factors from a panel study." Social Psychology Quarterly 49: 219–227.
Thornton, Arland, Duane F. Alwin, and Donald Camburn
    1983   "Causes and consequences of sex-role attitude change." American Sociological Review 48:211–227.
United States Department of Labor
    1988   Twenty Facts on Women Workers, Office of the Secretary, Women's Bureau. Washington, D.C.: Government Printing Office.
Welch, Susan
    1975   "Support among women for the issues of the women's movement." Sociological Quarterly 16:216–227.

Questions for Understanding and Critical Thinking

1. From your own experience, do you think education primarily enlightens people or reproduces inequalities in society? Explain your answer.
2. How does education take on a different meaning for women and men?
3. Why might additional years of education contribute to people's ability to recognize gender inequality but have little influence on their endorsement of group-based remedies for such inequality?

PART TWO

Suggestions for Further Reading

Ballantine, Jeanne H. 1993. *The Sociology of Education: A Systematic Analysis* (3rd ed.). Englewood Cliffs, NJ: Prentice-Hall.

Bourdieu, Pierre, and Jean-Claude Passeron. 1990. *Reproduction in Education, Society and Culture*. Newbury Park, CA: Sage.

Churchill, Ward. 1994. *Indians Are Us? Culture and Genocide in Native North America*. Monroe, ME: Common Courage Press.

Cookson, Peter W., Jr., and Caroline Hodges Persell. 1985. *Preparing for Power: America's Elite Boarding Schools*. New York: Basic Books.

Eder, Donna, with Catherine Colleen Evans and Stephen Parker. 1995. *School Talk: Gender and Adolescent Culture*. New Brunswick, NJ: Rutgers University Press.

Frankenberg, Ruth. 1993. *The Social Construction of Whiteness: White Women, Race Matters*. Minneapolis: University of Minnesota Press.

hooks, bell. 1994. *Teaching to Transgress: Education as the Practice of Freedom*. New York: Routledge.

———. 1995. *Killing Rage: Ending Racism*. New York: Henry Holt.

Kimmel, Michael S., and Michael A. Messner (Eds.). 1995. *Men's Lives* (3rd ed.). Boston: Allyn and Bacon.

Kozol, Jonathan. 1991. *Savage Inequalities: Children in America's Schools*. New York: Crown.

MacLeod, Jay. 1995. *Ain't No Makin' It: Aspirations and Attainment in a Low-Income Neighborhood*. Boulder, CO: Westview.

Messner, Michael A. 1992. *Power at Play: Sports and the Problem of Masculinity*. Boston: Beacon Press.

Navarrette, Ruben, Jr. 1993. *A Darker Shade of Crimson: Odyssey of a Harvard Chicano*. New York: Bantam.

Sadker, Myra, and David Sadker. 1994. *Failing at Fairness: How America's Schools Cheat Girls*. New York: Scribner.

Thompson, Becky W. 1994. *A Hunger So Wide and So Deep: American Women Speak Out on Eating Problems*. Minneapolis: University of Minnesota Press.

Thorne, Barrie. 1993. *Gender Play: Girls and Boys in School*. New Brunswick, NJ: Rutgers University Press.

Weis, Lois, and Michelle Fine (Eds.). 1993. *Beyond Silenced Voices: Class, Race, and Gender in United States Schools*. Albany: State University of New York Press.

PART THREE

Discrimination, Resistance, and Social Change

Every day that you live as a black person you're reminded how you're perceived in society. You walk the streets at night; white people cross the streets. I've seen white couples and individuals dart in front of cars to not be on the same side of the street.

　　—An African American student, Article 23

You don't need to look at [the job applicant's] address to know where they're from; it's how people come across; they don't know how to behave in an office.

　　—A clerical employer discussing job applicants
　　who live in a housing project, Article 24

I could do bad by myself. . . . If we get married and he's working, then he lose his job, I'm going to stand by him and everything. I don't want to marry nobody that don't have nothing going for themselves . . . I don't see no future . . . I could do bad by myself.

　　—Renee, Article 22

Many citizens of these United States still long to live in a society where beloved community can be formed—where loving ties of care and knowing bind us together in our differences. We cannot surrender that longing—if we do we will never see an end to racism.

　　—bell hooks, Article 27

THESE PERSONAL NARRATIVES highlight the pressing and pervasive nature of racism, sexism, and class inequalities in the United States. In Part One, we discussed race, class, and gender as interlocking systems of privilege and oppression. In Part Two, we examined the development of racial-ethnic, class, and gender identities and how people learn—through families, peers, sports, and education—about diversity and inequality in society. In Part Three, we analyze the process of discrimination as it is rooted in racism, sexism, and class oppression. We also discuss the consequences of discrimination in people's lives, their resistance to oppression, and prospects for social change. We begin with a closer look at the dynamics of racism, sexism, and class oppression.

Racism, Sexism, and Class Oppression

Racism is a system of beliefs and behaviors embedded in the power relations of a society whereby members of a subordinate racial-ethnic group are oppressed and exploited because they possess cultural, psychological, and/or physical characteristics that members of a dominant racial-ethnic group deem to be inferior (see Blauner, 1972). Based on this definition, racism in the United States has two major components: (1) prejudice and individual discriminatory actions of white people directed against people of color and (2) organizational and structural discrimination that is embedded in social institutions and enacted—either intentionally or unintentionally—by participants as they perform their everyday roles.

Racism is fueled by prejudice. In this context, **prejudice** refers to a deep-seated belief that one's own racial-ethnic group is superior and should be privileged, while other groups are judged to be inferior and thus deserving of subordination or oppression. Based on Gordon Allport's (1958) classic study on prejudice, sociologist Joe R. Feagin (Article 23) points out that prejudice at the individual level can be expressed along a continuum of actions that range from avoidance to exclusion or rejection, or even to attack. However, racism also is backed by power and resources: It may be enforced and maintained by the legal, cultural, religious, educational, economic, political, environmental, and military institutions of society. Control of power and resources enables dominant group members to perpetuate "white-skin privilege" for their own benefit (Feagin and Feagin, 1996).

Racist behavior is very complex; however, as Rita Chaudhry Sethi points out in Article 20, "media sensationalism, political expedience, intellectual laziness, and legal constraints" often conspire to pare down the image of racism to one that narrowly defines its forms, perpetrators, and victims. For example, racism commonly is viewed only in the stark polarity of black/white conflict. According to Sethi, this narrowly defined focus does not take into account race-based offenses experienced by members of such racial-ethnic groups as Asian Americans, especially those from South Asia. Not only do white Americans typically reject Asian American claims of racial victimization (due to stereotypes of the so-called model minority) but also other people of color may believe *real* racism has not been suffered by Asian Americans due to their alleged economic privilege or perceived whiteness. As Sethi suggests, such beliefs make cross-ethnic coalition building virtually impossible. Sethi posits that dominant racial-ethnic group members ultimately benefit from divisiveness among subordinate racial-ethnic groups when their members view each other—and not members of the dominant group—as the source of racial bias.

In Article 24, sociologists Kathryn M. Neckerman and Joleen Kirschenman note that some research on white/black interaction suggests that "classic racism—the view of people of color as undifferentiated" may have declined in recent years; however, race relations between strangers still remain tense and commonly are shaded with fear, suspicion, and moral contempt (see Blauner,

1989; Anderson, 1990). All people of color experience oppression based on racism, but women of color experience a duality of discrimination based on both racism and sexism.

Sexism **is a system of beliefs and behaviors embedded in the power relations of a society whereby persons of one sex, usually female, are oppressed and dominated by members of the other sex, usually male, based on the subordinate group's alleged inferiority.** Components of sexism toward women include (1) prejudice against women; (2) derogatory stereotypes that reinforce, complement, or justify the prejudice; and (3) discriminatory behavior, such as actions that keep women subordinate through categoric exclusion or segregation. Sociologists Nijole V. Benokraitis and Joe R. Feagin explain, "Modern sexism involves both antifemale prejudices and stereotypes and the *power* men have to implement them in the everyday practices of discrimination" (1995:39).

Sexism is backed by power and resources in the home, school, workplace, and public spaces. In public places, for example, women have different experiences than do men, particularly when they appear alone. In Article 21, sociologist Carol Brooks Gardner documents how women who may have made progress in their occupations, education, and home life nonetheless are objects of inferior treatment by men in public places. Harassment occurs in the form of catcalls, evaluative "compliments," and verbal contacts that subtly go astray when gender—not the business at hand—becomes a topic. Women also have greater fear of crime because of their perceived vulnerability to men in public places.

Sexism thrives in patriarchal societies where men are thought to be the natural leaders, heads of state, and corporate executives, and where women's natural roles are seen as followers, wives, mothers, and secretaries—positions that are supportive of and subordinate to the dominant roles of men. Reminiscent of W. E. B. Du Bois's analysis of African Americans' "double consciousness" (see Article 3), author Marilyn Frye suggests that women's oppression in patriarchal societies produces the "double bind—situations in which options are reduced to a very few and all of them expose one to penalty, censure or deprivation" (1983:2). As Frye explains:

> *It is often a requirement upon oppressed people that we smile and be cheerful. If we comply, we signal our docility and our acquiescence in our situation. We need not, then, be taken note of. . . . On the other hand, anything but the sunniest countenance exposes us to being perceived as mean, bitter, angry, or dangerous . . . which is enough to cost one one's livelihood . . . [or] to result in rape, arrest, beating and murder. (1983:2)*

Carol Brooks Gardner's analysis of crime-prevention advice given to women (Article 21) supports the assertion that women are oppressed in ways such as behavioral and appearance norms that bind and constrain them. For example, communicative acts between women and men in public are heavily *appearance dependent*—relying on appraisal of the physical look, manner, non-verbal communication, and dress of the other. Women, more than men, are required to focus on presentation strategies that communicate their ability to deal with harassment and crime. According to Gardner, recommended crime-prevention strategies—such as pretending that one has an escort or companion, restricting apparel choices and emotional expressions, and taking precautionary measures before appearing in public—actually limit women's freedom and mobility and may inadvertently project messages of dependency and lack of skill. Other characteristics of women—including race/ethnicity, ability/disability, and class—also affect how women will experience public places. Extremely wealthy women may be protected from public harassment and criminal victimization by personnel (limousine drivers, doormen at residences and businesses, personal security guards, etc.) who are paid to protect them, but women in middle- and lower-income categories typically must deal with public life without such human barricades.

Class oppression refers to the ability of members of an elite (upper or capitalist) class to command three main sources of domination: (1) control over the primary means of economic activity, typically involving ownership or management of the means of production; (2) control over the means of state administration (the government) and coercion (lawmaking and law enforcement); and (3) control over the means of communication and persuasion (such as media and telecommunications) (Miliband, 1989). According to political science scholar Ralph Miliband, the elite class controls most of the wealth and income that prevail in capitalist societies.

Wealth is the value of all of a person's or family's economic assets, including income, personal property, and income-producing property. Today, a majority of the wealthiest people in the United States inherited their money: Some inheritors are more than three generations removed from the original fortune (see Allen, 1987; Odendahl, 1990). By the early 1990s, four categories of wealth existed in the United States:

1. The *super-rich* (0.5 percent of households), who own 35 percent of the nation's wealth, with net assets averaging almost $9 million
2. The *very rich* (the next 0.5 percent of households), who own about 7 percent of the nation's wealth, with net assets ranging from $1.4 million to $2.5 million
3. The *rich* (9 percent of households), who own 30 percent of the wealth, with net assets of a little over $400,000
4. *Everybody else* (the bottom 90 percent), who own about 28 percent of the nation's wealth.

By 1995, the holdings of super-rich households were estimated to have risen from 35 percent to almost 40 percent of all assets in the nation (stocks, bonds, cash, life insurance policies, paintings, jewelry, and other tangible assets) (Rothchild, 1995). This change reflects a growing trend toward greater wealth inequality that began in the early 1980s and has continued into the 1990s.

Although redistribution of wealth has benefited persons at the top of the class structure, it also has affected the average holdings of the lower-middle and bottom wealth groups by about 30 percent. Beginning in the 1980s, the rich got richer and the poor and middle classes got further behind. Some wealthy people choose to translate their vast economic resources into political power; however, others choose to enjoy personal and social power that they derive from the ease and privileges their wealth affords them and from the limited power they wield over those whom they employ in their personal service (Miliband, 1989).

Wealth accumulation varies by racial-ethnic group. In a recent study of wealth and racial inequality among whites and African Americans, sociologists Melvin L. Oliver and Thomas M. Shapiro found that equally positioned whites and African Americans have highly unequal amounts of wealth:

> *Matching whites and blacks on key individual factors correlated with asset acquisition demonstrated the gnawing persistence of large magnitudes of wealth difference. . . . If white and black households shared all the wealth-associated characteristics we examined, blacks would still confront a $43,000 net worth handicap! (1995:174)*

In their analysis, Oliver and Shapiro demonstrate the continuing significance of race in the wealth accumulation process, especially in regard to two key ingredients: (1) racial differences in housing and mortgage markets and (2) racial differences in inheritance and other intergenerational transfers. The racialization of state policy (see Article 1 by Howard Winant) has contributed to racial differences in housing and mortgage markets by perpetuating residential segregation and producing a lower net worth of properties owned by some African American families. Although overtly racially biased federal housing, tax, and transportation policies were eliminated in the late 1960s, an extremely high degree of racial segregation remains today in residential communities. However, segregated housing is not a choice most African Americans freely make; it is a condition that results from racial steering, redlining (the systematic refusal by some lenders to make loans on property in certain neighborhoods based on their racial-ethnic composition), hostile white attitudes, and discrimination by mortgage lenders (Feagin and Sikes, 1994).

Racial differences in inheritance and other intergenerational transfers also contribute significantly to inequalities in the wealth accumulation process between whites and African Americans. Asset poverty is passed from one generation to the next in African American families, no matter how much occupational attainment or mobility they achieve. According to Oliver and Shapiro (1995), the problem may be attributed to disparities at three levels of inheritance: cultural capital, milestone events, and traditional bequests. As discussed in Part Two, cultural capital especially is important in childhood; a family's wealth may be used to enhance children's education, cultural experiences, and social networks. Intergenerational wealth transfer also occurs at milestone events in young people's lives, such as beginning college, getting married, buying a first house, or having a child, when parents contribute money or in-kind assistance (such as child care). Obviously, a well-off family has a greater ability to make larger contributions that ease children's financial burden and limit their future debt. Wealth also is passed on through traditional bequests at the death of parents or grandparents. Oliver and Shapiro suggest that inheritance among white Americans and African Americans differs for several reasons:

> *Segregation blocked access to education, decent jobs, and livable wages among the grandparents and parents of blacks born before the late 1960s, effectively preventing them from building up much wealth. Until the late 1960s few older black Americans had accrued any savings to speak of, as they likely had working-class jobs. Without savings no wealth could be built up. (1995:152)*

As contrasted with wealth, ***income* refers to the economic gain derived from wages, salaries, income transfers** (governmental aid such as Aid to Families with Dependent Children [AFDC]), **and ownership of property** (Beeghley, 1989). In the United States, money—in the form of both wealth and income—is very unevenly distributed. For example, in 1992, the wealthiest 20 percent of U.S. households received almost 50 percent of all income, whereas the poorest 20 percent of households received less than 4 percent of all income. The top 5 percent alone received 19 percent of all income—an amount greater than was received by the bottom 40 percent of all households. The difference becomes even more striking when one considers that the after-tax (spendable) income of the top 1 percent of U.S. families rose from $202,809 to $403,402 between 1977 and 1992, and the income of the bottom one-fifth fell from $8,495 in 1977 to $7,555 in 1992 (Fisher, 1992).

Income distribution also varies by race/ethnicity. In 1993, the median family income for African Americans was $21,232, as compared with $25,382 for Latinos/Latinas, $35,329 for whites, and $41,984 for Asian Americans and Pacific Islanders. Over half of African American (64 percent) and Latino/Latina (61.4 percent) households fall within the lowest two income categories; slightly over one-third (36.7 percent) of whites are in these categories (U.S. Bureau of the Census, 1994).

Across racial-ethnic lines, differences in the median income of married couples and female-headed households are striking. The proportion of children living in mother-only families increased from 8 percent in 1960 to 22 percent in 1996, and single parents account for half of all families earning less than $10,000 a year (Boroughs, 1996). Although most poor female-headed families are African American, about two out of every five poor female-headed families with children are white (Schein, 1995). Most poor single mothers and their children rely on income transfers such as AFDC and subsidized school-lunch programs for their economic survival. For those never married, poverty-level African American mothers in sociologist Robin L. Jarrett's study (Article 22), economic marginality is a long-term problem without easy resolution.

Two models—one cultural, the other structural—have been advanced to explain persistent poverty, especially among African Americans in central cities. As Jarrett (1994) explains, cultural explanations commonly assign the cause of poverty and the presence of a growing so-called underclass to *deviant values* that allegedly have contributed to changing African American household and family formation patterns. According to the cultural explanation, "ghetto-specific norms differ from their mainstream counterparts, positively endorsing single motherhood, out-of-wedlock childbearing, welfare dependency, male irresponsibility, criminal behavior, low mobility aspirations, and, more generally, family instability" (Jarrett, 1994:32). Accordingly, family breakdown locks central-city residents, especially unmarried mothers, in a cycle of poverty.

Unlike cultural explanations of poverty, structural perspectives argue that demographic shifts in household and family formation patterns reflect larger, *macrostructural economic transformation,* including the decline in entry-level jobs, the relocation of jobs away from the central city, and the mismatch between job requirements and employee skills. According to sociologist William J. Wilson (1987), poverty and all other central-city social problems are rooted in male joblessness. Wilson finds a direct relationship between the declining employment opportunities of African American men and the rapid growth of single-parent, female-headed households in the central city. Thus, a shortage of eligible African American men, brought about by declining economic conditions, impedes the construction and maintenance of mainstream family patterns and forces African American women to forego marriage, bear children out of wedlock, head their own households, and rely on welfare.

At the same time, women heads of households in central cities have few, if any, options for moving out of poverty, as organizational psychologist Virginia E. Schein explains:

> *Without the opportunity to earn an income sufficient to support a family, there is no way to move beyond poverty. An income opportunity is one that provides the possibility of earning a family wage with good benefits, offers a good chance of increased earnings over time, and has possibilities for growth in skills and advancement. (1995:123)*

According to sociologist William Kornblum (1991), African Americans who live in central cities do not lack family values; rather, they lack opportunities in the mainstream U.S. occupational structure. Respondents in Jarrett's (1994) study knew, for example, that they did not have the income opportunities, and most expressed a desire to return to school and acquire the necessary skills to get a steady job with a living wage, as compared to work that typically paid less than the cost for a babysitter and transportation to work. They also knew that economic factors contributed to their decision to forego marriage. Economic profiles of potential marital partners mirrored economic conditions in society in that the men frequently were unemployed, underemployed, or relegated to insecure jobs, such as car-wash attendants, fast-food clerks, and street peddlers in the *secondary labor market*—**the sector of the labor market that consists of low-paying jobs with few benefits and very little job security or possibility for future advancement.** By contrast, jobs in the *primary labor market* **are well paid with good benefits and have some degree of security and the possibility of future advancement.** Jobs in the primary labor market typically are held by white, middle- and upper-income individuals, primarily white Anglo-Saxon Protestant men.

For individuals and families at the bottom of the highly stratified U.S. class structure, class oppression diminishes *life chances*—**the extent to which persons within a particular layer of stratification have access to important scarce resources.** Persons with high income and/or substantial wealth have more control over their own lives. They have greater access to goods and services; they can afford better housing, more education, and a wider range of medical services. Persons with less income, especially those living in poverty, must spend their limited resources to acquire the basic necessities of life. Throughout U.S. history, discrimination based on race, class, and gender has exacerbated the problem of social inequality and oppression.

Discrimination

According to a report issued by the U.S. Commission on Civil Rights (1981), most people think of discrimination at the level of prejudiced individual attitudes and behavior. As previously defined, *prejudice* refers to a deep-seated belief that one's own racial-ethnic group is superior and should be privileged, while other groups are judged to be inferior and thus deserving of subordination or oppression. Although open and intentional prejudice persists in the United States, discriminatory behavior also may be hidden and sometimes unintentional.

Discrimination **refers to actions or practices of dominant group members (or their representatives) that have a harmful impact on members of a subordinate group.** Discrimination varies in how it is carried out: Individuals may act on their own or they may operate within the context of large-scale organizations and institutions, such as schools, churches, corporations, and governmental agencies. *Individual discrimination* **consists of one-on-one acts by members of the dominant group that harm members of the subordinate group or their property** (Carmichael and Hamilton, 1967). For example, a New York taxi driver may refuse to pick up African American passengers after dark or a white couple may cross a street to avoid walking past an African American college student. In Article 23, sociologist Joe R. Feagin documents individual discrimination perpetrated against middle-class African Americans while they were in the course of their daily activities in public places. By contrast, *institutional discrimination* **is the day-to-day practices of organizations and institutions that have a harmful impact on members of subordinate groups.** In Article 24, for example, sociologists Kathryn M. Neckerman and Joleen Kirschenman highlight how employers may use racially biased hiring strategies that negatively affect the employment chances of central-city African Americans. According to Neckerman and Kirschenman, employers may direct their recruitment efforts to white neighborhoods and avoid recruitment sources that would bring them a disproportionately central-city African American labor force. Job interviews and skills testing also may be used to screen out African American job applicants. Although institutional discrimination takes place in organizations, it is carried out by the individuals who implement the policies and procedures.

Four major types of discrimination have been identified:

1. *Isolate discrimination* is harmful action taken *intentionally* by a dominant group member against a member of a subordinate group. This type of discrimination occurs without the support of other members of the dominant group in the immediate social or community context. For example, a respondent in Feagin's (Article 23) study describes how a store proprietor in an "old, white neighborhood" would not sell a snowball (i.e., crushed ice covered with flavored syrup in a paper cone) to an African American man and his son unless they went to a little window outside the store where people could come up and order things while other (white) customers were served inside the store.

2. *Small-group discrimination* is harmful action *intentionally* taken by a limited number of dominant-group members who act together to injure or deny something to members of subordinate groups. This type of discrimination is not supported by existing norms or other dominant-group members in the immediate social or community context. For example, one of Feagin's (Article 23) respondents described a university student parade where a small group of white fraternity boys, who were waving a Confederate flag, yelled racist epithets as they passed a group of African American students watching the parade.

3. *Direct institutionalized discrimination* is an organizationally prescribed or community-prescribed action that *intentionally* has a differential and negative impact on members of subordinate groups. These actions are routinely carried out by a number of dominant-group members based on norms of the immediate organization or community context. Intentional exclusion of people of color from public accommodations is an example of this type of discrimination. In 1996, the death of Cynthia Wiggins, a 17-year-old African American woman, called attention to a practice of several malls in Buffalo, New York, whereby city buses (from the central city) were not allowed to make stops for passengers on mall property. Each day, Wiggins, a single mother, rode the bus for 50 minutes from her central-city neighborhood to work as a cashier at a fish and chips restaurant at the Walden Galleria Mall, located in a white suburb. One day, Wiggins was crossing the busy highway between the bus stop and the mall when she was hit by a 10-ton dump truck and subsequently died of her injuries (Barnes, 1996:33). According to Margaret Weir, a senior fellow at the Brookings Institution, the mall's practices are hardly unique:

> There is a tendency [for suburbs] to want to form separate localities so you can
> regulate who lives there and who shops there. . . . Communities can't do it by

racial restrictions because that's illegal. But they can do it through other rules and regulations. (quoted in Barnes, 1996:33)

Although many types of direct institutionalized discrimination are illegal, vestiges of such discrimination remain in hiring practices (see Article 24) and rejection actions, such as poor service in public accommodations (see Article 23).

4. *Indirect institutionalized discrimination* refers to practices that have a harmful impact on subordinate group members even though the organizational- or community-prescribed norms or regulations guiding these actions initially were established with no intent to harm. For example, in Article 24, Neckerman and Kirschenman suggest that job interviews routinely used by most employers may have a negative and differential impact on central-city African American applicants because such interviews are biased in favor of people who are friendly, articulate, and share common understandings of appropriate interaction and conversational style (i.e., shared culture) with prospective employers. According to Neckerman and Kirschenman, central-city African American job applicants with limited work experience and little familiarity with the white, middle-class world are likely to have difficulty in the typical job interview because they may have to justify a spotty work record or may find that misunderstanding and suspicion undermine rapport and hamper communication between the interviewer and the interviewee.

Discrimination at the organizational level cuts across class lines and affects middle-class and poverty-level African Americans alike. For example, credit policies of banks and lending institutions may prevent middle-class African Americans from acquiring mortgage monies and loans, as previously suggested by Oliver and Shapiro (1995) and Feagin and Sikes (1994). If there were no past-in-present forms of discrimination and if people of color had lived in the same neighborhoods as whites for decades, there would be no racially segregated minority neighborhoods that could be redlined and to which mortgage money could be denied on the basis of their being high-risk minority neighborhoods.

Similarly, in her analysis of African American professional women in Article 25, sociologist Elizabeth Higginbotham identified two factors—gender stereotypes and racial discrimination—that continue to contribute to the greater concentration of African American women in public, rather than private, sector employment. According to Higginbotham, more white women are able to move into the private sector—typically having higher-paid positions that offer more job security and opportunities for upward mobility—but African American women, even with advanced degrees, still struggle with racial discrimination and informal barriers to occupational advancement. African American women continue to be steered into training for traditionally female occupations and to be discouraged from attempting innovative careers. As a result, their professional training—often as teachers, social workers, nurses, or librarians—commonly keeps them dependent on the public sector for employment. In addition, rigid racial barriers limit their options in the private sector.

African American women trained in traditionally male-dominated fields are more likely to find jobs in the public sector where less racial bias tends to exist in hiring practices.

Social psychologist Philomena Essed (1991) refers to the interactive effect of racism and sexism in the exploitation of women of color as *gendered racism.* From this approach, jobs may be race typed and gender typed; high-paying primary sector jobs commonly are monopolized by middle- and upper-income white men, whereas people of color and most white women tend to hold jobs in the secondary sector of the labor market. Recall, for example, Article 15 in Part Two about elite boarding schools that suggested that "old boy" networks in business and education are built on years of friendship and social contact among white males that may begin in their boarding school days, continue in prestigious Ivy League colleges and universities, and follow them into careers and throughout life. According to a U.S. Commission on Civil Rights report:

> *Discrimination against minorities and women must now be viewed as an interlocking process involving the attitudes and actions of individuals and the organizations and social structures that guide individual behavior. That process, started by past events, now routinely bestows privileges, favors, and advantages on white males and imposes disadvantages and penalties on minorities and women. This process is also self-perpetuating. Many normal, seemingly neutral operations of our society create stereotyped expectations that justify unequal results, unequal results in one area foster inequalities in opportunity and accomplishments in others; the lack of opportunity and accomplishment confirms the original prejudices or engender new ones that fuel the normal operations generating unequal results. (1981:12)*

According to the commission report, no single factor is sufficient to explain the process of discrimination, and no single means will suffice to eliminate it. In Part Three, we will focus first on people's attempts to resist race, class, and gender oppression. Then we will examine several suggestions for lessening inequalities based on race, class, and gender in the next century.

Resistance and Social Change

When people think about discriminatory practices in U.S. society, many are overcome with a feeling of powerlessness regarding their ability to bring about social change. This concern is understandable; people are faced with systemic patterns of discrimination that maintain the power and privilege of dominant group members while perpetuating powerlessness and oppression of subordinate group members. Can people's actions make a difference? Should everyone be committed to improving racial-ethnic, class, and gender relations in the United States even if some people believe—either accurately or inaccurately—that they benefit from existing structures of inequality? At least four divergent viewpoints on the current state of racism, sexism, and class oppression in the United States can be identified.

The first perspective might be called *hyper-optimism* because this outlook assumes inequalities based on race, class, and gender largely have been vanquished (e.g., "Things are much better today than in the past"). Racism, sexism, and class inequalities are viewed as old problems that people continue to dredge up in an effort to keep affirmative action and social welfare programs alive.

A second perspective might be referred to as *hyper-pessimism* because this approach assumes no reduction in inequalities can ever occur because of white supremacy, capitalism, and/or patriarchy. This outlook assumes that race, class, and gender relations have become so divisive, polarized, and antagonistic that the only resolution is cultural nationalism and/or separatism. According to advocates of cultural nationalism, people of color can best promote their own interests through separation from the U.S. mainstream. From this perspective, African American and Latina/Latino communities should establish their own schools, businesses, and security forces to meet their own needs. Rooted in the Black Panther and Muslim movements of the 1960s and 1970s, cultural nationalism today is represented by spokespersons and organizations such as Louis Farrakhan and his Nation of Islam. Separatism is evidenced in African American immersion schools, for example, where students are taught about African American culture and heritage as well as techniques to overcome racial obstacles.

The issue of voluntary racial-ethnic separation of schools is not new. Late in the eighteenth century, for example, Boston's African American community first debated whether the educational interests of its children could be better served in separate institutions, as opposed to racially mixed schools (Brown, 1995). The separatism debate reemerged in the 1980s when some analysts suggested that the African American male is an endangered species (e.g., due to high rates of suicide and homicide) and thus in need of specialized instruction available only through separate classrooms or academies (Leavy, 1983). Although cities such as New York, Detroit, and Milwaukee operate schools that emphasize African American culture and heritage, enrollment is formally open to anyone in the respective school system who wishes to apply (Brown, 1995).

The issue of voluntary segregation of schools by gender also has been debated for many years. While critics argue that single-sex schools constitute gender-based discrimination, advocates of single-sex schools cite evidence that girls in single-sex schools have higher self-esteem, are more interested in nontraditional subjects such as science and math, and are less likely to stereotype jobs and careers by gender (Riordan, 1990; Hollinger, 1993). In regard to higher education, other studies have found that women's colleges help women develop self-confidence and assertiveness and attain more degrees in nontraditional fields such as economics, life science, physical science, and mathematics. Majors in these fields may lead to medical school or doctoral programs in the natural sciences, where women have been underrepresented for many years (see Tidball, 1985, 1986, 1989). By contrast, mixed results have been reported regarding all-male education. Although boys in single-sex schools appear to be more interested in nontraditional subjects such as literature and art (Hollinger,

1993), researchers also have found higher incidences of sexism among teachers and students in male-only schools (Lee, Marks, and Byrd, 1993).

A third perspective on the current state of racism and sexism might be thought of as *defensiveness*. Persons who hold this outlook tend to acknowledge that racism and sexism exist but feel that *they* had no part in producing such problems and thus have no responsibility for reducing oppression. Consider, for example, this letter from a student:

> *I have a question. I am a 19-year-old white male, and what I want to know is where I fit into all this? I have never been racist or sexist in my life, but I'm the bad guy? I know minorities and women have been discriminated against for centuries, but not by me!! So sometimes it bothers me that everyone assumes me (white males) as the criminal. I think there are better reasons to like (or dislike) people on a PERSONAL basis, because, either someone is nice or they are an ass, you know what I mean? (author's personal files)*

As this student suggests, he views racism and sexism as individual behavior that he had no part in, not as a *systemic problem* that requires societal change. According to some analysts, this outlook is based on *sincere fictions*—personal beliefs that are a reflection of larger societal mythologies, such as "I am not a racist" or "I have never discriminated against anyone," even when these are inaccurate perceptions (Feagin and Vera, 1995).

A final perspective on racism and sexism might be described as an approach that *calls for democracy, equality, and justice*. Individuals who advocate this viewpoint acknowledge the systemic nature of racism, sexism, and class inequalities but call for people to organize against oppression. In Article 26, journalism scholar Robert Jensen suggests that adoption of feminist theory can help both men and women understand the politics of their personal problems and come to terms with those problems:

> *Feminism provides an approach to society that allows women and men to better understand the world in which they live and to apply insights about gender to other struggles in life, both in the private and public spheres. (1995:116)*

According to Jensen, the abolition of patriarchy can only begin when men take feminism seriously and personally:

> *The primary goal of a feminist-based male identity politics is not just improving men's lives, but changing structures of power to end the oppression of women and children, as well as aid resistance to other forms of oppression in culture. (1995:123)*

Finally, bell hooks describes in Article 27 her hope for a *"beloved community*—where race would be transcended, forgotten, where no one would see skin color" (p. 263). According to hooks, people cannot give up on Martin Luther King's idea that a *beloved community* can be formed because "if we do we will never see an end to racism." hooks believes that hope for the future rests in small circles of love that people manage to form in their individual lives and that represent a concrete reminder that such a community is not impossible—that people can educate themselves for critical consciousness in ways that enable them to let go of white supremacist assumptions and values. She poses the question "Where do we go from here?" and responds:

> *To live in anti-racist society we must collectively renew our commitment to a democratic vision of racial justice and equality. Pursuing that vision we create a culture where* beloved community *flourishes and is sustained. . . .*
>
> *Like all* beloved communities *we affirm our differences. It is this generous spirit of affirmation that gives us the courage to challenge one another, to work through misunderstandings, especially those that have to do with race and racism. In a* beloved community *solidarity and trust are grounded in profound commitment to a shared vision. (pp. 271–272)*

As a new century approaches, do you think it would be possible to diminish racism, sexism, and class oppression in the United States? According to sociologist Stephen Steinberg, the United States has never had the political will to address issues until there is mounting pressure to do so:

> *This nation has never had the political will to address the legacy of slavery until forced by events to do so. As in the past, the catalyst for change will be "the mounting pressure" that emanates from those segments of the black society that have little reason to acquiesce in the racial status quo. It has yet to be seen exactly what form resistance and protest will take. . . .*
>
> *Our nation has chosen to canonize the Martin Luther King who, in his celebrated "I Have a Dream" oration, projected a racial nirvana in some indefinite future. But let us also remember the King who in the same speech said: "The whirlwinds of revolt will continue to shake the foundations of our nation until the bright day of justice emerges." (King, 1992; Steinberg, 1995:219–220)*

What do you think it might take to bring about a *beloved community* without invidious distinctions based on race, class, and gender inequalities in the United States?

References

Allen, Michael Patrick. 1987. *The Founding Fortunes: A New Anatomy of the Super-Rich Families in America*. New York: Dutton.

Allport, Gordon. 1958. *The Nature of Prejudice* (abridged ed.). New York: Doubleday/Anchor.

Anderson, Elijah. 1990. *Streetwise: Race, Class, and Change in an Urban Community*. Chicago: University of Chicago Press.

Barnes, Edward. 1996. "Can't Get There from Here." *Time* (February 19):33.

Beeghley, Leonard. 1989. *The Structure of Social Stratification in the United States.* Boston: Allyn and Bacon.

Benokraitis, Nijole V., and Joe R. Feagin. 1995. *Modern Sexism: Blatant, Subtle, and Covert Discrimination* (2nd ed.). Englewood Cliffs, NJ: Prentice Hall.

Blauner, Bob. 1989. *Black Lives, White Lives: Three Decades of Race Relations in America.* Berkeley: University of California Press.

Blauner, Robert. 1972. *Racial Oppression in America.* New York: Harper and Row.

Boroughs, Don L. 1996. "Winter of Discontent." *U.S. News and World Report* (January 22):47–54.

Brown, Kevin. 1995. "African-American Immersion Schools: Paradoxes of Race and Public Education," in Richard Delgado (Ed.), *Critical Race Theory: The Cutting Edge* (pp. 373–386). Philadelphia: Temple University Press.

Carmichael, Stokely, and Charles V. Hamilton. 1967. *Black Power: The Politics of Liberation on American Education.* New York: Random House.

Essed, Philomena. 1991. *Understanding Everyday Racism.* Newbury Park, CA: Sage.

Feagin, Joe R., and Clairece Booher Feagin. 1996. *Racial and Ethnic Relations* (5th ed.). Upper Saddle River, NJ: Prentice Hall.

_____ , and Melvin P. Sikes. 1994. *Living with Racism: The Black Middle-Class Experience.* Boston: Beacon Press.

_____ , and Hernan Vera. 1995. *White Racism: The Basics.* New York: Routledge.

Fisher, Anne B. 1992. "The New Debate Over the Very Rich." *Fortune* (June 29):42–54.

Frye, Marilyn. 1983. *The Politics of Reality.* Trumansburg, NY: The Crossing Press.

Hollinger, Debra (Ed.). 1993. *Single-Sex Schooling: Perspectives from Practice and Research.* Washington, DC: Office of Educational Research and Improvement, Department of Education.

Jarrett, Robin L. 1994. "Living Poor: Family Life among Single Parent, African-American Women." *Social Problems,* 41(1):30–49.

Jensen, Robert. 1995. "Men's Lives and Feminist Theory." *Race, Gender, and Class,* 2(2):111–125.

King, Martin Luther, Jr. 1992. *I Have a Dream: Writing and Speeches that Changed the World.* Edited by James Melvin Washington (p. 103). New York: HarperCollins.

Kornblum, William. 1991. "Who Is the Underclass?" *Dissent* 38(Spring):202–211.

Leavy, Walter. 1983. "Is The Black Man an Endangered Species?" *Ebony* (August):41.

Lee, Valeria, Helen Marks, and Tina Byrd. 1993. "Sexism in Single-Sex and Coeducational Secondary School Classrooms," *Sociology of Education* (July).

Miliband, Ralph. 1989. *Divided Societies: Class Struggle in Contemporary Capitalism.* Oxford: Oxford University Press.

Odendahl, Teresa. 1990. *Charity Begins at Home: Generosity and Self-Interest among the Philanthropic Elite.* New York: Basic Books.

Oliver, Melvin L., and Thomas M. Shapiro. 1995. *Black Wealth/White Wealth: A New Perspective on Racial Inequality.* New York: Routledge.

Riordan, Cornelius. 1990. *Girls and Boys in School: Together or Separate.* New York: Teachers College, Columbia University.

Rothchild, John. 1995. "Wealth: Static Wages, Except for the Rich." *Time* (January 30):60–61.

Schein, Virginia E. 1995. *Working from the Margins: Voices of Mothers in Poverty.* Ithaca, NY: Cornell University Press.

Steinberg, Stephen. 1995. *Turning Back: The Retreat from Racial Injustice in American Thought and Policy.* Boston: Beacon Press.

Tidball, Elizabeth. 1985. "Baccalaureate Origins of Entrants into Medical Schools." *Journal of Higher Education,* 56(4):385–401.

_____ . 1986. "Baccalaureate Origins of Recent Natural Science Doctorates." *Journal of Higher Education,* 57(6):606–620.

_____ . 1989. "Women's Colleges: Exceptional Conditions, Not Exceptional Talent, Produce High Achievers," in Carol Pearson, Donna Shavlik, and Judith Touchton (Eds.), *Educating the Majority: Women Challenge Tradition in Higher Education.* New York: Macmillan.

U.S. Bureau of the Census. 1994. "How We're Changing." *Current Population Reports, Special Studies,* Series P-23, No. 188 (December). Washington, DC: U.S. Government Printing Office.

U.S. Commission on Civil Rights. 1981. "The Problem: Discrimination." *Affirmative Action in the 1980's,* 65(January):9–15. Washington, DC: U.S. Government Printing Office.

Wilson, William J. 1987. *The Truly Disadvantaged: The Inner City, The Underclass, and Public Policy.* Chicago: University of Chicago Press.

ARTICLE 20 _____

In this article, author Rita Chaudhry Sethi examines racism directed against Asian Americans and explains why some whites and other persons of color often do not believe that Asian Americans have been the objects of racial victimization. According to Sethi, a more inclusive paradigm is needed for analysis of the experiences of Asian Americans, particularly South Asians. She notes that Asian Americans may be discriminated against on the basis of accents, subversive stereotyping, perceived religious fanaticism, and other cultural beliefs and practices that allegedly differ from those of dominant racial-ethnic group members.

Looking Ahead

1. How does racial discrimination against Asian Americans differ from that perpetrated against members of other racial-ethnic subordinate groups?
2. Why are racism and economic tension intertwined in the experiences of many Asian Americans?
3. What does the case study of the Dotbusters of Jersey City say about the current state of racial-ethnic relations in the United States?

Smells Like Racism

A Plan for Mobilizing against Anti-Asian Bias

◆ *Rita Chaudhry Sethi*

When I started my first job after college, Steve Riley, an African American activist, asked me: "So, how do you feel being black?" I confessed, "I am not black." "In America," Steve responded, "if you're not white, you're black."

U.S. discourse on racism is generally framed in these simplistic terms: the stark polarity of black/white conflict. As it is propagated, it embraces none of the true complexities of racist behavior. Media sensationalism, political expedience, intellectual laziness, and legal constraints conspire to narrow the scope of cognizable racism. What remains is a pared-down image of racism, one that delimits the definition of its forms, its perpetrators, and, especially, its victims. Divergent experiences are only included in the hierarchy of racial crimes when they sufficiently resemble the caricature. Race-based offenses that do not conform to this model are permitted to exist and fester without

Source: From "Smells Like Racism" by Rita Chaudhry Sethi, pp. 235–250, in Karin Guillar-San Juan (Ed.), *The State of Asian America: Activism and Resistance in the 1990s.* Copyright © 1994 by Karin Guillar-San Juan. Reprinted with permission from the publisher, South End Press, 116 Saint Botolph Street, Boston, MA 02115.

remedy by legal recourse, collective retribution, or even moral indignation.

Asians' experiences exist in the penumbra of actionable racial affronts. Our cultural, linguistic, religious, national, and color differences do not, as one might imagine, form the basis for a modified paradigm of racism; rather, they exist on the periphery of offensiveness. The racial insults we suffer are usually trivialized; our reactions are dismissed as hypersensitivity or regarded as a source of amusement. The response to a scene where a Korean-owned store is being destroyed with a bat in the 1993 film, *Falling Down* (a xenophobic and racist diatribe on urban life)[1] reflects how mainstream America/American culture responds to the phenomenon of anti-Asian violence:

> There was, in the theater where I saw the film, a good deal of appreciative laughter and a smattering of applause during this scene, which of course flunks the most obvious test of comparative racism: imagine a black or an Orthodox Jew, say, in that Korean's place and you imagine the theater's screen being ripped from the walls. Asians, like Arabs, remain safe targets for the movies' casual racism.[2]

The perpetuation of the caricature of racism is attributable to several complex and symbiotic causes. First, Asians often do not ascribe racist motivation to the discrimination they suffer, or they have felt that they could suffer the injustice of racial intolerance, in return for being later compensated by the fruits of economic success. Second, many Asians do not identify with other people of color. Sucheta Mazumdar posits that South Asians exclude themselves from efforts at political mobilization because of their rigid self-perception as Aryan, not as people of color.[3]

The final and most determinative factor, however, is the perspective that excludes the experiences of Asians (and other people of color) from the rubric of racism. Whites would deny us our right to speak out against majority prejudice, partially because it tarnishes their image of Asians as "model" minorities; other people of color would deny us the same because of monopolistic sentiments that they alone endure real racism.

For example, a poll conducted by *The Wall Street Journal* and NBC News revealed that "most American voters thought that Asian Americans did not suffer discrimination" but in fact received too many "special advantages."[4] Similarly, when crimes against Asians were on the rise in housing projects in San Francisco, the Housing Authority was loathe to label the crimes as racially motivated, despite the clear racial bias involved.[5] The Deputy Director of the Oakland Housing Authority's response to the issue was: "There may be some issues of race in it, but it's largely an issue of people who don't speak English feeling very isolated and not having a support structure to deal with what's happening to them."[6]

Other minorities reject Asian claims of racial victimization by pointing to economic privilege or perceived whiteness.[7] Such rejections even occur among different Asian groups. Chinese Americans in San Francisco attempted to classify Indians as white for the purposes of the California Minority Business Enterprise Statute: "If you are a white, male buyer in the City, all else being equal, would you buy from another Caucasian [i.e. Indian] or from a person of the Mongolian race?"[8]

The perspective of some people of color that there is a monopoly on oppression is debilitating to an effort at cross-ethnic coalition building. Our experiences are truly distinct, and our battles will in turn be unique; but if we are to achieve a community, we must begin to educate ourselves about our common denominator as well as our different histories and struggles. Ranking and diminishing relative subjugation and discrimination will only subvert our goal of unity.

Naheed Islam expresses this sentiment in part of a poem addressed to African American women:

> *Ah Sister! What have they done to us! Separated, segregated, unable to love one another, to cross the color line. I am not trying to cash in on your chains. I have my own. The rape, plunder, pain of dislocation is not yours alone. We have different histories, different voices, different ways of expressing our anger, but they used the same bullets to reach us all.*[9]

The combination of white America refusing to acknowledge anti-Asian discrimination, and minority America minimizing anti-Asian discrimination foists a formidable burden upon Asians: to combat our own internalized racial alienation, and to fight extrinsic racial classifications by both whites and other minority groups. It also renders overly simplistic those suggestions that if South Asians simply became "sufficiently politicized" they could overcome fragmentation in the struggle by people of color.[11]

As activists, a narrow-minded construct of racism impairs our political initiatives to use racism as a banner that unites all people of color in a common struggle.[10] The mainstream use of the word "racism" does not embrace Asian experiences, and we are not able to include ourselves in a definition that minimizes our encounters with racism. Participation in an anti-racism campaign, therefore, is necessarily limited to those involved in a battle against racism that fits within the confines of the black/white paradigm, and conversely relegates anti-Asian racism to a lesser realm in terms of both exposure and horribleness.

We need to be more sophisticated in our analysis of racism, and less equivocal in our condemnation. In doing so, we will expand the base of opposition against anti-Asian racism, and forge an alliance against all its myriad forms. The first step in this process is for Asians to apply a racial analysis to our lives. This involves developing a greater understanding of how racism has operated socially and institutionally in this country against ourselves and other people of color, as well as acknowledging our own complicity; and secondly, accepting ourselves as people of color, with a shared history of being targeted as visibly Other. Only then can we act in solidarity with other efforts at ending racism.

ANTI-ASIAN RACISM: FASHIONING A MORE INCLUSIVE PARADIGM

Racism takes on manifold creative and insidious expressions. Intra-racism, racism among different racial communities, and internalized racism all complicate an easy understanding of the phenomenon. My project here is to uncover shrouded racism perpetrated against Asians, particularly South Asians, in an attempt to broaden the use of the term.

Accent

It is only since 1992 that the Courts have begun to realize the legitimacy of discrimination based upon accent.[12] Immigrants, primarily those not of European descent,[13] suffer heightened racism because of their accents, including job discrimination and perpetual taunting and caricaturization. This is a severe and pervasive form of racism that is often not acknowledged as racist, or even offensive. Even among Asians there is a high degree of denial about the accent discrimination that is attributable to race. In a letter to the *New York Times,* an Asian man blithely encouraged immigrants to maintain their accents, without acknowledging the potential discrimination that we face, though he personally was "linguistically gifted" with an "American accent." The man wrote, "Fellow immigrants, don't worry about the way you speak until Peter Jennings eliminates his Canadian accent."[14]

Accent discrimination is linked directly to American jingoism, and its accompanying virulently anti-immigrant undertones. In the aforementioned movie *Falling Down*, the protagonist has the following exchange with a Korean grocer:

Mr. Lee: Drink eighty-five cent. You pay or go.
Foster: This "fie." I don't understand a "fie." There's a "v" in the word. It's "fie-vah." You don't got "v's" in China?
Mr. Lee: Not Chinese. I'm Korean.
Foster: Whatever. You come to my country, you take my money, you don't even have the grace to learn my language?[15]

A person's accent is yet another symbol of otherness, but it is one that even U.S.-born minorities do not regard as a target for race-based discrimination. Language is implicitly linked with race, and must be treated as such.

Subversive Stereotyping

The myths that are built based on the commonality of race are meant to depersonalize and simplify people. To many, the Indian Persona is that of a greedy, unethical, cheap immigrant. This stereotype is reflected in popular culture, where its appearance gives it credibility, thereby reinforcing the image. In the television comedy, *The Simpsons,* a purportedly politically sensitive program, one of the characters is a South Asian owner of a convenience store. In one episode, in an effort to make a sale, he says, "I'll sell you expired baby food for a nickel off." Similarly, in the program, *Star Trek: Deep Space Nine,* an alien race called the Firengi (Hindi for Foreigner) are proprietors and sleazy entrepreneurs who take advantage of any opportunity for wealth, regardless of the moral cost.[16]

These constructs are reified in everyday life as people respond to Indians as if they have certain inherent qualities. Indian physicians, for example, are perceived as shoddy practitioners, who are greedy and disinterested in the health of their patients. In successful medical malpractice suits, Indian doctors are routinely required to pay higher penalties.[17] Similarly, in the now-famous "East Side Butcher" case, where an Indian doctor was convicted of performing illegal abortions, there was no racial analysis despite the fact that no one had been prosecuted for that crime in New York State since the early 1980s despite the fact that hundreds of illegal abortions are performed annually.[18] Another Indian doctor, less than two weeks later, was found guilty of violations in her mammography practice and fined the largest amount in New York State history in such a case. One can not help but wonder if these convictions were, at least in part, motivated by the stereotype of the Indian immigrant.[19]

The Onus

A white, liberal woman once asked my friend Ritu if she wasn't being overly sensitive for taking offense when people put their feet near her face (a high insult in Indian culture), when she could not fairly expect people to understand her culture. The onus is always on us, as outsiders, to explain and justify our culture while also being expected to know and understand majority culture.[20] Constant cultural slights about cows, bindis and Gandhi are deemed appropriate by the majority while we are expected to subjugate expression of our culture to an understanding and acceptance of American culture. As another example, the swastika is an extremely common, ancient Hindu symbol. However, Hindus cannot wear or display the swastika in America because of Hitler's appropriation of it, and the expectation that we suppress our cultural symbols in an attempt to understand the affront to Jewish Americans. The assumption that it is our normative responsibility to make our culture secondary is racist because it suggests that one culture should be more free to express itself than another.

Religious Fanaticism

Eastern religions are commonly perceived as fraudulent, cultish, and fanatical; they are rarely perceived as equally legitimate as the spiritual doctrines of the Judeo-Christian tradition. The story of immaculate conception is accepted as plausible, while the multi-armed, multi-headed God is an impossible fantasy. Hinduism is portrayed as Hare Krishnas chanting with shaved heads and orange robes; and Islam is characterized as a rigid, violent, military religion. These hyperbolic characterizations are responsible for the fear of religion that causes local communities to refuse to permit places of worship in their neighborhoods.[21]

Western appropriation of Hindu terms reflects the perception of religion as charlatanical; the words have been reshaped through their use in the English language with an edge of irreverence or disbelief.

	Hindu Meaning	*English Use*
1. Guru	Religious teacher	Purported head; self-designated leader
2. Nirvana	Freedom from endless cycle of rebirth	Psychedelic ecstasy; drug-induced high
3. Pundit	Religious scholar	One with claimed knowledge
4. Mantra	A meditative tool; repetition of word or phrase	Mindless chant

Similarly, during times of political crisis (the 1991 Persian Gulf War; the February 1993 World Trade Center bombing), Islam has been the object of derision as a dangerous and destructive religion. After the suspects from the World Trade Center bombing were identified as Muslims, the media, the FBI and mainstream America responded with gross anti-Muslim rhetoric. A Professor in Virginia pointed out the ignorant conflation of the entire Muslim population into one extremist monolith:

> *Not all Islamic revivalists are Islamic fundamentalists, and not all Islamic fundamentalists are political activists, and not all Islamic political activists are radical and prone to violence.*[22]

Muslims have linked these characteristics of their religion to racial demonization.[23] *The Post* carried a headline entitled "The Face of Hate" with the face of a dark-skinned, bearded man of South Asian or Middle Eastern descent (the accused bomber). Similarly, the *New York Times* described the work of courtroom artists: "the defendant's beakish nose, hollow cheeks, cropped beard and the sideways tilt of his head."[24] In an Op-Ed piece in the *New York Times,* one Muslim responded to this description: "Such racial stereotyping serves nothing except to feed an existing hate and fear."[25]

Indicia of Culturalness

Indicia that identify us as other are generally used as vehicles for discrimination; with East Asians, eye-shape provides the target for racial harassment. South Asians' unique attributes are warped for use as racist artillery: attire (we are towel heads and wear loin cloths and sheets); costume (we are dotheads); and odor (we are unclean and smelly).

◆ ◆ ◆

When we explore racism, and its effect upon different ethnic and cultural groups, we must also examine the unique ways that specific groups experience racism, and the more neutral proxies and buzzwords used to signify race.

Class Conflicts/Economic Envy

Racism and economic tension are inextricable because race discrimination against Asians has often been manifested as class competition, and vice versa. Since the early 1800s, when Asians became a source of cheap labor for the railroads, we have been an economic threat. As Asians have more recently been portrayed as the prosperous minority, the favored child of America, there has inevitably been sibling rivalry. When auto workers beat up Vincent Chin, was it Japanese competition in the auto industry or unbridled racism that motivated the murderers? When African-Americans targeted Korean-owned stores in the riots in Los Angeles after the Rodney King verdict, was it the economic hardship of the inner city and perceived Asian advantages or was it simply racism? The answer is that race and class are inseparable because of the inherent difficulty in identifying the primary or motivating factor; any racial analysis must consider economic scapegoating as an avenue for racial harassment and racial victimization as an excuse for expressing economic tensions.

Conceptual and Perspective Differences

When an immigrant perspective clashes with a white American perpsective, the conflict should be considered a racial one. Values such as individuality, privacy, confrontation, competition, and challeling the status quo are considered positive and healthy; however, these components of the liberal state are not necessarily virtues elsewhere. When Hawaiian children do not respond to competitive models of teaching, but thrive in group activities; and when Punjabi children defer to authority, rather than challenge their teachers out of intellectual "curiosity," they are harmed by their inability to function in an essentially and uniquely "American" world. Identifying the differences in perspective and lifestyle between Asian immigrants and Americans will help in recognizing arenas in which we will be at a cultural/racial disadvantage.[26]

A Case Study in Anti-Asian Racism: The Dotbusters of Jersey City

In early fall of 1986, Asian Indians in New Jersey were the targets of racial terrorism. Houses and businesses were vandalized, and graffitied with racial slurs, women had their saris pulled, Indians on the street were harassed and assaulted, and a 28-year-old man was beaten into a coma. The *Jersey Journal* received and printed a letter from a group calling themselves the Dotbusters threatening all Asian Indians in Jersey City, and promising to drive them out of Jersey City. Teenagers in Dickinson High School were found with Dotbuster IDs. In spite of the obvious danger to the community, the police were unresponsive and denied that any Indians should truly be concerned.

The most heinous incident was the murder of Navroze Mody, a 30-year-old Citicorp executive. Navroze was bludgeoned to death with bricks by a group of young Latinos. Long after he had lost consciousness, he was repeatedly propped up and beaten further. His white companion was not touched. Four of the eleven attackers were indicted for manslaughter; two of the indicted were also accused of assaulting two Indian students two weeks before killing Navroze.

Despite the context in which the murder occurred, the incident was not generally perceived as racist in motive by the mainstream, the press, or the Indian community. The ways that Indians were targeted made it convenient to try to find other names for their encounters with racism. Their experiences were unrecognizable as the caricature of racism, and there was a collective refusal to be expansive and open-minded in interpreting what was happening.

The tone for the general characterization of the crime as not racially motivated was set by Hudson County Prosecutor, Paul DePascale, assigned to Mody's case. Although he conceded that: "There was no apparent motive for the assault other than the fact that the victim was an Asian American,"[27] he refused to pursue criminal charges for racial bias.[28]

The press, a reflection of mainstream sentiment, was reluctant to label the crime as racial in nature. Even the *Village Voice,* a liberal newspaper, carried a story asking above the headline: "Was his [Navroze Mody's] murder racially motivated?"[29] One newspaper accepted the racial motive by qualifying it as a "new" racism/"new" bigotry. The defendants' supporters saw no racial animus against Indians in the crime, inquiring instead: "Do you think there would be justice if it was the other way around? If the Indian were alive and the Puerto Rican dead?"[30]

Indians-at-large were mystified about the source of the anti-Asian wave of violence and found it difficult to accept as pure racism. People looked for other potential justifications and alternative labels.[31] One community leader remarked, "We pay our taxes," and characterized the Indian community as "faultless immigrants" in an effort to distinguish Asian Indians from African Americans and Latinos.[32] A second-generation Indian lawyer characterized such attacks as "national origin" discrimination, rather than racism.[33] Such denial prevented Asian Indians from making the obvious connection to other groups victimized because of their race.

The uncommonness of the anti-Indian discrimination obfuscated the real racism that rested at its core. Economic envy was the most obvious non-racial analysis proffered for escalating crimes against Asians. One Jersey City resident commented: "I've been in this country all my life and they come here and plop down $200,000 for a house."[34] Part of the infamous Dotbuster letter contained similar comments to journalist Ronald Leir: "You say that Indians are good businessmen. Well I suppose if I had 15 people living in my apartment I'd be able to save money too."[35]

Another major source of attack was traditional Indian attire. According to one community leader: "The number two factor for racism is that we look different."[36] Similarly, the hate group, the Dotbusters, takes its name from the cosmetic dot, or bindi, worn by many Indian women on their foreheads.

Finally, Indian languages and residential clustering create a sense of exclusive cohesiveness that threatens Jersey City's non-Asian communities. Anything that represented the insular-seeming culture was the object of harassment and hatred. Indian religion and cuisine were mocked, and Indians were repeatedly characterized as smelly (due to the lingering scents of cooking spice).

Despite the heinousness of the crime, the Mody case, and anti-Indian violence, did not receive sufficient public attention or outrage. During the same time that the case was being tried, the Howard Beach case[37] was in the headlines of all major newspapers. Of the four Howard Beach attackers, three received manslaughter convictions; of the eleven attackers in the Mody case, three were convicted of aggravated assault, and one of simple assault. Perhaps it was because Asian Indians did not know how to employ the political system that the verdicts returned did not fit the crimes committed. Perhaps it was because the attackers were also minorities.

But the main reason why justice was not served was because the racism that Indians were enduring did not fit the neat, American paradigm for racial violence.

. . . We can no longer see the world in black and white, where "those who don't fit the color scheme become shadows."[38] Lessons from our battles with bigotry should convince us that our understanding of it and the machinery we have built to fight it are hopelessly obsolete. Denying the richness of our community of people of color ultimately undermines the objective of unity, and hampers our political work combatting racism. During the late '80s, the left fought to find a common ground for people of color to coalesce; however, it is now the time to refine our collective mission to truly encompass the range of diversity among us. Any movement forged upon the principles of equality and tolerance can only be legitimate if it represents its margins.

NOTES

1. While the film generated much debate about the possible ironic intent of its stereotyping, the reactions of moviegoers showed that the irony was lost on most audiences.

2. Godfrey Cheshire, complete citation for article not available.

3. Mazumdar, Sucheta, "Race and Racism: South Asians in the United States" *Frontiers of Asian American Studies.*

4. Polner, Murray, "Asian-Americans Say They Are Treated Like Foreigners," *The New York Times,* March 7, 1993, Section B, p. 1.

5. Racial slurs were rampant (including "Go home, Chinaman" and accent harassment) and tension between the Asian and African American community was worsening. The fact that the perpetrators were African American might have contributed to the general reluctance to characterize these crimes as racially motivated. Again, this reflects an inability, or an unwillingness, to intellectually digest racism between non-white races, as it falls outside of the narrow black/white paradigm.

6. Chin, Steven A. "Asians Terrorized in Housing Projects" *San Francisco Examiner,* January 17, 1993, B1.

7. Witness this morsel of divisiveness: In Miami, where large Latino and African American populations co-exist, a Cuban woman was sworn in as State Attorney General. Many in the African American community were dismayed by this decision, and responded by stripping Cubans of their "rank" as a minority. One black lawyer commented: "Cubans are really 'white people whose native language is Spanish' and others agreed that Cuban Americans should be "disqualified because they have higher income levels than other minorities." Certainly there is complexity in this conflict; however, the net result is that people who could be in alliance based on race are divided. Rohter, Larry. "Black-Cuban Rift Extends to Florida Law School" *The New York Times;* March 19, 1993; B16L.

8. Transcript of San Francisco Board of Supervisors Special Session of Economic and Social Policy Committee April 30, 1991.

9. Islam, Naheed. "Untitled" from *Smell This,* an official publication of The Center for Racial Education, Berkeley, CA 1991.

10. Here, and throughout my chapter, I am operating within the constructs of our existing political reality. I am not addressing the normative question of whether people of color should be in coalition against racism, but given that it has been our primary organizing principle, how can we be more effective and inclusive?

11. Mazumdar, *supra* at p. 36.

12. Interestingly, the case was brought by the EEOC while under the tenure of Joy Cherian, a naturalized Indian. The Commission's 1980 guidelines covering this type of discrimination were written by an Indian, and the case was brought by an Indian plaintiff. Is that what it takes to obtain recognition of the racism that we experience?

13. The Executive Assistant for the Commissioner noted: "If an employer has an applicant who speaks with a French accent . . . or with an English accent, they say, 'How cute.' But if he speaks with a Hispanic accent they say, 'What's wrong with this guy?'"

14. Letter to the editor from Yan Hong Krompacky. "Immigrants, Don't Be In Such a Hurry to Shed Your Accents." *The New York Times,* March 4, 1993.

15. Foster then proceeds to demolish Mr. Lee's grocery store with a bat, in much the same way that Japanese cars were hatefully demolished just before Vincent Chin's death.

16. That such stereotypes exist in two programs that are perceived as being among the more progressive on television is itself indicative of the continuing denial that anti-Asian racism exists.

17. According to several medical malpractice attorneys.

18. This was exacerbated further by the fact that Dr. Hayat's sentence was so severe that even the District Attorney's Office had expected less and was "pleasantly surprised." Perez-Pena, Richard, "Prison Term for Doctor Convicted in Abortions" *The New York Times,* June 15, 1993, p. B1.

19. These stereotypes find expression everywhere. I was haggling for a pair of earrings in Times Square, and the vendor asked me if I was Indian. When I replied that I was, he responded, "Oh, I should have guessed. Indians don't want to take anything out of their pockets."

20. In an effort to better integrate into American culture, and mend relations with ethnic groups in New York City, Korean grocers are taking seminars to learn to smile more frequently, supposedly rare in their culture. *The New York Times,* March 22, 1993.

21. "It's the Hindus! Circle the Zoning Laws." Viewpoint by Bob Weiner, *Newsday,* April 26, 1993, p. 40.

22. Steinfeld, Peter. "Many Varieties of Fundamentalism." *The New York Times,* no date. An even better response was: [the World Trade bomber suspects's] "variety of fundamentalism was not any more representative of Islam than the people in Waco are representative of [mainstream] Christianity." *Id.*

23. Op Ed Letter to Editor "Don't Let Trade Center Blast Ignite Witch Hunt," March 23, 1993.

24. "Surprises in a Crowded Courtroom," Moustafa Bayamai, March 5, 1993.

25. *Ibid.*

26. Many Asians find themselves in low-ranking jobs in the corporate world because their skills have little application in the old boy cultural network. This is due in part to different concepts of authority and competition, as much as it is pure racial bigotry. My point is that the two should be viewed together to truly understand the full flourish of racism.

27. Vicente, Raul Jr., "Cops Arrest Two As Dotbusters." *Gold Coast,* March 24–March 31, 1988, p. 4.

28. His failure to label this as a racially-motivated crime may in fact be racially motivated. In March of 1988 there was opposition by Inter Departmental Minority Police Action Council in Jersey City to his appointment as city's acting police director because of alleged discrimination against a black woman officer. "Minority Cops Blast Director," *Gold Coast,* March 31, 1988, p. 7.

29. "Racial Terror on The Gold Coast" *The Village Voice,* January 26, 1988.

30. *Jersey Journal,* 3/1/88.

31. The collective denial precluded group solutions. Around the same time in Elmhurst 25 African American and Indian families were "preyed" upon in Queens. However, Indians were uninterested in forging an alliance with the African American community to fight ongoing racial harassment. Pais, Arthur, "Long Island Families Were Apathetic and Tearful When Harassed," *India Abroad,* July 31, 1987, p. 1.

32. Walt, Vivienne, "A New Racism Gets Violent in New Jersey," *Newsday,* 4/6/88, p. 5.

33. Spoken at the Strategy Session for the case of Dr. Kaushal Sharan, March 28, 1993, by a representative of the *Indian American Magazine.*

34. Walt, Vivienne, "A New Racism Gets Violent in New Jersey," *Newsday,* 4/6/88, p. 5.

35. Letter to *Jersey Journal* on August 5, 1987.

36. Walt, Vivienne, "A New Racism Gets Violent in New Jersey," *Newsday,* p. 5.

37. 1986 attack by white youths in Queens where a group of African Americans were stranded; one person died when he was chased onto a highway by the mob.

38. Zia, Helen, "Another American Racism," *The New York Times* letter to the editor.

Questions for Understanding and Critical Thinking

1. Why does Sethi argue that people must no longer see the world in terms of merely black and white?

2. What examples does Sethi give of how media, especially films and television programs, may get away with stereotyping Asian Americans in a manner that would be unacceptable if similar images were directed against other persons of color?

3. Why does Sethi argue that, when an immigrant perspective clashes with a white American perspective, the conflict should be considered a racial one?

ARTICLE 21 _____

Sociologist Carol Brooks Gardner's research focuses on gender, public harassment, and crime. For over a decade, she has documented the many types of indignity visited on white women and other situationally disadvantaged people—including persons of color and persons with disabilities—in public places in the United States. In this article, Gardner shows how women are oppressed by discrimination in public places and the kinds of advice they receive about crime prevention.

Carol Brooks Gardner is associate professor of sociology and women's studies at Indiana University, Indianapolis. Her research interests include sex and gender, community and urban sociology, and sociology of mental health.

Looking Ahead

1. How are public places different for women than for men?
2. What is the *situated self* and how is it related to communication in public places?
3. What strategies do women employ to achieve safety in public places?
4. How are women (and their acquaintances) affected by measures women believe they must employ to prevent harassment and criminal victimization?

Safe Conduct

Women, Crime, and Self in Public Places

◆ *Carol Brooks Gardner*

Women have different experiences in public places than do men, particularly when they appear alone. Belying the U.S. middle-class ideal of an egalitarian etiquette for public places (Goffman 1963, 1971), analysis of actual contact shows that public places are dotted with contacts that envince judgments of status and discrimination no less finely tuned and expressive than those envinced in private regions (Gardner 1980, 1983, 1988).

Although many social categories receive treatment in public places demonstrably different from those expected norms of middle-class etiquette (people with disabilities, children, gay people, and ethnic minorities are among these), the situation of women in public is striking. Women may have made considerable progress in occupation, education, and home life; yet, in public places they are regularly subject to inferior treat-

Source: From Carol Brooks Gardner, "Safe Conduct: Women, Crime, and Self in Public Places: Elite Education and Social Reproduction." © 1990 by the Society for the Study of Social Problems. Reprinted from *Social Problems*, Vol. 37, No. 3, August 1990, pp. 311–328, by permission.

ment by men in the form, for instance, of catcalls, evaluative "compliments," and verbal contacts that subtly go astray when gender, not the business at hand, becomes a topic (Gardner 1980, 1983, 1988, 1989).

Besides these routine ways that women can experience public places differently from men, there is the more dramatic case of crime in public. Researchers remark that, though men experience crime in higher numbers, women report greater fear of crime (Balkin 1979; Brown, Flanagan, McLeod 1984; Clemente and Kleiman 1977; Dubow 1979; Riger and Gordon 1981). The place of gender-role expectations in this difference is crucial (Hindelang, Gottfredson, and Garofalo 1978; Janoff-Bulman and Frieze 1987; Maxfield 1984). In public, fear of rape is a cardinal fear for women (Riger and Gordon 1981), since public places are the sites for most stranger rape (Ledray 1986). Women are never sure which of a man's activities are precursors to rape or other crime, and commonly class together any public harassment with public harassment preceding rape or other crimes (Grahame 1985; Kelly 1987). Popular advice and folk wisdom also can influence women's conduct in public, the way the are perceived, or the way they perceive themselves (Heath 1984; Brunvand 1981; Wachs 1988). Women's alleged responsibility for their own victimization has led them to define part of their task as "becoming streetwise," "taking necessary precautions," and "preventing crime" (S. Edwards 1987; Radford 1987).[1]

In this paper, I discuss the character of advice to women with regard to crime prevention in public and the character of women's beliefs about crime-preventive behavior. My goal is conjecture about women's situation. In addition to my own experience, I use two types of empirical materials to illustrate this essay: first, a review of the popular literature about crime prevention for women written in the last twenty years; and second, a set of 25 in-depth interviews with women about crime in public. I argue that the nature of both advice and experience is importantly related to possibilities for communication in public places in U.S. culture generally. For women, both advice and experience combine to affect the particular incarnation of the self appropriate to the situation of being in public places—a socially situated self, as Goffman defines it (1963:112).

This situated self appropriate to public places is supported, in addition to other elements, by various sets of strategies of presentation and impression management that may be thought of as rhetorics (Ball 1967). A rhetoric, sociologically speaking is a "vocabulary of limited purpose," whose set of symbols communicates a particular set of meanings directed and arranged to present a specific impression. These vocabularies are visual and verbal, and they may appeal to other senses as well (Ball 1967:296). Such a rhetoric serves to legitimize and neutralize what otherwise might be seen as deviant (Ball 1967). In particular, women who wish to prevent crime in public are encouraged to take up a typical rhetoric that imputes limited competence. Correspondingly, the situated self they are encouraged to present is characterized by this rhetoric, which connotes ineptness rather than skill, apprehension rather than ability, a self debased rather than revered. My goal is not to judge the advice literature on my informants' activities as wise or unwise, but to contemplate the type of self that they can foster in women and suggest how the activities of that self can be played out given the general character of public places.

I begin by discussing the empirical materials I use here, then specify some pertinent general features of communication in public places, features I later suggest are at variance with the advice rhetoric aimed at helping prevent crime. Next, I discuss three elements of the rhetoric of limited competence offered to crime-conscious women in public. Finally, I describe how rhetorical strategies contribute to the situated selves women and men present in public and help to sustain the informal social control of public places.

EMPIRICAL MATERIALS

The empirical materials I use to illustrate this essay come from two sources: a survey of popular literature directed toward women about crime prevention, and interviews with 25 women residents of Santa Fe, New Mexico in 1987.

I read all articles listed in *Reader's Guide to Periodical Literature* for the period 1970–1989 involving self-defense, crime prevention, women and crime, and women and rape and assault. Under similar headings and titles, I also read all books listed in *Books in Print* for the period 1965–1989, extending the period to gain more authors and perspectives.

This literature, perhaps partly the congealing of a folklore already in place, itself reveals gender stereotypes even in its broad dimensions. For example, there continue to be many books and articles directed to women in the name of street crime prevention. There is no complementary male-directed literature: when crime-prevention books for men are written, they are on self-defense skills. Some advice books for women are simply directed to the men who, it is assumed, will be their teachers (Tegner, 1965:201–16).

Though there is also a general, non-gender-specific literature on crime prevention and self-defense, the subset of literature directed at women stands apart in the extremity of measures advised. The asymmetry may be sound: perhaps any street harassment is more traumatic for women, who express more fear of crime in the first place; there is certainly no equal for men of women's generalized fear of rape.

Of course, I can claim no causal relationship here between these particular articles and the feelings and actions of informants with whom I spoke. Instead, I use the literature as a body of normative beliefs about women, crime, and conduct in public places. It represents what is available for, not necessarily what is taken up by, women in the culture. It is a remarkably consistent body of beliefs at that. It is also one that, in general, my informants said they knew.

The women I interviewed were from Santa Fe, New Mexico, a small but cosmopolitan city of some 52,000 residents. The interviewees were all middle-class. I interviewed these 25 women as part of a larger project studying gender behavior in public places that involved, ultimately, interviews with nearly one hundred women. I approached these 25 informants in various public places in the city, often as a tag-end to a casual conversation, greeting, or service encounter, and asked them if they would be willing to be interviewed. No woman refused, but the resulting pool is, of course, a convenience sample rather than one systematically representative of the women of the city, much less of U.S. women as a whole. Had I used a sample of poor minority women living in high-crime areas, for example, I would probably have culled a more explicit shared set of folk wisdom in response to sure, not likely, crimes, and a more extreme set of responses in terms of weaponry. Certainly, too, such a sample would have had more direct experience as crime victims. They might also have expressed a set of strategies for dealing with crime similar to those of their male counterparts.

The interviews were freeform and in depth, concentrating on public places as possible sites for crime. I asked informants about their perceptions of crime in public places in the city; their experience with crime, with near-crime, and with events they did not think of as crime but were nevertheless distasteful. I asked about their understandings of what to do in case of street crime and whether they ever had put these beliefs into practice. I also asked about their sources of information.

Interviews lasted from one to 3 1/2 hours; the average interview was about two hours. Twenty of the 25 women had Anglo surnames, and five had Hispanic surnames. For the most part, these were young women: 16 were between 20 and 35, seven were between 36 and 45; only two were over 60. Twelve were married or living with a man. Six had had formal self-defense training, either in a woman's self-defense class or through classes in martial arts; two others had attempted to train themselves in self-defense through books or videos; all but one identified themselves as purposive readers of literature on women and self-defense in, for example, newspapers and women's magazines. Three women identified themselves as victims of crime: one was a rape survivor; two others had experienced home robberies.

THE SELF AND COMMUNICATION IN PUBLIC PLACES

As an arena for face-to-face interaction, communication between strangers in public places exhibits some general characteristics that are distinct from communication between acquaintances in public and from much communication in private places. This constellation of characteristics shapes possibilities for interaction that do and can occur, not only for women interested in preventing crime but for all other citizens as well.

In what follows, I briefly sketch the communication characteristics most relevant to the situation of the woman and crime prevention in public places. This communication influences what Goffman has spoken of as the situated self appropriate to public places. With *situated self*, Goffman implies a self as something constituted according to the social situation of the moment, rather than as any stable, trans-situational possession. A self is, in effect, loaned to its putative owner and defined in part by the social control requirements of particular situations (Goffman 1961:149–52). In problematic social situations, the relevant self develops strategies for coping that can be expressed as rhetorics. Yet these rhetorics will be modified by the nature of communication possible or thought proper to social situations. Thus, any rhetoric involving crime prevention will be modified by the character of communication possible and thought proper in a particular setting.

Communication Characteristics

Communicative acts between individuals in public are heavily *appearance dependent*. That is, they rely on appraisal of the physical look, manner, nonverbal communication, and dress of the other—what Goffman has referred to as an appreciation of "body idiom" (Goffman 1963:33–34). It is understood that, all other things being equal, the citizen will attempt to give the best possible appearance in public.[2] Public places function as front regions (Goffman 1973:107–23), where performances are expected to be cut and polished, where impressions of proper decorum are expressed by adhering to more formal standards of dress, permissible sound levels, and prescribed activities and attitudes. In this way, an etiquette manual will tell a woman that the way she looks in public signifies "the way she wants to be seen by the world" (Geng 1971:76–77), and all citizens will be advised to restrict conspicuous activities such as kissing and smoking (Vanderbilt 1972:246–47, 316–18).

With only appearance to rely on, however, inescapable stereotypy results, as, for example, when a Korean-American in a black neighborhood is the object of catcalls that recapitulate stereotypes of Asian Americans (Navarro 1990), or a black who enters a Korean-American business experiences behavior reflecting stereotypes of blacks (Sims 1990). Or a citizen sometimes feels strangers fix reliably on blatant symbols of a status peripheral to the "real" self, as when a woman using an electric wheelchair says strangers bypass usual greetings to offer remarks on her chair (Gardner 1990).

Clearly, appearance dependence favors those whose appearance connotes statuses held in high regard; with regard to crime, it favors those taken stereotypically to be no easy victims or who can manipulate appearance to suggest strength or imperviousness to assault. Using traditional stereotypes, women will be seen by strangers as less capable of retaliation than men. As aspiring criminals will have to depend on judgments of appearance to select prospective victims, so those who seek to escape victimization must depend on assessment of strangers' appearance and manipulation of their own in order to avoid crime. One way to cope with crime in public therefore will be to develop an array of behavioral strategies that are also appearance dependent; alternatively, people will curtail others' visual access in order to prevent being judged a suitable target. The latter tack is taken in a small way by donning sunglasses that foil, among other things, a criminal judging one fearful and therefore an easy mark; similarly, a car may be used as a visual shell to both stymie appraisal of one's vulnerability and provide a physical baffle to intrusion.

Implicitly, then, in public the visual channel is preferred as an avenue of communication. A corollary of this appearance dependence is that silence is normative and speech between strangers is routinized and brief, and, aside from certain heavily scripted greetings or comments on the weather, is to be stimulated only by unusual circumstances. If talk is limited, routine, and warranted, then the citizen who fears crime will have no ordinary way to ascertain who is, and who is not, a potential foe—nor will seeming and actual foes have clear ways in which to make their identities less ambiguous.

Communication in public between strangers is also typically *transitory;* i.e., it is relatively fleeting compared to communication between acquaintances or communication in private places. It is also typically *episodic:* Face-to-face communication between strangers is interspersed with vacuum periods where contact is neither made nor attempted. Both these characteristics influence those fleeting contacts that are made, which therefore appear in relief and can become highly charged with meaning. Such brief, disjointed events will be all the person interested in preventing crime will have to judge the situation by; similarly they will be all the aspiring criminal will have to select a suitable target. Transitory and episodic communication can also favor purposeful strategies that cannot be sustained for long, as when a crime-fearing woman manages momentarily to adopt a no-nonsense expression.

Communication in public places also involves what Goffman (1963:20–21) refers to as *multiple social realities*. This phrase reflects the capacity of this one larger setting to host other, overlapping behavior settings—that is, a variety of individuals with highly differentiated motives, needs, wants, and agendas, as well as individuals from a great variety of social categories. Therefore, it is impossible to predict whether or not the given flow on a city street is likely to include someone with criminal intent. If one espouses a crime-preventive attitude or engages in crime-preventive strategies, it is hard to predict when this attitude or these strategies should be curtailed or suspended. At the same time, one's contact with even an innocuous-seeming stranger is necessarily history-less, so that suspicion can bleed onto even those one has no reason to fear.

Beliefs about Public Places

Coupled with these characteristics of communication in public places are certain normative ideas about what everyday life in public places is or should be like. First, much face-to-face communication between strangers is felt to be *insignificant.* In general, public places are transitways to other regions, not loci of interest in themselves; laws against loitering, lolling, and vagrancy exist in part to ensure that public places remain waystations, not goals. Our feeling that events in public places are insignificant co-exists with an obligation to present an appearance typically more formal than can be presented in the "relaxed" settings of private places. Second, these communications are believed to be *egalitarian* in character, expressive of the effective ceasefire that exists between strangers even of varying classes, racial groups, and genders. Much of our etiquette of public places is based on this second notion. It argues that we suspend personal interests, tastes, and involvements in order to effect a courtesy and openness owed to all (Benton 1956:15, 96–114; Martin 1982:99–100, 250–52, 280–81; Post 1969: 91–96).

Likewise, we feel that public places are not—nor, rightly, should they be—owned by any single group, and that, aside from certain strongly territorial neighborhoods, no one individual or group has rights of control over strangers; these feelings mean that we are all, in a sense, trespassers when in public.

However, they also mean that the personal space of ill-meaning others will abut our own, and that we have as little apparent right to prepare a defense as they have to prepare an offense.[3] Because of these general yet seldom explicated beliefs, we may have vague dissatisfaction with canons of advice that involve extensive manipulation of events or appearances in public places—as crime prevention advice can seem to do.

We can also come to feel that individuals who attribute deep meaning to the small interchanges of face-to-face communication there make too much of what is, after all, trifling.[4] At the same time, these general features of communication in public places and our general feelings about the nature of public places importantly color the informal social control that is exerted there, making it necessarily random, brief, and directed to all—as impersonal, in fact, as public courtesy and goodwill are expected to be.

These same characteristics of and our feelings about communication in public places color the strategies that can be and are advised to those who would avoid crime. I will suggest that any crime-preventive rhetoric, however, will be somewhat at odds with other constituents of the general situated self we believe is appropriate to public places.

SAFETY, PUBLIC PLACES, AND THE RHETORIC OF LIMITED COMPETENCE

Prescriptions to women in public places as to how to achieve safety are framed in terms of a rhetoric of limited competence, that is, a series of presentational strategies that project dependency and lack of skill. Further, this rhetoric of limited competence is by nature ambiguous (Zimmerman 1981:52): at the same time that it intends to communicate women's ability to deal with urban crime, it also communicates dependency and lack of skill.

The strategies that make up this rhetoric, part of the wisdom of the young urban woman in particular, about prudent behavior when on streets and even near home often ostensibly offer women ways to avoid harm. Yet they also advise women to adopt behavior that results in a profaned self, that is, a self that has unworthy qualities. This is much at odds with the understanding that one's public appearance should be one's best appearance. Thus, the situated self appropriate to public places when a woman believes she is "preventing crime" can come to seem to her ridiculous, and the presentation process can seem impractical as well.

The Apparent Escort

One key precaution for public behavior counsels the woman alone in public simply not to be alone or, at least, not to seem alone. There are several levels at and degrees to which this injunction can be observed, ranging from what is thought of as simple prudence (such as reluctance or refusal to go out at night unless accompanied), to common customs of deception (such as wearing a wedding ring when one is unmarried to ward off unwanted men), to more wide-ranging methods (such as pretending one has a roommate to confer safety when one does not). I discuss how first the advice literature, then my informants, explained these strategies.

The advice literature often recommends engineering an escort by, for instance, having "a male fellow employee escort you to your car and see you safely started—you might even drive him back to the office" (Barthol 1979:102), or even managing to be near a male by, for example, standing near the occupied ticket or toll booth in a subway station or near a police officer (Field 1980;

112); walking close to a group of people walking, if they look safe and are not all males (Barthol 1979:99); never being embarrassed to ask a friend to accompany one home (Wegman 1978:57). Formal "ride switchboards" and "escort services" for women alone at night achieve the same goals (Rockwood and Thom 1979:82).

The women I interviewed often said they should effect a male escort, since attackers will presumably shy away from this strengthened front. This strategy is one that even non-crime-conscious women say they choose for the ease it confers when in public. Women sometimes engineer accompaniment, even planning in advance. A lawyer in her fifties said she kept up a friendship with a neighborhood woman of whom she was not too fond in order to have someone "to go to the movies with, to have a drink with, or just to keep me company when I take out the garbage." A grade school teacher in her thirties who lived alone with her two small children once had been followed home, robbed, and nearly raped. She had a well-worked-out network of female and male acquaintances—one who could be counted on to take in a play with her, another who walked her to the store, a third whose car was at her beck and call—that she reciprocally "paid back"—though not in kind—by pet-sitting or baking cakes or breads. A graduate student in her twenties who lived with a boyfriend, with a less-organized network of escorts, commented that at some times she felt these were "unfortunately instrumental friendships," but appreciated also that she had little choice.

If a woman were to undertake some measures of impression management the advice literature recommends, she would appear to be self-plus-companion, or woman near a person who could be enlisted as companion if need be. The woman who stands near a convenient police officer seems to be protected, yet is not truly accompanied, of course; she mimics co-presence. In yet other cases, however, the crime-advice literature suggests a woman imply a companion, i.e., give the impression of being accompanied (and presumably protected) by displaying, not a man who is or seems a companion, but evidence of a man, for example, by telling a woman to place a man's hat or pipe on the seat of her parked car to indicate she "might be accompanied on her return" (Berman 1980:247).

A few women said they employed some of these strategies, though they also expressed some discomfort or awkwardness at discussing them. A married college professor in her thirties, whose three grown sons provide her with useful artifacts for these misleading signals of male co-presence or availability, referred to them laughingly as "male spoor." She added that she felt odd at using them. A homemaker in her fifties related that, having read such a recommendation, she borrowed her brother's spare hat and gloves; she was surprised to discover that they allayed her fears, and she found herself anxious when they were accidently removed from her car during cleaning: she had converted the items of clothing into talismans of safety. She was now embarrassed at her emotional investment in them. Other informants used a variety of expressions— "weird," "odd," "funny," "dishonest," and the like—to describe discomfort with these practices.

Women sometimes effectively create a companion male by enacting the role themselves. These strategies, by the way, are not a part of the advice literature. Interestingly, these women spoke of the measures, not as uncomfortably unusual, but as practically utilitarian. Though it might formally express a less competent or independent self, then, the rhetoric that women use need not always be experienced as such. In effect, a woman

who enacted the role of a protector becomes self *and* companion, emphasizing that, as her "real" female self, she is powerless when in public. In this spirit, some five informants said they wore slacks, especially dark slacks or jeans, flat shoes, and jacket or coat styles they felt were homologous with men's styles.

Women's primary rationale was not explicitly to "sham" male gender but to wear clothes that were "practical" for purposes of escaping notice, evading criminals, or practicing self-defense. One said that her purpose was not so much to seem male as not to seem female. A single mother in her thirties who often worked late as a hotel clerk said she always effected this style of dress, and cited its effect in public as a selling point: she "dressed like a man" and felt strangers were more likely to respect her if they felt it possible that she was a man. An art gallery owner in her thirties added that she tied her long hair at the nape of her neck in order to look less "feminine." A 24-year-old secretary who lived with her boyfriend and their toddler effectively withdrew signs of female gender rather than substituting male: she tried to leave no trace in her car "that it's a woman's car—no women's magazines, no clothes, none of my baby's toys or clothes." When using these strategies, informants did not express discomfort, perhaps because they were direct actions rather than deceptive use of symbols or attachment to them.

There are more traditional practices to indicate that a woman is protected by a man when in fact she is alone. Usually, these do not involve the woman in misrepresenting gender. She is not to suggest she is something she is not—i.e., a man—nor is she to destroy evidence that she is a woman. Instead, she should indicate, either truthfully or not, by use of verbal invocation or significant symbols that she has access to a man who could protect her if need be. The advice literature recommends practices such as suggesting a woman walk in the middle of the street at night and, if approached, "look up at one of the windows or down the block and yell, 'Hey, Tom, I thought we were going to meet on Elm Avenue,'" for a criminal will not be "sure if Tom is real or not" (Ingber 1987:140). Even when there is no special danger, companionship is not to be discarded lightly: a woman, when at the movies, is sometimes told to go with the companion who "decides to venture into the lobby to buy popcorn," since "It might turn out to be fun, and it's certainly safer" (Burg 1979:144). Speaking to or of an illusory male for effect is termed "the Invisible Man Routine" (Burg 1979:147–48). Some measures are to be played out with no audience at all, as when a woman is advised when in a hotel to leave the television playing softly while she is out and the do-not-disturb sign on the door (Burg 1979:147–48).

In this way, women informants said they sometimes purposefully mentioned a boyfriend or husband during a service encounter or public conversation with a male stranger, thereby also preventing pickups. Thus, a secretary in her twenties took care to mention her ex-husband, whom she could continue to invoke if she disliked or feared the man with whom she spoke, but of whom she would rapidly dispose verbally if she chose to encourage acquaintance. Women also perceived modest deceptions as allowable, such as wearing a wedding ring though unwed. One woman claimed the advantage of this method was its expressiveness to all men: it required no strategic insertion into a conversation otherwise about plumbing, the weather, or pizza delivery, only that she display her hand. A woman might claim both existence and availability, for example, by reporting, when talking on the phone, not only that she had a husband but that he was home.[5]

Informants said that such minor deceptions were suitable as routine precautions. In situations more directly menacing, a woman might take more active measures, as when the public realm threatened to encroach on the private. If she is home and a man claiming to be a repairperson knocks, a woman alone sometimes attempts to signal that a man is with her. She sometimes also attempts to signal that her home is occupied by a man while she is still on the street, involving tacks that occasionally make her feel "more than normally foolish," as reported a lawyer in her fifties who nevertheless says she does just such things. In the same way, a nurse in her thirties, who once believed a man was following her home, yelled up to her window, "Chet, honey, I'll get the door," and was chagrined to hear her dog Chet dutifully bark in response. An unmarried partner in a law firm, a woman in her forties, habitually yelled, "I'll get it honey," when her bell rang; once she had to explain to her conservative parents at the door that there was no honey after all.

Two young women, a cosmetology student and a secretary both in their twenties, noted that when they answered the phone at home they often took care to modulate their voices to a lower pitch; a criminal caller trying to discover a woman was home alone would thereby be misled. After the first turn at talk assured them a familiar caller, they resumed normal pitch. These examples were recounted with some embarrassment, because it was possible that they would be noticed and mocked by friends and relatives—as both had been.

Accompanied, a woman can feel obliged as a student of safety precautions to make her accompaniment as obvious as possible as often as possible. Evidence of solitude can become uncomfortable for her, based in part on actual experience when accompaniment is ambiguous. A homemaker in her thirties noted that when she and her husband were standing some three feet apart in a theater lobby and not engaged in conversation, a strange man stepped up to her, took her arm familiarly, and attempted to walk her away: "What he was going to do I don't know. Then my husband grabbed him by the collar and [the strange man] grinned very charmingly and walked away."

If women believe that they cannot experience public places unaccompanied, then it is also true that some women come to count men less as individuals than as protectors, functioning either well or poorly, a conception congruent with traditional ideas of gentlemanly behavior (see Hanmer and Saunders 1983). When effective, men are sometimes thought of as saviors; when ineffective, as failed gallants. In this vein, an unmarried graduate student said humorously that she thinks of her escorts on dates more as St. Bernards than as human beings; male escorts, especially at night, are the price paid for a life in public, says a department store clerk in her twenties who does not enjoy dating but wants to get out of the house. A third woman, a gay nurse in her thirties, takes a gay male friend when she goes to bars in a certain part of town for the safety she will then have; an irony is that she is the superior defender by martial arts training. Thus, the situated self that women are constrained to present can come to affect their judgment of effectiveness of a companion's performance.

I have said that purposeful attempts to suggest a man exists where none does imply that the situated self of the woman in public is weak. Some women went beyond the door, so to speak, and said they fantasied protective accompaniment at home, sometimes somewhat elaborately. In this way, a woman who worked as a hotel clerk admitted ruefully her conversations with her nonexistent companion began outside the door of her house, but continued after she entered and while she systematically checked for unwanted criminal companions room by room,

the conversation with the imaginary male interlocutor giving her heart. A single mother, she tried to mute them before her children, however, since she felt to act so was "a little odd." Another woman, a graduate student, said her initial words to her imaginary male roommate blended into talking to herself. A nurse reported that her briefly fabricated companion had had a name, habits in dress, and a preferred basketball team, all coincidentally her tastes also; her own actions reflected these tastes when, for instance, she picked out a tie of the sort that he would prefer and hung it deceptively on the bedroom door or left a Celtics game (not games involving other teams) blasting masculinity on the television when she had to go out at night.

Women sometimes say that, though they perform some of these measures, they feel they should apologize for them: they are "crazy" things to do, they make a woman feel "a little bizarre." This ritual accompaniment emphasizes to her that her "true" or "real" self provides insufficient protection for her own safety. She must create a tissue of a man, which can be suggested by the merest hints and evidences.

Caught up in these charades, however, other women report no discomfort. They speak humorously of their shadow mates, implying that they are not threats to a real self but strange rites required by the culture and not to be taken seriously. Perhaps a woman gains some sense of control over the situation of crime prevention if she can, in effect, design her own protector down to his tie. (On the beneficial and liberating aspects of imaginary others, see Caughey 1984).

It is not enough to note that, if women feel they have to engineer or mimic the presence of a man or suggest that they themselves are men, this is a sad commentary on modern urban life. Also important is the character of the situated self of public places that—according to some informants—such strategies create. Alone in public, women occasionally report that they still think of how safe they would feel or how much easier things in general would be, were they accompanied or were they male. Thus, a woman's time in public can be altered in ways unfamiliar to male citizens, in fact with strategies unfamiliar to most males. It is difficult to think of a situation where a man shams female accompaniment or female gender to ensure his safety, or where others advise him to do so.[6]

Profaning the Self in the Name of Safety

While behaving in a crime-conscious manner, women can come to feel constrained to present themselves in a way that belies their knowledge of proper female gender role behavior and proper public behavior in general, presenting an appearance whose worth they consciously denigrate rather than inflate. For the sake of preventing crime, women are advised to manipulate their dress and behavior in a number of ways that restrict apparel choices and emotional expressions, and require them to present something less than what otherwise would be considered their best possible appearance.

Minor strategies involve dress and manner; more major strategies are suggestions in the advice literature that, to deter crime, a woman should inform a man that she has some imperceptible—but loathsome—characteristic or disease or should enact a psychological or physically repulsive condition. Informants were aware of this range of crime-prevention wisdom, though by and large they put into practice only that involving appearance.

In general, the literature tells women in public to "dress with discretion so as not to stimulate interest" (*Good Housekeeping Magazine* 1972:193), or that "a woman is more likely to invite attack on the street if she is wearing tight, 'sexy' clothes. If you are heading for a party in a décolleté costume or an extra-brief skirt, it's best to ride up to the entrance rather than walk" (Hair and Baker 1970:94). Implicitly these cautions respond to the appearance dependence of communication in public. Whereas a woman wearing alluring clothing in a private context can use other communicative elements to assure others that she is not truly or only the sexually interested person she seems, the same woman in public lacks other communicative tools to mute the message clothing offers.[7]

Almost every woman I interviewed offered information about appearance, saying she tried to avoid "provocative" clothing that "invited" attacks from males, as well as an "inviting" manner. Most informants said they felt they should not behave in an over-friendly manner or in any way that suggests an over-friendly manner; that is, they should not employ a "sexy" walk or thrust their breasts out.

Some informants noted the drawbacks of dress and attitude manipulation: to succeed in making themselves unnoteworthy in public required an adjustment of appearance not worth the sacrifice. Certainly it violated expectations of other citizens in public as to appropriate female attire if a woman attempted to dress herself to look plain as a pie plate—all the more if she managed to be mistaken for a man. A grade school teacher, a warm and exuberant person, strongly felt that restrictions on one's manner were even more insidious: dressing differently was a surface measure, she thought, but damping her good humor undermined what was hers "naturally."

As well as manipulating dress and manner, women sometimes are told to avoid crime by making themselves too repulsive a target for approach. That the criminal will probably then turn to another woman as a target is apparently not to be a concern. In the literature, women are counseled to adopt "non-aggressive—but disgusting—behavior" (Wilson 1977:151); to claim "to be pregnant or epileptic or the carrier of a venereal disease" (Duckett 1982:68) or to have "herpes or even AIDS" (Kaye 1985:74); to "pretend to have an epileptic seizure, or fainting spell" (Berman 1980:247); to "faint or go limp; urinate, drool or even throw up" (Schraub 1979:153); to "quack like a duck" (Scribner 1988:69) or make sounds like a cow and flap her arms like an airplane (Pickering 198: 129). She is told not to be afraid to "make a scene [or] do anything to attract attention to yourself. That's exactly what you want" (Field 1980:120), though attracting attention to herself is not among the woman's desiderata in public places according to traditional norms (Benton 1956:8), nor is behaving "sexually aggressively" (Scribner 1988:69). She should "Act insane; eat grass, jump around, etc." (Krupp 1978:152); she should "Sing out loud. . . . Make a fool of yourself" (Kaye 1985:74). Some of this advice also is intended to disgust the potential criminal,[8] as when women are advised to tell rapists that they have venereal disease (Schraub 1979:153), even carrying an old penicillin bottle to bolster claims (Pickering 1983:121).

Informants reported knowing about, though very rarely putting into practice, this tack of purposefully inspiring disgust. Only one woman said she tried these more extreme tactics, a homemaker in her forties who effectively "gargled" and made noises at a man following her, but felt so foolish she was not sure her efforts were worthwhile. All such profanation requires a woman to present, not the more stringent definition of public comportment usually required of citizens, but a floridly flawed self. Here, the self is profaned because the actions are of such a nature as to make her seem out of role in

public, silly because overcautious or simply unfathomable.

Thus, informants reported that they would feel ridiculous or humiliated if they were to practice crime prevention by stimulating disgust. For example, a lawyer in her thirties mused on the possibility of telling an assailant she had AIDS or venereal disease and then having to further convincingly hypothesize how she came by these "repulsive" diseases. Because of these feelings, she concluded she could never pull off this strategy.

But some women said they had contemplated being purposefully repulsive when they felt threatened. Thinking the matter over at the time, they knew themselves to be poor deceivers to do so, whether because of inexperience or from overwhelming fear. Thus, a homemaker in her thirties, once confronted with a suspect man, decided to pretend to have an epileptic seizure, shortly thereafter remembering that she had no idea what such a seizure looked like. A nurse, who had been raped, offered that, "If anybody goes after me again, this [type of advice] won't help me. I'll be so scared I won't be able to spell AIDS, much less convince someone I've got it."

Such advice would indeed seem strange if offered to a man threatened with street violence. It is now a commonplace that an attractively dressed woman does not "cause" a man to rape her anymore than a well-dressed man causes a man to rob him. It is not so commonly noted that we do not advise men to fake insanity or to sham morally impugning disease with the alacrity that women are so advised. Of course, claims of sexually transmitted disease are aptly claimed when one fears sexual crimes like rape, not apt when one fears robbery.

The profanation of a woman's situated self in public places, then, results from beliefs she should either deliberately act ridiculous, inappropriately, or simply mute her personal attractions in hopes either of discomfiting her attacker or escaping his attention. At all levels, these strategies are at odds with the understandings that public places are regions where the individual presents a careful and "best" demeanor and look.

Anticipated Peril

A third type of distance from the normal citizens' situated self in public places is supplied by the advice to women and by their perception that they should take some measures of crime prevention in advance of actually appearing in public. Certain practices, in turn, bespeak an orientation to an action before that action is necessary. Evident precautions and planning contradict our general cultural feeling that events in public places are too trifling to warrant special thought and that an egalitarian civility prevails. Yet, tacitly appreciating the many social realities that public places contain and the impossibility of judging strangers with only transitory, episodic, and silent communications, women are also advised to extend their crime-consciousness back, before the actual moment of danger, in order to foil criminals. In effect, women are counseled to anticipate peril; some informants said they do just this, sometimes with awkward results.

The advice literature suggests there are some practices and some attitudes the woman should follow to prepare herself for the worst that might happen; moreover, she is to keep this advice in mind at all times: "Don't let down. Ever!" (Kaye 1985:74). Besides this general mental vigilance, there are preparations a woman can take to ward off or lessen the likelihood that she will become involved in danger, extending even to practices such as carrying a house key in her hand far in advance of when it will actually be needed (Schraub 1979:169), or position-

ing herself when she enters an elevator "near the control panel so you can hit the alarm button and as many floor buttons as possible if necessary" in case she is attacked (Krupp 1978:152).

Women are advised to take up many precautions in advance, sometimes far in advance, of trouble: a woman is told to carry her money in her bra (Barthol 1979:111), to hold her police whistle between her teeth as she walks home (Barthol 1979:111), to use her personal alarm "*before* a confrontation takes place, even if you're not sure you're in danger" (*Glamour Magazine* 1980:63). When a stranger enters an elevator she is on, she should pretend she has forgotten something and exit (*Today's Health Magazine* 1973); when on the street, she is told to scream or use her whistle "as soon as you *think* someone might be stalking you" (Berman 1980:247). Other citizens are certain to be puzzled, if not astounded, by such actions, as when a woman is told, if she thinks she is being followed, to run up and say "to a dependable soul: 'Hey Charlie, what's happening?'" (Krupp 1978:142).

Sometimes she must plan considerably ahead, as when she is told to choose her home with an eye to security (Wheeler 1982:69) or to get acquainted with her neighbors with a view toward enlisting them in case of danger (Bertram 1975:83). Such advice amounts to an honorable, not to say prudent, ulterior motive for making friends in the city.

Other long-range advice suggests that she make a list of dangerous public situations experienced by her and her friends and/or portrayed in local newspaper accounts for the last six months (Monkerud and Heiny 1980:14), that she mentally review crime-prevention techniques several times a day (Pickering 1983:7), that she make a calendar of self-defense practice times and a list of dangerous neighborhood features

(Griffith 1978:165–69, 174–75). Preparations must continue inside her home, where she can practice "knowing how to scream," but into a pillow pressed over her face (Barthol 1979:25). Or a woman can practice screams driving with the windows rolled up: "anyone watching thinks you are singing!" (Barthol 1979:25).

Many manipulations of appearance involve consideration far beyond the immediate situation of danger, as when the advice literature tells a woman to choose her clothes with regard to their running and escape potential (Burg 1979:121) or for their noiselessness. She should not, for example, wear shoes with "tap-tap" heels that will alert "everyone within a couple of blocks . . . that a female target approacheth!" (Barthol 1979:100–01).

With an eye to anticipating crime, informants reported following a number of strategies of both small and long duration. For example, a homemaker in her twenties said that, before she left the house, she always put her credit cards and large bills in her three-year-old's toy purse, reasoning that even if she were robbed her small daughter would not be; a nurse in her thirties transferred cash to a bra and a purse alarm to her pocket, judging the effect in the mirror to make sure there were no telling bulges. A lawyer in her thirties said she gave herself a "crime-check" in a full-length mirror each time she left her house, noting dress and presentation that might "invite" crime and, for each outfit, any handbag both match the outfit but not be "snatchable."

Some preparations were long-term and came to infect other ordinary, pleasurable parts of informants' lives. A 20-year-old homemaker regretted that she could no longer grow long nails, since she needed to be ready to fight an attacker if need be. A graduate student in her twenties with the opposite beliefs about nails regretted a need to

grow long nails to serve as weapons for self-defense, for they did not jibe with the professorial image to which she aspired. A cosmetology student felt that it took her "six times as long to find a house" because of her crime-preventive standards. A law partner in her forties enjoyed buying clothes when a teen but said the pleasure was now spoiled since she scrutinized potential purchases "with an eye to, 'will this provoke some depraved maniacal sadist to attack me?'"

Women sometimes took anticipatory walks through the street, mentally mapping common routes with an eye to potential help in case of danger. Compared to other citizens, they were overinvested in the act of public passage, commonly considered insignificant, warranting no practice runs, and as a result spontaneous. Evocatively, however, a married lawyer in her thirties described steps in thinking through a route or assessing an area and concluded, "I never go any place for the first time—I've been there already in my head." Plainly, there is the danger that erecting false events such as these will be inimical to the experiential integrity of the act itself, making it always a rehearsed one.

The woman who observes necessary strategies for anticipating peril when in public places is certain, sooner or later, to be vigilant when there is no cause. Given the extremity of the recommendations, this is likely to happen in some form or other many times daily. Sometimes, of course, she will not know circumspection is unneeded. Informants occasionally alluded to a low-grade guilt over their "paranoia" toward other citizens, who were seen in retrospect to have meant, or at least to have done, no harm to them. Sometimes they had been revealed to have had suspicions where none was warranted, as a secretary in her thirties was mocked by a man on the street for transparently carrying her keys "defensively," or the cosmetologist who stepped aside well in advance to avoid a man she feared, who then said to her, "You idiot."

When women anticipated peril from men they first took to be strangers, then turned out to know, they often reported feeling particularly "stupid." But one informant, a junior professor in her thirties, had a different attitude. After she nearly Mace'd her department chair, they both laughed, "then he started kidding me about what a paranoid I was, and that's where the laughter stopped. I apologize to no one for insuring that I stay alive."

In sum, measures advised by the rhetoric of limited competence sometimes respond to and sometimes contradict general features of communication in public places. Women informants reported taking pains to avoid crime when in public. Yet because they are fearful of crime and because the character of public places makes it impossible reliably to judge the many strangers one encounters, save by appearance, women need rely on what are necessarily quickly and clearly transmitted messages or on preparation that takes place outside of the region. Measures will likely be taken where unwarranted, so that a contingency of this rhetoric remains that either a stranger or an acquaintance can innocently rebuke the woman for strategies not immediately useful. The true culprit, of course, is not so much the advice she receives or the folk beliefs she bears, but the environing fear of crime.

Discussion

The significance of this rhetoric can be seen in terms of (1) its contribution to the situated self women present in public, including the possibility that crime consciousness will overwhelm the woman's other concerns in public places; (2) its relationship to an informal social control in public places; (3) its effect on the complementary situated self men must demonstrate in public.

In some ways, there is less discrepancy than might be suspected between the general situated self due public places and the rhetoric of crime prevention that is a part of it. In general, the situated self of public places subjects women to other imputations of limited competence and supplies them with a self regularly profaned, especially when they are youthful, by street remarks, by differential and commonly poorer treatment in shops and restaurants, by varying expectations of what items of information about the self a woman is obliged to disclose (Gardner 1980, 1983, 1988, 1989).

To some extent, the message of the rhetoric of limited competence is consistent with other experiences of the situated self of public places. Insofar as it is consistent, it emphasizes other negative experiences. At the same time, it makes more unlikely that women can achieve the egalitarian courtesy and trust that is, within limits, normative for public places in middle-class society. This carries an unpleasant connotation for women's place in society, suggesting that social control of women in public places both exists and is diffusely available for any man in public places. Indeed, it is exercised by men whether they intend it or not.

Part of women's status in public, then, is expressed by a heightened concern with crime, quite in contrast to the concerns reported by and advised for men. An examination of what I have called the rhetoric of limited competence shows how this is possible.

First, there is a great deal of anticipatory preparation, both mental and material, counseled for the woman who is going out. This vigilance, she often believes (and popular literature assures her), must typically be undertaken in a careful yet undetectable manner, conveying a masked strength that is appropriate also to her gender role. Added to the tasks of public presentation all citizens, she faces another: remaining intently aware of the many possible dangers of public life. The logical extension of circumspection that is the fate of the over-alert game-player has been dealt with at length by Erving Goffman under the topic of "Where the Action Is" (see Goffman 1967:149–270).

Thus, women who attempt to be crime conscious, and simultaneously who are attempting to give the appearance of attractive and casual self-contained noninvolvement in public, understandably find it a strain simultaneously to prime themselves to run, scream, enter the nearest building, stand in a carefully considered "safe" spot, walk in the middle of the street with dignity, and refuse apparently innocent (and perhaps actually innocent) requests for aid, matches, and information. A woman can experience public places primarily as an exercise in self-defense, spoiling other possible gains.

Beyond admonishing women to take up a possibly burdensome menu of activities, the rhetoric of limited competence reinforces other negative informal social control women experience in public. As Radford (1987:43) suggests, a woman not seen to be controlled by one specific man in public can at will be controlled by any man. This informal control results in a wide scope of beliefs and actions by women, in response to the similarly wide band of behavior by men in public places that one writer has referred to as a "continuum of sexual violence" (Kelly 1987).

The experience of various types of negative control in public yields a situated self bounded in a neatly symbolic way by geography and site, as well as by circumstance and concern. Thus, beliefs about crime prevention could operate to keep women at home, where they are seen to be physically safer and less concerned with strategies of caution—and where, traditionally, they have

belonged. And this social control exists outside public places, extending itself to poison major life decisions such as choosing a home as well as possibly occupying some part of her time in private with worry or with strategizing.

A further effect of crime-prevention beliefs is the portrait they paint of men. The felt obligation to behave in a crime-conscious manner can undermine, subtly or not so subtly, women's trust in the majority of quite innocent men whom women observe or with whom they come into contact in public places. Likewise, men conscious of women's fears in public will in part understand women's actions there according to how they find themselves reflected in women's behavior toward them.

In consequence, men sometimes may decide to go out of their way to appear innocent by, for example, conspicuously smiling and tipping a hat to a woman they pass in a run-down area or by ending any small piece of legitimate contact such as helping a woman open a door or manage a package with functional brevity and businesslike manner—all to communicate, in effect, that, though other males are suspected of harm they themselves are not and, furthermore, that they are sensitive enough to take the woman's point of view into consideration (Mehlman 1987). In this way, a man with no intention to fondle women in the subway reports placing his hands on a conspicuous subway pole to broadcast his innocence (Goffman 1971:38).

Other men who realize women's fears may exploit them short of the point of actual crime. Thus, most informants said they suspected any public approach by a man of having the nefarious as well as the innocent potential; all the more so can they suspect approaches, such as catcalls or pinches, that breach middle-class etiquette or enact conduct usually disapproved, such as following a woman for a block or two. It is important to appreciate that women's fear of crime in public places does not spoil public places for women alone, but that it also spoils, in some larger sense, men for women and women for men and public places for everyone.

Finally, although my analysis is one that treats all of these measures of crime prevention from the point of view of their possible effects on the situated self a woman presents in public places, my analysis is not meant to suggest, of course, that there are alternate strategies possible that would leave women in public places both safe and evidently self-possessed. Indeed, the concern of many of the women I interviewed—as well presumably as many of the women who read the popular literature on crime prevention—is to avoid the chance of rape or murder at the hands of unknown men who will assault them in public or follow them from public places to their homes. To analyze the character of the situated selves that these women believe and are told they must present in public in order to prevent crime is by no means to denigrate those beliefs and that advice: it is merely to note that along with those beliefs and advice comes what women themselves have sometimes noted to be sadly necessary measures.

ENDNOTES

Research for this paper was supported by the President's Council of Indiana University, whom I thank. I also thank William Gronfein, the late Erving Goffman, and two anonymous reviewers for comments on previous versions of this paper. Versions of the study were presented at the 1987 International Symposium on Victimology in San Francisco and at the 1987 annual Sociologists for Women in Society meetings. Finally, I thank all of my interviewees for their help. Correspondence to: Gardner, Department of Sociology, Indiana University, Indianapolis, IN 46202.

1. Interestingly, there is also a contrary set of advice telling women in search of dates or husbands to turn casual contacts in public into grist for their mill, suggesting that they can recognize desirable men as well as men they need fear (Gallatin 1987; O'Connor and Silverman 1989; Sommerfield 1986).

2. This is true barring some general fear for theft of valuable goods. To hide one's assets becomes, then, a general rule of conduct whose prudence overwhelms the temptation toward conspicuous display.

3. Beliefs about insignificance and egalitarianism are fostered by some of the social scientific work on public places. Such work emphasizes the civility present there and treats breaches of civility as deviant. For example, Goffman emphasizes such quintessentially egalitarian rites as civil inattention, whereby individuals signal by means of a mutal glance, then a dropping of that glance, that due respect has been awarded and no harm is intended (1963:83–85). At the same time he relegates the flagrant disrespect some social categories receive in public to the deviant case of "exposed" positions (1963:125–28).

4. Of course, all I have said about the character of communication in public places with regard to women and crime may be as well said of the character of communication with regard to men in public places. An intriguing question for a future study, then, is the problem not of why women fear crime in public places but of why men do not.

5. Sometimes women understand the various threads of advice to be in conflict. Thus, an unmarried secretary in her thirties decided to wear a wedding ring in order to suggest an absent protector; on the other hand, she feared the ring was also a lure for thieves, and compromised by wearing it only during daytime. She felt that theft was not likely in the daytime, but being followed home would be.

6. More familiar are admonishments to men to practice self-defense measures with an eye to attackers they might meet, a concern more elaborately advised for women, however. Women are also advised to invent another shadow presence, that of the imagined harasser or attacker; in this way, crime-preventive advice collaborates by exhorting a woman actively and extensively to role-play assaults with the criminal.

7. To be sure, all citizens will have reason to look out for crime, and all are cautioned, in some locales and circumstances, to conceal assets in the name of crime prevention—as are all citizens on vacation in unfamiliar parts (Gieseking 1980) and as, increasingly, city-dwelling children are (Hechinger 1984). But concealing monetary assets—appropriately understood as not integral to the self—is different from concealing physical assets, for bodily features are highly associated with the individual's "real" self.

8. Tacitly, the advice also assumes certain social categories and states—the epileptic, the mentally disabled, the pregnant, the menstruating—are worthy of disgust.

REFERENCES

Balkin, Steven
1979 "Victimization rate, safety, and fear of crime." Social Problems 26:343–58.
Ball, Donald
1965 "Sarcasm as sociation: the rhetoric of interaction." Canadian Review of Sociology and Anthropology 2:190–98.
1967 "An abortion clinic ethnography." Social Problems 14:293–301.
Barthol, Robert
1979 Protect Yourself. Englewood Cliffs, N.J.: Prentice-Hall.
Benton, Frances
1956 Complete Etiquette. New York: Random House.
Berman, Clifford
1980 "Crime: how not to be a victim." Good Housekeeping Magazine, September, 247.
Bertram, Camille M.
1975 "Protection: how, when, where, and what to do." Harper's Bazaar Magazine, March, 83, 131.
Benton, Frances
1956 Complete Etiquette. New York: Random House.
Brown, Edward J., Timothy Flanagan, and Maureen McLeod (eds.)
1984 Sourcebook of Criminal Justice Statistics—1983. Washington, D.C.: U.S. Government Printing Office.
Brunvand, Jan Harold
1981 The Vanishing Hitchhiker: American Urban Legends and Their Meanings. New York: Norton.
Burg, Kathleen Keefe
1979 The Womanly Art of Self-Defense. New York: A & W Visual Library.
Caughey, John L.
1984 Imaginary Social Worlds. Lincoln, Neb.: University of Nebraska Press.
Clemente, Frank, and Michael B. Kleiman
1977 "Fear of crime in the United States: a multivariate analysis." Social Forces 56:519–31.
Dubow, Fred
1979 Reactions to Crime: A Critical Review of the Literature. Washington, D.C.: U.S. Government Printing Office.
Ducket, Joy
1982 "Rape prevention." Essence Magazine, September, 68.
Edmiston, Susan
1973 "Up from cowardice." Redbook Magazine, August 60–61, 162–63, 165.

Edwards, Audrey
1982 "How three quick-thinking women escaped danger." Essence Magazine, September, 72.
Edwards, Susan
1987 "'Provoking her own demise'." In Women, Violence and Social Control, ed. Jalna Hanmer and Mary Maynard, 152–68. Atlantic Highlands, N.J.: Humanities.
Field, Jill Nevel
1980 "Playing it safe: at home, on the street, in your car, on the bus or subway." Mademoiselle Magazine, September, 112, 120.
Gallatin, Dr. Martin
1987 How to Be Married One Year from Today: Lover Shopping for Men and Women. New York: Shapolsky Publishers.
Gardner, Carol Brooks
1980 "Passing by." Sociologist Inquiry, 50:328–56.
1983 "Aspects of gender behavior in public places in a small southwestern city." Unpublished Ph.D. dissertation, University of Pennsylvania.
1988 "Access information: private lies and public peril." Social Problems 35:384–97.
1989 Analyzing Gender in Public Places: Rethinking Goffman's Vision of Everyday Life. American Sociologist 20:42–56.
1990 "Kinship claims and competence claims: people with disabilities in public places." Paper to be given at American Sociological Association annual meeting. Washington, D.C.
Geng, Veronica
1971 "Scorn not the street compliment!" In Cosmopolitan's New Etiquette Guide, ed. Helen Gurley Brown, 75–79. North Hollywood, Calif.: Wilshire Book Company.
Gieseking, Hal
1980 "Special report: summer criminals." Travel/Holiday Magazine, June, 77–78.
Glamour Magazine
1980 "Should you carry a personal alarm?" March, 63.
Goffman, Erving
1961 Asylums. Chicago: Aldine.
1963 Behavior in Public Places. Glencoe, Ill.: Free Press.
1967 "Where the action is." In Interaction Ritual, 149–270. Garden City, N.Y.: Doubleday.
1971 Relations in Public. New York: Basic Books.
1973 Presentation of Self in Everyday Life. Woodstock, N.Y.: Overlook Press.
Good Housekeeping Magazine
1972 "Street-safety precautions every woman should follow," October, 193.

Grahame, Kamini Maraj
1985 "Sexual harassment." In No Safe Place, ed. Connie Guberman and Margie Wolfe, 111–30. Toronto: Women's Press.

Griffith, Liddon R.
1978 Mugging: You Can Protect Yourself. Englewood Cliffs, N.J.: Prentice-Hall.

Hair, Robert A., and Samm Sinclair Baker
1970 How to Protect Yourself Today. New York: Stein and Day.

Hanmer, Jalna, and Sheila Saunders
1983 "Blowing the cover of the protective male: a community study of violence to women." In The Public and the Private, ed. Eva Gamarnikow, Meg Stacey, Linda Imray, Audrey Middleton, Jalna Hanmer, Sheila Saunders, Patricia Allatt, Claire Ungerson, Ann Murcott, Marilyn Porter, Janet Finch, Peter Rushton, Hilary Graham, Laura McKee, and Margaret O'Brien. London: Heinemann.

Heath, Linda
1984 "Impact of newspaper crime reports on fear of crime: multimethodological investigation." Journal of Personality and Social Psychology 47:263–76.

Hechinger, Grace
1984 How to Raise a Street-Smart Child. New York: Facts on File.

Hindelang, Michael J., Michael R. Gottfredson, and James Garofalo
1978 The Victims of Personal Crime. Cambridge, Mass.: Ballinger.

Ingber, Diana
1987 "Staying safe: the smart woman's guide to self-defense." McCall's Magazine, March, 138, 140, 142.

Janoff-Bulman, Ronnie, and Irene Hanson Frieze
1987 "The role of gender in reactions to criminal victimization." In Gender and Stress, ed. Rosalind C. Barnett, Lois Biener, and Grace K. Baruch, 159–84. New York: Free Press.

Kaye, Elizabeth
1985 "Preventing robbery and rape." Harper's Bazaar Magazine, April 72, 74.

Kelly, Liz
1987 "The continuum of sexual violence." In Women, Violence, and Social Control, ed. Jalna Hanmer and Mary Maynard, 46–60. Atlantic Highlands, N.J.: Humanities.

Krupp, Charla
1978 "Solving your problem: 84 ways to feel safer." Mademoiselle Magazine, October, 142–43, 146, 152.

Ledray, Linda E.
1986 Recovering from Rape. New York: Holt.

Martin, Judith
1982 Miss Manners' Guide to Excruciatingly Correct Behavior. New York: Atheneum.

Maxfield, Michael G.
1984 "The limits of vulnerability in explaining fear of crime: a comparative neighborhood analysis." Research in Crime and Delinquency 21:233–50.

Mehlman, Peter
1987 "Male guilt." Glamour, April, 332.

Monkerud, Donald, and Mary Heiny
1980 Self-Defense for Women. Dubuque, Ia.: William C. Brown.

Navarro, Mireya
1990 "For busy storeowner, nearby protests have raised fear of misunderstanding." The New York Times, May 17.

O'Connor, Dr. Margaret, and Dr. Jane Silverman
1989 Finding Love: Creative Strategies for Finding Your Ideal Mate. New York: Crown.

Pickering, Michael C. V.
1983 A Manual for Women's Self-Defense. North Palm Beach, Fla.: The Athletic Institute.

Post, Elizabeth L.
1969 Emily Post's Etiquette. New York: Funk & Wagnalls.

Radford, Jill
1987 "Policing male violence—policing women." In Women, Violence, and Social Control, ed. Jalna Hanmer and Mary Maynard, 30–45. Atlantic Highlands, N.J.: Humanities.

Riger, Stephanie, and Margaret T. Gordon
1981 "The fear of rape: a study in social control." Journal of Social Issues 37:71–92.

Rockwood, Marcia, and Mary Thom
1979 "Making your block, office, parking lot, community rape-proof." Ms. Magazine, March, 79–82.

Schraub, Susan
1979 "Bazaar's anti-rape handbook." Harper's Bazaar Magazine, March, 152–53, 169.

Scribner, Marilyn
1988 Free to Fight Back. Wheaton, Ill.: Harold Shaw.

Sims, Calvin
1990 "Black shoppers call Korean merchants hostile and unfair." The New York Times, May 17.

Sommerfield, Diana
1986 Single, Straight Men: 106 Guaranteed Places to Find Them. New York: St. Martin's.

Tegner, Bruce
  1965   Bruce Tegner's Complete Book of Self-Defense. New York: Bantam.
Today's Health Magazine
  1973   "What a scream can do for you." June, 29–33, 64.
Vanderbilt, Amy
  1972   Amy Vanderbilt's Etiquette. Garden City, N.Y.: Doubleday.
Wachs, Eleanor
  1988   Crime-Victim Stories. Bloomington, Ind.: Indiana University Press.
Wegman, James
  1978   "How to be safe on the streets." Glamour, September, 57.

Wheeler, Elizabeth
  1982   "Protecting yourself." Essence Magazine, September, 69.
Wilson, Julie
  1977   "How to protect yourself." Harper's Bazaar Magazine, March, 93, 151.
Zimmerman, Mary K.
  1981   "The abortion clinic." In Social Psychology through Symbolic Interaction, ed. Gregory P. Stone and Harvey A. Farberman, 43–52. New York: Wiley.

Questions for Understanding and Critical Thinking

1. Why are women commonly more *fearful* of crime than men?
2. What does Gardner mean by her statement that communicative acts between individuals in public are heavily *appearance dependent?*
3. Why do women sometimes feel the need to pretend that they have an "apparent" male escort who protects them from other men? What does such a finding reflect pertaining to gender, women's subordinate roles, and violence and crime in society?
4. Why might lesbians, African American women, and women with disabilities be singled out for harassment or criminal victimization?
5. As a woman or man, have you experienced harassment or been the victim of crime in a public place? What rights do you think people should have in public places? What limitations, if any, should be placed on people's behavior in public?

ARTICLE 22 _____

Based on in-depth interviews with never-married, African American mothers, sociologist Robin L. Jarrett investigates the ways that poor women adapt to economic marginality. In the process, she describes structural explanations of poverty and links them to personal agency in understanding poverty among the poor. Jarrett also makes one more aware of how discrimination is deeply embedded in race, class, and gender relations in the United States.

Robin Jarrett is a sociology professor at Loyola University of Chicago. Her areas of specialization include family, sex and gender, community and urban sociology, and racial and ethnic minorities.

Looking Ahead

1. Why does Jarrett believe structural explanations of poverty should be expanded?
2. How do the ideals and realities of marriage compare for the women in Jarrett's study?
3. What are the major economic impediments to marriage experienced by the women in this study?
4. What coping and resistance strategies do the women employ in daily life?

Living Poor

Family Life among Single Parent, African-American Women

◆ *Robin L. Jarrett*

INTRODUCTION: "BUT WHERE ARE THE PEOPLE?"

In the years since the media's rediscovery of race and poverty in America's inner cities, much has been written about . . . low-income housing projects. . . . [They] have become must-stops for anyone writing about the nation's so-called "underclass." Yet for all the ink and air time devoted to them, it is amazing how little we still know about the people who live there. . . . [R]arely do we get to know the people of the projects as anything other than sociological types . . . one-dimensional portraits of third- or fourth-generation welfare mothers, violence-prone, drug-dealing gang members or street smart

Source: From Robin L. Jarrett, "Living Poor: Family Life Among Single Parent, African-American Women." © 1994 by the Society for the Study of Social Problems. Reprinted from *Social Problems*, Vol. 41, No. 1, February 1994, pp. 30–49, by permission.

man-children living by their wits. Seldom do writers dare to look beyond the sociology and statistics . . . to see people as individuals rather than as examples of predrawn stereotypes (Monroe 1991:1).

Recent increases in the number of households headed by poor African-American women, the result of non-marital, adolescent childbearing, have encouraged researchers to once again debate the relationship between family structure, race, and poverty. Like past discussions, both structural and cultural arguments have been advanced to explain changing household and family formation patterns. Recent quantitative studies (see Baca Zinn 1990b; Marks 1991; Patterson 1981 for an overview), as well as past ethnographic research (see Jarrett in press for an overview), offer support for the structural argument, challenging the cultural position. These data indicate that economic forces are closely correlated with female headship and non-marital childbearing among poor African-American women. The structural perspective correctly documents the link between economic forces and family patterns. But it obscures many of the processes associated with living in poverty.

This paper expands on the structural explanation by describing the ways that African-American women live in poverty, dynamically adapting to larger economic forces. I use qualitative interview data to explore the following question: How do poor African-American women, in their daily lives, respond to conditions of economic marginality?

This paper is divided into four sections. Section One provides an overview of the current issues regarding family life and poverty among African Americans. Substantive themes and explanatory frameworks derived from the "underclass debate" are critically discussed and compared to earlier discussions of poverty in the United States. Section Two describes the qualitative group interviews that were conducted with a sample of never-married, African-American mothers. These data are used to examine issues raised in Section One, concentrating on unmarried women because they figure so prominently in the underclass debate. Section Three presents empirical findings from the focus group interviews. Verbatim excerpts from these discussions are used to examine key components of the structural argument. Observations from the focus group study are also compared with earlier ethnographic and qualitative research to explore continuity in family patterns. Finally, Section Four explores the broader theoretical implications of the research. The discussion addresses how the focus group data elaborate on the structural explanation and offer direction for future research.

FAMILY STRUCTURE, RACE, AND POVERTY: "FEMALE HOUSEHOLDER, NO HUSBAND PRESENT"

At the heart of the deterioration of the fabric of Negro society is the deterioration of the Negro family. It is the fundamental source of the weakness of the Negro community. . . . In essence, the Negro community has been forced into a matriarchal structure which, because it is so out of line with the rest of the American society, seriously retards the progress of the group as a whole (Moynihan 1965:5, 29).

How could it be that, despite the combination of economic growth and huge increases in expenditures on the poor, the number of poor stopped shrinking in the early 1970s? . . . We have encountered a variety of explanations. . . . Now we have an additional explanation: the increasing prevalence of a certain type of family—a young mother with children and no husband present (Murray 1984:133).

Under the new rubric of the "underclass debate," researchers have returned to old questions of the relationship between family structure, race, and poverty (Katz 1989; Piven et al. 1987; Wilson and Aponte 1985). Little consensus exists in its key dimensions—such as size, origins, defining characteristics—or if, in fact, such a group exists. Most researchers, however, use the term "underclass" to convey a group of minority poor who represent a persistent and more dangerous form of poverty (see Auletta 1982; Glasgow 1980; Lemann 1986; Mead 1986; Murray 1984; Ricketts and Sawhill 1988).

Several distinct groups are hypothesized to comprise the underclass, such as criminals, hustlers in the underground economy, the chronically unemployed, and the long-term working poor, but households headed by women are cited as key contributors to its growth (Auletta 1982; Glasgow 1980; McLanahan, Garfinkel, and Watson 1988; Ricketts and Sawhill 1988; Wilson 1987). For example, demographic data indicate that the proportion of poor African-American families headed by women increased from 30 percent in 1959 to 72 percent in 1977—more than doubling in one generation. Since then it has remained slightly above 70 percent. Female heads of household comprised, respectively, one-third of the poor in 1982 and 71 percent of all poor African-American families (Wilson, 1987).

Two conceptual frameworks, the cultural and the structural, provide competing arguments to explain changes in family patterns. The cultural explanation maintains that changing household and family formation patterns among low-income African Americans are the result of deviant values. Researchers cite various factors generating distinctive values, but cultural formulations that stress the role of liberal welfare reforms in exacerbating deviant values have been particularly influential (Mead 1986; Murray 1984). The basic argument is that ghetto-specific norms differ from their mainstream counterparts, positively endorsing single motherhood, out-of-wedlock childbearing, welfare dependency, male irresponsibility, criminal behavior, low mobility aspirations, and, more generally, family instability (Auletta 1982; Lemann 1986; Mead 1986; Murray 1984; see also Cook and Curtin 1987 for an overview).

The structural explanation argues that demographic shifts in household and family formation patterns reflect larger economic trends. Researchers cite macro-structural changes in the economy—including the decline in entry-level jobs, the relocation of jobs away from the inner-city, and the mismatch between job requirements and employee skills—and parallel declines in rates of male employment, marriage, and childbearing within marriage as evidence of external or situational pressures on family life. The fundamental thesis is that economic factors impede the construction and maintenance of mainstream family patterns: they encourage poor African-American women to forego marriage, bear children out-of-wedlock, head their own households, and rely on welfare income (Darity and Meyers 1984; Joe 1984; Staples 1985; Testa et al. 1989; Wilson 1987).

Current discussions about poverty and the underclass are similar in two ways to the poverty discussions that took place from the early 1960s to the mid-1970s when such issues were last seriously discussed. Then, as now, both structural and cultural arguments were the dominant explanatory frameworks as researchers debated the competing role of economic and cultural factors. Furthermore, recent and past studies concentrate on family structure or, more precisely, household structure. During both periods, structural and cultural perspectives focused on the idea that particular family arrangements—either as a consequence or as a cause—were associated with poverty status (Lemann 1986; Lewis 1965, 1966; Mead 1986; Moynihan 1965; Murray 1984; Garfinkel and McLanahan 1986; Wilson 1987).

Current discussions about poverty differ, however, from earlier discussions, in three key ways: in the analytic focus of research studies; in the disciplines of theorists who propose explanatory frameworks; and in the types of evidence used to support conceptual claims. First, current poverty studies are primarily concerned with female headship and a variety of demographic correlates, particularly welfare (Bane and Ellwood 1984a, 1984b; Ellwood and Bane 1984; Garfinkel and McLanahan 1986; Murray 1984; Nichols-Casebolt 1988; see also Baca Zinn 1989, 1990b; Piven et al. 1987; and Wilson and Aponte 1985 for an overview). By contrast, research from the 1960s and 1970s was principally interested in how poor families coped and adapted to poverty (Aschenbrenner 1975; Hannerz 1969; Jeffers 1967; Lewis 1965, 1966; Rainwater 1970; Schulz 1969; Stack 1974).

Second, current conceptualizations of the cultural perspective derive largely from journalists (Auletta 1982; Lemann 1986; see also Marks 1991; Williams 1992a). By contrast, in previous decades, cultural formulations emanated from anthropologists and sociologists (Gans 1969; Hannerz 1969; Leacock 1971; Lewis 1965, 1966; Rainwater 1970; Stack 1974; Valentine 1968; see also Rainwater 1987 for an overview). During both periods, discussions of the structural position have come primarily from social scientists. Third, current poverty studies use demographic analyses to substantiate or challenge particular theoretical claims (Baca Zinn 1989; Williams 1992a). By contrast, during the 1960s and 1970s both ethnographic research (see Hannerz 1975; Jarrett in press; and Rainwater 1987 for an overview) and demographic analyses were used to assess the cultural and structural arguments (Wilson and Aponte 1985; Katz 1989).

Yet, both recent and past poverty research are similar in that they both rely on cultural and structural frameworks as the dominant explanations. They also demonstrate a continued concern with family structure as a key causal or explanatory variable. As a consequence of their differences, poverty researchers today know more about the demographic profiles of poor African-American families than about their internal dynamics; they more frequently respond to journalistic conceptualizations of cultural processes than those of anthropologists and sociologists; and they possess a wealth of quantitative data and a dearth of qualitative and ethnographic research to explore the issue of family life and poverty.

The evidence marshalled by myriad studies favors the structural argument and challenges the cultural argument. Reviews of longitudinal panel data that focus on the link between welfare and marital status, reproductive behavior, and living arrangements indicate that welfare has little or no effect on these behaviors (see Baca Zinn 1989; Ellwood and Bane 1984; Garfinkel and McLanahan 1986; Marks 1991; Patterson 1981). Nor do these data provide evidence for the intergenerational transfer of poverty and welfare dependence as a result of normative orientations (Baca Zinn 1989; Corcoran et al. 1985; McLanahan, Garfinkel, and Watson 1988; Wilson and Aponte 1985). Other quantitative studies demonstrate a strong relationship between male unemployment, female headship, and out-of-wedlock childbearing (Darity and Meyers 1984; Joe 1984; Staples 1985; Testa et al. 1989; Wilson 1987).

Ethnographic research, though largely untapped in the current debate, can contribute to the current discussion of poverty in several ways. First, it can add further support to the structural argument, as it can serve to describe in detail how economic factors impinge on family life and the ways that the poor respond to these conditions. These data also reveal that the poor share conventional aspirations concerning family life, rather than exhibit a deviant set of values (Anderson 1976; Jeffers 1967; Ladner 1971; Liebow 1967; Stack 1974; Valentine 1978; see also Jarrett in press). Furthermore, qualitative data are the most appropriate type to assess cultural arguments (Rainwater 1987) and to critique improper conceptualizations of cultural processes as formulated in the culture of poverty framework (Gans 1969; Leacock 1971; Lewis 1965, 1966; Rainwater 1970, 1987; Valentine 1968; see also Swidler 1986).

The structural perspective challenges the culture of poverty argument and documents the association between economic factors and family patterns. Nevertheless, it is flawed in two critical ways. First, it assumes the superiority of the two-parent household (Cerullo and Erlien 1986). The structural perspective uses an idealized, if not mythic, model of the nuclear family to assess poor African-American families (Reed 1988). Consequently, it fails to acknowledge the diversity of family forms as well as their viability among the poor and non-poor alike (Baca Zinn and Eitzen 1992; Thorne and Yalom 1982; Williams 1992b; see also Baca Zinn 1990a). Second, the structural perspective takes an economic deterministic position and ignores the role of human agency. It posits a direct and unmediated relationship between economic factors and family patterns. Moen's and Wethington's (1992:243) general critique of structural models is applicable: the inordinate concentration on external factors encourages the overgeneralized view that families are "at the mercy of forces

beyond their control, their responses constrained to the point of total conformity to structural forces." Consequently, we know little about how poor women actually respond to conditions of economic marginality.

Despite its conceptual limitations, the structural perspective has received consistent empirical support. This suggests that the continued rejuvenation of the cultural perspective reflects larger racial divisions within U.S. society, rather than actual findings from academic research (Gresham 1989; Wilkerson and Gresham 1989). Historically, poverty research has been permeated by political controversies based on speculation and stereotyping, rather than sound theories and methods (Davis and Davis 1989; Rainwater and Yancey 1967; Suttles 1976). These observations highlight the need to move beyond stagnant debates that center on improperly conceptualized cultural models (Gans 1969; Leacock 1971; Rainwater 1987; Swidler 1986) as well as on deterministic and overgeneralized structural models.

◆   ◆   ◆

SAMPLE AND METHODOLOGY: "RESEARCH TOUCHED BY HUMAN HANDS"

Qualitative methods . . . as they get close to the subjects of their research . . . necessarily reflect social reality from the bottom upwards (Finch 1986:113).

The data reported in this paper derive from a series of focus group interviews (see Jarrett 1993 for a detailed methodological discussion). The interviews were broadly conceived as an exploratory examination of how women in poor families adapt to conditions of poverty. I concentrated on various aspects of family life, including family formation patterns, household living arrangements, childcare and socialization patterns, intergenerational relations, male-female relations, and welfare, work, and social opportunities.

Ten focus groups, comprised of a total of 82 low-income African-American women, were conducted between January and July 1988. Each focus group session lasted approximately two hours and was held with groups of no more than 8–10 women. The tape recorded discussions were relatively unstructured but topically oriented, allowing for comparisons across groups. The ten focus group interviews conducted represent a larger than average number for such research projects and fell within the upper range for serious research (see Calder 1977; Hedges 1985).

The criteria for selection of the women was based on the profiles of women discussed in the current underclass debate. They included: (1) never-married mothers, (2) who received AFDC, and (3) lived in high poverty or economically transitional neighborhoods in the city of Chicago. Most of the women were in their early to middle twenties and began their childbearing careers as adolescents. A purposive sample was drawn from Chicago-area Head Start programs since such programs are located in low-income communities and serve women fitting the above profile.

A team of research assistants transcribed and coded the interviews thematically by topical area. The initial codes were based on the broad topical areas guiding the research but were expanded to include unanticipated information that emerged in the discussion. Once this task was completed, key issues and themes were identified for each area.

THE EMPIRICAL DATA: "IN THEIR OWN WORDS"

[T]he actor's 'own story,' is a live and vibrant message from 'down there,' telling us what it means to be a kind of person we have never met face to face (Becker 1970:70).

In this section, I present empirical data that offer insights on the lives of real women and that address the limitations of the structural framework. As a point of departure, I examine the normative and behavioral dimensions of familial roles among the sample of never-married, African-American mothers. The concentration on the conflict between norms and behaviors provides a dynamic example of how women who hold conventional aspirations concerning family patterns respond in their daily lives. Around this broad topic, I explore four issues: (1) Marriage, the ideal; (2) Marriage, the reality; (3) Economic impediments to conventional marriage; and (4) Alternatives to conventional marriage.

Marriage, the Ideal: "Everybody Wants to Be Married"

Women consistently professed adherence to mainstream patterns. For virtually all of the women interviewed, legal marriage was the cornerstone of conventional family life. Marriage represented a complex of behaviors, including independent household formation, economic independence, compatibility, and fidelity and commitment that were generally associated with the nuclear family. Representative excerpts from group members illustrate:

Independent Household Formation

We were talking about marriage and all of that. . . . We was staying with his mother. . . . I told him we'll get married and we'll get our own place.

He lives with his grandmother. I don't want to move into his grandmother's home. I live at my mother's. I don't want him to move in there. When we get married, I want us to live in our own house, something we can call ours.

Economic Independence

He asked me [to get married]. . . . We never did. It's more like we waiting to get more financial.

Charles, [my boyfriend] be half-stepping [financially]. That's why I'm not really ready for marriage.

I plan on getting married. But I would rather wait. He said he wanted to wait until he made 22. He works two jobs, but he said he want to wait until he gets a better job, where he can support both of us.

He's always nagging me to get married. I ask him: 'Are you going to be able to take me off aid and take care of all four of my children?' So when I say that he just laugh.

Compatibility

I think a person should never get married unless it's for love. . . . [If] you want to spend the rest of your life with that person, you all [should] have a good understanding. If you marry somebody just because you pregnant, just because you have four or five kids by them, or because society or whoever pressured you into it, you goin' to become mean and resentful. And if that person turns out to not be what you thought or that marriage turns out to be something less than you hoped it would be, it's not goin' to be worth it.

I'm not married to him so I can do what I want to do. But when I get married, I can't do it at all. But it's not supposed to be like that. He says: 'I pay all the bills.' But you don't get to boss me.

I don't want to marry him 'cause me and him would never get along; but I like him.

You know, I like him a whole lot. But then [my mother] say: 'Well then why you don't a marry him?' [It's] because . . . somehow our waves just won't click.

A lotta' time you can't get along with the children's father. . . . Me and Carmen's father could not get along, point blank. [I]t wasn't the money. It's not 'cause I didn't have a father; he had a father. We came from good homes. We just could not get along. We don't even know how we made the baby. [laughter]

Fidelity and Commitment

If I get married, I believe in being all the way faithful.

I want you to take care of me. I'm not looking to jump into bed and call this a marriage. I want you to love me, care for me, be there when I need you because I'm going to be there for you when you need me.

As soon as [men] get married and things change and he's looking for somebody else. Man! Why didn't they find that person before they marry you and you start going through all those changes.

Nita, a mother of two children provided one of the most eloquent statements on the meaning of marriage. She said:

I would love to be married. . . . I believe I would make a lovely wife. . . . I would just love to have the experience of being there married with a man. I imagine me and my children, my son basketball player . . . playing for the [Chicago] Bulls. My daughter . . . playing the piano, have a secretary job or going to college. . . . Me, I'm at home playing the wifely duties. This man, not a boy, coming home with his manly odors. . . . My husband comes home, takes off his work boots and have dinner. . . . I would like to have this *before I leave this earth, a husband, my home, my car.*

Likewise, Charmaine, who despite her own unmarried status, firmly asserted:

I think everybody wants to get married. Everybody wants to have somebody to work with them . . . and go through life with. . . . I would like to be married. . . . I want to be married. I'm not gonna lie. I really do.

Women, despite their insistent statements concerning the importance of marriage as the cornerstone of mainstream family life, were well aware of the unconventionality of their actual behaviors. Women openly acknowledged that their single status, non-marital childbearing, and in some cases, female-headship, diverged from mainstream household and family formation patterns. Tisha said with a mixture of humor and puzzlement:

Is this what it's supposed to be like? So, I'm going backwards. Most people say: 'Well, you go to school, you get married, and you have kids.' Well, I had my kids. I'm trying to go to school and maybe, somewhere along the line, I'm going to catch up with everybody else.

Natty, the mother of an active preschooler who periodically appeared at the door of the meeting room, further observed:

I really would like to have two children but I'm not married . . . and I would like to be married before I do have another child. . . . So maybe one day we might jump the broom or tie the knot or whatever.

Sherry's comments were similar:

I wanted to marry him because we had talked about it so long. . . . We always talked about it . . . gettin' married, then have our kids and stuff and everything.

Tisha's, Natty's, and Sherry's observations indicate that the desired sequence of events entails economic independence, then marriage, and, finally, childbearing.

Women's observations in this study are consistent with past ethnographic research (Aschenbrenner 1975; Clark 1983; Holloman and Lewis 1978; Ladner 1971; Stack 1974; see also Anderson 1976). Even in Lee Rainwater's (1970) study of the purportedly notorious Pruitt-Igoe housing project in St. Louis, impoverished residents routinely professed adherence to mainstream values concerning marriage and family. He observed:

The conventionality and ordinariness of Pruitt-Igoeans' conception of good family life is striking. Neither in our questionnaires nor in open-ended interviews or observational contexts did we find any consistent elaboration of an unconventional ideal. In the working class, a good family life is seen to have at its core a stable marriage between two people who love and respect each other and who rear their children in an adequate home, preferably one that has its own yard. If only things went right, according to most Pruitt-Igoeans, their family life would not differ from that of most Americans (Rainwater 1970:48).

Marriage, the Reality: "That's a Little White Girl's Dream"

Women were pessimistic about actually contracting family roles as defined in the mainstream manner. Their aspirations for conventional family roles were tempered by doubt and, in some cases, outright pessimism.

Karen's comment reflected her sense of uncertainty:

I would like to get married one day . . . to somebody that's as ready as I am. . . . But it's so scary out here. You scared to have a commitment with somebody, knowing he's not on the level. . . . They ready to get their life together; they looking for a future.

Denise and Chandra were most pessimistic about their chances for a conventional and stable family life:

I used to have this in my head, all my kids got the same daddy, get married have a house. That's a little white girl's dream. That stuff don't happen in real life. You don't get married and live happily ever after.

It doesn't work in that way. Just because you have a baby don't mean they gone stay with you. . . . Even if you married, that don't mean he gone stay with you; he could up and leave.

Even Dee Dee's initially firm assertions were laced with doubt:

I'm goin' to get married one day. I'm goin' to say I know I'm getting' married one day, if it is just for a month. I'm gettin' married, I know that. [laughter] I know I am . . . well maybe.

Earlier in their lives most of these women assumed that their household and formation patterns would follow conventional paths. Remaining single, bearing children outside of marriage, and heading a household were not foregone conclusions. Rather, pessimism about the viability of mainstream patterns grew out of their first-hand experiences. Women related conflictual and depriving situations that caused them to reassess their expectations.

Andrea described her attempt to forge a long-term relationship and its disappointing outcome:

I would rather live by myself, me and my two kids, because I used to stay with somebody. . . . Me and him did not work out. We used to have to go scrape up some food to eat. I would rather stay by myself.

Both Pat and Lisa, recount similar tribulations:

It makes me angry to think about it. . . . I go through changes [with him] and . . . sometimes I just throw up my hands in the air— excuse the expression—I just say 'Fuck it! Had it! I'm tired! Sometime I say: 'Man disappear!'

[Men cause] a lot of headache and heartache. . . . All the time you taking to set that man straight, you could be spending with your child. . . . Instead of having time with your kids, you got to get him together.

Kara, like Pat and Lisa, expressed feelings of frustration:

You want to see [men] do something one way and they don't see it that way. They want to do it the way they want to do it. . . . You get mad. You frustrated. It's just emotionally draining.

Women's experiences were augmented by the experiences of others. Through the processes of observation of and comparison to older women in the community, younger women gauged their chances of contracting ideal family forms. Comments from Regina and Tennye, respectively, illustrated this:

A good husband has a good job where I can stay home with the family, raise the kids like on TV. But then it's hard. You don't find too many, not like when our mothers was coming up.

I don't think I'll ever find a husband because of the way I feel. I want it like my mother had it. [My father] took care of us. She been married to him since she was sixteen. He took care of her, took her out of her mother's house. She had four kids, he took care of all the kids.

These comments suggest that even as younger women compare themselves with older women, conventional patterns remain their reference point. Women's views also signal their awareness of declining opportunities for attaining mainstream family patterns within impoverished African-American communities.

Women's first-hand experiences indicate a more general point. Economic forces are not experienced in impersonal ways; nor are they experienced by solitary individuals, as implied by the structural perspective. Economic constraints are, instead, mediated through social relationships and interaction processes. Individuals ponder their situations with others in similar circumstances. As a result of his own ethnographic work, Hannerz (1969) critiqued the mechanistic components of the structural argument:

> [I]t is made to look as if every couple were left on its own to work out anew a solution to problems which have confronted many of both their predecessors and their contemporaries in the black community (Hannerz 1969:76).

His comment also suggests that the generational persistence and reaffirmation of particular strategies occur because the socioeconomic conditions that support them are still operant (cf. Franklin 1988). This point is aptly illuminated by Myesha and Pam, whose circumstances mirrored their mothers':

> My father wasn't around. But you know he tried. . . . He calls [me] now. Well, with my boyfriend, he [may] stay by my side. If he leaves, he just leave. . . . So, if my mama could do it, I know I can raise Daniel [my son].

> My mother had eight of us. I sympathize with what she go through because she doesn't get any help. But she raised us all by herself and we doing okay. It's a lot of women that don't need no man to help raise her kids because I know I can take care of mine by myself.

Economic Impediments to Marriage: "I Could Do Bad by Myself"

The women's own interpretations concerning changes in household and family formation patterns are consistent with the structural explanation of poverty. Economic factors, according to women, played a prominent role in their decisions to forego marriage, bear children outside of marriage, and, in some cases, head households.

Iesha described how economic factors influenced her decisions. She said:

> I had a chance to get married when I first had my two [children]. We had planned the date and everything, go down to city hall. . . . When the day came along, I changed my mind. Right today I'm glad I did not marry him because he still ain't got no job. He still staying with his sister and look where I am. Ever since I done had a baby I been on my own. I haven't lived with no one but myself. I been paying bills now.

Renee, who was considering marriage to her current companion, also recounted how economic considerations influenced her decisions:

> I could do bad by myself. . . . If we get married and he's working, then he lose his job. I'm going to stand by him and everything. I don't want to marry nobody that don't have nothing going for themselves. . . . I don't see no future. . . . I could do bad by myself.

Cheryl echoed her views:

> As far as I'm concerned about marriage and kids, I want to be married; but I also want to be married to somebody who is responsible, who can give me somethin' out of life. . . . I would like that security.

Pat was even more direct in her preference for an economically stable mate:

If he's out of a job, he can't sit here too long. I can't do it alone. . . . I got to see a place where he's helping me. But if you don't help, I got no time.

Tina, who was currently uninvolved ("on my own"), further described the link between male economic marginality and marriage:

I wanted to get married when I first found out I was pregnant, but he didn't want to get married. And I'm glad that he didn't. . . . It would have been terrible; he wasn't working. Maybe that was one of the reasons why he did not want to get married.

Other qualitative and ethnographic studies also describe the depressing effect that economic pressures have on marriage among poor women and men (Aschenbrenner 1975; Liebow 1967; Hannerz 1969; Rainwater 1970; Stack 1974; Sullivan 1985). The absence of legal marriage or economically stable partnerships, however, did not preclude the formation of strong and stable male-female relationships. Many of the women were involved in a variety of unions. As previously described, some of these relationships were indeed conflictual. Others were remarkably stable, considering the economic constraints that both women and men faced. Several women described long-term relationships, some of which had endured for over a decade.

One said:

I'm not married. I got three kids. But their father is there with the kids. He been there since I was 16. . . . I been with the same guy since I was 16 years old and I'm still with him now. I only had really one man in my life.

Another one echoed:

We been together for so many years; I really think we could work it out. . . . I go over his house, me and the kids, and stay for weeks. Then we come back home.

Still another one underlined:

I been with my baby's father for 12 years. We still not married. So maybe one day we might jump the broom or tie the knot or whatever.

These comments are important because they identify the existence of strong alternative relationships that are not detected in demographic profiles that recognize only legal marriages. They also confirm the result of earlier ethnographic studies that identify a variety of male-female arrangements that exist outside of marriage (Aschenbrenner 1975; Jarrett 1992; Liebow 1967; Rainwater 1970; Schulz 1969; Stack 1974; Sullivan 1985). Such arrangements varied from casual friendships to fully committed partnerships. The information gathered from the focus groups and the detailed accounts resulting from ethnographic case studies suggest the need to explore the spousal and parental roles that men assume outside of marriage. These arrangements have significant implications for the support and well-being of women and children.

Women's decisions regarding household and family formation patterns were not surprising in light of the economic profiles of potential marital partners. Even when men worked, their employment options were limited. The prospective mates of the women interviewed were generally unemployed, underemployed, or relegated the most insecure jobs in the secondary labor market. Within the context of the larger discussion on perceptions of social and economic opportunities, women described the types of jobs their male companions and friends assumed. They included: car wash attendants; drug dealers;

fast food clerks; grocery store stock and bag clerks; informal car repairmen; lawn workers; street peddlers; and street salvage workers.

The focus group data thus confirm the structural explanation of poverty and its emphasis on economic factors, such as joblessness. But they also go beyond the primary concentration on the economic instability of men and its consequences for family maintenance. The focus group interviews indicate that women also considered their own resources in addition to those of the men. They assessed their own educational backgrounds, job experiences, welfare resources, and childcare arrangements. For example, women reviewed their educational qualifications and assessed their potential for economic independence.

Educational Attainment

As far as working, I have to be serious. I don't have any skills and I prefer to go to school . . . do something progressive, you know, to try to get off of [welfare].

Now I'm trying to go back to school 'cause when I dropped out . . . I was in the 11th grade and was pregnant. . . . I was pregnant with her then, so I had to leave school. . . . Now I'm trying to go back to school for nursing assistant, so I can get off all public aid: find somethin' else to do 'stead of being on welfare all my life.

I try to do what I can. And it's hard out there when you dropped out of high school or you may have a G.E.D. And you have a child . . . and then go and try to find a job.

Work Experiences

Contrary to common stereotypes, many of the women had worked. Women's past work experiences served to clarify the limitations of using the types of jobs available to them as a strategy of mobility. The women's com-

ments focused on low wages, job access, and job inflexibility.

Low Wages

It don't make sense to go to McDonald's to make 3.35 an hour when you know you got to pay 4 dollars an hour to baby-sit and you got to have bus fare.

If you got to get something, you need something that's going to pay something, that's going to make a difference and not take away from it. And you know when they had that discussion like that on Oprah [Winfrey talk show], they don't really see that. They tell you get out there. One girl get on there talking about she'll scrub the floor for 3.50 [an hour], but what it's going to do for you? You still losing out. You not bringing in as much as you get if you were at home.

Job Access

It was too far. . . . I would have to get up at 4 o'clock in the morning in order to be at work at seven. [I] leave work at 3:30 and still wouldn't make it home until 8 o'clock. And it was too far when I wasn't making anything. . . . I didn't have no time for my kids, no time for myself.

Job Inflexibility

[I] miss[ed] a day on the weekend and they fire[d] me. I didn't understand. They call me, but I wouldn't go back, because ain't no telling when I get sick like I was sick then. I told them no I didn't want it. And I been looking, putting in applications hoping that somebody call.

Welfare Experiences

Welfare, like low-wage jobs, also represented an institutionalized impediment to mobility. The women's comments highlighted the need for benefits, the stigma of public aid, welfare regulations, and their need for child-care.

Need for Benefits

If [public aid is] going to do something, I prefer if they would take me off but leave my kids on. Because they would need it more and I figure I can take care of myself a little bit more than they can. You need that medical for them.

One reason, seriously . . . that I do not want [public aid] to take my check [is] because I need my medical card. They can take the money, but I need that medical card and I need those food stamps.

Stigma of Public Aid

You got to go out there on your own using [your] public aid background . . . because a lot of companies not going to hire you because you coming from public aid.

Welfare Regulations

They give you the runaround for nothing. . . . This money not coming out . . . their pockets. . . . [I]t's not like it's coming out they paycheck every week. . . . It's coming from your parents paying they state taxes. . . . You trying to take care of your children the best way you can and this is one of the ways that you can take care of your children.

How you goin' to get ahead? Somebody needs to explain it to me. . . . I know a lot of people that graduated from college and stuff, they ain't got jobs. If you do get a job you got to know somebody. . . . Soon as you get the job guess who be on your back? Mr. A.D.C.

They make you go through so many changes . . . so many changes for nothing. . . . When I was goin' to school, they call [me for an appointment. I said:] 'Can I come after I get out of school?' [They said:]

'No, come now.' [I said:] 'I have finals.' [They said:] 'So, come or you will be cut off.'

Childcare Needs

Women, unlike men, had to factor childcare into their work schedules:

Well, I want to wait until my kids get about 5 [to work], so if something's going on [at the babysitter's] they can tell me. I don't want to be worried. I don't have nobody. I keep my own kids.

If I want to go out and get a job, I ain't going to pick any daycare in the city, because they ain't so safe either.

I just feel it was harder for a woman . . . with children . . . to find a job. When I was working it was always Keisha [my daughter], this, Keisha, that, Keisha this, that. She did this today; she scribled on my wall. . . . So, my mother died. I quit working. . . . I didn't have nobody to keep her. And so that was that.

As a result of their limited educational attainment, low-paying jobs, welfare disincentives, and childcare needs, most women came to perceive their economic options as severely limited. Consequently, when women sought other opportunities, they took both men's economic limitations and their own into account.

Alternatives to Conventional Marriage: "You Can Depend on Your Mama"

The focus group interviews expand on the structural explanation of poverty in yet another way. They serve to identify the strategic processes and sequences of events that follow women's decisions to forego marriage, bear children as single mothers, and in some cases, head households. Women responded to their poverty in three ways: they extended domestic and childcare responsibilities to multiple individuals; they relaxed paternal role expectations; and they assumed a flexible maternal role.

Domestic Kin Networks

The extension of domestic and childcare responsibilities beyond the nuclear family represented a primary response to economic marginality. Extended kin networks that centered around women provided assistance to single mothers and their children. For example, LaDawn, whose unintended pregnancy interrupted her plans to leave home, attend college, and get "real wild," described how living with her mother provides valuable support for her:

> When you money is gone and you at home with your mama, you don't have to worry about where you getting your next meal from because mama is always going to figure out a way how you can get your next meal. . . . And your mama would be there to depend on; you can depend on your mama.

Likewise, Rita, who currently lives alone with her son, also receives assistance from her mother and other female kin. She described the complex, but cooperative pattern, that characterizes the care of her child:

> Well, on the days Damen has school, my mother picks him up at night and keeps him at her house. And then when she goes to work in the morning, she takes him to my grandmother's house. And when my little sister gets out of school, she picks him up and takes him back to my mother's house. And then I go and pick him up.

Sheila, the mother of a preschooler and a newborn and who lives alone, described her situation:

> I had a hard struggle. I had to ask my mama for a lot of help. . . . I needed help for food . . . to go to school . . . help to watch my kids.

Ebony, who now lives alone, described the childcare benefits of living with her mother:

> I'm on my own. . . . I wish my mother would come stay with me . . . to help me out. Because when I was at home . . . it was things that she knew I didn't know nothing about. Why the baby crying so much. Well, you had it outside [the blanket] with no covers on. Letting me know so when the next [child] came I knew not to do this.

Diana also described the childcare benefits of living with her mother. She further hinted how her mother's assistance facilitates Diana's role as the primary caregiver:

> My mother gives me good advice . . . if something's wrong. [My twins] had the chicken pox. What am I gonna do? . . . They itching. What should I put on them? She helps me out that way. And I stays with my mother. Me and my mother sit down and talk. We don't have no kind of problems as far as her trying to raise [my kids].

The women's accounts in these focus group interviews are paralleled in similar ethnographic studies. Aschenbrenner (1975), Jarrett (1992), and Sullivan (1985), in their works, highlight the importance of grandmothers, as well as other women kin, in the lives of poor women and children. Grandmothers provide money on loan, childcare on a daily basis, and help with cooking and cleaning. These services allow some young mothers to finish school and get a job, staying off public assistance. Other qualitative studies provide comparable descriptions of supportive kin who provide care for poor children (Anderson 1990; Burton 1991;

Holloman and Lewis 1978; Liebow 1967; Stack 1974; Williams and Kornblum 1985; Zollar 1985). These examples are important in another way. They indicate that households labeled as female-headed are often embedded in larger kinship networks. Inter-household family arrangements and the domestic activities shared between them are usually overlooked in quantitative studies. Consequently, female-headship as a living arrangement and family as a set of social relationships that may transcend household boundaries are often confounded (Jarrett 1992; Stack 1974; Yanagisako 1979).

Expansion of the Paternal Role

Living in poverty issued yet other strategies. A second type of strategy concentrated on paternal role performance. Women lowered their expectations of men and extended the paternal role to non-biological fathers as ways of facilitating the involvement of men in childcare. Evaluations of paternal role performance that hinged on providing for the family economically were replaced by assessments that centered on men's efforts to find work and assist with day-to-day child welfare (see also Rainwater 1970). For example, Jaleesa, an ebulient mother of one child, said of her daughter's father:

> Even though he don't have a job, sometimes what counts is he spends time with his child. That child will think about that: 'Well, my father's here when my mother's not here.' [That child will] have someone else to turn to. And the father say: 'Well I ain't got no job. I ain't going to be around a child.' That's not all to it.

Anna, who openly proclaimed her strength in the face of many obstacles, echoed Jaleesa's sentiments:

> I got three kids all by him and he try to help out when he can. He's not working now but

[he] did try to help. And . . . he be going out looking for a job. I don't try to pressure. [Men] care about their kids. They wanna try to help.

Anita, who with her mother, forms a strong coalition around the care of her children, elaborated on Jaleesa's and Anna's comments:

> If he ain't out there trying to find a job doing something . . . he can be there with that baby, holding that baby, changing that baby's Pampers and let that mommy get rest or let her go out there and do what she have to do to support that baby.

According to Yvette, simply showing interest in one's child was positively evaluated:

> It's not what you do, it's how you do it. I don't expect him to buy my baby snowsuits and boots. . . [I]t's just the thought. When Keith's [my son's] birthday come around, [his father] ain't got to give him a quarter, he ain't got to send him a card. You could pick up the phone and wish him a happy birthday.

The way that poor unmarried fathers assist in their care of their children, both directly and indirectly, is also exemplified in Sullivan's (1985) ethnographic study. Men in his study provided food, clothing, and supervision for their children. Women's willingness to lower their expectations of their children's fathers reflected a fundamental reality. Most men lacked the resources to fully support their children. Yvette summarized this point aptly: "If they don't have it, they just don't have it. You can't get blood from a turnip."

Additionally, women extended the paternal role to men other than the biological fathers of their children. This strategy ensured that there was a male who provided nurturance and discipline, as well as economic support. For example, Alisha, asserted:

It's not a father, but a male image. . . . My daughter will mind my brother better than she do me. I will tell her to sit down, whereas I would probably have to tell her four or five times; whereas my brother will come in with that manly image and will say sit down one time and she be sitting down.

Debra, whose male companion is not the father of her child, provided another example:

It don't have to be blood to be like a father to somebody. . . . You can meet a man that will be a better father to your child than the natural father and it's nothing wrong with that.

LaDawn offered a similar view:

The guy I'm with is not my daughter's father; but he accepts my daughter. With him accepting and helping me out with her, that's all right. Most men they not going to do too much except maybe like buy her a little something, play with her and call it a day. But he accepts my daughter. And seeing that it is not his, I think that's a big responsibility. Because if I ask him for something for my daughter, he'll give it to me. So I figure that right there is a man.

Several ethnographic studies also provide examples of how non-biological fathers supply support for poor African-American children (Aschenbrenner 1975; Burton 1991; Holloman and Lewis 1978; Liebow 1967; Schulz 1969; Stack 1974; Sullivan 1985). These studies identify an array of male figures, such as uncles, grandfathers, neighbors, fictive kin, and male companions who played significant roles in the lives of many children.

Expansion of the Maternal Role

A third strategy used by women to facilitate the care of children entailed the expansion of the maternal role. Women, when necessary, broadened their role repertoire to include both expressive and instrumental role responsibilities. Irrespective of the presence or absence of men in the home, women expressed similar views about role flexibility. Under conditions of economic marginality women understood that at some point in their lives they would assume extensive household and family obligations.

Ethnographic research has consistently found that strong and competent mothers are greatly admired in low-income African-American communities (Aschenbrenner 1975; Ladner 1971; Rainwater 1970; Stack 1974). The focus group interviews provided corroboration. Women's comments illustrated their strength and competence as mothers. For example, Jeannie and Connie, who were currently living with the fathers of their children, respectively claimed:

It does not take a man to make those kids strong. When I tell my kids to do something, they going to look at me first.

I can be their mother and father and teach them values, teach them the right things. . . . I don't think they have to have a father in the home to teach them the right things.

Crystal, Sharon, and Shelly, who, currently were not living with male companions, individually asserted:

I can discipline [my children] myself. I have that bass in my voice. . . . I raise my voice and they'll . . . sit down. They'll mind me; they'll mind my mother.

I think a father should be around. But it can't always be. I'm raising my children by myself.

[My daughter] is well taken care of and I feel good about myself that I can give her everything she needs without his help.

In addition to describing how poor African-American women respond to conditions of poverty, the interviews highlighted the meanings that women attributed to the alternative family roles that they assumed. Motherhood, irrespective of women's single marital status, conferred them with a valued role. Moreover, women's ability to garner scarce resources, provide care for children, and in some cases, maintain households under stark conditions of poverty led to enhanced self-esteem. For example, Diane, mother of twin daughters, expressed her views on motherhood:

It's some fun parts in it and then you got some down parts when you got to do this and got to do that. But I enjoy my daughters. . . . They make me happy. . . . They're what get me up in the morning.

Lois, who cared for her children as well as her sister's, gave a similar view:

People compliment [me]: 'You really take time [with your kids].' Just because . . . I got three kids and not married, that don't mean I'm running the streets all the time. I'm at home helping my children.

Roberta, a mother of four children, who freely admitted that "sometimes my children drive me up the wall," also said:

I feel proud that I'm a mother. I'm going to see them grow up and get big. . . . The best thing about being a mother is having my kids close to me, knowing that I love them, and just to know that I'm going to be there for my kids if they ever need me.

Contrary to common assumptions, women's accounts described some of the positive consequences of heading one's own household. Tammy, who shares a small apartment with her mother, two sisters, and her children mused:

I never had a place of my own . . . [but] I'm ready for responsibility. I'm ready to raise my family by myself without my mother or sisters telling me: 'Well, you shouldn't do this, and you should do that'. . . . I'm ready to do it by myself, now.

Iesha, who lives alone with her children, elaborated:

The person that's out there on their own is more responsible. You have to think about they are actually taking care of their home now. If they're paying rent, light bill, gas bill, they got to be responsible.

Lareesa, who described how she has been labeled "slow" in school, offered one of the most articulate statements on the relationship between household independence and personal development:

I [and my son] live with my grandmother. . . . She says I have to listen to what she says because as long as I'm living under her roof, I got to obey her rules. . . . I'm not saying I'm grown [emphasis], grown [sic], but I want responsibility. That's just like taking an exam. If somebody gives you the answers, that's cheating me out of my life, if I can't do what I want, learn from myself.

DISCUSSION: "BRINGING PEOPLE BACK IN"

As I got to know and to absorb a great deal about the daily routines and the physical and social contexts of the lives of many parents and children, the logic of many of the choices and much of the behavior of these low-income families became clearer (Jeffers 1967:117).

The primary goal of this paper is to expand on the structural explanation of poverty. The structural perspective correctly documents changes in household and family formation patterns and the relationship of these changes to economic factors. Nevertheless, it ignores alternative family arrangements and omits the role of personal agency in understanding poverty among the poor. The focus group data address these two limitations by concentrating on African-American women's first-hand accounts of their lives. Women's narratives describe family arrangements that were, indeed, different from mainstream patterns but that were viable, nonetheless. Significantly, these differences in household and family formation patterns do not represent abandonment of conventional aspirations (see also Rainwater 1987; Staples 1985; Williams 1992b). Further, women's accounts highlight the active roles that they played in caring for children and maintaining households. Women do not mechanistically respond to economic forces. Rather, they assess their options and make choices that allow them to forge meaningful lives despite the harsh economic conditions in which they and their children find themselves.

The findings from the focus group interviews corroborate those from existing ethnographic studies. This underscores the importance of qualitative and ethnographic data, rather than quantitative census and survey data, for understanding family processes and dynamics. New qualitative data, such as that derived from the focus group interviews, serve several functions: they expand quantitative conceptualizations and interpretations; update our current understanding of family processes among poor African-American families; enhance our confidence in past studies; and counter the tendency to use past qualitative studies as timeless explanations (Williams 1992a).

The data derived from this study suggest several driections for future research. First, reseachers should look seriously at alterna-

tive family arrangements and cease to assume the superiority of mainstream family patterns. Certainly it is conceivable that a two-parent household with adequate economic resources provides more opportunities for its children than an impoverished family with inadequate resources. However, researchers should not automatically assume that *all* middle-class families are stable and that *all* low-income families are unstable (see, for example, Coontz 1992).

Second, researchers should explore issues of coping and adaptation among poor families, rather than just document female headship and its demographic correlates. We need to identify more precisely the family dynamics that allow poor African-American families to cope (or fail to cope) with economic marginality. We know from past ethnographic research that a variety of family and household strategies can exist under the same social and economic conditions (see, for example, Clark 1983; Jarrett in press; di Leonardo 1984). Thus, the most theoretically compelling studies will be those that identify variations in coping strategies and seek explanations for these differences.

Finally, researchers should focus on gender as a major orienting framework. Mainstream poverty research, in general, and structural arguments, in particular, concentrate on poor African-American women but give little sustained analysis to the implications of gender (Baca Zinn 1989; Mullings 1989). Research that uses gender as an analytic framework can potentially answer such questions as how the conditions of poverty impact gendered ideologies and gendered strategies among poor African-American women and men.

The focus group data serve to not only expand the structural explanation of poverty, but also to highlight the humanity of the people who are too starkly described by statistical profiles and policy regulations. Leslie's comments underscore this point:

Just because you poor, you want someone to love too. Just because you poor, you might have to live off welfare, that doesn't mean that you're not eligible to have children. Like once you reach a certain income that you not eligible to have children because you too poor.

REFERENCES

Anderson, Elijah
1976   A Place on the Corner. Chicago: University of Chicago Press.
1990   Streetwise: Race, Class, and Change in an Urban Community. Chicago: University of Chicago Press.
Aschenbrenner, Joyce
1975   Lifelines: Black Families in Chicago. New York: Holt, Rinehart and Winston.
Auletta, Ken
1982   The Underclass. New York: Random House.
Baca Zinn, Maxine
1989   "Family, race, and poverty in the eighties." Signs: Journal of Women in Culture and Society 14:856–874.
1990a   "Family, feminism, and race in America." Gender & Society 4:68–82.
1990b   "Minority families in crisis: The public discussion." In Women, Class, and the Feminist Imagination: A Socialist-Feminist Reader, eds. Karen Hansen and Ilene J. Philiipson, 363–379. Philadelphia: Temple University Press.
Baca Zinn, Maxine, and D. Stanley Eitzen
1992   Diversity in Families. New York: Harper and Row.
Bane, Mary Jo, and David T. Ellwood
1984a   "The dynamics of children's living arrangements." Working paper supported by a Department of Health and Human Services grant, contract No. HHS-100-82-0038.
1984b   "Single mothers and their living arrangements." Working paper supported by a Department of Health and Human Services grant, contract No. HHS-100-82-0038.
Becker, Howard S.
1970   "The life history and the scientific mosaic." In Sociological Work: Method and Substance, ed. Howard S. Becker, 63–73. Chicago: Aldine.

Burton, Linda M.
1991   "Caring for children." The American Enterprise May/June: 34–37.
Calder, Bobby J.
1977   "Focus groups and the nature of qualitative marketing research." Journal of Marketing Research 24:353–364.
Cerullo, Margaret, and Marla Erlien
1986   "Beyond the 'normal family:' A cultural critique of women's poverty." In For Crying Out Loud: Women and Poverty in the United States, eds. Rochelle Lefkowitz and Ann Withorn, 248–261. New York: The Pilgrim Press.
Clark, Reginald M.
1983   Family Life and School Achievement: Why Poor Black Children Succeed or Fail. Chicago: University of Chicago Press.
Cook, Thomas D., and Thomas Curtin
1987   "The mainstream and the underclass: Why are the differences so salient and the similarities so unobtrusive?" In Social Comparison, Social Justice, and Relative Deprivation: Theoretical, Empirical, and Policy Perspectives, eds. John C. Masters and William P. Smith, 218–264. Hillsdale, NJ: Erlbaum Associates.
Coontz, Stephanie
1992   The Way We Never Were: American Families and the Nostalgia Trap. New York: Basic Books.
Corcoran, Mary, Greg J. Duncan, Gerald Gurin, and Patricia Gurin
1985   "Myth and reality: The causes and persistence of poverty." Journal of Policy Analysis and Management 4:516–536.
Darity, William A., and Samuel L. Meyers
1984   "Does welfare dependency cause female headship? The case of the black family." Journal of Marriage and the Family 46:765–779.
Davis, Angela, with Fania Davis
1989   "Slaying the dream: The black family and the crisis of capitalism." In Women, Culture, and Politics, ed. Angela Y. Davis, 73–90. New York: Random House.
di Leonardo, Micaela
1984   The Varieties of Ethnic Experience: Kinship, Class, and Gender Among California Italian-Americans. Ithaca, NY: Cornell University Press.
Ellwood, David T., and Mary Jo Bane
1984   "The impact of AFDC on family structure and living arrangements." Working paper

prepared for the U.S. Department of Health and Human Services under grant no. 92A-82.

Finch, Janet
1986   Research and Policy: The Users of Qualitative Methods in Social and Educational Research. Philadelphia: Falmer Press.

Franklin, Donna L.
1988   "Race, class, and adolescent pregnancy: An ecological analysis." American Journal of Orthopsychiatry 58:339–354.

Gans, Herbert
1969   "Culture and class in the study of poverty: An approach to anti-poverty research." In On Understanding Poverty: Perspectives from the Social Sciences, ed. Daniel P. Moynihan, 201–208. New York: Basic Books.

Garfinkel, Irwin, and Sara McLanahan
1986   Single Mothers and Their Children: A New American Dilemma. Washington, D.C.: The Urban Institute.

Glasgow, Douglas C.
1980   The Black Underclass: Poverty, Unemployment, and Entrapment of Ghetto Youth. San Francisco: Jossey-Bass.

Gresham, Jewell Handy
1989   "White patriarchal supremacy: The politics of family in America." The Nation 249:116–122.

Hannerz, Ulf
1969   Soulside: Inquiries into Ghetto Culture and Community. New York: Columbia University Press.
1975   "Research in the black ghetto: A review of the sixties." Journal of Asian and African Studies 9:139–159.

Hedges, Alan
1985   "Group interviewing." In Applied Qualitative Research, ed. Robert Walker, 71–91. Vermont: Gower Publishing Co.

Holloman, Regina, and Fannie E. Lewis
1978   "The 'clan:' Case study of a black extended family in Chicago." In The Extended Family in Black Societies, eds. Dimitri Shimkin, Edith Shimkin, and Dennis A. Frate, 201–238. The Hague: Mouton

Jarrett, Robin L.
1992   "A family case study: An examination of the underclass debate." In Qualitative Methods in Family Research, eds. Jane Gilgun, Gerald Handel, and Kerry Daly, 172–197. Newbury Park, Calif.: Sage.

1993   "Focus group interviewing with low-income minority populations: A research experience." In Conducting Successful Focus Groups, ed. David Morgan, 184–201. Newbury Park, Calif.: Sage.

In press   "Community context, intrafamilial processes, and social mobility outcomes: Ethnographic contributions to the study of African-American families and children in poverty." In Ethnicity and Diversity, eds. Geraldine K. Brookings and Margaret B. Spencer. Hillsdale, NJ: Erlbaum.

Jeffers, Camille
1967   Living poor: A Participant Observer Study of Choices and Priorities. Ann Arbor, Mich.: Ann Arbor Publications.

Joe, Tom
1984   The 'Flip-Side' of Black Families Headed by Women: The Economic Status of Men. Center for the Study of Social Policy. Washington, D.C.

Katz, Michael
1989   The Undeserving Poor: From the War on Poverty to the War on Welfare. New York: Pantheon Books.

Ladner, Joyce
1971   Tomorrow's Tomorrow: The Black Woman. New York: Anchor Books.

Leacock, Eleanor Burke, ed.
1971   The Culture of Poverty: A Critique. New York: Simon and Schuster.

Lemann, Nicholas
1986   "The origins of the underclass." The Atlantic Monthly 258:31–55.

Lewis, Oscar
1965   "The culture of poverty." Scientific American 215:3–9.
1966   La Vida. New York: Random House.

Liebow, Elliott
1967   Tally's Corner: A Study of Negro Street Corner Men. Boston: Little, Brown.

McLanahan, Sara, Irwin Garfinkel, and Dorothy Watson
1988   "Family structure, poverty, and the underclass." In Urban Change and Poverty, eds. Michael G. McGeary and Lawrence Lynn, 102–147. Washington: National Academy Press.

Marks, Carol
1991   "The urban underclass." Annual Review of Sociology 17:445–466.

Mead, Lawrence
1986   Beyond Entitlement: The Social Obligations of Citizenship. New York: Free Press.

Moen, Phyllis, and Elaine Wethington
1992 "The concept of family adaptive strategies." Annual Review of Sociology 18:233–251.

Monroe, Sylvester
1991 "Some sense of hope." Chicago Tribune Book Review March 17:1, 4.

Moynihan, Daniel P.
1965 "The Negro family: The case for national action." Washington, D.C.: Office of Policy Planning and Research. U.S. Department of Labor.

Mullings, Leith
1989 "Gender and the application of anthropological knowledge to public policy in the United States." In Gender and Anthropology: Critical Reviews for Research and Teaching, ed. Sandra Morgen, 360–381. Washington, D.C.: American Anthropological Association.

Murray, Charles
1984 Losing Ground: American Social Policy, 1950–1980. New York: Basic Books.

Nichols-Casebolt, Ann M.
1988 "Black families headed by single mothers: Growing numbers and increasing poverty." Social Work 33:306–313.

Patterson, James T.
1981 America's Struggle Against Poverty, 1900–1980. Cambridge, Mass.: Harvard University Press.

Piven, Frances F., Barbara Ehrenreich, Richard Cloward, and Richard F. Block
1987 The Mean Season. New York: Pantheon Books.

Rainwater, Lee
1970 Behind Ghetto Walls: Black Families in a Federal Slum. Chicago: Aldine Publishing Company.
1987 Class, Culture, Poverty, and Welfare. Unpublished manuscripts.

Rainwater, Lee, and William L. Yancey, eds.
1967 The Moynihan Report and the Politics of Controversy. Cambridge, Mass.: M.I.T. Press.

Reed, Adolph Jr.
1988 "The liberal technocrat." The Nation 246:167–170.

Ricketts, Erol R., and Isabel V. Sawhill
1988 "Defining and measuring the underclass." Journal of Policy Analysis and Management 7:316–25.

Schulz, David
1969 Coming Up Black: Patterns of Ghetto Socialization. Englewood Cliffs, NJ: Prentice Hall.

Stack, Carol
1974 All Our Kin: Strategies for Survival in a Black Community. New York: Harper and Row.

Staples, Robert
1985 "Changes in black family structure: The conflict between family ideology and structural conditions." Journal of Marriage and the Family 47:1005–1013.

Sullivan, Mercer
1985 Teen Fathers in the Inner-City. New York: Ford Foundation.

Suttles, Gerald D.
1976 "Urban ethnography: Situational and normative accounts." Annual Review of Sociology 2:1–8.

Swidler, Ann
1986 "Culture in action: Symbols and strategies." American Sociological Review 51:273–286.

Testa, Mark, Nan Marie Astone, Marilyn Krogh, and Kathryn M. Neckerman
1989 "Employment and marriage among inner-city fathers." Annals of the American Academy of Politial and Social Sciences 501:79–91.

Thorne, Barrie, and Marilyn Yalom
1982 Rethinking the Family: Some Feminist Questions. New York: Longman.

Valentine, Betty Lou
1978 Hustling and other Hard Work: Life Styles of the Ghetto. New York: Free Press.

Valentine, Charles
1968 Culture and Poverty: Critique and Counter-Proposals. Chicago: University of Chicago Press.

Wilkerson, Margaret B., and Jewell Handy Gresham
1989 "The racialization of poverty." The Nation 249:126–132.

Williams, Brett
1992a "Commentary: Poverty among African-Americans in the urban United States." Human Organization 51:164–174.
1992b "Us and them." The Nation 255:371–372.

Williams, Terry, and William Kornblum
1985 Growing Up Poor. Lexington, Mass.: Lexington Books.

Wilson, William J.
1987 The Truly Disadvantaged: The Inner City, the Underclass, and Public Policy. Chicago: University of Chicago Press.

Wilson, William J., and Robert Aponte
1985 "Urban poverty." Annual Review of Sociology 11:231–258.

Yanagisako, Sylvia J.
  1979   "Family and household: The analysis of do-
         mestic groups." Annual Review of Anthro-
         pology 8:161–205.

Zollar, Ann C.
  1985   A Member of the Family: Strategies for
         Black Family Continuity. Chicago: Nelson-
         Hall.

Questions for Understanding and Critical Thinking

1. How do cultural and structural models of poverty differ? According to Jarrett, which model best explains the diversity of U.S. family life today? Why?
2. Why is the term *underclass* controversial?
3. Why does Jarrett suggest that people should not automatically assume that *all* middle-class families are stable and that *all* low-income families are unstable?
4. How is poverty among African American women in central cities linked with macrolevel race and gender discrimination and class oppression?

ARTICLE 23 _____

Sociologist Joe R. Feagin and a team of interviewers engaged in systematic field research to determine the causes and consequences of racism and discrimination among middle-class African Americans. Participants in their study were allowed to describe their lived experiences in their own words.

Joe Feagin is Graduate Research Professor in sociology at the University of Florida, Gainesville, and author of numerous articles and books on U.S. racial inequality and discrimination.

Looking Ahead

1. What kinds of discrimination in public accommodations are experienced by middle-class African Americans?
2. Has discrimination caused most middle-class African Americans to give up on the American dream? Why or why not?
3. How have African Americans resisted discrimination?
4. Why are police officers a major problem for many middle-class African Americans?

The Continuing Significance of Race
Antiblack Discrimination in Public Places

◆ *Joe R. Feagin*

Title II of the 1964 Civil Rights Act stipulates that "all persons shall be entitled to the full and equal enjoyment of the goods, services, facilities, privileges, advantages, and accommodations of any place of public accommodation . . . without discrimination or segregation on the ground of race, color, religion, or national origin." The public places emphasized in the act are restaurants, hotels, and motels, although racial discrimination occurs in many other public places. Those black Americans who would make the great-

est use of these public accommodations and certain other public places would be middle class, i.e., those with the requisite resources.

White public opinion and many scholars have accented the great progress against traditional discrimination recently made by the black middle class. A National Research Council report on black Americans noted that by the mid-1970s many Americans "believed that . . . the Civil Rights Act of 1964 had led to broad-scale elimination of discrimination against blacks in public accom-

Source: From Joe R. Feagin, "The Continuing Significance of Race: Antiblack Discrimination in Public Places" in *American Sociological Review,* 1991, 58, pp. 101–116. Reprinted by permission of the American Sociological Association.

modations" (Jaynes and Williams 1989, p. 84). In interviews with whites in the late 1970s and early 1980s, Blauner (1989, p. 197) found that all but one viewed the 1970s as an era of great racial progress for American race relations. With some exceptions (see Willie 1983; Collins 1983; Landry 1987), much recent analysis of middle-class blacks by social scientists has emphasized the massive progress made since 1964 in areas where there had been substantial barriers, including public accommodations. Racial discrimination as a continuing and major problem for middle-class blacks has been downplayed as analysts have turned to the various problems of the "underclass." For example, Wilson (1978, pp. 110–1) has argued that the growth of the black middle class since the 1960s is the result of improving economic conditions and of government civil rights laws, which virtually eliminated overt discrimination in the workplace and public accommodations. According to Wilson, the major problem of the 1964 Civil Rights Act is its failure to meet the problems of the black underclass (Wilson 1987, pp. 146–7).

Here I treat these assertions as problematic. Do middle-class black Americans still face hostile treatment in public accommodations and other public places? If so, what form does this discrimination take? Who are the perpetrators of this discrimination? What is the impact of the discrimination on its middle-class victims? How do middle-class blacks cope with such discrimination?

ASPECTS OF DISCRIMINATION

Discrimination can be defined in social-contextual terms as "actions or practices carried out by members of dominant racial or ethnic groups that have a differential and negative impact on members of subordinate racial and ethnic groups" (Feagin and Eckberg 1980, pp. 1–2). This differential treatment ranges from the blatant to the subtle (Feagin and Feagin 1986). Here I focus primarily on blatant discrimination by white Americans targeting middle-class blacks. Historically, discrimination against blacks has been one of the most serious forms of racial/ethnic discrimination in the United States and one of the most difficult to overcome, in part because of the institutionalized character of color coding. I focus on three important aspects of discrimination: (1) the variation in sites of discrimination; (2) the range of discriminatory actions; and (3) the range of responses by blacks to discrimination.

Sites of Discrimination

There is a spatial dimension to discrimination. The probability of experiencing racial hostility varies from the most private to the most public sites. If a black person is in a relatively protected site, such as with friends at home, the probability of experiencing hostility and discrimination is low. The probability increases as one moves from friendship settings to such outside sites as the workplace, where a black person typically has contacts with both acquaintances and strangers, providing an interactive context with greater potential for discrimination.

In most workplaces, middle-class status and its organizational resources provide some protection against certain categories of discrimination. This protection probably weakens as a black person moves from those work and school settings where he or she is well-known into public accommodations such as large stores and city restaurants where contacts are mainly with white strangers. On public streets blacks have the greatest public exposure to strangers and the least protection against overt discriminatory behavior, including violence. A key feature of these more public settings is that they often involve contacts with white strangers who react primarily on the basis of one ascribed characteristic. The study of the micro-life of interaction between strangers in public was pioneered by Goffman (1963; 1971) and his students, but few of their analyses have treated hostile discriminatory interaction in public places. A rare exception is the research by Gardner (1980; see also Gardner 1988), who documented the character and danger of passing remarks by men directed against women in unprotected public places. Gardner writes of women (and blacks) as "open persons," i.e., particularly vulnerable targets for harassment that violates the rules of public courtesy.

The Range of Discriminatory Actions

In his classic study, *The Nature of Prejudice,* Allport (1985, pp. 14–5) noted that prejudice can be expressed in a series of progressively more serious actions, ranging from antilocution to avoidance, exclusion, physical attack, and extermination. Allport's work suggests a continuum of actions from avoidance, to exclusion or rejection, to attack. In his travels in the South in the 1950s a white journalist who changed his skin color to black encountered discrimination in each of these categories (Griffin 1961). In my data, discrimination against middle-class blacks still ranges across this continuum: (1) avoidance actions, such as a white couple crossing the street when a black male approaches; (2) rejection actions, such as poor service in public accommodations; (3) verbal attacks, such as shouting racial epithets in the street; (4) physical threats and harassment by white police officers; and (5) physical threats and attacks by other whites, such as attacks by white supremacists in the street. Changing relations between blacks and whites in recent decades have expanded the repertoire of discrimination to include more subtle forms and to encompass discrimination in arenas from which blacks were formerly excluded, such as formerly all-white public accommodations.

Black Responses to Discrimination

Prior to societal desegregation in the 1960s much traditional discrimination, especially in the South, took the form of an asymmetrical "deference ritual" in which blacks were typically expected to respond to discriminating whites with great deference. According to Goffman (1956, p. 477) a deference ritual "functions as a symbolic means by which appreciation is regularly conveyed to a recipient." Such rituals can be seen in the obsequious words and gestures—the etiquette of race relations—that many blacks, including middle-class blacks, were forced to utilize to survive the rigors of segregation (Doyle 1937). However, not all responses in this period were deferential. From the late 1800s to the 1950s, numerous lynchings and other violence targeted blacks whose behavior was defined as too aggressive (Raper 1933). Blauner's (1989) respondents reported acquaintances reacting aggressively to discrimination prior to the 1960s.

Deference rituals can still be found today between some lower-income blacks and their white employers. In her northeastern study Rollins (1985, p. 157) found black maids regularly deferring to white employers. Today, most discriminatory interaction no longer involves much asymmetrical deference, at least for middle-class blacks. Even where whites expect substantial deference, most middle-class blacks do not oblige. For middle-class blacks contemporary discrimination has evolved beyond the asymmetrical deference rituals and "No Negros served" type of exclusion to patterns of black-contested discrimination. Discussing race and gender discrimination in Great Britain, Brittan and Maynard (1984) have suggested that today "the terms of oppression are not only dictated by history, culture, and the sexual and social division of labor. They are also profoundly shaped at the site of the oppression, and by the way in which oppressors and oppressed continuously have to renegotiate, reconstruct, and re-establish their relative positions in respect to benefits and power" (p. 7). Similarly, white mistreatment of black Americans today frequently encounters new coping strategies by blacks in the ongoing process of reconstructing patterns of racial interaction.

Middle-class strategies for coping with discrimination range from careful assessment to withdrawal, resigned acceptance, verbal confrontation, or physical confrontation. Later action might include a court suit. Assessing the situation is a first step. Some white observers have suggested that many middle-class blacks are paranoid about white discrimination and rush too quickly to charges of racism (Wieseltier 1989, June 5; for male views of female "paranoia" see Gardner 1988). But the daily reality may be just the opposite, as middle-class black Americans often evaluate a situation carefully before judging it discriminatory and taking additional action. This careful evaluation, based on past experiences (real or vicarious), not only prevents jumping to conclusions, but also reflects the hope that white behavior is not based on race, because an act not based on race is easier to endure. After evaluation one strategy is to leave the site of discrimination rather than to create a disturbance. Another is to ignore the discrimination and continue with the interaction, a "blocking" strategy similar to that Gardner (1980, p. 345) reported for women dealing with street remarks. In many situations resigned acceptance is the only realistic response. More confrontational responses to white actions include verbal reprimands and sarcasm, physical counterattacks, and filing lawsuits. Several strategies may be tried in any given discriminatory situation. In crafting these strategies middle-class blacks, in comparison with less privileged blacks, may draw on middle-class resources to fight discrimination.

THE RESEARCH STUDY

To examine discrimination, I draw primarily on 37 in-depth interviews from a larger study of 135 middle-class black Americans in Boston, Buffalo, Baltimore, Washington, D.C., Detroit, Houston, Dallas, Austin, San Antonio, Marshall, Las Vegas, and Los Angeles. The interviewing was done in 1988–1990; black interviewers were used. I began with respondents known as members of the black middle class to knowledgeable consultants in key cites. Snowball sampling from these multiple starting points was used to maximize diversity.

The questions in the research instrument were primarily designed to elicit detailed information on the general situations of the respondents and on the barriers encountered and managed in employment, education, and housing. There were no specific questions in the interview schedule on public accommodations or other public-place discrimination; the discussions of that discrimation were volunteered in answer to general questions about barriers to personal goals and coping strategies or in digressions in answers to specific questions on employment, education, and housing. These volunteered responses signal the importance of such events. While I report below mainly on the responses of the 37 respondents who detailed specific incidents of public discrimination, in interpreting the character and meaning of modern discrimination I also draw on some discussions in the larger sample of 135 interviews and in five supplementary and follow-up interviews of middle-class blacks conducted by the author and two black consultants.

"Middle class" was defined broadly as those holding a white-collar job (including those in professional, managerial, and clerical jobs), college students preparing for white-collar jobs, and owners of successful businesses. This definition is consistent with recent analyses of the black middle class (Landry 1987). The subsample of 37 middle-class blacks reporting public discrimination is fairly representative of the demographic character of the larger sample. The subsample's occupational distribution is broadly similar to the larger sample and includes nine corporate managers and executives, nine health care or other professionals, eight government officials, four college students, three journalists or broadcasters, two clerical or sales workers, one entrepreneur, and one retired person. The subsample is somewhat younger than the overall sample, with 35 percent under age 35 vs. 25 percent in the larger sample, 52 percent in the 35–50 bracket vs. 57 percent, and 11 percent over 50 years of age vs. 18 percent. The subsample is broadly comparable to the larger sample in income: 14 had incomes under $36,000, seven in the $36,000–55,000 range, and 16 in the $56,000 or more range. All respondents had at least a high school degree, and more than 90 percent had some college work. The subsample has a somewhat lower percentage of people with graduate work: 39 percent vs. 50 percent for the larger sample. Both samples have roughly equal proportions of men and women, and more than sixty percent of both samples reported residing in cities in the South or Southwest—37 percent of the overall sample and 34 percent of the subsample resided in the North or West.

DESCRIPTIVE PATTERNS

Among the 37 people in the subsample reporting specific instances of public-place discrimination, 24 reported 25 incidents involving public accommodations discrimination, and 15 reported 27 incidents involving

street discrimination. Some incidents included more than one important discriminatory action; the 52 incidents consisted of 62 distinguishable actions. The distribution of these 62 actions by broad type is shown in Table 1.

Although all types of mistreatment are reported, there is a strong relationship between type of discrimination and site, with rejection/poor-service discrimination being most common in public accommodations and verbal or physical threat discrimination by white citizens or police officers most likely in the street.

The reactions of these middle-class blacks reflect the site and type of discrimination. The important steps taken beyond careful assessments of the situation are shown in Table 2. (A dual response is recorded for one accommodations incident.)

The most common black responses to racial hostility in the street are withdrawal or a verbal reply. In many avoidance situations (e.g., a white couple crossing a street to avoid walking past a black college student) or attack situations (e.g., whites throwing beer cans from a passing car), a verbal response is

TABLE 1 / Percentage Distribution of Discriminatory Actions by Type and Site: Middle-Class Blacks in Selected Cities, 1988–1990

Type of Discriminatory Action	Site of Discriminatory Action	
	Public Accommodations	Street
Avoidance	3	7
Rejection/poor service	79	4
Verbal epithets	12	25
Police threats/harassment	3	46
Other threats/harassment	3	18
Total	100	100
Number of actions	34	28

TABLE 2 / Percentage Distribution of Primary Responses to Discriminatory Incidents by Type and Site: Middle-Class Blacks in Selected Cities, 1988–1990

Response to Discriminatory Incident	Site of Discriminatory Incident	
	Public Accommodations	Street
Withdrawal/exit	4	22
Resigned acceptance	23	7
Verbal response	69	59
Physical counterattack	4	7
Response unclear	—	4
Total	100	99
Number of responses	26	27

difficult because of the danger or the fleeting character of the hostility. A black victim often withdraws, endures this treatment with resigned acceptance, or replies with a quick verbal retort. In the case of police harassment, the response is limited by the danger, and resigned acceptance or mild verbal protests are likely responses. Rejection (poor service) in public accommodations provides an opportunity to fight back verbally—the most common responses to public accommodations discrimination are verbal counterattacks or resigned acceptance. Some black victims correct whites quietly, while others respond aggressively and lecture the assailant about the discrimination or threaten court action. A few retaliate physically. Examining materials in these 37 interviews and those in the larger sample, we will see that the depth and complexity of contemporary black middle-class responses to white discrimination accents the changing character of white-black interaction and the necessity of continual negotiation of the terms of that interaction.

RESPONSES TO DISCRIMINATION: PUBLIC ACCOMMODATIONS

Two Fundamental Strategies: Verbal Confrontation and Withdrawal

In the following account, a black news director at a major television station shows the interwoven character of discriminatory action and black response. The discrimination took the form of poor restaurant service, and the responses included both suggested withdrawal and verbal counterattack.

He [her boyfriend] was waiting to be seated. . . . He said, "You go to the bathroom and I'll get the table. . . ." He was standing there when I came back; he continued to stand there. The restaurant was almost empty. There were waiters, waitresses, and no one seated. And when I got back to him, he was ready to leave, and said, "Let's go." I said, "What happened to our table?" He wasn't seated. So I said, "No, we're not leaving, please." And he said, "No, I'm leaving." So we went outside, and we talked about it. And what I said to him was, you have to be aware of the possibilities that this is not the first time that this has happened at this restaurant or at other restaurants, but this is the first time it has happened to a black news director here or someone who could make an issue of it, or someone who is prepared to make an issue of it.

So we went back inside after I talked him into it and, to make a long story short, I had the manager come. I made most of the people who were there (while conducting myself professionally the whole time) aware that I was incensed at being treated this way. . . . I said, "Why do you think we weren't seated?" And the manager said, "Well, I don't really know." And I said, "Guess." He said, "Well I don't know, because you're black?" I said, "Bingo. Now isn't it funny that you didn't guess that I didn't have any money (and I opened up my purse) and I said "because I certainly have money. And isn't it odd that you didn't guess that it's because I couldn't pay for it because I've got two American Express cards and a Master Card right here. I think it's just funny that you would have assumed that it's because I'm black." . . . And then I took out my card and gave it to him and said, "If this happens again, or if I hear of this happening again, I will bring the full wrath of an entire news department down on this restaurant." And he just kind of looked at me. "Not [just] because I am personally offended. I am. But because you have no right to do what you did, and as a people we have lived a long time with having our rights abridged. . . ." There were probably three or four sets of diners in the restaurant and maybe five waiters/waitresses. They watched him standing there waiting to be seated. His reaction to it was that he wanted to leave. I understood why he would have reacted that way, because he felt that he was in no condition to be civil. He was ready to take the place apart and . . . sometimes it's appropriate to behave that way. We hadn't gone the first step before going on to the next step. He didn't feel that he could comfortably and calmly take the first step, and I did. So I just asked him to please get back in the restaurant with me, and then you don't have to say a word, and let me handle it from here. It took some convincing, but I had to appeal to his sense of, this is not just you, this is not just for you. We are finally in a position as black people where there are some of us who can genuinely get their attention. And if they don't want to do this because it's right for them to do it, then they'd better do it because they're afraid to do otherwise. If it's fear, then fine, instill the fear.

This example provides insight into the character of modern discrimination. The discrimination was not the "No Negroes" exclusion of the recent past, but rejection in the form of poor service by restaurant personnel. The black response indicates the change in black-white interaction since the 1950s and 1960s, for discrimination is handled with vigorous confrontation rather than deference. The aggressive black response and the white backtracking underscore Brittan and Maynard's (1984, p. 7) point that black-white interaction today is being renegotiated. It is possible that the white personnel defined the couple as "poor blacks" because of their jeans, although the jeans were fashionable and white patrons wear jeans. In comments not quoted here the news director rejects such an explanation. She forcefully articulates a theory of rights—a response that signals the critical impact of civil rights laws on the thinking of middle-class blacks. The news director articulates the American dream: she has worked hard, earned the money and credit cards, developed the appropriate middle-class behavior, and thus has under the law a *right* to be served. There is defensiveness in her actions too, for she feels a need to legitimate her status by showing her purse and credit cards. One important factor that enabled her to take such assertive action was her power to bring a TV news team to the restaurant. This power marks a change from a few decades ago when very few black Americans had the social or economic resources to fight back successfully.

This example underscores the complexity of the interaction in such situations, with two levels of negotiation evident. The negotiation between the respondent and her boyfriend on withdrawal vs. confrontation highlights the process of negotiating responses to discrimination and the difficulty in crafting such responses. Not only is there a process of dickering with whites within the discriminatory scene but also a negotiation between the blacks involved.

The confrontation strategy can be taken beyond immediate verbal confrontation to a more public confrontation. The president of a financial institution in a Middle Atlantic city brought unfavorable publicity to a restaurant with a pattern of poor service to blacks:

I took the staff here to a restaurant that had recently opened in the prestigious section of the city, and we waited while other people got waited on. And decided that after about a half hour that these people don't want to wait on us. I happened to have been in the same restaurant a couple of evenings earlier, and it took them about forty-five minutes before they came to wait on me and my guest. So, on the second incident, I said, this is not an isolated incident, this is a pattern, because I had spoken with some other people who had not been warmly received in the restaurant. So, I wrote a letter to the owners. I researched and found out who the owners were, wrote a letter to the owners and sent copies to the city papers. That's my way of expressing myself, and letting the world know. You have to let people, other than you and the owner, know. You have to let others know you're expressing your dismay at the discrimination, or the barrier that's presented to you. I met with the owners. Of course, they wanted to meet with their attorneys with me, because they wanted to sue me. I told them they're welcome to do so, I don't have a thing, but fine they can do it. It just happens that I knew their white attorney. And he more or less vouched that if I had some concern that it must have been legitimate in some form. When the principals came in—one of the people who didn't wait on me was one of the owners, who happened to be waiting on everybody else—we resolved the issue by them inviting me to come again. And if I was fairly treated, or if I would come on several occasions and if I was fairly

treated I would write a statement of retraction. I told them I would not write a retraction, I would write a statement with regard to how I was treated. Which I ultimately did. And I still go there today, and they speak to me, and I think the pattern is changed to a great degree.

This example also demonstrates the resources available to many middle-class black Americans. As a bank executive with connections in the white community, including the legal community, this respondent used his resources not only to bring discrimination to public attention but also to pressure a major change in behavior. He had the means to proceed beyond the local management to both the restaurant owners and the local newspapers. The detailed account provides additional insight into the black-white bargaining process. At first the white managers and owners, probably accustomed to acquiescence or withdrawal, vigorously resisted ending the blatant discrimination. But the verbal and other resources available to the respondent forced them to capitulate and participate in a negotiation process. The cost to the victor was substantial. As in the first incident, we see the time-consuming and energy-consuming nature of grappling with poor-service discrimination. Compared to whites entering the same places, black Americans face an extra burden when going into public accommodations putatively made hospitable by three decades of civil rights law protection.

The confrontation response is generally so costly in terms of time and energy that acquiescence or withdrawal are common options. An example of the exit response was provided by a utility company executive in an east coast city:

I can remember one time my husband had picked up our son . . . from camp; and he'd stopped at a little store in the neighborhood near the camp. It was hot, and he was going to buy him a snowball. And the proprietor of the store—this was a very old, white neighborhood, and it was just a little sundry store. But the proprietor said he had the little window where people could come up and order things. Well, my husband and son had gone into the store. And he told them, "Well, I can't give it to you here, but if you go outside to the window, I'll give it to you." And there were other [white] people in the store who'd been served [inside]. So, they just left and didn't buy anything.

Here the act seems a throwback to the South of the 1950s, where blacks were required to use the back or side of a store. This differential treatment in an older white neighborhood is also suggestive of the territorial character of racial relations in many cities. The black response to degradation here was not to confront the white person or to acquiesce abjectly, but rather to reject the poor service and leave. Unlike the previous examples, the impact on the white proprietor was negligible because there was no forced negotiation. This site differed from the two previous examples in that the service was probably not of long-term importance to the black family passing through the area. In the previous sites the possibility of returning to the restaurants, for business or pleasure, may have contributed to the choice of a confrontational response. The importance of the service is a likely variable affecting black responses to discrimination in public accommodations.

Discrimination in public accommodations can occur in many different settings. A school board member in a northern city commented on her experiences in retail stores:

[I have faced] harassment in stores, being followed around, being questioned about what are you going to purchase here. . . . I

was in an elite department store just this past Saturday and felt that I was being observed while I was window shopping. I in fact actually ended up purchasing something, but felt the entire time I was there—I was in blue jeans and sneakers, that's how I dress on a Saturday—I felt that I was being watched in the store as I was walking through the store, what business did I have there, what was I going to purchase, that kind of thing. . . . There are a few of those white people that won't put change in your hand, touch your skin—that doesn't need to go on. [Do you tell them that?] Oh, I do, I do. That is just so obvious. I usually [speak to them] if they're rude in the manner in which they deal with people. [What do they say about that?] Oh, stuff like, "Oh, excuse me." And some are really unconscious about it, say "Excuse me," and put the change in your hand, that's happened. But I've watched other people be rude, and I've been told to mind my own business. . . . [But you still do it?] Oh, sure, because for the most part I think that people do have to learn to think for themselves, and demand respect for themselves. . . . I find my best weapon of defense is to educate them, whether it's in the store, in a line at the bank, any situation, I teach them. And you take them by surprise because you tell them and show them what they should be doing, and what they should be saying and how they should be thinking. And they look at you because they don't know how to process you. They can't process it because you've just shown them how they should be living, and the fact that they are cheating themselves, really, because the racism is from fear. The racism is from lack of education.

This excessive surveillance of blacks' shopping was reported by several respondents in our study and in recent newspaper accounts (see Jaynes and Williams 1989, p. 140). Several white stereotypes seem to underlie the rejection discrimination in this instance—blacks are seen as shoplifters, as unclean, as disreputable poor. The excessive policing of black shoppers and the discourtesy of clerks illustrate the extra burden of being black in public places. No matter how affluent and influential, a black person cannot escape the stigma of being black, even while relaxing or shopping. There is the recurring strain of having to craft strategies for a broad range of discriminatory situations. Tailoring her confrontation to fit the particular discrimination, this respondent interrupted the normal flow of the interaction to call the whites to intersubjective account and make a one-way experience into a two-way experience. Forced into new situations, offending whites frequently do not know how "to process" such an aggressive response. Again we see how middle-class blacks can force a reconstruction of traditional responses by whites to blacks. The intensity of her discussion suggests that the attempt to "educate" whites comes with a heavy personal cost, for it is stressful to "psyche" oneself up for such incidents.

The problem of burdensome visibility and the inescapable racial stereotyping by whites was underscored in the reply of a physician in an east coast city to a question about whether she had encountered barriers:

> Yes. All the time. I hate it when you go places and [white] people . . . think that we work in housekeeping. Or they naturally assume that we came from a very poor background. . . . A lot of white people think that blacks are just here to serve them, and [that] we have not risen above the servant position.

Here the discriminatory treatment comes from the white traveller staying in a hotel. This incident exemplifies the omnipresence of the stigma of being black—a well-dressed physician staying in an expensive hotel cannot escape. Here and elsewhere in the interview her anger suggests a confrontation response to such situations.

Middle-class black parents often attempt to protect their children from racial hostility in public places, but they cannot always be successful. A manager at an electronics firm in the Southwest gave an account of his daughter's first encounter with a racial epithet. After describing racist graffiti on a neighborhood fence in the elite white suburb where he lives, he described an incident at a swimming pool:

> I'm talking over two hundred kids in this pool; not one black. I don't think you can go anywhere in the world during the summertime and not find some black kids in the swimming pool. . . . Now what's the worst thing that can happen to a ten-year-old girl in a swimming pool with all white kids? What's the worst thing that could happen? It happened. This little white guy called her a "nigger." Then called her a "motherfucker" and told her to "get out of the goddamn pool." . . . And what initiated that, they had these little inner tubes, they had about fifteen of them, and the pool owns them. So you just use them if they are vacant. So there was a tube setting up on the bank, she got it, jumped in and started playing in it. . . . And this little white guy decided he wanted it. But, he's supposed to get it, right? And he meant to get it, and she wouldn't give it to him, so out came all these racial slurs. So my action was first with the little boy. "You know you're not supposed to do that. Apologize right now. Okay, good. Now, Mr. Lifeguard, I want him out of this pool, and you're going to have to do better. You're going to have to do better, but he has to leave out of this pool and let his parents know, okay?"

Taking his daughter back the next day, he observed from behind a fence to make certain the lifeguard protected her. For many decades black adults and children were excluded from public pools in the South and Southwest, and many pools were closed during the early desegregation period. These accommodations have special significance for middle-class black Americans, and this may be one reason the father's reaction was so decisive. Perhaps the major reason for his swift action was because this was the first time that his daughter had been the victim of racial slurs. She was the victim of cutting racist epithets that for this black father, as doubtless for most black Americans, connote segregated institutions and violence against blacks. Children also face hostility in public accommodations and may never shake this kind of experience. At a rather early point, many black parents find it necessary to teach their children how to handle discriminatory incidents.

The verbal responses of middle-class blacks to stigmatization can take more subtle forms. An 80-year-old retired schoolteacher in a southern city recounted her response to a recent experience at a drapery shop:

> The last time I had some draperies done and asked about them at the drapery shop, a young man at that shop—when they called [to him], he asked, and I heard him— he said, "The job for that nigger woman." And I said to the person who was serving me, "Oh my goodness, I feel so sorry for that young man. I didn't know people were still using that sort of language and saying those sorts of things." And that's the way I deal with it. I don't know what you call that. Is that sarcasm? Sarcasm is pretty good. . . . Well I've done that several times. This being 1989 . . . I'm surprised that I find it in this day and time.

One white clerk translated the schoolteacher's color in a hostile way while the other apparently listened. Suggested here is the way many whites are content to watch overt racist behavior without intervening. The retired teacher's response contrasts with the more confrontational reactions of the previous examples, for she used what might be called "strategic indirection." With composure she directed a pointedly sarcastic remark to the clerk serving her. Mockery is a more subtle tactic blacks can use to contend with antilocution, and this tactic may be more common among older blacks. Later in her interview this angry woman characterizes such recurring racial incidents as the "little murders" that daily have made her life difficult.

Careful Situation Assessments

We have seen in the previous incidents some tendency for blacks to assess discriminatory incidents before they act. Among several respondents who discussed discrimination at retail stores, the manager of a career development organization in the Southwest indicated that a clear assessment of a situation usually precedes confrontations and is part of a repertoire of concatenated responses:

> If you're in a store—and let's say the person behind the counter is white—and you walk up to the counter, and a white person walks up to the counter, and you know you were there before the white customer, the person behind the counter knows you were there first, and it never fails, they always go, "Who's next." Ok. And what I've done, if they go ahead and serve the white person first, then I will immediately say, "Excuse me, I was here first, and we both know I was here first." . . . If they get away with it once, they're going to get away with it more than once, and then it's going to become something else. And you have to, you want to make sure that folks know that you're not being naive, that you really see through what's happening. Or if it's a job opportunity or something like that, too, [we should

do the] same thing. You first try to get a clear assessment of what's really going on and sift through the information, and then . . . go from there.

The executive's coping process typically begins with a sifting of information before deciding on further action. She usually opts for immediate action so that whites face the reality of their actions in a decisive way. Like the account of the school board member who noted that whites would sometimes not put money directly in her hand, this account illustrates another aspect of discrimination in public accommodations. For many whites racial hostility is imbedded in everyday actions, and there is a deep, perhaps subconscious, recoil response to black color and persona.

The complex process of evaluation and response is directed by a college dean, who commented generally on hotel and restaurant discrimination encountered as he travels across the United States:

When you're in a restaurant . . . you notice that blacks get seated near the kitchen. You notice that if it's a hotel, your room is near the elevator, or your room is always way down in a corner somewhere. You find that you are getting the undesirable rooms. And you come there early in the day and you don't see very many cars on the lot and they'll tell you that this is all we've got. Or you get the room that's got a bad television set. You know that you're being discriminated against. And of course you have to act accordingly. You have to tell them, "Okay, the room is fine, [but] this television set has got to go. Bring me another television set." So in my personal experience, I simply cannot sit and let them get away with it [discrimination] and not let them know that I know that that's what they are doing. . . .

When I face discrimination, first I take a long look at myself and try to determine whether or not I am seeing what I think I'm

seeing in 1989, and if it's something that I have an option [about]. In other words, if I'm at a store making a purchase, I'll simply walk away from it. If it's at a restaurant where I'm not getting good service, I first of all let the people know that I'm not getting good service, then I [may] walk away from it. But the thing that I have to do is to let people know that I know that I'm being singled out for a separate treatment. And then I might react in any number of ways— depending on where I am and how badly I want whatever it is that I'm there for.

This commentary adds another dimension to our understanding of public discrimination, its cumulative aspect. Blacks confront not just isolated incidents—such as a bad room in a luxury hotel once every few years—but a lifelong series of such incidents. Here again the omnipresence of careful assessments is underscored. The dean's interview highlights a major difficulty in being black—one must be constantly prepared to assess accurately and then decide on the appropriate response. This long-look approach may indicate that some middle-class blacks are so sensitive to white charges of hypersensitivity and paranoia that they err in the opposite direction and fail to see discrimination when it occurs. In addition, as one black graduate student at a leading white university in the Southwest put it: "I think that sometimes timely and appropriate responses to racially motivated acts and comments are lost due to the processing of the input." The "long look" can result in missed opportunities to respond to discrimination.

Using Middle-Class Resources for Protection

One advantage that middle-class blacks have over poorer blacks is the use of the resources of middle-class occupations. A professor at a major white university commented on the varying protection her middle-class status gives her at certain sites:

> If I'm in those areas that are fairly protected, within gatherings of my own group, other African Americans, or if I'm in the university where my status as a professor mediates against the way I might be perceived, mediates against the hostile perception, then it's fairly comfortable. . . . When I divide my life into encounters with the outside world, and of course that's ninety percent of my life, it's fairly consistently unpleasant at those sites where there's nothing that mediates between my race and what I have to do. For example, if I'm in a grocery store, if I'm in my car, which is a 1970 Chevrolet, a real old ugly car, all those things—being in a grocery store in casual clothes, or being in the car—sort of advertises something that doesn't have anything to do with my status as far as people I run into are concerned.
>
> Because I'm a large black woman, and I don't wear whatever class status I have, or whatever professional status [I have] in my appearance when I'm in the grocery store, I'm part of the mass of large black women shopping. For most whites, and even for some blacks, that translates into negative status. That means that they are free to treat me the way they treat most poor black people, because they can't tell by looking at me that I differ from that.

This professor notes the variation in discrimination in the sites through which she travels, from the most private to the most public. At home with friends she faces no problems, and at the university her professorial status gives her some protection from discrimination. The increase in unpleasant encounters as she moves into public accommodations sites such as grocery stores is attributed to the absence of mediating factors such as clear symbols of middle-class status—displaying the middle-class symbols may provide some protection against discrimination in public places.

An east coast news anchorperson reported a common middle-class experience of good service from retailers over the phone:

> And if I was seeking out a service, like renting a car, or buying something, I could get a wonderful, enthusiastic reaction to what I was doing. I would work that up to such a point that this person would probably shower me with roses once they got to see me. And then when I would show up, and they're surprised to see that I'm black, I sort of remind them in conversation how welcome my service was, to put the embarrassment on them, and I go through with my dealings. In fact, once my sister criticized me for putting [what] she calls my "white-on-white voice" on to get a rental car. But I needed a rental car and I knew that I could get it. I knew if I could get this guy to think that he was talking to some blonde, rather than, you know, so, but that's what he has to deal with. I don't have to deal with that, I want to get the car.

Being middle-class often means that you, as many blacks say, "sound white" over the phone. Over the phone middle-class blacks find they get fair treatment because the white person assumes the caller is white, while they receive poorer (or no) service in person. Race is the only added variable in such interpersonal contact situations. Moreover, some middle-class blacks intentionally use this phone-voice resource to secure their needs.

RESPONSES TO DISCRIMINATION: THE STREET

Reacting to White Strangers

As we move away from public accommodations settings to the usually less protected street sites, racial hostility can become more fleeting and severer, and thus black responses are often restricted. The most serious form of street discrimination is violence. Often the reasonable black response to street discrimination is withdrawal, resigned acceptance, or a quick verbal retort. The difficulty of responding to violence is seen in this report by a man working for a media surveying firm in a southern industrial city:

> *I was parked in front of this guy's house. . . . This guy puts his hands on the window and says, "Get out of the car, nigger." . . . So, I got out, and I thought, "Oh, this is what's going to happen here." And I'm talking fast. And they're, "What are you doing here?" And I'm, "This is who I am. I work with these people. This is the man we want to put in the survey." And I pointed to the house. And the guy said, "Well you have an out-of-state license tag, right?" "Yea." And he said, "If something happened to you, your people at home wouldn't know for a long time, would they?" . . . I said, "Look, I deal with a company that deals with television. [If] something happens to me, it's going to be a national thing. . . . So, they grab me by the lapel of my coat, and put me in front of my car. They put the blade on my zipper. And now I'm thinking about this guy that's in the truck [behind me], because now I'm thinking that I'm going to have to run somewhere. Where am I going to run? Go to the police? [laughs] So, after a while they bash up my headlight. And I drove [away].*

Stigmatized and physically attacked solely because of his color, this man faced verbal hostility and threats of death with courage. Cautiously drawing on his middle-class resources, he told the attackers his death would bring television crews to the town. This resource utilization is similar to that of the news director in the restaurant incident. Beyond this verbal threat his response had to be one of caution. For most whites threatened on the street, the police are a sought-after source of protection, but for black men this is often not the case.

At the other end of the street continuum is nonverbal harassment such as the "hate stare" that so traumatized Griffin (1961). In her research on street remarks, Gardner (1980) considered women and blacks particularly vulnerable targets for harassment. For the segregation years Henley (1978) has documented the ways in which many blacks regularly deferred to whites in public-place communications. Today obsequious deference is no longer a common response to harassment. A middle-class student with dark skin reported that on her way to university classes she had stopped at a bakery in a white residential area where very few blacks live or shop. A white couple in front of the store stared intently and hatefully at her as she crossed the sidewalk and entered and left the bakery. She reported that she had experienced this hate stare many times. The incident angered her for some days thereafter, in part because she had been unable to respond more actively to it.

In between the hate stare and violence are many other hostile actions. Most happen so fast that withdrawal, resigned acceptance, or an immediate verbal retort are the reasonable responses. The female professor quoted earlier described the fleeting character of harassment:

> *I was driving. This has [happened] so many times, but one night it was especially repugnant. I think it had to, with my son being in the car. It was about 9:30 at night, and as I've said, my car is old and very ugly, and I have been told by people shouting at intersections that it's the kind of car that people think of as a low-rider car, so they associate it with Mexican Americans, especially poor Mexican Americans. Well, we were sitting at*

an intersection waiting to make a turn, and a group of middle-class looking white boys drives up in a nice car. And they start shouting things at us in a real fake-sounding Mexican American accent, and I realized that they thought we were Mexican Americans. And I turned to look at them, and they started making obscene gestures and laughing at the car. And then one of them realized that I was black, and said, "Oh, it's just a nigger." And [they] drove away.

This incident illustrates the seldom-noted problems of "cross discrimination"—a black person may suffer from discrimination aimed at other people of color by whites unable to distinguish. The white hostility was guided by certain signals—and old car and dark skin—of minority-group status. The nighttime setting, by assuring anonymity, facilitated the hurling of racist epithets and heightened the negative impact on this woman, who found the harassment especially dangerous and repulsive because she was with her son. She drove away without replying. Later in the interview she notes angrily that in such incidents her ascribed characteristic of "blackness" takes precedence over her achieved middle-class characteristics and that the grouped thinking of racism obscures anything about her that is individual and unique.

For young middle-class blacks street harassment can generate shock and disbelief, as in the case of this college student who recounted a street encounter near her university in the Southwest:

I don't remember in high school being called a "nigger" before, and I can remember here being called a "nigger." [When was this?] In my freshman year, at a university student parade. There was a group of us, standing there, not knowing that this was not an event that a lot of black people went to! [laughs] You know, our dorm was going, and this was

something we were going to go to because we were students too! And we were standing out there and [there were] a group of white fraternity boys—I remember the southern flag—and a group of us, five or six of us, and they went past by us, before the parade had actually gotten underway. And one of them pointed and said, "Look at that bunch of niggers!" I remember thinking, "Surely he's not talking to us!" We didn't even use the word "nigger" in my house. . . . [How did you feel?] I think I wanted to cry. And my friends—they were from a southwestern city—they were ready to curse them, and I was just standing there with my mouth open. I think I wanted to cry. I could not believe it, because you get here and you think you're in an educated environment and you're dealing with educated people. And all of this backward country stuff . . . you think that kind of stuff is not going on, but it is.

The respondent's first coping response was to think the assailants were not speaking to her and her friends. Again we see the tendency for middle-class blacks to assess situations carefully and to give whites the benefit of the doubt. Her subsequent response was tearful acquiescence, but her friends were ready to react in a more aggressive way. The discriminators may have moved on before a considered response was possible. This episode points up the impact of destructive racial coding on young people and hints at the difficulty black parents face in socializing children for coping with white hostility. When I discussed these street incidents involving younger blacks with two older black respondents, one a southern civil rights activist and the other an Ivy-League professor, both noted the problem created for some middle-class black children by their well-intentioned parents trying to shelter them from racism.

It seems likely that for middle-class blacks the street is the site of recurring encounters with various types of white malevolence. A vivid example of the cumulative character and impact of this discrimination was given by another black student at a white university, who recounted his experiences walking home at night from a campus job to his apartment in a predominantly white residential area:

> So, even if you wanted to, it's difficult just to live a life where you don't come into conflict with others. Because every day you walk the streets, it's not even like once a week, once a month. It's every day you walk the streets. Every day that you live as a black person you're reminded how you're perceived in society. You walk the streets at night; white people cross the streets. I've seen white couples and individuals dart in front of cars to not be on the same side of the street. Just the other day, I was walking down the street, and this white female with a child, I saw her pass a young white male about 20 yards ahead. When she saw me, she quickly dragged the child and herself across the busy street. What is so funny is that this area has had an unknown white rapist in the area for about four years. [When I pass] white men tighten their grip on their women. I've seen people turn around and seem like they're going to take blows from me. The police constantly make circles around me as a I walk home, you know, for blocks. I'll walk, and they'll turn a block. And they'll come around me just to make sure, to find out where I'm going. So, every day you realize [you're black]. Even though you're not doing anything wrong; you're just existing. You're just a person. But you're a black person perceived in an unblack world. [This quote includes a clarification sentence from a follow-up interview.]

In a subsequent comment this respondent mentioned that he also endured white men hurling beer cans and epithets at him as he walked home. Again the cumulation of incidents is evident. Everyday street travel for young black middle-class males does not mean one isolated incident every few years.

Unable to "see" his middle-class symbols of college dress and books, white couples (as well as individuals) have crossed the street in front of cars to avoid walking near this modest-build black student, in a predominantly white neighborhood. Couples moving into defensive postures are doubtless reacting to the stigma of "black maleness." The student perceives such avoidance as racist, however, not because he is paranoid, but because he has previously encountered numerous examples of whites taking such defensive measures. Many whites view typical "street" criminals as black or minority males and probably see young black males as potentially dangerous (Graber 1980, p. 55). This would seem to be the motivation for some hostile treatment black males experience in public places. Some scholars have discussed white perceptions of black males as threatening and the justifiability of that perception (Warr forthcoming), but to my knowledge there has been no discussion in the literature of the negative impact of such perceptions on black males. This student reports that being treated as a pariah (in his words, a "criminal and a rapist") has caused him severe psychological problems. When I discussed this student's experiences with a prominent black journalist in a northeastern city, he reported that whites sometimes stop talking—and white women grab their purses—on downtown office-building elevators when he enters. These two men had somewhat different responses to such discrimination, one relatively passive and the other aggressive. In a follow-up interview the student reported that he rarely responded aggressively to the street encounters, apart from the occasional quick curse, because they happened too quickly. Echoing the black graduate student's comments about processing input and missed opportunities, he added: "I was basically analyzing and thinking too much about the incident." However, the journalist reacts more assertively; he described how he turns to whites in elevators and informs them, often with a smile, that they can continue talking or that he is not interested in their purses.

On occasion, black middle-class responses to street hostility from white strangers are even more aggressive. A woman who now runs her own successful business in a southwestern city described a car incident in front of a grocery store:

> We had a new car . . . and we stopped at 7-11 [store]. We were going to go out that night, and we were taking my son to a babysitter. . . . And we pulled up, and my husband was inside at the time. And this person, this Anglo couple, drove up, and they hit our car. It was a brand new car. So my husband came out. And the first thing they told us was what we got our car on **welfare**. Here we are able-bodied. He was a corporate executive. I had a decent job, it was a professional job, but it wasn't paying anything. But they looked at the car we were driving, and they made the assumption that we got it from welfare. I completely snapped; I physically abused that lady. I did. And I was trying to keep my husband from arguing with her husband until the police could come. . . . And when the police came they interrogated them; they didn't arrest us, because there was an off-duty cop who had seen the whole incident and said she provoked it.

Here we see how some whites perceive blacks, including middle-class blacks, in interracial situations. The verbal attack by the whites was laced with the stereotype about blacks as welfare chiselers. This brought forth an angry response from the black couple, which probably came as a surprise to the whites. This is another example of Brittan and Maynard's (1984, p. 7) point that discriminatory interaction is shaped today by the way in which oppressors and oppressed mediate their relative positions. Note too the role of the off-duty police officer. The respondent does not say whether the officer was white or black, but this detail suggests that certain contexts of discrimination have changed—in the past a (white) police officer would have sided with the whites. This respondent also underscores her and her husband's occupational achievements, highlighting her view that she has attained the American middle-class ideal. She is incensed that her obvious middle-class symbols did not protect her from verbal abuse.

The importance of middle-class resources in street encounters was dramatized in the comments of a parole officer in a major West Coast city. He recounted how he dealt with a racial epithet:

> I've been called "nigger" before, out in the streets when I was doing my job, and the individual went to jail. . . . [Ok, if he didn't call you a "nigger," would he have still gone to jail?] Probably not. [. . . Was the person white?] Yes, he was. And he had a partner with him, and his partner didn't say anything, and his partner jaywalked with him. However, since he uttered the racial slur, I stopped him and quizzed him about the laws. And jaywalking's against the law, so he went to jail.

On occasion, middle-class blacks have the ability to respond not only aggressively but authoritatively to street discrimination. This unusual response to an epithet was possible because the black man, unknown to his assailant, had police authority. This incident also illustrates a point made in the policing literature about the street-level discretion of police officers (Perry and Sornoff 1973). Jaywalking is normally a winked-at violation, as in the case of the assailant's companion. Yet this respondent was able to exercise his discretionary authority to punish a racial epithet.

Responses to Discrimination by White Police Officers

Most middle-class blacks do not have such governmental authority as their personal protection. In fact, white police officers are a major problem. Encounters with the police can be life-threatening and thus limit the range of responses. A television commentator recounted two cases of police harassment when he was working for a survey firm in the mid-1980s. In one of the incidents, which took place in a southern metropolis, he was stopped by several white officers:

> *"What are you doing here?" I tell them what I'm doing here. . . . And so me spread on top of my car. [What had you done?] Because I was in the neighborhood. I left this note on these peoples' house: "Here's who I am. You weren't here, and I will come back in thirty minutes." [Why were they searching you?] They don't know. To me, they're searching, I remember at that particular moment when this all was going down, there was a lot of reports about police crime on civilians. . . . It took four cops to shake me down, two police cars, so they had me up there spread out. I had a friend of mine with me who was making the call with me, because we were going to have dinner together, and he was black, and they had me up, and they had him outside. . . . They said, "Well, let's check you out." . . . And I'm talking to myself, and I'm not thinking about being at attention, with my arms spread on my Ford [a company car], and I'm sitting there talking to myself, "Man, this is crazy, this is crazy."*
>
> *[How are you feeling inside?] Scared, I mean real scared. [What did you think was going to happen to you?] I was going to go to*

> *jail. . . . Just because they picked me. Why would they stop me? It's like, if they can stop me, why wouldn't I go to jail, and I could sit in there for ten days before the judge sees me. I'm thinking all this crazy stuff. . . . Again, I'm talking to myself. And the guy takes his stick. And he doesn't whack me hard, but he does it with enough authority to let me know they mean business. "I told you stand still; now put your arms back out." And I've got this suit on, and the car's wet. And my friend's hysterical. He's outside the car. And they're checking him out. And he's like, "Man, just be cool, man." And he had tears in his eyes. And I'm like, oh, man, this is a nightmare. This is not supposed to happen to me. This is not my style! And so finally, this other cop comes up and says, "What have we got here Charlie?" "Oh, we've got a guy here. He's running through the neighborhood, and he doesn't want to do what we tell him. We might have to run him in." [You're "running through" the neighborhood?] Yeah, exactly, in a suit in the rain?! After they got through doing their thing and harassing me, I just said, "Man this has been a hell of a week."*
>
> *And I had tears in my eyes, but it wasn't tears of upset. It was tears of anger; it was tears of wanting to lash back. . . . What I thought to myself was, man, blacks have it real hard down here. I don't care if they're a broadcaster; I don't care if they're a businessman or a banker. . . . They don't have it any easier than the persons on skid row who get harassed by the police on a Friday or Saturday night.*

It seems likely that most black men—including middle-class black men—see white police officers as a major source of danger and death (See "Mood of Ghetto America" 1980, June 2, pp. 32–34; Louis Harris and Associates 1989; Roddy 1990, August 26). Scattered evidence suggests that by the time they are in their twenties, most black males, regardless of socioeconomic status, have been stopped by the police because "blackness" is considered a sign of possible criminality by police officers (Moss 1990; Roddy 1990, August 26). This treatment probably marks a dramatic contrast with the experiences of young white middle-class males. In the incident above the respondent and a friend experienced severe police maltreatment—detention for a lengthy period, threat of arrest, and the reality of physical violence. The coping response of the respondent was resigned acceptance somewhat similar to the deference rituals highlighted by Goffman. The middle-class suits and obvious corporate credentials (for example, survey questionnaires and company car) did not protect the two black men. The final comment suggests a disappointment that middle-class status brought no reprieve from police stigmatization and harassment.

Black women can also be the targets of police harassment. A professor at a major white university in the Southwest describes her encounters with the police:

When the cops pull me over because my car is old and ugly, they assume I've just robbed a convenience store. Or that's the excuse they give: "This car looks like a car used to rob a 7-11 [store]." And I've been pulled over six or seven times since I've been in this city—and I've been here two years now. Then I do what most black folks do. I try not to make any sudden moves so I'm not accidentally shot. Then I give them my identification. And I show them my university I.D. so they won't think that I'm someone that constitutes a threat, however they define it, so that I don't get arrested.

She adds:

[One problem with] being black in America is that you have to spend so much time thinking about stuff that most white people just don't even have to think about. I worry when I get pulled over by a cop. I worry because the person that I live with is a black male, and I have a teen-aged son. I worry what some white cop is going to think when he walks over to our car, because he's holding on to a gun. And I'm very aware of how many black folks accidentally get shot by cops. I worry when I walk into a store, that someone's going to think I'm in there shoplifting. And I have to worry about that because I'm not free to ignore it. And so, that thing that's supposed to be guaranteed to all Americans, the freedom to just be yourself is a fallacious idea. And I get resentful that I have to think about things that a lot of people, even my very close white friends whose politics are similar to mine, simply don't have to worry about.

This commentary about a number of encounters underscores the pyramiding character of discrimination. This prominent scholar has faced excessive surveillance by white police officers, who presumably view blacks as likely criminals. As in the previous example, there is great fear of white officers, but her response is somewhat different: She draws on her middle-class resources for protection; she cautiously interposes her middle-class status by pulling out a university I.D. card. In the verbal exchange her articulateness as a professor probably helps protect her. This assertive use of middle-class credentials in dealing with police marks a difference from the old asymmetrical deference rituals, in which highlighting middle-class status would be considered arrogant by white officers and increase the danger. Note, too, the explicit theory of rights that she, like many other middle-class blacks, holds as part of her American dream.

CONCLUSION

I have examined the sites of discrimination, the types of discriminatory acts, and the responses of the victims and have found the color stigma still to be very important in the public lives of affluent black Americans. The sites of racial discrimination range from relatively protected home sites, to less protected workplace and educational sites, to the even less protected public places. The 1964 Civil Rights Act guarantees that black Americans are "entitled to the full and equal enjoyment of the goods, services, facilities, privileges, advantages, and accommodations" in public accommodations. Yet the interviews indicate that deprivation of full enjoyment of public facilities is not a relic of the past; deprivation and discrimination in public accommodations persist. Middle-class black Americans remain vulnerable targets in public places. Prejudice-generated aggression in public places is, of course, not limited to black men and women—gay men and white women are also targets of street harassment (Benokraitis and Feagin 1986). Nonetheless, black women and men face an unusually broad range of discrimination on the street and in public accommodations.

The interviews highlight two significant aspects of the additive discrimination faced by black Americans in public places and elsewhere: (1) the cumulative character of an *individual's* experiences with discrimination; and (2) the *group's* accumulated historical experiences as perceived by the individual. A retired psychology professor who has worked in the Midwest and Southwest commented on the pyramiding of incidents:

> I don't think white people, generally, understand the full meaning of racist discriminatory behaviors directed toward Americans of African descent. They seem to see each act of discrimination or any act of violence as an "isolated" event. As a result, most white Americans cannot understand the strong reaction manifested by blacks when such events occur. They feel that blacks tend to "over-react." They forget that in most cases,

> we live lives of quiet desperation generated by a litany of daily large and small events that whether or not by design, remind us of our "place" in American society.

Particular instances of discrimination may seem minor to outside white observers when considered in isolation. But when blatant acts of avoidance, verbal harassment, and physical attack combine with subtle and covert slights, and these accumulate over months, years, and lifetimes, the impact on a black person is far more than the sum of the individual instances.

The historical context of contemporary discrimination was described by the retired psychologist, who argued that average white Americans

> . . . ignore the personal context of the stimulus. That is, they deny the historical impact that a negative act may have on an individual. "Nigger" to a white may simply be an epithet that should be ignored. To most blacks, the term brings into sharp and current focus all kinds of acts of racism—murder, rape, torture, denial of constitutional rights, insults, limited opportunity structure, economic problems, unequal justice under the law and a myriad of . . . other racist and discriminatory acts that occur daily in the lives of most Americans of African descent—including professional blacks.

Particular acts, even antilocution that might seem minor to white observers, are freighted not only with one's past experience of discrimination but also with centuries of racial discrimination directed at the entire group, vicarious oppression that still includes racially translated violence and denial of access to the American dream. Anti-black discrimination is a matter of racial-power inequality institutionalized in a variety of economic and social institutions over a long period of time. The microlevel events of public accommodations and public streets are not just rare and isolated encounters by individuals; they are recurring events reflecting an invasion of the microworld by the macroworld of historical racial subordination.

The cumulative impact of racial discrimination accounts for the special way that blacks have of looking at and evaluating interracial incidents. One respondent, a clerical employee at an adoption agency, described the "second eye" she uses:

> I think that it causes you to have to look at things from two different perspectives. You have to decide whether things that are done or slights that are made are made because you are black or they are made because the person is just rude, or unconcerned and uncaring. So it's kind of a situation where you're always kind of looking to see with a second eye or a second antenna just what's going on.

The language of "second eye" suggests that blacks look at white-black interaction through a lens colored by personal and group experience with cross-institutional and cross-generational discrimination. This sensitivity is not new, but is a current adaptation transcending, yet reminiscent of, the black sensitivity to the etiquette of racial relations in the old South (Doyle 1937). What many whites see as black "paranoia" (e.g., Wieseltier 1989, June 5) is simply a realistic sensitivity to white-black interaction created and constantly reinforced by the two types of cumulative discrimination cited above.

Blacks must be constantly aware of the repertoire of possible responses to chronic and burdensome discrimination. One older respondent spoke of having to put on her "shield" just before she leaves the house each morning. When quizzed, she said that for more than six decades, as she leaves her home, she has tried to be prepared for insults and discrimination in public places, even if nothing happens that day. This extraordinary burden of discrimination, evident in most of the 135 interviews in the larger sample, was eloquently described by the female professor who resented having to worry about life-threatening incidents that her "very close white friends . . . simply don't have to worry about." Another respondent was articulate on this point:

> . . . if you think of the mind as having one hundred ergs of energy, and the average man uses fifty percent of his energy dealing with the everyday problems of the world—just general kinds of things—then he has fifty percent more to do creative kinds of things that he wants to do. Now that's a white person. Now a black person also has one hundred ergs; he uses fifty percent the same way a white man does, dealing with what the white man has [to deal with], so he has fifty percent left. But he uses twenty-five percent fighting being black, [with] all the problems being black and what it means. Which means he really only has twenty-five percent to do what the white man has fifty percent to do, and he's expected to do just as much as the white man with that twenty-five percent. . . . So, that's kind of what happens. You just don't have as much energy left to do as much as you know you really could if you were free, [if] your mind were free.

The individual cost of coping with racial discrimination is great, and, as he says, you cannot accomplish as much as you could if you retained the energy wasted on discrimination. This is perhaps the most tragic cost of persisting discrimination in the United States. In spite of decades of civil rights legislation, black Americans have yet to attain the full promise of the American dream.

REFERENCES

Allport, Gordon. 1958. *The Nature of Prejudice.* Abridged. New York: Doubleday Anchor Books.

Benokraitis, Nijole and Joe R. Feagin. 1986. *Modern Sexism: Blatant, Subtle and Covert Discrimination.* Englewood Cliffs: Prentice-Hall.

Blauner, Bob. 1989. *Black Lives, White Lives*. Berkeley: University of California Press.

Brittan, Arthur and Mary Maynard. 1984. *Sexism, Racism and Oppression*. Oxford: Basil Blackwell.

Collins, Sheila M. 1983. "The Making of the Black Middle Class." *Social Problems* 30:369–81.

Doyle, Betram W. 1937. *The Etiquette of Race Relations in the South*. Port Washington, NY: Kennikat Press.

Feagin, Joe R. and Douglas Eckberg. 1980. "Prejudice and Discrimination." *Annual Review of Sociology* 6:1–20.

Feagin, Joe R. and Clariece Booher Feagin. 1986. *Discrimination American Style* (rev. ed.). Melbourne, FL: Krieger Publishing Co.

Gardner, Carol Brooks. 1980. "Passing By: Street Remarks, Address Rights, and the Urban Female." *Sociological Inquiry* 50:328–56.

————. 1988. "Access Information: Public Lies and Private Peril." *Social Problems* 35:384–97.

Goffman, Erving. 1956. "The Nature of Deference and Demeanor." *American Anthropologist* 58:473–502.

————. 1963. *Behavior in Public Places*. New York: Free Press.

————. 1971. *Relations in Public*. New York: Basic Books.

Graber, Doris A. 1980. *Crime News and the Public*. New York: Praeger.

Griffin, John Howard. 1961. *Black Like Me*. Boston: Houghton Mifflin.

Henley, Nancy M. 1978. *Body Politics*. Englewood Cliffs, N.J.: Prentice-Hall.

Jaynes, Gerald D. and Robin Williams, Jr. (eds.). 1989. *A Common Destiny: Blacks and American Society*. Washington, D.C.: National Academy Press.

Landry, Bart. 1987. *The New Black Middle Class*. Berkeley: University of California Press.

Louis Harris and Associates. 1989. *The Unfinished Agenda on Race in America*. New York: NAACP Legal Defense and Educational Fund.

"The Mood of Ghetto America." 1980, June 2. *Newsweek*, pp. 32–4.

Moss, E. Yvonne. 1990. "African Americans and the Administration of Justice." Pp. 79–86 in *Assessment of the Status of African-Americans*, edited by Wornie L. Reed. Boston: University of Massachusetts, William Monroe Trotter Institute.

Perry, David C. and Paula A. Sornoff. 1973. *Politics at the Street Level*. Beverly Hills: Sage.

Raper, Arthur F. 1933. *The Tragedy of Lynching*. Chapel Hill: University of North Carolina Press.

Roddy, Dennis B. 1990, August 26. "Perceptions Still Segregate Police, Black Community." *The Pittsburgh Press*, p. B1.

Rollins, Judith 1985. *Between Women*. Philadelphia: Temple University Press.

Warr, Mark. Forthcoming. "Dangerous Situations: Social Context and Fear of Victimization." *Social Forces*.

Wieseltier, Leon. 1989, June 5. "Scar Tissue." *New Republic*, pp. 19–20.

Willie, Charles. 1983. *Race, Ethnicity, and Socioeconomic Status*. Bayside: General Hall.

Wilson, William J. 1978. *The Declining Significance of Race*. Chicago: University of Chicago Press.

————. 1987. *The Truly Disadvantaged: The Inner City, the Underclass, and Public Policy*. Chicago: University of Chicago Press.

Questions for Understanding and Critical Thinking

1. How has "deference ritual" affected African Americans, especially in the South?

2. Why have security and surveillance measures in stores typically focused more on African Americans than on other customers? What myths and stereotypes exist regarding the social characteristics of shoplifters in the United States? What are the realities?

3. According to Feagin, how do some middle-class African Americans use the resources of their middle-class occupations to deal with discrimination?

4. What are some examples of street harassment against African Americans? Why do some whites feel more free to engage in street harassment than in other types of discrimination?

5. How does the cumulative impact of racial discrimination affect African Americans?

ARTICLE 24 _____

In this article, sociologists Kathryn M. Neckerman and Joleen Kirschenman describe how employers' hiring strategies affect the employment opportunities of African Americans who live in the central-city areas. According to the authors, job interviews are especially problematic for central-city residents who often lack work experience that is highlighted in such interviews. The article also explores how racial bias and class oppression affect the job opportunities of central-city African Americans.

Kathryn M. Neckerman and Joleen Kirschenman were affiliated with the Department of Sociology at the University of Chicago when they coauthored this article. Neckerman currently teaches sociology at Columbia University.

Looking Ahead

1. How does racial bias affect job recruitment?
2. Why are job interviews biased in favor of friendly, articulate people?
3. What part do formal skills tests play in the screening of applicants?
4. How have employers adapted to increasing skill demands and declining labor-force quality? Are these practices race and class neutral? Why or why not?

Hiring Strategies, Racial Bias, and Inner-City Workers

◆ *Kathryn M. Neckerman and Joleen Kirschenman*

Employers and black job applicants encounter one another in a specific context of race and class relations. Widespread publicity, emphasizing poor schools, drug use, crime, and welfare dependency, shapes the way city residents view the inner city and whom they associate with it. These perceptions shade the relations between black and white, middle class and poor, sometimes engendering suspicion, resentment, and misunderstanding (Anderson 1990).

Given the uncertainty that characterizes most hiring decisions, it is likely that these perceptions and strained relations influence employers' hiring practices. For instance, employers might recruit selectively in order to avoid inner-city residents because of expectations that they would be poor employ-

Source: From Kathryn M. Neckerman and Joleen Kirschenman, "Hiring Strategies, Racial Bias, and Inner-City Workers." © 1991 by the Society for the Study of Social Problems. Reprinted from *Social Problems*, Vol. 38, No. 4, November 1991, pp. 433–447, by permission.

ees. Race and class misunderstanding or tension might be manifest in the job interview itself. If hiring practices are largely subjective, the influence of these perceptions about the inner city may be even more influential than would otherwise be the case.

Using data from interviews with Chicago employers, we examine employers' hiring strategies and consider their potential for racial bias. We focus on three hiring practices: selective recruitment, job interviews, and employment tests. We examine employers' views of different categories of workers and the way these preconceptions guide their recruitment strategies, and then discuss employers' accounts of job interviews with inner-city blacks. Finally, we examine the relationship between employment testing and black representation in entry-level jobs. The research is exploratory. We cannot provide rigorous evidence about the extent of racial bias. However, our interview data lend themselves to a fine-grained description of patterns of racial bias in hiring strategies. The description can serve as the basis for future empirical work on the employment problems of disadvantaged minorities.

LITERATURE REVIEW: HIRING STRATEGIES AND RACIAL BIAS

While there has been sustained interest in the high joblessness of blacks in the United States, most research considers skill deficiencies or spatial mismatches in labor supply and demand rather than barriers to employment that exist in the hiring process. To the extent that research examines access to jobs, most studies focus on the use of networks in filling lower-skilled positions and on inner-city blacks' lack of access to job networks (Braddock and McPartland 1987, Wilson 1987). The following survey of the literature examines the hiring process in more detail and explores how racial bias might occur at different points, from recruitment of the applicant pool to screening and interviewing.

Selective Recruitment and Racial Bias

Employers' recruitment practices are influenced by many considerations, including cost and time. For instance, employers use personal networks to recruit because they are inexpensive and fast. Small firms, lacking elaborate personnel offices, are especially likely to use informal networks, while larger firms are more likely to supplement networks with recruitment through classified ads and other formal sources.

Because screening applicants is costly, employers have an incentive to recruit selectively, excluding potential applicants they view as unpromising. Selective recruitment might be based on "statistical discrimination" or the use of nonproductive characteristics such as race to predict productive characteristics that are more difficult to observe (Aigner and Cain 1977, Bielby and Baron 1986, Phelps 1972, Thurow 1975). Employers' expectations about the productivity of different groups may be influenced by past experience, prejudice, or the mass media. Selective recruitment might also, of course, be motivated by a "taste" for discrimination or a reluctance to hire, work with, or be served by members of a particular group (Becker 1957).

Previous research suggests that employers recruit selectively based on race, ethnicity, class, and neighborhood. Of these categories, race and ethnicity have received the most attention, and empirical research has documented less favorable treatment of black and Hispanic job applicants (e.g., Braddock and McPartland 1987, Cross et al.

1990, Culp and Dunson 1986). But employers also share the larger society's perceptions of the "underclass," associating crime, illiteracy, drug use, and poor work ethic with the inner-city black population. Thus, they may look for indicators of class and "space," or neighborhood of reference, among black workers (Kirschenman and Neckerman 1991). Studies find that employers evaluate the educational credentials and references of blacks differently depending on whether applicants are from the central city or the suburbs (Crain n.d.; see also Braddock et al. 1986). Other employers confound race, class, and "space," generalizing their negative perceptions of lower-class or inner-city workers to all black applicants (Kirschenman and Neckerman 1991).

Race Bias in the Job Interview

Almost all employers select new employees by using job interviews, usually in combination with other bases for screening such as test scores, work experience, references, and credentials. Job interviews are widely used despite psychological research showing little correlation between interviewer ratings of job applicants and measured skills or job performance.

Research on white-black interaction suggests that prejudice or cultural misunderstanding create difficulties for blacks, especially lower-class blacks who interview with white employers. While classic racism—the view of people of color as undifferentiated—has declined, race relations between strangers are often tense and shaded with fear, suspicion, and moral contempt (Blauner 1989; see also Anderson 1990). Those from different racial or ethnic groups lack the common experiences and conversation patterns that ease interaction in impersonal settings (Erickson 1975). Blacks and whites often misread each others' verbal and non-

verbal cues (Kochman 1983). These misunderstandings are exacerbated when class as well as race separates people (Berg forthcoming, Glasgow 1981).

In research on employment interviews, race itself typically has little or no effect on interviewers' ratings, but race is significantly associated with interviewer ratings of nonverbal cues such as facial expression, posture, and certain aspects of voice that are known to influence employers (Arvey 1979, Parsons and Liden 1984). In one field study, for instance, black job applicants were rated significantly less favorably than whites on posture, voice articulation, voice intensity, and eye contact (Parsons and Liden 1984). Behavior or language seen as inappropriate also lowered interviewer ratings of objective characteristics such as education and experience (Hollenbeck 1984).

Race Bias in Employment Testing

Employment tests have been used for decades to measure general aptitude and specific job skills. Testing is used in hiring for perhaps one out of four high-school-level positions, with tests more common in the public sector and less common in unionized firms (Braddock and McPartland 1987, Cohen and Pfeffer 1986, Hamilton and Roessner 1972). Estimates of test validity vary. A recent meta-analysis of studies of the General Aptitude Test Battery (GATB), a widely used test of cognitive and psychomotor skills, estimated a .19 correlation between test scores and job performance (Hartigan and Wigdor 1989).

Racial bias in hiring stemming from the use of employment tests has been a longstanding concern. In 1971, the *Griggs v. Duke Power* decision required that if employment tests or other apparently neutral means of screening were shown to have an adverse impact on the hiring of protected groups, the firm must demonstrate that the test is job-related. Employers have found it difficult to validate general aptitude tests to the courts' satisfaction and have lost most testing cases since 1971 (Burstein and Pitchford 1990). However, this litigation stimulated the research on test validation. The meta-analysis cited above found that the correlation between test scores and job performance ratings was lower for minority employees than for nonminority employees but that on average test scores did not underpredict minority job performance (Hartigan and Wigdor 1989). Tests of skills such as typing are more easily validated and have not been open to the same legal challenges.

Most research on employment testing simply compares test scores to job performance rather than comparing testing to other means of employee selection. Yet if employers do not test applicants, they may rely more heavily on selective recruitment or on subjective impressions in the job interview. Thus, even if tests introduced some racial bias, subjective means of screening might disadvantage minority applicants more. For instance, if employers base hiring decisions on their preconceptions about inner-city schools rather than on tests of individual job applicants, then *all* graduates of those schools might be screened out. This hypothesis is consistent with other research suggesting that formal job search methods work better for blacks than informal methods because the formal methods provide more objective criteria by which employers can evaluate job applicants (Holzer 1987).

THE CHICAGO EMPLOYER SURVEY

Our research is based on face-to-face interviews with 185 employers in Chicago and the surrounding Cook County. The sample was stratified by location, industry, and size, and firms were sampled in proportion to the distribution of employment in Cook County.[1] Inner-city firms were oversampled. Unless otherwise specified, all descriptive statistics presented here are weighted to adjust for oversampling in the inner city. As no comprehensive list exists of Chicago-area employers, the sampling frame was assembled from two directories of Illinois businesses, supplemented with the telephone book for categories of firms underrepresented in the business directories. The field period lasted from July 1988 to March 1989, and yielded a completion rate of 46 percent. In terms of industry and size, the completed sample's weighted distribution roughly matches the distribution of employment in Cook County.[2]

Our initial contacts and the majority of interviews themselves were conducted with the highest ranking official at the sampled establishment. The interviewers and respondents were not matched by race with the respondents. All of the interviewers were non-Hispanic white; 8.5 percent of the respondents were black, 1.5 percent were Hispanic, and the remainder were non-Hispanic white.

The interview schedule included both closed- and open-ended questions about employers' hiring and recruitment practices and about their perceptions of Chicago's labor force and business climate. Because of the many open-ended questions, we taped the interviews. Item nonresponse varied depending on the sensitivity and factual difficulty of the question, with most nonresponse due to lack of knowledge rather than refusal to answer. In addition, the length and detail of responses to open-ended questions varied widely. Some employers volunteered additional information in response to closed-ended questions, which provided useful context for interpretation of the survey results.

Most closed-ended questions focused on the "sample job," defined as the most typical entry-level position in the firm's modal category—sales, clerical, skilled, semi-skilled, unskilled, or service. Entry-level jobs were selected for study in order to focus on the employment of disadvantaged workers, many of whom are first-time job seekers with limited skills. Because we sampled firms by industry and size, we do not have a random sample of entry-level jobs. However, when we compared the occupational distribution of our sample jobs to that of Cook County (excluding professional, managerial, and technical categories), we found that the two distributions were quite similar. The sample job serves as the unit of analysis for the quantitative part of this research. In the text, employers are categorized based on these sample jobs.

The interview schedule included several questions that bear on issues of hiring strategies and racial bias. We asked closed-ended questions about the race and ethnicity of employees in the sample job, as well as about use of various recruitment sources, the importance of specific hiring criteria, and any credentials or skills required for the sample job. Additionally, in the context of a general discussion of the quality of the workforce and of inner-city problems, we asked employers to comment on the high unemployment rates of inner-city black men and women and on any differences they saw between immigrant and native-born workers and among black, white, and Hispanic workers. Although these questions do not permit systematic comparisons of employers' perceptions of white, black, and Hispanic workers, they yielded rich data on employers' views of minority workers, often a sensitive subject. Answers to the open-ended questions were examined in the context of each case, and some items were coded and tabulated.

Although we surveyed both city and suburban employers, for this discussion we examine quantitative data for city employers only. Preliminary analysis suggested that patterns for city and suburban employers differed, and we did not have enough cases for separate analysis of the latter. Excluding suburban cases left 137 cases for analysis, although missing data reduced the number of cases available for multivariate analysis to 118. For Table 2, we divided the occupations into four categories, (1) clerical, (2) sales and customer service, (3) skilled and craft, and (4) "blue-collar" or semiskilled, unskilled, and noncustomer service. Because of the heterogeneity of service occupations, we divided them between the sales and blue-collar categories. "Customer service"—including jobs such as waitress, tour guide, and theater usher—had hiring criteria that were similar to sales jobs; other service jobs such as cook and janitor were more similar to semi-skilled and unskilled blue-collar jobs.

HIRING STRATEGIES AND RACIAL BIAS

During the time of the survey, the main problem most employers faced was not quantity of job applicants, but "quality." Employers complained that Chicago's work force lacked both basic skills and job skills. They were also dissatisfied with work attitudes, with many saying that employees were not as loyal and hard-working as they once were. Also, employers' traditional ways of getting information about job applicants had become less useful. For example, respondents told us that a high school diploma was no longer a reliable indicator of good basic skills. In addition, the threat of lawsuits has made it increasingly difficult to get information from an applicant's previous employers.

In this context, careful screening has become both more important to employers and more difficult to do. To identify good workers, some employers screened applicants using skills tests, "integrity interviews," psychological profiles, and drug tests. Others tried to recruit selectively or used informal networks. Almost half of our respondents said that employee referrals were their best source of qualified applicants, and it has become more common for employers to pay recruitment bonuses to employees whose referrals are hired. One respondent estimated that he hired 80 percent of all employee referrals, compared to only 5 percent of all applicants attracted by a newspaper ad.

In the following sections, we examine the implications of these hiring strategies for black employment. We consider three ways of screening potential workers: selective recruitment, job interviews, and employment testing.

Selective Recruitment

More often than not, employers recruited selectively, limiting their search for job candidates rather than casting a wide net. Employers sometimes explained their recruitment strategies in terms of practicality, for instance the ease or low cost of using personal networks or the difficulty of screening the large number of applications yielded by newspaper ads. But far more often they said their recruitment strategies were intended to bring them better applicants. The criteria of applicant quality they expressed were formally race- and class-neutral, but the recruitment strategies designed to attract high-quality applicants were not. When employers targeted their recruitment efforts at neighborhoods or institutions, they avoided inner-city populations. In addition, selective recruiting was more widespread among employers in poor, black neighborhoods than among those located elsewhere. The perceptions that employers expressed of inner-city black workers are consistent with the interpretation that they avoid these applicants

because on average they expect them to be lower-quality workers.

One way of screening the applicant pool is by not advertising job openings in the newspapers. More than 40 percent of our respondents did not use newspaper advertising for their entry-level jobs, and those who did place ads often did so as a last resort after employee networks had been unsuccessful. Moreover, about two-thirds of all city employers who advertised used neighborhood, suburban, or ethnic papers in addition to or instead of the metropolitan papers. Using neighborhood or ethnic papers (here, "local" papers) allowed employers to target particular populations, usually white, ethnic, or Hispanic. For instance, one downtown law firm advertised in white ethnic neighborhoods because its residents were believed to have a better work ethic. On the other hand, a few white-collar employers told us they advertised jobs in the *Defender,* a black newspaper, because of a commitment to minority hiring or simply to "keep the numbers in balance." In most cases we cannot identify the specific neighborhoods which employers targeted because respondents were not asked for this detailed information. But the effect of recruiting from local papers is evident from the survey. City employers who advertised only in local papers averaged 16 percent black in the sample job, compared to 32 percent black for those who advertised in the metropolitan papers.

Recruiting based on the quality or location of schools also provided employers with a way of screening. A downtown employer, for instance, believed that youth from suburban schools had better writing skills. Although the firm advertised over the entire metropolitan area, suburban resumes received more attention. When employers volunteered which schools they recruited from, it was usually Catholic schools and those from the city's white northwest side neighborhoods. One manufacturer posted ads at a Catholic school as well as at two of the city's magnet technical schools. A downtown bank recruited from three northwest side Catholic schools. Recruitment from Catholic schools selects white students disproportionately, but this form of recruitment was not necessarily seen in racial terms. Black Catholic school students were also viewed as more desirable employees than black public school students.

On the other hand, the state employment service and welfare programs which disproportionately refer inner-city blacks were associated with low-quality applicants, or in one respondent's words, "the dregs of the year." Neither agency screened adequately, most employers felt, and as a result tended to send inappropriate or unqualified applicants. A manufacturer who had hired white workers through Job Corps criticized the program, saying that none of them had worked out: "As a group I would be prejudiced against them." Another said:

> Any time I've taken any recommendations from state agencies, city agencies, or welfare agencies I get really people who are not prepared to come to work on time, not prepared to see that a new job is carried through, that it's completed. I mean there just doesn't seem to be a work ethic involved in these people.

Most employers did not recruit through these agencies; only a third of all employers used the state employment agency, and 16 percent used welfare programs.

Employers in inner-city areas of the city were more likely than other employers to recruit selectively. For instance, they were less likely to recruit from schools or local newspapers (see Table 1). They tried to recruit the best of the local labor force by using labor market intermediaries such as informal networks or formal agencies to screen workers.

As other research has shown, because blacks were seen as higher-risk employees, the recommendations and information provided by these intermediaries could be especially important for them (Coverdill 1990). One respondent attributed her firm's success with black workers to their heavy use of employee referrals. Another said employers were likely to be wary of a black man "unless he's got an 'in.'" A large southside employer recruited local high school or college students and added, "It gets them in the door if they're children of university people we know."

Large inner-city employers were especially likely to use formal labor market intermediaries. An inner-city day labor agency was able to place many black workers although many clients preferred "carloads of Mexicans"; its manager attributed this success partly to a computerized record-keeping system:

> Having so much detail on each individual employee allows us to record in their files good performance and bad performance, and we're therefore much more able to discriminate between good workers and bad, much more so than our competitors, who would just take anybody off the street, and because they can't really monitor somebody's performance, why take a risk? Whereas we're in a position to take a risk, because if the person doesn't pan out, either he goes to a different job, or we tell him goodbye. . . . It's after they're on the payroll that you really do your screening.

An inner-city hospital developed a "feeder network" into nearby elementary and high schools, funding tutors, child care for teen mothers, and other educational assistance, and providing information about health care careers for those who went on to college. The hospital used its feeder system to "draw the best talent on the top to us. . . . They've already got the work ethic down, they've been

TABLE 1 / Recruitment Practices: Percent of Employers Using Each Recruitment Source or Screening Mechanism, by Type of Neighborhood

	Downtown	Nonpoor White	Poor Black	Other	Total
Recruitment Sources					
Ask employees	93.3	85.6	93.3	83.3	88.8
Use schools	47.9	47.7	36.7	29.2	44.1
Illinois Job Service	30.3	33.3	40.0	31.3	32.5
Private employment agencies	39.5	19.7	23.3	8.3	25.5
Community groups	21.0	34.1	30.0	20.8	27.1
Welfare programs	11.8	19.7	20.0	14.6	16.1
Newspaper, media ads	69.7	59.1	40.0	39.6	58.4
Metropolitan papers	39.0	14.7	16.7	8.3	22.6
Local papers	2.9	18.3	0.0	22.9	11.6
Metropolitan and local	23.8	17.4	23.3	8.3	18.8
Walk-ins	63.0	83.3	73.3	75.0	73.9
Referrals from union	11.8	11.4	30.0	6.3	12.5
Help-wanted signs	10.1	14.4	33.3	20.8	15.5
Best source:					
Ask employees	42.1	46.8	36.7	36.4	42.6
Newspaper, media ads	29.9	24.2	26.7	18.2	25.6
Formal Prerequisites					
No formal prerequisites	26.2	42.3	57.1	54.2	39.9
Education only	24.3	26.0	7.1	4.2	20.3
Formal skills test only	15.0	22.8	29.0	25.0	20.6
Education and skills test	34.6	8.9	10.7	16.7	19.3
Unweighted N	42	52	13	23	130

Source: Chicago Employer Survey. Community areas classified as "Nonpoor white" were those with 50 percent or more white residents and 20 percent or less poor households. Areas classified as "Poor black" were those with 50 percent or more black residents and more than 20 percent poor households. Newspaper categories do not sum to total percent using newspapers because of missing responses among those who used newspapers.

dealing with both school and work, we also know what's going on with the schooling, the grades and all." The hospital also recruited staff through community job programs and employee networks, but not newspapers. "If you are just a cold applicant," the hospital's representative said, "chances of you getting in are almost nil."

Inner-city employers not large enough to develop these extensive screening mechanisms were at a disadvantage. One inner-city retailer said that young workers were disrespectful and prone to steal; she added,

"I think I'm getting the best of what I've got to select from, and they're still no good. And other people in the same line of business say the same thing. I know the guy at the gas station, the guy who runs the Burger King, and all of us say the same thing." Even these smaller employers tried less elaborate means of screening. The retailer just cited recruited some employees through a youth mentoring program. A fast food manager sent prospective workers to a distant suburb for training as a way of selecting the most motivated.

The interviews suggest that selective recruitment designed to attract higher-quality applicants disproportionately screens out inner-city blacks. Employers' perceptions of inner-city black workers are consistent with the interpretation that at least some do this deliberately. "The blacks that are employed are just not as good, not that there aren't good blacks, but it's a smaller percent than it would be of whites, for whatever reasons, cultural things, or family background, whatever," said one respondent. Table 2 shows the coded responses to a question inquiring about reasons for the high joblessness of inner-city black workers. Although this question was implicitly comparative, it did not elicit perceptions about workers of other ethnic backgrounds. Employers were especially likely to say that inner-city blacks lacked the work ethic, had a bad attitude toward work, and were unreliable; they also expected them to lack skills, especially basic skills. About half said that these workers had a poor work ethic. In the words of employers: "they don't want to work," "they don't know how to work," "they cannot handle the simplest of tasks," and "they come late and leave early." About 40 percent said inner-city black workers had attitude problems, including a bad attitude toward work as well as apathy

and arrogance: "They've got an attitude problem. They want to be catered to. . . . they want it handed to them, they don't want to do anything." Another respondent said that black men have a "chip on their shoulder; [they] resent being told what to do." One third of all employers said black workers tended to be undependable, "here today, gone tomorrow."

These perceptions of inner-city black workers are likely to underlie much of the selective recruitment discussed earlier. It is impossible for us to say whether employers avoid these applicants because of their race or their class, or for some other reason; race and class are so confounded in a setting like Chicago. But the effect of selective recruitment is to screen out disadvantaged black workers.

Social Interaction in the Job Interview

Virtually all employers interviewed job applicants, using these interviews to assess a wide range of qualities including literacy, values, common sense, integrity, dependability, intelligence, and character. Although they acknowledged the subjectivity of selection through interviews, they were confident their real world experience gave them the

TABLE 2 / Percent of Employers Making the Following Observations about Inner-City Black Workers, by Occupation

	Customer Service	Clerical	Craft	Blue-Collar	Total
Lack of job skills	14.3	12.5	35.5	7.7	13.2
Lack of basic skills	65.3	50.7	64.5	40.2	50.4
Lack of work ethic	49.0	50.0	45.2	43.6	47.2
Lack of dependability	28.6	26.4	32.3	42.7	32.8
Bad attitudes	28.6	43.7	41.9	33.3	37.8
Lack of interpersonal skills	14.3	9.7	9.7	4.3	8.5
Unweighted N	21	53	13	50	137

Source: Chicago Employer Survey. These figures were coded and tabulated from the open-ended questions about inner-city black men and women.

ability to spot good workers. The interview may take on particular importance for inner-city black applicants. Potentially, it is an arena in which they might overcome the negative images associated with their race or other markers such as neighborhood or school. One respondent described his bad experiences with black employees, but added that not all blacks were bad workers: "Well, you know when you talk to somebody you can tell a certain amount of something." Another noted that if she interviewed someone from the projects, "I would really spend a lot of time on prior work history and the types of things, the tasks that their job [requires]." These employers, and perhaps others, gave greater weight to the interview when applicants were poor or black.

Discussion of past work experience is generally an important aspect of the job interview. Searching for indications of dependability and willingness to work, employers said they probed reasons for gaps in applicants' work records. Unemployment itself did not disqualify an applicant with an acceptable excuse, such as illness or family responsibilities, and the interview provided a chance for an applicant to justify his or her work history.

In addition to relatively straightforward questions about work experience, employers often developed their own subjective "tests" of productivity and character. For instance, a manufacturer of transportation equipment asked if applicants had a "personal philosophy about work, a personal work ethic." Another manufacturer used the interview to judge "how the person looks at life, you know, is it what's in it for me or . . . is it a positive attitude." Much depended on the "gut reaction" of the employer. When one respondent was hired, she described how she and the recruiter "just clicked. I had the stuff, but also we just, just clicked. It's real important." Many paid attention to how ex-

pressive or open an applicant was. A law firm supervisor scorned the textbook job interview methods, saying what mattered to her was how "casual, frank, and honest" people were. A real estate developer looked for "someone that appears to sit up straight, talk expressively . . . [who] appears to be intelligent, articulate, forthcoming with their answers—you don't have to drag every word out of them." A hotelier, looking for desk clerks who could handle stress, said "I think you can determine that from how forthright they are in the interview."

Complicating interaction during the job interview is many employers' distrust of job applicants in general, and perhaps minority applicants in particular. Employers complained that some applicants lied about their work record and skills. Lying on applications was one common reason for rejecting applicants at a security firm: "Well, you know, you lied about your driver's license. They have previously been suspended or a couple of your references said they don't even know you or you said you went to a certain school, you didn't go to this particular school." A clerical employer complained, "They'll come in, say they type 50, 60 words a minute, and you put them on a typewriter and they type 20. Or they'll say they have computer experience, and then it turns out they don't know what a cursor is." Another said, "They've gotten to be so good at conning people that it's just frightening." Such falsification was mentioned more often by employers who saw many minority applicants, and one respondent said that black men were more likely to falsify their applications.

Other research suggests that inner-city black applicants experience difficulty in job interview interactions, and indeed, we heard some explicit criticisms of how inner-city blacks interview. Most common were complaints about applicants dressed in shabby or inappropriate clothing or coming late to interviews. But some respondents said more generally that inner-city blacks, especially men, did not know how to interview: they "aren't prepared; they don't have the enthusiasm"; they were belligerent or had "a chip on their shoulder"; they didn't know dates of employment or provided inconsistent information. One respondent commented that black men were not willing to "play the game" or to "follow the rules."

Our question about whether employers might be wary of poor people or those from the projects drew similar responses: applicants from a poor neighborhood did not know how to present themselves. A manufacturer said that project residents would be favorably evaluated if they had a positive attitude, but that they were not well equipped to "come in and really sell themselves." A clerical employer commented, "You don't need to look at the address to know where they're from; it's how people come across; they don't know how to behave in an office." A number of respondents remarked on cultural differences between inner-city blacks and the middle-class whites who dominate in business settings. Inner-city residents come from "a different world," said one manufacturer; "we don't realize that their rules are very different than ours."

It is obvious that job interviews are biased in favor of people who are friendly and articulate. But we find evidence that interviewing well goes beyond interpersonal skills to common understandings of appropriate interaction and conversational style—in short, shared culture. Job applicants must be sensitive to verbal and nonverbal cues and to the hidden agenda underlying interviewers' questions. They may be called upon to talk about abstract matters such as philosophy of work. And in discussing their past work experience, potentially an awkward subject for inner-city applicants with few previous jobs,

they must be forthcoming and honest. Because inner-city blacks have trouble with this interaction, heavy reliance on the interview to assess qualities such as honesty, intelligence, reliability, and so on is likely to disadvantage them.

Skills Tests and Black Representation

About 40 percent of the Chicago employers used formal skills tests to screen for the sample job. It is likely that this high incidence of testing is associated with city employers' distrust of the Chicago public school system and the quality of the city labor force. Only 30 percent of suburban firms in our survey used skills tests. Use of formal skills tests was much more common among clerical employers than among anyone else. More than half of all white-collar employers used conventional tests, measuring skills such as language, spelling, composition, math, typing, and filing speed. The clerical tests ranged from standard typing tests to "matching words in columns and seeing whether they know their ABCs" for filing.

Blue-collar employers also gave tests, most often informally. Skilled and craft employers often asked prospective employees to name tools or perform a given task. A precision tool manufacturer thought certification was helpful, "But most everything's going to come out on the test anyway; no matter what kind of paper people bring in, when he sets them up out there and they make the piece, it'll show." Employers of semi-skilled or unskilled blue-collar workers often screened for basic skills informally, observing how well employees filled out job applications; a few required a high school diploma as a proxy for literacy. Some had simple tests embedded in job application forms. A transportation employer described his firm's hiring process: "They fill out an application, which includes a little test—see whether they can read, write, and add." Another employer "sit[s] them down at a machine, [to] see how well they can do."

When employers have relatively objective means of getting information about job candidates, we would expect them to place less weight on more subjective and presumably more racially-biased hiring strategies. The previous two sections provide evidence that screening through selective recruitment or job interviews, both relatively subjective, disadvantage inner-city black applicants. In this section we ask whether employers who use skills tests have higher proportions of blacks in the sample job. Although our previous discussion emphasized both race and class, limitations of our data prevent us from analyzing the percent of inner-city or poor black workers in the sample job.

Considering only the bivariate relationship, we find that employers who tested job applicants for skills, either formally or informally, averaged 37.9 percent black in the sample job compared with 25.0 percent black among employers who did not test. But these figures are confounded by firm size. Larger firms were more likely to use skills tests and had higher proportions of black workers. It is also likely that other characteristics such as occupation or neighborhood composition confound the association between skills tests and black representation. To control for the influence of these variables, we performed an ordinary least squares (OLS) regression using percent black in the sample job as the dependent variable.

Variables used in the regression are described in Table 3, and their means, standard deviations, and ranges are shown in Table 4. Dummy variables for craft occupations and secretarial occupations were included in the regression. Other occupational dummy variables were tested as part of a specification search but did not approach significance.[3]

Regression results are shown in Table 4. Skills testing continued to be positively associated with percent black in the sample job when firm size, percent black in the neighborhood, and occupation were controlled. The "test" variable was just short of statistical significance at the .05 level. Examination of regression diagnostics indicated little problem with multicollinearity or outliers, although some heteroskedasticity may be present.[4] The percent black in the community area and the dummy variable indicating craft occupations were statistically significant. The significance of percent black in the community area, which has the largest effect of any of the variables, indicates the importance of firm location for work force composition and lends indirect support to the spatial "mismatch" hypothesis. The negative association between craft occupations and percent black is likely to reflect long-standing patterns of discrimination in the skilled trades.

TABLE 3 / Variables Included in Analysis of Percent Black in Sample Job

Firm size	Establishment size at survey date, divided by 100.
% black in area	Percent of Community Area residents who are black, using 1980 Census figures for the area in which the firm is located. Chicago Community Areas are aggregations of roughly 10-20 census tracts.
Skilled occupation	Coded "1" when the sample job is a skilled or craft occupation.
Clerical job	Coded "1" when the sample job is secretary or typist.
Test	Coded "1" for employers who give formal or informal skills test.

TABLE 4 / OLS Regression of Percent Black in Sample Job ($N = 118$)

I. Unweighted Descriptive Statistics for Variables Included in Analysis

	Mean	Standard Deviation	Minimum	Maximum
Proportion black in job	.318	.312	.00	1.00
Firm size	4.509	13.412	.08	110.00
Proportion black in area	.246	.294	.00	.98
Craft	.076	.267	.00	1.00
Secretarial	.110	.314	.00	1.00
Test	.551	.500	.00	1.00

Correlation Coefficients

	Proportion Black in Job	Firm Size	Proportion Black in Area	Craft	Secretarial	Test
Proportion black in job	1.000					
Firm size	.166	1.000				
Proportion black in area	.504	.020	1.000			
Craft	− .189	− .068	− .001	1.000		
Secretarial	− .037	− .087	.008	− .101	1.000	
Test	.196	.166	.031	− .126	.209	1.000

II. OLS Regression on Percent Black in Sample Job

	Coefficient	T-Statistic	Significance
Firm size	.003	1.410	.161
Proportion black in area	.527	6.452	.000
Craft	−.198	−2.174	.031
Secretarial	−.081	−1.026	.307
Test	.099	1.959	.053
Constant	.146	3.457	.001
Adjusted R squared		.306	

Note: The firm size variable is the number of employees divided by 100.

The results presented here show that Chicago employers who test for skills, either formally or informally, tend to have higher proportions of blacks in the sample job than employers who do not test. These findings must be interpreted cautiously because there are alternative explanations for which we could not adequately test. For instance, it is possible that these employers test for skills because they attract more black applicants. It might also be that their hiring criteria differ from those of employers who do not test. However, our results suggest the need for future research to address these issues.

CONCLUSION

Our evidence suggests that negative preconceptions and strained race relations both hamper inner-city black workers in the labor market. Many respondents perceived inner-city black workers to be deficient in work ethic and work attitudes, as well as in skills. Employers commonly directed their recruitment to white neighborhoods and Catholic or magnet schools and avoided recruiting from city-wide newspapers and public agencies because they believed these recruiting strategies brought them better workers. By design or not, these practices excluded blacks disproportionately from their applicant pool.

The job interview could be an opportunity for inner-city black job applicants to counter these negative stereotypes. But inner-city black job seekers with limited work experience and little familiarity with the white, middle-class world are also likely to have difficulty in the typical job interview. A spotty work record will have to be justified; misunderstanding and suspicion may undermine rapport and hamper communication. However qualified they are for the job, inner-city black applicants are more likely to fail subjective "tests" of productivity given during the interview.

Finally, employers who use skills tests have on average a higher proportion of black workers in the sample job than employers who do not test. Again, our results do not indicate that skills tests involve no racial bias but simply that skills tests are less biased than more subjective means of assessing job applicants. It should be emphasized that the survey on which these results were based took place in the context of legal restrictions on the use of employment tests and in a particular social context. The findings may not be generalizable to the time before these legal restrictions were enacted, nor do they indicate the likely effects of lifting these restrictions.

Our study was restricted to entry-level jobs and excluded professional, managerial, and technical positions; therefore, our results cannot be generalized to higher-level positions or to promotion rather than hiring. It is possible that promotion decisions are less prone to racial bias because employers have more information about individual job performance and need not guess about productivity based on markers such as race or class. Consistent with this, one study shows that educational credentials are more influential in hiring than in promotion (Bills 1988). On the other hand, to the extent that higher-level positions require contact with clients, supervision of staff, or interaction with executive or professional personnel, then the hiring criteria are likely to emphasize social skills and cultural compatibility, and promotion decisions may be more subjective. More research will be needed to distinguish these two effects.

The ways some employers have adapted to increasing skill demands and declining labor force quality are not race- or class-neutral. By directing recruitment away from inner-city neighborhoods, employers may provide themselves with a higher-skilled applicant pool but at the expense of qualified inner-city applicants. Attention should be given to ways that inner-city residents can demonstrate their competence, whether through certification by schools, screening by labor market intermediaries, or more extensive testing by employers. If rewards are not forthcoming for those who do improve their educational and work skills, inner-city residents' motivation to get education and training is likely to diminish.

Although we have emphasized the role of racial bias in the hiring process, the findings of this study are consistent with other interpretations of inner-city residents' employment problems. Problems of skills mismatch are evident in employers' concern with "quality" not "quantity" of applicants. Researchers' criticisms of the quality of ghetto schools are certainly echoed by employers. Finally, this work supports the emphasis others have given to job networks, suggesting that personal and institutional "connections" may be even more important in the inner city than they are elsewhere.

ENDNOTES

1. Given our focus on employment opportunities, the purpose of the design was to yield a sample that approximately matched the distribution of employment in Cook County. For instance, if 5 percent of Cook County jobs were in large, inner-city manufacturing firms, then 5 percent of the interviews should be in large, inner-city manufacturing firms. The sample necessary underrepresents small *firms*, but does so in order to gain a more representative picture of employment opportunities. For more information, see the Final Report available from the authors.

2. About 22 percent of employers we contacted refused to take part. We did not have the resources to pursue all potential respondents who were willing to be interviewed. Halfway through the field period, we set a minimum of 40 percent completion rate in all industry-by-location categories and stopped pursuing unresolved cases in categories with completion rates higher than 40 percent. Response rates by industry, firm size, and location were monitored, and special efforts were made to pursue cases in categories with low completion rates.

3. Variables tested include dummy variables for bank tellers, semi-skilled and unskilled laborers, and service workers, as well as the two variables in the final specification. The number of occupational dummy variables that could be included at once was limited because multicollinearity resulted when several were included together in the model. The inclusion of these variables did not substantially change the coefficients for firm size, skills testing, or percent black in the neighborhood. Also tested was a dummy variable for race of respondent. In our data, race of employer was highly correlated with percent black in the community area, firm size, and the skills test variable, and inclusion of the variable raised the condition index to 47, indicating serious multicollinearity. In analyses not shown, we also ran the regression without the minority employers and found the results substantially unchanged.

4. A condition index of 26 indicated no serious problems with multicollinearity. Several outliers and influential cases were identified; running the regression without these cases produced coefficient estimates slightly larger than those presented here, and with higher levels of significance. Inspection of residuals indicated that the linear specification was appropriate. The residuals plots also revealed some heteroskedasticity, so the significance tests may not be reliable. Substituting a generalized least squares model for OLS did not seem warranted for this simple descriptive exercise.

REFERENCES

Aigner, Dennis J., and Glen C. Cain
1977 "Statistical theories of discrimination in the labor market." Industrial and Labor Relations Review 30:175–87.

Anderson, Elijah
1990 Streetwise: Race, Class, and Change in an Urban Community. Chicago: University of Chicago Press.

Arvey, Richard D.
1979 "Unfair discrimination in the employment interview: Legal and psychological aspects." Psychological Bulletin 86:736–765.

Becker, Gary S.
1957 The Economics of Discrimination. Chicago: University of Chicago Press.

Berg, Linnea
Forth-   Ph.D. Dissertation. Evanston, Ill.: North-
coming   western University.

Bielby, William T., and James N. Baron
1986 "Men and women at work: Sex segregation and statistical discrimination." American Journal of Sociology 91:759–799.

Bills, David B.
1988 "Educational credentials and promotions: Does schooling do more than get you in the door?" Sociology of Education 61:52–60.

Blauner, Bob
1989 Black Lives, White Lives: Three Decades of Race Relations in America. Berkeley, Calif.: University of California Press.

Braddock, Jomills Henry, II, and James M. McPartland
1987 "How minorities continue to be excluded from equal employment opportunities: Research on labor market and institutional barriers." Journal of Social Issues 43:5–39.

Braddock, Jomills Henry, II, Robert L. Crain, James M. McPartland, and R. L. Dawkins
1986 "Applicant race and job placement decisions: A national survey experiment." International Journal of Sociology and Social Policy 6:3–24.

Burstein, Paul, and Susan Pitchford
1990 "Social-scientific and legal challenges to education and test requirements in employment." Social Problems 37:243–57.

Cohen, Yinon, and Jeffrey Pfeffer
1986   "Organizational hiring standards." Administrative Science Quarterly 31:1–24.

Coverdill, James E.
1990   "Personal contacts and youth employment." Unpublished Manuscript. Evanston, Ill.: Northwestern University.

Cross, Henry, G. Kewnney, J. Mell, and W. Zimmerman
1990   Employer Hiring Practices: The Differential Treatment of Hispanic and Anglo Job Seekers. Washington, D.C.: Urban Institute Press, Report 90-4.

Crain, Robert L.
n.d.   "The quality of American high school graduates: What personnel officers say and do about it." Baltimore, Maryland: The Johns Hopkins University, Center for the Social Organization of Schools.

Culp, Jerome, and Bruce H. Dunson
1986   "Brothers of a different color: A preliminary look at employer treatment of white and black youth." In The Black Youth Employment Crisis, ed. Richard B. Freeman and Harry J. Holzer, 233–259. Chicago: University of Chicago Press.

Erickson, Frederick
1975   "Gatekeeping and the melting pot: Interaction in counseling encounters." Harvard Educational Review 45:44–70.

Glasgow, Douglas G.
1981   The Black Underclass: Poverty, Unemployment and Entrapment of Ghetto Youth. New York: Vintage Press.

Hamilton, Gloria Shaw, and J. David Roessner
1972   "How employers screen disadvantaged job applicants." Monthly Labor Review 94: 14–21.

Hartigan, John A., and Alexandra K. Wigdor, eds.
1989   Fairness in Employment Testing: Validity Generalization, Minority Issues, and the General Aptitude Test Battery. Washington, D.C.: National Academy Press.

Hollenbeck, Kevin
1984   Hiring Decisions: An Analysis of Columbus Employer Assessments of Youthful Job Applicants. Columbus, Ohio: Ohio State University, National Center for Research on Vocational Education.

Holzer, Harry
1987   "Informal job search and black youth unemployment." American Economic Review 77:466–52.

Kirschenman, Joleen, and Kathryn M. Neckerman
1991   "We'd love to hire them but . . .": The meaning of race to employers." In The Urban Underclass, ed. Christopher Jencks and Paul Peterson, 203–232. Washington, D.C.: Brookings.

Kochman, Thomas
1983   Black and White Styles of Conflict. Chicago: University of Chicago Press.

Parsons, Charles, and Robert C. Liden
1984   "Interviewer perceptions of applicant qualifications: A multivariate field study of demographic characteristics and nonverbal cues." Journal of Applied Psychology 69: 557–568.

Phelps, Edmund
1972   "The statistical theory of racism and sexism." American Economic Review 62: 659–61.

Thurow, Lester
1975   Generating Inequality. New York: Basic Books.

Turner, Margery Austin, Michael Fix, and Raymond J. Struyk
1991   "Opportunities denied, opportunities diminished: Discrimination in hiring." Project report. Washington, D.C.: The Urban Institute.

Wilson, William Julius
1987   The Truly Disadvantaged: The Inner City, the Underclass, and Public Policy. Chicago: University of Chicago Press.

Questions for Understanding and Critical Thinking

1. Why did many of the employers in this study not advertise job openings in the newspapers?
2. What characteristics do employers tend to attribute to central-city African American job applicants?

3. How do Neckerman and Kirschenman support their assertion that some skills tests may be less biased against central-city African Americans than other, more subjective means of assessing job applicants?

4. Do the assumptions and conclusions of this study confirm or refute widely held stereotypes about the unemployed, such as their laziness or lack of desire to get a job? Why or why not?

ARTICLE 25 _____

In her research, sociologist Elizabeth Higginbotham debunks a widely held belief that professional African American women who have achieved middle-class status now "have it all." According to Higginbotham, African American women, even with advanced degrees, still struggle with racial discrimination and informal barriers to occupational advancement. Both gender and racial discrimination play a role in the occupational distribution of African American professional women, who primarily are employed in the public sector.

Elizabeth Higginbotham is acting director of the Center for Research on Women and Professor of Sociology at the University of Memphis.

Looking Ahead

1. Why is it important to investigate how both race and class interact to shape the lives of males and females?
2. What patterns of discrimination are evident in the history of employment for educated African American women?
3. How have the structural barriers experienced by African American women changed in recent decades? How have they remained the same?

Black Professional Women

Job Ceilings and Employment Sectors

◆ *Elizabeth Higginbotham*

Myths and stereotypes about the success of educated Black women, many promoted by misleading news reports of major trends, mask important employment problems faced by members of this group (Sokoloff 1992). The limited social science research on the plight of middle-class Black women makes fertile ground for myths about their success and stereotypes about their abilities to handle all situations. In reality, this is not a population exempt from problems on the job. Research on the employment status of educated Black women can be important in addressing the nature of contemporary racism in America and how it impacts people of color who are members of the middle class.

This [article] explores the employment status of Black professional women.[1] Throughout the twentieth century, there has been a tiny elite of educated Afro-American women employed in professional and man-

Source: From Elizabeth Higginbotham, "Black Professional Women: Job Ceilings and Employment Sectors," pp. 113–131 in *Women of Color in U.S. Society,* edited by Maxine Baca Zinn and Bonnie Thornton Dill. © 1994 by Temple University. Reprinted by permission of Temple University Press.

agerial positions. Since the 1970s, this population has experienced significant growth. In 1984, 14.3 percent of full-time, year-round employed Black women were in professional, technical, and kindred specialties, and 5.4 percent were managers, officials, and proprietors (U.S. Department of Labor 1984). They constituted nearly a fifth of all full-time, year-round employed Black women sixteen years and older. They are employed in a variety of occupations, but the majority—even today—are primary and secondary teachers, social workers, librarians, school counselors, and nurses. Since the 1970s, the number of Black women in traditionally male professions, such as attorney, accountant, physician, dentist, and minister, has increased, but the majority continue to be clustered in traditionally female professional and managerial positions (Kilson 1977; Sokoloff 1987, 1992; Wallace 1980).

The more education a woman has, the more likely she is to be employed. Thus, while a minority of Black women have college educations—about 5 percent of Black women over twenty-five years of age—this is the group most likely to be in the labor force (Jones 1986).

Some scholars might argue that the size of this group of Black women in professional and managerial positions is evidence that racial and sexual barriers can be scaled by the talented. From another perspective, educated Black women's employment patterns reveal a history of racial discrimination. During most of this century, the majority of employed professional and managerial Black women have worked either in the public sector (city, county, state, and federal government) or for small independent agencies and employers in the Black community (Higginbotham 1987; Hine 1989).

This [article] provides details of the contemporary employment patterns of Black and White women to illustrate segmentation or clustering of professional and managerial women along racial lines. It addresses the question: What form does racial stratification take in this post–Civil Rights era? The concepts of job ceilings and employment sectors are used to illustrate shifting patterns of racism in the labor market options of professional and managerial Black women. These concepts are useful in evaluating the recent progress made by Black women.

THE BLACK MIDDLE CLASS

The traditional social science practice is to view social class as status rankings. New scholarship offers a definition that views social class as opposing structural positions in the social organization of production. Different social classes do not represent different ranks in a social hierarchy but denote shared structural positions with regard to ownership of the means of production, level and degree of authority in the workplace, or the performance of mental or manual labor. From this perspective, the middle class is defined to include the small traditional groups of self-employed shopkeepers and independent farmers, and the numerically larger group of professionals, managers, and administrators. This group, frequently referred to as the professional-managerial class (see Walker 1979), performs the mental labor necessary to control the labor and lives of the working class. In the modern industrial capitalist state, it is designated as middle class because of its position between labor and capital. The primary role of the middle class is to plan, manage, and monitor the work of others. Its members have greater incomes, prestige, and education than other workers, but the social relations of dominance and subordination are key in defining their social class position (Braverman 1974; Poulantzas 1974; Ehrenreich and Ehrenreich 1979; Vanneman and Cannon 1987).

While Black women and men in middle-class positions enjoy many class advantages, they are still members of a racially devalued group. Understanding the middle class of a racially oppressed group requires a perspective that can investigate how both race and class interact to shape the lives of males and females. Racial oppression may be shared within the racial minority community but mediated by one's position within the class hierarchy (Barrera 1979). Both working-class and middle-class Afro-Americans are segmented and limited to the least remunerative and prestigious occupations, relative to Whites within their social class. Working-class Black men and women were denied access to many industrial, clerical, and sales jobs because these positions were reserved for Whites. Black men and women were readily able to find work in jobs that White people did not want. In the case of Black women, in the first half of the century they were employed primarily as domestics, and later gained access to service work, factory work, and some clerical and sales jobs (Amott and Matthaei 1991; Jones 1984).

Historically, Black middle-class men and women who occupied professional positions served their racial communities. These positions are often shunned by White professionals. Even today, most middle-class Black people teach and provide health and human services, and professional and managerial services to other Black people. The size and affluence of the Black community is a factor in the growth of the Black middle class (Drake and Cayton 1970; Landry 1987). Gender also plays a significant role in access to professional occupations.

GENDER DIFFERENCES IN JOB CEILINGS FOR BLACK AMERICANS

As noted above, patterns of discrimination are evident in the history of employment for educated Black women and men. The concept of job ceilings helps clarify practices prior to the 1960s. Contrasting employment patterns between the public and private sectors best describes discriminatory patterns after the passage of Civil Rights legislation.

Job ceilings are the racially specific caps or ceilings placed on the occupational mobility of targeted groups. This form of economic oppression can be maintained by formal or informal practices. The results are the same. Black people are denied the opportunity to fill certain jobs, even if they are qualified, because employers have decided that this particular work is closed to Black Americans. Over the years, Black Americans have learned to watch for subtle changes or cracks in this ceiling.

Job ceilings, institutionalized early in this century, were instrumental in excluding Black people from many industrial jobs—both positions they might have held in the past and new jobs that were opening up. Job ceilings were very effective means of keeping Black people in low-wage manual jobs—the lowest of all working-class employment.

In *Black Metropolis*, St. Clair Drake and Horace Cayton (1970) talked in detail about the job ceiling in Chicago in the 1920s and 1930s:

> *Between the First World War and the Depression, the bulk of the Negro population became concentrated in the lower-paid, menial, hazardous, and relatively unpleasant jobs. The employment policy of individual firms, trade-union restrictions, and racial discrimination in training and promotion made it exceedingly difficult for them to secure employment in the skilled trades, in clerical and sales work, and as foremen and managers. Certain entire industries had a "lily-white" policy—notably the public utilities, the electrical manufacturing industry, and the city's banks and offices. (p. 112)*

The job ceiling was not unique to Chicago. It was a fundamental part of the labor market in urban and rural communities, both in the North and in the South (Hine 1989). Its existence prohibited Black males and females from following occupational mobility patterns open to both native-born White Americans and White immigrants. Over time, even first- and second-generation White immigrants were able to move from menial jobs into unskilled and semiskilled factory work. The next generation might proceed into skilled industrial work and sometimes eventually into white-collar positions.

With this established channel closed to them, Black American men and women had to find alternative routes out of the low-wage jobs in private household work, janitorial and custodial services, laundry work, and the other positions in which they could seek employment. A few Black men and women, with the support of their families or through their own efforts, were able to carve out an alternative course to better employment. They struggled to get an education, most often in traditionally Black institutions.

Acquiring a college education was often a route around the job ceiling for Black males and females. An education gave the credentials to qualify for middle-class positions. In this way, some Black people could bypass the ceiling and move to the next floor. That floor consisted of white-collar professional and managerial positions, primarily within the minority community.

For Black women, a college education did not guarantee a better livelihood than domestic or other low-wage service work. The Black females who obtained a college education, even an advanced degree, found another layer of obstacles in front of them. In a racially segmented society, even middle-class occupational positions are shaped by racism (and in the case of women, also sexism). So

Black women who had the education to merit employment in middle-class professional jobs still faced race and sex barriers to securing satisfying and economically rewarding work in the middle class.

Prior to World War II, gender restrictions shaped the professions for which Black women could prepare and practice. Black women seeking higher education were steered into primary and secondary school teaching, nursing, social work, and library sciences (Hine 1989; Jones 1985). Gender also shaped the options of Black men. They were directed into medicine and dentistry, the ministry and business, as well as teaching. These gender-specific trends were noted by earlier social science researchers (Cuthbert 1942; Johnson 1969; Noble 1956). Black males and females were expected to practice their gender-specific professions within a racially segregated society.

On the whole, educational training equipped Black men for professional occupations in which they could be self-employed or work within Black institutions. With medical or dental training, they could set up independent or joint practices as physicians and dentists, in which they saw mostly Black patients—and in large communities, they were able to develop successful enterprises. As ministers, Black men were directly responsible to a congregation—if it was a large congregation, they could gain economic security. Some Black men moved into providing insurance and other services to the Black population. And other Black men found employment in traditionally Black educational institutions, where they were somewhat removed from the racist policies and practices in the White-dominated labor market.

College-educated Black women faced a different prospect. They were discouraged from pursuing traditionally male occupations and directed into developing female professions (Hine 1989). Thus, Black women were not educated for professions that enabled them to set up their own businesses or independent practices. Nurses do not set up individual practices; they are hired to work for doctors or employed in hospitals or clinics. Teachers do not recruit their own students; they are hired by public or private school systems. Librarians do not run their own institutions; they are hired to work in libraries operated by the city, the county, or an educational facility. And social workers do not go into business for themselves; they are hired by human service agencies in the private or public sector. Gender barriers, along with race and class obstructions in both educational institutions and the labor market, complicated Black women's securing professional employment (Higginbotham 1987; Hine 1989; Jones 1985). A college education often prepared them for occupations where they still faced a racial job ceiling.

And Black women did confront rigid job ceilings. Many Northern cities did not hire Black people for professional positions in their schools, clinics, hospitals, libraries, and other agencies. In the South, some public sector jobs were set aside for Black people, because Jim Crow policies dictated segregated facilities. This was particularly the case in the teaching field, where Afro-Americans had a monopoly on positions in Black schools, and during the Depression in public health and voluntary health operations (Hine 1989). North of the Mason-Dixon Line, city and county employment policies regarding Black professionals were very mixed. De facto segregation was usually the rule for designating where children were schooled, but cities differed in whether they would hire Black teachers to staff the facilities used to educate Black children (Tyack 1974). Black nurses could not find employment outside of Black hospitals and private homes. Because they were not trained for professions that could be translated into independent entrepreneurial prac-

tices, Black females were dependent on salaries and wages. Thus, employment prospects for educated Black women were contingent upon city and county hiring policies to staff public institutions.

For these reasons, the numbers of Black professional and managerial women remained small and lagged behind the percentages of White women in these occupations. The percentage of Black women employed as professional, technical, or kindred workers increased from 4.3 in 1940 to 5.3 in 1950, 7.7 in 1960, and to 15.3 percent by 1980. Despite the increase among professionals, the number of Black women in managerial positions did not exceed 1.4 percent until 1980, when it reached 4.2 percent (Higginbotham 1987).

EMPLOYMENT SECTORS: BLACK PROFESSIONAL WOMEN'S PLACE

Legislation against race and sex discrimination challenged many of the arbitrary practices, such as job ceilings. Since the mid-1960s, more educated Black people have found jobs in the professions for which they have credentials. This has meant an increase in the numbers of Black women in professional and managerial positions, as well as their employment in a wider range of occupations (Kilson 1977; Sokoloff 1992; Westcott 1982). Yet, Civil Rights legislation did not dismantle the racism that is a critical part of the labor market. Empirical research indicates that the occupational positions of educated Black women are still problematic (Higginbotham 1987; Sokoloff 1987, 1988, 1992). They continue to face employment barriers, but the discrimination has taken a new form. Now Black women find themselves limited to employment in certain sectors of the labor market.

Recent scholarship, especially work by Sharon Collins (1983), indicates that Black employees in professional and managerial positions are concentrated in the public sector. When they are in the private sector, Black middle-class employees are in the marginal areas of production (such as personnel, public relations, and the like). These observations are supported by reports from Black managers in the private sector (Bascom 1987; Fulbright 1986).

In an earlier work (Higginbotham 1987), I discussed how contemporary professional Black women remain concentrated in the traditionally female professions of teacher, social worker, nurse, librarian, and so forth. Recently, a significant number of Black women, as well as their White sisters, have broken into new occupations—those traditionally dominated by males. Today, there are more Black and White women who are physicians, dentists, lawyers, accountants,

and managers in both small and large firms. Indeed, if one looks at broad occupational categories, the degree of sex segregation in the professional labor market has declined since the 1970s (Sokoloff 1987, 1988, 1992). If one looks below the surface, one can identify how racism remains embedded in the social structure. Instead of being evenly split between the private and public sectors, the majority of professional and managerial Black women are employed in the public sector. Census data reveal that in fourteen of the fifteen Standard Metropolitan Statistical Areas (SMSAs) with the largest Black populations, the majority of Black professional and managerial women are employed in the public sector (see Table 1).[2] In each of the same fifteen metropolitan areas, the majority of White professional and managerial women were employed in the private sector.[3]

TABLE 1 / Sectoral Distribution of Women Managerial and Professional Specialty Workers for Fifteen SMSAs, 1980

SMSA	Black				Non-Black			
	N	Public (%)	Private (%)	Other (%)[a]	N	Public (%)	Private (%)	Other (%)
Atlanta	18,479	55.7	42.5	1.8	81,998	34.8	60.3	4.9
Baltimore	19,902	72.3	26.9	0.8	79,351	40.4	55.1	4.4
Chicago	44,066	53.8	44.8	1.4	268,359	26.6	69.0	4.4
Cleveland	10,835	53.8	44.0	2.1	65,049	30.0	65.9	4.1
Dallas	11,308	54.8	42.6	2.6	122,666	32.2	62.0	5.8
Detroit	24,257	59.3	39.1	1.5	127,661	33.7	62.1	4.2
Houston	19,418	55.5	42.4	2.1	114,954	30.8	63.5	5.7
Los Angeles	36,119	47.6	49.3	3.1	299,395	27.3	64.9	7.9
Memphis	9,040	71.7	27.0	1.3	26,633	34.6	60.3	5.1
Miami	9,679	60.3	38.2	1.5	59,261	26.7	66.9	6.4
Newark	14,208	55.2	43.6	1.2	78,532	33.5	62.1	4.4
New Orleans	11,446	65.8	32.8	1.4	36,259	31.5	63.7	4.9
New York	67,026	49.3	48.8	1.8	697,395	34.4	59.8	5.8
Philadelphia	25,273	56.0	42.2	1.8	164,890	29.2	65.6	4.6
St. Louis	12,939	58.2	40.3	1.4	81,959	29.3	66.3	4.4
Mean Percentage	15.4	57.9	40.3	1.7	84.6	31.7	63.2	5.1

[a]Includes self-employed and unpaid family workers.

Source: U.S. Bureau of the Census, *Census of Population 1980*, vol. 1, *Characteristics of the Population* (Washington, D.C.: U.S. Government Printing Office, 1983), ch. D, "Detailed Population Characteristics," Table 220.

For example, in the Memphis metropolitan area, Black women are about 25.3 percent of the females employed in professional and managerial occupations, and 71.7 percent are employed in the public sector; only 34.5 percent of White professional and managerial women are so employed. Likewise, 60.4 percent of White professional and managerial women work in the private sector, while only 27 percent of Black women in those same occupations do so. This is a common pattern for both Northern and Southern cities.

In the metropolitan area of Newark, New Jersey, Black women constitute 15 percent of women employed in professional and managerial occupations. In 1980, 55.2 percent of these Black women worked in the public sector, while only 33.7 percent of White professional and managerial women did so. And 61.8 percent of White women worked in the private sector, while only 43.6 percent of the Black professional and managerial women did. This is very interesting, in light of the fact that about the same percentages of Black and White professional and managerial women in the Newark metropolitan area are teachers, counselors, and librarians (34 percent)—they are just employed in different sectors. While 82.1 percent of the Black teachers, librarians, and counselors in Newark are employed in the public sector, 70.3 percent of the White women in the same occupations are employed there (Higginbotham 1987).

In the New York City metropolitan area, Black professional women are more evenly distributed in public (49.3 percent) and private (48.8 percent) sector work. With many corporate headquarters and larger numbers of private schools, social service agencies, and hospitals, one might expect that Black women would have more options in the private sector than might be found in either Newark or Memphis. But White women also have these options. In the Big Apple, only 26.6 percent of White professional and managerial women were employed in the public sector and 66.5 percent were in the private sector. New York ranks third, behind Chicago and Miami, in the concentration of White professional and managerial women in the private sector. The figures for other cities in the nation are similar, with only a slight regional variation—Southern cities have somewhat higher concentrations of Black professional women in public sector employment. Los Angeles is the only city where the majority of Black professional women are in the private sector.

The 1980 census indicates that many educated Black women are working as professionals and managers, but they are mostly likely to be public school teachers, city and county health advocates, city welfare workers, public librarians, city attorneys, public defenders, city and county managers and administrators, and faculty members of public community and four-year colleges and universities. Professional Black women are less likely to work for major corporate law firms, teach at private educational institutions on any level, or serve on the medical staff of private hospitals than are their White counterparts. These data encourage us to ask questions about the nature and extent of progress for Black professional women.

The search for explanations of the continued clustering of Black professional and managerial women in the public sector reveals two major factors. First, educated Black women continue to be concentrated in traditionally female occupations—jobs that are primarily dependent upon the public sector for employment. Indeed, the majority of our teachers, librarians, social workers, and so forth are employed by city, state, and county governments. In Southern cities, outside of Atlanta and Miami, professional and managerial women, both Black and White, are clustered in traditionally female occupations, especially primary and secondary school teaching.

The second factor is racism—a racism that persists from an earlier era but takes on new forms in this post–Civil Rights age (Omi and Winant 1987). The distribution of employed Black and White professional and managerial women in public and private sectors provides the means for examining differences in the structural barriers women face in the labor market.

A DECADE OF PROGRESS?

An examination of 1970 census data on the sector distribution of Black and non-Black women for the same fifteen SMSAs reveals that in fourteen of the fifteen SMSAs used in the previous analysis, the majority of Black professional women were employed in the public sector, while the majority of non-Black women were found in the private sector (see Table 2). In 1970, it was New York, not Los Angeles, that was the exception. For the same fifteen SMSAs, the mean percent of Black women in the public sector was 61.5, 3.5 percentage points higher than the 1980 mean. In 1970, the mean percentage of non-Black professional and managerial specialty women in the public sector was 37.8, 6.1 percentage points higher than the 1980 figures for non-Blacks. Thus a comparison of the 1970 and 1980 census figures, even with the limitations of the data, indicates that a smaller percentage of professional and managerial women, both Black and White, are employed in the public sector.

TABLE 2 / Sectoral Distribution of Women Managerial and Professional Workers for Fifteen SMSAs, 1970

SMSA	Black				Non-Black			
	N	Public (%)	Private (%)	Other (%)[a]	N	Public (%)	Private (%)	Other (%)
Atlanta	6,973	68.5	29.0	2.5	37,105	43.0	50.6	6.1
Baltimore	10,461	72.6	24.4	2.9	45,591	45.0	49.2	5.8
Chicago	21,239	59.2	38.0	2.7	162,771	34.3	60.5	5.2
Cleveland	6,390	59.4	36.2	4.4	45,162	37.3	57.6	5.1
Dallas	4,709	51.8	42.9	5.3	40,668	34.9	56.8	8.4
Detroit	12,920	57.8	39.2	3.0	80,224	41.3	53.3	5.4
Houston	7,516	53.0	41.1	5.9	47,090	35.7	55.4	8.9
Los Angeles	17,429	58.0	37.4	4.6	194,433	36.2	54.8	9.0
Memphis	4,772	76.8	20.0	3.2	14,742	43.1	49.5	7.4
Miami	3,120	68.9	27.7	3.4	30,161	34.0	57.8	8.2
Newark	6,550	55.9	40.7	3.4	46,450	40.4	53.9	5.7
New Orleans	5,450	68.5	28.6	2.9	21,331	34.4	57.1	8.5
New York	41,131	49.2	47.5	3.3	317,389	36.5	57.1	6.3
Philadelphia	14,772	58.7	38.3	3.1	106,796	35.2	58.4	6.4
St. Louis	7,357	63.8	33.2	3.0	54,666	36.0	56.0	5.9
Mean Percentage	13.7	61.5	34.9	3.6	86.3	37.8	55.2	6.8

[a]Includes self-employed and unpaid family workers.

Source: U.S. Bureau of the Census, *Census of Population 1970*, vol. 1, *Characteristics of the Population* (Washington, D.C.: U.S. Government Printing Office, 1973), "Detailed Population Characteristics," Table 173.

Table 3 reports the percentage point change in the sector distribution of women in professional and managerial specialty occupations between 1970 and 1980 for the fifteen SMSAs. The last column reveals that there have been small but significant gains in the percentage of Black women employed in professional and managerial positions. These data reinforce other findings about the progress Black women made during the decade (Sokoloff 1988, 1992; Westcott 1982). But a closer look at the percentage increases and decreases in the public and private sectors indicates that change is not uniform for all professional and managerial women.

In the majority of the metropolitan areas, the percentages of non-Black women (the majority of this population is White, but it includes Asian American, Latina, and Native American women) in the private sector have grown considerably. This progress is due to the entrance of women into traditionally male occupations, which are more likely to be found in the private sector, and increasing opportunities to perform traditionally female work in the private sector (private schools, private hospitals, and private colleges and universities).

Even in Memphis, private sector employment for White professional and managerial women increased by 10.8 percentage points.[4] A few other cities also witnessed significant growth in the percentages of non-Black women in the private sector: 10.3 percentage points for St. Louis, 11.1 percentage points for Miami, 8.8 in Detroit, and in many other metropolitan areas, increases in the range of five to nine percentage points.

TABLE 3 / Percent Change in the Sectoral Distribution of Women Managerial/Professional Specialty Workers for Fifteen SMSAs, 1970–1980

	Public		Private		Other[a]		Total Change
SMSA	Black	Non-Black	Black	Non-Black	Black	Non-Black	Black[b]
Atlanta	− 12.8	− 8.2	+ 13.5	+ 9.7	− 0.7	− 1.2	+ 2.6
Baltimore	− 0.3	− 0.6	+ 2.5	+ 5.9	− 2.1	− 1.4	+ 1.3
Chicago	− 5.4	− 7.6	+ 6.8	+ 8.3	− 1.3	− 0.8	+ 2.6
Cleveland	− 5.6	− 7.3	+ 7.8	+ 8.3	− 2.3	− 1.0	+ 1.9
Dallas	+ 3.0	− 2.7	− 0.3	+ 5.2	− 2.7	− 2.6	− 0.7
Detroit	+ 1.5	− 7.6	− 0.1	+ 8.8	− 1.5	− 1.2	+ 2.1
Houston	+ 2.5	− 4.9	+ 1.3	+ 8.1	− 3.8	− 3.2	+ 0.6
Los Angeles	− 10.4	− 8.9	+ 11.9	+ 11.1	− 1.5	− 1.1	+ 2.6
Memphis	− 5.1	− 8.5	+ 7.0	+ 10.8	− 1.9	− 2.3	+ 0.9
Miami	− 8.6	− 7.3	+ 10.5	+ 11.1	− 1.9	− 1.8	+ 4.6
Newark	− 0.7	− 6.9	+ 2.9	+ 8.2	− 2.2	− 1.3	+ 2.9
New Orleans	− 2.7	− 2.9	+ 4.2	+ 6.6	− 1.5	− 3.6	+ 3.7
New York	+ 0.1	− 2.1	+ 1.3	+ 2.7	− 1.5	− 0.5	− 2.7
Philadelphia	− 2.7	− 6.0	+ 3.9	+ 7.2	− 1.3	− 1.8	+ 1.1
St. Louis	− 5.6	− 6.7	+ 7.1	+ 10.3	− 1.6	− 1.5	+ 1.7
Mean Percentage	− 3.2	− 5.9	+ 5.4	+ 8.2	− 1.8	− 1.6	+ 1.7

[a]Includes self-employed and unpaid family workers.

[b]Represents percentage point change in Black/non-Black composition of all women managerial and professional specialty workers.

The mean percentage point increase in private sector employment for non-Black women across the fifteen SMSAs was 8.15.

Black professional and managerial women have also made serious inroads into the private sector since 1970. Yet, in all but two metropolitan areas, their progress lags behind their non-Black sisters. Only in Atlanta and Los Angeles did Black women have larger percentage point increases in private sector employment than did non-Black women. Both of these are Sunbelt cities where there were large increases in private sector employment for non-Black women as well.

The more common pattern saw smaller changes for Black women than non-Black women. Houston, another Sunbelt city, had a small increase for Black women (1.3 percentage points), but a significant shift of 8.1 percentage points for non-Black women. In Baltimore, Newark, New York, and Philadelphia, Black professional and managerial women had percentage point increases below 4. In the metropolitan areas of Chicago, Memphis, and Cleveland, Black professional women increased their percentages in private sector employment by 6.8, 7.0, and 7.8, respectively. Table 3 provides evidence that Black women are moving out of public sector employment in many metropolitan areas, but that movement is slower than that of their non-Black counterparts. The mean percentage point increase in private sector employment for Black women across the fifteen SMSAs is 5.4, considerably lower than the figure for non-Black women of 8.2.

In two SMSAs, the concentration of Black managerial and professional specialty women in the private sector declined. In Dallas, the percent of Black women in these occupations who were employed in the private sector declined by 0.3 percentage point while non-Black women increased by 5.2 percentage points. In Detroit, Black women's concentration in the private sector declined by 0.1 percentage point while non-Black women's concentration in the private sector increased by 8.8 percentage points. It is evident that educated White women made more significant progress than educated Black women. Racism does not disappear when one gets an education and a middle-class occupation. These data provide one means of detailing the racial constraints faced by Black women in professional and managerial employment.

CONCLUSION

Black women as well as White women are gaining access to education in traditionally male fields. Once they finish this training, they enter a racist and sexist labor market. With only one major discriminatory barrier, more White than Black women are able to enter the private sector. Thus, some research indicates that dominant culture women are moving into the upper levels of the middle class while Black women are lagging behind (Landry 1987). Black women, even with advanced degrees, still struggle with racial discrimination and informal barriers to occupational advancement. Instead of the myth of the advantages of being a double minority, both Black and female (Epstein 1972), Fulbright's (1986) research indicates that there are no advantages to being both Black and female for managers; instead, there are additional constraints. The case can also be made for Black women in traditionally female fields. Even when women remain in traditionally female occupations, White women are able to practice these professions in the private sector, especially private schools and agencies (Higginbotham 1987).

Both gender and racial discrimination play a role in the occupational distribution of Black women. First, Black women continue to be steered into training for traditionally female occupations and discouraged from attempting innovative careers. Thus, their professional training keeps them dependent upon the public sector for employment as teachers, social workers, nurses, and librarians. Second, rigid racial barriers that limit Black people's employment options in the private sector, in both male- and female-dominated occupations, keep their numbers in the private sector low. Therefore more Black women, even those trained in traditionally male fields, find jobs in the public sector because there is less discrimination in hiring in this segment of the labor market.

These data prompt many other questions about the quality of work life for Black professional and managerial women. What does it mean to be employed in the public sector in metropolitan areas today? In the light of city, county, and state fiscal problems and reduced commitments to human services, the prospects appear grim. Many public school teachers are demanding more police protection in the schools and the institutionalization of faculty and student identification cards, as well as insisting upon smaller class sizes and more materials. In many urban communities there are additional demands to raise teachers' salaries and provide greater fringe benefits, but on the whole, working conditions are equally critical work issues for many primary and secondary public school faculty members.

In the light of these tensions and the decreasing desirability of public schools as places to work, many Black teachers are finding they have few alternatives in the labor market. Many are returning to universities for retraining to increase their employment options. Others are redefining their goals and planning to work their twenty, twenty-five, or thirty years until retirement—with the hope that the financial cushion of a pension will enable them to begin second careers.

Similar issues confront human service workers in health and social service agencies. Budget cuts have resulted in significant reductions in staffing—leaving the remaining employees with high caseloads and impossible tasks. Such individuals are lucky to be able to keep their jobs during an era when the delivery of services to poor and working-class people is not a priority. Yet they face daily frustrations on the job. As the data suggest, many of the professional and managerial people working under such conditions are Black women and other people of color.

These current realities suggest that public sector professional employment, especially for women in traditionally female occupations, is not the prize it appeared to be in the 1950s and 1960s (Block et al. 1987). In an earlier age, women employed as teachers, social workers, and nurses in public schools and city agencies had excellent salaries, decent fringe benefits, and vacations. They also could easily return to their professions after their childbearing years. Even where professional public sector employees have been able to keep their wages on a par with private sector employees in their metropolitan areas, the conditions of work have deteriorated. These realities may provide the motivation to leave the public sector. If so, we must ask if each public sector professional employee has the same chance of securing comparable work in the private sector. These data suggest that White women might be more successful in seeking new employment options outside the public sector.

These data should encourage detailed investigations of the progress of Black, White, Latina, Asian American, and Native American professional and managerial women in the private sector. As a nation, we celebrate the impact of the Civil Rights and women's movements and the passage of federal guidelines in opening corporate doors for women and racial minorities, yet these gains are fragile in the face of indifferent federal administrations (Collins 1983). Given these shifts, how do professional and managerial women survive in the private sector? Perhaps a major obstacle for many is gaining access to private sector jobs.

The racial barriers faced by educated Black women are different from the blanket opposition to hiring Black people in professional and managerial positions that characterized the early part of this century. There has been significant progress in both access to higher education and employment options. The persistence of racism can result in a middle class that is segmented along racial lines. Black professionals, managers, and administrators are clustered in the public sector. In their positions they serve clients in public schools, local welfare agencies, public hospitals, public defender's offices, and other human service agencies. Many of these clients are poor and working class, and many are Black people or other people of color. Meanwhile, non-Black women (especially White women) are increasing their numbers in private sector employment. Are Black professionals, particularly women, trapped in public sector employment? In these middle-class positions, are they professionals relegated to jobs, wages, and working conditions that mirror the racial segmentation in traditional working-class occupations?

I addressed the persistence of racial restrictions in the employment options for Black professional and managerial women. Indeed, the findings suggest that one way to explore racial discrimination is to observe racial differences in access to jobs in employment sectors. There are many other issues that merit exploration, especially the day-to-day experiences of Black and other women of color in professional and managerial positions in different occupations and sectors.

With a grounding in theory—especially a theoretical approach that recognizes that racism is still with us—and with solid empirical tools, we can build an exemplary scholarship of people of color across social class lines. Armed with both theory and data, we can uncover evidence that highlights the intersection of race, gender, and class. This scholarship can praise the diligence and persistence of female and male members of the Afro-American community. It can also portray the costs of racism for this population. Knowledge such as this will help us know ourselves and understand the larger problems that we confront as we continue to struggle against racism and sexism in all their forms.

ENDNOTES

Acknowledgments: I wish to thank Lynn Weber, Betty Wiley, Jobe Henry, Jr., and Sandra Marion for their help in preparing this [article]. I would also like to acknowledge the comments of the editors, Maxine Baca Zinn and Bonnie Thornton Dill.

1. This discussion does not include Black women who are in the middle class solely by virtue of marriage. Black women married to professional and managerial men but not employed in the labor force faced different circumstances.

2. This study does not include the District of Columbia because it is a major metropolitan area where a significant number of all residents are employed in the public sector.

3. In 1970, the data on occupational distribution by SMSA categorized workers as either Black or non-Black; thus, the non-Black figures included Asian American, Latina, and Native American women as well as White women. This makes the status of non-racially oppressed White women difficult to ascertain. Better data on White and Black women are available for 1980 and those data are used here in the text. In Table 1, data for Black and non-Black women are used to facilitate comparisons with 1970 data.

4. Memphis has a small Asian American, Latino, and Native American population; thus we can assume that the vast majority of the non-Black population is White.

REFERENCES

Amott, Teresa, and Julie A. Matthaei. 1991. *Race, Gender, and Work: A Multicultural Economic History of Women in the United States.* Boston: South End Press.

Barrera, Mario. 1979. *Race and Class in the Southwest.* Notre Dame, Ind.: University of Notre Dame Press.

Bascom, Lionel. 1987. "Breaking Through Middle-Management Barrier." *Crisis,* April/May, pp. 13–16, 61, 64.

Block, Fred, Richard Cloward, Barbara Ehrenreich, and Frances Fox Piven. 1987. *The Mean Season: The Attack on the Welfare State.* New York: Pantheon.

Braverman, Harry. 1974. *Labor and Monopoly Capital.* New York: Monthly Review Press.

Collins, Sharon. 1983. "The Making of the Black Middle Class." *Social Problems* 30(April):369–382.

Cuthbert, Marion. 1942. *Education and Marginality.* New York: Stratford Press.

Davis, George, and Glegg Watson. 1982. *Black Life in Corporate America.* Garden City, N.Y.: Anchor Press/Doubleday.

Drake, St. Clair, and Horace Cayton. 1970. *Black Metropolis.* New York: Harper Torchbooks.

Ehrenreich, Barbara, and John Ehrenreich. 1979. "The Professional and Managerial Class." Pp. 5–25 in *Between Labor and Capital,* Pat Walker, ed. Boston: South End Press.

Epstein, Cynthia F. 1973. "The Positive Effect of the Multiple Negative: Explaining the Success of Professional Black Women." *American Journal of Sociology* 78(January):912–933.

Fulbright, Karen. 1986. "The Myth of the Double-Advantage: Black Female Managers." Pp. 33–45 in *Slipping Through the Cracks: The Status of Black Women,* Margaret C. Simm and Julianne Malveaux, eds. New Brunswick, N.J.: Transaction Press.

Higginbotham, Elizabeth. 1987. "Employment for Black Professional Women in the Twentieth Century." Pp. 73–91 in *Ingredients for Women's Employment Policy,* Christine Bose and Glenna Spitze, eds. Albany: State University of New York Press.

Hine, Darlene Clark. 1989. *Black Women in White: Racial Conflict and Cooperation in the Nursing Profession, 1890–1950.* Bloomington: Indiana University Press.

Johnson, Charles, 1969. *The Negro College Graduate.* College Park, Md.: McGrath.

Jones, Barbara A. P. 1986. "Black Women and Labor Force Participation: An Analysis of Sluggish Growth Rates." Pp. 11–31 in *Slipping Through the Cracks: The Status of Black Women,* Margaret C. Simm and Julianne Malveaux, eds. New Brunswick, N.J.: Transaction Press.

Jones, Jacqueline. 1985. *Labor of Love, Labor of Sorrow: Black Women, Work and the Family from Slavery to the Present.* New York: Basic Books.

Kilson, Marion. 1977. "Black Women in the Professions." *Monthly Labor Review* 100(May):38–41.

Landry, Bart. 1987. *The New Black Middle Class.* Berkeley: University of California Press.

Noble, Jeanne. 1956. *The Negro Women's College Education.* New York: Teachers College, Columbia University.

Omi, Michael, and Howard Winant. 1987. *Racial Formation in the United States.* New York: Routledge.

Poulantzas, Nicos. 1974. *Classes in Contemporary Society.* London: New Left Books.

Sokoloff, Natalie. 1987. "Black and White Women in the Professions: A Contradictory Process." Pp. 53–72 in *Ingredients for Women's Employment Policy,* Christine Bose and Glenna Spitze, eds. Albany: State University of New York Press.

_____. 1988. "Evaluating Gains and Losses of Black and White Women and Men in the Professions, 1960–1980." *Social Problems* 35(February):36–53.

_____. 1992. *Black Women and White Women in the Professions.* New York: Routledge.

Tyack, David B. 1974. *The One Best System: A History of American Education.* Cambridge, Mass.: Harvard University Press.

United States Bureau of the Census. 1973. *Census of Population 1970.* Vol. 1, *Characteristics of the Population.* Washington, D.C.: U.S. Government Printing Office.

_____. 1983. *Census of Population 1980.* Vol. 1, *Characteristics of the Population.* Washington, D.C.: U.S. Government Printing Office.

United States Department of Labor, Bureau of Labor Statistics. 1984. *Employment and Earnings* 31 (December). Washington, D.C.: U.S. Government Printing Office.

Vanneman, Reeve, and Lynn Weber Cannon. 1987. *The American Perception of Class.* Philadelphia: Temple University Press.

Walker, Pat, ed. 1979. *Between Labor and Capital.* Boston: South End Press.

Wallace, Phyllis. 1980. *Black Women in the Labor Force.* Cambridge, Mass.: MIT Press.

Westcott, Diane Nilsen. 1982. "Blacks in the 1970's: Did They Scale the Job Ladder?" *Monthly Labor Review* 105(June):29–38.

Questions for Understanding and Critical Thinking

1. Where are the majority of professional and managerial African American women employed? What explanation does Higginbotham give for this fact?
2. How does employment differ in the public and private sectors?
3. Why might African American professional women be at greater risk in public-sector, rather than private-sector, employment?
4. How are racial barriers faced today by educated African American women different from those experienced by previous generations of African Americans?

ARTICLE 26

Robert Jensen suggests that *feminist theory*—a perspective that focuses attention on the importance of gender as an element of social structure—can help men and women understand the politics of their personal problems and come to terms with those problems. According to Jensen, equality for women and men requires that patriarchy be abolished, and this process can begin only when men take feminism seriously and personally.

Robert Jensen teaches journalism at the University of Texas at Austin, where he has been actively involved in feminist scholarship and women's studies.

Looking Ahead

1. What benefit does feminism offer men?
2. How does Jensen distinguish between "progressive male identity politics" and the men's rights movement?
3. What is the primary goal of feminist-based male identity politics?

Men's Lives and Feminist Theory

◆ *Robert Jensen*

The two main points of this essay may seem self-evident or simplistic to feminists, but they are important for men to consider: (1) For men who are messed up (that is, facing problems related to their emotional lives, sexuality, their place in society, and gender politics—in other words, me and virtually every other man I have ever met) feminism offers the best route to understanding the politics of such personal problems and coming to terms with those problems. (2) If men accept the first point, feminism will confront and confuse us about ourselves, and our job is to embrace, not run, from that challenge. Put more simply: Men need to (1) take feminism seriously, and (2) take it personally, for

their own sake as well as in the interests of justice.

While these may seem like common-sense observations, they are not easy for men to come to terms with. When I began studying feminism six years ago, I did not immediately realize that feminism explained not only men's oppression of women, but my own isolation, alienation, and pain. Nor did I realize that I could understand myself through feminism without denying my participation in the oppression of women or falsely equating men's and women's problems. While I understood that the personal is political, I was slow to realize that the phrase applied not only to women but to me; it

Source: From Robert Jensen, "Men's Lives and Feminist Theory," in *Race, Gender & Class* (Jean Belkhir, editor), Volume 2, No. 2, Winter 1995, pp. 111–125. Reprinted by permission.

took time for me to understand that feminism required me to not only criticize patriarchal constructions of masculinity in the abstract, but to be unrelenting in my critique of my own behavior.

I was socialized and trained to be a man in this culture, and like most men, I learned my lessons well. Feminism helps me reject patriarchal constructions of masculinity and, at the same time, reminds me that my identity was formed within that patriarchal construction. For me to both help myself and make good on my commitments to feminism, I must confront that male identity in a responsible and politically progressive manner using feminist theory. If I want to understand myself and my society, I must be willing to apply, in ways that can be difficult and distressing, a feminist critique to my life, and to leave that process open to evaluation by women. This approach differs from the goals and methods of the men's movement (see various critiques in Hagan 1992); I suggest men should reject being part of any men's movements and and—for their own sake as well as the sake of women, children, and the world—engage feminism.

I am not suggesting that women in general, or feminists in particular, should focus more on men's pain or that women have an obligation to like and trust men who advertise themselves as pro-feminist. However, the common goal of liberation can connect men and women; I come to feminist theory with the realization that my future as a fully moral and responsible human being depends on women's liberation.

While this essay is rooted in personal experience, my goal is not to use it as a confessional or hold myself up as a model; I do not write to cast myself as one of the "good guys," distinct from non-feminist men. Instead, I want to use my own admittedly stumbling progress toward these goals to make some tentative claims about this liber-

atory process. I will begin with a short discussion of identity politics and the contemporary men's movement, then move on to explain why men should take feminism seriously and personally.

MALE IDENTITY

"Identity politics," as it is commonly used, suggests that group identities can be the basis of analysis and action. This essay is a call for a progressive male identity politics that uses a feminist critique of male power and male sexuality, and that requires of men an honest engagement with their lives and a commitment to real change. Because we usually think of identity politics as a way for marginalized groups, such as African-Americans or lesbians and gays, to resist oppressive power, it may seem odd to talk of a progressive identity politics for heterosexual men. My male identity gives me privilege and protects me: What kind of liberatory identity politics can a straight white boy have?

By a progressive male identity politics, I mean the process of understanding one's social location and practicing a politics informed by that understanding. Identity is not static and dictated by biology, but is the product of the obstacles or privileges that the culture in which one lives attaches to one's characteristics. Identity politics need not be essentialist or falsely totalizing, but simply an acknowledgment of the pattern of those obstacles and privileges. If we view identity as a strategy for action, not as an essentialist marker, we can focus on how all oppressions in this culture are interlocking, mutually reinforcing, and based on some similar dynamics of domination and subordination. Identity politics is often criticized for turning people inward, toward themselves and others in their groups, and for inhibiting coalition-building. But rather than fragmenting resistance to oppression, an understanding of politics informed by identity can produce solidarity. In my own life, feminism was the first critical approach I discovered, and what I learned about power and oppression from feminist theory led me to a new understanding of racism, heterosexism, and the workings of class/wealth privilege.

Understanding identity in this way makes it possible that a man might choose to become a traitor to his privilege, to take an anti-patriarchal stance and do whatever work in resistance that one finds meaningful. Resistance to institutionalized sexism (which implies and demands, I think, resistance to white supremacy, heterosexism, and class-based oppression as well) is obviously not the only option, nor is it the most popular option with men. My goal is to find a way to persuade men that their identity politics should be based on a feminist critique, which is no small task in this culture. One of the hurdles is to convince men that feminism is not crude "male-bashing." To some men, any feminist criticism will be perceived that way, and countering that image is difficult. But in six years of interaction with feminists, including a number of lesbian and radical feminists, I have never been bashed. I have been held accountable for my behavior, and I have been told when my presence in a group was not preferred. I have not always felt comfortable listening to feminist critiques, of men or of me, but I have never been attacked, harassed, or intimidated simply for being a man. Whatever criticism I have received has been offered, if not kindly, at least clearly without malice.

A commitment to feminism is plainly not the only avenue open to men. A man might recognize his various forms of privilege and decide to actively work to shore up that privilege by being, if not anti-feminist, at least non-feminist. This is the approach of the men's rights movement, which casts men as the victims of women's liberation movements and of men's lack of attention to their own needs. The men's movement is right in identifying the way in which some men are hurt by rigid gender norms, but this analysis often fails to distinguish between the suffering of those who, as a class, hold power and the oppression of those who don't. Many men are miserable in this culture, and that misery is sometimes tied to gender politics. Being miserable, however, is not the same as being oppressed (Frye 1983, 1). When men experience things that we could call oppression, they are tied to other systems of power, such as racism, class/ wealth privilege, and heterosexism. None of these systems work wholly separately, but men are not oppressed along a gender axis; men are not oppressed *as men* in contemporary U.S. culture (Clatterbaugh 1992). For example, men often point out that because they have been the only ones drafted into military service, they are oppressed (Farrell 1993, Chapter 5). This ignores the fact that certain men created and maintained a system in which only men are drafted and that men hold the vast majority of positions of power in the military. While it makes sense to talk about the way in which elite men tend to impose the duty of killing and dying disproportionately on poor or non-white men—to inject a class or race analysis—it is nonsensical to suggest that men are oppressed as men.

A less political path for men who want to obscure the real-life consequences of sexism for men and women is what is commonly called the mythopoetic wing of the men's movement, but which might more accurately be called a form of "masculinist nationalism . . . a reconstellation of patriarchal rules and roles and an attempt to consolidate cockocratic power in response to challenges from the women's movement" (Caputi and MacKenzie 1992, 71–72). These men acknowledge the problems with traditional gender roles—"the images of adult manhood given by the popular culture are worn out; a man can no longer depend on them" (Bly 1990, ix)—and pay lip service to women's problems—how the "dark side of men" has resulted in the "devaluation and humiliation of women" (Bly 1990, x). The mythopoetic men's movement understands that traditional markers of masculinity—repression of emotion and vulnerability, a need to control and dominate—are destructive. But in its commitment to Bly's celebration of the "Wild Man"—to the idea that being a man is centrally about a power and strength that flows from an essential "deep" masculinity— the men's movement undercuts its own project. While some of these men believe that the solution to sexism lies in rescuing the concept of masculinity from crude machismo, my concern is that in a deeply entrenched patriarchal system, men's obsession with masculinity—no matter how it is reconceptualized—usually ends up reinforcing male power. Michael Kimmel (1992, 12) points out that this movement is the latest attempt by men in American culture, in response to women's movements, "to create islands of untainted masculinity" rather than examine critically the claim that there are essential characteristics of the masculine. Said another way by Bell Hooks (1992, 112), the emphasis of these men seems to be "more on the production of a kind of masculinity that can be safely expressed within patriarchal boundaries" than a critique of patriarchy.

The anti-patriarchal position which I take is rooted not only in feminist theory but in a growing body of literature by men who embrace the insights of feminist theorists and activists. In general, these men reject essentialist explanations for men's behavior and view masculinity and femininity as social constructions (Kimmel 1987a, 13). The way in which societies value some characteristics and denigrate others, and define those

characteristics as male or female, is not natural, biological, or inevitable. Men have the ability to resist negative definitions of masculinity and change behaviors, and to challenge the notion that a single definition of masculinity should exist. As Patrick Hopkins (1992, 128) puts it: "personally do not want to be a 'real man' or even an 'unreal man.' I want to be unmanned altogether. I want to evaluate courses of behavior and desire open to me on their pragmatic consequences not on their appropriateness to my 'sex.' . . . I want to betray gender."

Many of these pro-feminist writers also point out the uncertain and contradictory nature of masculinity. Kimmel (1987b, 237) suggests that the "compulsive masculinity" common in American life—marked by "violence, aggression, extreme competitiveness, a gnawing insecurity"— is "a masculinity that must always prove itself and that is always in doubt," hence the frantic drive by men to control their environments. Along with the privileges of male dominance come isolation, alienation, and pain (Kaufman 1993).

Masculinity itself is marked with hierarchies; young, effeminate, and gay men, for example, are subordinated by other men. Carrigan, Connell and Lee (1987) call the dominant definition of maleness "hegemonic masculinity." While most men don't live up to the macho-cowboy ideal of that definition, most men are responsible in some way for maintaining that hegemonic model and most men benefit from the institutionalization of men's dominance over women that comes with the model.

Echoing the theme of this paper, these writers suggest it is in men's interest to work toward a new definition of what it means to be a man, which requires a personal investment and commitment—acknowledging the "me in "me(n)," as Joseph Boone puts it (1990), and resisting the temptation to talk in abstractions instead of in one's own voice from one's own gendered body.

From here forward, I will defend the notion that feminism is a better route for men to come to terms with their own lives. This self-interest argument is not meant to obscure the more important argument about the oppressive nature of patriarchal values and structures, and the injustice of sexism. Numerous feminist works eloquently make the case for gender equality and against patriarchy on moral and political grounds (Frye 1983). My approach here stems from the observation that a justice argument does not always persuade people with power to give up some of that power. As Marilyn Frye put it in an informal seminar at the University of Minnesota in 1991, if you have your foot on someone's head, you shouldn't have to be told that it is right to take it off. If the oppressor can't see that, she pointed out, it's difficult to convince him of it through an argument about justice.

TAKING FEMINISM SERIOUSLY

The deeper and more fundamental the critique of an unjust system, the more difficult it may be to persuade privileged people to be part of the dismantling of their privilege. In this sense, I think most men do "get it"; while they may profess confusion about what women want from them, they understand at some level the nature of the feminist critique and the things at stake. If taken seriously, feminism requires men to evaluate not only the politics of public patriarchy, but their conduct in private, especially in the bedroom. Men, understandably, are often reluctant to do that, precisely because they "get it" (in the sense of understanding) and want to keep "getting it" (in the sense of consuming women's sexuality).

However, a clear presentation of feminism that appeals to men's self-interest—while making it clear that the feminist movement is focused on women's lives and that feminists aren't obligated to take care of men—can be effective. Feminism can help us answer many of our questions, ease our pain, heal our wounds, and allow us to be decent people because it is not just about concern for "women's issues" and it is not just a theory of gender relations; feminism also is an explanation and critique of the domination/subordination dynamic that structures power relations in this society. Feminism provides an approach to society that allows women and men to better understand the world in which they live and to apply insights about gender to other struggles in life, both in the private and public spheres (beginning with the realization that the private/public dichotomy is problematic). Two examples, based on common concerns in the men's movement, illustrate this. One is about what is often called "the father wound," and the other has to do with intimacy and sexuality.

Many contemporary men lived with fathers who were emotionally repressed, unable to nurture, absent, cruel, and physically and/or sexually abusive-father-as-terrorist. I have what I take to be a fairly typical experience here, a father who could not deal with his own emotions, could not control his anger, and generally was more trouble to me as a child than he was worth. My mother played out the passive/aggressive counterpart to her unfeeling and abusive husband, and had her own equally important role in my emotional problems as a child and young adult. That quick sketch obscures, of course, a complex network of relationships, and for my purposes here more detail about those emotional problems is not crucial. My point is that some men take this kind of scenario and cast the father as victim, the son as victim, and the mother as, at best, an unimportant bystander or, at worst, an active agent in retarding the development of the son's male identity.

Feminism gives me a much different take on it. There was a power discrepancy in my house: My father had it, and my mother didn't. Because of that, my father's personal failings dictated the tone of our lives. My mother—shaped herself by similar abuses of power in her childhood, constrained by cultural expectations, and lacking certain kinds of social, political, economic, or physical power—slipped into a role that both exacerbated the problems caused by my father and created other problems. Gender politics structured those roles and relationships, and for many reasons neither my mother nor father had the resources to move beyond those constraints. Neither of them can be held accountable for the system into which they were born, but both are responsible for their behavior. The key difference, however, was that the power differential gave my father more choices. Some men in his position made better choices. Some women made better choices than my mother, as well, but it is important to remember that my mother acted in reaction to the power my father, and other men, had wielded.

This analysis is important because it allows me to see how the ways in which I suffered at the hands of my father and my mother were directly tied to the systematic, institutionalized, and unjust distribution of power in my family and in the culture. The root of the problem was the power my father could wield in a patriarchal family and culture. If my father were to analyze his family history, I believe he would come to similar conclusions about his parents; I don't want to ignore the ways in which my father suffered as a child and continues to suffer because of that. The father wound, for both him and me, is real, and the resolution of it is important. But feminist theory can help a man heal the father wound, and make clear

not only his mother's involvement in the creation of wounds, but the nature of his mother's wounds.

My first example of the value of feminist theory to men—coping with problems with parents—suggests that men will benefit directly and immediately with a feminist critique. My second example, problems with intimacy and sex with women, is less optimistic for the short term. However, feminism, especially radical critiques of male sexuality, hold promise. The work of feminist critics (e.g., Dworkin 1988) argues that the central dynamic of sexuality in patriarchy is domination and subordination, sex as the exercise of power and a form of control. As Dworkin (1987, 63) writes: "The normal fuck by a normal man is taken to be an act of invasion and ownership undertaken in a mode of predation; colonializing, forceful (manly) or nearly violent; the sexual act that by its nature makes her his." That conception of sex is, I believe, deeply rooted in the bodies of the vast majority of contemporary men. Any effort to reconstruct a more healthy sexuality that is not overtly politicized—that is, does not foreground questions of the play of power along gender, sexual orientation, and race axes—will fail.

My experience has shown me that the task of untangling myself from the norms of patriarchal sex and rebuilding an egalitarian sexuality is extraordinarily difficult. In this sense, I acknowledge that trying to persuade men to accept a deep critique of patriarchal sex is complicated by my inability to articulate specific alternatives. In my life, I have gradually become more aware that the core sexual lessons I learned as a child and young man in this culture were about objectifying and consuming women and their sexuality. This is fundamentally about being trained in a way of seeing women, to view them first and foremost not as human beings but as collections of body parts to be evaluated for their sexual possibilities. That statement is hardly ground-breaking; feminists have been pointing this out for decades. What I want to contribute to the discussion is an admission that overcoming that training, learning a new way of seeing, is more difficult than most of us want to admit. Despite some intellectual and emotional progress, I feel as if my sexuality is still rooted in the same way of seeing. I have made progress, some of it occurring as I write this and some of it encouraging, but that progress also sometimes seems minor in face of the journey that lies ahead.

So, if I am correct about the nature of the work ahead, and if I can't pretend to promise men that such work can be accomplished easily, what stake do men have in changing? What if, a man might ask, my body and I can't find a way to feel comfortable about sex? My only answer is that if, while I struggle to expand my sense of the erotic and find new language to use (see Lorde 1984; Heyward 1989), I am forced to choose between patriarchal-sex and no-sex, no-sex is the better choice. Those are not the only alternatives, of course, and I would hope that such a choice would be only temporary, but in this struggle feminist theory sustains me. Once I understood even the barest outline of feminism, I realized why I had always felt vaguely uncomfortable about sex, why my use of pornography and consumption of women's sexuality had always left me feeling empty. Long before I had read a word of feminist theory, that feeling was with me, and from talking with other men I know that I am not idiosyncratic in this. Feminist theory helped me understand that empty feeling: Sex based on domination over another feels bad to me. No matter how sensitive I was, no matter how much attention I paid to my partner's pleasure, there was no way for me to totally repress the understanding in my body that my sexuality was built on the ob-

jectification and commodification of women and a need for control. Feminist theory did not create that feeling in me; feminist theory merely helped me understand it. Having a name and explanation for it didn't clear up the problem, just as ignoring the problem didn't make it go away. No matter how confusing and troubling it has been to sort through my sexual responses and life choices, I gladly choose that confusion and pain to the unnamed confusion and pain of a sexual life built on a need for power that is ultimately unsatisfying.

One purpose of this essay is to contribute to breaking down the silence among men on these issues. Michael Kimmel suggests that men face a "general confusion about how we experience our sexualities, a confusion that remains fixed in place because of our inability to talk frankly and openly with other men about our sexualities" (1990, 3). Confusion and fear are lessened, though not necessarily eliminated, by such open talk.

TAKING FEMINISM PERSONALLY

So, when I talk about male identity politics, I do not mean the politics of men identifying their gender privilege and protecting it through various overt and covert mechanisms. I am interested in how men can be aware of their gender privilege, question it, and act as a traitor to that male privilege. I suggest we do that not only because it is the ethically and politically responsible thing to do, but because it will help us make sense of our own lives, even if at times that makes life seem confusing, tentative, undefined, and frightening. The only things more confusing and frightening, I would argue, are an unreflective commitment to patriarchy and the various strategies to pretend that the multiple oppressions that patriarchy supports don't really exist.

This work requires a willingness to confront not only the workings of patriarchy in the abstract, but one's own life in the most particular. I have not always done that, even after I identified myself as being committed to feminism. I am not convinced that most pro-feminist men do that. I believe men sometimes ally themselves with feminist theory or causes as a cover; once on the "right side," they feel protected from scrutiny themselves. Explaining her unwillingness to let men call themselves "feminists," Cleage (1993, 28) argues that the label: "tends to lead to smugness, self-satisfaction and the feeling that the man who is struggling to overcome his own sexism and the sexism of his brothers has somehow achieved a more exalted status, a safe conduct pass that allows him to be a little less rigorous on himself, having demonstrated his good intentions."

Maintaining an intense level of self-scrutiny, preferably within a supportive and honest community, is crucial to successful pro-feminist engagement. While I may fall short at times, it must be a central goal. When we evade that task, we are more prone to fall into the trap Cleage describes. Again, a personal example is useful here. I have suggested that male sexual training focuses on a quest for domination and control over women, an approach to sex that John Stoltenberg (1989, 9) has accurately labeled "rapist ethics." The implication is that men in contemporary culture are trained to be rapists, which suggests that to not rape takes effort. If that is true, and I think it is, then the inescapable conclusion is that most men have raped or tried to rape. By that, I don't mean that most men are guilty of rape as it is legally defined, but rather that "normal" sexual activity has rape-like qualities (MacKinnon 1989, 146). To take such a claim seriously is disturbing, and requires an examination of one's sexual history, but such

an examination offers the best chance for positive change for individuals and society. Let me recount part of my self-examination.

Have I ever raped or tried to rape a woman? For the first 30 years of my life, I would have said no, without qualification. For four years after that, I typically said that I thought I had never raped, but that a complete answer required the input of the women with whom I had been sexually active. Now, I tend to answer with a simple yes, but that "yes" requires explanation and context.

First, a specific case. As a young adult I dated for several months a woman whom I will call Sue here. As the relationship became more serious, I made it clear I thought sexual intercourse was appropriate. Sue was hesitant, but talked about it in a way that suggested she agreed that sex of that nature was to be expected. Through a variety of delaying tactics on her part, however, we never reached that point. On occasion, I pressured her on the subject, pushing the level of intimacy as far as I could. I took this lack of intercourse to be an indication of some serious flaw, either in the relationship or in her. For a variety of reasons, some related to sex and some not, Sue and I stopped seeing each other.

Were my sexual advances attempted rape? Legally they were not, but politically and morally, I think I can be said to have tried to rape her. One was my willingness to take a lack of a vocal objection—the lack of a clearly stated "no"—to be consent, rather than assuming that any sexual contact should begin with mutual consent that comes out of human connection and communication. When I pressed physical contact and she resisted in subtle and covert ways, I often chose not to acknowledge her resistance. I always stopped short of forced intercourse, but that doesn't change the rape-like nature of the interaction.

Complicating the case even more is the fact that at the time I knew her, Sue was working with a therapist to address a troubled family history. She talked to me in guarded ways about an abusive father and angry brothers. Looking back on those conversations through a feminist lens—paying attention to what she said and didn't say—I now think it likely that Sue was an incest survivor. While I have no way of knowing that for sure, what I have learned in the past five years about family dynamics, sexual abuse, and gender suggests to me that the abuse she lived through in her family was sexualized. Assuming that to be true, my actions with her are even more problematic because of the common effects of childhood abuse on adult sexuality. That is not meant to stereotype adult survivors of childhood abuse as passive individuals waiting to be revictimized, but to acknowledge the way in which childhood abuse complicates questions of desire and agency in adults. It is impossible for me to know how Sue felt about what I saw as "harmless" inquiries and "gentle" nudges, but I can judge my inability to understand her situation as a failure. I had a moral responsibility to listen and an epistemic responsibility (Code 1987) to understand her abusive history and how those experiences likely framed her view of sex and intimacy, or to ask for more information when I didn't understand. Instead, I ignored or minimized what she said, preferring to pursue my own sexual interests. As a man, not only did I have the power to ignore her needs and interests, but the sexual script I was trained to follow called for such behavior. The fact that I stopped short of a legal definition of rape doesn't absolve me from the level of sexual intrusion that I did commit. In Frye's terms (1983, 67), I looked at Sue with an "arrogant eye," organizing everything I saw with reference to myself and my interests. The arrogant male perceiver shapes

women to fit his mold, and when Sue didn't fit, I saw it as something wrong with her. As Frye (1983, 70) reminds us, such perception is not only wrong, it is coercive, a fundamental kind of harm, "a maiming which impairs a person's ability to defend herself."

What is the value of this examination of my sexual history? If I believe that the patriarchal construction of sex as dominance is politically and morally wrong, then I have an obligation to apply that belief to my life. Evaluating my past is crucial to understanding where I stand today; understanding my past is part of understanding patriarchy. Such understanding creates the possibility not only of personal change but of expanding our knowledge as a society. What I have learned from this self-reflection, and from conversation with others about it, is that separating men into two groups, rapists and non-rapists, can divert us from the deeper critique (Funk 1993). Some men rape in violent and terrifying ways that society condemns and, on rare occasions, actually punishes. But many men have engaged in sexual acts in which their pleasure is connected to the objectification of women, the expression of power as sex, and the eroticization of dominance. One way to avoid confronting that critique is to reason that (1) rape is something bad men do, so (2) if I raped, then I am one of the bad men, but (3) I know that I am not one of the bad men, so (4) I do not rape, and therefore (5) I do not have to critically evaluate my own sexual practices. Feminist critiques of sexuality make a compelling case that the first premise is simply false. When I began to take seriously that critique, I began to understand myself better.

I am not suggesting that I have completed this process of evaluating my life, or that the process ever ends; it is a lifetime commitment. I argue only that it is an integral part of a commitment to feminist theory and politics. This kind of engagement with my male identity has strengthened my understanding of the feminist critique. It has been, and continues to be, difficult and painful. But it also has allowed me to grow, intellectually and personally, by acknowledging feminist insights that theory and practice are not separate, that experience is an important element of theorizing, that the public-private distinction is false.

I could live as a man working in feminist theory in the academy and avoid evaluating my own life, always talking about "men" and "men's violence" and "patriarchy" as if I lived outside of those terms. I could, in a sense, float between genders, critiquing other men and not myself, but such an approach would be based on a lie. So, if a man accepts my argument that feminism can help him make sense of his life and starts down that path, it is crucial to "take it personally" and not back away from the application of feminist theory to his own life. To back away would guarantee that the abstract engagement with theory fails to spur personal development.

CONCLUSION

Some men, and women, may object that my argument overgeneralizes about men's experience, especially men's sexual experiences. Men have told me that they do not believe they were taught rapist ethics, or that they had moved beyond crude locker-room machismo. Others have told me they do not have the problems with intimacy and emotion that I have referred to. I can accept these observations and still argue for the importance of my generalizations. First, no man in mainstream contemporary U.S. culture escapes sexist training. Sexism is institutionalized; sexist behaviors and values are widely seen as normal or natural and continue unless there is active intervention to counter them. If that is true, then men have an oblig-

ation to explore the ways in which that sexist training may have taken root in their bodies. And even if a man could completely erase any trace of sexism from his life, the culture continues to offer a kind of "default" identity. In the absence of an open refutation of traditional masculinity, the culture gives men an identity that assumes male dominance. With that default identity come privileges that one cannot always refuse to accept; they are part of being male in this culture.

I do not want to appear self-denigrating or falsely humble with this analysis. In arguing that men should acknowledge the way in which their identity is tied to patriarchy, I do not want to suggest that men cannot change, that all men are equally culpable, or that I do not realize the ways in which I have successfully combated my patriarchal training. I believe that I am a better human being than I was a decade ago, with far fewer instances in which I fail to live up to feminist ideals. I believe that I do better in this area than the majority of men in this country. I try to acknowledge my successes as well as my failures. However, I know that none of that would be possible if I had not engaged, and continue to engage, in the male identity politics that I suggest here: intense self-evaluation, with help and feedback from like-minded people.

My goal has been to write a personal but not depoliticized essay. The primary goal of a feminist-based male identity politics is not just improving men's lives, but changing structures of power to end the oppression of women and children, as well as aid resistance to other forms of oppression in the culture. As I have suggested, while the answer to men's questions and quandaries about gender politics can be found in feminist theory, the answers are not easy, just as they are not easy for women. As Connell (1987, 282) puts it: "Breaking down the gender system means, to some extent, tearing down what is most constitutive of one's own emotions, and occupying strange and ill-explained places in social space."

It is not easy to occupy that strange space, and I realize that my argument may not persuade many men. What I have written has little power unless the man reading it feels in his body and heart some of what I have talked about. It is an argument that fails if it works only at the intellectual level, which is both its strength and weakness. By bringing my own life into this essay, I hope that men who read it will be encouraged to engage feminism. I also hope that those who do will continue the conversation, so that the gaps in my understanding—both emotional and intellectual—might be filled.

REFERENCES

Bly, Robert. 1990. *Iron John*. Reading, MA: Addison-Wesley.

Boone, Joseph A. 1990. "Of Me(n) and Feminism: Who(se) Is the Sex That Writes?" In Boone and Michael Cadden, eds. *Engendering Men: The Question of Male Feminist Criticism* (pp. 11–25). New York: Routledge.

Caputi, Jane, and Gordene O. MacKenzie. 1992. "Pumping Iron John." In Kay Leigh Hagan, ed., *Women Respond to the Men's Movement* (pp. 69–81). San Francisco: Pandora/HarperCollins.

Carrigan, Tim, Bob Connell, and John Lee. 1987. "Hard and Heavy: Toward a New Sociology of Masculinity." In Michael Kaufman, ed., *Beyond Patriarchy* (pp. 139–192). Toronto: Oxford University Press.

Clatterbaugh, Kenneth. 1992. "The Oppression Debate in Sexual Politics." In Larry May and Robert A. Strikwerda, eds., *Rethinking Masculinity* (pp. 169–190). Lanham, MD: Rowman & Littlefield.

Cleage, Pearl. 1993. *Deals with the Devil and Other Reasons to Riot*. New York: Ballantine.

Code, Lorraine. 1987. *Epistemic Responsibility*. Hanover, NH: University Press of New England.

Connell, R. W. 1987. *Gender and Power: Society, the Person and Sexual Politics*. Stanford: Stanford University Press.

Dworkin, Andrea. 1988. *Letters from a War Zone: Writings 1976–1987*. London: Secker & Warburg.

Dworkin, Andrea. 1987. *Intercourse*. New York: Free Press.

Farrell, Warren. 1993. *The Myth of Male Power: Why Men Are the Disposable Sex*. New York: Simon & Schuster.

Frye, Marilyn. 1983. *The Politics of Reality*. Freedom, CA: Crossing Press.

Funk, Rus Ervin. 1993. *Stopping Rape: A Challenge for Men*. Philadelphia: New Society.

Hagan, Kay Leigh, ed. 1992. *Women Respond to the Men's Movement*. San Francisco: Pandora/HarperCollins.

Heyward, Carter. 1989. *Touching Our Strength: The Erotic as Power and the Love of God*. San Francisco: Harper & Row.

hooks, bell. 1992. "Men in Feminist Struggle—The Necessary Movement." In Kay Leigh Hagan, ed., *Women Respond to the Men's Movement* (pp. 111–117). San Francisco: Pandora/HarperCollins.

Hopkins, Patrick D. 1992. "Gender Treachery: Homophobia, Masculinity, and Threatened Identities." In Larry May and Robert A. Strikwerda, eds., *Rethinking Masculinity* (pp. 111–131). Lanham, MD: Rowman & Littlefield.

Kaufman, Michael. 1993. *Cracking the Armour: Power, Pain and the Lives of Men*. Toronto: Viking/Penguin.

Kimmel, Michael S. 1992. "Introduction." In Kimmel and Thomas E. Mosmiller, eds., *Against the Tide: Pro-Feminist Men in the United States, 1776–1990* (pp. 1–51). Boston: Beacon.

Kimmel, Michael S. 1990. "Introduction: Guilty Pleasures—Pornography in Men's Lives." In Kimmel, ed., *Men Confront Pornography* (pp. 1–22). New York: Crown.

Kimmel, Michael S. 1987a. "Rethinking 'Masculinity': New Directions in Research." In Kimmel, ed., *Changing Men: New Directions in Research on Men and Masculinity*. (pp. 9–24). Newbury Park, CA: Sage.

Kimmel, Michael S. 1987b. "The Cult of Masculinity: American Social Character and the Legacy of the Cowboy." In Michael Kaufman, ed., *Beyond Patriarchy* (pp. 235–249). Toronto: Oxford University Press.

Lerner, Gerda. 1986. *The Creation of Patriarchy*. New York: Oxford University Press.

Lorde, Audre. 1984. "Uses of the Erotic: The Erotic as Power." In *Sister Outsider* (pp. 53–59). Freedom, CA: Crossing Press.

MacKinnon, Catharine A. 1989. *Toward a Feminist Theory of the State*. Cambridge: Harvard University Press.

May, Larry, and Robert Strikwerda. 1994. "Men in Groups: Collective Responsibility for Rape." *Hypatia* 9(2):134–151.

Stoltenberg, John. 1993. *The End of Manhood*. New York: Dutton.

Stoltenberg, John. 1989. *Refusing to Be a Man: Essays on Sex and Justice*. Portland: Breitenbush Books.

Questions for Understanding and Critical Thinking

1. How can feminism help men understand the politics of personal problems and come to terms with those problems?
2. What are the characteristics of *compulsive masculinity?*
3. Why would privileged people want to be part of the dismantling of their privilege?
4. Do you agree with Jensen's assessment that male sexual training focuses on a quest for domination and control over women? Why or why not?

ARTICLE 27 _____

Author and African American scholar bell hooks is an articulate spokesperson regarding the persistence of racism in U.S. society. hooks suggests that racism cannot be thought of solely as overt behavior; instead, one must look behind the facade of contemporary life to see that racism is an institutionalized system, based on skin color, that privileges white people and disadvantages people of color. In this article, hooks suggests that people cannot give up on the dream of a *"beloved community* where race would be transcended, forgotten, where no one would see skin color."

bell hooks is Distinguished Professor of English at City College in New York. This article is reprinted from her recent book *Killing Rage: Ending Racism.*

Looking Ahead

1. Who originated the idea of a *beloved community?*
2. How successful does hooks believe people have been in establishing this dream?
3. Why does hooks believe that it is not necessary to eradicate race, class, and cultural difference before a *beloved community* can be formed?

Beloved Community

A World without Racism

◆ *bell hooks*

Some days it is just hard to accept that racism can still be such a powerful dominating force in all our lives. When I remember all that black and white folks together have sacrificed to challenge and change white supremacy, when I remember the individuals who gave their lives to the cause of racial justice, my heart is deeply saddened that we have not fulfilled their shared dream of ending racism, of creating a new culture, a place for the *beloved community.* Early on in his work for civil rights, long before his consciousness had been deeply radicalized by resistance to militarism and global Western imperialism, Martin Luther King imagined a *beloved community* where race would be transcended, forgotten, where no one would see skin color. This dream has not been realized. From its inception it was a flawed vision. The flaw, however, was not the imagining of a *beloved community;* it was the insistence that such a community could exist only if we erased and forgot racial difference.

Many citizens of these United States still long to live in a society where *beloved community* can be formed—where loving ties of care and knowing bind us together in our differences. We cannot surrender that longing—if we do we will never see an end to racism. These days it is an untalked-about longing. Most folks in this society have become so cynical about ending racism, so convinced that solidarity across racial differences can never be a reality, that they make no effort to build community. Those of us who are not cynical, who still cherish the vision of *beloved community,* sustain our conviction that we need such bonding not because we cling to utopian fantasies but because we have struggled all our lives to create this community. In my blackness I have struggled together with white comrades in the segregated South. Sharing that struggle we came to know deeply, intimately, with all our minds and hearts that we can all divest of racism and white supremacy if we so desire. We divest through our commitment to and engagement with anti-racist struggle. Even though that commitment was first made in the mind and heart, it is realized by concrete action, by anti-racist living and being.

Over the years my love and admiration for those black and white southerners in my hometown who worked together to realize racial justice deepens, as does their love of me. We have gone off from that time of legalized segregation to create intimate lives for ourselves that include loving engagement with all races and ethnicities. The small circles of love we have managed to form in our individual lives represent a concrete realistic reminder that *beloved community* is not a dream, that it already exists for those of us who have done the work of educating ourselves for critical consciousness in ways that

enabled a letting go of white supremacist assumptions and values. The process of decolonization (unlearning white supremacy by divesting of white privilege if we were white or vestiges of internalized racism if we were black) transformed our minds and our habits of being.

In the segregated South those black and white folks who struggled together for racial justice (many of whom grounded their actions not in radical politics but in religious conviction) were bound by a shared belief in the transformative power of love. Understanding that love was the antithesis of the will to dominate and subjugate, we allowed that longing to know love, to love one another, to radicalize us politically. That love was not sentimental. It did not blind us to the reality that racism was deeply systemic and that only by realizing that love in concrete political actions that might involve sacrifice, even the surrender of one's life, would white supremacy be fundamentally challenged. We knew the sweetness of *beloved community.*

What those of us who have not died now know, that generations before us did not grasp, was that *beloved community* is formed not by the eradication of difference but by its affirmation, by each of us claiming the identities and cultural legacies that shape who we are and how we live in the world. To form *beloved community* we do not surrender ties to precious origins. We deepen those bondings by connecting them with an anti-racist struggle which is at heart always a movement to disrupt that clinging to cultural legacies that demands investment in notions of racial purity, authenticity, nationalist fundamentalism. The notion that differences of skin color, class background, and cultural heritage must be erased for justice and equality to prevail is a brand of popular false consciousness that helps keep racist thinking and action intact. Most folks are threatened by the notion that they must give up allegiances to specific cultural legacies in order to have harmony. Such suspicion is healthy. Unfortunately, as long as our society holds up a vision of democracy that requires the surrender of bonds and ties to legacies folks hold dear, challenging racism and white supremacy will seem like an action that diminishes and destabilizes.

The misguided idea that one must give up cultural allegiance to create harmony positively emerged from religious freedom fighters whose faith urged them to let go attachment to the things of this world (status, ethnicity, national allegiances) in order to be one with God. Negatively, it has been appropriated by the enemies of anti-racist struggle to further tensions between different racial groups, to breed fundamentalist and nationalistic feelings and support for racial separatism. Since the notion that we should all forsake attachment to race and/or cultural identity and be "just humans" within the framework of white supremacy has usually meant that subordinate groups must surrender their identities, beliefs, values and assimilate by adopting the values and beliefs of privileged-class whites, rather than promoting racial harmony this thinking has created a fierce cultural protectionism. That conservative force that sees itself as refusing assimilation expresses itself in the call for cultural nationalism, for disenfranchised groups to embrace separatism. This is why black leaders who espouse black separatism are gaining political power. Many black people fear that white commodification and appropriation of blackness is a neo-colonial strategy of cultural genocide that threatens to destroy our cultural legacy. That fear is not ungrounded. Black people, however, are misguided in thinking that nationalist fundamentalism is the best or only way to either preserve our heritage or to make a meaningful political response to ending racism.

In actuality, the growth of nationalist separatist thinking among black people is an extreme expression of collective cynicism about ending white supremacy. The assumption that white folks will never cease to be racist represents a refusal to privilege the history of those whites (however few) who have been willing to give their lives to the struggle for racial justice over that of white folks who maintain racist thinking—sometimes without even knowing that they hold racist assumptions. Since white supremacist attitudes and values permeate every aspect of the culture, most white folks are unconsciously absorbing the ideology of white supremacy. Since they do not realize this socialization is taking place, many of them feel that they are not racist. When these feelings are rooted in denial, the first stage of anti-racist struggle has to be breaking that denial. This is one of the primary distinctions between the generation of white folks who were raised in the midst of white supremacist apartheid, who witnessed firsthand the brutal dehumanization of black people and who knew that "racism" permeated the culture, and this contemporary generation that either engages in historical amnesia or does not remember. Prior to desegregation, few whites would have been as arrogantly convinced that they are not racists as are most whites today, some of whom never come into contact with black people. During civil rights struggle, it was commonly understood that whites seeking to live in an anti-racist world measured their progress and their commitment by their interactions with black people. How can a white person assume he or she is not racist if that assumption has not been concretely realized in interaction? It was precisely the astute recognition on the part of freedom fighters working for racial justice that anti-racist habits of being were best cultivated in situations of interaction that was at the heart of every vision of non-racist community.

Concurrently, most white Americans who believed or believe that racism is ethically and morally wrong centered their anti-racist struggle around the desire to commune with black folks. Today many white people who see themselves as non-racist are comfortable with lives where they have no contact with black people or where fear is their first response in any encounter with blackness. This "fear" is the first sign of the internalization in the white psyche of white supremacist sentiments. It serves to mask white power and privilege. In the past the affirmation of white supremacy in everyday life was declared via assertions of hatred and/or power (i.e., public and private subordination and humiliation of black folks—the white wife who sits at her dining table eating a nice lunch while the maid eats standing in the kitchen, the white male employer paying black workers less and calling them by obscene names); in our contemporary times white belief in black inferiority is most often registered by the assertion of power. Yet that power is often obscured by white focus on fear. The fear whites direct at blacks is rooted in the racist assumption that the darker race is inherently deprived, dangerous, and willing to obtain what they desire by any means necessary. Since it is assumed that whenever fear is present one is less powerful, cultivating in whites fear of blacks is a useful neocolonial strategy as it obscures the reality that whites do much more harm to blacks daily than vice versa. It also encourages white people to believe that they do not hold power over blacks even as their ability to project fear when there is no danger is an act of denial that indicates their complicity with white supremacist thinking. Those white people who consciously break with racist thinking know that there is no concrete reality to suggest that they should be more fearful of blacks than other people, since white folks, like blacks, are likely to be

harmed by people of the same race. Let me give a useful example. When I worked as an assistant professor at an Ivy League university one of my white female students was raped by a black man. Even though she had been deeply committed to anti-racist work before the rape, during her period of recovery she found that she was fearing all black men. Her commitment to anti-racist struggle led her to interrogate that fear, and she realized that had she been raped by a white male, she would not have felt all white males were responsible and should be feared. Seeing her fear of all black males as a regressive expression of white racism, she let it go. The will to be vigilant emerged from both her commitment to ending racism and her will to be in loving community with black folks. Not abandoning that longing for community is a perspective we must all embrace if racism is to end.

More than ever before in our history, black Americans are succumbing to and internalizing the racist assumption that there can be no meaningful bonds of intimacy between blacks and whites. It is fascinating to explore why it is that black people trapped in the worst situation of racial oppression—enslavement—had the foresight to see that it would be disempowering for them to lose sight of the capacity of white people to transform themselves and divest of white supremacy, even as many black folks today who in no way suffer such extreme racist oppression and exploitation are convinced that white people will not repudiate racism. Contemporary black folks, like their white counterparts, have passively accepted the internalization of white supremacist assumptions. Organized white supremacists have always taught that there can never be trust and intimacy between the superior white race and the inferior black race. When black people internalize these sentiments, no resistance to white supremacy is taking place;

rather we become complicit in spreading racist notions. It does not matter that so many black people feel white people will never repudiate racism because of being daily assaulted by white denial and refusal of accountability. We must not allow the actions of white folks who blindly endorse racism to determine the direction of our resistance. Like our white allies in struggle we must consistently keep the faith, by always sharing the truth that white people can be anti-racist, that racism is not some immutable character flaw.

Of course many white people are comfortable with a rhetoric of race that suggests racism cannot be changed, that all white people are "inherently racist" simply because they are born and raised in this society. Such misguided thinking socializes white people both to remain ignorant of the way in which white supremacist attitudes are learned and to assume a posture of learned helplessness as though they have no agency—no capacity to resist this thinking. Luckily we have many autobiographies by white folks committed to anti-racist struggle that provide documentary testimony that many of these individuals repudiated racism when they were children. Far from passively accepting it as inherent, they instinctively felt it was wrong. Many of them witnessed bizarre acts of white racist aggression towards black folks in everyday life and responded to the injustice of the situation. Sadly, in our times so many white folks are easily convinced by racist whites and black folks who have internalized racism that they can never be really free of racism.

These feelings also then obscure the reality of white privilege. As long as white folks are taught to accept racism as "natural" then they do not have to see themselves as consciously creating a racist society by their actions, by their political choices. This means as well that they do not have to face the way

in which acting in a racist manner ensures the maintenance of white privilege. Indeed, denying their agency allows them to believe white privilege does not exist even as they daily exercise it. If the young white woman who had been raped had chosen to hold all black males accountable for what happened, she would have been exercising white privilege and reinforcing the structure of racist thought which teaches that all black people are alike. Unfortunately, so many white people are eager to believe racism cannot be changed because internalizing that assumption downplays the issue of accountability. No responsibility need be taken for not changing something if it is perceived as immutable. To accept racism as a system of domination that can be changed would demand that everyone who sees him- or herself as embracing a vision of racial social equality would be required to assert anti-racist habits of being. We know from histories both present and past that white people (and everyone else) who commit themselves to living in anti-racist ways need to make sacrifices, to courageously endure the uncomfortable to challenge and change.

Whites, people of color, and black folks are reluctant to commit themselves fully and deeply to an anti-racist struggle that is ongoing because there is such a pervasive feeling of hopelessness—a conviction that nothing will ever change. How any of us can continue to hold those feelings when we study the history of racism in this society and see how much has changed makes no logical sense. Clearly we have not gone far enough. In the late sixties, Martin Luther King posed the question "Where do we go from here?" To live in anti-racist society we must collectively renew our commitment to a democratic vision of racial justice and equality. Pursuing that vision we create a culture where *beloved community* flourishes and is sustained. Those of use who know the joy of being with folks from all walks of life, all races, who are fundamentally anti-racist in their habits of being, need to give public testimony. We need to share not only what we have experienced but the conditions of change that make such an experience possible. The interracial circle of love that I know can happen because each individual present in it has made his or her own commitment to living an anti-racist life and to furthering the struggle to end white supremacy will become a reality for everyone only if those of us who have created these communities share how they emerge in our lives and the strategies we use to sustain them. Our devout commitment to building diverse communities is central. These commitments to anti-racist living are just one expression of who we are and what we share with one another but they form the foundation of that sharing. Like all *beloved communities* we affirm our differences. It is this generous spirit of affirmation that gives us the courage to challenge one another, to work through misunderstandings, especially those that have to do with race and racism. In a *beloved community* solidarity and trust are grounded in profound commitment to a shared vision. Those of us who are always anti-racist long for a world in which everyone can form a *beloved community* where borders can be crossed and cultural hybridity celebrated. Anyone can begin to make such a community by truly seeking to live in an anti-racist world. If that longing guides our vision and our actions, the new culture will be born and anti-racist communities of resistance will emerge everywhere. That is where we must go from here.

Questions for Understanding and Critical Thinking

1. Have people in the United States given up on the idea of living in a *beloved community?* Why or why not?

2. What evidence can you cite to support hooks's assertion that many people have "become so cynical about ending racism . . . that they make no effort to build community"? What evidence can you cite that contradicts this assertion?

3. Why does hooks believe nationalist separatism is growing in momentum in the United States?

4. Do you think a *beloved community* such as hooks describes will be formed in the United States during your lifetime? Why or why not?

PART THREE

Suggestions for Further Reading

Aguilar-San Juan, Karin (Ed.). 1994. *The State of Asian America: Activism and Resistance in the 1990s.* Boston: South End Press.

Baca Zinn, Maxine, and Bonnie Thornton Dill (Eds.). 1994. *Women of Color in U.S. Society.* Philadelphia: Temple University Press.

Benokraitis, Nijole V., and Joe R. Feagin. 1995. *Modern Sexism: Blatant, Subtle, and Covert Discrimination* (2nd ed.). Englewood Cliffs, NJ: Prentice Hall.

Gans, Herbert J. 1995. *The War Against the Poor: The Underclass and Antipoverty Policy.* New York: Basic Books.

Gardner, Carol Brooks. 1995. *Passing By: Gender and Public Harassment.* Berkeley: University of California Press.

Hacker, Andrew. 1995. *Two Nations: Black and White, Separate, Hostile, Unequal* (expanded ed.). New York: Ballantine.

Hochschild, Jennifer L. 1995. *Facing Up to the American Dream: Race, Class, and the Soul of the Nation.* Princeton, NJ: Princeton University Press.

Kurz, Demie. 1995. *For Richer, For Poorer: Mothers Confront Divorce.* New York: Routledge.

Oliver, Melvin L., and Thomas M. Shapiro. 1995. *Black Wealth/White Wealth: A New Perspective on Racial Inequality.* New York: Routledge.

Schein, Virginia E. 1995. *Working from the Margins: Voices of Mothers in Poverty.* Ithaca, NY: Cornell University Press.

Steinberg, Stephen. 1995. *Turning Back: The Retreat from Racial Justice in American Thought and Policy.* Boston: Beacon Press.

Author Index

Note: Page numbers of articles by respective authors are in *italic* type.

Subject Index

Notes: Page numbers of articles are in *italic* type.

A *t* following a page number indicates that the subject is referenced in a table.

Ability grouping. *See* Tracking

Accent, as basis for discrimination, 317–318

Accounting for Cosmetic Surgery: The Accomplishment of Gender (Dull and West), *90–105*

Activism, 250

Admissions policies, at Ivy League schools, 228–231, 229*t*, 230*t*

admissions directors, 231–232

admissions process, 232–235

Adult socialization and black identity, 175–176

African American professional women, 405–416

education and, 406

employment sectors, place in, 409–412, 410*t*

gender differences in job ceilings for, 407–409

job ceilings for, 407–409

middle class, 406–407

progress of, in employment sectors, 412–414, 412*t*, 413*t*

African Americans. *See also* Black movement

antiblack discrimination in public places, 366–386

aspects of discrimination against, 367–369

assessing a discriminatory situation, 376–377

black maleness stigma and, 381

body image and, 189–193

Civil Rights Act of 1964, 366–367, 385

deference ritual and, 368–369

descriptive patterns of discrimination, 370–371, 370*t*, 371*t*

employment options for women, 308–309

employment rates at McDonald's, 112–113

family values and, 305–306

gender construct of, 86, 87

gender differences in job ceilings for, 407–409

hiring strategies and. *See* Hiring strategies

hypertension among, 44–45

income and, 304

master status and skin color, 41–43

middle-class resources as protection against discrimination, 377–378

police brutality and, 383–384

racial identity among, 173–184, 180*t*, 181*t*

range of discriminatory actions against, 368

responses to discrimination, 311–312, 368–369, 371–384

single-parent families. *See* Single-parent families

sites of discrimination against, 367–368

Social Register listings, 78

socialization and, 131–132, 136–137, 173–184, 180*t*, 181*t*

Souls of Black Folk (Du Bois), *The, 48–53*

street harassment of, 378–383

tracking and, 276

wealth and, 303–304

women professionals. *See* African American professional women

Age, and socialization, 176, 180*t*, 181*t*

Agents of socialization, 129–130

American Indians. *See* Native Americans

American system of education, 225–226. *See also* Education

American views on weight, 199–200

Anorexia, and body image, 187–200

Antiblack discrimination. *See* African Americans

Anticipated peril, 336–338

Anticipatory socialization, 133

Apartheid, 10

Apparent escort, 330–334

Invisible Man Routine, 332

Appearance-dependent interaction, 301–302, 327–328

Ascribed status

and ethnicity, 8

and race, 6

Asian Americans.

See also Indians

accent as basis for discrimination, 317–318

bias against, 315–322

discrimination within different Asian groups, 316

as model minorities, 316

as safe target for discrimination, 316

Social Register listings, 78

Assessing discriminatory situation, 376–377

Assimilation, 39–46

domination model of, 41–44

hypertension and, 44–45

without domination, 43

Attire, as basis for discrimination, 319, 397

Bartering, between private schools and Ivy League schools, 225, 231. *See also* Charters

Ivy League admissions process, 232–235

Behavior, resistance to moral reform and, 265–266

Belief systems

about public places, 329

gender-based, 20, 282–293, 283*t*, 288*t*, 291*t*

443